HAUNTED SKIES

VOLUME NINE   **1981-1986**

HAUNTED SKIES VOLUME 9 1981-1986

Copyright © 2013 John Hanson & Dawn Holloway. All rights reserved.

First paperback edition printed 2013 in the United Kingdom.

A catalogue record for this book is available from the British Library.

ISBN 978-0-9574944-2-8

Published by
Haunted Skies Publishing

For more copies of this book, *please email:* johndawn1@sky.com

Telephone: 0121 445 0340

Designed and typeset by Bob Tibbitts ~ (iSET)

Printed in Great Britain

FOREWORD
By Nick Redfern

T HERE is an old phrase that goes like this: 'They don't make them like that anymore.' Well, I'm going to amend that by saying: 'They don't make them like this anymore!' What am I talking about? The very book you are now holding in your hands, that's what.

The 9th (yes, 9th!) volume in the still-ongoing series of *Haunted Skies* books, by John Hanson and Dawn Holloway, is a fantastic addition to the previous eight titles, packed with case after case of reported UFO activity, many previously unknown or barely touched on elsewhere, and all given the excellent Hanson-Holloway treatment.

When I said that they don't make them like this anymore, I mean in terms of the sheer number of events, the detail given to studying and commenting on those same events, and the classic nature of the incidents that John and Dawn place under the microscope.

It must be said that many of today's UFO-themed books (and authors) are guilty of simply regurgitating old, tired and worn-out cases, and downloading the most inaccurate nonsense from the Internet.

Fortunately, our authors prefer to do things the proper way. You know: actually leaving the house and getting out into the field and interviewing people, tracking down sources, finding witnesses to decades-old cases, and pursuing their quarry in true detective-style.

Doing so works far better than simply copying and pasting reams of material from this website or from that blog. *Haunted Skies*, Volume 9, then, is very much old-school Ufology – and I mean that as a 100 percent complement.

Covering 1981 to 1986, the book is not just a joy to read; it's packed with an incredible number of visuals, many of which are in full colour. Those visuals include images of old newspaper and magazine articles, eyewitnesses, locations of encounters, government files, letters from officialdom, and much more.

But, it's the cases that really count. You'll be pleased to know that Dawn and John's latest title is jammed with cases that will both intrigue and amaze.

We're talking about – among numerous other things – early '1980s' encounters involving the so-called Black Triangle-style of UFOs, a fascinating saucer-landing on the Derbyshire/Yorkshire border, highly significant alien abduction reports with 'missing time' components, unexplained lights seen over mystery-filled Wiltshire, and a near-collision between a UFO and a nuclear submarine.

On top of that, there's the curious saga of the bowler-hat-wearing 'Man in Black' (and his vanishing, equally black, old car), sinister and disturbing goings-on in the dark depths of Hopwas Woods (a place I know very well!), a couple of intriguing cases of a 'British Roswell' variety (including very weird and still-unresolved affairs from both Ireland and Wales), and a batch of notable reports from UFO-saturated Warminster. And let's not forget the mysterious circumstances surrounding 'The Man On The Moon', and the enigmatic fallings of strange things from the sky.

With that all said, I'll add in conclusion: I have a great deal of admiration for John and Dawn. When they began the *Haunted Skies* project, they had a vision and a drive to create a series of books that would chronicle, to a near-infinite degree, the many and varied UFO encounters reported all across the UK since the 1940s. And, I'm very pleased to see, and to say, that they still have that vision and drive.

Unlike so many other researchers who have given up the chase, or fallen by the wayside, our authors are still marching on, still uncovering treasure-trove upon treasure-trove of material, and still informing, enlightening, and entertaining us – in equal, thought-provoking measures.

Read this book from cover to cover – it's a hugely important piece of work.

Nick Redfern is the author of many books, including *The Real Men in Black* and *Contactees*.

INTRODUCTION

IN our 9th Volume of *Haunted Skies* we examine the UFO events which occurred between 1980 and 1986 in the skies, and occasionally on the ground, of all manner of strange events – important enough to be brought to the attention of The Lord Hill Norton, whom we wrote to wondering why such a prominent figure had taken an interest in a matter, which still attracts ridicule to this present day. In one of a number of letters sent to us, he gave this reply:

> *"My position is and always has been that there are physical objects, almost certainly not man-made, regularly detected in Earth's atmosphere. I want to know what they are, who, or what is directing them and what is their purpose."*

Many people whom we came across over the intervening years felt frustrated with the *apparent* indifference adopted by the MOD, who have always declined to be drawn into any discussion over sightings of UFOs brought to their attention, and seek to convince us that the majority of UFO sightings can be explained and that as they are of no Defence significance, they are of no interest.

At the time of final preparation of this Volume, beginning in December 2009, and completion 2013, there has been the closure of Air Desk 2a, at the MOD, as part of a cost-cutting exercise, which may give the impression that UFOs are no longer of any importance to the authorities. In the *Sun* newspaper, dated 7th November 2012, Dr. David Clarke published his views on the UFO subject in an article, entitled 'CLOSED ENCOUNTERS OF THE THIRD KIND', which he seeks to convince us that the majority of UFO sightings can be explained away. I (John Hanson) felt I had to respond to this and wrote a letter to the *Sun*, but it was never published – although I left the comment on-line.

This is what I had to say:

As a retired Police Officer, who served for nearly 30 years in the West Midlands Police Force, I have to say that I have no recollection of any UFO sightings brought to my attention during that time. If somebody had, I would have considered them candidates for psychiatric help, or suffering from delusions, or the worse for drink.

In 1995, my son – now a Detective Inspector but then a Police Constable – and his female colleague, witnessed a saucer-shaped object hovering over a tree in Stirchley, Birmingham, following a report from members of the public (which included a doctor) of an unidentified object seen moving over the City Centre.

Up to then I was sceptical of such matters but decided, out of curiosity, to conduct my own research into the subject, wondering if I would find any evidence of such phenomena. I spent the next 15 years unearthing original sighting reports from members of the public, along with my partner, Dawn Holloway – speaking to people who had reported seeing something highly unusual. As far as I remember, out of all those thousands of people – which included many retired RAF pilots, who I have interviewed over the years – not one of them ever claimed to have seen any aliens, or have been abducted. All they wanted to tell me was what they had seen. What I made of it was up to me.

It has taken us all of these years just to document, on a day-by-day basis, those events which are contained in a number of books, entitled *Haunted Skies* (Volume 1-6) and we have only just completed Volume 7 (1978-1979) of over 400 pages! In the early days, many national newspapers asked us for books and promised us a review. So far this has not happened.

We have hundreds, if not thousands, of incidents relating to reports of UFO activity, right up to the present date They often fall into the following categories . . .

1. UFO 'displays'

2. Sightings of structured objects

3. Complaints by motorists who have been followed by UFOs.

4. Others who claim to have suffered physical or mental trauma, following the sightings of UFOs, this of course includes Close Encounters, whether at home or in a vehicle.

We do not claim that aliens or UFOs exist. What we do claim is that there is irrefutable evidence of phenomena which is more likely to be indigenous to our planet, rather than the incursions of any extraterrestrial life-force. We also feel that this evidence should be preserved, as it forms a very important part of our social history, and will continue to do so, if only to salute the courage of so many who have decided, often in the face of ridicule, to tell us of their experiences.

In our opinion, they surely exist; if they did not, the evidence would indicate otherwise, and we would not have written any of these Volumes. However, common sense dictates that *they are of interest* and always have been. How can they not be of interest? Our *apparent* inability to determine the nature of what UFOs represent, and where they come from, should not prevent us asking questions about something to which we deserve an answer.

We felt that *Haunted Skies* had now come of age, both in size and its presentation of colour images. We also felt that wherever possible (within reason) we would continue to publish brief details of UFO sightings from other countries, if they were judged of relevance and supplemented reported British UFO activity.

ACKNOWLEDGEMENTS

Gordon Creighton – formerly the editor of FSR (*Flying Saucer Review*) – a distinguished diplomat, whose knowledge of UFOs was second to none. We felt privileged when he invited us to be consultants, following a visit to his house in Rickmansworth, Hertfordshire, to discuss the publication of *Haunted Skies*, and granted us permission to refer to some of the sightings contained within FSR.

Sadly, Gordon passed away some years ago. We were honoured to attend his funeral and would also like to thank his son, Philip Creighton, for permission to refer to cases contained within the magazine.

Brenda Butler – for allowing us access to an enormous wealth of tape-recorded interviews, photographs, personal diaries, and sighting reports, obtained while running the East Anglian Paranormal Research Association, with Ron West.

Margaret Ellen Fry (*now a firm friend*) – author/ head of The Welsh Federation of Independent Ufologists and member of Contact UK – for her assistance, understanding, and the opportunity to share not only her many personal experiences but access to investigations into reported UFO activity, going back to the 1950s.

We would like to thank **Philip Mantle** for his encouragement, assistance and supplying us with many rare photographs of other researchers, including Mark and Graham Birdsall, together with original case files relating to investigations carried out by the Yorkshire UFO Society.

Daniel Goring – former editor of *Earth-link* magazine – a specialist in his own field, responsible for many investigations, during the 1970s, around the London and Essex areas, for his assistance and allowing us to quote from specific sightings contained within the magazines. He has also put us in touch with many witnesses and UFO researchers, including **Bill Eden, Phyllis Mooney** and **Edward Harris**. Daniel has also provided us with a considerable number of previously unpublished sighting reports from around the mid to later part of the 20th Century, and should be praised for his commitment in recording for posterity, the events covered by his group.

Ivan W. Bunn of the *Lantern* magazine series – We would like to thank you for all your help in allowing us access to research and investigations into reported UFO activity, over the years.

Nicholas Maloret, of WATSUP – We would like to thank him for his continuing encouragement and permission to refer to a number of investigations conducted by him, and other members of the organisation.

Peter Tate, Bristol UFO Researcher – Thank you for your immense assistance and for providing us with various documents and sighting reports, researched by you over the years, including personal letters from Arthur Shuttlewood. He is best remembered for those scintillating late night conversations, discussing UFOs in his own imitable style, interspersed with liberal doses of humour, now gone but certainly not forgotten.

Ian Mrzyglod, of *Probe* – We would like to thank him for advice and assistance, and allowing us to refer to a number of UFO sightings investigated by his group. Also thanks to **Marty Moffat**, and others, for the loan of photographs.

Matt Lyons, head of BUFORA, for his continued support and encouragement with producing the *Haunted Skies* series of books. He is a credit to the organisation.

Omar Fowler – previously with SIGAP (Surrey Investigation of Anomalous Phenomena) – now PRA, Derby (Phenomenon Research Association) and consultant for *Flying Saucer Review* – for allowing us permission to refer to some of your investigations into sighting of UFO reports brought to your attention.

Malcolm Robinson, SPI (Scottish Phenomena Investigations) for his assistance.

Tony Pace, previously head of UFO Investigations for BUFORA – for advice and encouragement, over many years, and allowing us to include details from him and **Roger Stanway's** investigations into reported UFO activity in the Staffordshire area.

Bob Tibbitts – of CUFORG (Coventry UFO Research Group) – who has allowed us access to the group's archives, and for personal letters and his typesetting and design work.

Those delightful ladies – **Kathleen Smith** and **Pat Smith** – along with Pat's then husband, **Fred Smith,** previously members of the of the Isle of Wight UFO Society. They were responsible, together with **John Feakins** and **Rose** and **Leonard Cramp**, for producing over 80 early UFO magazines (UFOLOG) cataloguing UFO activity over the British Isles, during the mid 20th Century. Thank you, Kath, for entrusting us with a staggering amount of personal letters and UFO files, collected by you and other members, which would have been lost from history if it had not been for your dedication in cataloguing such matters. Sadly, Kath passed away a few years ago – now gone, but not forgotten.

We would also like to thank **Wayne Mason, David Sankey, Steven Franklin, David Bryant, Jason Chapman, Robert Townsend** and others, who have furnished us with illustrations for use in Volume 9.

Finally, special thanks to our much loved dog, Maude, who accompanied us. Sadly, she passed away on the 18th May 2009. If we have forgotten anyone, we apologise and will include them in the credits for Volume 10 of *Haunted Skies*.

Vicky Hanson and Maude

1981

In this year the Thatcher government withdraws plans to close down 23 mines, after negotiations with National Union of Mineworkers.
Buckingham Palace announces the engagement of Prince of Wales and 19-year-old Lady Diana Spencer.

In the spring, riots break out in Brixton; many of the police are injured. During the summer, rioting breaks out in London, Birmingham, Leeds, and many other towns and cities.

Bucks Fizz is the winner of the Eurovision Song Contest with the song *Making Your Mind Up*, while the Academy Award-winning film *Chariots of Fire* is released.

On the 29th July, the wedding of Charles, Prince of Wales, and Lady Diana Spencer takes place at St. Paul's Cathedral. More than 30 million viewers watch the wedding on television – the second highest television audience of all time in Britain.

Petrol costs £1.32 a gallon, average price of a house £24,000.

First flight of USA Space Shuttle Columbia takes place. IBM in US launches its first PC, which uses Microsoft Software MS DOS, the term 'internet' is first mentioned.

JANUARY 1981

COUPLE TELL OF FRIGHTENING JOURNEY, WHILE DRIVING THROUGH WARWICKSHIRE

Also includes – Coventry man sights mysterious object over City • London man describes what he saw over Hackney • Triangular UFO seen over London airspace A cigar-shaped UFO seen by USAF Security at RAF Woodbridge • A farmer's wife comes across landed object – was it a UFO, or is there a more rational explanation? *Abroad:* Multi witness sighting of triangular-shaped object in Arizona USA.

UFO over Warwickshire

IN January 1981, Peter Higgins and his girlfriend – Lynn Simmonds – were driving home to Kenilworth, in Warwickshire, at 10pm, when they noticed:

> ". . . a red and blue stationary 'light' in the sky, which suddenly dropped downward, as if about to land. As we drove past it – now just off the ground, we saw the two 'lights' formed part of a large cigar-shaped object, partly illuminated along its length by a number of smaller lights rotating around the centre of the 'body'. Our curiosity turned to fear, so we switched off the car lights and drove away. Upon looking back, we were horrified to see the UFO was actually following us. When we reached Kenilworth, we were astounded to see it hovering over a parade of shops. Suddenly, in a flash of light, it disappeared!

(Source: Gary Lanham, UFOSIS)

UFO over Coventry

Michael Newark, from Coventry, told of an incident he witnessed, during 1981, on a sunny day with a clear blue sky, while playing football with his son against the side of the house.

> *"I sighted a long object moving against the wind, heading from north to south, at a height of some 80ft; it reminded me of a plastic sheet running backwards and forwards. I estimated it was about 7ft wide by 12ft long, and oblong in shape. It then changed direction – now moving west to east – which allowed me to obtain a closer look at the rear of the object, which showed a dark spot in its centre, two thirds of the way along its back and what appeared to be an 'edge' pass over the top of the object every few seconds before re-appearing from the underneath. Within a short time the object was out of sight. It seemed alive – that's the only way I can describe it. It was undoubtedly one of the strangest things I had ever seen before, or since."*

(Source: Personal interview/*Ovni*, July/August 2003/Mr. Omar Fowler, PRA)

UFO over Warwickshire

Two people were driving from Stourbridge, along the A491, during the evening of 5th January 1981, when they saw a stationary yellow 'light' in the sky, which began to approach them. As it passed overhead, they were astonished to see:

> *". . . an oval-shaped metallic object, showing a light at each end. Within minutes, the object was out of view – just a tiny yellow light in the sky."*

(Source: Mark Pritchard, UFOSIS)

UFO over London

Paul Anderson was between 15-17 years of age and living with his mother, Ivy, in a ground floor council flat at 24, Kent Court, South Hackney, next to Queensbridge Road, during the early 1980s.

One evening he arrived home, at around 9pm, but was unable to get into the flat as he didn't have a key. After several knocks on the front door, and receiving no answer (although the lights were on) he presumed his mother was probably in Bill's house next door, at number 25, as they were on good terms with him.

Paul decided to make his way to Bill's flat. As he was about to walk left, into Bill's pathway, his attention was drawn to a high-pitched wailing sound – child-like, in some way – that was coming from upstairs in the block, a little further down on the top landing. His first thoughts were could it have been children? – Unusual, as to his knowledge, there were no children up there.

> *"I began to sense a spiralling movement directly above me, which at first, made me think that someone was shaking a carpet over the top balcony, creating a swirling, distorted image. The sounds along the top landing had distinctly given way to a contrasting silence, as I began to study intently, this rather unusual pattern of movement, which clearly was not a carpet being shaken over the balcony, but something much higher up – higher than the balcony – and it*

was moving fast, spiralling erratically above Kent Court, which is 33ft high. I speculated on whether it was possibly some dark grey pigeons from the roof, fluttering and flying around in a circle formation, but at that time in the evening, seemed very odd indeed. Then, to my sudden amazement, from this dark rotating movement, began to emerge a very solid structure, spinning itself in complete silence, almost indistinguishable against the Hackney night sky.

It started to slow down, quickly, in a very controlled manner. It reached a pace of rotation that enabled me to see into its curved inner structure very clearly. It was a concaved-shaped design of strong dull-dark grey metal. Its appearance was so strikingly dull that it matched the very sky itself that it was spinning in.

To see how this object used this perfect camouflage was very impressive indeed. The dull grey metal, turning in the sky up there in the heavens, spiralling around like a piece of magic before my eyes, rotating steadily, behaving like an inner-drum of a washing machine, and with a Saint Paul's cathedral inner globe presence, had magnificence about it. Although this object was displaying this incredible technology in front of my eyes, it also had an ancient, timeless aura.

Paul Anderson and his mother, Ivy

Pau's neighbour, 'Bill'

Paul, remembering what he saw at 24, Kent Court, in South Hackney

I could really sense some very strong powerful mechanics pulsating through this heavy looking structure, enabling it to somehow remain stationary above Kent Court. I gazed in absolute wonder at this spinning, concave spectacle in the sky, which suddenly moved slowly and gently backwards."

At this point, because of the building (Kent Court) which was directly in front of him, he lost sight of it and was left staring up into a blank sky.

He immediately headed for Bill's house and vibrantly tapped away on the front door. After being let in, he told his mother and Bill what he had just seen! They were visibly shocked, but listened with great interest, realising how sincere he was, although Bill was sceptical about what he had actually seen.

Paul pulled the living room curtain to one side, with its view towards the south-west area of the sky from this window, which was the direction the object had moved into just before he lost sight of it, and encouraged his mother and Bill to come over to the window.

His heart sank with immense disappointment and puzzlement, wondering where the object had gone. Only 20 seconds previously, the most stunning and most mysterious airborne object he had ever seen had manifested itself over Kent Court in a most dramatic fashion, and then apparently disappeared into thin air! The sky was empty and clear with absolutely no sign of anything unusual.

UFO over Essex

On 7th January 1981, David William Taylor of Hillcrest Road, Hornchurch – a telephone engineer by occupation – was with three friends, standing around a bonfire in Devonshire Road, Seven Kings, Ilford, Essex, at 8pm, when a long cylindrical-shaped object was seen in the sky, moving in a straight line through the sky.

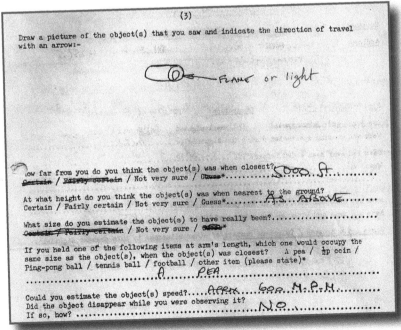

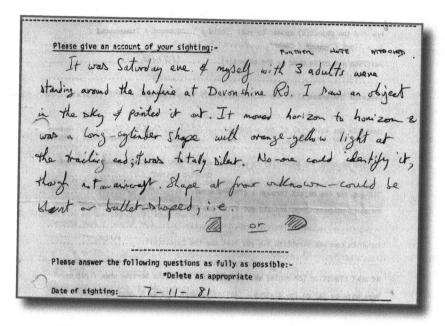

Please give an account of your sighting:-

It was Saturday eve & myself with 3 adults were standing around the bonfire at Devonshire Rd. I saw an object in the sky & pointed it out. It moved horizon to horizon & was a long-cylinder shape with orange-yellow light at the trailing end; it was totaly silent. No-one could identify it, though not an aircraft. Shape at front unknown — could be blunt or bullet-shaped, i.e.

Date of sighting: 7 – 11 – 81

UFO landing – France

At 5pm on 8th January 1981, Mr. Nicolai – a gardener from Trans-en-Provence, France – saw a metallic disc-shaped object, making a whistling sound, land with a hard thump in the garden. He described it as being:

> ". . . 8ft by 6ft in size, and had four openings on the underside. It also had a thick band around the middle section of the object."

The incident was reported to the police and was later investigated by GEPAN – the French Government's scientific team of UFO investigators. The physical traces included evidence of vegetation and soil heating, skid marks, and circular ground marks. The chemical analysis revealed that the soil had been heated to temperatures not in excess of 600° Celsius.

(Source: Jacques Vallee, *Confrontations: A Scientist's Search for Alien Contact*)

UFO over Tilbury, Kent

Three days later on the 11th January 1981, Tilbury crane driver – Mr. Simon Fitzgerald, was travelling to work from Grays, in Essex, along Dock Road, Marshfoot, at 6.30am, when he saw an object, which he described as:

> ". . . far too bright to be an aircraft, showing two bright lights, and a green one surrounded by a glare. I stopped at the side of the road and watched it before it went out of sight."

(Source: Dan Goring, *Earth-link*)

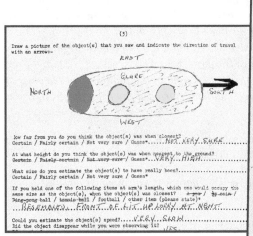

(3)

Draw a picture of the object(s) that you saw and indicate the direction of travel with an arrow:-

How far from you do you think the object(s) was when closest? Certain / Fairly certain / Not very sure / Guess*...... NOT VERY SURE

At what height do you think the object(s) was when nearest to the ground? Certain / Fairly certain / Not very sure / Guess*.... VERY HIGH

What size do you estimate the object(s) to have really been?.....................

Certain / Fairly certain / Not very sure / Guess*

If you held one of the following items at arm's length, which one would occupy the same size as the object(s), when the object(s) was closest? A pea / 5p coin / Ping-pong ball / tennis ball / football / other item (please state)*

RESEMBLED FRONT OF LIT UP LORRY AT NIGHT

Could you estimate the object(s) speed?.... VERY SLOW
Did the object disappear while you were observing it? YES

Case No. 1981-1-1
1981-1-1

ESSEX UFO STUDY GROUP

Unidentified Flying Object Sighting Report Form

Please give an account of your sighting:-

I was traveling to work to "Tilbury Power Station" on Sunday morning on the 11-1-81, at about 6-30 AM when I saw this object in the sky, at first I thought it was an aircraft looking again I realized it was too bright a light for a plane, and there were no flashing lights and no sound. It resembled two bright lights, and a green light surrounded by a glare, it was traveling from "North" to "South" approaching the "Kent coast." The Green light was facing the North end, I stopped my moped at the side of the Road for about a couple of minutes to watch, then suddenly it vanished I did'nt see it any more

---

Please answer the following questions as fully as possible:-
*Delete as appropriate

Date of sighting: 11·1·81

Time of day:. MORNING... B.S.T.(Daylight saving)/G.M.T.*

How many objects did you see?.... ONE

Where were you when you saw the object(s)?Exact location MARSHFOOT, DOCK ROAD, APPROACHING TILBURY, ESSEX.

How long was the object(s) in sight for?.... TWENTY TO TWENTY FIVE FEET
Certain/Fairly certain/Not very sure/Guess*

Was the object(s) in sight continuously? Yes/No*.... YES

Did the object(s) while under observation:

Move in front of anything / Move behind anything / Remain visible in the sky all the time*

Any other comments on this? THEN SUDDENLY DISAPPEARED

UFO over London

Just after midnight on 16th January 1981, Eric Kempson and his brother-in-law, Tony Nicholls, were driving along Shooters Hill, London, when they saw:

> "... a black Delta-shaped object, showing a number of coloured lights underneath. From out of the UFO's base projected a powerful beam of light that illuminated the road. I cannot say what it was that we saw, but I am convinced it was no aircraft, helicopter, or weather balloon."

In the same year, a Delta-shaped UFO was seen by Bradford resident Christine Cunnington, who was at her home address with her fiancée William Nicholls, and sister, checking out a new telescope, when:

> "We saw what looked like a huge Delta-winged aircraft, gliding noiselessly, over the roof of our house, heading south-west, towards Halifax, showing a number of red lights along the back of each wing."

(Source: Personal interview)

Triangular UFO over Arizona

Workers on a repair gang at the Morenci copper-smelting plant, in Arizona, claim a massive spacecraft swooped on the factory, in January 1981. It seemed to be examining one of the two 650ft smokestacks by beaming a light ray down it. The four men, who were repairing the other stack, said the UFO was shaped like a boomerang, and as big as four football fields. It had 12 small red lights on its surface, in addition to a large white searchlight beam underneath.

"It just sort of stopped in mid-air above the smokestack and shone the big light right into it", said workman Randall Rogers, 20. His colleague, Larry Mortensen added, *"I have never seen an airplane hover like that. I got the feeling that it wasn't aggressive. Certainly it did nothing to frighten us."* A third member of the gang, Kent Davis, said: *". . . that during examination of the stack, one of the red lights at the edge of the 'boomerang' suddenly darted away from the craft, like a rocket."*

The UFO was also seen by 100 members of a high school marching band, holding a practice session on the football field of Morenci High School, just over a mile away. Director Bruce Smith said:

"I looked up and saw all these lights in the shape of a 'V'. There was no sound. It hovered for a few minutes then disappeared high into the sky."

Frustratingly we were unable to identify what date this happened in January, but found other accounts involving what appears to be the identical sighting, which was reported to have taken place on 23rd October 1980 – this time the director of the band was Bruce Allen.

"The whole band saw it and there must have been thirty to forty parents in the stands who saw it too; the kids were pretty excited. It was some type of object, shaped like a 'V' or a boomerang, outlined in different colored lights. It didn't make a sound. It was real big. It looked like the entire sky above the field was filled with this object. It was bigger than any airplane, even a 747. It just roamed clockwise, slowly, above the field as we were rehearsing. It stayed there for the entire rehearsal, almost as if it were watching us. It seemed like it was checking out what was going on down here. It was going very slow. I've never seen anything like it before. As the kids were leaving after practice, I turned the field lights off and looked up and the object was gone."

Kris Windsor (17):

"It was a bunch of lights, with a big one in the middle. Everybody was looking up. At first, everybody got kind of scared but we had to keep on rehearsing."

Tim Pingleton (18):

"I saw a string of lights in a triangular shape, like a boomerang. It was about three hundred yards long. It looked like it would go forward, stop, and stay there for about three minutes, then take off and not go very fast at all, then stop and go forward again. I wasn't frightened but the fact that it stopped right over us was sort of weird. I saw it again later on, farther off at an angle."

Allen, who had been band director at the school for ten years, said the sighting began a few minutes after seven on the night of 23rd October 1980, and lasted for nearly an hour. Shortly before it appeared over the school, five maintenance workers saw it over the huge Phelps-Dodge copper smelter – a mile west of the school, on the other side of a mountain. *"We were just going to lunch, about five minutes to seven, when we noticed something big flying directly toward us"*, said Randall Lee Rogers, (21) – a repairman.

"It was sort of boomerang-shaped. There were twelve red lights on it and a big searchlight

right in front. It was, maybe, the size of a football field. We saw it fly down right over us, until it was right over the smokestack."

The smelter had two 600ft tall smokestacks, about 140ft apart. The tops of the stacks were 23ft in diameter.

One other sighting in the area was notable. On a Monday night, early in December 1980, Opal Ray was attending a *Tupperware* party at home, ten miles south of Clifton. She and several other women were standing outside the house, waiting for a guest to arrive, when an object passed over the house.

Mrs. Ray said:

"It was a triangle and had red lights on each point. It went directly over us and it was low enough that you could see the bottom. It looked like hardwood planking, about three or four inches wide, like a hardwood floor. It scared me, and hovered over the house before shooting away."

Her description of the object was somewhat similar to what Kathryn Bezjian and her husband saw from their home in Eureka Springs, Arkansas, three years earlier. A large object passed over their house, making a low humming sound.

Mrs. Bezjian said:

"As it got directly over us, the bottom of it was diamond-shaped. It looked like raw wood. In the middle of this diamond was a red light, a signal-like light like you'd see on any plane, and up underneath it were three or four small red lights."

Many UFO sightings occurred in that part of Arizona in December 1980, mainly in nearby Clifton, just several miles south of Morenci. *"There have been several different sightings but the main one was on the night of December 10"*, said a Clifton businessman, who also had this to say:

"I feel sure that at least a thousand people saw these objects. I saw three lights or objects in formation, of triangular shape that kind of floated over this area, four times. We watched it for a couple of hours. It made a thirty-mile circle around Clifton and was, maybe, a mile high. The second time around, two objects left the main body at a high rate of speed, and I never saw them come back. It kind of made the hair stand up on the back of your head. We didn't hear anything that sounded like jets. It sounded more like a sewing machine motor, a little buzzing sound. It was definitely something I had never seen before and we see jets and planes through here all the time. My son-in-law thought he saw lights in a cabin one time, but I didn't see it. Many people are reluctant to say anything about these things, because they're afraid people will think they're kind of squirrelly."

We emailed the local newspaper and Morenci Library hoping to obtain newspaper articles about this but never received any acknowledgements. **(Source: *FSR*, Volume 31, No. 6, 1986)**

UFO over Kingswinford

On the evening of 15th January 1981, a motorist and his companion were on their way from Stourbridge to Wolverhampton, along the A491, when they stopped at a set of traffic lights in Kingswinford, at which point a bright yellow 'light' in the sky caught their attention. When the traffic lights changed to green, they pulled the car off the side of the road, and got out to take closer look. The 'light' then began to move slowly towards their position, heading in a southern direction. As it passed overhead they were astonished to see an oval-shaped object, with a metallic surface, showing a blue and red light at each end. The object then headed away and was soon only visible as a yellow 'light' in the sky. **(Source: UFOSIS)**

UFO over Woodbridge, Suffolk

USAF Serviceman Steve La Plume was on duty at the East Gate of RAF Woodbridge, with Wendell Palmer, one evening in January 1981.

> *"We saw an object darting across the sky, continually changing course and altitude, in a series of up and down movements – almost too fast for the eye to catch – and contacted Security Control by radio, explaining what we were seeing. A short time later, Colonel Halt and General Williams arrived but, by then, there was nothing to be seen.*
>
> *After about 30 minutes, the UFO returned – now much closer, allowing us to see it was cigar-shaped, showing green, red and blue, lights on its underside. As it passed overhead, it illuminated the forest floor underneath it. What really annoyed me was that I couldn't remember what happened next. I have no memory of the object moving out of sight, or disappearing. We decided not to report the second sighting, fearing ridicule."*

Steve La Plume

(Source: Personal interview)

Landed UFO

At 7am on 21st January 1981, a farmer's wife, living at Birdfield Farm – smallholding on the South Yorkshire/ Derbyshire border, close to the B6054 road – happened to look through the window, when she saw:

> *"... something looking like a tent resting on the ground, about 8ft in height but more conical in structure, with a single apex, metallic-grey in colour. In front were three white blotches, like sacks or eggs apparently attached to it."*

At 8.30am she left to do some shopping. On her return there was nothing to be seen. She then contacted the farmer on whose land the object had been observed, and was told he had no knowledge of anything like she described on his land. Unfortunately, details of the incident were not made available for investigation until 13 months later, following a visit to the location by Richard Adams and

© R. Adams & P. Fuller

Paul Fuller. Rather surprisingly, they discovered an area, roughly 11ft by 11ft of disturbed furrowed soil, containing three depressions, approximately 4ins deep. **(Source: Paul Fuller/Jenny Randles)**

UFOs over Bath

Three days later, at 6pm on 24th January 1981, a cluster of five 'golf ball'-sized lights, forming an oblong shape, were seen moving slowly across the sky over Bathampton, near Bath, in front of a much larger object, by local antiques dealer Maureen Woodgate, who was on her way home.

According to the report, submitted on the same day to the British UFO Society, Maureen says she observed the objects for between 10 and 20 minutes.

> *"The lights/objects stopped for a few minutes before carrying on with their journey, at which point I left the scene as I needed to get petrol"*

(Source: British UFO Society)

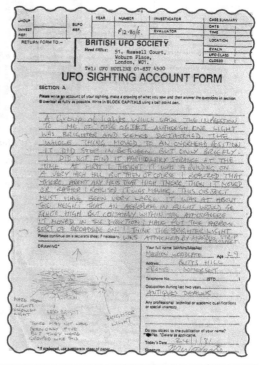

On 25th January 1981, a hovering cigar, or spindle-shaped object, was seen performing darting motions across the sky over Chatsworth, USA. It is said that numerous photographs were taken.

(Source: *The UFO Evidence,* Volume II, Section VII)

UFO over Italy

Three days later, at 5.30am, a 'disc' was sighted manoeuvring over some woods and landing behind some trees in Colle Maddalena, Italy. A burnt circle of grass and some charred tree branches were later found at the landing site. **(Source: *ITACAT,* Italian UFO Catalogue)**

FEBRUARY 1981

EX-POLICEWOMAN SIGHTS HUGE CRAFT, FOLLOWED BY PARANORMAL HAPPENINGS

Also includes – Bristol groundsman sights UFO • A Yorkshire woman describes a terrifying ordeal, involving alien abduction. *Abroad:* Humanoids seen by babysitter in USA • Pilot aboard aircraft tells of being paced by UFOs • An American woman encounters 7ft tall humanoids and alleges abduction.

UFOs over Kent

O N 13th February 1981, ex-policewoman Maureen Hall – a friend of Ronald and Margaret Fry's, and BUFORA Secretary – was driving back to Dartford, in Kent, with her husband, Michael, when they sighted strange 'lights' moving up and down in the sky.

They pulled up near to the village of Hale, close to what is now the M25 ring road, and stood watching the lights, which kept appearing over a field by the roadside. After continuing on their journey, they were surprised to see a huge dark craft hovering over a wooded area, close to the Hale roundabout, near to an underground military base.

As the object passed overhead, Maureen had a very strange sensation.

When the couple arrived home, Maureen felt as if something, or someone, was pushing her towards the kitchen sink. This was followed by the sighting of a 'man' near the doorway. When her husband went over to confront 'him', 'he' vanished.

Coincidentally, the following day, Margaret Fry was on her way home, after leaving the hairdressers at the Pantiles, Bexleyheath, at 4.45pm, in company with her husband, Ron, when she noticed what she first thought was the setting sun,

> *". . . but instead of sinking in the sky it rose up and increased in size, swirling like a Catherine wheel. I ran up Littleheath Road and saw a young man in a white sports car, on a driveway, heading off after the object – now moving towards the direction of Plumstead. Ron and I gave chase, but lost of the sight of the object."*

Close Encounter – USA

At 1.45am on 14th February 1981, a 17-year-old girl from Greensburg, PA, was baby-sitting when she spotted an object hovering at treetop level, about 50ft away.

> *"The object was silent and had three white lights, forming the point of an equilateral triangle. It appeared to be a triangular object made out of a dark coloured metal. Above one of the lights there was a large transparent window, separated by thin metallic-like partitions. A dull beam of light descended slowly from the object's base and to the ground. Inside the craft two humanoid beings could be seen. They had very large heads, oriental like eyes, gill like ears, and two holes instead of a nose. One appeared to be sitting and the other standing behind an instrument panel. The panel was white and had several black and greyish circular controls. The humanoid that was standing had a long thin neck, smooth white skin, and normal looking arms; he stared at me with pupil-less white eyes."*

The girl became spellbound and felt compelled to stare at the beings for 15 minutes. She then reluctantly went back to the living room and did not see the object depart.

(Source: HC addition # 724 Source: Bob Gribble, *Mufon Journal*)

UFOs over Bristol

At 5pm on 14th February 1981, Mr. Rodney Holbrook – employed as a groundsman, at Canford Park, Westbury-on-Trym – was in the process of finishing work, when he sighted what he thought was an air balloon, until he realised there was no basket underneath.

> *"It was a large, black, slowly revolving sphere, with a square block on top, and travelling at about 25mph over Southmead, Bristol, at a height I estimated to be 350-550ft, before it disappeared behind some trees."*

Enquiries made by the Probe UFO investigation group – Ian Mrzyglod, and his fellow members – Mike Seager and Terry Chivers – at various airports and balloon organisations, failed to identify what this object could have been … (not forgetting various shaped balloons – then used to promote certain businesses in the Bristol area, which included the British Gas flame, Robertson's 'Golly', and a giant Peanut man!) – Clearly not the answer, on this occasion. **(Source: Personal interview/*Probe*)**

© Rodney Holbrook

PROBE

M.A.U.F.O.G

UFO Research Organisation

16 Marigold Walk,
Ashton,
Bristol. BS3 2PD.

Tel, 0272 666270
646710

SR1.A. UFO SIGHTING REPORT FORM: INITIAL STAGE

Please complete this form to the best of your knowledge, and if unsure on any particular points, please state "Don't know".

WITNESS

Full name (Mr/Mrs/Miss/Ms) RODNEY FRANCIS HOLBROOK Age 32

Address 19 AMBLESIDE AVE, SOUTHMEAD, BRISTOL BS10 6HA

Current Occupation GROUNDSMAN Telephone No 508077 (STD)

LOCATION

Location of Witness CANFORD PARK, WESTBURY-ON-TRYM, BRISTOL

Day & Date of Sighting SAT. 14th FEB. 1981 Time of Initial Sighting 5 o'clock

Description of Weather Conditions COLD SUNNY CLEAR SKY AND NO WIND

THE SIGHTING

No. of Objects 1 Colour BLACK Shape SEE DRAWING

Sounds NONE Odours NONE Estimated Speed 25 MPH

Did the Object(s) appear solid? YES Apparent Size NOT SHORE

Describe the Movement of the Object(s) AT STEADY SPEED, TURNING SLOWLY AROUND

Estimated Distance ALMOST ABOVE Estimated Angle of Elevation TURNS & CHANGE

Estimated Altitude at Beginning 550 FT & at End 350 FT Brightness NONE

Direction When First Seen SOUTH Last Seen NORTH Duration of Sighting 1 MINUTE!

Attention of the Witness Drawn to the Object Because REALIZED IT WAS NOT A HOT AIR BALLOON HAS FIRST THOUGHT How Did the Sighting End? DISAPPEARD OVER TREES AND OUT OF SITE

Any Unusual Environmental Effects? No APPARENT EFFECTS

GENERAL

To Whom and When Was the Sighting Reported? To YOU ON MONDAY 16th FEB 81

Was Anyone Else Present? NO Did They See It?

Have You Had Any Previous Sightings? NO Were Any Photographs Taken? NO

DRAWING: (PLEASE MARK DIRECTION OF MOTION WITH ARROWS).
Colour if Possible.

It was round, but has it turned slowly around another part would show, as seen in drawing. the drawings may not be that good object hard to describe

what side view may have looked like

Allegation of Abduction – USA

At 2am on 15th February 1981, a girl from Franklin, Ohio was awoken after a brilliant white light filled her room.

She got out of bed and looked through the window to see a bright hovering disc-shaped object.

Under hypnosis she recalled being taken onboard by *"several seven-foot tall humanoids, with pointed chins and yellow cat like eyes"*. She was examined and was told by the aliens that they came from a planet called Antares. This is all the information we have at the present time. No doubt the reader may wish to continue their own research into the matter, bearing in mind the nature of the allegation, sadly it is becoming increasingly more difficult to track down original files as time goes by.

(Source: HC addition # 1092/ Brad Steiger, *The UFO Abductors*, Type: G)

UFO paces Airliner – February 1981

At 9.24pm on 25th February 1981, an Aeroflot YAK-40 airliner, flying north-west of Tallinn, Estonia, was paced by two orange, elongated objects. The UFOs flew parallel to the plane and then approached from 70° to the right. The crew saw four orange lights on the first object and three lights on the other one. After three minutes, the first object executed a turn to the right, then to the left. The second object repeated the manoeuvre and followed after the first, some six to eight minutes later.

(Source: Richard F. Haines, Project Delta: *A Study of Multiple UFO*)

MARCH 1981

MYSTERIOUS 'GLOBES OF FIRE' CRASH ONTO PARKED CARS, BEFORE FLYING AWAY!

Also includes – A Birmingham woman (known to the author) sights cigar-shaped object over the *Man on the Moon Public* House – was there a connection with a local Top Secret bunker nearby?

AT 7pm on 12th March 1981, a blue flashing saucer-shaped object was sighted above the horizon, at Stockton-on-Tees, by a schoolgirl.

(Source: *North East Evening Gazette* – 'Schoolgirl sees 'saucer')

Fireballs over Romsley, Worcestershire

A number of orange 'balls of fire' were seen raining down over Romsley – a small suburb, high on the hill, overlooking the Worcestershire countryside – during early March 1981. The incident caused some of the people, living nearby, to come running out of their houses and throw buckets of water over the vehicles to dowse the flames, after some of the burning objects fell onto the roofs of parked vehicles. Another witness spoke of seeing one of the flaming 'globes' heading towards the Birmingham area, at an estimated speed of 15mph. Despite fairly lengthy enquiries, we were unable to identify the amount of damage and speak to the persons concerned – not that it detracts from what appears to be a genuine but puzzling report. Were they the bi-product of some bizarre atmospheric conditions, or flaming meteorites from outer space? This was not the last time we to hear of similarly described objects, as the reader will see.

(Source: *Birmingham Evening Mail*, 14.3.81)

'Flying Saucer' over Birmingham

At 9pm on 17th March 1981, Mrs. Gillian Gilbert, living on the Redditch Road, Kings Norton, Birmingham, was waiting for her son to arrive home, after having mislaid the house keys.

"It was a cold and wet evening, with quite a wind. My son came up to me and shouted to come and have a look at something in the sky that he could see. I thought he was trying to play me up, because he had told me earlier in the week that he had seen a 'flying saucer'. I wasn't feeling in the mood for jokes but decided to humour him and glanced across the sky, when I was shocked to see this orange cigar-shaped object, slowly moving a few hundred feet above the traffic island, at the junction with Redditch Road and West Heath/Redhill Road, over the Man on the Moon *Public House. I was rooted to the spot with fear, and could only watch as it moved slowly over the roof of a nearby factory."*

The nearby factory, owned by the Central Electricity Board, rumoured locally to be the site of a *Top Secret Civil Defence bunker, was demolished in 2007, and houses built on the land.

Above: Man on the Moon pub. Below: Houses built on the site above the secret bunker and Central Electricity Board building.

*In the early 1950s, the Government planned to protect essential communications by building a series of hardened underground telephone exchanges. These were designed to protect the chain of communications, even if a Hiroshima-sized atomic bomb destroyed the city above. Due to advances in weapons, they were obsolete by the time they were complete. However, they still played an important part in national communications. There are three known exchanges, London (Kingsway), Manchester (Guardian) and Birmingham (Anchor). There are reports of a similar centre in Glasgow, although this is so far unconfirmed.

Anchor takes its name from the Birmingham Assay Office, which is above the exchange, the mark for Birmingham being an anchor. It was the largest of the three underground exchanges packed with equipment, handling 250,000 automatic calls a day. Construction of the new exchange started in 1953, with a cover story that a new underground rail network was being built. Work progressed until 1956, when the public were told the project was no longer economic; instead Birmingham got its underpasses through the city to help relieve congestion. Nobody had realised that an underground exchange and tunnel system 100ft below Newhall Street had been completed at a cost of £4m.

The construction entrance was near Moor Street Station, where a slip road in the middle of the dual carriageway took a road down into the tunnel complex to get large construction equipment into the site. Once work had finished, this entrance was sealed off and the public were able to use the slip road to reach Moor Street station on the other side of the dual carriageway. This former entrance no longer exists, following the re-development in Digbeth.

The main way into 'Anchor' was by lift at the rear of Telephone House. This was situated between Lionel Street and Fleet Street; there was a strict security check before entering the exchange. Another entrance was by a staircase across the road in Newhall Street. At the bottom of the lift there was a heavy blast door, weighing about two tonnes, which could seal the entrance to the exchange if required. There was also a large concrete block that could be used to seal the ventilation shaft. Some of the tunnels also had airtight doors for added protection.

The main exchange at Anchor was one upper level with another set of stairs going down further to the deeper level cable tunnels which lead off, unlit, into the distance. At the bottom of the lift shaft, tunnels lead off in several directions to different parts of the exchange, a left turn to the repeaters and right the auto.

The main tunnel used is about the same dimensions as the London underground, running from Anchor to Midland ATE in Hill Street, from there the tunnel continued under New Street Station and on to the exchange in Essex Street. The tunnels carried many cables supported on metal racks set into the walls. The main part of Anchor housed the generator hall, the exchange being DC powered, for safety reasons; the mains transformers and high voltage switch gear were air cooled instead of the normal oil cooling. Anchor was the first exchange in the UK to get fluorescent lighting. Electricity was supplied from its own sub station keeping the three generators for standby in case the main power was to fail. Also in the exchange was the domestic accommodation including kitchens, sleeping quarters, canteen, mess room and offices along many corridors.

Water for the complex and cooling system came from a 300ft deep artesian well. The air conditioning and cooling system was considered very important in case the tunnels were blocked, so that the air cooled equipment could remain running for long periods of time without overheating. It was the first post office installation to be fitted with air conditioning controlling temperature and humidity.

Waste water and sewage was pumped up to the street sewers above. The tunnel walls were constructed of thick concrete blast proof sections, with an anti spall mesh. This was not completely waterproof and allowed some water into the complex. At the time the main exchange was above the water table, although some of the cable tunnels needed continuous pumping to keep them dry. Today the exchange is below the water table, which has now raised 50ft, following the demise of local heavy industry and breweries that once used large quantities of water. The main serving station for all the CEGB (Central Electricity Generating Board) circuits was situated in Redhill Road, just outside Kings Norton, connecting their emergency control centre and their bunker. The bunker is situated amongst residential houses and appears to be a semi sunken structure The ventilation and ducting can be seen, but because of the large control centre all around, it is hard to tell where the bunker ends. Anchor was only once put on standby during its lifetime; this was during the Cuba crisis, in 1962. All ordinary engineers were replaced with chosen managers and no women were allowed.

(Source: Wikipedia)

Author: The view from what was the back of my house!

"Coincidently I (John) used to live at 593, Redditch Road, Kings Norton. At the rear of the garden was the perimeter wall enclosing a large factory block; the building was well illuminated but very few people were seen. Local rumours spoke of it being a Civil Defence bunker. I mentioned this building to a man whom I met, while in the Police. He was the manager of a telephone exchange at the Rotunda, in the Bull Ring, Birmingham. He told me that this building was connected to the City Centre and served as a nuclear fallout shelter for the chosen responsible few in Government, should a nuclear strike take place. There was a 'D' notice on all of this, which was removed some years ago.

Another man, known to me personally – then a regular visitor to Birmingham Library – told of being in the car park, one afternoon, when a door opened in the wall and some men came out. He was so intrigued, he waited for the right opportunity and then slipped through the door and found himself in a vast underground city, with shops and telephone boxes, with one subtle difference – there were no other people down there, apart from what appeared to be maintenance crew. At some stage he was stopped by a blacked out car and, after being unable to produce ID, was escorted back to the library entrance door, and warned of dire consequences should he come back... as for the UFO, was it attracted to the electrical energy used in the complex? Not forgetting other sightings which had taken place locally, over the years – ironically, not too far from the Man on the Moon Public House."

A short distance away, along Wast Hills Road, just off Redhill Road, Kings Norton, was the scene of another strange sighting – this time involving a Council employee, on his way to work, who was driving towards the *Man on the Moon* Public House, at 6.30am. He heard a heavy crackling noise, followed by the failure of the vehicle's electrics.

"Puzzled, I got out and opened the bonnet, trying to discover what the fault was. I happened to look upwards and see a silver, cigar-shaped object, silently moving overhead. When it had gone I tried the car, which started straightaway."

(Source: Personal interview)

APRIL 1981

BLACK TRIANGULAR OBJECT HOVERS OVER MOTORIST

Also includes – Strange light follows a Swindon woman, while on her way home
A close encounter in Lancashire, involving local youths, who came face-to-face with a
creature after a UFO is seen • A mysterious light is seen circling Bold Power Station,
Merseyside • Did a UFO collide with a Nuclear Submarine off the Solent?

Black Triangular UFO

IN the adjoining County of Worcestershire, Jane Lewis – a housewife from Redditch (previously sceptical of UFOs) – was to change her mind when driving past the ancient *Washford Mill* Public House, just off the A453 Birmingham to Alcester Road, at 11.30pm, in April 1981.

> *"I was flabbergasted to see this gigantic black triangular object, hovering a few hundred feet off the ground, showing a single fixed white light at its centre. Other car drivers had stopped to look. I have to admit it really frightened me. It's something I don't speak about with people generally, as it brings back the fear I felt at the time."*

(Source: Personal interview)

Strange 'light' over Swindon

At 8.45pm on 7th April 1981, Julie Wilson, aged 17, was walking along Mildenhall Way, Penhill, Swindon, and had just passed some flats, to her left, when she noticed a luminous green oval 'light', shining through bushes at the side of the road – so bright that she had difficulty in looking at it for any period of time.

Feeling very uneasy, she began to run along the path and had covered about 30 metres, when she glanced behind her and saw that the 'light' was now apparently much closer and larger, but still behind the bushes. Frightened, she started to run but stopped and looked behind, her curiosity overcoming her fear, when she saw, some 35 metres behind her:

> *". . . a door-shaped light, positioned just above the path, I estimated to be 4ft wide by 10ft high, showing a bright white centre with a greenish hue around the vertical edges, moving towards me at walking speed."*

Julie continued running and, at a point near the junction with Stapleford Way, she stopped to look back again, but the 'light' had gone – the whole incident being over in 30 seconds. The incident subsequently caught the attention of the SCUFORI UFO Group, who launched an investigation into the matter and considered a number of options, which included meteorological phenomena, reflections, and a helicopter.

Further enquiries made revealed that at the time of the incident, a Gazelle helicopter – equipped with a bright searchlight and showing normal navigation lights, consisting of a red light on its port, with a green light on the starboard side and a flashing red light on the tail – was flying over the general area of Penhill, although the 'helicopter' explanation was considered but not accepted unequivocally. After all, the witness never reported any down draft and only one single light. Clearly it was therefore impossible to arrive at a satisfactory conclusion for what occurred that evening.

Was there any connection with a report of supernatural apparitions being seen by a family living in Penhill Drive, Swindon, during the 1990s, who asked the Council to be re-housed? Apparently the previous occupier was a Spiritualist.

(Source: *Swindon Advertiser*, 8th April 1981/Martin Shipp, SCUFORI)

Close Encounter, Lancashire

The *Rossendale Free Press* newspaper, dated 11th April 1981, told of having been contacted by Simon Haworth (13) and Mark Ashworth (16) of New Church Bacup, Lancashire. The boys claimed that they had seen a 6ft high orange cigar-shaped object, covered with lights, hovering in the sky before dropping down behind a nearby wall. The boys looked over the wall, but there was nothing there.

They decided to make their way home but encountered a creature, described as 5ft tall, shaped like a tenpin bowling pin.

Mark said:

> *"It had no eyes, mouth or ears – only a lump, like a small swelling on one side of its head. There was a long black shiny garment hanging over the 'body' it appeared to float along."*

It was said that the boys arrived home in a terrified condition.

Some years ago we spoke to Mark, who told us he still had the 'shivers' when he thought about what they had seen. **(Source: Alan Bramhill)**

At 10.30pm on 13th April 1981, a bright orange and red object was seen in the sky over Guisborough, by local resident – Mr. Neil Swinburne of Leyland Road, Skelton, before heading into cloud making a loud rumbling noise. **(Source: *North Eastern Gazette*, 15.4.1981 – 'Did anyone see sky object?')**

UFO over Bradford, Yorkshire

At 9.40pm on 15th April 1981, Graham Townsend from Bradford, Yorkshire, was walking past Idle Cricket Ground with his friend, Andrew Swift, when they saw a bright yellow 'globe' in the sky,

> *". . . moving from side-to-side in one continual movement across the sky, at a height of about*

1,000ft; around the 'globe' could be seen spiky points of light, flashing on and off – then it shot across the sky so fast that the eye could hardly register, before halting in mid-air – now seen as globe-like in appearance – before being lost from view ."

Following publicity in the local newspaper, Graham was contacted by Mr. and Mrs. Yeatman from Thorpe Edge, Idle.

They told him of having seen a yellow *'ball of fire'* in the sky that they took to be a helicopter or aircraft, with a light fitted underneath but realised this was not the explanation.

According to Graham, a number of UFOs were reported over St. Helens, in Lancashire, the next day.

Warminster Sky Watch

In the same month Probe Group publicity Officer Terry Chivers had occasion to write to the editor of the *Wiltshire Times* in response to a letter published by the newspaper from UFO Researcher Ken Rogers who suggested an official sky watch point should be sited outside Warminster. Mr Chivers also described the UFO scene as being "virtually dead," fortunately we are pleased to say that while the area in longer

```
                                                              17/4/81.
The Editor,
Wiltshire Times,
15 Duke Street,
Trowbridge,
Wiltshire. BA14 8EF.


                    FOR PUBLICATION


Dear Editor,

I am writing in response to Mr. Ken Rogers' letter which you printed last week regarding
the setting up of an official skywatch point for UFO-spotting. His arguments for such
a point were that the farmers at Cradle and Starr Hills, Warminster, have been troubled
by thousands of people in the past by skywatchers from all over the world and it is now
time to watch from somewhere else.

The reason that I am writing is that the farmers only had to put up with crowds years
ago, and that today, Cradle Hill is deserted save for a few people on an occassional
Saturday night, and Starr Hill has been 'off-limits' to skywatchers for the last five
or so years ever since the hay barn was set alight by vandals.

In our opinion, the UFO scene is virtually dead as far as Warminster in concerned; you
only have to speak to the majority of the locals to find that out, and the farmers only
have to suffer when people try and revive the 'old days' by publicising 'skywatch pants'
to attempt to attract visitors to the town.

If left alone, the hills will gradually become deserted more often until the UFO era
is eventually forgotten and the farmers will be troubled no more. So don't put the cat
among the pidgeons Mr. Rogers and cause unnecessary problems for the farmers by trying
to create UFOs as a tourist attraction for Warminster. As Mr. Rogers said in his letter,
it was 16 years ago when UFOs were seen over the town..... not today.

Yours sincerely,



Terry P. Chivers
Publicity Officer           PROBE,
                            8 Eden Grove,
                            Whitley,
                            Melksham,
                            Wiltshire.
```

thronged with sky watchers, thanks to people like Kevin Goodman sky watches are still being arranged annually. We are delighted to learn that Terry made his own visit to this locality to meet up with the former head of Probe – Ian Mrzyglod.

UFO over Bold Power Station, Merseyside

On 16th April 1981, Beryl Jones – a resident of a first floor flat at Mount Pleasant Avenue, Parr Street, overlooking Bold Power Station, St. Helens, Merseyside – noticed a strange *'light'* flying around the Power Station, at 8.50pm, and brought it to the attention of her boyfriend – Alan Thomas, who suggested it was probably an aircraft, although he was curious as to why it was only showing one light.

A short time later, the blue/green *'light'* started to move eastwards, towards Sherdley Park. In doing so it appeared to change shape from *'globe'* to *'cigar'* – now radiating outwards, with all the colours of the rainbow.

As a result of the incident being brought to the attention of Brian Fishwicke – a UFO Investigator for MIGAP, he made

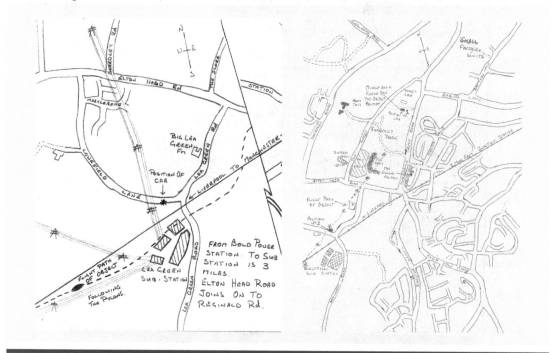

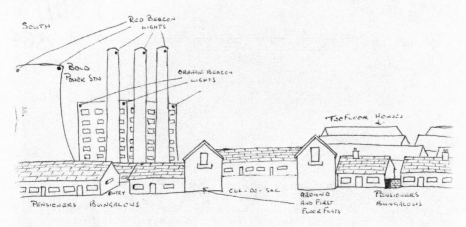

VIEW FROM BERYL JONES LIVING ROOM WINDOW

On Thursday (16/4/81) evening a large Cigar Shaped object was seen near Bold Power Station. A Miss Beryl Jones had seen the object, she rang MIGAP member Bill Alcock (he use to be a neighbour of Miss Jones) as she was talking to Bill, she said that she could still see the object. Bill then rang me and told me what had been said, he asked me if I could see the power station and the object. I went outside to have a look, but I couldn't see either, I got back to Bill and told him that I couldn't but that I would give my brother a ring, who lives a mile away from the power station.

I rang him and asked him to go outside and look towards the power station to see if he could see something unusual. After a while, my brother came back to the phone, he said that he could see an object coming from the station and heading towards Sherdley Park in an easterly direction. I rang Bill and tolf him that my brother had seen the object and now it had moved off towards Sherdley Park. Bill said that he would ring MIGAP member Bob Ellaby, he lives opposite the park, he said that he would get back to me. At this point, I rang Beryl Jones to see if she could still see the object. She said that the object had moved towards Sherdley Park.

My neighbour from across the road had just pulled up, I went out to tell him about the sighting, he said that he would take me to the park to see the object. I told him that I was waiting for a phone call and that if the offer still stood, that I would go with him after. The phone rang, it was Bill, he said that Bob wasn't in, but his wife Jean had gone out and seen the object over the park. I told him that I would be going to the park to see if I could see the object. John and I went to the park, it is roughley four miles away, we arrived at the park around 2130hrs. We parked the car on the target golf car park, we could see the object just above the height of the trees opposite. It was moving away from us in a south westerly direction, after about five minutes, the object had gone out of sight behind the trees. We decided to move to another location to see if we could still see it.

We headed out towards Lea Green, this is a fairly high spot and this would give us a clear view of the object. As we got to Lea Green, we could see the object in the far distance, it seemed to be following the power pylons in a south westerly direction. If the object had continued on its course, it would have took it over to Cohnar's Quay.

16/4/81
564

<u>Interview with Miss Beryl Jones</u>
<u>Thursday 23rd April 1981</u>
<u>0245hrs.</u>

I had arranged to go and see Beryl four days earlier, but I couldn't keep
the appointment, so we arranged it for the 23/4/81.   I arrived at her
flat at 0240hrs, she invited me in an apologised for having the ironing
out, she said that I was a little early.   While she was clearing away, I
decided to make a couple of sketches of the area looking out of her living
room window.   Being on the first floor, she has a good clear view of the
power station, I also took some compass readings, eventually she had finished
clearing the ironing.   She made us a cup of coffee then we got on with the
interview.

<u>The Interview.</u>   "On Thursday evening, 16th April.   I was lying on the
settee watching television, the reason I was lying down was
because a couple of days previous I had hurt my back and
the doctor told me to take it easy.

"My boy friend Alan was with me, as I was lying there, I
saw through the window a bright light over towards the power
station, I don't draw the curtains because no one can see
into the flat.   Anyway, the light seemed to be flying around
the power station, I looked at the clock, the time was 2055hrs,
I asked Alan to look towards the power station and asked him
if he could see something.   He said do you mean that plane
that is circling around the power station.   I then said that
was a funny looking plane with only one light visible.
Anyway, we continued to watch it, after a while I thought I
would give one of my ex-neighbours a ring, (Bob Ellaby) I
knew he had something to do with a UFO group.   His wife Jean
answered the phone and said that Bob was out, but she gave
me Billy Alcocks number, he too use to live near me. I gave
him a ring and told him what I had seen.   I put the phone
down and we both continued to watch the object.

"After a while the object started going towards Sherdley Park,
(east).   Then you rang asking me what the object was doing
and I told you that it had just gone to the park.   As the
object was moving away, it seemed to change shape.   It resembled a cigar and it also began to change colour from a bluey
green to all the colours of the rainbow.   We had been watching
the object for roughley ¼ to 1 hour before it went out of
view.   The night sky was full of stars and very clear.
You will see on the sighting form that I ticked off: The object
changed brightness, Flickered, Throbbed and started to pulsate.

"Then it moved off towards the park, where we lost sight of it.

"I have never had any psychic experiences. I don't like to mention this, but Alan said that after the sighting that I had began to talk in my sleep, you see, Alan lives with me. He siad that I was saying that it is all silver."

I asked her what she had been dreaming about, she went on to say that, she was standing by the side of a field, then suddenly she could see a kind of a silver substance coming over the grass, she said that it resembled Mercury. The silver stuff was coming toward sher and that it started going over the fence surrounding the field, it was at this point that she woke up. That is the only weird experience that she had had since the sighting.

Since the Thursday evening sighting, she said that she had seen the object on the following Friday night 17/4/81 and the Saturday night 18/4/81, over the Easter holidays, but since that week-end, she has never seen it since.

On the Saturday evening 18/4/81, I was on night duty at the Fire Station and around 2100hrs, I received a phone call from my neighbour, John. He said that he was out at the front of his house with his car and that he had seen the object again, he said that it was travelling in a westerly dire ction.

After arriving back to Miss Jones' flat, after a social evening, Miss Jones pointed out an object in the sky. It appeared to change colours as we watched it. Once inside the flat we again noticed that the object was still there and that its colour continued to change from red to blue to yellow. We watched it for some more time before it faded from view.

use an additional piece of paper if space is insufficient.

2. Draw a picture of object seen.	3. Name. T.M. STANTON
	Address. TORTWOOD GDNS. RAINHILL STOERS, RAINHILL, PRESCOT.
	Tel No. O51- 2b
(circle)	4. Occupation.
But this kept changing colour.	Assistant Laboratory technician
	5. When did you see the object. 19th April 1981
	6. What time was it when you saw the object. appox 11 O'clock

I WAS SITTING ON THE COUCH WHEN BERYL ASKED ME TO LOOK OUT OF THE WINDOW AT, WHAT AT FIRST SIGHT, LOOKED LIKE A STAR, LOOKING AT IT MORE CLOSELY, IT APPEARED TO MOVE SLIGHTLY, UP AND DOWN, AND SIDE TO SIDE, AS WELL AS CHANGING COLOURS AT RANDOM. IT STAYED IN THE SAME PLACE FOR APPROXIMATELY 45 mins AND THEN DIMINISHED VERY QUICKLY.

NB SINCE THIS SIGHTING THERE HAVE BEEN SEVERAL OTHERS, FROM THE SAME PLACE, AND IN THE SAME DIRECTION GENERALLY.

use an additional piece of paper if space is insufficient.

2. Draw a picture of object seen.	3. Name. A. THOMAS
	Address. , MOUNT PLEASANT AVE, PARR, ST. HELENS
(circle)	Tel. No. 242
	4. Occupation. TECHNICIAN
	5. When did you see the object. 18TH. APRIL 81,
	6. What time was it when you saw the object

his way to the park, arriving there at 9.30pm, accompanied by an ex-neighbour of Beryl's, who had been the one to contact him.

> *"We parked the car on the Target Golf Car Park and could see the object just above the height of the trees opposite, moving away from us in a south-westerly direction, before it was lost from sight behind our line of vision.*
>
> *We headed out towards Lea Green – a fairly high spot, where we stood and watched the object – now in the far distance, apparently following the electricity pylons, towards the south-west."*

The following day, Brian contacted the Power Station and confirmed the helicopter used by them was not flying that night. On 18th April 1981, Brian was on night duty at the Fire Station, when he received a telephone call to say that the UFO had been seen at 9pm, heading in a westerly direction across the sky. Further conversation revealed that a bright yellow and orange colour object was seen hovering under cloud above Skelton, before shooting away into the cloud, making a rumbling noise. According to another witness, the object was seen apparently following the pylon cables between Skelton Green and over the Leyland Estate.

(Source: *North Eastern Gazette*, 20.4.1981)

Did a UFO collide with Nuclear Submarine?

Bill Jordan wrote to us about what he witnessed, which happened around the time he read about a collision at sea, off The Solent, involving a Nuclear powered submarine, after a blue light was seen under the water. Unfortunately, we were unable to identify when and where this happened, but he believes it took place in early 1981.

> *"I am still baffled by what I witnessed; I know it took place at around the same time as the collision at sea, when the conning tower was found to be damaged. I'm not saying there is any connection with UFOs, but I do know that there were lots of reports of strange lights seen over Swannage and the Isle of Wight. I was outside the house, one afternoon, when I happened to look upwards and see what looked like a huge lump of concrete descending towards me. I was so frightened I thought it was going to crash into the house and kill me. I crouched down, fearing the worst – nothing. I gingerly got to my feet and looked up, seeing it motionless in the sky, a couple of hundred feet above my head, resting on what appeared to be some kind of white steam – then, like a bullet, it went off across the sky. A few days later, when I had recovered my composure, I wrote to a UFO Group, in London, enclosing an illustration of the object. They wrote back, offering me a T-shirt for two pounds fifty. I didn't bother after that – until now."*

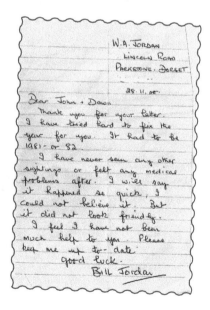

Formation of UFOs over Lincolnshire

At 10.50pm on 22nd April 1981, a keen astronomer from Ashby, Scunthorpe, was viewing the night sky through a pair of 16 x 50 binoculars, when he saw six small UFOs, with a larger red light beneath them, creating a triangular formation, travelling horizontally across the sky.

MAY 1981

UFO SEEN OVER HANTS BY GLIDER PILOT

Also includes – UFO seen over Hampshire • UFO sighted by Russian Astronaut
Fin-shaped UFO over farmer's field, Worcestershire • Peculiar marks found in the
ground near Ipswich, Suffolk, by groundsman • Wigan couple sight strange black
craft while out driving • Falls of coins at a church in Reddish, Manchester

UFO over Hampshire – May 1981

AT 3.15pm on 2nd May 1981, Mr. R. Whittaker of Church Crookham, Aldershot, Hampshire, was flying in a glider, approximately two miles south-west of Lasham Airfield, at a height of 2,500ft, when he noticed a silver coloured object in the sky, moving towards him.

"It looked like a car hubcap. As it passed me, I wondered if it was a balloon and decided to follow it and make sure it was just that. As I approached the object it started to turn to my right and I saw it side-on, now shaped like a rugby ball. After making one turn in a clockwise direction, the object moved away, southwards, and was soon lost from view. I still thought it might have been a balloon, but couldn't understand why it had turned around me when I followed it."

(Source: *FSR*, Volume 27, No.1)

UFO sighted by Russian astronaut

On 5th May 1981, while aboard the Salyut-6 Space Station, Cosmonaut Major General Vladimir Kovalyonok, had an encounter during the Mission.

In an interview conducted with Michael Hesemann, at the International UFO Congress, in 2002, Vladimir said:

"Many cosmonauts have seen phenomena which are far beyond the experiences of earthmen. For ten years I never spoke on such things. The encounter you asked me about happened on May 5, 1981, at about 6pm, during the mission. At that time we were over the area of South

Africa, moving towards the area of the Indian Ocean. I just made some gymnastic exercises, when I saw in front of me, through a porthole, an object which I could not explain. It is impossible to determine distances in space.

A small object can appear large and far away and the other way around. Sometimes a cloud of dust appears like a large object. Anyway, I saw this object and then something happened I could not explain – something impossible, according to the laws of physics. The object had this shape, elliptical, and flew with us. From a frontal view it looked like it would rotate in flight direction.

I called my partner Viktor Savinykh to take a look at the unidentified object in space. It was hard to determine the size and the speed of an object in space. That is why I cannot say exactly, which size it actually was. Savinykh prepared to take a picture of it. It only flew straight, but then a kind of explosion happened, very beautiful to watch, of golden light. This was the first part. Then, one or two seconds later, a second explosion followed somewhere else and two spheres appeared, golden and very beautiful. After this explosion I just saw white smoke, then a cloud-like sphere. Before we entered the darkness, we flew through the terminator, the twilight-zone between day and night. We flew eastwards, and when we entered the darkness of the Earth shadow, I could not see them any longer. The two spheres never returned. It was reminiscent of a dumb-bell. I reported about it to the Mission Control immediately."

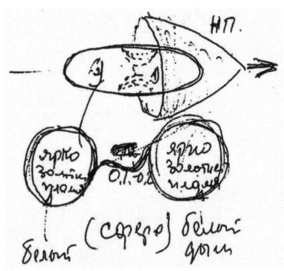

Cosmonaut Major General Vladimir Kovalyonok and diagram of the object he saw in space

Essex Constabulary – Force order on reporting of UFOs

On 6th May 1981, PC 417 B. Cordroy from the Essex Constabulary contacted UFO Investigator – Bill Eden, of the Essex UFO Group to tell him:

> *"I was on duty in Cow Lane, Great Chesterford, Essex, carrying out a check of unoccupied property, at 10pm, when I noticed a 'bright light', 45° off the horizon – completely motionless in the sky. I decided to investigate further and followed the object – now moving and pear-shaped, with its widest part facing the horizon – along the B184 road. It then dropped slightly and changed to a horizontal slither of light, giving off a yellowish glow."*

The officer showed Bill a copy of the report, preceded by the caption: '**In response to Force Order of 13th February 1978, AWC Ops'** which were, instructions issued to police officers on the reporting of UFOs.

(Source: Dan Goring, *Earth-link*)

UFO over Wolverhampton

According to MOD declassified reports (in 2009) during 1981, a policeman reported something odd hovering above Wolverhampton's New Cross Hospital, described as:

> *". . . about two feet long and 18 inches wide', and '. . . like an inverted meat dish, flying through the air, with an 18-inch arm descending underneath."*

UFO over farmers field, Bromsgrove

On 9th May 1981, Mr. Woodford from Dodford, near Bromsgrove, Worcestershire, was looking out of the bedroom window, overlooking fields at the rear of his house, at 9am, when he saw what he took to be a white goose above the winter barley, about 200ft away. Puzzled, he picked up a pair of binoculars and then shouted out for his wife to come and have a look. Mrs. Woodford looked through the lens and saw:

". . . a bright pear-shaped object, about 3-4ft across, hovering just above the crop, with what looked like a fin projecting out of its base."

The couple watched as it slowly moved upwards, towards the East, reaching a height of 60ft off the ground, and after completing a circle, dropped downwards, once again, hovering a little higher above the crop than before – almost as if it was actually going to land. Instead, it rose upwards over a 4ft fence, with great precision, as if under control.

Mr. Woodford rushed out of the house and gave chase in his Land Rover, while Mrs. Woodford dialled 999 for the Police, who arrived a short time later, and took some details from them.

"We later received a reply from the MOD, who said that they were unable to offer any explanation. In a way, I'm glad my husband didn't catch up with it, as I was concerned about his personal safety."

(Source: Personal interview/Crystal Hogben)

UFOs seen over Cornwall

At 1am on 11th May 1981, Nursery school supervisor – Sandy Tsan from Penzance, in Cornwall – was at her home address, during the late evening, when she noticed a bright 'globe of light', motionless in the night sky. A few minutes later three other identical objects appeared, forming a straight line.

Mrs. Tsan, who admitted to having been shaken by the experience, watched them for about 25mins – until they faded away.   (**Source:** *Earth-link*)

Strange lights over Wiltshire – strange marks found in field

At 1am on 11th May 1981, Mrs. Scott (58) from Edencroft, Haresfield, Highworth, near Swindon, Wiltshire, happened to glance out of the bedroom window, when she saw:

> *". . . a yellow light, shaped like half a plane, moving across the sky in a northerly direction; a few seconds late, it was out of view."*

Immediately afterwards she noticed three petal-shaped lights, each of which consisted of four separate lights, in a field about a quarter of a mile away, completely stationary. This was followed by what looked like a searchlight, which seemed to be moving between the lights. About 6-7 minutes later, they disappeared from view. Mrs. Scott then went back to bed.

Mrs. Scott contacted Terry Amey – who was a member of the Swindon-based UFO group (SCUFORI) – on 12th May, and told him what she had seen. He then contacted a colleague – Martin Shipp – and the two men made their way to the site, after having contacted the landowner for permission. They discovered several strange marks in the field (which normally contains a herd of cows) where the lights had been seen.

Polaroid photos were taken of the scene, after discounting that poachers were responsible. However, enquiries made with another farmer revealed that he and his farmhands were out rounding up cows, using a Land Rover with a damaged front wing, at the time when the sighting took place. This excellent piece of detective work, conducted by the two men, identified correctly the cause of a sighting that might well have been blown out of all proportion by the media, with allegations of aliens landing and abductions of livestock.

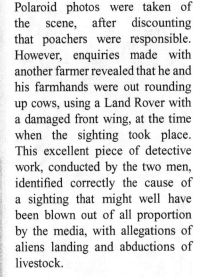

the light took about three seconds to travel an angular span of 90°, which is rather fast for any aircraft!

It was first thought that an aircraft was indeed responsible for this part of the sighting, as it is in the direction of the approach route for aircraft landing at RAF Brize Norton. However, a much more likely explanation comes not from the air but from the ground. As already stated, a landrover was being used to round up a herd of cows. This landrover is only driven on private land, and therefore does not have to comply with MOT regulations. The front headlight on the passenger side is totally out of line due to collision damage. In fact, it points up into the air at an angle of about 30°. It is believed that the witness saw the light beam from this misaligned headlight sweep across the electrical wires which run parallel to her window 150 metres away, as the vehicle turned around. These wires, although slightly lower than the light was reported to have been seen, travel in the same direction. Another point to note is that the landrover was to the right of the witness, with the wires to the left of it, and so the headlight would move across the wires from right to left, much as the witness described.

Strange marks found in field – Ipswich, Suffolk

Two days later, on 13th May 1981, Ipswich grounds man – Peter Parish – was out patrolling at Foxhall, Ipswich, at lunchtime, when he came across a number of strange depressions in the ground, consisting of:

> *". . . a cross, cut into the sandy ground, measuring 18ins in diameter and a few inches deep, with 8 small circular holes, 2-6ins in diameter. In addition to this was the extraordinary discovery of a series of spiralling grooves around the sides of nearby ferns, closest to the holes, creating an impression that whatever had been used to extract the soil from the holes had caught the sides of the stems in its operation."*

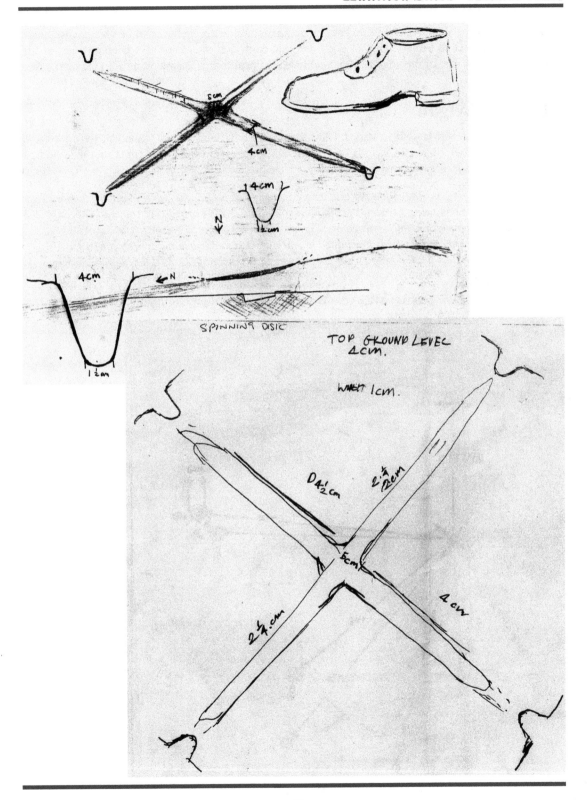

During a visit to the area, over 20 years later, in company with Peter, believed to be an ancient mound, similar in appearance to Silbury, Hill, in Wiltshire, (although this would not have been obvious, at first glance, as the south side of the ridge had been removed by local farmers, some years ago) the marks were still there.

UFO over Wigan

Five days later, on 18th May 1981, Miss J. Clayton and her boyfriend, Kevin Campbell, were travelling along Simms Road, Billinge Hill, Wigan, at 2.30am, when they noticed a bright 'light' in the sky, larger than any star. Curious, they stopped the car.

> *"At first it was moving sideways and then started to descend, the white light becoming brighter – now showing a variety of colours surrounding it. My boyfriend got out and I began to feel frightened, thinking it was going to crash. Kevin asked me to get out of the car. When I did, the 'light' moved upwards and halted in mid-air, for about two minutes. We heard a quiet engine noise start up, followed by the appearance of two headlights. As it flew overhead, we were able to see it clearly. It looked like a black plane."*

(Source: MIGAP – Merseyside Investigation Group into Aerial Phenomena)

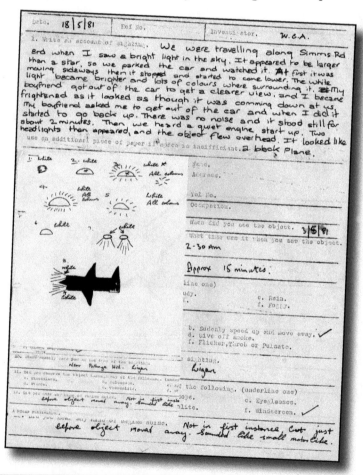

UFOs - A LOAD OF BALONEY? by Lionel Beer

When I took part in a 'phone-in' programme on LBC (London Broadcasting Company) on 19th May, 1981, one caller dogmatically informed us that UFOs were a "load of baloney" and couldn't possibly be visitors from outer space. He implied that anyone who 'believed' in them needed their head examined. Well I am not in the believing business, but I do regard UFOs as a subject worthy of serious scientific study. Millions of people the world over have reported strange objects or lights that they were unable to identify, and ufologists are interested in determining the cause of all these reports. Perhaps our LBC caller would maintain that life-peer Lord Kings Norton, an engineer and scientist with a long association with terrestrial flying machines and a distinguished public service career, needs his head examined? Kings Norton, although adopting a sceptical approach to UFOs is nonetheless President of the British UFO Research Association (BUFORA). He is a prominent member of the 'House of Lords All-Party UFO Study Group', which is open to MPs (Patrick Wall MP is a regular attender). The 'Lords Group' was formed following a three-hour debate on UFOs in the Chamber on 18th January 1979, initiated by the Earl of Clancarty. Clancarty, BUFORA Vice-President and founder of an international UFO group called 'Contact', has written five popular UFO books under his other name of Brinsley Le Poer Trench. Even Woolworths sell them! The 'Lords Group' has held frequent meetings with speakers from the USA, Canada, Denmark, Spain and Italy. In May 1981, Fred Hoyle, distinguished astronomer and author of sci-fi stories like 'A for Andromeda', addressed their Lordships. The Duke of Edinburgh is known to have had a passing interest in UFOs for many years and recently expressed interest in attending a meeting at the House of Lords. Lord Clancarty commented: "It has given the subject a marvellous Fillip!"

Both their Lordships along with several hundred ufologists attended the 2nd London International UFO Congress at the Mount Royal Hotel, Marble Arch over the Spring 1981 Bank Holiday, a premier event in the UFO buffs' diary. Delegates came from Reykjavik, Toronto, Washington, etc., and a Soviet Air Attache was also said to have been present! Dr. Bruce Maccabee, an optical physicist from the USA whose work for the US Navy is classified, outlined new information gleaned from the American intelligence agencies (FBI, CIA etc). There have been some startling attempts by the US Air Force in years past to track and detain UFOs, not to mention landing cases. What information there is has been prised out of the authorities using the full weight of the Freedom of Information Act. Pressure groups argue that we badly need a FOI Act in the U.K. but both Tory and Labour governments have been patronisingly obstructive.

There are rumours that a UFO and its small dead 'humanoid' occupants crashed near the Roswell Air Force Base in New Mexico in 1947. After being held at other bases, it is suggested that the 'remains' are now housed at the McDill A.F.B. in Florida, or at the CIA compound at Langley Field, Virginia.

Radio phone-in on the UFO subject

Another item of UFO Memorabilia is presented from the archives of BUFORA President Lionel Beer, who took part in a radio phone-in for the London Broadcasting Company on the 26th of May 1981.

Lionel Beer, seen here with 'Haunted Skies' co-author Dawn Holloway

Apports at Reddish, Greater Manchester

Apports can include all manner of earthly objects descending to the ground. We have already discussed our own experiences in Rendlesham Forest, involving the fall of single stones, in Volume 8 of *Haunted Skies,* and the much larger stones, which fell through the sky over Thornton Road, Washwood Heath, in Birmingham.

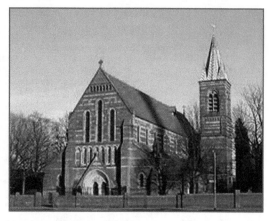

On the morning of 28th May 1981, a young girl claimed that she had been walking through the churchyard of St. Elizabeth's Church, Reddish, situated between Manchester and Stockport, when a 50 pence piece fell from the sky in front of her.

As a result of this, presumably she told other children who made their way to the Church, where they recovered (it is said) many pounds worth of change. The owner of the local sweet shop, who no doubt became suspicious about the increase of sales at his shop, contacted Reverend Graham Marshall at the Church, wondering if the poor box had been broken into.

Reverend Marshall had a look around the churchyard and recovered money to the value of over a pound – which may not sound a lot now, but was considerable in those days.

Dan Goring, of *Earth-Link,* contacted the Reverend and spoke to him about the matter.

> *"He confirmed all of the details and said that during his talks with some of the children, they told him they would hear a 'tinkling' sound, followed by the discovery of a coin on the ground. Only in one case did a girl claim she had seen one falling."*

Reverend Marshall said:

> *"It's been quite an attraction for them with up to ten or a dozen coins falling at a time I reckon the local children probably had the richer pickings before me. Some of the children told me the coins were found embedded in the ground by their edges, I'm don't think the coins fell from a great height, because the children heard a tinkling noise when they fell"*

One explanation which was quickly discounted suggested the coins might have fallen from a magpie's nest or dropped by a bird flying overhead.

In April 2013 we e-mailed Angie the current Reverend at St Elizabeth's hoping that she might have had a photograph of the Reverend Marshall but she was unable to help or prepared to comment on the matter.

St. Elizabeth's Church was used as a set for the wedding of Ashley Peacock and Maxine Heavey in the TV soap *Coronation Street*. The Church also featured as the setting for the BBC children's drama *Clay* broadcast on CBBC. Extensive modifications to the vestry and interior of the Church were required to change it into a Catholic Church set in 1960's Tyneside.

(Source: Personal interview by Dan Goring/*Stockport Express*, 4.6.1981/Wikipedia 2013)

Coins and Stones thrown

On March 24, 1963 at Brooklyn, Wellington, New Zealand, 1963 a guest house was inexplicably battered by a hail of stones and a few coins. Police were called and unsuccessfully searched for the perpetrator of the assault, which lasted for seven hours. Windows were smashed and people were struck, but none injured. The coins included New Zealand pennies and a large copper coin. The mysterious attack occurred again for two more nights, and then stopped.

Many people will have heard of angel hair, which is believed to be a by product of a UFO sighting, but how many people will be aware that even in the mid 20th Century, the following items were recorded as falling to earth, by Charles Fort – alabaster, algae, animal matter, anthracite, ants, arrows, ash, asbestos, axes, basalt, beef, birds, blood, blood like rain, blue ice, bricks, buss substance, charcoal, cinders clinkers, coal, coffee beans, coke, coloured hail, disks, earthy matter, edible substance, eels, fish, flesh, fibres, fireballs, flakes, flint objects, foul jelly, frogs, fungus, gelatinous jelly, glutinous drops, grey powder, green stones, hair, hay, high grade steel, ice large, jelly fish, larvae, lichen, lizards, lung tissue, metal objects, metals, mud, nickel, nitric acid, oil, organic matter, paper, perfumed matter, pink substance, receptacles, seeds, shells, silk, snails slag, snakes, soot, spiders, stones starch, steel, sulphur, turpentine, turtles, unknown metals, vegetable matter, wood, worms.

One would probably accept that some of the items named may well have been swept up into the sky by severe weather conditions but objects of weight such as coins and stones seem unlikely especially in calm and tranquil conditions.

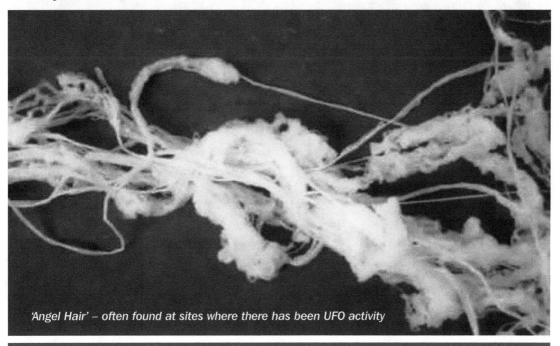

'Angel Hair' – often found at sites where there has been UFO activity

JUNE 1981

MYSTERIOUS FALLS OF STONES

Includes – Investigation into Thornton Road, Birmingham, by police – householders
terrified over two year period • Witchcraft at Hopwas Wood, Tamworth?
Also includes – Triangular UFO, seen over Smethwick
Truck lifted off the ground by UFO in USA

Falls of stones

REPORTED incidents involving the falls of stones and other items go back centuries. In the absence of any rational explanation, they are often explained away as the result of poltergeist activity. They have been reported as appearing out of nowhere to strike the outside of houses, or falling inside sealed rooms. Another line of thought is that poltergeist activity interferes with the brain's electromagnetic energy, subconsciously causing the person to lift up inanimate objects, such as coins, or stones, without them even knowing.

Incidents relating to complaints of spontaneous materialisation of objects, however bizarre and unlikely they first appear, is impossible to believe unless you, yourself, experience the disquieting thud, as a warm stone falls inexplicably onto the ground in front of you, wielded by an invisible person, or agency as we can testify personally .

Prior to outlining events which involved the considerable resources of the West Midlands Police over a two year period in an unsuccessful bid to catch the offenders, it may be of some importance to briefly look back through history at other incidents involving the inexplicable movements of stones.

1841 – *The London Times*, 16th September

The Newspaper described complaints of windows being broken by an 'unseen agent' at the detached home of Mrs. Charton – resident of Sutton Courthouse, Sutton Lane, Chiswick. Two Police Constables, assisted by members of the public, carried out surveillance to catch the persons responsible, but were unsuccessful in preventing windows from being broken at the front and back of the house, which was surrounded by high walls.

1843 – *The Times*, 18ᵗʰ January

At Livet, in France, two girls were out picking up leaves when stones of different colours showered down on them slowly and harmlessly. It is said that their parents arrived and also witnessed the same phenomena. Priests and doctors were called and were gently 'stoned'; this only took place at one spot, and only when the girls were there. A few days later, it stopped. **(Source: *The Book of the Dammed*, Charles Fort)**

1887 – At Appleby, Westmorland

A large, round, wet pebble from a nearby stream crashed through the window of the Mill House, Appleby, Westmorland. This was followed by a number of other stones, which caused extensive damage to fittings and furniture. **(Source: *Poltergeist Over Britain*, Harry Price)**

1925 – Rumania

Rumanian peasant girl Eleanor Zugun (12) was plagued by falling stones. It became so bad that her parents even sent her to a mental home. The stones, which were being moved from a nearby brook, crashed through the window. A priest, who was called, marked the stones with a cross and threw them back outside. However, they were thrown back again with even more ferocity.

(Source: *Phenomena: A Book Of Wonders* – John Michell, Robert J.M. Rickard)

1928 – Sumatra

The renowned paranormal investigator – Ivan T. Sanderson – told of an incident in Sumatra, in 1928, which happened while sitting on the veranda of an estate house as a guest, one evening. A shiny black pebble dropped onto the veranda out of nowhere. Dozens more followed. Sanderson, who was familiar with the phenomenon, tried an experiment. He had the stones gathered up and marked with chalk, paint, or whatever else could be used. The stones were then thrown back out randomly into the garden and shrubbery. *"We must have thrown over a dozen such marked stones; within a minute they were all back! Nobody, with a powerful flashlight or super-eyesight, could have found those little stones in that tangled mess . . . and thrown them back onto the veranda. Yet, they came back, all duly marked by us!*

1943 – Oakland, California

In August of that year Mrs. Irene Fellows finally called the police, after two weeks of stones pelting her house at various times of the day. At first sceptical, the police inquiry became serious when their investigation clearly identified the pockmarks of the falling stones on Mrs. Fellows' roof and walls, and by the litter of stones on her lawn. Mrs. Fellows and members of her family were frequently hit by the stones, although to no serious injury. The thorough police investigation could offer no explanation for the stones, which seemed to materialise out of nothingness. **(Source: WWW.2013)**

1944 – *London Sunday Pictorial*, 9ᵗʰ October:
'Bulldozer Frees poltergeists'

A bulldozer belonging to the US Army was used to widen a road in Great Leighs, Essex, leading to Boreham Airbase, in order that military vehicles could use the road; a large stone, which local myths believed was pinning down the spirit of a local witch, known as the Witch of Scrapefaggot Green, was moved out of the way in Drachett Lane. This was followed by a number or mysterious events, which included sheep found outside their still secure pens (with no visible means of how this had happened). A builder found his scaffold poles spread all over his yard. Decorators found their heavy paint pots and tools missing, when they turned up for work at a cottage. (The paint pots were later found under a bed in the attic) The *church bells rang of their own accord, at midnight, and the church clock was found to be two hours slow.

Cows stopped giving milk, chickens stopped laying eggs and three geese disappeared without a trace. A chicken that belonged to no one was found dead in a water barrel. Daily the turmoil grew, until a reporter for the *Sunday Pictorial* arrived on the scene and witnessed one event himself. At the village tavern, the *Dog and Gun*, a large stone turned up on the doorstep. The landlord – Bill Reynolds – said he had not seen it before and did not know where it had come from. After he and the reporter struggled to move it out of the way, he stated it would take at least three strong men to lift it.

Harry Price, of the London University Council for Psychical Investigation, was called in and he suggested the stone be put back, which it was, at midnight on 11th October 1944. This stopped the manifestations from occurring, with one last exception – a woman, who kept rabbits, found they had been placed into a chicken coup.

Records show details of an alleged [our word] witch, from Great Leighs, by the name of Ann Hewghes, who was brought to trial at Chelmsford Assizes, in 1621, for the murder of her husband and various misdemeanors, performed on the nights of the witches Sabbath. Ann was found guilty and condemned to death at the stake. She was then buried at the same location and covered by a stone to keep her down. As crossroads were traditionally the burial places of witches. Bones and ashes were said to have been found beneath the stone at Scrapefaggots Green – an old Essex name for a witch, modern accounts spell this as Scrapfaggot Green. **(Source: WWW Internet 2013)**

1973 – Skaneateles, New York

Most often, a particular house is the target for this phenomenon, but in this highly unusual case, two fishermen became the victims of the falling stones – a paranormal storm that followed wherever they went! The rain of pebbles began as they were finishing their fishing expedition and followed them as they made their way to their car. The shower ceased for a while, then resumed when they stopped briefly on their way home. Deciding they needed a drink, they went to a bar, and when they came out some time later, the rain of pebbles began again. As they were about to go their separate ways in their hometown of Liverpool (about 25 miles north-east of Skaneateles), the little stones dropped on them one last time. **(Source: WWW.2013)**

1975 – *London Sunday Express*, 4th May: Who built thousands of piles of stones in a Cotswold field?

Just as strange and perhaps even more bizarre was the discovery of thousands of small piles of stones, found on a barley field belonging to Farmer Mr. Peter Lipiatt of Widden Hill Farm, Chipping Sodbury, in Gloucestershire. It was estimated that the work involved would have taken people a lifetime to build.

---

*2012 At Exhall, in Warwickshire, the Church clock was stripped down for cleaning. At a given time, the clock continued to strike the hour, which is impossible – no wonder the man concerned who had laid out all the springs and incumbent parts for examination was very frightened. **(Source: Chris Hanson)**

1981 – Thornton Road, Washwood Heath Birmingham

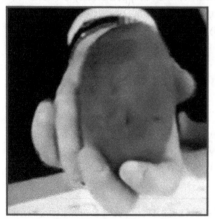

One of the apported stones

In Sir Arthur Clarke's book, entitled: *World of Strange Powers*, by John Fairley & Simon Welfare (published in 1984 by Book Club Associates) they outlined that investigations were made into the matter by the West Midlands Police, during early 1981, and included interviews with some of the officers, including Detective Sergeant Brian Laurie and Chief Inspector Leonard George

Len Turley

Turley, who is shown holding some of the stones at Bromford Police Station. Chief Inspector Turley said:

> *"My team has spent more than 3,500 hours in a fruitless investigation. In that time the police had solved five murders, but the file on Thornton Road was still frustratingly open."*

Three homes – numbers 32, 34 and 36 – bore the brunt of the damage, with rear windows continually smashed and roofs damaged. At the height of the trouble, residents placed chicken wire over windows and erected corrugated sheeting. In May, 1982, the *Birmingham Mail* reported: *'As dusk falls tonight on a Midland suburban road, frightened residents will check their barricades and prepare to fend-off yet another mystery attack on their homes.'*

The article was accompanied by a picture of Evelyn Malcolm, with the tin hat she wore for protection. Other householders wore safety helmets and laced cotton thread around their gardens to see if it would be broken by the culprits. Amazingly, despite their properties being trashed, the cords were never snapped. The home of Geoffrey Sidebotham and sister, Gwyneth Donnelly, sustained the worst damage. They still live at 36 – the home they shared with their parents.

In 2012, the *Birmingham Evening Mail* interviewed the couple as an update to the events that had taken place, now over 30 years ago. Geoffrey, aged 67, said:

> *"I'm still very bitter. It was an absolute nightmare and hastened the death of my mother, without a doubt."*

His mother, crippled with arthritis and emphysema, died in 1982. Geoffrey worked nights for the 'Co-op', so was not present when windows were put through, but he was sceptical about the ghostly claims.

> *"Someone – not something – did it, and got away with it. It upset the whole household. There were police everywhere, even in the trees, freezing"* he recalled.

> *"Windows were smashed every night by stones. As soon as you replaced one, it would be put through again. One bed was covered in glass. We weren't fully insured, so it cost a fortune."*

Gwyneth wept as she recalled the nightly torment. The 64 year-old said:

> *"It took my mother's life. I can remember a stone coming through the window and landing right by her wheelchair. I used to go to bed with a Bible under my pillow and prayed every night for it to stop. A vicar came to our house and he was convinced it was the work of vandals."*

Police never bought into the poltergeist theory, believing the culprit was using a giant catapult to bombard houses from a 200-yard distance. In December 1981, Supt. Baden Skitt vowed officers would get their man.

> *"We have devoted know-how and manpower of major murder hunt proportions. We are not treating it as a game. A very serious crime is being committed. The culprit holds all the aces, but we will get him in the end. He will slip up."*

Geoffrey Sidebotham: *"After all those years, I would still like to get to the bottom of it."*

Natalie Holford was just 17 when the attacks started at her home, number 32.

> *"Nowadays, I believe very much in psychic things. I just wish I knew then what I know*

now. At the time, I said there was someone who knew what was going on – but I'm more open-minded now. It was like being stalked, as if someone was watching us. The police would leave here at 2am and by the time they had reached the police station, there would be another attack. You could hear the stones rolling down the roof. It was so weird. It always happened when you were falling asleep. I was studying for my 'A' Levels, at the time, and it took its toll on me. My 'A' Levels were rubbish. It got to the point where you couldn't sleep; you were just waiting for something to happen . . . It was happening so regularly. There were police everywhere and they even put a camera in one of our rooms. My mum was at her wits' end; it was the lack of sleep."

We contacted Simon Welfare – the Producer of Arthur C. Clarke's TV programme, who told us:

"After such a long interval, I'm afraid I have no information on the story. I do remember that it struck us as being very odd, at the time. However, unlike many anomalous falls, we did think – without having any proof whatsoever – that the stones were being thrown by people. This would chime in with the fact that many poltergeist cases have later shown to have been the work of people, who, for whatever reason, have wanted to cause mischief."

PC Dave Cross aka 'The Vicar'

We decided to make further enquiries into the matter after we learnt that the operation had incurred many hundreds of Police man hours spent on nightly surveillance, using sophisticated night cameras, in an unsuccessful bid to catch the culprits responsible. First of all, we identified the names of the officers who had been in charge of the operation, as a result of liaison with retired PC Dave Cross known to his colleagues as 'The Vicar', (then the custodian of the Police Museum, at Sparkhill, Birmingham)

Next, we decided to visit Thornton Road, Washwood Heath, expecting to find some drab Victorian houses in an eerie 'period' setting, but were surprised to discover a row of semi-detached houses, built (from the look of them) around the 1930s. Seizing the moment, we knocked on the door of the house concerned and were surprised to discover that the original witness Natalie was still living there.

Natalie told us,

"It all started late one evening, in early 1981. I can't be sure of the exact date. I was in bed, when I heard the sound of my stepfather – John Johnson – as he entered the house, followed by the noises made by someone scrambling over the glass veranda roof that joins onto the next door neighbour's house. I realised that someone was up to no good and telephoned the police, who arrived a short time after. I later heard that somebody was arrested after abandoning a stolen car on the Washwood Heath Road. He must have thought there was an entrance between the houses.

From then onwards the problems started, usually at about the same time, when, just as I was going off to sleep, I would hear the sound of what I later found out to be a piece of brick, or smooth stone, dropping down onto the roof above me, and then rolling down the tiles onto the ground. You can imagine how unnerving this was. I naturally wondered if there was a connection with the stolen car business.

My bedroom was at the rear of the house and, as the problems persisted, with stones striking the window glass, we were forced to erect some protection around the windows, as time went on. Mind you, we weren't the only ones. Mr. Malcolm, who lived with his mother, next door, at 30, also complained about stones striking his house, so did Mrs. Lee, although she passed away some years ago (1999).

In reply to your question about other strange incidents that may have some bearing on what happened, I did have a frightening experience in 1968/1969, when I saw what I took to be a black 'figure', wearing what looked to be a hat, actually floating in the air just outside the house, although when I told my mother and father about it, they dismissed it as a dream. It was only in later years, when I became aware of the publicity given to the 'Men in Black' cult, did I realise the similarity with what I had seen.

There was also a German bomb that exploded just in the back garden, near the house. You can still see the dip in the ground. Apart from that, we were a normal happy family. At the time, I was studying for my 'A' levels and, while still intrigued by what happened, I can't understand why it went on for so long, unless it was some sort of reprisal against us for reporting the matter to the police.

I remember, on another occasion, when the police had left watching the house, a stone struck the back window, 15 minutes later, while I was putting the cat out. Incidents like these weren't uncommon."

Deborah James – who was then living a few doors away from Natalie, told of arriving home, late one evening,

"... when to my great surprise a stone fell through the sky onto the ground – almost as if thrown by invisible hands. I never saw anyone do it."

Police Constable Brian Russell – now a Police Sergeant, stationed at West Midlands Police, Lloyd House – was one of the first officers we spoke to about his memories of the events which took place at Thornton Road.

". . . still clear in my mind because they were so unusual. I recall a conversation held with D.I. Bennett, from Bromford Lane, who vowed to catch the prankster, after various Police operations set-up to identify the culprit, had failed. As there were three houses affected by the blight of stone throwing, it was decided to place two officers into each back garden, equipped with infra-red night sights – quite bulky apparatus, in contrast to the much lighter ones now in use. I took up my position in the rear garden of the middle house (Natalie's house) – a property which had received a higher rate of damage than its neighbours alongside. Sometime in the early hours, I heard what sounded like footsteps coming towards me. I alerted my colleague. When we peered through the night scope, there was nothing to be seen – then, to my great surprise, the embankment we were sat on, at the rear of the garden, shook – as if having a tremor. I'd had enough. I ran away from the scene, very frightened, and made my way on foot to Bromford Lane Police Station, where I told D.I. Bennett, in no uncertain terms, what had happened, refusing to go back there again. Ironically, my rapid exit from the locality had caused some of the officers to believe I was chasing the offender!"

Police Constable 'Ted' Newey –

> *"I was one of a number of Officers who took part in regular night-time surveillance, at the rear of houses in Thornton Road, Alum Rock, during the early 1980s. On one occasion, I was accompanied by PC Trevor Robinson, and sat in the back garden against the rear fence, which was made up of what looked like old railway sleepers, on what was a bitterly cold night. Suddenly, we heard this noise – like someone, or something, striking the wooden sleepers with a lump hammer, behind us. I turned around, expecting the worst – there was nobody to be seen – just that awful noise, which eventually faded away. Things became so bad that the Police asked a Royal Artillery Officer to attend the scene and advise them, from the trajectory of the falling stones, to pinpoint where they were coming from. What I found odd was that despite marking the stones on the ground, by numbering them, none of these were ever thrown at the premises. On another occasion, I was staggered to see a rain of stones, approximately 50-60 of them, falling through the air onto the ground – many of which were the size of eggs; others, as big as your hands – all of them smooth and clean."*

Inspector Robert Moon –

> *"I was one of those hapless officers, who worked the case in question. I spent a few nights lying under a tarpaulin, trying to fathom out where the missiles were coming from – to no avail, although I did hear things dropping down onto the ground but never saw where they were coming from. If my memory serves me right, similar incidents happened in the same locality, some years later. I can confirm that they were not rocks, but mainly small and polished – the sort of stones you would find on a shingle beach, rather than inland."*

Gil Howard, Retired Police Constable –

> *"In 1981, 1 was the 'gaffer's clerk' at Bromford Lane, which covered the Thornton Road area. I can remember arranging the rosters, so that Officers could stay the night in one of the rear garden sheds of a house, close to the property under observation. Despite many man hours nothing conclusive ever came to light, although I thought it odd.*
>
> *D.I. Johnson's brother lived in one of the affected houses. All sorts of theories were put forward by the public, which included a Roman catapult, firing projectiles from Hodge Hill Common – its trajectories worked out by a local mathematician. Chief Inspector Len Turley had a biscuit tin on the window in his office, containing a number of stones recovered from the scene. I know Arthur C. Clarke covered the incident is his book, suggesting some sort of paranormal connection, but the police would never have been able to get away with this explanation. It was put down to a neighbour dispute."*

We took careful note of what everybody had told us, believing there was far more to this matter than we would ever know. We suspected the stones had been warm when picked up, although nobody actually mentions this important fact.

The stones shown in Sir Arthur Clarke's book appeared smooth, round and polished, pebble like in appearance, apparently free from any debris one may have expected if they had had been picked up from a soil bed, in a garden. The majority of the stones had been thrown from the rear, towards the backhouse, on occasion striking the houses on either side of Natalie's house, creating an impression that the offender was pelting two or three houses with stones, when it appears Natalie's house was the 'target' which faced the nightly barrage.

Some of the stones were checked for fingerprints but none were found, nor any marks, differentiating them from other stones found in the gardens of nearby houses. They looked, according to one officer, as if they had been washed before being thrown. One local man – Chris Martin, spent many hours outside with his tin helmet, watching and waiting – to no avail. Other residents feared going out at night.

We could not help but wonder if there was any connection with these ongoing disturbances and the discovery of a number of broken marble gravestones, purchased legitimately, some years prior to the stone throwing, used to construct a rockery and garden path at the rear of the property concerned, which may have some bearing on what took place.

We discovered an amazing coincidence between the officer in charge – Detective Inspector Dennis Johnson, an ex-Crime Squad Officer and his brother – John Johnson, who lived at the house with Natalie. Oddly, although we were told that *Birmingham Evening Mail* had publicised many stories about the Thornton Road 'stone thrower', we found nothing on file at the Central Library.

At the height of the problems, Chief Inspector Len Turley, in charge of the investigation, spoke of his frustration. He said:

> *"We have spent more than 1,000 man hours on this case. We are keeping an open mind about the whole thing. We don't know why it's gone on for so long. If we even knew the reason for it, we would be one step nearer."*

In late April 2013, we made a second visit to Thornton Road, where we took some photographs of the street and then knocked on the door of Geoffrey Sidebotham hoping to interview him but were given short thrift by a younger man who after enquiring about the nature of our visit slammed the door in our faces after we explained further!

Even now it is said householders are unable to decide whether they were in the midst of poltergeist activity or simply victims of vandalism. Ironically, we were ourselves to experience the fall of a stone on more than one occasion, during visits to Rendlesham Forest, in Suffolk, some years later (See *Haunted Skies* Volume 8). The fact that these stones fell to earth with a thud, and were quite warm to the touch, is something we are unable to explain, to this present date, however, there is a vast difference to what we experienced in the forest and what took place in Thornton Road – the sheer size of the stones!

Sadly we learnt that Len Turley passed away on 9th May 2012, aged 77 years. His wife remembers many aspects of the case that puzzled her husband, who was unable to identify the source of the stones, despite many hours spent by officers working night duty.

On 11th May 2013, we visited Len's wife, Doreen Turley – a charming lady – who spoke fondly of Len and of his career, which began when he joined Staffordshire County Police as cadet, after leaving school. After passing the Sergeant's exam, he was promoted and was the first Crime Prevention Officer for Staffordshire County. Their son also served as a Police Officer. He recently retired at 54.

Doreen:

> *"Len didn't talk much about what he did in the police, and remained open-minded as to the cause. He remarked, on more than one occasion, that the police couldn't explain what was happening in Thornton Road but that it was continuing to happen."*

Doreen Turley

The West Midlands Ghost Club

Ghostly figure, witches coven, buried treasure and falling stones in Staffordshire?

Over the years we had occasionally spoken to Nick Duffy, one of the founder members of the West Midlands Ghost Club, about the mysterious events that took place in Thornton Road, and other incidents involving reports of paranormal disturbances.

In 2007 Steve Chew – a member of The West Midlands Ghost Club – received a report, from a family friend, of a tall, ghostly figure, dressed like a priest or vicar, seen in the *Hopwas Wood area of Tamworth Staffordshire, which vanished in front of his eyes. The Club made a visit to the location in 2009, wondering if there was any substance to this sighting and rumours in local folklore, which claimed the area was haunted by the ghost of a small child. Research into the locality revealed that the *Tamworth Herald* had published an article in 1984 *'Strange midnight ritual round a fire – police swoop on naked 'witches' in the woods'* where they told of the arrest of sixteen people by the police, during the Solstice weekend. These people claimed they were witches….

'Naked 'witches' had to end their secret midnight ritual when police moved into an isolated clearing in Hopwas Woods, near Tamworth. The 16 startled witches – six of them women – were dancing and chanting around a fire. They spent the rest of the night in the cells at Tamworth police station, because officers suspected they were in possession of drugs. It is understood that the witches claimed they were part of the international Silver Star organisation and were celebrating the weekend's summer solstice – the longest day.

Nick Duffy

Police were called to the woods in the early hours of Saturday, after a car was heard making its way along a narrow track. In a clearing on army-owned land at the heart of the firing range danger area, police found the naked dancers with a supply of food and drink, and equipment thought to have included a chalice and a sword. Police reinforcements were sent to the scene and some officers stayed to guard the site throughout the night.

The witches, aged from the early 20s to nearly 50, are thought to be mainly from the Tamworth area. But it is believed some had travelled from as far as the West Country for the ritual gathering.

Superintendent Don Robinson, Tamworth's police chief, said:

"All 16 people agreed to come to the police station voluntarily, so that we could check out their identities and the account they had given of themselves. We then suspected they were in possession of drugs and they were detained so that we could inquire into that aspect. We are now considering the question of proceedings under the Drugs Act. As far as we can make out, no offences were committed, other than the possible drug offences."

When they were discovered, the witches are understood to have told police that their presence had desecrated the coven's 'sacred ground', but Superintendent Robinson said they had co-operated with the police in the investigation. Yesterday a Tamworth clergyman, who is an expert on the Occult, said he had heard for a long time about a coven of witches meeting in Hopwas Woods. The Rev. David Shearer, Minister of Coton Green Evangelical Church, said:

"I would have no doubt that the people involved in the incident at the weekend are witches. Witches – white or black – are all worshippers of Satan, and part of the Occult. There is no such thing as witches working for good. I wouldn't be at all surprised if there is more than one witch's coven meeting in the Tamworth area."

In a further follow-up article on the subject, it was revealed, by some of the occultists involved, that ceremonies had allegedly been taking place in Hopwas Woods over the past 12 years.

Hopwas Wood – the setting for naked cavorting!

First metal plate found

In December 2010, a further visit was made to Hopwas-Hayes Wood. While scanning a section of the woods, far removed from the main A51 Lichfield Road, John Conway picked-up a strong signal from his metal detector.

He was amazed to find what appeared to be a sizeable, copper plate, some 11ins by 8ins, located approximately 6ins down. The soil in the area concerned is very black in colour and appears to have a somewhat 'oily' property to it. John wondered if the heavy 6mm thick object may have been some form of 'knock-down target', possibly left there after military usage of the area. (Part of the woodland was apparently used by the Ministry of Defence in the past). However, on further scrutiny, it was clear that some form of markings were on it. Further cleaning revealed the sizeable 'star' emblem, raised on its surface, and other 'occult-related' designs and script.

Because of such an intriguing find, the West Midlands Ghost Club contacted the *Tamworth Herald* and told them of the find. They published the following article:

Tamworth Herald, Dec 9th 2010 – 'Mysterious Artefact Baffles Ghost Hunters Exploring Ancient Woods':

'Evidence has emerged of occult activity in Hopwas after a 'copper plate' featuring engraved magical symbols was dug up in the village's ancient woodland. The rectangular tablet, which features an illustration of a star alongside mystical writing, was found buried about four inches below the ground in Hopwas Woods last Saturday.

It was dug up by investigators from the West Midlands Ghost Club, who had been researching old stories of witchcraft and haunting in the area. Intrigued members of the club are now appealing for more information about the artefact and an explanation of what the symbols might mean.

John Conway said he discovered the tablet while using a metal detector at the site as part of his research into the area's mystical past and described the find as "totally unexpected and intriguing". Our interest in Hopwas came about two years back, because we had heard a couple of ghost stories from the area. On checking up on the history, we heard about things going on in Hopwas Woods. We visited the wood with a metal detector – the purpose of the visit being to get an overview of the area concerned and, potentially, find evidence of some form of magical practices. We did not notice at first, but we were in the centre of a natural circle of quite old trees. We initially thought what we'd found was simply a thick piece of copper sheet, but, upon further scrutiny, we found it was deeply etched with peculiar symbols and writing, quite evidently of an occult-related nature. After cleaning up and polishing the item, the magical symbols could be seen, but he said he realised the 'ethical' implications of digging up a potentially sacred item. We realise someone has put something there purposefully. If they want to contact us privately, we would be quite happy to hand it back.'

In 1984, reports of naked 'witches' in the woods emerged after a raid by police, in which several people were detained. At the time, the leader of the group, part of The Order of the Silver Star, spoke out and defended the group's actions. Members denied being witches and described themselves as 'serious occultists' who had been using the woods since the early 1970s. During rituals, they claimed they 'connected with the stars and planets'.

Nick Duffy told us that the first article resulted in the group being inundated with general enquiries – many from the general Tamworth area, others from overseas, including the USA and Australia. Within a short period, the story also became a firm favourite on the internet blog circuit, being covered by a variety of pages, many of which were of 'Pagan' origin.

Following comments made on the *Tamworth Herald* website itself, the club received a number of responses, which included one suggestion that the West Midlands Ghost Club had actually 'invented' the story/discovery as some form of publicity stunt!

Nick Duffy:

> *"One of the more interesting responses received during this period was from a young man, who informed us that he had apparently discovered part of a mysterious looking statue, while out walking in Hopwas Woods, some time earlier."*

Tamworth Herald, January 7th – 'Another Mysterious Artefact Is Dug Up In 'Witches' Woods':

'Further evidence of occult activity in Hopwas has emerged following the discovery of another buried artefact in the village's woodland. An Egyptian-style clay statuette has been uncovered by Tamworth man Andrew Lee – who contacted the Herald after reading about the discovery of an engraved copper tablet, with magical writing, which was found in Hopwas Woods last month.

And mystery continues to surround the copper plate after a language enthusiast produced a transliteration of the symbols, which surrounded an image of a star. Mr Lee said: "I found [the small clay statue] last year while walking my dad's dogs around Hopwas Woods. I found it when one of the dogs started sniffing around a dead bird at the bottom of a tree. While I was shooing away the dog, I saw the thing buried face down in the ground."

He added: "At first I thought it was a piece of pottery, but when I dug it out, I got quite excited that it was a whole figure."

The statue, which shows signs of weathering, is thought to be of the Egyptian jackal-headed god Anubis. He is said to be a protector of the deceased and their tombs, and is associated with mummification and the afterlife.

Mr Lee said: "I thought it might be good to show it, as it's been sitting in the cupboard, wrapped in newspaper, for months. Perhaps there might be others who have things lying around they've found there in the past."

The copper plate was discovered by investigators from the West Midlands Ghost Club, after researching old stories of witchcraft and haunting in the area. John Conway, who discovered the tablet with his metal detector, revealed the translation to the Herald this week.

He said the language and runes, some difficult to decipher, were Enochian, used in the 16th Century by noted occultist John Dee. It reads: 'BAGLE (for) PAPNOOR (to this remembrance); I (is) DOVIOM (probably a name); LONSHI (the power); OL (I, the maker) UMPLIF (our strength) OGG BIGLIAD (in our comforter)'. It is from an ancient tract, called the 7th Enochian key, which reads: 'For to his remembrance, is given power, and our strength'.

Mr. Conway said: "We have had lot of interest, and even from American occultists who were interested in obtaining photographs of the item. It is just a matter of interest for us, but we can do very little with it. We could take it back to where we found it, or we could return it to the proper owners." '

Falling stones?

Nick Duffy:

> *"While walking around the clearing concerned, both group members present individually reported hearing loud, thumping noises, seemingly close at hand and, apparently, occurring on the ground nearby!? By all intent and purpose, it seemed as if someone were possibly hurling something akin to heavy stones in their direction – though no rocks or any form of physical movement/presence could be detected to account for the noises experienced. While taking a general look around the area concerned, one of the group members saw a small, orange light – some 20 or so feet distant – seemingly in the process of falling to the ground from a height of around two feet. The effect looked very much like someone dropping a cigarette end to the ground, though the light 'appeared' at the two feet level and travelled directly ground-ward. No one present during the visit were smokers, so those present were at a total loss as to what the effect might have been? Nothing else of any potential interest was noted during the visit."*

Another plate found

Incredibly the group was to learn of another incident, involving the recovery of a similar plate by Mr. Joe Smith, from Hopwas Woods, some ten years previously.

> *"During that day I had spent about three or four hours in the woods – it was only when I made my way back from the furthest edge of the wood, that faces the farmer's field, that I got quite a strong signal. The plate itself was only about a foot deep,*

and at first just seemed to be a sheet of metal but there were a few grooves and marks in it, so I decided to take it home to clean it up, thinking that it would be an old box cover of some kind. When I cleaned the plate, there were strange symbols etched into the front."

(Source: Nick Duffy and members of the West Midlands Ghost Club)

1894 – A stone throwing mystery solved?

During the reign of Queen Victoria, Enmore a suburb west of Sydney, New South Wales, Australia attracted media attention in May of that year, when

*Hopwas is recorded in the Domesday Book as "The King holds Opewas; there are three hides; the arable land is six carucates. In demesne there is a mill of thirteen shillings and four pence rent; and eleven villans and two bordars employ five ploughs. Here are thirty acres of meadow, a wood six furlongs in length and three in breadth. The whole was valued aforetime and then at 40s."

30 police officers spent seven days trying to catch the offender, after stones were thrown at the house of Police Constable McCann and his wife. Stones were marked and placed in the yard. When these were thrown back, they caused suspicion to fall onto the adopted daughter (12) of the couple. She told the officers she had been compelled to hurl the missiles 'after being instructed to do so in her dreams', and that she did not believe she was doing anything wrong. The girl was returned to an industrial school. One is bound to think there is more to this than meets the eye and that justice was unfairly done.

(Source: *The Press*, 29.5.1894)

1901 – Manila, New Zealand

Andrew Michie's house at Glenbarra, near Manila, New Zealand, situated on a grassy plain in a lonely spot, fronted by a small watercourse, fringed by oak trees, was the target of bombardment by stones, over many nights running. The damage included a door smashed off its hinge, windows broken, the iron roof dented, and slabs splintered. Despite observations kept, the culprit was not found. A Mr. Hartley and Hetherington, who were described as 'marsupial shooters', struck camp near the house and were asked to assist; on one occasion, a missile shot through the front door, striking one of the daughters on the head and inflicting a nasty abrasion. The police were called out and conducted a search with trackers, but were unsuccessful. A pair or trousers and a comb were left outside, one night. The following morning, half of the trousers and half of the comb were found to be missing. These were returned, a few evenings later, tied to a stone that landed on the roof. Mr. Michie – a boundary rider – offered a £10 reward for the 'elucidation of the mystery', which was increased to £20, by Mr. Park – the owner of the station.

(Source: *Poverty Bay Herald*, 9.9.1901/*The Advertiser* (Adelaide, National Library of New Zealand)

1910 – Port Melbourne

The police were engaged, over several weeks, in an unsuccessful attempt to solve a stone throwing mystery, at Port Melbourne. Three houses in Princess Street were regularly bombarded, between midnight and 7.00am. Showers of large stones fell, smashing windows, crockery, and furniture. One woman was struck a blow by a half brick. The police themselves came under attack. **(Source: Colonist, 16.12.1910)**

1921 – Gurya, Sydney, Australia

During April, the home of a resident was subjected to nightly stone throwing and mysterious rapping noises. The police and residents failed to find the culprit. A resident of the property – a little girl – was taken to one of the rooms, accompanied by the police and asked "*Is that you?*" (Her sister – who had died recently); she received a message to the affirmative. Further damage was reported at the location by large stones falling, causing damage, and shutters wrenched from their hinges. The girl was taken away, and over 70 people surrounded the house, on what was a wet night, but no stones fell. The following morning, as motor cars approached the house, a large stone struck a tree. An examination of the stone revealed a red cross on it. The girl was brought back to the house and guarded by four men. Shortly afterwards, a stone came through the bedroom window and landed on the bed. The stones then began to strike the house, but the phenomena eventually came to an end.

(Source: *Hawera and Normanby Star*, New Zealand, 15.4.1921/*New Zealand Herald*, 19.4.1921)

Triangular UFO over Smethwick

It appears that there was little evidence of UFO activity for June 1981, in contrast to other months. A search of our comprehensive files revealed little information, although declassified records released by the Public Records Office, thirty years later, told of a triangular UFO sighted in Smethwick, during June 1981.

The unidentified eyewitness wrote:

> *"I was walking the dog around the estate, and had stopped to chat to a neighbour. I commented it was a pleasant evening and looked up at the sky and saw a triangular object passing overhead. It was approximately 30ft in length, with a dark grey fuselage. At the rear were two huge orange lights."*

Truck lifted off the ground by UFO – Texas, USA

At 2.10pm on 12th June 1981, Robert Gomez was the driver of a tanker truck, containing 165 gallons of water in the tank, heading west along Highway 665, toward Alice, when he sighted a bright object in the sky. He first thought it was an aircraft, until it increased in brightness and stopped in mid-air. He described it as:

> *". . . being domed, disc-shaped, brilliant white in colour, and showing a dark ring around the rim, with another dark ring around its centre."*

Gomez felt the truck slowing down and tried to accelerate, but was shocked to discover the truck had apparently been lifted about a foot off the ground. Although his AM radio had stopped working, his CB radio was still active – so he reported what was happening to his dispatcher. Shortly afterwards, the UFO disappeared into the clouds. Smoke was discovered coming out of the water tank valve, which now showed 55 pounds of pressure on the gauge. He opened the valve, to drain the remaining water, but only steam came out.

(Sources: Richard Hall, *Uninvited Guests*, p313-314/ *MUFON UFO Journal*, January 1982/ Richard Hall, *The UFO Evidence, Volume II: A Thirty-Year Report*, p276)

This was not the only occasion when a vehicle was lifted off the ground by a UFO.

In Pennsylvania, USA, a woman's car was lifted 2-3ft off the ground. Even more terrifying was an account given to us by a Police Sergeant, from Oxfordshire, whose vehicle was lifted upside-down and slammed into the road, while on duty, one early morning more on this in a later chapter.

At 12.20am, the 13th June 1981 a spinning, transparent cone, three metres in length, touched down on the ground in Chia-Li, Taiwan. It expelled a mist – then took off and shot away to the north.

(Source: Paul Dong, Wendelle Stevens, *UFOs over Modern China*)

UFO LIFTS WOMAN'S CAR

T. Scott Crain Jr.

Pennsylvania State Section Director for MUFON (Mutual UFO Network, Seguin, Texas)

At 8.50 p.m. on the night of October 15, 1983, Catherine Burk, 67, was driving home from Altoona, Pennsylvania, after visiting her family, when she encountered an unusual object in the sky. As she approached her turn-off to Bellwood, travelling north on Route 220, she describes seeing out of the passenger side window a bright, silvery disc, that was flat on top, about 24 feet in diameter, coming towards her from the south-east. The object was approximately 30 feet off the ground and emitted a "fast hum", that was "sharp" like the sound of a "helicopter landing". As the object passed over the top of her car, it lifted her 1976 *Chevrolet Malibu* up on two wheels. The left side of her car was lifted approximately two to three feet off the road and was held there while she was still going down the road for nearly three seconds. As Mrs. Burk attempted to lean towards the passenger side of her automobile to bring it level again, the object moved away, dropping her vehicle back on the road with a terrific bounce. *"I couldn't get control of the car. I was sliding over the seat,"* Mrs. Burk said, who ended up almost under the dashboard when the car came down. When Mrs Burk regained control of her vehicle, she pulled off the highway. The object moved north-west towards Bellwood as it disappeared behind the ridge. It took her 20 to 25 minutes to re-start her vehicle, and every time she had to stop on the way home, it cut out.

Reported to Police

Mrs. Burk's daughter telephoned to her later that evening to see if she had got home safely. When she discovered how upset her mother was, she called Bellwood Police. Bellwood Police Chief Gregory Ciaccio took down Mrs. Burk's account of the affair, and reported that she was "visibly shaking and . . . was not drinking". Ciaccio reported that he saw no visible damage to the car.

Catherine Burk describes UFO encounter (Photo courtesy of Larry G. McKee)

I was the principal investigator of this case, for the Mutual UFO Network. I interviewed Mrs. Burk first on the telephone on October 26, 1983 and then had a personal visit with her on November 5, 1983. The witness appeared to me to be sincere and honest, and not the type of person to concoct this type of story. She doesn't watch movies or read books about UFOs, and was inclined to think that what she had observed was "something the Government had constructed". Although there may have been other witnesses to the object in the Bellwood area, I have not yet located any. However, Stan Gordon, MUFON's State Director for Pennsylvania, says similar type UFO reports have been made in this State over the past few months.

Injuries to witness

As a result of being jarred around in her car, Mrs. Burk is still being treated at Mercy Hospital in Altoona for a number of ailments. She was still wearing a neck brace on November 5, her shoulder was sore, she may have suffered spinal problems, she may have chest injuries (X-Rays were taken) and her hearing is impaired in her right ear.

Mrs. Burk was employed as a telephone operator in a nursing home for 10 years, and currently works part time as a security guard for homes in the Sylvan Hills development in Altoona.

Mrs. Burk was frightened by her experience and now all she wants to do is to put the incident behind her.

This case has recently been examined in the MUFON JOURNAL, but I feel that it deserves a larger audience and will be of interest to readers of FSR.

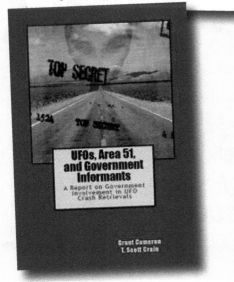

TOP SECRET

UFOs, Area 51, and Government Informants

A Report on Government Involvement in UFO Crash Retrievals

Grant Cameron T. Scott Crain

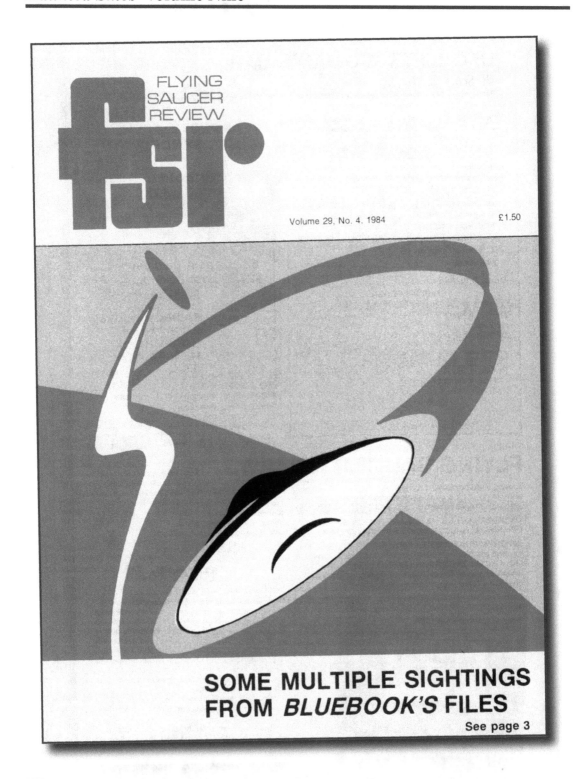

JULY 1981

UFO SIGHTED BY NEWSPAPER BOY

Also includes – UFO seen flying over Warminster by housewife.
Was it a balloon, or something else? • Philip Mantle and Andy Roberts conduct
lengthy investigation into claims by Yorkshire woman of alien abductions, in 1987,
going back many years.
ABDUCTION ON THE A5 – Two women describe journey, while driving home
from a Shropshire nightclub along the A5 – a road synonymous with sightings
of strange aerial craft. A rare opportunity to learn, first-hand, from the women
concerned what they saw, and the result of regression and what those
sessions revealed • A Gloucestershire man sights UFO over M50 Motorway and
believes that he was taken against his will by aliens • A motorist and his wife
experience some strange smells and then sight UFO over Pepperbox Hill, Wiltshire.
Abroad – Ringed UFO over Tibet • UFOs sighted over Greece • In Finland, two men –
out fishing – report close encounter, followed by missing time

UFO over Ashbury

AT 6.45am on 9th July 1981, schoolboy Wayne Disbury was out on his 'paper round', when he noticed a bright white object on the ground, close to the B4000 road, which runs between Shrivenham and Ashbury, leading to the village of Kingstone Winslow. Thinking it was a plastic bag, he continued on his 'round'.

At 7.35am, Michael Winley – a member of the Royal Observer Corps – was driving to work along the B4000, heading towards Ashbury, when he noticed two horses in the field acting in an agitated manner. Thinking they were being worried by a dog, he stopped his car and got out, ready to chase off the animal.

> *"I was surprised to see a bright object on the ground, near to the horses, and assumed it might have been a meteorological balloon, and went over to pick it up. As I did so, the object*

– resembling a dustbin lid in shape, 2-3ft in diameter, chrome top and black base, funnel or tube protruding from its centre, showing what looked like a small truncated cone on its front, with a number of small indentations around its perimeter – rose vertically upwards, between 150-200ft off the ground, and flew silently over my head, and descended, before coming to a halt, approximately 70ft off the ground."

A business colleague of Mr. Winley's – Kevin Clarke – was driving along the same stretch of road, when he noticed Mr. Winley's car, and pulled up at 7.45am. Curious as to what was going on, he made his way over the field and was astonished to see the object hovering in the air.

A few minutes later, another workmate – Raymond Millin – also turned up. He and the other two men stood watching it before it moved off towards the direction of Idstone, parallel to the B4000 – until lost from view.

At 8.05am, Mr. & Mrs. Richardson, accompanied by Mr. & Mrs. Case, were travelling along the B4000, towards Swindon, in the opposite direction to the other witnesses, when they saw a small object approaching their position, 2-300 yards away, travelling slowly (no more than 10mph) described as being:

'. . . 2ft in diameter by 8ins deep, a light metallic colour (mottled on top) with a dark base, showing indentations'.

Mr. Richardson also noticed a small hollow tube sticking out of the base, although the others did not see this. He then stopped the car adjacent to the field, and got out, in time to see it pass directly overhead, 15-20ft up – apparently, as if to land. At this stage, he decided to continue his journey to work.

The incident was later brought to the attention of Marty Moffat, of the SCUFORI UFO Group, who launched a thorough investigation into the matter, wondering whether a remote control balloon could have been responsible, but finally concluded, in view of the lack of any further information, to classify it as an unidentified object.

UFO over Warminster

At 7.50pm on 14th July 1981, a silver balloon-shaped object was seen heading across the sky, over Warminster, by Olive Doreen Stevens, who was sat in the living room of her home at Downlands, Cop Heap. Mrs. Stevens contacted the Police, at Warminster, who sent an officer around to interview her.

View from Mrs Stevens' window, looking approximately south-west. The UFO has been drawn on by Mrs Stevens and amended only to show the upper and lower segments, by Ian Mrzyglod. The application of a felt-pen has caused the drawn object to depict a larger UFO than was actually seen. At same distance as the balloon, this object, as drawn, would resemble something more in the order of approximately 6ft. The motion of the object was a steady level flight from right to left and it disappeared behind the house to the left of the picture.

PROBE
M.A.U.F.O.G.

16 Marigold Walk,
Ashton,
Bristol. BS3 2PD.

UFO Research Organisation

Tel. 0272 666270
646710

SR1.A.   UFO SIGHTING REPORT FORM: INITIAL STAGE

Please complete this form to the best of your knowledge, and if unsure on any particular points, please state "Don't know".

WITNESS

Full name (Mr/Mrs/Miss/Ms)..OLIVE DOREEN STEVENS...................... Age..66...
Address...21..THE DOWNLANDS...WARMINSTER...WILTS..........................
Current Occupation..MARRIED WOMAN.......... Telephone No.24041...(STD) 0985.

LOCATION

Location of Witness...21..THE DOWNLANDS...WARMINSTER...........................
Day & Date of Sighting.14th JULY 1981.(TUESDAY)..... Time of Initial Sighting.1950 HRS...
Description of Weather Conditions..CLOUDY...VISIBILITY GOOD...........................

THE SIGHTING

No. of Objects..ONE........ Colour.SILVER ABOVE. RED BELOW. Shape.......... DISC SHAPE
Sounds..NO SOUND............. Odours..NO ODOUR......... Estimated Speed.SEE BELOW
Did the Object(s) appear solid?..YES...... Apparent Size.TWO-FOUR FEET IN DIAMETER
Describe the Movement of the Object(s).SIDEWAYS..RIGHT..TO..LEFT......
Estimated Distance.150-200 YARDS..... Estimated Angle of Elevation.EYE LEVEL..
Estimated Altitude at Beginning.DON'T KNOW & at End.SAME.. Brightness..NONE...
Direction When First Seen.WEST... Last Seen.S/EAST. Duration of Sighting.10-15 SECONDS
Attention of the Witness Drawn to the Object Because MOVED. ACROSS WINDOW I WAS FACING
.... How Did the Sighting End? DISAPPEARED. BEHIND. ROOF. OF. HOUSE...
Any Unusual Environmental Effects?..NO..........................

GENERAL

To Whom and When Was the Sighting Reported? PROBE. ON 18th JULY. 1981...........
Was Anyone Else Present?..NO............. Did They See It?..N/A.......
Have You Had Any Previous Sightings?..NO....... Were Any Photographs Taken?..NO......

DRAWING: (PLEASE MARK DIRECTION OF MOTION WITH ARROWS). * at the about the speed
Colour if Possible.   of the helicopters we see here quite
                                            frequently.

S. EAST   W

12

The gas filled balloon that was released along the same flight path taken by the UFO

SR1.B.   ACCOUNT OF THE INCIDENT (and any items not covered by
previous questions).

*...I was watching television & a programme called
"My Music" had been on for about ten minutes.
In facing the television I also face a large picture
window which looks out over Warminster Cora House &
approx. 350-400 feet above sea level on the side of
Cophens. I first caught a glimpse of the object
out of the corner of my eye & then I saw that it
was flying in a direct line & at a steady pace I got
up & went to the window & watched it until it
disappeared out of sight behind the roof of a house.
It appeared to be power motivated & flying west
to S. East over Warminster at a distance of approx.
150-200 yards.*

If you do not wish your name to be published, mark 'X' in the box. ⊠

This information is acurate to the best of my knowledge:

Signature. *N. Stevens* ....   Date *23rd July 1981* ....

The matter was then passed by the police to the Probe UFO Group, who conducted a thorough investigation, carried out by Ian Mrzyglod, his wife – Julie, and other members, including the purchase of a gas filled balloon that was released along the same flight path taken by the UFO, at the home of the witness, revealing that Mrs. Stevens had probably seen a silver balloon, moving across the sky, which she accepted as being the explanation.

Although we may not necessarily agree with some of the findings of the group, one cannot help but admire the professional way in which Ian Mrzyglod and his colleagues conducted not only themselves, but their investigations into matters such as these.   **(Source: Ian Mrzyglod/Marty Moffat, *Probe*/SCUFORI)**

Introduction

After unsuccessful attempts to come to some arrangement with the Wiltshire Constabulary whereupon they would furnish us with details of UFO sightings reported to them from the public, we were more than surprised to receive a telephone call from the Warminster Police Station informing us of this sighting.

We had visited this police station during our efforts as described above and did have a meeting with the Chief Superintendant a few weeks prior to the call. We had asked to see details of another case which occurred in Warminster, which had also been reported to the Warminster police, and that is why we found ourselves in the police station itself. Happily, we did obtain the information we required on the older case, this particular case not yet having taken place.

From that meeting it seems that we won the confidence of the Warminster police, for despite the negative response from the Chief Constable, based in Devizes, we received, via the telephone call, all the necessary details of this case. It involved a 66 year old lady, who through her living-room window, witnessed a small disc-shaped object traverse from right to left just across the street at the end of the garden. The object, shaped more like a lens, was red underneath and silver on top. She immediately contacted the police who thought it of sufficient interest to pay the witness a personal visit. After their visit they contacted us.

The Witness

Mrs. Olive Stevens is aged 66 and is very intelligent. She is also very active and alert, something that is not common with people of that age. She is very house-proud and the house is kept in imaculate order, possibly reflecting her desire to be precise and acurate. She answered the questions on the Sighting Report Form very boldly, stating facts that the average person would not hope to know, such as the height of the house above sea level. She also answered questions very quickly during the inter-view and knew what she wanted to say. Mrs. Stevens was perfectly aware of where the object first appeared and where it finally disappeared, and provided the basic plain facts of the incident.

Although some of the estimations given by Mrs. Stevens on the completed SR1 form are erroneous, she did not alter any information over the entire investigation. These errors in estimation are more than common with most people, and even the trained eye cannot always acurately guess heights and distances, and therefore were treated as significant.

Mrs. Stevens had no idea whatsoever what the object was, and was looking for us to explain it rather than confirm it as a UFO. She has never read any literature on UFOs, except for the numerous press reports of Warminster's famous apparent UFO activity.

The Location

The Downlands, off Cop Heap Lane, Warminster, is a very select upper-class residential area, seeluded from the rest of the town. It has its own drive with a large ranch-type gate leading on to Cop Heap Lane which gives the impression that the Downlands residents could shut themselves off from anyone else by simply closing it.

The sighting was made from the living room of No. 21 The Downlands, Warminster, which overlooks the back garden and then across Warminster itself. The house is situated about half-way up the Downlands estate which is itself built on a slope. No. 21 is about 135 metres above sea-level so quite a good view is visible from the living room. At the end of the garden, there is a steep drop on to Cop Heap Lane, of about twelve feet. This is made up of hedgerow and several small trees. A telegraph pole is also situated centrally at the end of the garden in the street. All these objects moment-arily obscured the object as it moved from right to left, it finally disappearing behind a house some 35 yards away.

The Sighting

At 1950 hrs BST, Mrs. Olive Stevens was sat in the living room of her house watching television, "My Music" to be exact. The date was 14th July 1981, and Mrs. Stevens explains in her own words: " In facing the television I also face a large picture window which looks out over Warminster. Our house is approx 350-400 feet above sea-level on the side of Cop Heap. I first caught a glimpse of the object out of the corner of my eye, and when I saw that it was flying in a direct line and at steady pace, I got up and went to the window and watched it until it disappeared out of sight behind the roof of a house. It appeared to be power motivated and flying West to South East over Warminster at a distance of approx 150-200 yards."

Mrs. Stevens first saw the object as it appeared between the second tree in from the right on photograph A, and the telegraph pole, moving in a straight line from right to left. It was travelling in an ESE direction and completed its visible transition in a time of between 10 and 15 seconds.

No sound was heard from the object and there appeared to be no environmental effects. Weather conditions were dull.

The Investigation

On 20th July, after hearing of the sighting via Warminster police, a sighting report form was sent to Mrs. Stevens together with an SAE. This was duly completed on 23rd July and returned a few days later. On 31st, Ian and Julie Mrzyglod drove to Warminster after having first spoken to Mrs. Stevens to arrange a suitable time, and interviewed her about the sighting.

A series of photographs was also taken from the living room, looking through the picture window (double-glazed), and another series through the open window. Whilst there Mrs. Stevens (OS) was shown PROBE's size test frame No 2 (F2) and was asked to use this in an effort to determine an approximate size of the object. OS held the frame at arm's length, which was 61cm, and selected the 10mm disc as a close representation of the object against the background where it was seen. At this point, no firm distance had been established, so measurements were taken (as best as possible) from the front of the house, to the rear of the house opposite behind which the object had vanished. This distance was approx 35 yards.

Using calculations, it was estimated that the object measured slightly less than 2 feet in diameter.

Two days later, PROBE member Bill Ryder was contacted in order to obtain precise weather conditions for the time of the sighting. It was initially thought that the red underside colouring of the object was due to sun reflection from it being near sunset. Unfortunately, Mrs. Stevens' summary of the weather conditions on the report form as 'cloudy - visibilty good'. The concise weather report bore out this as there was a great deal of cloud at a height of between 2000 and 3000 feet. As OS had said, visibilty was good, actually 30 km. So the object did not reflect sunset, and it was indeed coloured red itself.

Because of the small size of the object, model aircraft had to be checked out. It must be pointed out that due to the information already obtained at this stage it was felt unnecessary to check out aircraft movements etc, and this aspect of the investigation procedure was omitted. However, after telephoning the Warminster Tourist Information Centre for information on model aircraft clubs, the library had to be contacted. IM could not obtain any information from the Tourist Information as they did not keep such records and suggested that the library be contacted.

The Warminster Library proved a little more helpful but could not provide IM with any addresses. Apparently there used to be one some years ago, and they only operated from Keevil aerodrome. No-one flew model aircraft over or around the town. This avenue of enquiry had to be dropped also.

It was quite fortunate that IM was reading the then current issue of PEGASUS (May/June 1981), as this featured a short article by Richard Colborne on silver balloons. It described a newly-marketed balloon that is made of a thin plastic/aluminium laminate and is inflated by gas(helium or balloon gas). They are silver, but also available in other colours and are highly reflective.

IM attempted to contact Richard Colborne through SIGAP, who produce PEGASUS, but discovered that he was in Mexico. This halted investigation in this area, as this enquiry was to establish a manufacturer who could supply such a balloon.

This proved unfortunate as all calculations were directing the investigation toward the balloon theory. Because an approximate distance from the window had been established, namely 35 yards - perhaps 40, the speed of the object could then be determined. Put down on paper, using OS figures from the sighting report form (10-15 seconds) it transpired that it travelled at a speed of between 5 and 7 miles per hour. Its direction was in order of that of the wind, which itself was a 10 knot westerly. In terms of miles, 10 knots roughly equalls to 11.5 miles per hour, and it did not seem odd for an object to be carried at a speed of, say 6 mph, by a wind travelling at 11.5 mph - after allowing for drag (wind resistance and mass).

Meanwhile, OS had drawn the object onto the photograph after two attempts. Firstly, she had placed it too high and it had to be erased with TIPPEX whitener. Her second attempt, although more correctly positioned was far too large compared with the actual size of the object. It was felt that this did not matter too much because the actual figures were available on paper. IM later amended the drawn object, with the permission of OS, to show the division of the silver and red colours.

Several telephone calls were made by Julie Mrzyglod to toy shops in Avon and Wiltshire to try and trace manufacturers of these balloons, which bore more of a resemblance to seamed cushions than traditional balloons. All that could be ascertained is that no shops contacted stocked such items but were well-aware of their existance. Some shops themselves were endeavouring to purchase some but could not find a supplier. It was suggested by some shops that the balloons could perhaps be bought from market dealers, or shop-doorway sellers, but none in Bristol were selling them.

At that time, several reports of small discs were being reported around the country and SCUFORI, the Swindon group were involved in a mini-flap in which several groups of witnesses all saw small siver cushion-like discs hovering in the Swindon area. They too were also looking for a supplier until one of their members obtained an advert from a circular to shop-owners. This advert was offering silver balloons, and the name, address and London telephone number was relayed to IM.

The company, FAIRLANE (UK) LTD, were telephoned on 7th October by IM, and after explaining the reason for wanting to obtain a sample balloon (especially a silver/red one) Fairlane agreed to send one free of charge. Actually they sent four, including a silver/red one as promised, together with a silver/yellow balloon, and two all-silver balloons - one of these heart-shaped. A letter of thanks was sent on 9th October, the day they arrived.

The next problem was obtaining a suitable gas to inflate them, as ordinary air did not make them bouyant. SCUFORI tried several gases including CALOR, and they tried hot air. The only answer was to hire a BALLOON GAS cylinder from BOC Ltd in Bristol. SCUFORI, as it was in their own interest as well, agreed to pay half the costs which totalled £18. The balloons could now be inflated easily and several photographs were taken for future reference.

The Reconstruction

On Sunday 18th October, a pre-arranged visit was made to Warminster and IM called upon OS and her husband, explaining what was about to happen. OS was told that a gas-filled balloon would be sent up into the air and retained by a length of cotton, at the bottom of her garden in the street. The balloon was sent aloft on the opposite side of Cop Heap Lane, as near to the assumed flight-path of the object. A set of photographs were taken of the balloon from the living room. OS agreed that what she was looking at then was very possibly what she had originally seen.

Mrs. Stevens was quite satisfied that she had originally seen a gas-filled plastic silver/red balloon, floating with the wind, fly past her window. PROBE were also satisfied that she may have seen one of these balloons.

Further tests were carried out on Cradle Hill, Warminster later that afternoon to record on film the actions of these balloons when not retained with thread. The article in PEGASUS explained that these balloons would rise in the air until they found their own ceiling – something that would be essential if such a balloon was the culprit, as Mrs. Stevens' object definitely maintained a level course, neither rising nor dropping.

A balloon was filled as much as possible with the gas and sent aloft with no restraining thread and it slowly lifted up into the air. It also kept an even keel and certainly resembled a 'common flying saucer' as it ascended. At about 200 feet, an extremely rough estimation, the balloon did level out as if it had found its own ceiling – in this case about 700 feet above sea-level – but it was freshly inflated to its maximum. The object that OS watched had reached a ceiling of roughly 400 feet above sea level (about 20 feet above the road) but there is no way of knowing how long it had been inflated and for how long it had been drifting. The balloon which had been sent aloft afterwards ascended further – perhaps caught in a thermal – and drifted in a south east direction towards Battlesbury Hill. It eventually vanished from sight because of its height but mainly due to its distance away from the observers.

It is a fact that that balloon would eventually descend as the gas escaped from it, as it did when tested overnight indoors. When left against the ceiling of the room at night, it was found on the floor in the morning – still inflated but not holding a sufficient quantity of balloon gas to make it lighter-than-air. Therefore it is quite possible that OS had witnesses a balloon that had been released perhaps a few hours earlier, somewhere west of Warminster. It had by that time lost some of its gas and had descended to a much lower height. It is not impossible that the balloon which had been released on Cradle Hill had not dropped a few hours later and was then drifting at roof-top level somewhere around Salisbury.

Some of this is obviously speculation, but enough experimentation has been carried out to support these theories. The actions of the balloons have been recorded on still photographs for later use should any similar cases require them, and these actions go a long way toward explaining what was seen over Warminster on 14th July 1981. Of course it cannot be proven that OS definitely saw a balloon, but the suggested explanation seems both logical and plausible. PROBE, along with the witness, are happy to accept this theory and apply it to this particular case. Until the time when perhaps should more information be available on this case, this file has been therefore closed with the evaluation of <u>EXPLAINED</u>.

Conclusion

Mrs. Stevens was quite satisfied that she had originally seen a gas-filled plastic silver/red balloon, floating with the wind, fly past her window. PROBE were also satisfied that she may have seen one of these balloons.

Further tests were carried out on Cradle Hill, Warminster later that afternoon to record on film the actions of these balloons when not retained with thread. The article in PEGASUS explained that these balloons would rise in the air until they found their own ceiling - something that would be essential if such a balloon was the culprit, as Mrs. Stevens' object definitely maintained a level course, neither rising nor dropping.

A balloon was filled as much as possible with the gas and sent aloft with no restraining thread and it slowly lifted up into the air. It also kept an even keel and certainly resembled a 'common flying saucer' as it ascended. At about 200 feet, an extremely rough estimation, the balloon did level out as if it had found its own ceiling - in this case about 700 feet above sea-level - but it was freshly inflated to its maximum. The object that OS watched had reached a ceiling of roughly 400 feet above sea level (about 20 feet above the road) but there is no way of knowing how long it had been inflated and for how long it had been drifting. The balloon which had been sent aloft afterwards ascended further - perhaps caught in a thermal - and drifted in a south east direction towards Battlesbury Hill. It eventually vanished from sight because of its height but mainly due to its distance away from the observers.

It is a fact that that balloon would eventually descend as the gas escaped from it, as it did when tested overnight indoors. When left against the ceiling of the room at night, it was found on the floor in the morning - still inflated but not holding a sufficient quantity of balloon gas to make it lighter-than-air. Therefore it is quite possible that OS had witnessed a balloon that had been released perhaps a few hours earlier, somewhere west of Warminster. It had by that time lost some of its gas and had descended to a much lower height. It is not impossible that the balloon which had been released on Cradle Hill had not dropped a few hours later and was then drifting at roof-top level somewhere around Salisbury.

Some of this is obviously speculation, but enough experimentation has been carried out to support these theories. The actions of the balloons have been recorded on still photographs for later use should any similar cases require them, and these actions go a long way toward explaining what was seen over Warminster on 14th July 1981. Of course it cannot be proven that OS definitely saw a balloon, but the suggested explanation seems both logical and plausible. PROBE, along with the witness, are happy to accept this theory and apply it to this particular case. Until the time when perhaps should more information be available on this case, this file has been therefore closed with the evaluation of EXPLAINED.

Ian Mrzyglod   Julie Mrzyglod

24th October 1981

5

Alien Abduction – Birstall, West Yorkshire

An opportunity to examine one such report, following detailed investigation by Philip Mantle and Andy Roberts, began in July 1987. It was first brought to the notice of Philip, by way of telephone messages left for him at his home address, on his return from holiday. Phil telephoned the woman – Jane Murphy (22) from Highfield Grange, Birstall, and held a brief conversation with her, during which she spoke of having seen aliens in her house over a period of the last 12 years.

Phil:

> *"I must admit that, at first, I thought I was dealing with a hoaxer, or someone who was mentally unbalanced, but agreed to see her on the 30th July."*

On that date the two men went to the house in Birstall, West Yorkshire, and after introductions, Jane explained what had taken place, which was one of many interviews conducted during visits to see her.

1976

Jane:

> *"One night, while in bed, the room was filled with red light, accompanied by a whirring noise. The next day, when I*

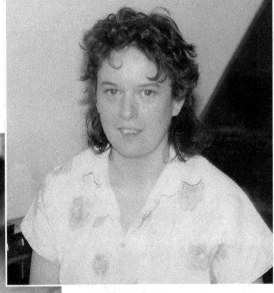

Photograph of Jane Murphy taken at her home on August 11th, 1987. Photograph taken by Philip Mantle

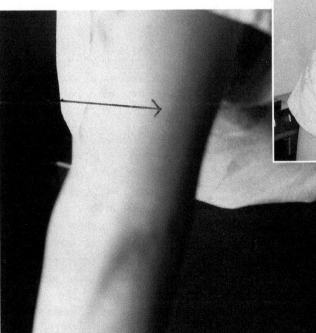

Photograph of Jane's arm taken on 11th August, 198. The mark on Jane's arm was so small that it is not visible on this photograph. An arrow indicates the approximate position of the mark

> *got up, I heard on the local radio station of some UFO sightings which had taken place around the area, and wondered if they were connected with what I had experienced."*

The fields where Jane Murphy encountered the 'spaceship' and was abducted in March 1981. These photographs were taken in September 1987 by Philip Mantle. According to Jane, the factory in the centre of the photograph was not built at the time of her abduction experience. To date (September 1987) this fact has yet to be verified. These fields are only a short distance from Jane's present address, and although there are houses and a farm nearby, as well as the factory, they are off the beaten track somewhat.

Jane was asked to describe the aliens she met. Initially she could only remember their eyes, which were completely black, or blue in colour, and larger than human ones.

> *"Their hair was like doll's hair. They were human in appearance, but not quite human. They were about 7ft tall; there were both male and female species of the aliens, although I did not notice any physical extremities as the ones which distinguish male and female humans."*

1981

In March, Jane, who had retired to bed late, suddenly awoke to find herself standing in a field, feeling very cold and wet. She then noticed a huge metallic object, hovering over the field. Suddenly, a group of 'figures' (as many as 10) approached her. The 'figures' were vaguely humanoid, but for some reason Jane found herself unable to focus on them.

> *"One of the 'figures' had a cloth in his hand and put it over my face. I pretended to be unconscious but they injected me; I blacked out. I acted as if I was asleep, but 'they' weren't fooled; the next thing I knew was being injected in the arm and then lost consciousness. I was then aware of being on a couch or a table. I was instructed to wash in a type of shower or bath, apparently constructed to hold a human being in shape. My sexual organs were examined. I was then led to a table close to the 'aliens', on the top of which was a number of what looked like 'sweets' displayed. I took one, and was about to eat another, when I was told quite forcibly, by one of the aliens, not to."*

Status report update – Andy Roberts, September 1987: (extract)

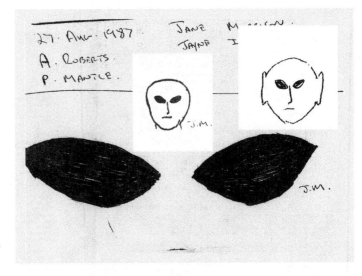

"Phil and I have interviewed Jane five times for period of between 30-90 minutes. She appears to be a repeater witness, although many of her experiences have taken place in a type of lucid dream. She also alleges that several members of the family have had UFO related experiences. I do not think she is attempting to hoax us on a conscious level. She has never asked for any publicity and has insisted we keep her details confidential. The overall details of the case fit reasonably well into the general abduction scenario. She has been to see her doctor and psychiatrist because of the unsettling nature of the experiences. Whatever the case, Jane appears to be giving us UFO related information which is complex and little known amongst most people outside the UFO community. If she believes these experiences to be true then the question remains, where is she is getting this information from?"

2.8.1989 – Philip Mantle:

"Until we gain the assistance of reputable social scientists then we will remain as the only avenue open to such people who have undergone strange experiences, the origins of which we amateurs can only guess at. We are the last port of call for such people and I will not turn my back on them"

We decided not to include the whole of those documents owing to lack of space in this book, there is no reason to disbelieve what Jane has claimed, she is one of many that has sustained a traumatic experience of almost unbelievable terrifying proportions involving intelligences who appear to exist alongside us. Both Phil and Andy felt in their final summary that they were dealing with a genuine and sincere woman rather than any deliberate hoax.

(HC addition # 1992, Source: Carl Nagaitis, Philip Mantle, *Without Consent,* Type: G)

Jane was shown the inside of the 'spaceship' during her tour, and saw what she believes were female aliens, drinking, but that no conversation took place. Her recollection of this incident is vague, according to Phil and Andy. The two men were startled when Jane described an act of sexual intercourse with one of the aliens, who had lain on top of her. Although no penetration had taken place, Jane was adamant that sex had occurred. After the event she later noticed a small mark on her arm, which had not been there before.

The Abduction Experience of Jane Murphy

Introduction

It was my pleasure to meet Jane on June 21st, 1988, after having read the transcript of the interview carried out by Phil--ip Mantle and Andy Roberts in August, 1987.

In a short note which I wrote a little later, I gave my im--pression of Jane, who struck me as a thoroughly down-to-earth individual, free of any overt eccentric or neurotic behaviour traits.

As a parapsychologist, I couldn't help comparing her experi--ences with out-of-body experiences and her description of the alien abduction seemed akin to accounts of astral travelling, which are not uncommon in the occult literature.

I welcome this opportunity to comment more fully on this case.

The Main Facts and their Interpretation.

Jane draws a distinction between those occasions when, as she says, 'it's really happening' and the many dreams she has had of being taken on the spaceship, being made pregnant by the aliens, having pre-natal examinations, having the baby there, being threatened with harm if she talks about her experiences to others, having minor surgical incisions and so on.

She has had a series of disturbing and frightening encount--ers, the main elements of which are as follows.

1. At age sixteen, her bedroom glowed red and a humming noise accompanied it. She says that she was not asleep, but she may have been in a hypnopompic state, in which anomalous percept--ions can occur. The next morning there were radio reports of UFO sightings in the locality the previous night.

2. Between sixteen and twentyone, she reports many dreams of UFOs; usually five or six at a time in formation.

3. At age twentyone, after the birth of her child, she claims she was abducted by aliens into a UFO near her mother's home. Because she was terrified, she was injected with a sedative. Ater an alien had sex with her, she took a bath and was ex--amined by the aliens. She claims she saw other humans who had also been abducted. Once they were finished with her, she found herself easily into bed immediately. She woke up at once and noticed it was 6.30.a.m. Both she and her spouse notic--ed a new mark on her arm the next day and claims that this is where she had been injected.

John W. Shaw

Training Consultant
Chartered Psychologist
Senior Lecturer
Manchester University
and
Associate Professor
Columbia Pacific University (UK Faculty)

Hollybush Farm
Newtown
Biddulph Park
Biddulph
Staffordshire. ST8 7SW

0782 517444

16th August 1988.

Dear Philip,

Thank you for your recent letters. I very much appreciated the various reports and articles which you sent me and reading them has helped me to put my encounter with Jane Murphy into perspective. The more one thinks about such experiences, the more psychological possibilities emerge.

In elaborating upon JM's experience, I should stress that my explanation is not intended as an explanation of all abductee experiences. 'Psychological' explanations, as Westrum points out, are not always adequate. However, in Jane's case, since there is no evidence that she was physically absent from her home during the supposed abduction, a psychological explanation becomes more tenable. I admit that the physical symptoms she suffered after several of the encounters such as stomach ache, vaginal infection, physical marks and scars, suggest that she was physically present during the abduction.

However, I think one need not draw this conclusion. Some evidence, and associated theorising, suggests that the physical body is part of a "Chinese box" arrangement in which astral and spiritual counterparts of the physical are to be found. Certain types of paranormal healing suggest that changes in the physical body can be brought about without the supposed 'healer' being physically present. I refer particularly, but not exclusively, to absent healing and also to the Chapman/Lang phenomena, of which you may have heard.

The strongest evidence for this theory is, however, to be found in the many reports of OOBES, especially many reports of the subjects' own physical body being perceived from a different position, e.g. near the ceiling of the bedroom, operating theatre or whatever. The fact that the sensory system operates during such dislocation, and also memory, is important, especially if one is to account for the reports which Jane and other abductees bring back.

One of the most striking points of evidence of 'bilocation' (which is not the same as OOBE, but is clearly related) is recounted in the recent book "The Geller Effect" by Uri Geller and Guy Lyon Playfair (pp 250-2). I think you should try to get hold of this and read the section in question.

Mr Alan Dormer.
Bramfield Road
Rayleigh, Essex,

9/1/07

Dear Hanson,

read with much interest your article in the Southend Standard 5th January about UFOS. I have hesitated about contacting you because I am not looking for any kind of publicity good or bad, but I have decided to tell you what I saw if it helps your project. Back in the early 80's about the time John Lennon was killed, I was travelling to work with a friend at about 6 o'clock in the evening,(friend has since died). We were travelling down the A13 to London where we worked in a bank doing night security when suddenly I said to my friend look at that, coming towards us was a disc shaped object silver greyish in colour, I guess it was about 10feet by 10 feet it would have fitted easily into my living room, it was traveling very slowly no more than about 50-60 miles per hour, and only about 40-50 feet above the ground, it did'nt seem to care if anyone saw it. There was no sign of exhaust fumes, or flames coming from it, it did'nt seem to make any noise at all, I did,nt see any windows in it, and it only seemed very flat looking, no space for any passenger, maybe it was guided from another sorce somewhere. The disc flew past the car on my side, I was the passenger, it was so close you could almost touch it, I would have given anything for a camera any camera it was that close. I turned my head to watch it go past and as I did I noticed other cars behind watching it also, but I don't remember us moving, it seemed as though we had pulled into the kirb but I don't remember my friend breaking. Suddenly the disc turned onto it's side so that the bottom was facing me, and again there did'nt seem to be any windows, as it turned it started to accelerate and disappeared from my view. I said to my friend did you see that, I can't believe it. But my friend who was ever the sceptic said, it must be kids larking about,and I said, how could kids throw something in the air as big as a car. Then we just seemed to carry on down the A13, but I don't recall my friend starting the car, but as I mentioned, I don't remember him stopping in the kirb, it seems that moment in time seems a blank, did We, did'nt we, sought of thing. I never saw any reports in the local papers, but I know others did see what I saw. As I said at the beginning, I am not looking for any kind of publicity. I have sent you this story to help you if it can. Best wishes for your project.

Yours Sincerely.

Alan Dormer

Date/Time	:	1981 @ 02.40 Hrs
Location	:	A45 Road between Flore and Northampton
Witness	:	Mr.Michael White
Source	:	LUFOS (Northampton Branch)
Investigators	:	Diane Shepherd

Description

I was travelling in my car when I turned left at the A45 junction with Stanpole village towards Northampton. I then became aware of a very bright object on my left hovering in the sky. As I moved slowly it moved slowly easterly, keeping at the same distance, believing it to be a helicopter possibly in distress I slowed down almost to a stop, listening for noise. There was none and I thought my eyes were deceiving me, it was raining gently and I was looking at the object through raindrops on my sunroof.

I remember looking in my mirrors for other cars, noticing also the time of day, by this time the object had altered position in the sky to a point where I saw it through the windscreen. I wound open my sunroof and passenger's window, getting wet I increased speed at which point the object did likewise, but very quickly also gaining height then stopping.

Increasing my speed it stayed in view, it then started to move back slowly towards my direction at the same altitude and stopped in the sky. I stopped too, I wished for other witnesses at this point, there were none. At this point I was looking at it with my naked eye, I had just passed Upton church, then at a fantastic speed it moved in a south-easterly direction across my line of forward vision.

I wound down my driver's window and closed the sunroof as I was getting wet, the object then stopped and hovered to my right at a greater distance than the Easterly Stance. I accelerated to approximately 40mph it too then gained fantastic speed in a Easterly direction, I turned in a Northerly direction and looking back it was just a bright 'pin-head'.

I caught sight of it on two more occasions when proceeding across Kingsthorpe Mill. My experience had been so intense that I found myself mistakenly in the driveway of my old house from where I had moved some three years earlier.

About three weeks later, I read a piece in the Northampton Evening Newspaper. The 'Chronicle & Echo' was appealing on behalf of two readers for confirmation from any other readers. They had reported to the columnist, seeing a fast moving light some three weeks earlier and they thought they were seeing things. As this sighting seemed to coincide with the timing and general description of my own experience, I replied to the appeal indicating my positive experience.

Several days later, Jane began to suffer from stomach ache, which then developed into a vaginal infection. She went to see her local doctor, who proscribed medication. However, as this failed to clear the problem, Jane went to the hospital where they gave her further medication which eventually cleared the infection, although this took three months.

Phil sent us a file of documents, containing approximately 100 pages, which relates to the interviews conducted by him and Andy Roberts. The file also included opinions expressed by John. W. Shaw a chartered psychologist and then senior lecture at Manchester University who was asked to comment following interviews held with Jane.

The A5

The A5 is a major road in England and Wales. It runs for about 260 miles (420 km) (including sections concurrent with other designations) from London, England, to Holyhead, Wales, following, in part, a section of the Roman Iter III route, which linked Lodnon and Dover and later took the Anglo-Saxon name of Watling Street.

This stretch of road was to provide the backcloth for a number of UFO sightings, brought to our attention, over the years. Some of them involved motorists, who told of being followed by strange lights. We were to hear of all manner of strange reports, which occasionally involved complaints of medical ailments that occurred shortly after the event. This included a complaint by a Birmingham lorry driver, who sustained scratches to his face, after a strange object hovered over the cab, of his vehicle while near the Welsh Border in the 1990s.

Close Encounter over A5, Shropshire

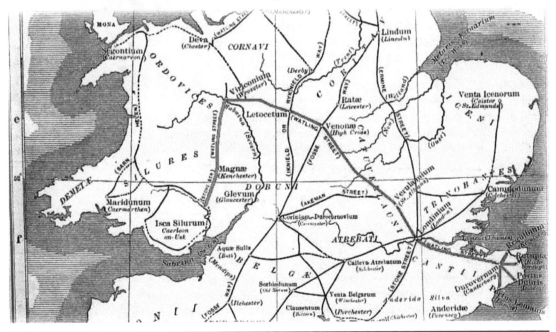

In 1978, Valerie Walters (23) was working at the Granada Bingo Hall and Social Club in Wellington, Shropshire, when she became friends with fellow worker Rosemary Hawkins (23). Through the friendship Valerie met Vivien Heyward (24), Rosie's next door neighbour, and the three of them began to go out socially.

During the early morning of the 16th July 1981, Valerie, Rosemary and Vivien were travelling home from a night club, at Shrewsbury, along a stretch of the A5, when they sighted a UFO. Their subsequent story of what happened was to bathe them in a glare of publicity and lead to many personal interviews on TV, and radio. Unfortunately, it was also to attract the attention of the tabloid newspapers. One example showed the girls as terrified victims, being strapped to their chairs by their alien captors, others even more graphic. We wrote to Valerie, in 2003, and she agreed to talk to us. During another visit to her; a couple of years later, we spoke to Valerie and Rosemary. In May 2013 we saw Valerie once again when we discussed the matter again.

On 15th July 1981, Valerie, Vivien, Rosemary, and Joan Copp, arranged a night out at the 'over 25s dance' at Tiffanys Nightclub, in Shrewsbury (renamed Park Lane). They would travel there in Vivien's car – a white 'Hillman Avenger' – and meet up with other girls they knew.

Rosemary and Vivien called for Valerie, at 8.30pm. The three of them went to pick-up Joan, who told them she had changed her mind about going out, which Valerie thought out of character for her, as she had seemed keen enough earlier in the day. After arriving at the club, they found their other friends already there and purchased some soft drinks, rather than alcoholic beverage, because of the cost.

Valerie thought it seemed an odd evening because they had forgotten that, instead of the usual cabaret act, there was a brass band playing, (The Zutphen Brass Band) but decided to stay on for the 'disco', which started at 11.30pm, rather than leaving. At about 1.00am the group noticed two men, by the bar, dressed in white trousers and white shirts, like cricketers, who appeared interested in striking up a conversation with them.

One of them came over and asked the group if they had a car and, if so, whether anyone was going back to Telford. He then asked Vivien if she could give them a lift to Wellington. She declined, as she had never met them before and after the usual cheeky banter, he rejoined his companion.

Valerie and Rosemary

A few moments later, when the girls looked up, the two men then went into the gent's toilets and were not seen again, which struck them as strange, as they never saw them leave through the exit door?

Sighting of the UFO

Valerie:

> *"When we left the club, just after 2am, Vivien was driving, with Rosemary sitting in the front passenger seat, with me sat behind her in the rear passenger side. As we drove through the town, we saw four men working on a gas main, at the side of the road, which seemed odd at that time of the morning. They were dressed like workmen and only one of them was wearing*

a hard hat; their clothes reminded me of the 1970s pop group – *The Village People!*

Just before we reached The Horseshoe *Public House, on our right, a taxi overtook us, driving fast, and caused Vivienne to swerve onto the grass verge at the side of the road, in order to avoid a collision.*

*We continued on our journey over the bridge, past the old Abbey, on the left, then through Abbey Foregate, past Shrewsbury College, and drove onto the A5. As we drove through *Atcham, Vivien remarked on how quiet everything had gone. I put this down to a bored and disappointing evening – something we all agreed on.*

Valerie indicating the location of the incident

By now I had began to feel drowsy. As we went around the next bend in the road, I saw some lights in the distance. I first thought they must have been either car lights, or a helicopter from RAF Shawbury, and settled down again. As we went past the turning for Uppington and Walcott, I was aroused by Vivien calling out, 'What are those lights?'

I sat up and leaned forward. A mixture of emotions coursed through me – excitement and fear. I looked out of the front window and saw, slightly to the left of the car and in front of us, the base of a strange 'craft', hovering a couple of hundred feet in the air above, forming a perfect circle, with two red lights in the middle and four very bright yellow/white lights spaced evenly around the inner rim of the outer edge, which illuminated a grey metallic surface in appearance, accompanied by a low buzzing noise coming from it, despite the car engine running.

I heard Vivien shout out, 'The car's losing power. There's something wrong with the engine'. I felt disorientated and, looking out of the window, had a notion there was something wrong with the landscape. It seemed different, as if we were travelling along an unfamiliar route. It was like something out of a science fiction film. Rosemary wanted to stop the car to get a closer look. Vivienne refused. She put her foot down hard, but things seemed to go into slow motion.

When I looked through the window again, I could see it quite low down in the field next to us, enabling me to see it sideways, when I saw a row of windows and a dome, which lit up the field below it, highlighting a nearby oak tree in its brilliance – then it was higher up in the sky, showing windows, dome, and bottom of the 'craft'. As it went upwards, the white lights dimmed, before it vanished from view. We seemed to have been watching it for only a few minutes, but found ourselves driving past the Shamrock Café, which was only a minute's drive from where we had first seen the UFO."

*Atcham is a village, ecclesiastical parish and civil parish in Shropshire, England. It is situated on the B4380 (the old A5) 5 miles south-east of Shrewsbury. The River Severn flows around the village. To the south is the village of Cross Houses and to the north-west the hamlet of Emstrey.

The girls decided to report the matter to the police and drove to Malinslee Police Station, at Telford, and told the officer what had happened. They were very disconcerted when he laughed at them, suggesting they must have seen a helicopter on night exercise from RAF Shawbury!

Allegation of missing time

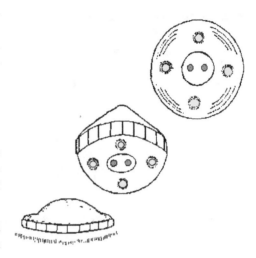

When Valerie arrived home at 3.25am, rather than the usual time of 2.30am, leading her to believe she was unable to account for twenty minutes or so of missing time, she told her husband, Steven, what had taken place.

The next morning, Valerie discovered Vivien had contacted the *Shropshire Star*, as a result of which an article about the matter was published on 17th July 1981.

Valerie:

> *"After the incident, I experienced some nosebleeds and discovered some raised lumps on the left-hand side of my body, which were not there previous to the incident. When I discussed this with Rosemary, I was astonished to find she had similar marks on her body. Fortunately, they disappeared within 2-3 years."*

After a few weeks had gone by without any further contact from the police, Steven purchased a copy of *The Unexplained*, which had details of a Manchester-based UFO organisation. Valerie wrote to them and received a visit from Stephen Banks, one of their investigators.

A séance takes place

A couple of weeks after the UFO sighting, on one of the regular 'girls' night in', attended by Rosemary, her daughter Fran, and neighbour Jane, Valerie asked Pauline, her mother-in-law – an experienced medium – whether she would be willing to set up a séance.

Valerie:

> "I poured a glass of wine for each of us and placed them on a coffee table, nearby, so that we could have a drink after the séance. We held hands and Pauline said a prayer of protection. Immediately, I felt myself going light-headed. My face was itchy as if I had cobwebs all over it. I realised I was about to go into a trance and pulled myself out of it. Pauline then began to talk in a male foreign voice. As she did so, her facial features changed. This was quite scary. I asked her to speak in English, which she did. Pauline's 'guide' said he was a Mexican Indian and that he was enjoying having a drink.
>
> He told Jane, who hadn't met Pauline before, that her father was very poorly with a heart condition and it would soon be time for him to leave the Earth plane. He also said that actor Leonard Rossiter, who played in Rising Damp, was going to have a heart attack. A few weeks later, both men passed away."

It was also disclosed that Natalie was going to lose her baby but that she would have more children (she was unaware that she was pregnant). Within a few weeks, Natalie had a miscarriage. The 'guide', now slurring his words, then told the group he was enjoying the drink and goodbyes were said.

Valerie:

> "When we turned around to get our drinks, all of the glasses were empty. How could this be? The circle had not been broken!"

In July 1981, Rosemary and Valerie travelled to Liverpool, where they were interviewed on *This Morning TV*, by Richard Madeley and Judy Finnegan. During the course of this programme, they also met John. E. Mack, Jim Bowen, and Michael York.

Offers of Regression

Valerie:

> "I had written to Jenny Randles, after seeing her address in a magazine that my husband had bought for me. We were visited by a young man, named Stephen Banks, who had been sent out to investigate our UFO sighting. He was going through the evening's events with us, when he pointed out that there was some time missing! He suggested that we might like to try hypnotic regression to find out what had happened during the missing time.
>
> Harry Harris contacted us after reading Stephen's report with MUFORA, as a result of which our first hypnosis sessions took place in September 1981, when Harry Harris, Norman Collinson, Mike Sacks, and hypnotist – Dr. Joseph Jaffe, were present. In Christmas 1981 another session took place, involving just myself, Harry Harris and Dr. Albert Keller. In

*1982 all three of us met up with Harry Harris, and Dr. Davies. In 1991/2 Rosie and I had an idea that perhaps we would be able to overcome our fears by carrying out an experiment to hypnotize us together, which took place with Harry Harris, *Roy Dutton and Dr. Davies again.*

Valerie Walters in 2013

Hypnosis session autumn 1981

The first session, which was videoed by Harry, was conducted in the lounge of Harry's house at Timperley Cheshire and began with the two subjects being placed into a rapid trance-like state by a GP Doctor hypnotist. The Doctor then called Harry back into the room. He had only been told about them having been involved in a car crash and that they were experiencing problems in remembering details. He had not been told about the UFO connection. The Doctor then asked the girls about the circumstances of their road trip, in July 1981. They told of a 'craft' blocking the road ahead of them and of being approached by small creatures, who had gone to the nearside passenger door and, it appears, had tried to drag Rosemary out of the car. Rosemary began to become agitated at this point. The Doctor checked her pulse and told

---

*Roy known to the authors is a retired aerospace engineer, who has long nurtured the theory (backed up by convincing evidence) that UFO sightings and close encounters can be plotted in accordance with now identified age old programmes, using the sun and selected stars as sources of reference, which Roy believes was originally set-up to facilitate long-term monitoring of our species by fully automated craft. He has written a book, which we recommend, entitled UFOs in Reality (T.R. Dutton, Author House, UK, 2011)

Rosemary Hawkins in 2013

her to sleep. The GP then began to question Valerie, who spoke of seeing Vivienne staring straight ahead in the car,

> *"In the moonlight I saw small human-like creatures, moving towards the car and approaching the passenger door. The door was opened. Rosemary screamed that they were trying to pull her out and was resisting furiously. A black mist enveloped her and she was gone. I remember climbing out of the car. Vivienne was still comatose. I was aware of walking through an open gate into the field, feeling completely bewildered. I felt a pair of hands placed on my shoulders from the rear, and a strong masculine voice said to me 'Don't be afraid'."*

Hypnosis session March 1991

This took place on the 24th March 1991, and involved Harry, Roy Dutton, Linda Taylor, and now Elaine (Rosemary's sister) who had been asked to take on the role of asking questions of the two women, following the initial introduction made by the therapist. Once again, the two women became agitated during conversation about when 'they' had tried to remove Rosemary from the car. After assurance that what they were remembering was not happening now, Rosemary became calm and spoke freely, describing her fight with the entities during her removal from the vehicle, and then being enveloped by a black mist. She then told of finding herself in a strange white room, with white lights, containing just a table.

The White Room

Elaine then asked Valerie to tell her what happened. Valerie described the events leading up to the sighting of the UFO.

> *"It was like being sucked up into a vacuum, or lift. I couldn't catch my breath. I found myself in a white, wedge-shaped room. The walls were like metal and I could hear shuffling, and saw a man and woman in the room."*

Valerie asked them where Rosemary was; she was told Rosemary was being examined, at which point Valerie remarked that they were now touching her clothes and hair.

Valerie:

> *"The 'woman', whoever she was, had, by now, put on my shoes and was trying to make me laugh by hobbling around in them."*

Elaine then switched back to Rosemary and asked her what happened next in the white room. Rosemary said she was very frightened.

> *"I was stood near the wall, not daring to move – then I was told to get onto the table. I don't want to but know I must. I could hear a shuffling sound. Six of them – round heads, with no faces – like robots, appeared all around me. They moved as if on rollers, or castors. I knew they weren't going to harm me. I had to go with them through a door and down a corridor, along which I could see strange things – like machinery. I was told not to describe this as it would betray them. [See Ros Reynolds-Parham's experience, 1982, for engine plans – was there a connection?] I then entered a small, narrow room; it had doors, windows, and two beds. In an oblong room I could see Valerie. I was then 'floated' horizontally into this room, accompanied by six of the little 'robots' and placed onto a bed next to Valerie, who was asleep."*

The two women then pieced together the following account of what took place. A tall man, with dark eyes and long hair, wearing a green gown, entered the room. He placed one hand on Rosemary's left hand, the other on Valerie's right arm, and telepathically communicated with both women, accompanied by an overwhelming sense of well-being.

When asked why they thought this was happening to them, they replied:

> *"The man is trying to demonstrate this form of communication was possible."*

When asked why Vivienne was not included, 'he' said that

> *"Vivienne wasn't strong enough to cope with it, we are not the only ones that this has happened to, and the purpose was one of learning."*

The Aliens' homeland and the next stage

According to Roy Dutton, the following part was the most exciting part of the session. When asked if the creatures had given them any information about where they had come from, Rosemary replied:

"You wouldn't understand."

Pressed further, she told of having seen something like a map but she was unable to draw it.

"Not like a road map – like a black window, with shapes on it."

At this point the hypnotherapist asked them to remember every detail of the map, so that they could draw it afterwards.

Further recall took place and included conversation about being

"floated from our respective beds, along two small side-by-side tunnels (powered by a machine that didn't need a motor) with a light at the end. The 'man' was waiting for us . . . smelt disinfectant . . . have to go on . . . they are unable to influence humans, who had come to a realisation first . . . lots of other people had gone through these experiences and they would know when the time was right . . . out of the tunnels . . . now lying on two tables . . . given sweet medicinal drink, about half a cup full, to counteract the effect of the machine."

At this point, the two women said that there were now three other people in the room. Further questioning failed to identify who these were, at which stage Rosemary began to become agitated, so the session was brought to a halt.

Hypnosis session March 1991 – A map is drawn

On April 24th 1991, the respective parties assembled once again at Harry's house. The two women were taken back to the strange rooms and questioned about the 'tunnels', but became very confused and refused to answer any further questions.

Roy asked the hypnotist if he could speak to them, and was given permission to do so. He told them that he had made a full transcript of the converservations and was puzzled why they were now reluctant to answer the questions.

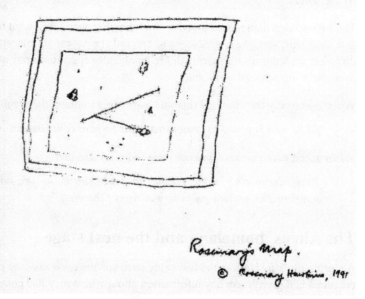

Rosemary replied: *"You haven't asked the right questions"*.

Roy asked them some questions about the map and handed a pencil and pad to Rosemary, who was then asked to try and draw what she could remember of the map, which she agreed to, and was then awoken. The minutes ticked by as Rosemary struggled to draw the diagram, but eventually, she finished and handed the map back to Roy. Valerie was asked to do the same. The session then came to a close.

Rosemary's map.
© *Rosemary Hawkins, 1991*

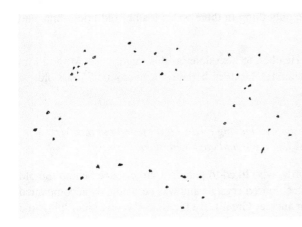

We were to come across a number of other similar incidents, involving interaction between motorists and UFOs along the A5, as the years passed. Frustratingly we were to see, time after time again, the way in which the Press responded to reports of this nature, continuing to 'poke fun' at people who should be praised for having the courage to come forward and tell of their experiences. If we were talking of one individual case, involving people of questionable mentality, it would be easy to prejudge, but we are not. For far too long, people have had to endure the stigma associated with reports such as these.

Valerie and Rosemary are to be commended for having the courage to come forward and stand up in the face of ridicule to tell what happened. It was a privilege to meet them and speak to others at length, like Lynda Jones from Didsbury, Manchester, who was to find herself in a similar situation in 1979.

In 1982 Vivienne, a nurse by profession, went to Canada to work as a children's nanny – neither Rosemary nor Valerie ever heard from her again, and have no idea where she is to this present date.

Objects moving of their own accord

In 1992, Rosemary was employed as a part-time bar person at the *Shropshire Lad* Public House, close to where she lived at Malinslee. Valerie happened to call in one lunchtime for a drink, and was at the bar, chatting to Rosemary, when the drinks tray on the bar top flew up into the air, did a somersault, and landed on the floor beside Valerie. It is alleged that the pub was haunted. Was there a connection with this, or with the two girls? The answer to the question may lie with another mysterious incident that occurred at Rosemary's house, a couple of weeks later, when after hearing a crashing noise in the kitchen, Rosemary discovered one of the kitchen cupboards open, and all the baking tins spread over the kitchen floor.

Early years and an invisible friend

It should come of no surprise to the reader to learn that Valerie had a background history of strange happenings. Her earliest memories go back to the age of four, when she and her sister found themselves outside the house, sitting on a wooden bench at the top of the road, after being 'floated' out of the house.

On one occasion the two girls were found by their mother, who was puzzled as to how they managed to get through the locked doors, and chastised Valerie for unlocking them. In addition, Valerie told of having an invisible friend, named Heather, with whom she used to play in the next door neighbour's shed – which was little used.

> *"Heather would go off somewhere to a building that seemed shiny and made of glass, where we would play games with other children and a small lady. She was very old and had long, curly, red hair. I called her Pixie. There was a large chest in the shed that contained many books, although I couldn't read at the time."*

According to Valerie, her parents often told her off for going missing. When she explained where she had been, they said they had looked in the shed and the only thing in there was a load of old bric-a-brac and that no books were seen.

Valerie was instructed not to mention her 'friend', Heather, to next door, as this might upset Mr and Mrs Wall, who lived in the next row of cottages. Their daughter, Heather, had died aged around 5 years old.

Valerie:

> *"Heather came to see me, one day, and said she was moving away. I later found out that Mr and Mrs Wall had moved to Liverpool. I think her spirit had gone with them."*

Valerie continued to see 'Pixie' for a while afterwards, who liked to play in a large space behind the old chest in her grandmother's room. 'Pixie' played with coloured crystals and was occasionally accompanied by a gentleman, wearing a long white robe (like an ancient Greek). By the time she was nine, 'playtime with Pixie' had ceased.

Thirty years later, in 1992, Valerie purchased a rag doll for her daughter, Vicky (2). She named it 'Diddib'. Another doll was supplied to Vicky and she was asked what she wanted to call it. 'Heather' was her answer!

In 2002, on another trip to Liverpool, Valerie was part of a group that made a visit to the two Cathedrals and Albert Docks. While sat down, having a rest, she heard a voice say:

> *"I don't think you'll recognise me, because you were very young when you moved away from Church Road. My name is Mrs Wall. My family used to live by your grandparents. I recognised you, because you are so much like mom that I thought you was Barbara."*

Present day: New buildings where the 'Shamrock Café' used to be

Valerie has spent considerable time researching not only into the UFO subject but the paranormal and synchronicities which abound all around us in everyday life. The amount of coincidences is mind-boggling and she tells of many precognitions, either through memory flash or strange dreams, about events many of which were to come true.

Rosemary also claims to have had her share of similar psychic experiences.

Space prevents us from including all of Valerie's written work in this Volume. We have condensed the gist of what transpired during the sessions of regression, which were carried out with the women concerned, rather than reproducing fuller testimonials of fairly lengthy text. We wish Valerie and Rosemary the best for the future and felt privileged that they allowed us to 'write-up' their account of something, or someone, whose influence (whether alien, or not) still captivates not only theirs but our interest to this present day.

The Wrekin and Calendar Stone

Valerie believes there may be a connection between UFO sightings and the nearby Wrekin Hill once home to an ancient hill fort which is a famous Shropshire landmark? Historian George Evans and expert on the Wrekin, believes this was a sacred mountain, which was used to identify the spring, summer and autumn equinox. He has himself observed the way in which, at certain times of the year, the 'Calendar stone' – a shaft of light – would come through the rocks and rest on another rock for about ten minutes, before disappearing.

(Sources: As above, 'Close Encounter at the Shamrock Café', *News of the World*, August 1983– Keith Beabey and Pippa Sibley, personal interviews with Valerie and Rosemary/Jenny Randles & Norman Oliver, BUFORA/*New Bufora Journal*, Issue No. 7, April 2003, *Shropshire Star*, July 17, 1981)

Alien abductions

It became clear, from the number of UFO sightings brought our attention, over the years, that some of the people involved, many of whom had seen something totally out of the ordinary would ultimately try to forget the incident after realising efforts to convince others only attracted ridicule.

It seemed a lifetime ago that Tony Dodd has asked us to visit Janet, from Stourport, Worcestershire, whose allegation of abduction had been published in the *News of the World*. How unprepared and so naive I (John) truly was then!

We have often wondered if sightings of UFOs, now generally accepted as everyday occurrences, form a preliminary stage that may lead to an abduction experience. Some of the people whom we spoke to, over the years, who had sighted UFOs, particularly at close range, would tell of additional occurrences of 'high strangeness' that happened afterwards, but would fail to connect these manifestations with the original UFO incident, believing there was a vast gulf between the sighting of UFOs in the sky and paranormal events on the ground. In fact, eminent researchers maintain the likelihood of a strong association between the paranormal and UFO phenomena.

Sometimes, presumably stemming from the degree of UFO 'exposure' to the field of energy that surround them, people have and will continue to, claim allegations of what they interpret as alien abduction, involving being taken against their will by non-human entities and then subjected to complex physical and psychological procedures.

Whilst we cannot prove the abduction process involves alien beings who carry out medical examinations of their human victims as claimed by so many people worldwide, it is clear a process of behaviour in itself completely alien to our normal way of life continues to take place – this should concern us all.

Often those reports will speak of a forced medical examination of their reproductive system. Abductees sometimes claim to have been warned against environmental abuse and the dangers of nuclear weapons. While many of these experiences are described as terrifying, some have been viewed as pleasurable or transformative.

Due to this lack of any substantial physical evidence, most scientists and psychiatrists dismiss the reports of abduction as deception, suggestibility (fantasy-proneness, false-memory syndrome) personality, sleep phenomena, psychopathology, psychodynamic therapy and other environmental factors.

We accept we are not scientists or trained academics in the field of mental health, but we remain curious why, if these scientific explanations provide the answer to allegations of abduction, what part does the UFO sighting take place in all of this as these appear to be the stimulus which orchestrates a process of behaviour ending with an allegation of something far more serious than strange lights in the sky?

If UFOs did not exist, then it would be easier to dismiss such claims. As reported in the *Harvard University Gazette*, in 1992, Dr. John Edward Mack investigated over 800 claimed abductees and spent countless therapeutic hours with these individuals. He declared, *"The majority of abductees do not appear to be deluded, confabulating, lying, self-dramatizing, or suffering from a clear mental illness."*

Some abduction reports are quite detailed. An entire subculture has developed around the subject, with support groups and a detailed mythos explaining the reasons for abductions – The various aliens (Greys, Reptilians, "Nordics" and so on) are said to have specific roles, origins, and motivations. Abduction claimants do not always attempt to explain the phenomenon, but some take independent research interest in it themselves and explain the lack of greater awareness of alien abduction as the result of either extraterrestrial or governmental interest in cover-up. We can only say that we have met people who claim to have been the victim of such abductions, and that their trauma is real and painful.

There appears to be a misconception that the abduction phenomenon is a fundamentally new one and began with sightings of UFOs back in the 1940's and the realisation some following 20 years later that these 'craft' contained occupants. Whilst the reader may have their own opinions about this we do not believe that the majority of UFO incursions are attributable in extraterrestrial origin, but feel 'they' are indigenous to the home planet – Earth.

The problems arise with determining how long 'they' have been here – where that leaves the human race in the scheme of things we are not sure! Personally we believe they represent a modern chapter in the history book of human presence on this planet, which involved recorded sightings of flying vehicles and creatures which have been seen in the skies, going back many thousands of years.

1942

Other incidents over the years of interest brought too our attention included a report from a postmistress living in the Oswestry area. She was cycling home to Ellesmere (5miles north east of Oswestry) after a dance at 11.30pm in 1942, on what was fine dry night. As she approached 'tunnel bank' leading to Welshampton she alighted from the cycle due to the steep slope and carried on through a wooded area with a steep descent into a canal on the other side. She noticed two white lights like car headlights hugging the ground low down moving at speed along the gulley. *"They made no sound and came within feet of me and then moved past disappearing instantly as they did so"*

(Source: Jenny Randles Radio Shropshire phone in 1992/*Northern UFO News* April 1993)

1975

At 1.45am on 20th February 1975 a brightly lit object, shaped like a bowl, pursued a car being driven by a farmer's wife, near Tern Hill Shropshire, described as *'swinging from side to side, before moving away'*. One is bound to ponder, in light of the above reports, whether there is far more to these incidents than we shall ever know, sometimes it is not about what happened at the time (important as that might be) but what happened afterwards.

Close encounter in Kentucky USA

Another extraordinary UFO sighting caught our attention which also involved three women this time from Kentucky in the United States. We emailed the library and local newspaper seeking any further information on this matter, but received no answers from any of these sources. It is well worth contrasting with what Valerie, Vivien and Rosemary experienced although this one occurred four years previous to theirs, on 6th January 1976.

The February first issue of the *Kentucky Advocate,* published at Danville, Kentucky, published an article relating to UFO sightings in that general area. It included a report from Ms Louise Smith (44), Ms Mona Stafford (35) and Mrs Elaine Thomas (48), who were driving home to Liberty from a late dinner at *The Redwoods Restaurant*, located five miles north of Stanford.

At a point about one mile south of Stanford, they saw a huge disc-shaped object, which was metallic gray, with a white glowing dome. A row of red lights rotated around the middle and underneath were three or four red and yellow lights that burned steadily. A bluish beam of light issued from the bottom.

When the women arrived home in Liberty, it was 1.25am. Having left the restaurant at 11.15pm, they should have arrived home by midnight, indicating there was a time loss of about one hour and 25mins. The *Kentucky Advocate* article was forwarded to APRO Field Investigator (Aerial Phenomena Research

3 Women Are Abducted by a Massive UFO

... Lie Detector and Hypnosis Confirm Their Chilling Account

By BOB PRATT

In one of the strangest, most terrifying UFO encounters of all time, three Kentucky women were taken out of their car and subjected to torturous physical examinations by mysterious beings.

Their incredible ordeal has been verified by police lie detector tests and separate hypnotic sessions conducted by a top university professor.

The women — all lifelong churchgoers with excellent reputations — remember seeing a huge flying saucer swoop down toward them as they were driving along a country road. Suddenly they felt an awesome force take control of their car — until it was hurtling along at 85 miles an hour.

Then came a strange 80-minute blank in their lives — a baffling gap that the women found impossible to explain. The gap ended with their next conscious memory . . . driving into a town eight miles away from the original sighting.

It took deep hypnosis to unlock the secrets of those missing 80 minutes. The explanation that emerged was a fascinating story of abduction.

In a trance, each woman told of being removed from the car and held prisoner in a strange chamber. Each also was forced to undergo a frightening and painful examination before finding herself back in the car.

And investigators who probed the case found there was physical evidence to confirm the trio's experience — each woman suffered a bizarre

ORDEAL: Friends (from left) Elaine Thomas, Mona Stafford and Louise Smith were driving along when UFO swooped on them. Then came an 80-minute blank unexplained until the three underwent hypnosis.

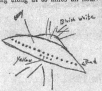

DRAWING of UFO by Louise Smith was almost identical to those done by the other two women, though all were in different rooms at the time.

underneath." The UFO stopped ahead of them — then circled around behind their car. Suddenly the auto picked up speed. Louise found she couldn't control it.

"This is one of the most convincing UFO cases on record," declared UFO expert Len Stringfield, a director of the Mutual UFO Network and an investigator for the prestigious Center for UFO Studies.

Dr. R. Leo Sprinkle, a veteran hypnotist who conducted the hypnosis sessions, said he firmly believes the women described "real" experiences while hypnotized.

"It is very difficult for people to lie under hypnosis," noted Dr. Sprinkle, associate professor of psychology at the University of Wyoming.

"And when three people in separate hypnotic sessions all agree on the essential parts in their account, the chance they have lied is beyond all reasonable possibility."

The three women — Elaine Thomas, 48; Louise Smith, 44; and Mona Stafford, 35 — have lived in and near Liberty, Ky., most of their lives. Two are grandmothers and the third, Mona Stafford, is the mother of a 17-year-old.

They were returning from a late supper in Stanford, 29 miles from home, when their nightmare began at 11:30 p.m. last January 6. Suddenly, a mile west of the city, a large disc-shaped object hurtled into view.

"It was as big as a football field!" recalled Louise, who was driving. "It was metallic gray with a glowing white dome, a row of red lights around the middle and three or four red and yellow lights

85 miles an hour! The others screamed to slow down — but I held my foot in the air to show them it wasn't even on the gas pedal!" Louise said.

Then some awesome force began dragging the car backward . . . and at that point came the 80-minute gap in the trio's memories. Their next conscious memory was of seeing a street light as they entered Hustonville — eight miles from where they'd seen the UFO.

The frightened women immediately drove to Louise's home in Liberty. They should have arrived around midnight — but it was 1:25 a.m. "An hour and 20 minutes, maybe longer, was missing — time we couldn't account for," Louise said.

Louise's neck hurt, so she asked Mona to look at it. Mona found a strange red mark "like a fresh burn that hadn't blistered, three inches long and an inch wide. Elaine's neck had the same mark and so did mine."

The terrified women summoned a next-door neighbor, Lowell Lee, and told him their story. He sent them into separate rooms to draw a sketch of the UFO. The drawings were almost identical.

The red marks vanished two days later. But the hour and twenty minutes they'd lost continued to puzzle them . . . until The ENQUIRER had them hypnotized on two separate occasions in July.

During the hypnotic sessions, all three vividly recalled what had happened to them, from

the time their car was pulled backward until they reached Hustonville.

Elaine Thomas remembered lying on her back in a long, narrow incubator-like chamber while beings — "dark figures, small, looked about four feet high" — kept passing by and looking in at her.

She said a blunt instrument was pressed hard against her chest, causing considerable pain. At the same time, something was encircling her throat — and each time she tried to speak, she was choked into silence. Elaine cried softly at times under hypnosis.

"Something is pressing on my throat! Like hands, all over, all around . . . I see shadows as they pass by . . . pressure on my chest . . . they won't let me breathe! I can't get away!"

Louise Smith said she was in a "hot, dark" place and something was placed over her face. She begged the beings to let her see them, and once she was allowed to look — but quickly closed her eyes because whatever she saw was frightening. Even under hypnosis Louise can't remember what the beings looked like.

Reliving her experience hypnotically, Louise gasped out: "Help me, Lord, please! . . . (sobbing) . . . It's so dark . . . I'm scared. Get that off my face . . . let go my arm . . . I want to get up but I can't . . ."

At one point she cried out: "Please, I can't do NO MORE! . . . I'm so weak . . . I want to die! Please don't! (sobbing) . . . Don't touch me!" And later: "Can I go home now? (smiling) . . . I'm going fast, so fast! . . . I see a light . . . it's a street light!"

Mona Stafford remembered lying on a bed in what seemed to be an operating room, her right arm pinned down by

HYPNOTIZED Elaine Thomas describes her ordeal aboard the UFO to Dr. R. Leo Sprinkle.

some invisible force, while three or four figures in white gowns sat around her bed. She doesn't recall their features.

Mona believed she was being tortured. She said that once her eyes felt as though they were being jerked out of her head, and another time her stomach felt as if it were being blown up like a balloon.

"My head hurts, my eyes hurt so bad . . ." she said. ". . . I see an eye . . . it's kinda like crystal . . . it just bursts out into light or something . . . My head feels like it's tied down . . . it's hurting, it's numb . . ."

At one point she screamed: "Ooh! He's coming at me! . . . Ooh, they're pulling at me, they're pulling my feet! My feet are being bent backwards. Twisted. I CAN'T TAKE NO MORE!"

The women were given lie detector tests by Detective James Young, senior polygraph examiner for the Lexington, Ky., Police Dept. and vice-president of the state polygraph association. Afterward, Young said in a signed statement:

"It is my opinion that these women actually believe they did experience an encounter."

Dr. Sprinkle, who hypnotized all three women twice, added: "It is quite obvious these women have specific impressions which indicate to them that they were being observed and handled by strange beings.

"In my opinion, it would be very difficult if not impossible for these women to fake their impressions. The impressions during the 'loss-of-time' experience are similar to those of other UFO witnesses who apparently have experienced abduction and examination."

Sheriff Bill Norris of Lincoln County, where the women saw the UFO, told The ENQUIRER that during January there had been "a number of UFO sightings in the county."

$1,000,000 REWARD

ONE MILLION DOLLARS! That's how much money The ENQUIRER is offering for positive proof that UFOs come from outer space and are not a natural phenomenon.

The final judges on claims for this huge reward are: Tom Clark, a former Attorney General and U.S. Supreme Court Justice, and Francis Bergan, former New York Court of Appeals Judge.

All evidence we receive will be screened by our editors, by Jim Lorenzen, international director of the Aerial Phenomena Research Organization (APRO) and by Jack Acuff, head of the National Investigations Committee on Aerial Phenomena (NICAP).

Claims with the most convincing evidence will be submitted to The ENQUIRER's Blue Ribbon Panel on UFOs, made up of top scientists and educators. If they

agree unanimously that the UFO in evidence is not a natural phenomenon and came from outer space, they'll pass the case to our two final judges.

If both judges approve the award, The ENQUIRER will present a check for $1 million to the person or persons who supplied the evidence.

The ENQUIRER also offers awards of up to $10,000 each year to anyone judged by the Blue Ribbon Panel to have supplied the most scientifically valuable evidence on UFOs, though not the proof required for the $1 million reward.

This offer is valid throughout the world and good until June 30, 1977, unless extended by The ENQUIRER. It shall not be construed as an inducement to betray any military secrets of the United States. Mail all evidence to: UFO Reward, NATIONAL ENQUIRER, Lantana, Fla. 33464.

Page 49 NATIONAL ENQUIRER

Organization) Bill Terry – who went to see the women, as a result of which he felt abduction had taken place and that the usual hypnosis procedures should be utilized. The matter was then brought to the attention of Dr. R. Leo Sprinkle – APROs consultant in psychology, who went to see the women on the weekend of the 6th March 1976.

The event

On the evening in question, Mrs. Louise Smith, employed as an extension assistant for the Casey County Extension Office, left work at the usual time and went home. She then got into her 1967 Chevrolet, purchased that day, and drove to a service station to fill up with fuel for the next day.

Mona Stafford, who was driving by, spotted Louise's car and pulled her car into the station, whereupon Mrs. Smith asked her if she would accompany her home and help her with some tailoring. The two ladies, each in her own car, drove to the Smith trailer home and set about the task. At about 8pm, Mrs. Thomas dropped by and the three lapsed into conversation about their favourite subject: art. Mrs. Stafford had planned to go to her sister's home to have her hair done and at about 9pm, said she had better call her sister because it was getting late and, besides, it was her (Mona's) birthday.

When Mrs. Smith learned about the birthday, she suggested they go over to *The Redwoods* for a late dinner and a birthday celebration. Also, there was a painting on the wall of the restaurant which she had wanted to sketch. The restaurant, incidentally, is the only restaurant open at that time of night in the area.

The three drove the 29 miles to the restaurant, had their dinner and then pulled out sketch pads and went to work. A man at the restaurant asked Mrs Smith to sketch him, which she did, and then she realised that it was getting late, so the three paid their bill and left. Mrs Smith drove, Mona sat in the middle of the front seat, with Mrs Thomas on her right by the passenger window.

Mona Stafford Drawing

Mona was the first to sight the object, which was descending from their right to the left, and asked Louise to speed up as she thought it was a plane about to crash and she wanted to help any survivors. Mrs Smith saw it clearly, but Mrs Thomas didn't see it until it had stopped at treetop level, at what they estimated to be one hundred yards ahead of them. All of the women said the object was huge, Louise describing it *"as big as a football field"*, while Mrs Stafford said it was at least as large as two houses.

Mrs Smith said that the object rocked gently for perhaps two seconds, at which time she estimated its size, for it extended beyond the edges of the road and over the fields on both sides. Then the thing moved across the road to their left, circling behind and above some houses, and then apparently came back to the highway and swung in behind the car.

At a point in their journey, about a quarter of a mile beyond the houses, the inside of the car was lit up with a bluish light, which came from behind. Mrs Smith said that at first she thought it was a state trooper, approaching from behind, but realised, almost immediately, that it wasn't. At this point, Louise and Mona were near panic. The car began to pull to the left and Louise screamed at Mona to help her control it. The speedometer was registering 85mph and both Mona and Mrs Thomas shouted at Mrs Smith to slow down. Louise held her foot in the air to show them and said, *"I don't have my foot on the accelerator and I can't stop it!"* Mona reached over and grabbed the wheel and they fought the force together. Then, quite suddenly, the women experienced a burning sensation in their eyes and Louise later described an additional pain, which seemed to *"go right through the top of my head! It was almost unbearable!"*

The next sensation was that of some force pulling the car backward. Also, they got the feeling that the car was going over a series of 'speed bumps' (raised ridges in a road, which are meant to keep the speed of automobiles to a minimum). Mrs Thomas began urging Louise to stop, so that she could get a good look at the object, but Mona and Louise were too terrified. Elaine had only a glimpse of the object, as it circled to their left then around behind her and was later to comment about the object's beauty. *"I can't describe it"*, she said, *"I've never seen red that beautiful. I wanted to get out and look at it."*

Then, the women said they saw a strange, wide, lighted road, stretching as far as they could see, ahead of them. At the same moment Mona noted a red light on the instrument panel, which indicated that the engine had stalled, despite the sensation they were moving very fast.

At what seemed to be a split second later, the women saw a street light ahead and realised that they were coming into Hustonville, a full eight miles beyond, where they had encountered the strange aircraft. They wondered among themselves how they had reached there so fast, and then became quiet while they proceeded on into Liberty.

When they arrived at Mrs Smith's trailer, they all went inside. Mrs Smith went into the bathroom, took off her glasses and splashed water on her face, whereupon her hands and face began to burn with searing pain. All three had a red mark on the backs of their necks, measuring about three inches long and one inch wide, with clearly defined edges, giving the appearance of a new burn before it blisters. Louise and Elaine's marks were centrally located between the bases of their skulls and the top of the back, whereas Mona's was located to the left, behind her ear. They could not account for the marks, which disappeared two days later. All three were experiencing burning and tearing of their eyes, but Mona Stafford had a much more severe case of conjunctivitis (an inflammation of the conjunctiva membrane of the eyes).

Prior to washing her hands, Louise had taken off her watch and was startled to see that the hands of her watch were moving at an accelerated rate of speed, the minute hand moving at the speed of a second hand, and the hour hand was moving also. Upon experiencing the pain of the water on her hands and face, she forgot about the phenomena of the watch and does not recall when it returned to normal or when she reset it.

Concluding that something was wrong, the three ladies went next door to the home of Mr Lowell Lee, and told him what they had seen. He asked them to go into separate rooms and sketch the object and, when finished, he found the resulting sketches to be almost identical.

Although all the women had trouble with their eyes, only Mona Stafford sought medical help, as her problem was so severe. The doctor who examined her found no explanation for the pain and tearing but gave her some eye drops, which helped very little.

Bill Terry, accompanied by Dr Sprinkle, proceeded to Mrs Smith's home. They were met by a number of investigators from CUFOS and MUFON, who felt as they had been 'first' on the case APRO should not be allowed to entered. Dr Sprinkle decided to contact APRO Headquarters for a decision on how to proceed next.

It was finally decided Dr Sprinkle would conduct the hypnotic sessions, but that there would have to be a mutual agreement concerning the release of the story.

A summary of Dr Leo Sprinkle's findings . . .

Mrs. Smith *". . . suffered much as she relived the experience. The behaviours, e.g., weeping, moaning, tossing her head, shuddering and shaking, etc., were evident to those of us who observed her, especially as she seemed to 'relive' an experience of a fluid material covering her face. Her smile, and evident relief in 'seeing the street light' at the end of her hour and one-half loss-of-time experience was dramatic and indicated that she was 'safe' in the car, once again, and returning home with her friends."*

Dr Leo Sprinkle

Sprinkle then goes on to recount Louise's claim that her pet parakeet, who, according to her claims and the claims of others who observed the bird, refused to have anything to do with her after the UFO experience. Others could approach the bird and it would not react wildly; however, whenever Louise came close to the bird, the bird would flutter and move away from her. The bird died within weeks after the UFO experience.

Mona Stafford *". . . responded well to the hypnotic suggestions and she was able to describe impressions which led her to believe that she had been taken out of the car, and that she was alone on a white table or bed. She saw a large 'eye', which seemed to be observing her. She felt as if a bright* *white light was shining on her and that there was 'power' or energy, which transfixed her and held her to the table or bed. She experienced a variety of physiological reactions, including the impressions that her right arm was pinned or fastened; her left leg forced back under her, with pain to the ankle and foot; pressure on the fingers of the left hand, as if they were forced or squeezed in some way; a feeling of being examined by four or five short humanoids, who sat around in 'surgical masks' and 'surgical garments' while observing her. At one point, she sensed that she was either experiencing out-of-the-body travel, or else she was waiting outside a large room, in which she could view another person – probably a woman – lying on a white bed, or observation table. She perceived a long tunnel or a view of the sky – as if she had been transported to an area inside a large mountain or volcano. Although she wept and moaned and experienced a great deal of fatigue as a result of the 'reliving' of the experience, she felt better the next day; she expressed the belief to me that she now had a better*

understanding of what happened during the loss-of-time experience.

Mrs Thomas had been rather quiet during the initial interview in March 1976, although it was obvious that she is perceptive and aware of other people's attitudes and feelings. Like the others, she has lost weight, but she has also experienced some personality changes. She dresses a bit more colourfully now, and she is more willing to talk and to share her ideas with others. She, too, experienced a similar reaction during the hypnotic techniques: she apparently was responding well to suggestions to go deeper; when she 'relived' the UFO experience, she experienced a great deal of emotional reaction. Her main impression was that she was taken away from her two friends, and that she was placed in a 'chamber', with a window on the side. She seemed to recall figures which moved back and forth in front of the window of the chamber – as if she were being observed. Her impression was that the observers were four feet tall humanoids, with dark eyes and grey skin. One disturbing aspect of the experience was the memory that she had some kind of contraption or 'covering' that was placed around her neck; whenever she tried to speak, or think, the contraption or 'covering' was tightened, and she experienced a choking sensation during these moments. At first, Mrs Thomas interpreted the memories as indication that she was being choked by hands, or that she was being prevented from calling out to her friends; later, however, she came to the tentative conclusion that an experiment was being conducted, and the experiment was to learn more about her intellectual and emotional processes. She recalled a 'bullet-shaped' object, about an inch and one half in diameter, being placed on her left chest; she previously had experienced pain and a red spot at that location.

During the polygraph examination, and during the initial hypnotic sessions, each UFO witness was interviewed separately from the other witnesses. After the initial description of impressions, the women were invited to attend the additional hypnosis sessions, so that each woman could observe the reaction of the other two women. During these sessions, there was much emotional reaction, which seemed to arise from two conditions: the compassion of the witnesses for their friend, who was 'reliving' the experience and releasing emotional reactions to the experience; also, it seems as if the description by one witness would 'trigger' a memory on the part of another witness, even if the experiences seemed to be 'similar' or 'different'.

Certain similarities were observed: a feeling of anxiety on the part of each witness regarding a specific aspect of the experience. For Ms Smith, it was the 'wall' and the 'gate' beyond, which she was afraid to 'move psychologically'; for Ms Stafford it was the 'eye' which she observed and the impression that something evil or bad would be learned if she allowed the eye to 'control' her; for Ms Thomas, it was the 'blackness' which seemed to be the feared condition or cause for anxiety. Each woman seemed to experience the impression that she had been taken out of the car and placed elsewhere, without her friends and without verbal communication. For Ms Smith, the lack of verbal communication was most distressing, although she had the feeling of 'mental communication' that she would be returned after the 'experiment'.

Differences were noted in that each woman seemed to have a somewhat different kind of 'examination' and in a different 'location'. Ms Smith did not have a clear impression of the location, although she did recall a feeling of lying down and being examined; Ms Stafford had the impression of being in a 'volcano or mountainside', with a room in which a bright light was shining on a white table, with white clothed persons, or humanoids, sitting around and observing her; Mrs. Thomas recalled impressions of being in the dark chamber with grey light, permitting a view of the humanoids, who were apparently observing her."

In his conclusive paragraphs, Dr. Sprinkle reports:

"In my opinion, each woman is describing a 'real' experience, and they are using their intelligence and perceptivity as accurately as possible, in order to describe the impressions which they obtained during the hypnotic regressions session. Although there is uncertainty about their impressions, especially in regard to how each person could be transported out of the car and relocated in the car, the impressions during the 'loss of time' experience are similar to those of other UFO witnesses who apparently have experienced an abduction and examination during their UFO sighting.

Although it is not possible to claim absolutely that a physical examination and abduction has taken place, I believe that the tentative hypothesis of abduction and examination is the best hypothesis to explain the apparent loss-of-time experience, the apparent physical and emotional reactions of the witnesses to the UFO sighting: the anxiety and the reactions of the witnesses to their experiences which have occurred after their UFO sighting.

When I called the women on 26th July 1976 , they told me they were re-experiencing some of the original symptoms, e.g., fatigue, listlessness, sensitivity to skin, burning feeling on the face and eyes, fluid discharge, etc, following on from the events of 6th January 1976.

I tried to reassure the ladies that it is not an uncommon experience in hypnotic regression that persons — after 'reliving' earlier emotional experiences — may re-experience some of the symptoms which accompany those emotional reactions.

In my opinion, the UFO experiences of these women are a good example of the type of apparent abduction and examination which seems to be occurring to more UFO witnesses. I believe that the investigation could be continued with the hopes of obtaining further information about their experiences. The women have cooperated sincerely and openly in describing their reactions to the UFO sighting and loss-of-time experience, and the polygraph examination and hypnotic regression sessions have been useful in uncovering their impressions of the UFO sighting and subsequent events.

I believe the case is a good example of UFO experiences, because of the number and character of the witnesses . . . and because of the results of further investigation through polygraph examinations and hypnotic regression sessions."

Dr Sprinkle also mentioned that Mrs Stafford had been having trouble sleeping, and would not stay at home; she would either go to her parents' home or that of a friend, or curl up on the floor to sleep. She also repeatedly claimed that she would not live *'to see another birthday'*. Hopefully this is only a fear and not a portent of things to come.

On the 1ˢᵗ August 1976, Mrs Smith was overcome by an inexplicable urge to return to the scene of the original sighting. She got out of her car, and 'heard' the words: *'feel of your hands'*. When she did so, she realised that three rings, which she habitually wore – a small gold ring, a pearl ring, and a gold ring, with onyx and a small diamond – were gone.

On the 26th September, Mrs Smith walked out of her trailer home and found the onyx and diamond ring lying close by. Inexplicably, she scooped up the ring, walked to the creek which runs by her home, and threw it into the water.

(Source: *APRO Bulletin*, Vol. 25 No. 4 Oct 1976)

In 2013 we contacted Roberta Smith a charming lady and State Director, of the Kentucky branch of MUFON with regard to this matter hoping that she may have some additional information regarding the incident. Roberta told us that she had no more than what was posted on the internet, other than Louise Smith who was her husband's first cousin had passed away several years ago.

Roberta Smith, State Director, Kentucky Branch, MUFON

"She never would talk to any of the family about her abduction. The last time we heard anything from Mona, she was not in good health, and we do not know her personally. The other lady has passed away also. But these were three outstanding ladies in the community, they just happened to be in the wrong place at the wrong time. I was not married to my husband when this abduction happened, and did not learn of it until years after the incident. The place where these ladies lived and were abducted is only about 30-35 miles from where my aunt and many relatives live. There are, what we call 'knobs' between them. Knobs are taller than hills and shorter than mountains. After learning of this incident, I remember that back at that time, there was a wave of UFO sightings in this area. Everyone was seeing them. This went on for over a week. It was the talk of the community, it is a rural area. I only wish there was more info I could give you concerning the Stanford Abduction, but as I said, I came into the Smith family after this happened.

I have asked several family members about it, and they all said she wouldn't talk about it and the only thing they knew was what they read from reports and newspapers. I am sorry, but I have never seen this drawing by Mona. I would assume that Mona has the copyright, but I do not know Mona personally and know of no way, at the moment, to contact her. I think there is something unusual about her drawing. As far as I know, the car was not taken into the craft, only the three women. I did not know that Mona was an artist, but Louise was a very good one. Someone in the family stated that Louise had several paintings she had done, but they had been stolen."

An examination of the NICAP Files reveals a staggering number of UFO sightings for this year. One is bound to wonder just how many other 'victims' there were, not only in the USA, but the UK – this is quite frightening and makes a mockery of statements made assuring us that the majority of UFO reports can be explained rationally away. These sightings were not about reports of lights in the sky, but a variety of strange objects seen by civilians and police officers – they included, a silver sphere seen over Goldstone Tracking Station, Barstow California.

A 'Flying Saucer' seen Florida

A token sample for the February period of 1976 shows us the following information. February 10th – High Spring, Florida, 11pm. A woman living near Lake City called the sheriff's office to report a "flying saucer." Sheriff Deputies were dispatched to investigate and reported seeing a UFO hovering about 500 to 600 feet in the air. Different colored lights were flashing from what looked like a glass dome. Florida highway patrol troopers also observed the object before it moved out of sight.

(**Source:** *UFO Investigator,* **July 1976**)

Motorist paced by UFO, Alabama

February 18, 1976; Near Okatchee, 8pm Two women driving in a rural area reported that lights high in the sky paced their car for 13-14 miles from Chatchee to Lincoln, Alabama. Near Okatchee, Alabama they saw a large orange object in the woods near the ground to their left. Their CB radio stopped working, making no static, no sound at all. Two objects then followed them until they reached Lincoln, Alabama, where the UFOs approached to within 300-400 feet. The women saw five objects at this point. After passing through Lincoln, the objects stopped pacing the car and the CB radio suddenly started working. The two objects that had paced the car were egg-shaped and glowing with a fluorescent light.

(**Sources: CUFOS investigation file May 17, 1976- Mark Rodeghier, *'UFO Reports Involving Vehicle Interference case'* CUFOS**)

UFO activity over the Shropshire area

It has never been our intention to include too many other UFO sighting reports from intended future volumes of *Haunted Skies*, as this would interrupt the chronology of what our books are all about. However, there will be occasions when we feel this rule should be broken, in order for the reader to be given the opportunity to learn of other sightings that may be of relevance at this particular stage, rather than waiting for a future volume.

We decided to include brief details of incidents from around the Shropshire area, some of which have already been covered at more length in previous volumes, and a UFO sighting, which was only brought to our attention recently from a Gloucestershire man, that was to leave him traumatised to this present day. His testimony should be compared to that of the women from Shropshire and their (Kentucky) USA counterparts as there appears to be similarities.

The Shropshire area has been the subject of many sightings. They include (briefly) a report by teacher Jerry Richmond, who was returning home from Bridgnorth, at 1.30am on 25th July 1968. As he neared Hilton, on the Bridgnorth to Wolverhampton Road, he saw an elliptical-shaped object, estimated to be a hundred feet long, rise up into the air from a behind a clump of trees, about 30-40 yards away.

He was then followed for 9 miles by the object, which resembled a helicopter/cigar in shape.

Also there was a close encounter which took place on 12th April 1969, involving a female teacher, living a few miles outside Bridgnorth, who came across a landed UFO, with three 'figures' next to it. An examination of the ground, later, by Derek Samson, revealed a triangular-shaped mark on the ground. (Full details of these two incidents can be found in the relevant volume of *Haunted Skies*.)

UFO Landing near Bridgnorth, Shropshire

Some years ago we spoke to Patrick Rollason – a retired West Mercia Police Officer – about what he witnessed, while a village 'bobby', stationed at Bridgnorth Police Station, Shropshire, in May 1987. Pat told of having received a telephone call from Captain Robbie Evans, owner of the Wyken Estate, who reported having seen a strange red glow in the sky over Chempshill Coppice, near Worfield, Bridgnorth – an area of mature woodland, forming part of the Davenport Estate.

Davenport House

"I decided to visit the locality myself, wondering whether there was any connection with the nearby RAF base, at Cosford, or the local Halfpenny Green Airport. As I was about to get into the police car, I was aware of a loud humming noise resonating in the air – like an electrical buzzing – but thought no more of it at the time. I made my way to high ground overlooking the area concerned, close to Rindleford – a tiny hamlet, near Worfield – which gave me a clear view over the countryside. I was shocked to see a grey saucer-shaped object, making a quiet humming noise, similar to what I had heard when leaving the police station.

I estimated it to be 100-200ft across, with a dome on top, hovering over a field. Projecting from underneath the 'saucer' were three beams of orange light – diffused, rather than bright. I stood watching for a few minutes, feeling the hairs standing up on the back of my neck – then the humming noise increased in pitch to a droning noise. The next thing that happened was that it shot

An area of Davenport Estate, the scene of the incident

off at terrific speed and out-of-sight. By now dusk was beginning to fall. I decided to leave any further investigation until the next morning. When I returned to the scene, the following day, I came across a local shepherd, Tommy Perry, who told me something odd had happened in the field because 'Moss', his dog, was too frightened to go anywhere near the area.

We walked across the field, toward some trees, and discovered a huge area of dried grass, formed in a big circle; my impression being, through examination of the ground, was that it

*looked as if the circle had been created not through the application of any heat, but as if all
the moisture had been sucked out of the ground only on the inside of the circle, in complete
contrast to untouched plant growth on the outside."*

Pat told us he had submitted a full report of the incident to his supervising
officer, a copy of which was also sent to the MoD, and that he was later
contacted by Mr. Mike Pryce – a reporter for *The Worcester Evening News*,
who interviewed him, details later being published in that Newspaper.

We contacted Mr. Pryce, who told us he remembered the incident very well
because it was so unusual, although he regretted having not visited the locality
himself. Pat gave us details of another witness – a lady then employed in the
police canteen, at Bridgnorth who was a passenger on a bus passing the scene
at the time. Unfortunately, we were unable to interview the lady concerned, due
to health problems, but her son confirmed to us that his mother had certainly
seen something very strange, while a passenger on the bus, along with several
other passengers. We wrote to the MoD, seeking further information about
any UFO incidents that had occurred in May 1987, in the Shropshire area.
They told us they had no knowledge of any UFO reports during that particular
period.

In 2013 we spoke to Pat's wife, Mary, who told us that the UFO sighting was
the subject of conversation over the years, but that Patrick had passed away on
the 5th April 2010, at Worcester Royal Hospital. He would no doubt have been
pleased that his story was eventually published. **(Source: Personal interviews)**

Patrick Rollason

Further research

In May 2013 we went to see Roger Murphy – the owner of Davenport Estate. He was very helpful and
suggested we contact local farmers – Richard and James Tudor – about their knowledge of Captain Robbie
Evans.

We spoke to Mrs. Tudor, who confirmed she had knowledge of a Robin Evans, who had employed Geoffrey
Davies as the manager of Wyken estate, but she had never heard of him being referred to as Captain Robbie
Evans, although there was no doubt this was the same man. As a result of further enquires we spoke to
Geoffrey Davies:

Jeff Davies:

> *"I knew Robert Evans. His rank was actually a Major, but the locals called him Captain.
> He didn't like the Christian name, and called himself Robin. He passed away in July 1986.
> This could not have happened in 1987. I never heard Robin talk about any UFO incident
> all the time I knew him. As for Tommy Perry, I think he was dead before I came to Wyken, in
> 1974. The best bet is to speak to his son, Roy Perry, whose son, Andrew, works for the Tudors.
> Robin was unmarried and, apart from a brother, had no immediate family. I have a photo,
> somewhere, with him on it. I will try to find it. I knew Pat Rollason. He wasn't our regular
> 'Bobby', but I met Pat when we had some trouble up here."*

There is no reason to doubt the veracity of the report given by the officer; the problem is that incident could
not have happened in 1987, taking into consideration what Mrs. Tudor, Geoffrey Davies, and others have

told us. We shall never know when this happened, but are puzzled why Pat Rollason left it for so many years before contacting the newspaper, who published the matter in July 1987.

We now know that Tom Perry passed away in 1981, so it had to be some before that. We also learnt that the conversation regarding the problem with the dog did happen and that 'Moss' refused to go into the field. Unfortunately, the newspaper cutting never specified a year – just May. The fact that the article was published in July 1986 would indicate this was current to that year when in fact this was not the case.

UFO seen over Clee Hill, 1996

At 11.30pm on 16th September 1996, Roger and Rosemary Wise from Bridgnorth, Shropshire, were driving home along the Telford Road, when Rosemary exclaimed: *"What's that?"* pointing upwards into the sky.

Roger:

> *"I looked out of the window and saw this huge 'craft', moving slowly through the sky, low down, at about 2,000ft. I slowed the car down, so as not to lose sight of it – now visible quite clearly as somewhat rectangular in appearance, showing a number of illuminated 'portholes' along its side. Suddenly the front of the object changed from dim to very bright, followed by the amazing sight of a 'saucer' or disc-shaped object, about a fifth in size of the larger object, being ejected into the sky, which flew silently towards the west of Clee Hill and disappeared over the horizon, followed by the larger 'craft' – close enough to make out individual detail on it.*

(Source: Personal interview)

UFO over Telford, 2003

At 8.30am on 10th February 2003, Telford resident – Sue Harding – was taking the dog for her usual morning walk.

> *"I met up with a young woman with her dog, and they began to play. The sky was very clear and I looked up to see birds circling – gulls and crows. Above them was what I initially*

thought was a buzzard, as they are fairly commonly sighted. I soon realised that it was not a bird; it was a blue object, deep blue, and almost had a glassy appearance. Its leading edge was curved, almost semicircular, and the inside edge had a feathered or fronded effect. We established that it was not a kite, as it was travelling too fast, but not so fast that we didn't get a good look. Every few seconds the object would rotate and, as it did so, three lights – all a lighter blue than the object itself – would flash and then it would continue flying, curved edge first. It was soon heading out of range on a constant course and speed, still rotating every few seconds. It is difficult to gauge the altitude, maybe about 250 ft above the ground."

(Source: Personal interview)

Close Encounter over M50, Gloucestershire, 15th February 1995

We felt the reader should be given the opportunity of seeing for themselves the similarities between what Rosemary, Val, and Joan experienced, and another incident brought to our attention, in 2012, by retired Gloucestershire police officer – Trent Davis (who had sighted a triangular UFO hovering over the police radio transmission tower, above Cleeve Hill, Cheltenham, in 1974, followed by frightening memory flashbacks, involving examination by alien beings).

In late April 2013 we met up with John – now retired, and living with his wife and family in Newent Gloucestershire who asked us not to reveal his real identity, fearing unwarranted ridicule and attention.

Although his sighting covers four separate incidents that took place, in the early to mid 1990s, it is the third which is of importance and far more serious in its implications, as it relates to a close encounter which still haunts John to this present day.

While Val and Rosemary now interpret what happened to them as a benevolent experience, John sees it differently. He struggles to make sense of something completely out of the normal, hardly helped by having had to deal with it on his own, over the years, after having reported it to Robin Cole, of Circular Forum – the Cheltenham-based group – on 16th May 1996, at 10.15pm.

John:

"My first UFO sighting took place on the 4th July 1991. I had been working nights at a factory on the Ashburton estate, Ross-on-Wye (manufacturing military parts for the MOD). I was taking a break outside, at 4am, looking over towards Safeways Supermarket, on a bright summer's morning. The Moon was showing in a blue sky; no stars could be seen. I noticed a pinprick of light, like a small star under the Moon, which began to increase in size and move closer towards me, before eventually halting. It then 'switched off' and in its place appeared a silent saucer-shaped object, showing a red light underneath, and white, green, and blue lights, around the outer edge. I watched it for several minutes, and then went inside and

View over the factoy

shouted for Harry, a colleague, to come outside and see it. However, he was loading some press work and couldn't come immediately. I ran back outside; it was still there, but now accompanied by an identical 'craft'. I estimated they were hovering over the Motorway, between Wilton roundabout and the area of the Gateway depot. By the time Harry came out, they had gone."

'John'

The second sighting occurred in July 1994, when the factory relocated to Alton Road, Ross-on-Wye. John was on the 2pm-10pm shift. At about 9pm, he was outside with some other workers, taking a break, looking at half-a-dozen air balloons moving across the sky.

> *"I turned to my left and saw (and heard) – about 45° off the horizon – an aircraft, leaving a vapour trail behind it, on what was a perfectly blue sky – warm, with many swallows and swifts flying around. I turned around and glanced at Ponts Hill, at the back of the factory, and was astonished to see, high in the sky, a similar object (that I was to see in 1995) showing lights around its periphery. I pointed it out to one of the women there. She laughed and said it was either a satellite, or UFO! Within minutes, it had gone."*

The Third and most dramatic event

The most dramatic and life changing incident took place at 9.45pm on 15th February 1995, while John was driving home, having left work at 9.30pm. This was a regular journey taken over the last seven years, and covers a distance of nine-and-a-quarter miles, normally taking 15mins maximum. The journey is split into 1.8miles: by-pass to M50, at Ross-on-Wye, three-and-three-quarter miles motorway, along the M50, four miles along the Newent to Gorsley B4224 road, and then home.

"I arrived at the roundabout at the M50, Travellers Rest end, at 9.40pm, on what was a dark but clear night. I looked across the valley through a gap in the hedge, towards Ponts Hill, which is on the far horizon, about 10-12miles away, and saw a bright 'light' in what was a starless night. Due to a hedge at the side of the road, I lost sight of it momentarily. On the other side of the road, two cars and a small van were just leaving the M50 on the opposite side. I looked again across the valley, through a gap, seeing the bridge that gives access over the

"View of direction I travelled home on 15-2-1995. First bridge from Travellers Rest roundabout on M50 I saw light heading towards me. Long gap in hedge before bridge . . . second gap."

"View from bridge – UFO flightpath, down to the abduction point between two blue signposts."

"The point where the voice warned me: 'Unsafe', 'Unsafe'; after telling me to 'pull over and you can get a better look' – last point before abduction."

M50 leading to Rudhall and Weston- under-Penyard in the valley, and noticed the bright 'light' was now low down and racing across fields facing me.

I first thought that it must be a helicopter, or aircraft, but once again lost sight of it, due to the side of the road. As I came out of the other side of the bridge, an intense 'light' dropped down onto my car; it wasn't like a searchlight and I could still see the dipped headlights of the car. This light flooded the inside of the car; I looked and saw, with utmost astonishment, a 'craft' pacing my vehicle, at about 50mph. I switched off the radio, put the car in neutral, and pressed the driver's side window down. I put my head out and looked up and saw an intense white 'light', showing a dark circular patch in the middle. Whether this 'patch' was a hole in the underside of the object, which I estimated, to be 80ft above me, and the length of two double-decker buses, I cannot say.

Suddenly, I heard a voice in my head, saying 'Pull over and you can get a better look'. I looked along the hard shoulder for a safe place to stop, as told. At this point, as the hard shoulder disappears, due to a small road which runs underneath the motorway, there are warning barriers. Straightaway, I heard the voice again – 'Unsafe, Unsafe'. I started to pull over, feeling that my actions were being guided by some form of hypnotic control, rather than my own free will. From the bridge to this point it takes about 20secs, during which time the light, 'craft', object – call it what you will – was now positioned above the car and between the rock faces of the opposing motorway lanes. I believe this was the time when I was abducted, as in the blink of an eye – almost like watching a frame jump in a film – I was back again and aware of my surroundings. The car was in 5th gear and I am driving at 50mph; everything seemed normal, when I heard a voice, saying, 'Don't stop now – keep going. There is no traffic either side of the motorway. Keep going.' I remember saying out aloud to myself 'Where's the light?', but it was now all over."

"Last point at which I saw the UFO, heading towards me as I went under bridge."

"Part of the rock face leading to the start of the abduction."

SECTION A | STATEMENT | 19/5/96

1) Give a full account of what you saw, including a sketch if possible. (Continue on a separate sheet if required)

MY THIRD SIGHTING AND MOST DRAMATIC INCIDENT TO DATE. IT HAPPENED ON THE EVENING OF THE 15TH FEBRUARY 1995 ON WEDNESDAY. I LEFT WORK AT EXACTLY 9.30 P.M. IN THE EVENING TO GO HOME, FROM THE MAIN FACTORY AT ALTON ROAD ROSS-ON-WYE. THE JOURNEY WHICH I TAKE HOME IS ABOUT 9¼ MILES. I HAVE BEEN TRAVELLING THIS ROAD FOR 7 YEARS. THE SAME ROUTE EVERYDAY. THIS JOURNEY SHOULD TAKE NO MORE THAN 15 MINUTES MAXIMUM. IT CONSISTS OF 1.8 MILE BYPASS TO M.50. AT ROSS-ON-WYE 3¾ MILES MOTORWAY M50 AND 4 MILES ON THE NEWENT/ GORSLEY B4224. I ARRIVED AT THE ROUNDABOUT AT THE M.50. TRAVELLERS REST END AT APPROXIMATELY 9.40 P.M. IT WAS DARK BUT CLEAR. I LOOKED ACROSS THE VALLEY THROUGH A GAP IN THE HEDGE TOWARDS PONTS-HILL ON THE FAR HORIZEN ABOUT 10-12 MILES, LOW DOWN WAS A LARGE BRIGHT LIGHT. IN AN OTHER WISE STAR LESS NIGHT SKY.

P.T.O.

SECTION B | LOCATION & ENVIRONMENT

1) Date of sighting: 15/2/95   2) Local Time: 9-40 P.M. (AM/PM?)

3) Immediate Locality/Town: ROSS-ON-WYE M.50. NEAR TRAVELLERS REST INN

4) County: HEREFORDSHIRE

Give details as to where exactly you were, and what you were doing when the sighting occurred:
DRIVING ALONG THE M.50. AT THE ROSS-ON-WYE END NEAR THE TRAVELLERS REST ROUNDABOUT INCIDENT HAPPENED AT AND BEYOND THE FIRST MOTORWAY BRIDGE.

Describe the general landscape and landmarks, and whether it was urban, rural, or otherwise:
SIGHTED FIRST THROUGH GAP IN HEDGE TOWARDS PONTS-HILL HORIZEN SECOND GAP IN HEDGE. SEEN STREAMING ACROSS FIELDS TOWARDS BRIDGE FROM THAT DIRECTION. INCIDENT AT BRIDGE (FIRST) (RURAL)

Was it day or night? (If dawn/dusk, describe it, indicating in favour of day or night):
(NIGHT) BUT CLEAR NO STARS.

Can you indicate the following weather conditions at the time.

Cloud	Wind:	Rain:
CLOUDY	NONE	NONE
Temperature: COLD.	Humidity: —	Visibility: GOOD

LOST SIGHT OF IT BECAUSE OF ANOTHER HEDGE. TWO CARS AND A SMALL VAN WERE JUST LEAVING THE M.50. ON THE OPPOSITE SIDE. I LOOKED AGAIN ACROSS THE VALLEY THROUGH A GAP WHICH IS OPEN RIGHT UP TO THE FIRST BRIDGE. THIS BRIDGE GIVES ACCESS OVER THE M.50. AND LEADS TO RUDHALL AND WESTON-UNDER-PENYARD IN THE VALLEY. IT TAKES APPROXIMATELY 25-30 SECONDS TO GET TO THIS BRIDGE FROM THE ROUNDABOUT. THE BRIGHT LIGHT IS NOW DOWN BELOW THE HORIZEN AND IS RACING ACROSS THE FIELDS IN THE VALLEY FACING ME. AS I HAD SEEN A SIMILAR BRIGHT LIGHT IN MY FIRST SIGHTING, 1991. IT BOTHERED ME. BUT TRYING TO PUT THIS WORRY TO ONE SIDE I CONCLUDED THAT IT MUST BE AN HELECOPTER OR SUCH LIKE. JUST AS I LOST SIGHT OF IT BY GOING UNDER THE BRIDGE. I SAW IT BANK AT HIGH SPEED. AS I CAME OUT FROM THE OTHER SIDE OF THE BRIDGE A BRIGHT AND INTENSE LIGHT DESCENDED UPON ME VERY QUICKLY. THIS LIGHT DID NOT AT ANY TIME PROJECT VERY FAR OUT, LIKE A SPOTLIGHT OR TORCH BEAM. I COULD STILL SEE THE DIPPED BEAMS OF MY CAR LIGHTS AHEAD OF ME. IT INFILTRATED THE INTERIOR OF MY CAR. THE CRAFT HAD NOW SLOWED TO THE SPEED OF MY CAR ABOUT 50 M.P.H. FROM VERY HIGH SPEED TO NEARLY NOTHING. I PUT THE RADIO OFF PUT THE CAR IN NEUTRAL TO CUT THE ENGINE NOISE. I PRESSED THE DRIVERS SIDE WINDOW BUTTON WHICH AUTOMATICLY POWERS DOWN. I PUT MY HEAD OUT OF THE WINDOW AND LOOKED UP I WAS GREETED BY AN EERIE INTENSE LIGHT WITH A DARK CIRCULAR PATCH IN THE MIDDLE.

I DON'T KNOW WHETHER THIS WAS A HOLE IN THE UNDERSIDE OF THE CRAFT. THERE WAS NO NOISE (NOT HELECOPTER OR PLANE) THE LIGHT AS IN THE FIRST SIGHTING COMPLETLY ENVELOPED THE CRAFT. IT APPEARS FLUORESCENT A BIT LIKE AN AURA AROUND THE OUTSIDE OF THE CRAFT. BUT IT SHIMMERED WHEN YOU LOOKED AT IT. I ONLY HAD A FEW SECONDS TO SEE THIS AND ESTIMATED THAT IT WAS ABOUT 80 FT. ABOVE ME. AND ABOUT 2 BUS LENGTHS WIDE. (DIAMETRE) I AM NOW FIDGETING ABOUT IN THE CAR AS THE LIGHT IS BOTHERING ME. ALL OF A SUDDEN I HEAR A VOICE IN MY HEAD SAYING.

"PULL OVER AND YOU CAN GET A BETTER LOOK!"

I WENT FROM WORRYING ABOUT THE LIGHT AND BEING AGGITATED TO TOTALY DOCILE. LOOKING STRAIGHT AHEAD NOT AT ALL CONCERNED ABOUT THE ENCROACHING LIGHT. THAT WAS DESCENDING ON ME. I LOOKED ALONG THE HARD SHOULDER FOR A SAFE PLACE TO STOP AS I HAD BEEN TOLD

AT THIS POINT. THE HARD SHOULDER DISAPPEARE A SMALL ROAD RUNS UNDERNEATH THE MOTORWAY. A BARRIER WITH WARNING POSTS APPEARS IN FRONT OF ME. A VOICE WARNS "UNSAFE" "UNSAFE" THE CAR AS I START TO PULL OVER. I STRAIGHTEN UP TAKING NOTICE OF THE VOICE. I AM SURE THESE VOICES ARE SOME SORT OF TELEPATHY. IT'S AS IF THEY CAN SEE THROUGH MY EYES EVERYTHING THAT IS GOING ON, AND ARE GUIDING ME. I AM UNDER SOME FORM OF HYPNOTIC CONTROL. I CAN SEE EVERYTHING THAT IS GOING ON. BUT I HAVE TO OBEY THE VOICE.

FROM THE BRIDGE TO THIS POINT IT TAKES ABOUT 20-26 SECONDS EVERYTHING IS HAPPENING VERY QUICKLY. THE CRAFT HAS TO DESCEND BETWEEN TWO ROCK FACES AND POSITION ITSELF ABOVE MY CAR AS WELL AS FITTING BETWEEN THE FOUR LANES OF THE CARRIAGWAY. IT IS LARGE BUT HAS FANTASTIC CONTROL. IT IS AT THIS POINT I THINK I WAS ABDUCTED. IT WAS AS IF I BLINKED MY EYES AND I WAS BACK AGAIN.

(3) THE ONLY THING I CAN COMPARE THIS WITH IS IF YOU ARE WATCHING A VERY GOOD FILM AND IT JUMPS A FRAME. YOU NOTICE SOMETHING BUT BECAUSE YOU ARE ENGROSSED IN THE STORY IT APPEARES CONTINUES.

I AM NOW LOOKING STRAIGHT AHEAD ON THE SAME BIT OF ROAD. THE CAR IS IN GEAR NOW (5TH) I AM DOING ABOUT 50 M.P.H. I AM STILL NOT BOTHERED ABOUT THE LIGHT. EVERY THING APPEARES NORMAL AND ANOTHER VOICE SAYS. "DON'T STOP NOW." "KEEP GOING." "THERE IS NO TRAFFIC EITHER SIDE OF THE MOTORWAY." "KEEP GOING."

I ESTIMATE IT WAS BETWEEN 5-10 SECONDS AFTER THIS THAT I CAME OUT OF THE HYPNOTIC STATE AND THE CRAFT HAD GONE. THEY HAD RELEASED MY MIND. I EXCLAIMED ALOUD "WHERE'S THE LIGHT." "WHERE'S THE LIGHT." NOT REALIZING IT WAS ALL OVER. THEY HAD GONE.

(4) I CONTINUED DRIVING AS I HAD BEEN TOLD BUT I WAS NOW COMPLETLY CONSCIOUS AND IN CONTROL. I NOTED THERE WAS NO TRAFFIC WHAT SO EVER AS I HAD BEEN TOLD. AND I KEPT GOING. WHEN I REACHED THE SLIP ROAD AT THE GORSLEY TURN OFF (B4221) I STOPPED BEFORE TURNING ON TO THE B4221 FOR NEWENT. I PUT THE HAZARD LIGHTS ON GOT OUT OF MY CAR LOOKED ACROSS THE MOTORWAY AT A SMALL WOOD OPPOSITE. I SAW LIGHTS GOING DOWN BEYOND THE WOOD BUT COULD NOT SWEAR THAT THEY WERE THE SAME LIGHTS THAT HAD PLAGUED ME EARLIER. STILL NO TRAFFIC. I GOT BACK INTO MY CAR. PUT THE HAZARD LIGHTS OFF PUT MY SEAT BELT ON AND THEN NOTICED MY DIGITAL CLOCK WAS READING 10-22 P.M. THAT MEANT THAT A 3½ MILE JOURNEY WHICH WOULD NORMALY TAKE 3-4 MINUTES TOOK 40 MINUTES. I REMEMBER FEELING PLEASED WHEN I SAW THE LIGHTS OF A CAR COMING FROM GORSLEY GOLF CLUB.

(5) THE FIRST CAR I HAD SEEN SINCE ENTERING M.50. AS THE CAR PASSED I PULLED OUT BEHIND IT BUT IT TURNED RIGHT ONTO THE MOTORWAY TO ROSS-ON-WYE. I CONTINUED HOME ARRIVING AT ABOUT 10-35 P.M. STILL WONDERING WHAT HAD HAPPENED. THE LIGHT STILL HAUNTING ME. WHICH IT DOES TO THIS DAY. I CHECKED THE CAR OVER AND MYSELF TO SEE IF I HAD BEEN INVOLVED IN ANY FORM OF ACCIDENT. NO DAMAGE TO THE CAR AND NO MARKS ON MY BODY.

THE ONLY EXPLAINATION TO THE LACK OF TRAFFIC ON THE MOTORWAY AND LOSS OF TIME, WOULD BE IF I HAD BEEN TAKEN WHEN THERE WAS A LULL IN THE TRAFFIC AND PUT BACK WHEN THERE WAS A LULL IN THE TRAFFIC. 40 MINUTES BEING LOST INSIDE THE CRAFT FOR WHAT PURPOSE I DO NOT KNOW. MY CONCLUSION IS. I WAS TAKEN BY A U.F.O. SIMILAR OR THE SAME AS DESCRIBED IN MY EARLIER SIGHTINGS WITH ITS OUTER LIGHT ON. THIS LIGHT

(6) ACTING AS A TYPE OF STROBE GIVING IT A SHIMMERING OR PULSING EFFECT, THUS HYPNOTIZING ME, WHILE TAKING THE CAR AND MYSELF UP INTO ITS HULL AND THEN UP INTO THE SKY OUT OF SIGHT. FOR 40 MINUTES, TO DO WHAT EVER THEY HAD TO DO TO ME AND THEN BRINGING ME BACK TO EXACTLY THE SAME SPOT ON THE MOTORWAY. TO CONTINUE MY JOURNEY.

I THINK U.F.O's ARE USEING MOTORWAYS AS EASY ACCESS FOR ABDUCTIONS AND NOW THAT THE AMERICAN AIR-FORCE HAS GONE ITS LEFT THE GATE WIDE OPEN FOR THEM. TO DO WHAT THEY WANT. UP UNTILL 199D MY FIRST SIGHTING WHERE I SAW TWO CRAFT. I HAD NEVER SEEN ANYTHING IN 47 YEARS OF MY LIFE.

P.S. WHEN I ARRIVED HOME AT ABOUT 10-35 P.M. MY WIFE WAS IN BED ASLEEP SO WAS MY YOUNGEST SON STEPHEN IN HIS BED ASLEEP.

(In our interview with John, he told us he heard the voice say *"Don't be afraid . . . don't be afraid"*. This was not in his original 'write-up', as sent to *Circular Forum*, which contained over forty pages of script.)

John continued on his journey and then turned off at the Gorsley sign (B4221) for Newent. He stopped the car briefly, to look over a small wood, where he saw some 'lights' going down behind the wood, but wasn't sure if this was connected with what he had had just experienced. He looked at his watch; it was showing 10.22pm, which meant that a short journey, that normally takes a few minutes, had lasted 40 minutes. John noticed the lights of a car, heading away from Gorsley Golf Club. This was the first vehicle he had seen since entering the M50. He arrived home at 10.35pm, still wondering what had happened to him. After checking the car over for any damage, or injuries caused to him, there were none.

His wife and one of his three sons were in bed, the other away, the third watching TV. When John attempted to tell his son what had transpired, his son told him to wait until the football had finished! When the match finished, John explained what had taken place to his son, who couldn't understand why it had taken him such a long time to arrive home.

John pondered then (as he has continued to do so now, nearly 20 years later) whether the complete vehicle was lifted up into the 'craft', before being brought back down onto the road. He cannot understand why the incident happened during a lull in traffic, and then being 'put back' when there was another lull, as the Motorway is normally quite busy at that period of time.

John believes he was medically examined during the abduction process, and over the months and years that followed, he experienced flashbacks of what took place, many of which caused him considerable trauma. In addition, he began to notice some very bizarre synchronicities in his life. They included the number *22. John tells of various incidents that involve this number being brought to his attention.

They included:

1. While travelling up the Motorway a stone flew up and smashed his windscreen, at 2.22pm.

2. He was driving along the road when a vehicle cut in aggressively in front of him. The number plate showed 22.

3. One of the lottery dice used at work for the firm's syndicate went missing. This was found under the fridge, at home.

4. Templates used at work showed the number 22.

5. During a visit to a shop in Gloucester, to collect a new fridge, he discovered his car had been stolen. The thieves had left another stolen car in its place – its registration number was 22 SKY. We feel that this may be just a complete coincidence but if this was the case what were the chances of the car being abandoned and later found by the police in Battledown Approach, Cheltenham near where the Circular Forum had their meetings!

---

*In Numerology all numbers are reduced down to the vibration of a single digit, for example a 25 is reduced to a 7 (2 + 5 = 7) and 18 becomes a 9 (1 + 8 = 9). However, in Numerology 11 & 22 require unique attention. These are called the 'Master Numbers'. A person with an Expression or Life Path that reduces down fully to an 11 or 22 are said to be endowed with special gifts of high-level inspiration and leadership, but their life may also be very challenging and highly paradoxical. For instance, Michael Jordan, Bill Clinton, and Tim McGraw, are number 11s, and John Assaraf, Dean Martin, and Sir Richard Branson are 22s.

John contacted Robin Cole of the Cheltenham based group *Circular Forum UFO Group* on the 16th of May, 1996 and spoke to him at length about what he had experienced. His account to Robin (as published in the 1st edition of the magazine) was identical to what he told us in 2013.

The information was passed to Tony Dodd director of investigations for *Quest*, then on to Nick Pope, before being paassed on to Professor Mack at Harvard University for analysis. Co-incidentally, there was even a reference to myself (John Hanson) in the magazine, as giving a talk about UFOs on the 19th February 1997 – how time flies!

Publicity was given to this incident in the local newspapers . . .

It was clear from John's agitated behaviour during the time we spent with him talking about his experience, that he still remains baffled by the nature of exactly what occurred. We both felt there was more he could tell us, but we suspected it was of a highly personal nature and were not inclined to pursue our suspicions that this may have had something to do with what happened aboard the 'craft'.

John also reported that following the incident there were occasions when normal everyday objects could trigger off a flash of disturbing memory associated with what took place after the UFO event. This was found to be a recurring theme in the backgrounds of so many people that we had spoken to over the years.

In the book *Abduction*, based on his work with over 100 abductees, John Mack states:

UFO experts examine 'alien abduction' case

NEWENT: LEADING UFO investigators are studying claims that a man from the Forest of Dean area was abducted by aliens.

He experienced vivid flashbacks and may be suffering post traumatic stress disorder. The man, not identified to guard him from ridicule, reported his case to paranormal group Circular Forum last year.

He said the incident had happened while he was driving on the M50 near Newent 15 months before.

While emerging from under a bridge, an 80ft tall bright white object which was about the width of the motorway hovered overhead.

The man pulled over, and next remembers driving in the middle lane 40 minutes later.

Months afterwards he began having flashbacks and recalled the object having a "fast strobe" effect which could have hypnotised him.

He remembers being observed by beings and lying inside a large white room.

Cheltenham-based Circular Forum has contacted several respected experts from UFO groups for their views.

Paperwork and a video interview were dispatched to Tony Dodd, director of investigations for Quest, which publishes UFO magazine, and Nick Pope, a former UFO desk officer with the Ministry of Defence.

Robin Cole, forum head of investigations, said the case was sensitive and complex. No conclusions had been reached.

> *"We can continue to try to make the phenomenon fit the world as we have known it, jamming it into a kind of Procrustean bed of consensus reality. Or we can acknowledge that the world might be other than we have known it. Then we are free to see where our thinking leads us. I have spent countless hours trying to find alternate explanations that would not require the major shift in my worldview that I have had to face . . . but no familiar theory or explanation has come even close to accounting for the basic features of the abduction phenomenon."*

Dawn and I felt John was a very genuine man, who has suffered what he feels is a frightening ordeal, for which no answers can be found. He is one of many thousands (if not millions) worldwide that has been plunged into a frightening ordeal which appears to be outside the remit of everyday life. He yearns for answers as to what it was exactly that he encountered along that stretch of lonely road all those years ago and is still affected by the experience to this present day. We wish him well and hope he finds some peace in eventually coming to terms with what took place.

What should be of real concern to us are the after-effects experienced by people who have been apparently exposed to the energies radiated by these objects. Whether, in some of those cases, there is any physical foundation to the allegations made by people who claim they have been the victims of alien abduction is a question we cannot answer. If at the end of the day these experiences have all happened in the mind, rather than through physical interaction, one is bound to wonder how do we explain the prevalence of strange marks found on the body, later, and mysterious medical ailments, which arise after the incident and not before? As Gordon Creighton said, many times over: *"Even if you are a sceptic, reports of UFO sightings and abductions are still the greatest phenomena of all time!"*

John cites an example of everyday common objects that can cause a flashback – a cycle and marks on wood. Some people may find this the butt of humour, but be assured – if it happened to them, they wouldn't be laughing and we might be writing up about them as well!

*Our records for July 1991 revealed (brief details) a disc-shaped object, seen in Scotland on 8th July 1991, a black lozenge-shaped object, seen by the co-pilot of a Boeing Aircraft en route to Gatwick, London, and on the 15th, a UFO was seen hovering over Tawsmead Copse, Wiltshire. In the same month an acorn-shaped object was captured on photo, by Dawn Holloway, at the same location following the discovery of a crop formation.

A check of February 1995 failed to reveal any UFO sightings for the 15th February 1995. We had details of a triangular object, captured on photograph on the 8th February by a police officer, at Old Trafford, a 'shambling creature' seen in the Cannock area on the 18th, and a triangular set of lights over Derbyshire, on 26th February. Unfortunately no other reports from around M50/Gloucester area, which would have been of interest, not only to us but to John. Not that this is needed to corroborate the event which befell him.

UFO over Somerset

Carole Brown of Tatworth, South Chard, Somerset, was taking the family dog for a walk, at 10.20pm on 22nd July 1981, when she saw:

> *". . . a circular red/orange 'light', moving across the sky, behind nearby trees. I watched it for five minutes – then it stopped and reversed along its course and was gone."*

(Source: *Probe*)

*Further information will be found in the appropriate later volume of Haunted Skies.

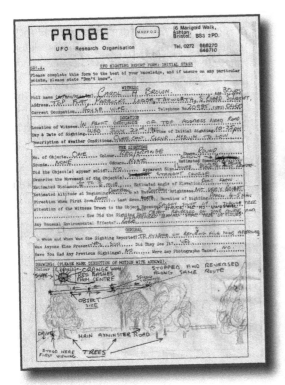

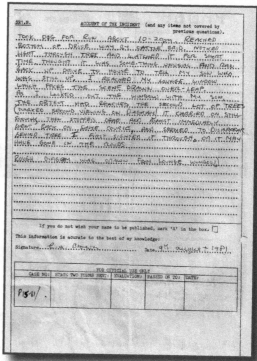

Strange smelling UFO, Wiltshire

The following day at 3.45am on 30th July 1981, Mr. & Mrs. Hopgood and their two children – Karen (14) and Helen (13) – from Southampton, were driving to Wales, via Salisbury, hoping to avoid any traffic along the route.

After passing the Cadnam roundabout, still in a holiday frame of mind, their mood changed when a peculiar smell – like sewage – pervaded the car, which they presumed was crop fertilization taking place nearby.

While passing Wellam, another smell, this time like strong coffee, entered the inside of the car. Mystified, they continued on their journey, proceeding along an incline, known as Pepperbox Hill, on the way to Salisbury. A couple of a hundred yards on the road, Mr. Hopgood saw a pinkish offside rear light, which he first took to be the tail lights of a lorry in front of him, thinking the other tail light wasn't working. As their car drew closer, the 'light' moved to the other side of the road

> *"I decided to get past it and put my foot down, but then I realised the 'light' had to be at least 10ft off the ground.*
>
> *I grew excited, not knowing what exactly was in front of us. Oddly, I never thought it might have been a UFO. By now I was moving at 70mph, trying to build up the speed to get past, and was able to see a red 'ball of light' – the size of a lorry tyre – about 80 yards away from us. As we approached the summit of the hill, the 'light' rose up to a height of about 40ft and disappeared over the top of the hill."*

Relieved, the family drove on, but as they neared Salisbury, a few minutes later, that all pervading smell of sewage, once again, entered the car. This faded away, to be replaced by the smell of lemons – the atmosphere now heavy with static electricity. As they approached Warminster, with day breaking, things returned to normal. They never saw the object again.

(Source: Omar Fowler, SIGAP/PRA)

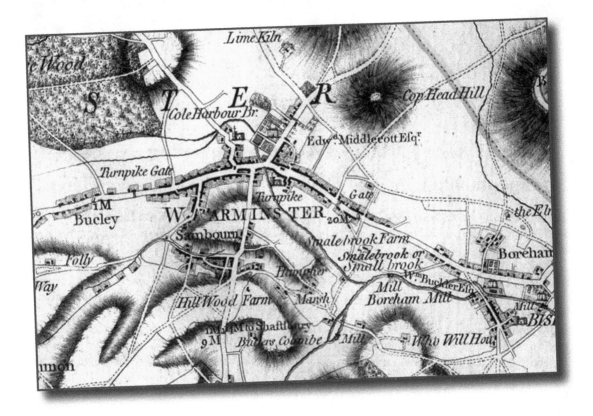

AUGUST 1981

TRIANGULAR UFO SEEN OVER SOUTH YORKSHIRE

Also includes – Police officer sights domed UFO over Bridgend • Wigan housewife sights revolving 'light' over town • A 'wonderful experience' for a Stoke-on-Trent housewife and her husband

UFOs reported

ACCORDING to a telephone 'UFO hotline', set up in August 1981, in the Batley area of South Yorkshire, a number of calls were made, reporting the sighting of UFOs in the Derbyshire area. They included, *'a large triangular object, covered with small lights, seen moving over fields, at Bonsall Moor'*, *'an object, displaying eight bright lights'*, seen at the rear of a family home, at Hasland, Chesterfield (of which it was said three photographs were taken), and a sighting by a Leeds couple, who were driving along the M1 Motorway, between Junction 25 and 27, when they saw, *'a large circular object, hovering over the Motorway, which lit up the road before landing in a nearby field'*.

(Source: Dronfield Gazette, 20.9.1981 –
'UFOs spotted in Derbyshire')

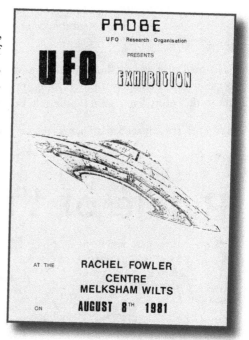

PROBE
UFO Research Organisation

PRESENTS

UFO EXHIBITION

AT THE RACHEL FOWLER
CENTRE
MELKSHAM WILTS

ON AUGUST 8ᵀᴴ 1981

UFOs over Bridgend

On 22nd August 1981, Police Constable David Harris, of the South Wales Constabulary, was on night patrol, driving along the main road, at Lewiston, Bridgend, with another officer, when they noticed a dome-shaped object, with a strip of green light at either side, surrounded in haze, hovering over mountains to their left, in the direction of Dolau Ifan Ddu Farm, Blackmill, at 12.20am.

"I stopped the car, intending to get out and have a closer look, my curiosity aroused, but changed my mind when I realised how agitated my partner had become – probably because whatever the object, it was hovering over the village where his family lived. Although we checked out the surrounding area, including the mountain tops of Mynydd y Gaer, we never sighted the strange 'craft' again.

Following newspaper publicity given to the incident, I was contacted by a Mrs. Evans-Delve, who told me that she had been driving along the road between Bryncethin and Blackmill, with her mother, just after 11.30pm, during the early 1980s, when she sighted a gigantic cigar-shaped object, with a glowing 'red tail', in the sky. By the time she brought her mother's attention to it, the object was out of view.

As they drove past Blackmill Hospital they then saw it again, hovering over a nearby railway line. To their amazement, the UFO then slowly moved over and took up a hovering position, just above their vehicle, as they continued on their journey. When they reached Lewiston, Mrs. Evans-Delve pulled into a bus stop, intending to confront whatever it was, but was prevented from doing so by her mother.

To the amazement of the two women concerned, the UFO became charged with lights and appeared to turn over, changing shape into a 'silver disc', with lights all around its base, before moving away at a phenomenal speed, disappearing from view within seconds. Mrs. Evans-Delve also told me that she discovered UFOs had been sighted, the following day, over St Athan. Although I cannot confirm that this incident was connected with what we saw, I believe, from the information supplied to me by Mrs. Evans-Delve, that it may well have been the same UFO."

Mrs. Evans-Delve was not the only person to witness the shape shifting characteristics of a UFO. Ambulance men on patrol in Hungerford, Berkshire, reported sighting an extremely bright *'light'* moving over the countryside, before being seen to split into two.

The two halves then headed off across the sky, side by side – lost from view, as they went over the horizon.

SUNDAY EXPRESS 9-8-81

Riddle of the night fireball

Sunday Express Reporter

IT WAS a fine night as the two ambulancemen stood looking skyward for shooting stars.

Suddenly they were startled by a ball of fire hurtling across the darkness overhead. Three seconds later it had vanished. But what caused it remains a mystery.

The ambulance men, Roger Dicks and Graham Brunsden, saw the blazing object at about 11 pm while on duty at Hungerford, Berkshire, ambulance station.

Mr Dicks said: " We thought at first it was an aircraft on fire. it was about 1,000 feet up at a distance of between three and four miles.

" We expected our telephones would soon be ringing. But nothing happened. And the local police said they had had no reports of a crash in the area."

The ambulancemen say that the blazing object was travelling horizontally across the sky and trailing smoke.

It made no sound, but before it disappeared, it seemed to separate into two halves, with the second half travelling at a lower altitude.

Mr Dicks, who has a science degree, said : " It is a complete mystery. But I can't help feeling the object was man-made—about the size of a garden shed.

" So far, however, I have not found anything to account for it. And nobody else has reported seeing it."

UFO over Wigan, Lancashire

During the evening of the 27th August 1981, residents in the Billinge and Garswood area of Wigan, Lancashire, sighted a large conical-shaped craft flying overhead in the sky. The object circled the area for 45mins, at an estimated height of 1,000ft, and those who viewed it through binoculars said it had a number of lights on it. Mrs Parkin, of Crookhurst Drive, said:

> *"It continually changed colour from red to blue. Through a pair of binoculars we could see it was revolving and appeared to be conical. We've never seen anything like it before; it was very unusual. There were, perhaps, a couple of aircraft in the area, but we could hear them and this object was soundless."*

The Civil Aviation Authority, Police, Manchester Air Traffic Control, Jodrell Bank, and the Manchester Meteorological Department were unable to explain the sightings.

Cone-shaped UFO over Stoke-on-Trent

In August 1981, Marion Connolly of Fenton, Stoke-on-Trent, was awoken during the early hours of the morning by a humming sound. On going to the window and looking out over the nearby Fenton Park, she was amazed to see a luminous object heading towards the house, and shouted for her husband to come and see it. The couple watched the UFO, spellbound, with its blinding light, as it passed over the house, and rushed to the window, opposite, in time to see:

> *". . . a cone-shaped rear, not round, like the front. We both felt it was a wonderful experience and a privilege. We did wonder if it had taken-off from the park, after landing, and it had been the noise which awoke me."*

(Source: Irene Bott/Graham Allen, SUFOG)

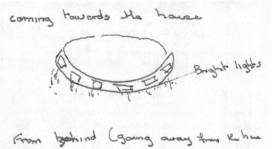

Unidentified Flying Objects Studies Investigation Service

Tel.No) 021-422-3949

Our ref.

Chairman: Geoffrey L.Westwood

E.Westley Tel.707-0254
B.Taylor   Tel.422-3949
****

Please reply in this instance to:

Editor-Ufosis,
731 Hagley Road West,
Quinton,
 Birmingham B32 1AJ.

Your ref.

Date. September 81
  News sheet No.9

NEXT UFOSIS MEETING IS ON THE 11th SEPT.FRIDAY AT DR.JOHNSON HOUSE,
BULL STREET.START : 6.30 - 7.00PM - Finish 9.30PM. Room 2.

1.Agenda for meeting: Apologies,Minutes of last meeting,Matters arising,
                         Any other buisness ....

2.UFOSIS has decided to run certain projects with the object of building
up as much useful information as possible.Adrian Potter has agreed to
make a start on cataloguing aircraft and their lighting patterns.If
other members would like to take on a project from the following list
will you let me know or Eric Westley either by letter or at the next
meeting 11/9/81.

Astronomical Data ,Satellite info. , Meteorological data ,
Airship movements , Bird Migration , Signal Flare areas or any other
useful information which you might consider to be of help to the group.

3.To supplement the trips to Warminster for skywatching and other purposes
the Investigations Co-ordinator would like all members to try an exper-
iment.Sometime during the hours of darkness on the week-end
September 1981 spend half/one hour outside,completing the enclosed
Skywatch Report Form.The idea being that any object you see to note
down in the appropriate column the relevant information.
Note:Column 2&3 are degrees clockwise from North.
     Column 4.Imagine the sky as a flat wall and give the "o'clock" re-
             ading of any moving objects line of flight.
     Column 6&7 Give approx. size and brightness relative to a bright
             star.
     Column 8 Make any relevant comments.
     Column 9 IGNORE
     Column 10 put your initial.
Please return completed form to E.W.Westley,10 Alexander Road,Acocks
Green,Birmingham B27 6HE or bring it with you to the meeting on the 11th
Sept.

Warminster Trip. Ufosis have a trip planed for Cradle Hill,Warminster
on the 3rd October 81.Start off approx. 11am.The idea being that members
inform me or Eric Westley either by letter or at the next meeting,we can
then organise transport for whoever is interested in going.Obviously
a member who has a car will be able to take 3/4 other members down and
share the cost of petrol,this has been done in the past and has worked
out very well.Anyone who is interested please let us know so we can sort
the transport out.Departure back from Warminster will be around 11.30-
midnight depending on the weather.

Space Shuttle. STS-2(Space Transportation System) is scheduled to lift
off from the U.S. on September 30th,Truly and Engle are the crew for
this mission.

U.F.O.S.I.S

SEPTEMBER 1981

CIGAR-SHAPED OBJECTS SEEN IN SKY OVER TODMORDEN

Also includes – Denise Bishop, from Plymouth, reports having been burnt by UFO after sighting, investigated by Bob Boyd • Crescent-shaped UFO over Bradford • 'Beautiful silver diamond-shaped object' seen by woman and her children, in Lowestoft sky, near USAF airbase • Triangular UFO seen in sky, over Edinburgh

UFO over Todmorden

IN September 1981, a cigar-shaped object was seen over Todmorden, in Yorkshire, over several nights, by police and members of the public. At 1.15pm on 3rd September 1981, Jacqueline Bice (32) was driving home from Swindon to Highworth, in Wiltshire, accompanied by her friend, Louis Wykes (17). After leaving the A419 dual carriageway, they turned onto the B4109 (which links Blunsdon with Highworth) when they noticed a bright blue *'mass of light'* apparently flashing to their right in the sky, 25°off the horizon, shining through bushes, which lit up the sky a few miles from each side of it.

Burnt by UFO

At 3am on 11th September 1981, Plymouth-based UFO Researcher, Bob Boyd, received a phone call from a man, who told him about an incident involving his girlfriend's sister, which had taken place a few hours previously, and that he had contacted the police, who advised him this was not a matter they were able to deal with and had given him Bob's telephone number.

> *"I felt that I should see the girl immediately, amid dire warnings from my wife, and went out to see the girl, Denise Bishop – then 23 years old, and an accounts clerk, whom I found to be a very calm, self-possessed, girl. She had never thought about UFOs, and had not read any books on the subject. I interviewed her from 3.15 until 5am, and took a couple of black and white photographs (the last on the film) of the burn to her hand."*

Denise:

> *"I was coming into my house, at approximately 11.15pm. As I approached the corner of the bungalow, in Weston Hill, Plymouth, I thought I saw some lights behind the house. As I got*

to the back door, allowing me to see up the hill behind our house, I saw an enormous unlit and dark metallic grey UFO, hovering above the houses on top of the hill. Coming from underneath the object, and shining down on the rooftops beneath it, were six or seven broad shafts of light. These were lovely pastel shades of pink and purple and also white. I saw all this in an instant and I was terrified. I hurriedly reached for the door but as I put my hand on the handle, from the unlit side of the ship, a lime green pencil beam of light came down and hit the back of my hand. As soon as it hit my hand, I couldn't move. I was stopped dead in my tracks.

The beam stayed on my hand for at least 30 seconds, in which time I could only stand and watch the UFO. I was very frightened, although the UFO was a fantastic sight to see. It was huge and silent. In fact, the whole area seemed very quiet. The green beam, which didn't give off any illumination – like a 'rod of light' – then switched off and I continued to open the door. It was as if a film had been stopped, then started again.

I had been stopped in mid-stride and when the beam went off, it continued the same movement. I opened the door and rushed into the house. As I did so, the UFO lifted into the sky slightly, and moved away and out of my sight. Rubbing my hand, I ran in and told my sister.

We went back outside but there was nothing to be seen. Coming in again, my sister examined my hand but there was nothing there. I went and sat down and, a few minutes later, my sister's dog sniffed my hand, making it sting. On looking at it I noticed spots of blood and, after washing it, saw it was a burn.

At 2.30am, my sister's boyfriend John Greenwell came in and said we must report it to the police. He phoned the police but they couldn't help, except to give us Bob Boyd's number."

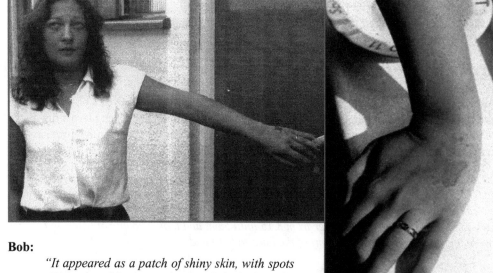

Bob:

"It appeared as a patch of shiny skin, with spots of blood and bruising about it. It looked as if a patch of skin had been removed, exposing the

shiny, new skin beneath. I tried to get Denise to go to the casualty ward at a local hospital, but she refused. When she complained that the wound was hurting, I told her to put her hand in cold water but this made it worse. Antiseptic cream was put on and this gave some relief. Denise had calmed down somewhat, but said she was terrified when the incident happened. Her first words to me were "Will they come back to get me?" "What if it had been on my face or eyes?" and "Why me?" She was very frightened. After talking and allaying her fears somewhat, we called it a night."

John Greenwell decided to carry out some enquiries at local houses, close to where the incident had taken place, and spoke to a Suzanne Meakin from Bridwell Road, Weston Mill, who told him that shortly after 11pm, her dog had bolted out of the room and up the stairs. He then lay down for some time and refused to move the behavior being completely out of character for him. Mr. & Mrs. Gardner, of Bridwell Road, were other witnesses who were interviewed by Bob after the initial visit by John. They said that between 11pm and 11.30pm their toy poodle had ran about gathering up all her toys, and taking them to a fabric kennel, and then sat in the kennel clearly agitated and very nervous.

On 16th September 1981, Denise attended a meeting held by the Plymouth Group, and showed them her burnt hand, before leaving for a holiday in Canada. Bob asked her if she had any objection to him publicizing details of the case, to which she agreed but asked him to keep her name confidential. (By this time the burn had a fully formed scab. Two weeks later the scab was gone, leaving a red mark – like a pale birth mark)

On 28th October, Roger Malone of the *Western Herald*, published the story of Denise – 'Attacked By A Spaceship' – and showed the photographs of her and the burn to her hand.

Bob:

> *"This shows a patch of white on the back of Denise's hand. Whether the whiteness of the burn was enhanced by the overhead light, at the time the photo was taken, or whether the wound had some sort of glow to it, I cant say"*

The following day, after the article had been published, Denise received a call from Elsie of Weston Mill Hill, who told her that she had seen the UFO. Elsie was later interviewed and spoke of seeing the object emitting three beams of light.

In December 1981, Derek Mansell, of Contact UK, told Bob that a copy of his report had been passed to a consultant at a leading hospital, who believed, from his examination, that the lesion showed the features of a laser burn.   **(Source: Bob Boyd, Plymouth UFO Group)**

UFO over Bradford

At 6.55pm on 20th September 1981, trainee teacher – Frances Bowtell from Baildon, Bradford, sighted a stationary 'blob' of light in the north-west direction of the sky. Curious, she fetched a pair of binoculars and looked through, but after seeing nothing of any note, decided to halt the observations some 20 minutes later.

> *"As I was about to stop looking, thinking it was some sort of extra bright star in the sky, all of a sudden, it split into three parts – now showing what looked like a small white cloud, with a crescent shape below it. Underneath that was a small faint light."*

(Source: *Bradford Telegraph*, 25.9.81 – 'Three In One Light Puzzle')

Spinning UFO over Cleveland

Shortly after sunset on 21st September 1981, a large spinning object, with 'coloured rings of light' around it, constantly changing from red, green, blue and white, was sighted in the north-eastern part of the sky from the Roseworth Estate, Stockton-on-Tees, Cleveland, by a number of people, after it was first sighted by David Muldowney (11) and his friend – Brian McDowell. Telephone enquiries with Teesside Airport revealed no knowledge of any UFO being plotted on their radar.

(Source: *North Evening Gazette*, 22.9.81 – 'Strange Lights In The Sky')

UFO over Lowestoft Suffolk

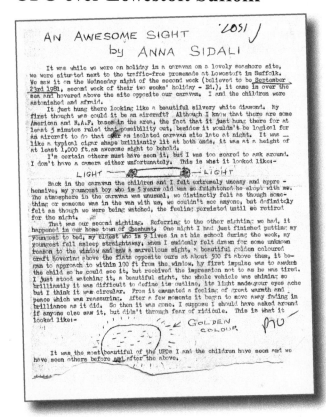

Two days later, on the 23rd September 1981, Anna Sidali and her children were on holiday at Lowestoft, in Suffolk, taking a breath of fresh air, before night fell, when:

"I noticed a beautiful silver, diamond-shaped object, appear in the sky. I wondered if it had anything to do with the nearby USAF Airbase when, all of sudden, it was overhead. Frightened, I took the children and ran inside. The oddest thing is that I felt as if we were being watched. It's difficult to explain, but the sighting took place against a backcloth of oppressive atmosphere."

(Source: Ivan W. Bunn)

Triangular UFO over Edinburgh

At 10.45pm on 24th September 1981, Henry Duncan and his daughter were out walking the family dog, at Wester Hailes, Edinburgh – a cold and frosty evening, with no wind – when they were astonished to see:

". . . a distinct metallic grey colour, triangular-shaped object, with a bright red 'disc of light' in each corner, 900-1,800ft off the ground. After hovering briefly in the sky, it shot off Northwest, towards Edinburgh Airport, wobbling in the air as it did so."

(Source: Dan Goring, *Earth-link*, October 1982/*BUFORA Bulletin*, No. 3, March 1982)

OCTOBER 1981

HUGE GOLDEN LIGHT SEEN OVER HASTINGS – WERE HELICOPTERS SCRAMBLED?

Also includes – Cigar-shaped object then seen by residents • Triangular-shaped object seen in sky, over Chester, by various witnesses • Flying black 'doughnut' seen over Kidderminster • Cigar-shaped UFO seen hovering over motorway junction at Huyton, Liverpool, by factory workers • Two boys out night-time fishing, in Suffolk, sight UFO over sea • Mysterious flashes seen in the sky, over Shipley, Yorkshire A large, coloured 'disc' over Worthing, and strange 'plank like' objects seen in the sky over Keighley

'Flying Cigar' over Hastings – October 1981

COLIN Carey was walking his dog along Plynlimmon Road, Hastings, at 9pm on 4th October 1981, when he happened to notice a large bright yellow light, with a white centre, moving across the sky, between two houses. By the time he had ran to high ground, there was no sign of it.

At 9.15pm Matilda Antell (65) of Bristol Way, Hastings, felt compelled to go to the window and have a look out. When she did so, she saw a huge golden light in the sky, about the size of a dinner plate, over Church-in-the-Wood, Hollington, which kept changing shape into a cross, then cigar, moving backwards and forwards.

> "Suddenly, six or seven aircraft appeared (I think they were helicopters) at which point the object formed its own cloud. Thinking it had gone, I continued to watch and was astonished to see it come out again and radiate this golden light. It then increased in size and moved closer, showing other coloured lights. I phoned my daughter-in-law, Janette, to come to the house and have a look."

Janette arrived and scanned the sky, but by then there was nothing to be seen. However, after ten minutes of observations, she was rewarded when a cigar-shaped object came out of a white haze, along with a pyramidal shaped one, flashing with lights all around it.

"There were blue lights around it as well, with lots of aircraft flying through the sky. When they approached the object, it disappeared behind its own cloud. I was shaking after what I had witnessed. I have seen the moon in different states. This was no moon."

This explanation, by the Royal Greenwich Observatory, was rejected – they suggested the couple had misidentified the moon!

Triangular UFO over Chester

At 9.20pm, the same evening, a resident living in Blacon, near Chester, was waiting for the cat to come in, when:

"I saw this object in the sky, moving slowly towards us. I called my husband. It looked like an egg in shape, encased in glittering lights. As it passed overhead, it changed into a triangular shape. We watched as it headed away, before briefly halting in mid-air, a few hundred feet away."

Another witness was Mr. W. Morle also from Blacon, Chester.

"I was on the way to the off-license, at 9.20pm, in my car, when my wife tapped on the window and asked me to look at something in the sky. I got out of the car and saw, almost overhead, a row of brilliant white, pulsating lights, forming a triangle, approximately 15ft on each side, with a base of 10ft, moving slowly through the air – no more than 10-15mph, completely silently. When it reached the outskirts of Chester, it tilted to the right, as if observing something."

(Source: British UFO Society/ *News of Hastings,* **8.10.81 – 'Hastings UFO Moonlight, Says Observatory')**

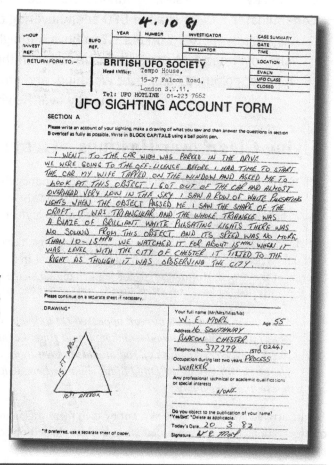

Doughnut-shaped UFO over Kidderminster

During the afternoon of 5th October 1981, people living in Stone – a small village, near Kidderminster, Worcestershire –

contacted the police, after sighting an object, resembling a black doughnut, flying across the sky, at an estimated height of 2,000ft. Others described is as looking like:

> "... a rotating flat cylinder, 35ft in diameter, with a shimmering black metallic underside and silvery top, last seen heading in a north-east direction, skimming over the top of power cables."

(Source: Crystal Hogben, *Magic Saucer*, Kidderminster)

Cigar-shaped UFO over Liverpool

On 10th October 1981, two factory workers from Huyton, near Liverpool, were on their way to purchase some fish and chips from a mobile food van, parked in Crompton Road, at 10.50pm, when they were staggered by the sight of a huge 'glowing cigar', with a number of lighted windows along its side, hovering over the nearby junction of the M62/M57 Motorways. Transfixed, they sat watching, unable to believe their eyes. When they eventually returned to the factory, they discussed the matter but decided against reporting it at that stage, fearing ridicule.

(Source: Brian Fishwicke, MIGAP)

Mrs. C. Sullivan from Bradford, Yorkshire, was sat in a queue of traffic, waiting for traffic lights to change on the Otley Road junction with Shipley, at 9.10am on 13th October 1981, when she saw:

> "... two bright silver lights, joined in the middle, positioned halfway down the side of the Wrose TV Mast. After a few minutes, they sped off – now looking almost like a black tube – before disappearing from view."

(Source: Graham Birdsall/Derek Mansell, Contact UK/ *Earth-link Magazine*, October 1982)

UFOs over Suffolk, Lancashire and Sussex

At 2am on 29th October 1981, Kevin Grimsby (16) from Hollesley, on the Suffolk coast, was out night fishing with a friend, when they saw:

> "... a silvery object flickering and pulsating with light – the size of a car – hanging a few hundred feet above the sea, giving off a faint hum."

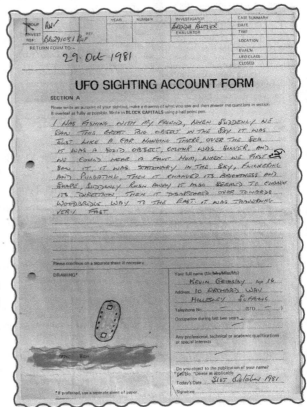

30/10/81 24

Simon spots UFO

By COLIN CLARK

WORTHING POLICE have notified the Royal Air Force at West Drayton about an unidentified flying object which terrified a 13-year-old Worthing schoolboy and 'put the fear of God' into his father.

Mr Derek Stenning, 36-year-old odd-job man, of 359 Tarring Road, Worthing, was driving home from Patching at 7.30 p.m. on Friday when his son Simon spotted what he described as 'a large coloured disc hovering above a clump of trees on the north of the A27.'

Simon, a Durrington High School pupil, told me, 'One half was red and the other white and the two colours kept flashing alternately.'

The red and white lights also transposed their position as they flashed.

Sped away

It had two exhaust-type projections from which sparks were appearing, he said.

As he pointed out the object to his father it suddenly rose in the air and 'seemed to come toards the car' as it crossed the A27, he claimed.

Then it accelerated away towards the sea 'at an incredible speed.'

The experience which lasted under one minute, left Simon terrified. 'When I got out of the car at home my legs were all shaky,' he said.

Fear

Even Simon's father admitted, 'It put the fear of God into me. This was unlike anything I have seen.'

A Ministry of Defence spokesman told me, on Monday, 'The sighting will be investigated. If there is a whisper of something strange, we will dig a little further.'

After hovering for 15 minutes, it moved away towards the direction of Woodbridge, and was soon just a speck in the sky.

(Source: Brenda Butler)

UFO over Shipley

Eric Booth from Nab Wood, near Shipley, Yorkshire awoke for no apparent reason, at 3.40am on 29th October 1981. On going to the window he saw something with three lights, hovering between trees, in Nab Wood.

> *"Every ten minutes there was a huge flash – like a camera flash going off. I awoke my wife, Julie, and we watched it for about 30 minutes, until it clouded over and disappeared."*

(Source: *Telegraph and Argus* – 'Eric tells about UF0 mystery', 29.10.1981)

Plank-shaped UFOs over Keighley

Pensioner Betty Banks, from South Street, Keighley, was preparing an early morning drink on the 29th October 1981, when she looked out of the window and saw:

> *". . . two plank-shaped objects in the sky, showing a brilliant light. The lights then went out and the objects contracted into a ball shape – like hedgehogs, curling up – before gradually fading away."*

'Flying Disc' over Worthing

The following day, Derek Stenning, from Worthing, was driving home with his son, Simon, at 7.30pm, when they sighted a large coloured 'disc', alternately flashing red and white lights, with two exhaust type projections, from which sparks were appearing as it hovered over a clump of trees, North of the A27.

> *"It then suddenly rose upwards and seemed to approach us, before crossing the road, accelerating towards the sea at an incredible speed."*

The father and son, considerably shaken by the experience, later reported it to the MoD, who was quoted as saying:

> *"The sighting will be investigated. If there is a whisper of something strange, we will dig a little deeper."*

(Source: *Worthing Gazette*, 30.10.1981 – 'Simon Spots UFO')

NOVEMBER 1981

UFO SIGHTING OVER RAF WOODBRIDGE

Also includes – Orange pulsating object seen over Lancashire • Police Inspector's wife sights UFO over Hampshire – she believes they are about to land • UFO, with searchlight, over Ilford, Essex, seen by local woman • Mushroom-shaped UFO over Bradford • 'Gigantic dragonfly' seen over Weymouth • Duke of Edinburgh takes evasive action after another airliner sights UFO

UFO over RAF Woodbridge, Suffolk

IN early November 1981, security personnel at RAF Woodbridge, reported to their Base Commander of having seen *'a huge cigar-shaped object, estimated to be 100yds long and 50ft in diameter, move over from the coast, float silently over the Base, and complete a 'figure of eight' movement over the Control Tower, before heading back out to sea'.*

Colonel Charles Halt:

> *"Many of the Security Police had seen unexplained things at RAF Woodbridge. Several personally told of seeing 'East End Charlie' (as they called him). He appeared to be a World War Two aviator that wandered near the back gate. One particular event occurred on Guy Fawkes Night, in 1981, when a large cigar-shaped craft floated silently over the Airfield and circled the Air Traffic Tower before drifting off."*

(Source: Personal interview/Brenda Butler)

UFOs over Lancashire & Yorkshire

On 8th November 1981, Mrs. June Smith was at her home address in Heather Rise, High Moor, Scouthead, Oldham, watching late night TV, at 1.15am, when she saw an oval-shaped object in the sky, leaving a vapour trail behind it.

"It stopped over Scouthead, somewhere near the radio mast at Wharmton. It was larger than a helicopter and appeared pulsating. The colours on it kept changing from orange to red. I awoke my husband who watched it with me. All of a sudden it shot off across the sky, heading in an eastern direction, very fast, before disappearing from view."

(Source: BUFOS)

On 12th November 1981 (approximately), Mary Robinson and her husband, Keith, were with two friends, driving towards Keighley, when they saw a brilliantly-lit object (apparently revolving) hovering above trees, near the Currergate Restaurant, near Steeton. Frightened, Mary told her husband to drive on. This was, we understand, one of many similar sightings which took place around the Aire Valley and Bradford areas, during the same month.

On 14th November 1981, an object, showing at least seven large spikes of light radiating outwards from it, was seen over Low Moor, Bradford, by Mrs. Alma Metcalfe and her husband, at 6pm. To the couple's surprise, a smaller version broke away from it, followed by another one. All three then headed off towards the Richard Dunn Centre.

UFO over Hampshire

On the evening of 15th November 1981, Jan Dawson – the wife of a Police Inspector, from Horton Heath, Hampshire – noticed a 40ft long object, apparently probing the ground of a nearby field with what looked like laser beams of light.

She telephoned a neighbour, who came around immediately, and the couple sat there watching.

Jan:

"We saw two flashing lights – one red, the other white – 30-40ft apart. One of them began to change shape – then a small piercing light appeared to go from the darkness, between the red and white lights, down to the ground and back up again. This happened twice. I was extremely frightened. Within a short space of time, the lights were now close to the bottom of the garden – now wider apart and appearing to hover. They gave me an impression that they were looking for somewhere to land. I telephoned my mother while this was happening and told her what we were

seeing. One of the lights began to change shape; I was so frightened I dropped the phone down. The object then rose up above the 8 acre field and vanished from sight."

Jan then telephoned her husband, Peter, who was on duty at Eastleigh Police Station, to tell him about it. He later said:

> *"It is obvious my wife was telling a perfectly genuine story. She is not given to drink, fantasizing, or making things up. Quite often there are logical explanations for these sightings. This is probably one of the few which doesn't have a logical explanation."*

(Source: Personal interview/Tony Jones, Wessex Association for the Study of Unexplained Phenomena [WATSUP]/*unidentified newspaper* – 'Wife's Terror Over Flashing Lights UFO', 15.12.1981)

UFO over London

Raja Samy (11) and his mother were driving home, after having delivered some presents, when they noticed three small shiny 'dots' in the sky, over Leytonstone, London, on the evening of 17th November 1981. These were soon joined by a number of other 'dots' and 'bars of light', which were seen to form a 'saucer' shape in the sky. **(Source: Crystal Hogben, *Magic Saucer*)**

UFO over Essex

At 5.30pm on 19th November 1981, Dorothy Margaret Dark of Goodmayes, Ilford, Essex, was on her way home from work, when she noticed a bright stationary object in the sky, over the corner of the local park.

> *"It was drizzling with rain and dark at the time; no stars were visible. This light was the only thing in the sky. It was projecting a searchlight onto the clouds above. As it moved away, the alternating bright and dim lights gave an impression that it was revolving. It passed silently over the house before disappearing, at which point I heard a purring sound."*

(Source: Essex UFO Study Group)

UFO over Redcar

Also on 19th November 1981, an object, described as resembling *'a drainpipe, with lights all around it'*, was seen passing across the face of the moon, over Redcar.

(Source: *North Eastern Gazette*, 19.11.1981 – 'Drainpipe, or UFO?)

Strange 'craft' over Weymouth

Two days later, on 21st November 1981, Weymouth man – Mr. Jack Smith – was on his way home, halfway between Salisbury and Blandford, when he saw:

> *". . . what looked like a gigantic dragonfly, with a basket underneath; I had a look through binoculars and saw a pilot in the open cockpit."*

(Source: *Dorset Evening Echo*, 20th November 1981)

Mushroom-shaped UFO

A massive bright mushroom-shaped light was seen hovering in the sky, at 4pm on 25th November 1981, over Wrose, a few miles from Bradford City Centre, by Baildon resident – Julie Bettison, who watched it for a minute before it dimmed and moved upwards into cloud, where it was lost from sight.

(Source: *Bradford Telegraph and Argus*, 26.11.1981)

Silver UFO over Pontefract

On 30th November 1981, a spherical, silver object, was seen *'tilting and moving upwards across the sky, surrounded by a red glow, with blue and green lights'*, over Pontefract, at 10.45pm, by retired RAF Serviceman Gordon Walker and his son, Ian, who called the police. An officer arrived and looked at the UFO through a pair of high-powered binoculars and commented, *"I've been on night duty for 20 years and never seen anything like it before."*

(Source: *The Sunday Mirror*, 6.12.81 – 'Police In A New UFO Riddle')

Prince Philip and a near-miss with UFO

On 30th November 1981, The *ITV News at Ten* channel disclosed that the Duke of Edinburgh, who was piloting an 'Andover' of the Queen's flight, was involved in a 300mph near-miss with a Boeing 747, which was changing course to avoid a UFO, after having taken-off from Heathrow Airport on the 27th November 1981.

(Source: *The Times*, 1.12.1981)

DECEMBER 1981

UFOs over Suffolk

L INDA Jarvis was walking to Saxmundham, in Suffolk, at 4pm on 22nd December 1981, when she noticed:

". . . four, silver, round objects (the size of a ten pence piece) in the sky, travelling in a horizontal line in a north to south direction, stopping and starting in flight, as well as changing shape as they did so. Within five minutes, they had dropped in the sky behind houses, and that was the last I saw of them."

(Source: Brenda Butler & Ron West)

1982

WORLD EVENTS

The Commodore 64 8-bit home computer is launched by Commodore International Las Vegas it becomes the all-time best-selling single personal computer model. Air Florida Flight 90 crashes into Washington, D.C.'s 14th Street Bridge and falls into the Potomac River, killing 78.

First computer virus, the Elk Cloner, infects Apple II computers via floppy disk. London-based Laker Airways collapses, leaving 6,000 stranded passengers and debts of $270 million.

An Argentine scrap metal dealer raises the Argentine flag in Georgia. Argentina invades and occupies the Islands. Argentina's Invasion of South Georgia April 26, British retake South Georgia during Operation Paraquet.

Prince William is born at St Mary's Hospital in Paddington, West London. President Ronald Reagan becomes the first American chief executive to address a joint session of the Parliament Women's Peace Protest at Greenham Common: 30,000 women hold hands and form a human chain around the 14.5 km (9 mile) perimeter fence.

Petrol costs £1.67 pence a gallon.
(Source: Wikipedia)

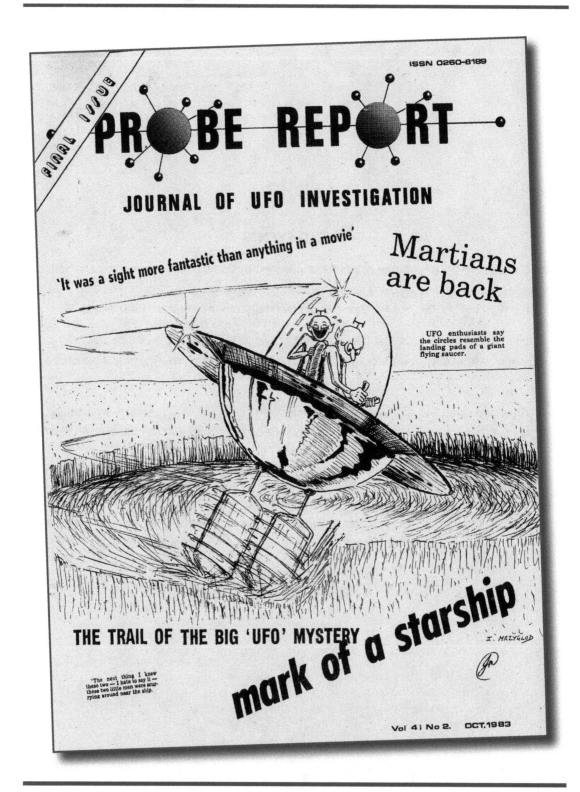

JANUARY 1982

COUPLE REPORT BEING CHASED BY UFO

Also includes – Close Encounter for Lancashire woman and her mother, followed by a confrontation with the 'Men in Black' • Strange figures seen in the bedroom by a Portsmouth woman

UFOs over Lincolnshire

AT 8.30pm on 2nd January 1982, a whole *'formation of objects'* were seen passing through the air, over Lincolnshire, heading towards the village of Saxilby. Within seconds, after completing a sharp turn, they were lost from sight. **(Source: Richard Thompson)**

Other strange phenomena included a report of 25 sheep found mutilated and headless at Rossendale, Lancashire, at the turn of the year. Armed police searched the area but never found the culprits.

(Source: TV interview with Bob Rickard, *'Pebble Mill at One'*, 22.2.1982/ *Northern UFO News*, Feb. 1982)

UFO over Herefordshire

A Worcestershire couple wrote to us with regard to what they witnessed, while travelling along the A44, towards Kington, Herefordshire, just after 6pm, in early January 1982.

"We saw what we thought might have been a helicopter, performing low level exercises, a few miles away. Curious, we stopped the car and got out to have a closer look, when we realised, from its movements, it was no helicopter or aircraft. Unsure of what to do, or who to contact, we resumed our journey towards Kington. All of a sudden, a luminous object appeared on our left-hand side, low down in the sky, approximately a few hundred yards away – as if following a parallel course to our vehicle. As we approached Kington, whatever

it was, just disappeared from sight. Relieved, we continued on our journey but were shocked to see it as we drove out of the village. Once again, the object paced us. Frightened, we just drove on. When we reached *Bredenbury, twenty-two miles later, it shot off across the sky in a 'blur of light' and headed towards the Malvern Hills, at a terrific speed"

(Source: Personal interview)

Close Encounter, Lancashire & MIB

At 7pm on 10th January 1982, Southport, Lancashire woman – Linda Taylor – was driving along the East Lancashire road, with her mother in the back seat, when they noticed a huge *'light'* over the road, behind some trees, performing strange zigzag movements, before it suddenly shot up into the sky and disappeared.

All of sudden, the car began to lose speed. Linda changed down a gear and applied her foot on the accelerator. The car began to vibrate, the lights flashing on and off – clearly, there was something very wrong.

Then, in front of her vehicle, appeared an old-fashioned 1930s style black car, showing a small oval window in the rear. The car was unlit, and had no number plate, with its rear bumper almost touching the front of her car.

"I could see the driver. He was a very large figure, with broad shoulders, dressed in dark clothing, with a bowler hat. Through the old-fashioned oval back window, my mother shouted, 'Look out, we are going to crash into it'. I changed down into second gear, to avoid crashing into it, and opened the window, thinking to shout at the man, and saw a UFO covered in lights, each about five feet in diameter – all different colours. I screamed and put my head back inside the car. As I did that, the car in front vanished."

Linda Taylor with Harry Harris studying a map of area of the encounter

Linda pulled onto the forecourt of a garage, just before the M63 Motorway, and watched, with her mother, the huge *'light'* in the sky, which actually began to circle the garage.

"It was as if time stood still. I am sure it circled us, three times, although my mum thought it was only once – then it stopped above a tree, made a quick movement, tilted, and began to vibrate, before rising upwards into the sky."

*We were to come across a number of other reports, involving sightings from motorists driving along the Worcestershire/Herefordshire borders, over the years. A more recent example took place at 4am on the 22nd of November 1997 when two police officers watched a spherical green object in the overcast sky for approximately one minute as it passed over Bredenbury, apparently descending in height after originally seen in the western direction. **(Source: MOD Files, defe-24-1990)**

By the time Linda arrived home, after dropping off her mother, at Hulme, she realised it was nearly an hour later than it should have been. Very shaken by what had taken place, and feeling nauseous, she knocked on the front door.

After opening the door, her husband took one look at her and thought she had been involved in an accident.

> *"I told him to phone my mother, to find out what had happened, and went straight to the toilet, where I was violently sick. I then noticed my legs were covered in strange black and red marks. They disappeared, the following day. I kept quiet about what had happened for 9 months, but after seeing a TV documentary about UFOs, contacted UFO researchers Michael Sacks and Harry Harris, who arranged to have me hypnotically regressed."*

Unfortunately, this failed to reveal any details concerning what had happened, during the missing hour. Enquiries made with the MOD, to ascertain if any other UFOs had been tracked on radar that night, proved unsuccessful.

Other witnesses to strange things seen in the sky were Muriel Upton and Althea Richards, from the Isle of Wight. What they saw was later explained away as being Venus!

(Source: MAPIT/Orbis Publishing, *The Unexplained/Marvels and Mysterious UFOs*)

27.1.82.

Venus holds clue to golden UFO

27/1/82

SOLENT Coastguards have come up with the probable identity of an "Unidentified Flying Object" involved in a close encounter with two pensioners in the Isle of Wight.

Miss Muriel Upton and her companion Miss Alathea Richards spoke of their feelings of "fear and excitement" as they watched a gold coloured globe in the western sky above their home in Wilberforce Road, Brighstone.

"It appeared to have poles sticking out of the side of the circular shape and was stationary at first, and then dropped slowly down," said Miss Upton.

"Then it turned a very bright red, lighting the sky around it before disappearing as if someone had turned off a switch."

According to coastguards at the Needles the women were probably watching another planet rather than witnessing a visit from outer space.

"Venus is very bright at the moment and sets about three hours after the sun in the western sky. That looks very gold before turning a bright red colour.

"We have had a number of reports recently, including one from a warship that reported what the crew were convinced was a red flare.

"It seems the most likely explanation. The poles the lady spoke of could well have been created by refraction of light."

Bedroom visitors, Portsmouth – and crop marks discovered in nearby field

Illustrating the distinct possibility that, on occasion, there appears to be little difference between what some people would claim as a paranormal experience, involving ghostly figures seen and a bedroom visitation, describing an incursion by alien entities, this was brought to our notice by Nick Maloret – formerly a member of the Wessex-based group, WATSUP. Nick, who has assisted the authors with advice and a steady stream of previously unpublished reports over the years, was to tell of a very strange incident which involved his brother's (Gerard) wife – Joan, aged 24 at the time, during 1965.

Above: The family bungalow at Cowplain, where the strange incident occurred.

Below (left) Nick Maloret and (right) brother Gerard with wife Joan and family.

The couple lived in a bungalow at Hart Plain Avenue, Cowplain, near Portsmouth, Hampshire, with their daughter, Claire, who was just under one year old. At the time the area was still rural, with adjoining fields used for keeping livestock, before the Wecock Farm Housing estate was built.

Joan:

"There was a bedroom at the back of the bungalow; in front was a patio and garden, backing onto further gardens. Street lighting was minimal. The locality was normally pitch-black when I had to get up, in the middle of the night, to feed the baby."

Sometime between midnight and the early hours of one morning, in September or October 1965, Joan was awoken by a bright light illuminating the windows – strong enough to penetrate through the closed curtains.

Baby Claire (seen above) and Joan (below) at the rear of the bungalow in the 1960s. The window where the beings were seen is on the left hand side.

"Two shadows appeared; at first blob-shaped, and then materialising into heads, bodies and arms, showing hands with three fingers. The size of these 'persons', or whatever they were, was similar to that of a child, about 4ft tall. They had what I can only describe as 'pointy at the top' heads, with a thick torso beneath. The arms were extremely thin and long in

proportion to their bodies; these were trailing over the window frame – like feelers, jointed in an odd manner. The 'fingers' seemed to be testing the window sill, as if seeking a way of opening it and entering the room. In the seconds it took to register what was going on, I grabbed my baby and yelled for my husband, who, although waking briefly, promptly fell asleep! [In later conversation,

INTERPRETATION OF THE SCENE. ENDORSED BY THE WITNESS

THE SILHOUETTED FORMS WERE ESTIMATED TO BE NO MORE THAN 4 FT. TALL.

'JOAN MALORET'S SKETCH

after the event, he remembered seeing a strange light]. *After further unsuccessful attempts to wake him up, I fled the room with Claire in my arms. I then turned on all the house lights, wondering if 'they' were intrigued by the baby. I went into the kitchen and was relieved to see the outside illumination had gone."*

Joan spent the rest of the night unable to relax, and continually moving around the house. At about 5am, she and husband Gerry, who was now aware of his wife's experience, ventured outside to see if there were any suspicious marks around the window, or some evidence of the night-time intruders. Although nothing was apparent around the house, they were shocked to see a huge circle of scorched grass, about the size of an average garden, in the adjacent field.

Joan, who was extremely unsettled for some time after the event, still finds it difficult to talk about an experience which puzzles her to this present day. She did not report it to anybody, fearing (not unnaturally) that nobody would believe her, and feeling the safety of the baby was of paramount importance.

Nick also established, through conversation with other people in the locality, that horses kept in the field, were often found wandering in people's back gardens, and suggested to Joan that these may have been the shapes she saw. Joan accepted, on occasion, that she and Gerard had found cows and horses straying onto the drive of their bungalow, but this was totally different to what she had experienced. Is it sheer coincidence that about a quarter of a mile away from the family home was the source of other complaints of ghostly behaviour – on the nearby Wecock Farm Estate – in 1977?

GHOSTLY HAND AT WORK AT NUMBER 13

THE NEWS (PORTSMOUTH) 5 FEBRUARY 1977

Susan Vickerstaff (21), with one piece of evidence of an unidentified presence at her home at Partridge Gardens, Wecock; a cracked mirror which was damaged when it 'jumped off' a shelf.

THE NEWS (PORTSMOUTH) 8 FEBRUARY 1977

Something spooky this way comes

Mrs. Cripps with Darren and the family's mastiff, Carlo.

Road map of the Cowplain area. The school, Robin Gardens, Puffin Walk and Partridge Gardens, along with Eagle Avenue (which I assume to be a renaming of a continuation of Hart Plain Avenue) were not in existence in 1965. The school occupies the site of the original 'Wecock Farm'.

Nick Maloret:

> *"In 1977, myself and other members of the WATSUP Group, visited Mrs. Cripps – a resident of one of the two houses concerned, in Partridge Gardens – after she had reported a number of strange occurrences in the house.*
>
> *These houses border the same field as the homes in Hart Plain Avenue. Mrs. Cripps told us that she had seen a white 'figure' float past her kitchen window. I have to wonder if the site on which these homes were built on might provide us with a clue as to why the manifestations took place, understanding the association between paranormal events and ancient sites. On a visit to the area on the 12th March 2013, I was able to determine the section of field containing the scorched circle had been built over, or covered by gardens."*

Nick remains intigued by the strange marks he photographed on the back window.

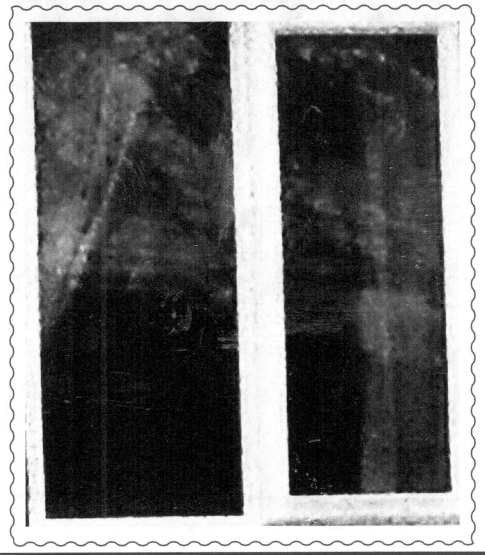

N⬨RTHERN UF⬨ NEWS

Publication of NUFON....
Edited by: JENNY RANDLES

UFO RESEARCH NORTH
Cover Design: IAN MRZYGLOD

Address:- 8 Whitethroat Walk Birchwood Warrington Cheshire WA3 6PQ

Number 112
MAR / APR 1985

Northern UFO News

Subscription for 1985 issues £5.40

Printed by IMPRESS (Bristol)

IN THIS ISSUE:-

Usual features plus What is the BUFORA NIC?
(pp 2-3), Anamnesis update (pp 5-6), Tapping
the hidden cases (SSPR Research) (pp 6),
SCOOP! - The corn-field wrecker in action!
(p.8).Cases from:- Derbyshire, Northumbria
and Scotland (pp 8-12) CASE HISTORIES:-
Northants CE4 "Repeater" & Scotland weird
one! (pp 13-16): Rendlesham update (p.16)

FEBRUARY 1982

MYSTERIOUS OBJECT CRASHES ONTO GROUND
AT MAIDENHEAD

Also includes – 'V'-shaped formation of lights, seen over Birkenhead

UFO landing, Maidenhead

AS dawn broke on 13th February 1982, people living in Halifax Road, Maidenhead, Berkshire, were awoken by the sound of an explosion, as an unidentified flying object crashed into the concrete path, close to the back garden of the Whelan family, followed by orange flames and clouds of smoke being seen.

After a number of 999 calls were made to the Emergency Services, the Fire Brigade rushed to the scene. When they had extinguished the fire, they discovered a football sized, jagged rock-like substance, smouldering in a crater, and decided to call the police, who carried out an examination of the scene and commented that they had never witnessed anything like it before. We contacted retired Police Sergeant William Bell, who had attended the incident. He said:

> *"I don't recollect any verbal conversations made, following my visits to the scene, but I do remember the location of the incident to be in the centre of a front garden concrete path, a few feet away from the public footpath. There was an indentation in the concrete, about 6-10ins in diameter, consistent with rapid burning. It was raining at the time. I later heard it was caused by a substance, such as phosphorous or carbide material, being placed onto the concrete and being ignited by the rain."*

Dan Goring, who 'wrote-up' the incident in an edition of *Earth-link*, believes it was a *'ball of sodium'* – an explanation denied by Mrs. Whelan. We spoke to her and she promised to send us a photo taken after sending her a postal order but never heard any more; perhaps this was lost in the post? We learnt that the substance was sent to Aldermaston Laboratory for analysis, although the result is not known.

(Source: Dan Goring, *Earth-link*)

UFO over Derbyshire

A soldier who had served in Bosnia contacted BUFORA, in 1996, wishing to bring their attention to a sighting he had in 1982, when aged 10 and living in Littleover, Derby.

> *"At about 2am, I was awoken by this loud buzzing noise. I looked out of the window and saw this object, hovering over fields at the rear of the house. It had a flashing light on each corner – red, yellow, and green. It was so low I could see a definite shape to it. I was frightened and ran into my parents' bedroom. I was unable to sleep for the rest of the night."*

(Source: *UFO Times*, **July/August 1996**)

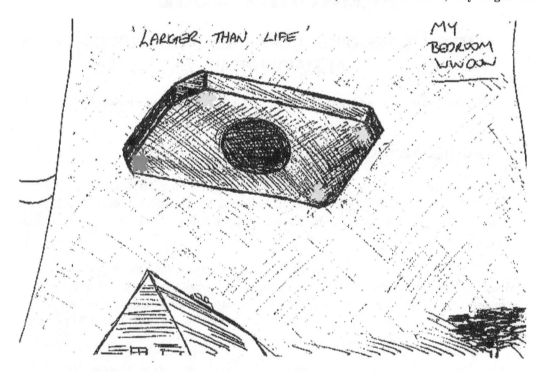

Wing-shaped UFO over Birkenhead

A resident of Birkenhead was walking to meet a friend at a local bus stop, in February 1982, at 7.30pm, and happened to look up into the sky, when he saw a series of bright lights apparently moving in a straight line.

> *"As they approached closer, I saw they formed a 'V'-shaped formation. The lights were white/slightly bluish, as they passed overhead. I formed an impression they were attached to a larger object which blotted out the sky as it moved overhead, the only sound being a slight 'swish'. I estimated there were approximately 20-30 lights underneath what looked like a huge 'flying wing', or Boomerang-shaped object."*

(Source: Omar Fowler, PRA, Page 6, *OVNI*, July/August, 2003)

Was there a connection with what Tommy Dunsford saw in 1960? Sadly Tommy has passed away, but his sketches and sighting lives on.

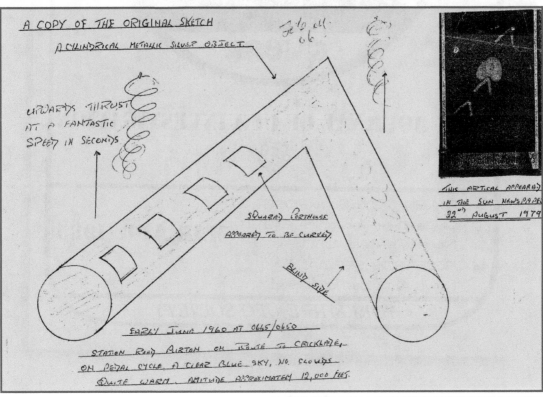

A COPY OF THE ORIGINAL SKETCH

A CYLINDRICAL METALLIC SILVER OBJECT

UPWARDS THRUST AT A FANTASTIC SPEED IN SECONDS

SQUARED PORTHOLES APPEARED TO BE CURVED

BLIND SIDE

THIS ARTICAL APPEARED IN THE SUN NEWSPAPER 22nd AUGUST 1979

EARLY JUNE 1960 AT 0645/0650 STATION ROAD AIRTON ON ROUTE TO CRICKLADE, ON PEDAL CYCLE, A CLEAR BLUE SKY, NO CLOUDS. QUITE WARM. ALTITUDE APPROXIMATELY 12,000 FEET.

CONFERENCE 85 REVIEW

ONFERENC
kshire UFO Soci
EKING THE TR

quest

THE JOURNAL OF UFO INVESTIGATION

- □ RALPH NOYES ex-DS8
- □ UFOs Over Yorkshire - 1913!
- □ Norway's 'fake' UFO
- □ RESEARCH SPECIAL !

News, Articles, Features.

MAR APR 1985

YORKSHIRE UFO SOCIETY

MARCH 1982

WOMAN MOTORIST ENDURES CLOSE ENCOUNTER AT SKIPTON

Also includes – Motorist and family report being chased by UFO • Northumbria woman sights UFO • Police Officers are called out • Another UFO sighting takes place, involving Police – this time in Milton Keynes

Close Encounter, Skipton

A BUSINESSWOMAN, living near Skipton, was travelling from Morecambe to Skipton, at 10.30pm on 4th March 1982 – a regular journey made, normally lasting an hour, along the A65 Keighley-Kendall road – accompanied by her dog. As they reached an area close to Standrise Plantation, which rises over the tops of Elslack Moor, two brightly coloured 'balls of light' – one red, the other green – swooped downwards over the car.

She first thought it was a lorry, trying to overtake, and then realised this could not be the case, as the lights were now above the car. Suddenly, a white *'beam of light'* (about 30ft in diameter) dropped down, lighting up the roadside and grass verges. This was followed by the sound of the car engine, revving. After having travelled about a mile, still enveloped in these mysterious *'lights'*, they saw a lorry approaching, at which point the *'lights'* went out and were never seen again.

According to the husband:

> *"They were about the size of a football and kept pace with the car, at window height. We were very frightened; the dog cowered in the back, while the children cried. My wife screamed at me to turn the car and drive back home. When I did this, the object came after us. After a short time, they finally went away and that was the last we saw of them."*

After arriving home, the wife felt physically and mentally drained – a condition that persisted for a further week. Her journey had taken 95 minutes instead of the usual hour. The next day she discovered a rash on her back and chest. She contacted the police, to report the incident. They telephoned Graham Birdsall and his brother, Mark, of the Yorkshire UFO Society. After interviewing the woman, they offered her the opportunity of using hypnotic regression to discover what had happened during the interval of 30 minutes of reported missing time, to which she agreed.

Graham (left) and Mark Birdsall

Following a number of regressions by a qualified hypnotist, from Lancashire, the woman suddenly began to talk to the investigators – as if some outside force was using her as a means of communication, and incredibly engaged in conversations that lasted over dozens of recorded pages, including a question put to her, *"Have we got enemies?"*, to which she answered, *"Yes, from far away from out there. They are evil, evil, evil"*.

The woman eventually underwent three hypnosis sessions, in the course of which she mentioned contact with aliens who had supposedly been visiting Earth for centuries. During one of the sessions an entity, calling itself Zeus, supposedly spoke through her.

According to the *Yorkshire Post*, who published details of this incident, in September 1983, the information supplied by this highly intelligent woman was to lead to other enquiries, involving Greece and Africa, although the nature of the enquiries and the whereabouts of the mass of documentation obtained during the enquiry are not known.

As a result of what took place, they contacted Yorkshire UFO Society – run by Graham and Mark Birdsall – who carried out an investigation into the matter, after being promised that they would not identify the family, who had asked for confidentiality, fearing ridicule. The family refused to travel along the same road again and found another route.

Source: *Yorkshire Evening Post*, September 1983 – 'Close Encounter On The A65 Road/ Philip Mantle, Yorkshire UFO Society/Tony Dodd)

UFO over Northumbria

Northumbrian housewife – Violet Cardew, from West Denton, had just let the dogs out, at 11.30pm on 8th March 1982, when she noticed an object in the sky:

> "... showing red, green, white and blue lights, with what appeared to be red sparks falling from one side".

Violet alerted her husband and dialled 999 for the police. Constable David Parking and PC Bob Taylor arrived and, although sceptical to begin with, soon changed their minds when they saw the UFO for themselves. After about an hour, the object was lost from view, west of Newcastle, as it appeared to land by the 'Wall' (Hadrian's Wall).

Northumbria Police confirmed both officers had submitted a full report into what they had seen, and added:

> *"There is no indication of what it might have been."*

(Source: *Newcastle Evening Chronicle*, **9.3.82 – 'We saw UFO Say Constables')**

On 11th March 1982, a strange object was seen during the early hours of the morning, over Glebe Way, Hornchurch, Essex, by Mr. John Sylina. This was later reported to Dan Goring of the Essex based Group who arranged for him to be interviewed.

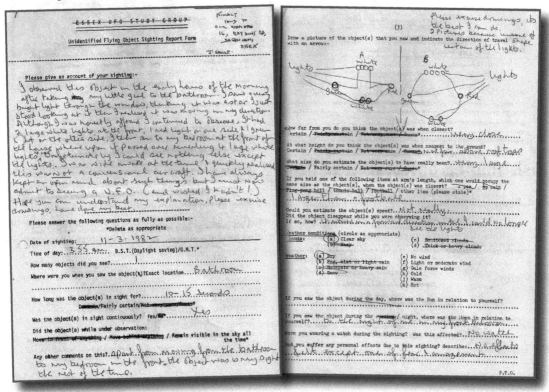

In the middle of the same month the BUFORA UFO Conference took place.

Fish-shaped object over Milton Keynes

At 4.40am on 24th March 1982, Police Sergeant Ian Victory and PC Anthony Underwood were on mobile patrol in the Fishermead area of Milton Keynes, when they saw some unusual orange *'lights'* in the sky. Curious, they stopped and got out, watching, in amazement, as *'a yellow lozenge-shaped object, illuminating enough light to show some sort of structure below it'*, was seen.

PS Victory:

> *"I have no idea what it was, but there is no way I imagined it. The frustrating thing is that if you had told me you had seen it, I would not have believed you."*

PC Underwood:

> *"It was almost sort of fish-shaped, moving very slowly, and passed overhead. I thought I could see some sort of structure – like girders – on the underside. We could hear a noise – like a quiet humming, throbbing, sound. It had small lights on each side, red and bluish-*

white, with two bright white front 'headlamps'." [How often had we heard that description, over the years?]

Another witness was milk rounds man – Richard Waite, who was passing the traffic roundabout, at Chaffron Way, and Saxon Street, Milton Keynes, at 4.45am, when he noticed the two Police Officers stood outside their vehicle, pointing up into the sky. The Officers asked him what he thought of the object in the sky.

Richard looked and saw:

". . . a rectangular array of lights of a yellowish hue, with three blue flashing lights at the edges, accompanied by a slight humming sound. I watched with them, as it went off towards Bletchley and out of sight."

**Source:
Jenny Randles,
Director of
Investigations,
BUFORA/*The Sun*
– 'Beat Cops Have
Close Encounters',
25.3.1982/
*Milton Keynes
Mirror*, 31.3.1982
– 'You Can't Park
That Flying Saucer
Here – Move it'**

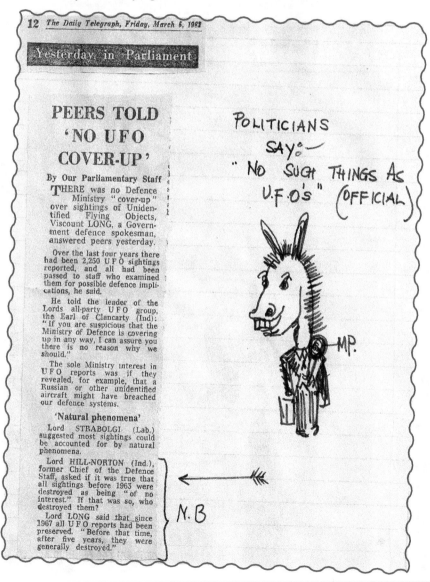

'Lord Crackpot' and the great cosmic cover-up

DAILY STAR 30-3-82

By GERRY BROWN

SKY-WATCHING peer Lord Clancarty doesn't just SUSPECT that flying saucers and beings from outer space are visiting Britain—he's "damned sure" of it.

And, what's more, he has literally THOUSANDS of sightings from all over the world to back his claims.

But the guardians of Whitehall's innermost secrets are implacably opposed to most of his ideas and theories.

They insist the 70-year-old peer is nothing more than a time-wasting eccentric.

Each time they receive one of his pestering letters, they groan and flinch, duck and dive.

But the correspondence is difficult to ignore when it comes on House of Lords note-paper from William Brinsley le Poer Trench, eighth Earl of Clancarty.

And next week it could become impossible to ignore if he succeeds in enlisting the House of Lords in his campaign.

This long - running feud between him and the keepers of locked filing cabinets is no mere administrative quarrel.

It is a tussle of cosmic inter - galactic proportions.

The men from the Ministry who monitor Britain's skies insist we are being visited by nothing more sinister than twinkling meteorites, wayward balloons and sparks of badly behaved lightning.

Lord Clancarty: "It's a Whitehall cover-up"

sightings over Britain between 1978 and 1981.

The earl is no wild-eyed newcomer to the ranks of flying saucer enthusiasts.

that, I've developed a thick skin, and those tactics don't bother me in the least.

In fact, he's sure it's all part of a deliberate cover-up.

"There are literally hundreds of sightings in Britain every year, and I accept that the vast majority of them can be explained by aircraft, balloons and tricks of the light," he says.

"But there is still a solid body of unexplained evidence which cannot be dismissed lightly.

"It's Government policy to try to pour cold water on the reports of these sightings."

five flying saucers with them, and gave Eisenhower a display of their flying skills and their supernatural abilities to become invisible then reappear.

"But that meeting decided it would all be too much of a sudden shock for mankind to cope with, and they agreed to break the news gently over the course of many years.

Nuclear

"UFO's have been making more and more frequent appearances over Earth since we exploded our first nuclear bomb, and they are often spotted flying close to our nuclear power installations."

SPOTTED ... over New Zealand, Dec. '78

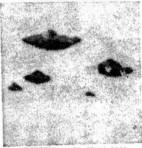

SPOTTED ... Sheffield 1963

On 30th March 1982, the *Daily Star* published a very derogatory article about Lord Clancarty. Sadly, 35 years later, little has changed with the attitude of the tabloids towards the UFO subject.

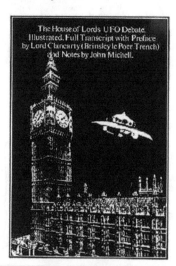

APRIL 1982

APRIL FOOLS' DAY UFO, OR NOT?

Also includes – UFO sighted over Wharmston Mast, Lancashire • Close encounter at Dorking, Surrey • Couple chased by cigar-shaped UFO, on the same evening that a similar object was sighted over Todmorden.

UFO over Southampton

ON 1st April 1982, a black doughnut-shaped object was seen crossing the sky, at 9.30am, over Bitterne, Southampton, by Mrs K. Alexander, who described it as having a hole (or concave part in the middle) visible, as it occasionally flipped over in flight. Although one is tempted to ponder on whether this was an April Fools' Day joke, it doesn't appear to be the case, but we may be wrong, not forgetting other sightings of a similar object seen in other parts of the UK.

UFO over Lancashire

At 4.45am on 17th April 1982, Gordon Walters (77) of Co-operative Street, Upper Mill, near Oldham, Lancashire, sighted an unusual bright *'light'* in the sky, near Wharmston Mast. Mrs. Marjorie Walters (60) later told UFO investigators from the British UFO Society that she had seen a similar object, in the same position, on 19th, 20th, and 24th April 1982.

Close encounter – Dorking, Surrey

Peter Mackerell – an HGV Driver, of Dorking, Surrey – described his encounter, which also took place on 17th April 1982.

> *"I was driving along the A25 from Guildford to Dorking, on Saturday, with my fiancée, when I saw two bright white lights in the distance,*

1.4.82.

Strange object flies past

FLYING OBJECTS

A SOUTHAMPTON family were left shaken and stunned after a strange object flew past their home at about 9.30am this morning.

The black doughnut-shaped object flew soundlessly over the Alexander family's home at West End Road, Bitterne, heading in a north-easterly direction and maintaining a constant height and speed.

"Sometimes it would flip over and we could see the hole or concave part in the middle," said Mrs. K. Alexander.

Mrs. Alexander, who was alerted to the strange object by her 12-year-old daughter, said the object was too small to have been a plane or a helicopter.

"I would just like to know if anyone else saw anything like the thing we saw." she said.

hovering above some trees. When we reached the clump of trees [Grid reference TQ134484, 5 miles from Pitch Hill – scene of other UFO reports] *the light was powerful enough to shine around the trunks of the trees. I just continued driving; then the lights were above us. I slowed down, as we turned the corner, wondering what they were. We soon found out, when we saw this huge shape – like a fat cigar, with red and green lights on the front, and green square lights running down the sides. I drove up the kerb in surprise, and when we got to the other end of the 'cigar', having driven underneath it, I saw two massive jet-like burners, glowing about a hundred feet above us.*"

Mrs. Christine Mackerell corroborated what had happened. She told of the light-hearted banter with Peter, after having first seen the two white lights, thinking they may have been headlights – an attitude that was to change drastically, when Peter shouted out, *"It's a UFO"*.

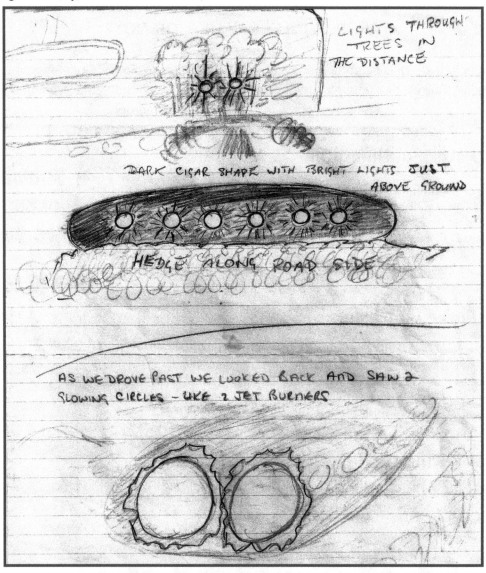

"Immediately, my legs went to jelly. I was petrified. I said, 'Go back, go back', and we went past it. I looked back and saw these two great big orange jet burners. I was so scared – it was eerie, horrible, unbelievable, and evil looking shape. I wanted to go home, but Peter decided to turn around and have another look. When he did so, whatever it was had gone."

Christine and Peter continued on their journey, noting, with some surprise, that cars started to appear again on the road

"because all the time we were on the road, there hadn't been a single car drive past, and there was this eerie stillness".

The couple reported the matter to the police, who advised them to ring the UFO desk at Gatwick Airport. When they rang the Airport they were told that no such department existed!

(Source: Personal interviews/*FSR*, Volume 38, No. 3 (Captain Gordon Millington, Retd. BA Hons., Consultant to *FSR*/Omar Fowler, SIGAP)

Cigar-shaped UFO over Todmorden

On the same evening, Gary and Les Barker, from Todmorden, South Yorkshire, were driving over the Moors, at 10pm, near to Walsden, when they saw the silhouette of a dark pylon-shaped object in the sky, followed by the car lights inexplicably cutting out. Incredibly, Gary's wife, Gladys, also reported having sighted what appears to have been a similar UFO, over the Ashenhurst area of Todmorden. Another witness was Lora McArthur, of Ashenhurst, who first heard of a UFO being seen in the area on her CB radio. At first, she thought it to be a joke but went outside and saw, along with a number of other people, a cigar-shaped object, revolving in the sky. *"It showed different coloured lights – like disco lights – which seemed to split up the thing."*

On the 17th of April a strange light was seen in the sky close to the Wharmton radio transmitter, by Gordon Walters. This was one of many sightings of similar objects over the tower during this period.

On 18th and 19th April 1982, further sightings of UFOs were reported around the same area, involving over a hundred people, sparking off considerable newspaper interest.

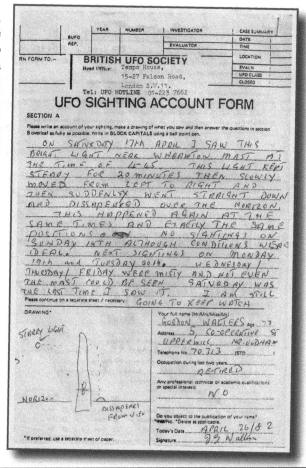

The sightings were later explained away as being misidentification of a star, although others suggested that what people had seen were *'earthquake lights'* – an unusual luminous aerial phenomenon, often seen as white, blue, or orange lights, which appear in the sky close to areas of tectonic stress, sometimes lasting several seconds – a hypothesis backed up by reports of a colossal boom heard all over the Calder Valley, at 4.30pm on 20th April 1982, causing hundreds of people to run out into the streets, as their houses shook.

(Sources: *Hebden Bridge Times/Todmorden News*, 23.4.82 – 'Disco In The Sky Puzzles 100',
'Have The Space Invaders Returned To Calder Valley?')

ET GO HOME—scientists want down-to-earth approach

UFOs—craft from outer space, weather balloons or the sightings of a feverish imagination?

Expert Jerry Randles is among those now treating the subject in a rigorous scientific manner. Nicholas Leonard spoke to her about her work:

Flying saucers: pilots afraid to report them

JENNY RANDLES, Director of Investigations at the British UFO Research Association, and Peter Warrington, an expert astronomer, have written a fascinating book called 'Science and the UFOs' (Blackwell, £12.50 sterling), which without any of the usual mystique, analyses in rigorous fashion the present state of knowledge about UFOs.

We found out about it by pure accident, simply because we were investigating an.

A sober American pilot called Kenneth Arnold saw a curious formation of disc-like objects over Mount Rainier in Washington State on June 24, 1947.

He told the media that they looked to be 'flying like saucers skipping over waters. The 'flying saucer' phenomenon had begun.

In the 38 years since then, some 8,000 sightings of UFOs (Unidentified Flying Objects) and other inexplicable phenomena in the sky have been reported in Britain alone.

Recent research suggest that is more

Much 'ufology' is carried out by enthusiasts with axes to grind. It is a subject which attracts cranks and fanatics.

Recently, however, the topic has been rising up the credibility pole in respectable scientific circles.

The revelations of sub-atomic physics have made experts much less willing than they were to declare that anything is 'impossible'. If the Einstein theories of time, space and energy are correct, then many 'impossible' phenomena may prove to have a scientific explanation.

MAY 1982

TERRIYFYING CLOSE ENCOUNTER FOR HEREFORDSHIRE WOMAN

Also includes – 'Triangle of lights' seen over Attlebridge • Dave Bezer and his investigations into UFOs

Close Encounter, Herefordshire

MRS Janet Fitzpatrick, BSC (Hons) was driving home at 10.45pm, on 2nd May 1982,

". . . along the Kington to Hereford road, at 10.45 pm, with my two young children, when I noticed a cluster of 'lights' floating above the ground, on the opposite side of the field. They seemed to be interested in something on the ground – that's the impression I felt. As I drove on, within a few seconds, there were six of these 'lights' hovering four to eight feet off the ground, close to the car.

Each 'light' was made up of a pair of bright white lights, joined together by a brightly lit but fuzzy rod – 'like a stem waving in the wind', possibly reaching the ground – although I was unable to confirm that. They came right up to the side of the hedge in a group, looking inwards from the other side of the hedge, which separated the road from the field – then, in a horrifying movement, they formed in a line – almost as if they were queuing up to have a look at us. I sat there mesmerized. What else could I do? It sounds absurd, but I knew, then, that they were interested in us but meant no harm. I continued on my journey, turning onto the main road. Suddenly, two great flashes of light illuminated the field and they were gone.

When I arrived home, with the children fast asleep, I got out of the car and was unable to stop shaking for some considerable time, as a result of what I had viewed as a terrifying experience."

Over the years we were to come across many accounts, involving UFOs seen following vehicles, particularly in the Hereford and Worcester areas. We did not know what to make of this report; it seemed to be in a category all of its own. We had not come across anything like it before, (although we had by now come across many sightings of UFOs around the County) but saw no reason to disbelieve what Janet – a well educated and intelligent woman – had courageously told us.

'Triangle of Lights' – Attlebridge

Norwich man – Mr George Steel, was driving through Attlebridge, with his girlfriend – Cheryl Sadd (now his wife) at 11pm on 24th May 1982, when the couple saw:

> *". . . a 'triangle of orange, red and blue, lights', hanging in the air, approximately 200ft off the ground, about a quarter-of-a-mile away".*

George stopped the car, his curiosity aroused. As he did so, the triangular mass of lights shot off across the sky, at phenomenal speed.

(Source: Brenda Butler/*Eastern Evening News*, 29.5.82 – 'Lights Riddle In Close Encounter For George')

Triangular lights seen, Norwich

FROM: Eastern Evening News 29/5/1982;

LIGHTS RIDDLE IN CLOSE ENCOUNTER FOR GEORGE

A young Norwich man encountered unexpected traffic on his way home through Attlebridge on Monday night. Mr. George Steel, 22, of 98 Stafford Street, Norwich, and his girlfriend Cheryl Sadd spotted a triangle of orange, red and blue lights hanging almost motionless about 200 feet above the ground.

"It was hovering in the middle of nowhere, only about a quarter of a mile away. When we stopped it seemed to sense we were there and just went off at amazing speed," said Mr.Steel who was on his way home on the main Fakenham to Norwich road just before 11pm.

He said he really wanted to know if anyone else had seen the lights. "I'm absolutely convinced it wasn't an aircraft. Call it a UFO, whatever you like" he said.

On the 24th of May 1982 we learned of a triangular object seen by a young Norwich man and his girlfriend.

UFO over Transmission mast

At 2.30am on 25th May 1982, Mr Robert Darraugh of Mossley, Tameside, was taking his early morning break, at Weldems factory, next to the Leeds and Liverpool Canal, when he saw a bright '*light*', with a blue tint, moving slowly through the air from its position at the side of Wharmton transmission mast.

> *"It looked to be about three inches in length from the ground, and reminded me of a fluorescent light tube, from where I and a colleague – Bob Bridden – were standing. The amazing thing was that we saw it again, the next morning, at the same time."*

An investigation held into the matter by Cheshire based UFO Researcher – Dave Bezer – revealed the likelihood that the two men may have seen an aircraft, passing across the face of the transmitter – a regular route taken by aircraft flying into Manchester Ringway Airport – although Dave remains mystified as to why they reported having watched the object for 20 minutes, when his observations on civilian aircraft, using this route, showed a flight time of eight minutes between appearing and disappearing from view.

Dave Bezer was to tell us of several other incidents, involving sightings of UFOs, during the 1980s. Some took place in the valley of Greenfield, and others on the Holmfirth road (the A635) – rumoured to be one of the most haunted roads in England, including a stretch of road which runs from the bottom of the Valley of Greenfield to Holmfirth – known, in more recent times, as where the victims of the Moors Murders were buried.

UFO stakeout! Strange person seen

On the night of 30th May 1982, while investigating a report of a UFO seen around the TV transmitter mast, situated on the top of Wharmton, Dave decided to carry out some observations near to the mast. The mast was situated on private land, so he decided to make his way to the high moorland of Greenfield. As it was a Sunday night before the Bank Holiday, it meant he could stay all night, not being at work the next day. Accompanied by his eldest son, David, he arrived in the Valley of Greenfield, that night, about 8.30 pm.

"We walked up past the paper mill and up to Dove Stone Reservoir, and then walked onto the road, which runs across the dam, and stood looking out across the open waters of the reservoir, from the end where the Yacht Club is situated.

I was talking to David about what I was going to be doing. I told him, 'You're OK to get some sleep in the tent'. There were still a few people walking about in this popular local beauty spot, so we decided to wait until it was a bit darker before we moved to where we were going.

The sun was just disappearing over the hilltop of Lydgate, when I became aware of a dark skinned youth, who stood behind us. He was wearing no shirt. As I looked at him I felt the hairs on the back of my neck stand up. There was something not right about him. I turned to David and said, 'Let's go'. The weather had been quite warm up to this stage, but it felt to be getting colder and the wind was beginning to get up – it had been calm until 'he' had appeared on the scene. We walked up the valley; it gets quite steep the higher up you go. As we reached the big square rock we call 'The Sugar Loaf', I decided to stop and change my plans. I had originally been planning to go to the top of 'Indians Head', but as we reached the spot I said to David, 'It's too windy to go any higher up. We'll pitch the tent here". The wind was so strong that we both had to lie on the ground sheet until we got it pegged down.

The 'youth' had followed us up the valley and was sitting on a rock across the river and kept beckoning me towards him. I resisted the invitation and just stood watching him. He then got up and set off towards the top of Dove Stone Moss, as it was nearly dark. Now, I thought, where the heck is he going? I got my binoculars out of my bag and was watching him move up the steep hillside, across the side of the hill. At a point near to the top of a dry stone, he vanished from view. I couldn't believe what I had just seen and kept looking for him, thinking he may have ducked down, but never saw him again."

JUNE 1982

HAYMAKERS ENCOUNTER UFO

Also includes – UFO seen over Hartley, in Kent, by Ex RAF Officer and his wife –
become disheartened with the attitude of the police and MOD.

June 1982 – UFO – Clapton, Somerset

ON 9th June 1982, a party of four people were in the process of making their way home, at 9.15pm, after having spent the day haymaking, at a farm midway between Midsomer Norton and Clapton, Somerset, when they became aware of a bright pink/red/orange colour object in the sky. Further observation revealed an oval object (sharply defined) with apparent lightly curved '*antennae*' protruding from its '*body*', slowly moving towards the position of the witnesses. Believing it was going to land, the party ran along the road, hoping to intercept it, but lost sight of it as it dropped down behind some trees. It then rose upwards and hovered briefly, before dropping down again. The peculiar rising and falling action went on for about 25 minutes. By 9.55pm, the incident was over.

(Source: *Probe*, **Robert Moore, Jenny Randles, Mr. S. Cambell and Mr. P. Taylor,
BUFORA case ref/82-030 IFO**)

UFO over Kent

Mr Berry – a former World War II RAF pilot, part-time instructor at a glider school, and antique dealer – was out walking with his wife, in a rural part of Kent, close to the family home, on 18th June 1982, when they saw:

> "... *an enormous pink-red object, descending slowly through the air, over the tops of trees, opposite, about 2miles away and about 1,000ft up in the air. It seemed to 'slowly solidify' before touching down on the ground. I estimated it was 200ft by 200ft in size. When the 'power shut off', the length was about 175ft.*"

The couple rushed home and telephoned Gravesend police, to report what they had seen. The officer kept Mr Berry on the phone for a long time and then asked the couple to call in at the Station the next morning, which they did. When they reminded the officer about the previous call, he denied all knowledge and asked for a form in triplicate to be sent to RAF Manston, as requested. Feeling very frustrated by the lack of interest and action the couple returned home, but were interviewed later by Margaret Fry, who was contacted by Desmond Smith – a newspaper reporter – after he learnt of what the couple had witnessed.

(Source: Margaret Fry)

Three days later a '*doughnut shaped object*' was sighted by the crew of an aircraft en rout from Gatwick to Corfu.

CONTACT (U.K.) 1982-6-1

REPORT FORM FOR U.F.O. SIGHTING (No. ....)

This organisation has been set up to investigate, collate and analyse reports of Unidentified Flying Objects. It will be of great value if you will kindly give precise details of your observation on the date of ....*12. JUNE. 1982*........

SECTION A.   FULL ACCOUNT OF OBSERVATION

On the evening of 18 June 1982 at 9.50 p.m my wife & I were making our way home down Briars Way, HARTLEY, KENT (NEAR DARTFORD) where we live. It was a typical June evening with a clear sky. Suddenly I became aware of an illuminated & strange shape, perhaps as large as a harvest moon, suspended in the sky in the N.E. and stationary over HARTLEY woods. Although I had served 6 years in World War II in Anti-Aircraft Command and had held a pilot's license I couldn't relate it to anything I had seen before. It was red/orange in colour and although solid it appeared translucent also and I could clearly make out its construction as if planks or spars had been used. It didn't radiate any light to earth but it was brilliant around its perimeter with especially bright lights at the ends of the construction. I don't know how long it was there but we observed it for a full minute before it descended behind the trees of HARTLEY woods These are 2 miles away. On reaching home. I telephoned the police at GRAVESEND

174

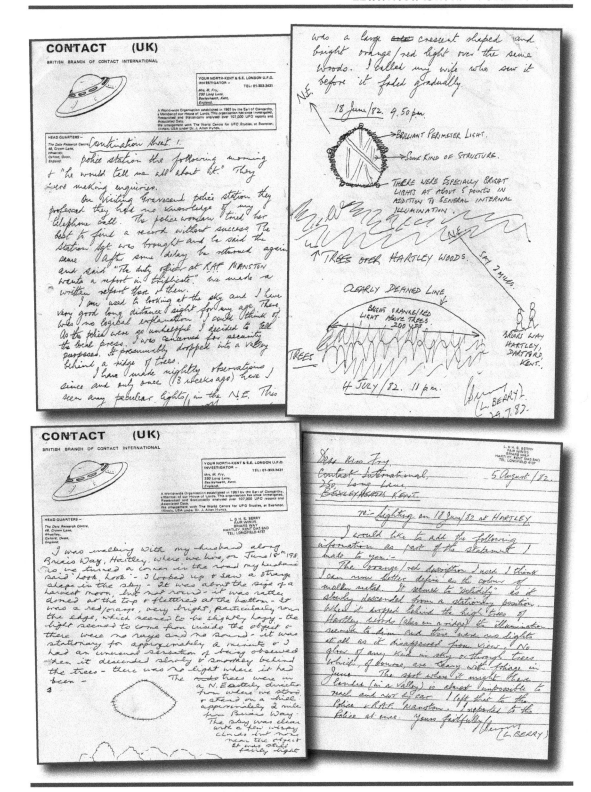

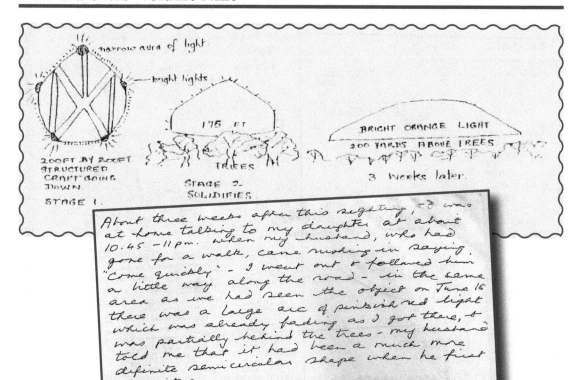

narrow aura of light

bright lights

175 FT

TREES

BRIGHT ORANGE LIGHT

200 YARDS ABOVE TREES

3 weeks later.

200FT BY 200FT
STRUCTURED
CRAFT GOING
DOWN

STAGE 1.

STAGE 2.
SOLIDIFIES

About three weeks after this sighting, I was at home talking to my daughter at about 10.45 - 11 pm. when my husband, who had gone for a walk, came rushing in saying, "Come quickly" - I went out & followed him a little way along the road - in the same area as we had seen the object on June 18. there was a large arc of pinkish red light which was already fading as I got there, & was partially behind the trees - my husband told me that it had been a much more definite semicircular shape when he first saw it -

HSylvia Berry.   July 29th 1982.

BRADFORD Telegraph & Argus Tuesday 22nd June 1982

Signs in the sky — a UFO

ANCIENT legends have it that a Royal birth is heralded by strange sightings in the sky.

A report is being passed to the Ministry of Defence today over the sighting by four Britons of an unidentified flying object while on a flight from Gatwick to Corfu yesterday.

The Dan-Air Boeing 737 with 130 passengers was near Brindisi, Italy, when the captain, his co-pilot and two passengers, who were visiting the flight deck at the time, saw "the object" about two miles away.

Capt. Len Schwaiger, 52, said: "We noticed a black shining object about the size of a car in the opposite direction about two miles away.

"It was rather doughnut shaped and appeared to be flat bottomed. We all watched it for about a minute."

The co-pilot, First Officer David Robertson, said: "The object appeared to have no aerodynamic shape and it may have had a small window on top."

Dan-Air said today that the pilots filed their report on their return to London last night. It will be passed on to the Ministry for analysis in the normal way.

"We get sightings from our pilots from time to time but not recently and to get one seen by four people at the same time is pretty unusual."

JULY 1982

Diamond-shaped lights over Oldham • Triangular UFO seen over London

Strange lights over Oldham

RUTH Dent, from Greenfield, near Oldham, had occasion to go to the bathroom, at 3.45am on 20th July 1982. As she moved out of the bedroom, Ruth involuntary looked out through the flat window and saw:

"...a very bright 'light' in the sky. Further inspection revealed three separate 'lights', joined together, just above the skyline of the War memorial. As it moved closer, it seemed to change shape – now diamond in appearance. When I looked again, after having been to the bathroom, it had gone."

(Source: Bolton UFO Society (BUFOS) Dave Bezer)

Triangular UFO over London

In July 1982, Chris Chord was living in a penthouse apartment, at West Halkin Street, in London.

"At 5pm, I happened to be walking into my bedroom, when I saw a 'black dot' in the distance. Within seconds, a huge 'black triangle' passed overhead at such a speed I thought I might have been imagining it, if it wasn't for the fact that the glass in the window was slightly vibrating. This happened before the 'black triangle' passed over. It was almost as if it was from another dimension – that's the only way I can explain it."

(Source: WWW.UFO Evidence/Personal interview)

1982, River Lea, Tottenham, London

© Copyright 2005 www.davidsankey.com

AUGUST 1982

GLASS BALL UFO SEEN TAKING UP WATER

Also includes – Silver UFO, showing panels, seen in sky over Stockport
UFO over Wigan • Spinning spokes of light UFO seen over Warminster, chased by
the witnesses • Dome-shaped object seen to land at Westbury, Wiltshire
Further reports of UFO activity over Oldham

UFO over River Rea

BRIAN Jessop was out with school friends, looking for anything of interest, after the River Rea, near Tottenham Locks, had been drained of water, during a clean-up exercise by the Local Authority, in August 1982.

"My friend told me he could hear a sucking noise, but I never heard anything. Suddenly, we saw an object hovering about 15ft above the water. It looked like a glass ball, 6ft in diameter, filled with smoke, showing a dim light in the centre. We watched as it slowly rose upwards, about a foot, and began to bounce up and down, before heading away across the sky. We were terrified and ran away. The next evening, we went back – our curiosity well and truly aroused – and heard barking, and saw two Thames Valley Police dog vans, parked nearby, with the officers shining their torches – as if looking for something. I'm still mystified by what it was we saw."

(Source: Personal interview)

Silver UFO

Stockport man – George Harvey (50) was walking through Stockport cemetery, near Nangreave Road, Heaviley, at 1.30pm on 10th August 1982, when he saw a strange object in the sky, covered with silver panels –

". . . and what appeared to be a misty skirt, or rim, on its underside, with a red light to the left and blue to the right. When it moved away, it stood on end and then turned back on its underside, before accelerating out of view, at great speed."

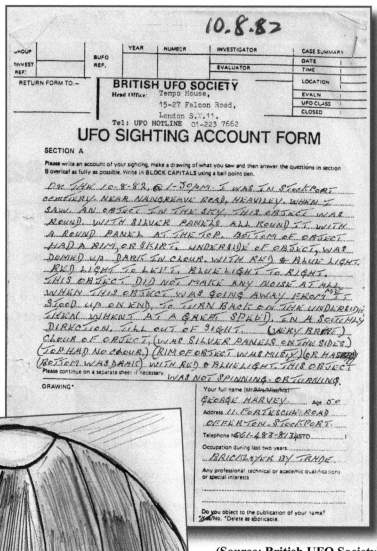

(Source: British UFO Society)

UFO over Wigan

At 9.10pm on 13th August 1982, Brian Lydon of Langdale Crescent, Abram, spotted three UFOs on this night.

The first was a small star-shaped object that hovered in mi-air above him. This was followed by:

". . . a massive thing, that was seen to move slowly towards the Plank Lane district of Leigh."

The third object, which seemed to originate from Winter Hill, forced Mr. Lydon to take cover, beneath some trees, as it hurtled towards him.

(Source: Bill Eatock)

UFO over Warminster

At 10pm on 20th August 1982, Miss Pat Reeves was sat with her three friends in the back garden of their Portway home, Warminster, near the West Wiltshire Golf Course – the scene of a number of UFO sightings, over the years – when they saw:

> *". . . whirling white 'spokes of light', heading through an overcast sky."*

They jumped into their car and made their way towards Upton Scudamore, where they saw the object hovering over Cow Down Hill, just off the A350 road.

> *"The 'spokes' were of appreciable thickness and rounded ends. In between the spokes – presumably attached to the rim of the central object – were 30 dim diffuse lights, like light bulbs. The size of the object*

was staggering – as big as Wembley Stadium, 2-3ft in the sky, at arm's length. It reminded us of the UFO seen in the film, 'Close Encounters'.

After a few minutes, all the lights went out. I shouted, 'Come back, please'. To my amazement, they came back on as the object reappeared in the sky, roughly over Cradle Hill, before reversing back along its original course, and took up a hovering position in the air again."

By this stage the others were beginning to become worried, following Pat's excited shouts directed at the UFO to land, at which point she agreed to leave the scene and made their way back home. Pat and her friends decided not to say anything, fearing ridicule. **(Source: Dan Goring, *Earth-link*)**

EVENING CHRONICLE, OLDHAM, MONDAY, AUGUST 16,

UFO HUNT CENTRES ON SADDLEWORTH

UFO sleuth David Bezer is trying to solve the mystery of a shining object which has been spotted several times in Saddleworth.

The bright, cylindrical-shaped object, has been seen on six occasions high at the side of the Wharmton television mast at Grasscroft.

Reflecting

"It's certainly very baffling. We have no idea what the object is," said 35-year-old David, an official investigator with the British UFO Society.

It was first spotted by a 77-year-old Uppermill man in April, and its last sighting was just before 3 a.m on May 26.

Now, David, of Stephens Road, Stalybridge, is anxious to trace anyone else who may have seen the mystery object.

"We have made exhaustive checks which have ruled out aircraft or the possibility of a star reflecting on the mast.

"On at least two occasions, the object hovered by the tower for about 20 minutes before moving away.

"It has been spotted from Uppermill and Mossley, and I would like to contact anyone who may have seen the shape," he added

"It is completely unexplained. The more information we can get, the better."

David can be contacted on 338 6068.

UFO landing, Wiltshire

Justin Bailey contacted us about what he witnessed in mid-August 1982.

> *"One night, after having retired to bed, I awoke and went to the bathroom to visit the toilet. As I did so I glanced at my clock, which showed 1.15am. As I passed my bedroom window, I noticed a strongly coloured orange object moving along the White Horse escarpment, from the direction of Warminster, towards the quarry area. At the time I was living in Elm Grove,*

and my window faced the hills, from which I could see the Badger Lane area, right along to the 'horse' itself. My best friend, at the time, lived in the old farmhouse adjacent to Leighton Sports Centre, in Westbury.

We spent every spare moment of days and nights up on the hills, woods, and indeed, the ranges themselves, looking for spent ammunition cartridges and the like. We even used to go up and watch the military exercises, when they took place, and, as such, were very used to the equipment, vehicles, aircraft and weapons, and associated noises, being used at the time.

In fact we were chased from the ranges, several times, after getting a little too close to the weaponry. The object was travelling at slow speed and showing a very bright strong orange glow from underneath – not a focussed beam, just an ambient glow. It eventually came to a field directly behind an old grove of trees that line a pathway along the front of grassy slopes, which was and still is visible against the surrounding trees. The line of large trees were clearly in silhouette as the object came in behind them, and where it appeared to land, leaving only its top half visible. It was what I'd call a classic UFO shape, with a domed top that was still glowing orange.

I could see the ridge line behind the top of the object; it must have been positioned in the field directly behind the grooved path and is not within the range boundary track. In fact, I can still place it as being 2/3rds of the way up the slope and halfway across the field itself, which is roughly equal to halfway along the tree line, which is how I judged its position. At this point I began to call for my parents – which did not go down well at all – and whilst trying to tell them to look at what I was seeing, my mum was informing me that she had work in the morning and was not getting out of bed.

The object itself had been stationary for approximately two minutes now, and I'd given up trying to convince my parents to look. At this point, as I turned back to look again, it lifted and gave off a large amount of bright orange light, which appeared to light the whole escarpment and was very intense, before disappearing at very high speed over the ranges back towards Warminster.

I had never seen anything move at such speed, military or not. My window was wide open and at no time was there any noise. Almost daily we saw and heard Chinooks, Lynx, Sea Kings, Hercules, A10s, tanks, and Apaches, moving over, and this was nothing I recognised. In fact, I clearly remember hearing the church bells ringing as I lay in bed afterwards, trying to go to sleep, and it being a still, cloud-free, night.

In the morning I sat down and told my parents what I had seen. They didn't believe me, at first, but apologised later, after hearing some reports on the radio of UFOs being seen in the area. Sadly, I've never encountered anything that I haven't been able to explain – from the strangely glowing rolling mists on the plains, to tricks of light through the atmosphere and strange weather effects – but I always have a camera to hand, just in case. I would be happy to show you the area it landed in, which is 10-15 minutes walk from the White Horse itself."

UFOs over Oldham

At 10.40pm on 25th August 1982, Oldham housewife – Mrs Susan Fink, went into her back garden, to check if any of the children's toys had been left out, when her attention was drawn to a large bright '*light*' in the sky. Thinking it was probably an aircraft (as the house lies under a flight path) her initial reaction was to dismiss the event, but she soon changed her mind when the looming '*light*' changed shape into a clear-cut triangle, with the base at the top.

"It then increased in size, causing the base to change shape, now resembling an upside-down ice cream cone. Two smaller lights then came from out of one side of the 'cone' and dropped downwards, under the base, one being larger than the other. The bottom of the cone

expanded, until it completely engulfed the two smaller objects, which changed shape, once again, to 'cigar', before accelerating away into the distance – now a tiny 'star' in the sky."

BUFOS **S**trange **E**ncounters

NAME ....Susan Fink............................ Mr/Mrs/Miss/Ms.

ADDRESS ....1 Croft Brow, Garden Suburbs....
....Oldham....................................

.... TEL: ....

AGE GROUP: 18 - 25, 26 - 39, 40 - 55, 56 - 70, 70+. AGE IF UNDER 18 ......

QUALIFICATIONS (Where relevant) ....

DATE OF ENCOUNTER ...25th August 1982....

TIME OBJECT/ENTITY FIRST SEEN ...2240....

PRECISE LOCATION OF WITNESS ..Back garden of a..
...House in Croft Brow, Garden Suburbs....
...Oldham....

ACCOUNT OF EXPERIENCE

On the night of Wednesday the 25th of August 1982 I went into my back garden to see if the children had left any toys in the garden. When my attention was drawn to a very bright light in the sky, as we live on a flight path at first I thought it was a plane But the light kept getting bigger, then it changed shape into a triangle, with the base at the top, then it tilted to the right until it came into a position with the base at the bottom. The light which was very bright and triangular in shape, was hazy around the edges, the light then grew in magnitude, and the base of the triangle began to change shape, it began to go round and ashape like a upside down ice-cream cone was observed after this two lights came out of the side of the upside down ice-cream cone and began to sink down the side until they where in a position below the base of triangle, they were cigar shaped and one was bigger than the other, then the bottom part of the cone began to grow until it completley engulfed the two smaller shapes and the larger shape took up the shape of a huge eliptical shape. It then appeared to exelerate away until was just like a very bright star then it disseapeared from view in the dark cloud on the distant horizon.

I AGREE THE ABOVE ACCOUNT IS ACCURATE.

MY NAME MAY/MAY NOT BE PUBLISHED.

Signature ...Susan Fink...

Date ...16/ 9 /82...

W   WEATHER CONDITIONS

Cloud	Moon/Stars	Precipitation	
0	Yes/No	——————	0.003
1/3	Yes/No	Rain/Hail/Snow	0.004
2/3	Yes/No	Rain/Hail/Snow	0.006
O/Cast	——	Rain/Hail/Snow	0.009

WITNESS DRAWING OF OBJECT/ENTITY

Mrs. Fink contacted the police to report the matter. As they seemed disinterested, she then rang Air Traffic Control, at Manchester Airport, who took details from her and promised to send them to Jodrell Bank. Feeling dissatisfied, she contacted the RAF, who gave her Dave Bezer's details – a point of some amusement to Dave, who wondered how they had obtained them. Enquiries made into the incident, revealed that the object had been seen over Failsworth – the site of several Ferranti Electronic Engineering factories – an interesting observation, bearing in mind the incident at Cairo Mill, Waterhead, Oldham (in 1972).

Just before midnight, on the same evening (25th August 1982) Mrs Phyllis Robinson was just about to close the curtains at her Oldham home, when she noticed:

> *". . . what I thought was an aircraft, coming in very low over the rooftops, but then realised it was much larger than what normally flies over, and stopped to watch, when I was surprised to see an object, resembling a railway carriage in appearance, with large portholes on its side, through which dazzling light projected. It then continued through the sky, heading towards Bardsley, and stopped for about thirty seconds, enabling me to see what looked like two huge searchlights, before turning slowly, at right angles, and heading towards Failsworth. I turned to speak to my husband. By that time, it was now climbing rapidly upwards – now a 'bright light', getting smaller – the whole thing over in just a few minutes."*

Dave Bezer, who investigated this matter, had this to say:

REPORT ON THE SIGHTING ACCOUNT OF MRS PHYLLIS ROBINSON
I first became involved with this account after the lady herself contacted me after seeing my name in a newspaper article conected with another sighting incident that involving Mrs FINK these two sites of these sightings being in close proximity to one another and both ladys where seen on the same night Mrs Robinson seems a very intelligent lady and is something of artist if some of the drawings that she showed me are anything to go by in fact she has drawn me a very exellent drawing of the object. present at the interview where Mrs Robinson and her husband who is a fanatic on areoplanes and his wife the witness to these sighting seems to have a great interest to. As she went to draw the bedroom curtains she caught sight of a very unusual object that appeared to be just above the roof tops of the houses across the road at the object which was cigar shaped and was flying at a angle of some 25 to 30 degrees one end being higher than the other which she describes as being like a huge railway carriage (full account on sheet) Site details follow O.S. position of witness NORTHINGS @ 403.05 EASTINGS 392.7. T he house terraced is situated on HATHERSHAW LANE this road being the A6104 a connectin road which joins the A627 with the main A62 (trunk) at failsworth this is road continuing on past the two FERRANTI ELECTRONIS which are just at the back of the A62. positeo n object was first seen in 244 it then moved across her field of vision to a bearing 184 which brought it into a position over the huge scool complex which is just down the road it then shot up in the air and dissapeared into the distance last seen bearing 220 the object was in view over Iris St for much of the incident. The A627 is the main Ashton-u-Lyne to Oldham road and the A62 is the main trunk road between Manchester and Huddersfield. Other things of possible interest on the site of these sightings is two Confectionary Factories PARK cCAKE Bakeries a small Res' a Mail Order Warehouse and in close proximity there are several dissused pit sites this area in the past was a very active area for mine workings in the pastI am putting this sheet in but I am going to look into this one much closer
Additional imformation on this sighting the mail order mill which is situated directly down the road from the witnesses house has 6 huge searchlights situated on the side and the back of the mill away from the witness which light up the mill yard at night there is a very great possiblity that these searchlights where reflected back on the clouds which were moving and giving the strange sighting effect but this is only a theory and is in no way conclusive but it is a possibillity thats has gotto be looked at in more detail when the darker nights come back again I believe the lighss where reflected of something but i have got to find out what it was to prove this theory.

Close encounter – Redcar, Cleveland

At 1.20am on 30th August 1982, Mr and Mrs George Philips of Frances Street, Redcar, Cleveland were awoken by the screams of their baby daughter, Sarah. Fearing the worst, the couple ran into the bedroom and picked up the child to calm her down. Eventually the baby went back to sleep, leaving the couple to return to bed.

The next morning, George recalled a strange dream in which he and his wife had not returned to bed after settling their daughter down but had seen a strange craft land on the concrete carport outside the house. He was stunned to discover that his wife had also experienced the same dream. The '*craft*' was described as being *"oval in shape, showing three landing legs, two antennae on top, and a row of bright lights around the middle"*. The couple also remembered (albeit somewhat vaguely) the arrival of two strange creatures seen ascending the stairs of the house. These were described as being, *"about 2ft high, almost childlike in size, wearing no clothing; they had pale skin, no hair or a nose"*. The couple both remember following the '*entities*' outside – not surprisingly, they were very frightened. They checked the baby's room and found a damp patch next to the cot. A sample was taken and discovered to be human urine; presumably one of them had wet themselves during the night

This was an incident that baffled both husband and wife. Some years later, they decided to contact the Independent UFO Network (formed in 1987) and discussed the matter with them, hoping for some answers.

In an interview conducted by Philip Mantle on the 6th October 1991, the couple were asked if they noticed any strange rashes or feeling sick, and of any dramatic changes in their life. The wife said she had been

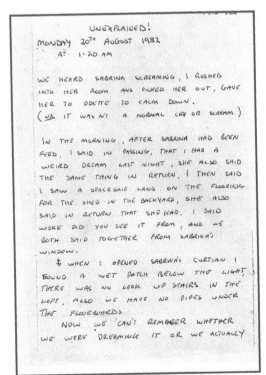

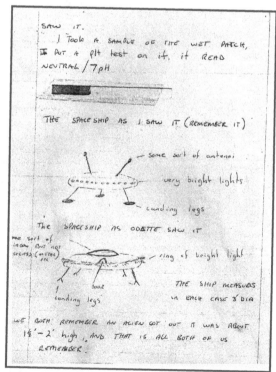

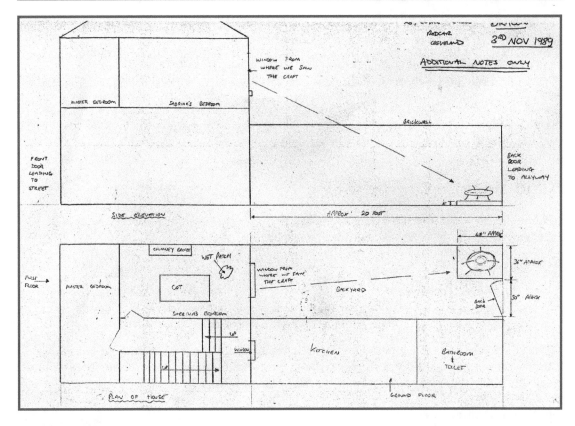

hysterical all afternoon, and for a couple of days afterwards, but there was no evidence of any great changes wrought in their lives following on from the incident.

It is not uncommon for people involved in Close Encounters to drastically alter their lifestyle – a course of action that appears to be precipitated by the event itself and a yearning for further contact.

George had a different story. He told of being struck with an unusual illness in November of that year, which was diagnosed as Polyarteritis Nodosa – a disease where the blood attacks the capillaries – and was in hospital for three months, recovering.

Philip then asked him about the security of the house and whether a burglar alarm was fitted. He was told they had no alarm – just bolts on the back door.

Hypnosis Regression

In a session conducted with Mrs Philips, she told of the baby screaming and of going to pick her up, at which point she realised George wasn't on the landing. She shouted for him, but there was no answer. She tells of looking out of the window with the baby held in both arms. She heard a noise coming from downstairs, and then sights something *'terrible'* on the stairs – *"It's small, it's pale skin is funny, it's alive"* – (compares it with a small child). She is asked about the eyes and the clothes *'it'* is wearing, but is unable to assist. *"It has no hair, no ears that I could see, and no sign of any nose."* Mrs Philips said she could only see it standing there and was frightening, as she had never seen anything like it before. *"There's one behind it."*

At this point she walked down the stairs, the two '*beings*' having now gone, and made her way to the front of the house – still looking for her husband. She made her way back to bed and found George asleep.

George could only say that he awoke in the night after hearing his daughter's screams, and looked out of the window where he thought he saw movement to the rear of the house. He went downstairs and opened the back door, saw nothing, and went back to bed.

Budd Hopkins

Incidents like these are frightening, and the people who have to endure them are left with some very disturbing questions, but no answers and often no support.

Budd Hopkins:

> *"A person will often find in the house evidence of a visit made by he or she outside which they have no memory of. In one particular case, a man woke up in the morning with the recollection that he had been outside, and of seeing figures in the room."*

We had the pleasure of talking to Budd Hopkins about matters such as these, during a lecture held in England, some years ago. He was the first to point out that he, himself, was once sceptical about the possibility of any abduction scenario, because it seemed impossible to believe. Like us, he had no reason not to disbelieve reports of UFO activity but was apprehensive about them containing occupants. It took him 20 years to change his mind!

He confirmed in many of the 'Close encounter' accounts given to him, that people had reported having experienced missing time, or the car they were travelling in sometimes ended up in the wrong direction (or discovering themselves dressed incorrectly, or items of clothing missing).

Budd also said:

> *"This was often followed by nightmares afterwards. In listening to these people you assume that something traumatic had occurred to them, so I enlisted the help of a couple of friends who were psychiatrists, psychologists, and others, to help us with hypnotic regressions, to look into these experiences that the people were unable to recall all the details of. We always ensured that the people who carried out the sessions of hypnosis were skeptics about the UFO phenomena and allegations of abductions. I don't think they ended up skeptics, but that's the way they began.*
>
> *As we examined more and more reports, we were able to see identical correlations of behaviour in the background history in the cases that we looked at. You have to accept you're dealing with a phenomenon that has an absolute core of reality about it.*
>
> *Most dramatically are the physical marks found on people's bodies after these experiences; they fall into various types. One is what we label as a scoop mark, which is a little round depression, about the size of my thumb nail or a little smaller, as if some sort of small object or tool has just removed a layer of cells.*

Another type is just a straight like surgical cut that can be anywhere from often a small inch or so, but down to maybe three and a half, four inches long, with little, if any, bleeding having taken place. Another set of these marks can be simply large bruises, especially on the insides of the thighs, as if some kind of gynecological stirrups had been used or something of that sort. Again, if this happens during the night, the person goes to bed unmarked and wakes up with these various cuts or whatever I've described, and some of them are extremely dramatic in appearance.

In one case a woman went to a doctor after one of these 'things' turned up on her back, after she made a report of having been abducted. The doctor insisted that she'd had surgery because there were, at regular intervals, little extensions along the cut. She denied this and told him she had discovered the problem after waking up. That is one basic, dramatic piece of evidence.

One of the most important things about abduction reports is that they originate from all over the World. If you asked the man on the street to explain what his perception of a UFO abduction is about; he may get one or two things right, but most people really don't have a clear idea of what is happening.

Trying to speculate as to what the ultimate meaning of all this is to the human race is very difficult. We know what they're doing, I think, beyond any doubt at this point. As to why they're doing it, that's speculation. It definitely seems to me, though, that what they're doing

Budd Hopkins and Dawn Holloway at a recent lecture held in Truro

is for their purposes, not for ours. Many people still appear to believe they are coming here to take us over. I don't see a sign of either one of those being true. They seem to be here for their own purposes. Now, they could take what they need – our DNA, our genetics. They could create their hybrids to solve some particular evolutionary problem that they may be facing. Who knows? And they could just simply leave and then leave us alone again, which would be quite wonderful.

But, I don't think it's possible to say. I don't have enough to go by, enough information, to say what they're here for. They're not here, that's for sure, to help us plug up the ozone layer hole. They're not here to take over our supermarkets. They're here for their own reasons. And I'm not sure what those are."

Ghostly events a short distance away – food for thought!

A search of the immediate locality for any other incidents of interest revealed details of what was reported as a ghostly manifestation, a few streets away. We cannot prove that there was a connection between what took place in Frances Street and the nearby Alfred Street, but would not be surprised if there was.

This took place at 2am, one morning in 1963, and involved Mrs Pamela Iredale and her nine-month-old baby, and her brother, Barry Gardner, who fled their terraced house in Alfred Street, Redcar.

Mrs. Iredale said, at the time:

"I just couldn't stand it any longer . . . I didn't believe in ghosts, but I wouldn't spend another night in that house for a fortune. I knew that an old lady had died there and I was used to hearing strange noises during the night, but thought nothing of them. Then the stairs began to creak as if someone was coming up them. For no apparent reason the baby's cot collapsed and the curtains fell to the floor. Then the living room door, which was fastened with a tight ball catch, began opening and shutting. There were no draughts and on one occasion it slammed and opened continuously for half an hour. I was so scared I locked myself in the bathroom and stayed there until it stopped. After that I asked a girlfriend to stay with me, but she said the house gave her the creeps and she moved out after a few days.

Last night's happenings were the last straw. I had just gone to bed and my brother was getting undressed in his room, when I saw this old woman with a lighted candle. She was dressed in a grey frock and had white curly hair. I was petrified and called out to Barry. It wasn't a dream. I wasn't even asleep. The room became icy cold. I gathered up baby Colin, and the three of us just fled the house. There is no way I will go back and live there again."

The property's owner – Mr George Smee, of Yeatby – confirmed his wife had died in the house and she was a small grey haired lady. He put the claims of a ghost down to a case of a vivid imagination.

(Source: *Now & Then*, **issue 19, July 2002)**

In the south east of Redcar is an aircraft listening post built in 1916 during the First World War as part of a regional defence system to detect approaching aircraft, principally Zeppelins, and give early warning. It is an example of an acoustic mirror, of which other examples can be found along the east coast of Britain. The mirror was used up until the invention of radar and although it was built on open fields today a modern housing estate now surrounds it. Only the concrete sound mirror remains and is now a Grade II listed building.

SEPTEMBER 1982

'BEAUTIFUL' UFO SIGHTED OVER SADDLEWORTH

Also includes – UFO seen over Cwmbran, Wales, by couple – typical response from MOD • A saucer-shaped object over Yorkshire • 'Cottage loaf' UFO seen over Gwent • A dome-shaped object over Oldham, seen by schoolboys and their grandmother • A UFO is seen to land on school grounds – the next day the pitch is dug up! • A 'black mass' seen over Lydgate Church, Oldham • Police Officers at Monmouth sight UFO • A report of a 'car stop' in Sudbury, Suffolk, and of what is claimed to have been an alien abduction, by a woman known to the authors Alert at RAF Alconbury, a 'T'-shaped UFO is seen by a local motorist, while out driving near the Base

September 1982 – UFO over Saddleworth

MR HEAP, of Uppermill, Saddleworth, was driving his car along Burnedge Lane, Saddleworth, at 10pm on 1st September 1982, with his wife in the front passenger seat, when she saw a pulsating, or shimmering, '*bright object*' moving across the sky, with rays projecting from it, on the end of which were small lights, glittering like diamonds.

> "*I tapped my husband on the arm and directed his attention towards the object. He stopped the car and we watched the 'lights' – now moving over Platting Road – not much higher than the top of the house. We then jumped back into the car and drove down into Oldham Road, to obtain a clearer view, but it had gone. It was, without doubt, one of the most beautiful things I had ever seen in my life.*"

Mr Heap was also interviewed with regard to this matter. He corroborated what his wife had seen, describing it as

> "*a huge, pulsating triangle of light – hazy at the edges*", and that it was "*a dry and clear night.*"

		YEAR	NUMBER	INVESTIGATOR	CASE SUMMARY	
OUP	BUFORA REF.				DATE	
VEST				EVALUATOR	TIME	
F:					LOCATION	
RETURN FORM TO:—					EVAL'N	
					UFO CLASS	
					CLOSED	

UFO SIGHTING ACCOUNT FORM

SECTION A

Please write an account of your sighting, make a drawing of what you saw and then answer the questions in section B overleaf as fully as possible. Write in **BLOCK CAPITALS** using a ball point pen.

WE HEARD OUR DAUGHTER (SABRINA) SCREAMING AT APPROX 01:20 am ON MONDAY 2ᵀᴴ AUGUST 1982. I RUSHED INTO HER ROOM AND PICKED HER OUT. I THEN GAVE HER TO MY WIFE (ODETTE) TO CALM HER DOWN (N.B. IT WASN'T A NORMAL SCREAM OR CRY) IN THE MORNING, I SAID IN PASSING TO ODETTE, THAT I HAD A WEIRD DREAM LAST NIGHT, SHE SAID THE SAME THING. I THEN SAID I SAW A SPACESHIP LAND ON THE FLOORING FOR THE SHED I WAS MAKING, IN THE BACKYARD, SHE ALSO SAID THE SAME THING. I THEN ASKED HER WHERE SHE SAW IT FROM, AND BOTH TOGETHER WE SAID FROM SABRINA'S BEDROOM WINDOW. WHEN WE WENT UPSTAIRS, WE FOUND A WET PATCH BELOW THE LIGHT, THERE WAS NO WATER LEAKING FROM THE ROOF OR CEILING, WE HAVE NO PIPES UNDER THE FLOOR BOARDS OR IN THE ROOF. AFTER ✱ SQUEEZING IT FROM THE CARPET I TESTED IT WITH A PH STICK RESULT WAS 7 PH. I BELIEVE ONE OF US WAS SO FRIGHTENED, THEY WET THEMSELVES (SABRINA WAS STILL IN NAPPIES) ALSO WE BOTH REMEMBER ONE OR TWO ALIENS COMING UP THE STAIRS, WE CAN'T REMEMBER RETURNING TO BED, WE DON'T KNOW HOW LONG WE WERE UP FOR, AND WE DON'T KNOW WHETHER WE HAD PHYSICAL CONTACT WITH THEM. THEY WERE ABOUT 1½ FEET 2 FEET HIGH — THE SPACESHIP WAS APPROX 3 FOOT DIA - RECKONING THE SIZE OF THE SHED FLOORING.

Please continue on a separate sheet if necessary.

DRAWING*

PHIL'S THING — ANTENNA — VERY BRIGHT LIGHTS

ODETTE'S THING — SOME SORT OF WINDOW BUT NOT GLASS MAYBE METAL — BRIGHT LIGHTS — DOOR

SEE ATTACHED (ROFF) NOTES TAKEN SHORTLY LATER PLUS AN EXTRA DRAWING TO SHOW ACTUAL POSITION AT OUR HOUSE

*If preferred, use a separate sheet of paper.

Your full name (Mr/Mrs/Miss/Ms) P & O.R. .... Age 27 — 25

Address.................... REDCAR CLEVELAND

Telephone No (0642) ..... (STD........)

Occupation during last two years....... INSTRUMENT ARTIFICER — HOUSEWIFE

Any professional, technical or academic qualifications or special interests
....
....

Do you object to the publication of your name?
*Yes/● *Delete as applicable.

Today's Date 3ᶜᴰ NOVEMBER 1989

Signature. P. & O.R.

Published by the British UFO Research Association (BUFORA LTD.) for the use of investigators throughout Great Britain. Further copies may be obtained from BUFORA Research Headquarters., Newchapel Observatory,

UFOs over Cwmbran, Wales

At 9pm on 14th September 1982, David Mason (32 years of age) – a printer by trade, from Cwmbran – was watching TV, when he noticed a 'bright light' in the sky and called his wife, Angela.

> *"My husband called me to the window to see an object on the mountain. There was a slight mist on the mountain, but the object was very bright, and just hovered. It seemed to be hazy around the edge, with another set of lights underneath. It looked as if it turned away, because the light got 'slimmer' – then returned. It did this twice and moved across the sky, at quite a speed, but then the 'light' was a lot smaller – then it disappeared."*

After the couple had telephoned the police, two officers arrived and made a written record of what they had seen, and promised to pass it onto the MOD. Details of the incident were later made public. An MOD spokesman was later quoted as saying:

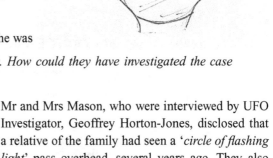

> *"Following these enquiries, we are satisfied there were no Defence implications."*

This attracted a comment from Mr Mason, who said he was

> *"surprised not to have heard from the MOD. How could they have investigated the case without interviewing me further".*

Angela and David Mason and their son Paul re-enact their experience

Mr and Mrs Mason, who were interviewed by UFO Investigator, Geoffrey Horton-Jones, disclosed that a relative of the family had seen a *'circle of flashing light'* pass overhead, several years ago. They also mentioned having seen *'jets of air coming from the object'*, before it shot away. A letter sent to the MOD, asking for any information about the incident, at Cwmbran, received the following answer:

> *"We received no reports of an unidentified flying object, near Cwmbran, on 14th September 1982, and as I have said before, we do not have the resources to search through files for any reports. The report we have received so far proved to be of no interest from a Defence point of view."*

(Source: *The Observer*, 4.3.1984, 'It's official – there are UFOs/Lionel Beer, BUFORA/ Letter to MOD)

UFO over West Yorkshire

At 9.30pm on 20th September 1982, a saucer-shaped object, showing four flashing red lights '*going around in circles*', heading towards Bradford, was seen by members of the Hodgson family, at Saltaire, near Shipley, West Yorkshire. (**Source:** *Telegraph and Argus*, 22.9.82)

UFO over Gwent

At 10.45pm, the same day, Mr and Mrs Beryl Spreadbury, from Newport, Gwent, were travelling along the B4236, Caerlow Road, heading towards Ponthir, when Beryl directed her husband Paul's attention to something in the sky.

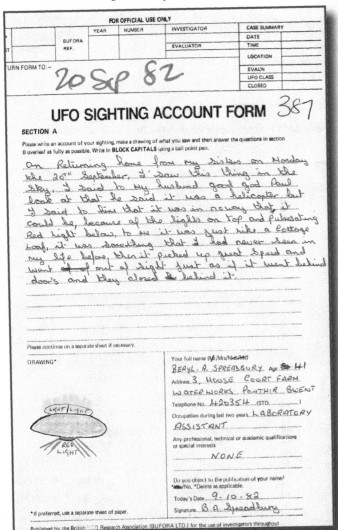

Paul:

"I saw what I first took to be a helicopter – then I realised this couldn't be the case. This 'thing' had two window-shaped, brilliant pulsating lights, a pulsating red light below, and looked like a cottage loaf.

Within seconds it accelerated away, in a blur of speed, and was out of sight – as if someone had opened an invisible door."

(**Source: Jenny Randles, BUFORA/ Geoffrey Horton-Jones**)

UFO lands on school grounds, Lancashire

From documents sent to us by Dave Bezer, we were to learn of another forgotten UFO incident, which took place during the long school holidays, in September 1982, involving Jillian Thwaites (13) – a pupil at Breeze Hill School, Glodwick – who was taking a short cut along Salford Street, to the top of the hill, at 8pm, when:

*"I saw an object on the ground, close to the school, displaying rows of coloured lights, made up of green and yellow on the top, with red lights below, before it shot upwards into the sky, changing colour to white as it did so, and headed off towards *Hartshead Pike."*

The following day, Jillian paid a visit to the school, her curiosity aroused, and found the area dug over by workmen, who were preparing an 'all weather pitch'. By the time local UFO Investigator – Dave Bezer – reached the scene, a few days later, after having been told of the matter, the pitch had been completed – which meant he was unable to obtain any soil samples.

It is of interest to discover that the incident was one of a number that took place along the same straight line of observations from the top of the hill, identified as North 404.2 – East 394.1 – Position of object on ground, North 404.2 – East 394.6 – Compass bearing 100.

Enquiries made into the incident revealed the object had been seen over Failsworth, the site of several Ferranti Electronic Engineering factories.

(Source: Dave Bezer)

More Oldham UFOs

At 8.15pm on 23rd September 1982, Carl Holt (13) was playing in his bedroom, with two other boys – Simon Young and Ian Wright – near Oldham, when they noticed a strange *'light'*, visible on the skyline, hovering over some trees on a golf course, east of the television mast.

After watching it, for a few minutes, the boys alerted the rest of the household, as a result of which they were joined by Mrs Sandra Holt, Mrs Nancy Ball (grandmother, visiting from Wales) and a Mrs Hilary Littleford, who saw:

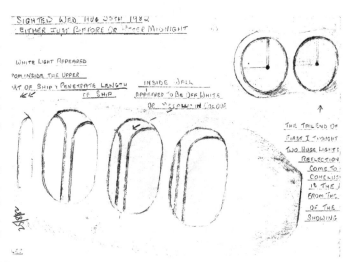

". . . a dome-shaped object, showing two bright lights; as it approached closer, three lights could be made out. It then appeared to stop still, tilt on its one side and cross behind the mast, revealing an underside illuminated by blue and red lights."

---

*The tower was rebuilt in 1863 by John Eaton to commemorate the marriage of HRH Albert Edward to Princess Alexandra, replacing a building that had been there since 1751.An inscription stone reused in the tower states "This Pike Was Rebuilt By Publick Contributions Anno Domini 1751 " In the 1930s the tower was open to the public and contained a sweet shop; it closed at the outbreak of the Second World War and the tower entrance was bricked up. There is a well on the summit enclosed by a stone slab. The inscription above the tower's entrance reads "Look well at me Before you go And See You nothing at me throw". Cairo Mill was also used by the Ferranti Company for many years. This was the scene of another UFO incident some years previously. On 31 August 2010, Breeze Hill School and Counthill School merged to become the Waterhead Academy. The campus was renamed Roxbury Campus until the academy moved to a third location in November 2012. Breeze Hill had intensive playing fields and an Astro-turf pitch, used for various sports both by students from the school and by the local community.

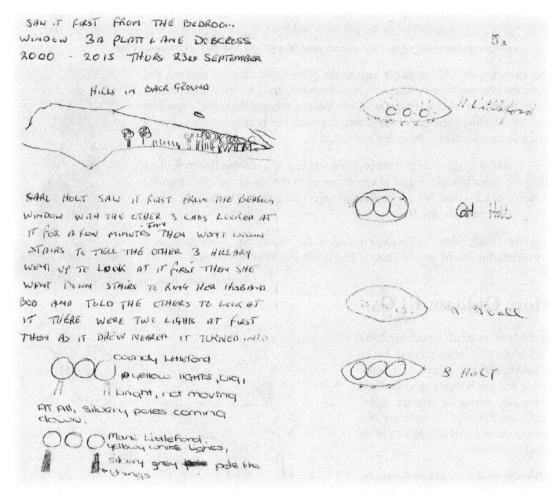

SAW IT FIRST FROM THE BEDROOM WINDOW 3A PLATT LANE DOBCROSS
2000 - 2015 THURS 23RD SEPTEMBER
5.

HILLS IN BACK GROUND

II Littleford

EARL HOLT SAW IT FIRST FROM THE BEDROOM WINDOW WITH THE OTHER 3 LADS LOOKED AT IT FOR A FEW MINUTES THEN WENT DOWN STAIRS TO TELL THE OTHER 3 HILLARY WENT UP TO LOOK AT IT FIRST THEN SHE WENT DOWN STAIRS TO RING HER HUSBAND BOB AND TOLD THE OTHERS TO LOOK AT IT THERE WERE TWO LIGHTS AT FIRST THEN AS IT DREW NEARER IT TURNED INTO

G1 Holt

candy Littleford
B yellow lights, big,
bright, not moving
AT ALL, silvery poles coming down.

II Beall

S Holt

More Littleford,
yellow white lights,
silvery grey pole like things

Mrs Littleford then rang her husband, Bob, who, with their children – Wendy and Marie – came outside and watched the three large, bright yellow '*lights*', in the sky. These were stationary to the left of the television mast, showing what appeared to be '*silver poles of light*', projecting downwards from underneath the objects, before moving slowly away into the distance.

Despite the incident being reported to the local newspaper – 'UFO sighting over Holt's?' local UFO researcher – Dave Bezer – believes there is a possibility that the family may have misidentified the '*lights*' as searchlights of an aircraft, travelling along a regular route near to where the sighting took place, following a light mist that had fallen onto the hills after heavy rain and sunny spells.

UFO over Saddleworth

Another incident involved a youth, aged 15, who was running home from Lydgate Church, down Stockport Road, after pantomime practice, at 9pm on 23rd September 1982. He noticed:

"*. . . a bright yellow/white 'triangle of light', low on the horizon, over the Quick Edge area*",

where Yates Farm and a scrap-yard are located.

Upon his arrival home, the teenager mentioned what he had witnessed to his mother, who then decided to take him back to the Church, as he had forgotten to bring home his script. After reaching the Church, the youth checked, but found no sign of the script and wondered if it might have fallen out of his pocket, so he and his mother set off, retracing the steps taken in the previous journey.

When they arrived at the same place where he had seen the unusual '*light*', his mother drew his attention to a strange '*yellow light*' she could see, heading slowly across the sky, from North to South. Further scrutiny revealed:

Lydgate Church

> "... *a dark, dome-shaped object with huge legs, like scaffolding poles, about 10ft in length, showing a red light on top, clearly illuminated against a backcloth of yellow light."*

At this point the lights, which had been left on in the family car, nearby, went out. Attempts to roll it down the hill to start it failed, as if the battery was completely flat. When they reached Popular Avenue, some yards away, the lights and engine came back on again. **(Source: Dave Bezer)**

Black mass, Oldham

UFO researcher – Dave Bezer, who was to find himself involved in a number of investigations of UFOs seen around the Saddleworth area, decided to pay a visit to Lydgate Church, one night, after having been told of an incident which had occurred at the location, involving a couple from Uppermill.

> "*I left my Mossley home, at 3am, taking my dog – 'Penny', with me. When we reached a point just above the Grange, the dog 'stopped dead' in its tracks and tried to move backwards. Obviously distraught, I looked up the road and noticed a jet black patch lying on top of the road. I shone my torch at it but the light failed to penetrate the black mass, although the beam illuminated the ground around it. I estimated the black mass to be 10ft in height and about 20-30ft in width. I sensed it was evil; I have no idea what this was and why it was there."*

Several days later Dave received a telephone call from somebody, who told him about an accident in which they had been involved. When he checked the location, it matched the same place in the road where he had seen the black mass. Was it sheer coincidence?

UFO over Monmouth

Police Constables – Simon Holder and Timothy Banks – were on patrol, in Monmouth, at 4am on 24th September 1982, when they saw a strange flickering blue and white '*light*' in the sky, pulsing red light.

'ELLO 'ELLO IS THAT A UFO?

PCs Holder and Banks—'scary' encounter.

STRANGE bright lights in the sky spotted by two policemen and an amateur astronomer have started a UFO mystery.

They say they saw a brilliant white object surrounded by red and blue flashing lights.

The constables, Simon Holder, 24, and Tim Banks, 25, said one of the red lights "broke away" and landed.

They were so convinced that their sighting was some sort of spaceship that they made an official report—and have been backed by their chief, Inspector.

Several incidents, all within 11 days of each other, happened in a triangle of South Wales near the Severn estuary, only five miles from a US arms depot.

Shot off

Close encounter one came when printer David Mason and his wife, Angela, spotted the UFO from the bedroom of their home in Cwmbran, Gwent.

David said: "It was about the same size as the Moon. Jets of air came from it. At first it hovered then it shot off at incredible speed."

Six nights later Paul and Beryl Spreadbury were driving to their Ponthir home when they saw what looked like a glowing cottage loaf.

Beryl said it moved slowly at first and then shot off.

Constables Holder and Banks spotted the lights while on a night patrol near Monmouth: PC Holder said:

By GEOFF KING

"One of the red lights moved away from the rest of the object and appeared to land.

"We got out of our van and just stood watching it for half an hour—it was quite scary." A few days later, amateur astronomer Roy Tredree of Whitchurch, near Monmouth, watched the lights through powerful binoculars.

"I honestly believe that this was something from another world," he said.

Now the British UFO Research Association has launched its own investigation.

Director Lionel Berr said: "This case has more credibility than most because the same thing has been reported independently by good witnesses."

Too many UFO calls

TWO Gwent policeman who reported a UFO landing have had so many telephone calls from UFO societies and the media in the United States that they have been told by their senior officers not to give any in-depth interviews.

Their report received world coverage. It appeared in newspapers and particularly in magazines devoted to space subjects.

They received calls from several American broadcasting stations and societies and from some people who said they were UFO buffs, all wanting them to descrive in detail what they saw.

The fact that they were policemen, that they put in an official report and that their sighting was confirmed by independent witnesses, tended for the incident to be regarded as authentic.

Chief Inspector Keith Harris, of Monmouth police, said "We would like to help but we do feel that the policemen's time can be used on more valuable things."

There were two more UFO reports in Gwent at the weekend.

Mrs Marian Mason, of West Rodien, Coed Eva, Cwmbran, told police she saw an object shaped like a flying saucer with a number of lights travelling from Thornhill towards Ty Coch. It then appeared to return and disappeared.

About two hours later Mr John Clarke, of Frome Walk, Bettws, reported to the police that a saucer-shaped object with red, green and blue lights had travelled from east Newport towards Cwmbran.

According to PC Holder:

"Two red lights fell from it to Earth. As they struck the ground there was a flash, followed by a blue light, which rose upwards and vanished at incredible speed. It was quite scary."

After reporting the matter, the officers were engulfed with enquiries from the media and UFO Groups (some as far away as Los Angeles) eager to interview them, as a result of which they were instructed not to give any further interviews.

At 8pm on 24th September 1982, an unusual *'light'* was seen in the sky over Cardiff, in Wales, by Mr R.L. Tredree (58) described as:

". . . showing a red light at each end – bright enough to illuminate the cloud as it headed eastwards, followed by a 'flash of light' as it disappeared from sight".

(Source: *Daily Mirror*, 25.9.82 – 'Close Encounter for two Bobbies' – 'Dawn Landing' – 'Riddle of multi-coloured spaceship'/*Western Daily Press*, 26.10.82 – 'Silence for UFO Pc's.'/*Sunday Mirror*, 3.10.1982, 'Ello', 'Ello' – Is that a UFO?/*South Wales Argus*, 16.10.82 – 'Buzz off plea from UFO spotters/BUFORA)

UFO over Suffolk

Between 7.15pm and 8.30pm on 26th September 1982, villagers living near Stowmarket, in Suffolk, noticed an orange-yellow *'light'* in the sky, that slowly changed colour to cream. This *'light'* changed colour and its intensity before gradually changing direction.

Mr Brian McDonald was one of the witnesses. He contacted the Police, who told him that the MOD would send him a statement form that would be passed to Dept DS8, where it *"would be checked from a security point of view."*

Another witness was Mr Martindale, of Needham Market. He thought the UFO was close to a field near Priestley Wood. **(Source: *East Anglia Daily Times*, 29.9.1982)**

UFOs over Wiltshire

At 8.30am on 27th September 1982, at Bottlesford, in Wiltshire, *"two star like objects, continually changing colour from gold to red"*, were seen moving across the eastern sky, in a series of *'snaking up and over'* movements, by Managing Director – Stephen Smith – who was stood outside his front door, talking to a neighbour. Although the objects were estimated to have been between 1-3 miles away, they caused the dog, next door, to begin howling. **(Source: Brenda Butler)**

This sighting took place near Hastings in East Sussex and was reported to Skysearch by Westfield resident, Mr. Ken Munday. Although the actual year and date cannot be ascertained (it took place sometime between 1982 - 1984) all other details are clearly remembered.

It was the month of September and Mr. Munday who was an insurance agent at the time, was undertaking his usual Wednesday night work visiting clients. On this occasion, he had to visit Hastings resident Mr. Bates. Unfortunately, at the onset of his visit, Mr Munday had accidentally locked his car keys in his car, however he did not realize this until much later. Realizing of Mr. Munday's predicament, Mr. Bates very kindly drove him to his home in Westfield where he collected a spare set of car keys. Then both men started off on the return journey to Mr. Bate's home. Returning along their outgoing route, they travelled on the A28. The time was 10.45 pm and they were approximately half a mile from the area called 'The Harrow' which is situated on the northern outshirts of Hastings. As the car approached a very sharp bend in the road both men were amazed to see a metallic object rising up in the air from the field in front of them.

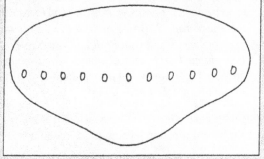

Mr. Munday stated the object that was reminiscent of an old type humming top was about thirty to forty feet in diameter and had orange lights around its girth.

As the men watched the object, it continued to rise, then travelled slowly to the right before accelerating, arching up over the road and around the bend towards the town of Battle.

But when Mr. Munday and Mr. Bates travelled around this bend, no sign of the object could be seen.

Alien Abduction – Sudbury, Suffolk

In late September 1982, Ros Reynolds-Parnham, from Little Clacton, Essex, and her boyfriend, at the time – Philip, decided to visit her relatives, in Corby, Northamptonshire, and were travelling along the A1902, at Sudbury, in Suffolk, near the village of Stoke by Clare.

> *"At 8pm, a horseshoe-shaped group of lights flew very low over the car, as we passed under some power cables. I remember the lights, the silence, and the blue tendrils bouncing off the cables. My first thought was it may have been a 'helicopter', but everything was wrong – its movement, speed, silence, etc. As we drove out through the town, through Long Melford, and headed along the Clare to Haverhill Road, it came back and zipped over the car, two or three times, scaring the pair of us. The 'thing' matched our speed and ran parallel with us, for some time, along the road.*
>
> *From the side it was a big, bright, egg-shaped light, with a faint set of smaller coloured lights rotating around inside. I guess it was between 50 and 100ft away and the whole thing was at least the size of the length of our car, as it negotiated the hedges and telegraph wires. Philip was so scared that he just looked straight ahead. The car suddenly acted as if it had run out of petrol and died, along with the lights. We both had an argument as to who would look under the bonnet, and then got out together – me to keep my eyes on this thing, as it hovered silently over the field. The next thing I knew was that we were both back in the car – the engine now running, and lights on, with the 'thing' still hovering. We basically felt very quiet and subdued, for want of a better explanation, and just drove off as fast as possible. We never spoke the rest of the way, or I do not think we did. We arrived at Corby – not at 10pm, as expected, but 1.30-1.45am!"*

Ros and Philip made their excuses, without even mentioning what had taken place, and returned home. Philip (for some reason only known to him) decided to hand paint the Ford Cortina a different colour, on the same day.

The following day, Ros (completely out of character) suffered a severe nosebleed (she never had one before, or since) a very bad burn mark on her chest, which has scarred, and a 'V'-shaped incision on her back. Her lifestyle, eating habits and personality, was to completely change dramatically, including an avid interest in drawings, writing, and typing, although generally feeling quite ill but fine before the UFO encounter.

> *"I gave up drinking and smoking and developed a craving for sweets. Even stranger, I began to write complex notes on how the Universe was formed, and wrote up the *engine plans of the 'spacecraft'. This was so unlike me. Eventually, we split up. For three years I was afraid to go outside. I split with Philip on very violent terms; he was never a violent person before. I sought medical help over some of the problems, but never mentioned my fears of it being possibly UFO, partly as I didn't admit it to myself, and partly as I was embarrassed and felt I would be laughed at as a fool."*

As a result of contacting a UFO organisation, who came to see her, it was suggested she be hypnotised, to extract further information regarding her encounter.

According to Ros:

> *"As the hypnotist started to put me under, a 'beam of light' appeared in the room. The video*

and audio equipment malfunctioned and spun around. The sceptic, who came to observe, was pinned to the chair with such force as to leave claw marks on his arms and all the clocks in the house stopped. I never got hypnotised, but they did bring in a psychic investigator."

Some of her memory has returned

"I was in a room with a large Perspex type pedestal table in the centre. I remember being led to it. I didn't struggle (don't know why not) and was laid down on the thing. I remember sensing the whole procedure was clinical – like the tagging, weighing and measuring, of a wild animal. The 'Greys' never spoke out aloud, just telepathically, and there was a taller, blond haired person – that's all I remember. I get very emotional if I try and remember more."

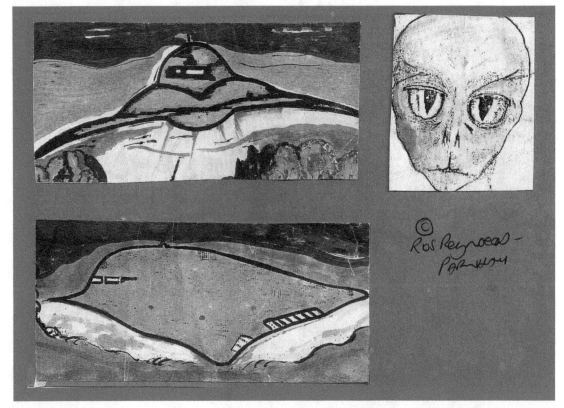

We have to say that we were astonished at the depth of detail shown in the *'engine plans'* of the *'craft'*, powered by a *'Rhubinium crystal'* – a power source unknown to our science, although curiously, Rubidium, discovered in 1861 (being a soft silvery-white element of the alkali group, which ignites spontaneously in the air) was considered for use in ion engines for space flight. **(Source: Personal interview)**

A boomerang-shaped object, fluorescent blue in colour, described as being hundreds of feet long, was seen floating between clouds, for a few minutes, over Sholing, Southampton, on the evening of 29th September 1982, by local resident – Mike Dowling. It then inclined towards the ground and took off, at tremendous speed, heading towards Southampton. Enquiries made with the police, to identify the object, proved unsuccessful. **(Source: *Unnamed Newspaper* – 'Giant Boomerang Appears')**

CLOSEST ENCOUNTER: Ros with an impression of one of the aliens. Right, the spot where she was abducted

By AMANDA WARD

NIGHT had closed in as Ros Reynolds-Parnham and her boyfriend Philip drove along a quiet country road to a relative's house. Then a light caught her eye.

Suddenly, a blazing shape was hovering above them. Terrified, Philip put his foot down — and everything went blank.

Four hours later, Ros came round to find herself back in the car, her head spinning, a gash on her neck throbbing.

Then she remembered. It was an experience too terrifying to believe.

Ros had been abducted and "raped" by aliens.

The ghastly encounter on the A1092 in Sudbury, Suffolk, has taken a terrible toll on Ros — and denied her the chance of motherhood. She says she has not had a period since the incident 14 years ago.

"I'm not a weirdo," says the 35-year-old show dog breeder who still shudders when she looks at the sky. "I'm telling the truth. I'm just so scared that they will come back."

Ros is not alone in her fears — she is one of Britain's 100 "abductees".

Now strange encounters and weird happenings are the basis of the new six-part BBC2 series *Secrets Of The Paranormal.*

Ros, of Essex, says: "After the abduction, I can remember being on a perspex pedestal in this pinky-grey oval room. I can't remember any doors. There was a bright light above

it. I just felt terror. I couldn't move, scream or faint. It was as if I was an onlooker. There were grey figures all around me.

"They had very large heads and big black eyes. They didn't have a nose, had a slit for a mouth, no ears and they were about 3ft 6ins. They smelled like rotten eggs. They had long, spidery hands with four fingers.

"These aliens were very cold, calculating and they did some experiments. I know they did something because of the scars at the top of my legs. I felt raped, abused, dirty. They were saying something about 'juice'."

Ros and experts believe her abductors were interested in finding out about the human reproductive system.

She says: "I don't know what they did to me but I haven't had a period since."

Ros's hand reaches up to touch the small white scar on her neck — the result, she says, of the four-hour examination. The incident occurred in

September 1982. Ros says: "Philip and I were driving to see his relatives when this horse-shoe shaped object, about the size of a helicopter, swooped down.

"It had multicoloured lights blazing underneath. At first I thought it might have been reflection of my glasses. It was really bright but there was no sound.

"We were terrified and Philip accelerated. Then the car died. I thought Philip was joking. I was in a blind panic and neither of us wanted to get out. I remember saying that I would count to three and we'd get out together."

THE next thing Ros knew was that she was back in the car, with the engine running.

"I felt a bit dopey but I just wanted to get out of there. We didn't say a word as we drove to our destination."

When the couple arrived it was 2am. They should have been there at 10pm. Ros says: "I woke up with a mark on my back and like a burn mark on

my neck. It kept itching." But there was something far more unsettling to come. "I began to 'sleep-write'. I'd get up in the night and draw things in dots. I looked at the first one and it was a pair of large eyes. Then I'd write strange formulas or type odd letters. I couldn't remember doing it."

Her symptoms got worse: "I got terrible headaches, as if someone was sticking a red-hot needle into my head. I'd also hear a noise at the same time, like a fax going off. I was backwards and forward to the doctor's but the only he gave me pills. I didn't take them. I didn't want to be drugged up."

The strain became too much and Ros and Philip split. She spiralled into despair.

She says: "Even now, I don't go to bed before 3am. I'm scared I'll start writing."

Last year the Ministry of Defence recorded 373 sightings of "aerial activity not immediately identifiable to the observer". That's compared to the 1994 figure of 350.

Philip Mantle of the British UFO Research Association (BUFORA) says: "Some abductees report seeing hieroglyphic type writing, or grey figures who smell like rotten eggs.

"More females are reporting this type of incident. Others report removal of sperm or ovum — perhaps for interbreeding. There are still many questions but this is one of the most convincing cases I've heard."

Ros shivers and says: "I ask myself why me? I know one thing — I won't go back to that road again."

● *FOR more information, call BUFORA on 01924 444049.*

Brits' close encounters

IF YOU find Ros's account difficult to believe, think again. There have been 100 recorded abductees in Britain in the past 50 years, says Philip Mantle of UFO researchers BUFORA.

Calls are coming into the 1,000-member association at a rate of one month.

Mr Mantle, who has also talked to countless abductees for his book *Without Consent*, believes alien kidnapping does happen.

He says: "It can happen to anyone, regardless of sex or where they live. We don't know why it happens, or why the people are chosen.

"But some of their accounts would really make your hair stand on end."

The night that Ros came face to face with a creature ● from the unknown

64/93

■ Eerie : How Ros pictured one of the aliens

■ Eerie : How Ros pictured one of the aliens

BY SHARON ASPLIN

ROS IS a normal woman — certainly not the sort to indulge in fantasies about little men from Mars or flying saucers.

But one evening she claims she was taken by force into an unidentified flying object and subjected to a terrifying examination by alien beings.

It was a difficult decision for Ros Reynolds-Parnham, 32, of Little Clacton, to speak publicly about her experiences. But she wants to reassure others who have undergone a similar ordeal and not leave them to go through the months of fear and doubt alone as she did.

Ros has now opened up to millions after appearing on the GMTV breakfast show and is eager for people to realise the seriousness behind her message.

Ten years ago Ros and her boyfriend of the time were travelling to see relatives. As they approached Sudbury Ros said she spotted a horse-shoe of bright lights in the sky, which noiselessly lowered over the car.

When they came to open countryside the lights returned two or three times and "locked" on to their vehicle. The car then went dead.

"We went out to discover what was wrong," she said. "As we had stopped so had the big light. It was very bright but it did not hurt your eyes – it is very difficult to describe."

Ros, who discovered only years later that she went inside the UFO, could not remember anything else. "All I know is we got on with our journey and when we got there we were three hours later than we should have been."

She had always been sceptical about UFOs but this started her thinking. She is now convinced things she had previously

ABDUCTED BY A UFO AN ESSEX WOMAN NEVER THOUGHT SHE WOULD HAVE THE CONFIDENCE OR COURAGE TO SPEAK ABOUT HER EXTRA-TERRESTRIAL ENCOUNTER . . . *UNTIL NOW*

seen and passed off as aeroplanes in the sky were probably alien craft. Three weeks later she had an urge to type and draw. In her sleep she drew maps of engine rooms and diagrams of how the earth was formed, and made notes about disasters and the truth behind great world mysteries, the future and how the earth was formed – all things she knew nothing about.

Ros says she has scars and other physical signs of her ordeal. She cannot have children because since that autumn night she has never had a monthly cycle.

"I got through being worried, I could not talk to anybody about it because I thought they would think I was a freak," she said. "I just bottled it up, I became a recluse for a while worrying about what had happened."

Eventually she managed to pull her life together again and then a few years ago saw an article in a local newspaper about an East Anglian UFO investigation team.

They arranged a hypnosis session at her Plough Corner home. It was a failure. "The video recording was wiped out, everything went wrong," she explained. "A bright beam of light came into the room and all the clocks stopped."

Through a mutual friend, she then got in touch with Mark Reynolds-Parnham. Mark claims he was born psychic and he uses his abilities to investigate cases like Ros. It was during the investigation the two fell in love and married.

Details of her experiences were pieced together in a second hypnosis session. Mark said his wife described four or five small aliens, around 3ft 6in to 4ft tall, who approached her and forced her to the craft.

Under hypnosis Mark realised Ros had been taken to an examination room and had become very agitated as the aliens undressed her and laid her on a table as they tried to study her.

What had happened, continued Mark, was a typical UFO abduction scenario, which had taken place with many people on this planet for many, many years.

Ros admits she is still frightened by what happened and is obviously embarrassed by what she revealed, as she had to leave the room while her husband talked about it.

Most people have been quite open-minded and compassionate about their claims, the couple said, and so far no-one has denounced them as crazy. "Some are very interested because they believe it and some are interested because they want to be convinced," said Mark.

"But we have never had anyone come up to us and say we are lying."

■ Anyone who wants help or perhaps something unusual explained should contact the Bufora office, a professional investigation and counselling service, on (0582) 763218.

I was ABDUCTED by six small aliens

Happy ending – Ros and Mark were abducted by aliens

UFO over RAF Alconbury

David Hall – a science teacher, living in Kent – contacted us in 2005, wishing to bring our attention to an incident that had taken place in 1982, involving the sighting of a gigantic UFO, while living in Godmanchester, Cambridgeshire.

> *"I was aged 18, at the time, and on my way home, one evening, at about 8.30pm, during the autumn of 1982, as it was dark. As I drove past RAF Alconbury, I noticed, from the warning signs placed outside the airbase, that security was high and that there was some sort of alert going on, with increased activity occurring inside the base itself.*
>
> *After seeing a police car travelling the other way, I tried, unsuccessfully, to tune the car radio into the police frequency, hoping to find out what was going on, at which stage I noticed a 'light' in the sky that I took to be a helicopter, at first, but as I approached an iron bridge I realised, from its shape, that this was no helicopter. I slammed on the brakes and got out of the car and looked up, astonished by the sight of a 'T'-shaped gigantic flying 'craft', rusty-brown in colour, with an exterior surface covered in huge panels. I watched as this 'craft' began to travel away, not point first, as one would have expected, but in a peculiar fluid motion, with complete disregard for what I perceived as the law of aerodynamics. I tried to follow it but had to give up because, although the object was travelling on a straight trajectory, I had to negotiate the twists and turns of the country roads."*

The reader will hear of other reports from around this location, one of them involved a local schoolgirl who had to obtain medical treatment for problems to her eyes following the passage of the object as it went over. Her courage for reporting the matter to the authorities was to lead to so much ridicule she ended up changing schools. The trauma of that event is still with her today.

On 30th September 1982, four separate UFO sightings were reported to the authorities, during a one hour period. They included two white flashing objects, seen over Pontypool, a blue and white flashing '*light*', at Pontnewydd, a bright blue '*light*', at Cwmbran, and a narrow green '*band of light*', over Pontypool.

UFOs over Gwent

Local Government Officer – Gloria Gauntlett, and her sister, Joanne, were talking to Mrs C. Davies, outside her house in Pontypool, Gwent, at 9.30pm on 30th September 1982.

> *"We noticed an unusual green light – like a searchlight, stationary in the clear sky above us, the brightness moving from one end to the other. About a minute later, the object vanished from sight."*

(Source: BUFORA/Lionel Beer)

405

GROUP /INVEST REF:	BUFORA REF.	YEAR	NUMBER	INVESTIGATOR	CASE SUMMARY	
					DATE	
				EVALUATOR	TIME	
					LOCATION	
RETURN FORM TO:-					EVAL'N	
					UFO CLASS	
					CLOSED	

UFO SIGHTING ACCOUNT FORM

SECTION A

Please write an account of your sighting, make a drawing of what you saw and then answer the questions in section B overleaf as fully as possible. Write in **BLOCK CAPITALS** using a ball point pen.

After leaving my friends house at 47 Golf Rd we stood for a short while talking on the drive, and on looking up at the sky I noticed an unusual green light, something like a fluorescent light or searchlight beam. After watching it for a short while it appeared to be moving, but on further observation I noticed that it was not moving only appeared to be, because the brightness moved from one end of the object to the other. As we stood looking at it, the object just disappeared as if it had been switched off. The sky at the time was quite clear with only a few scattered clouds.

Please continue on a separate sheet if necessary.

DRAWING*

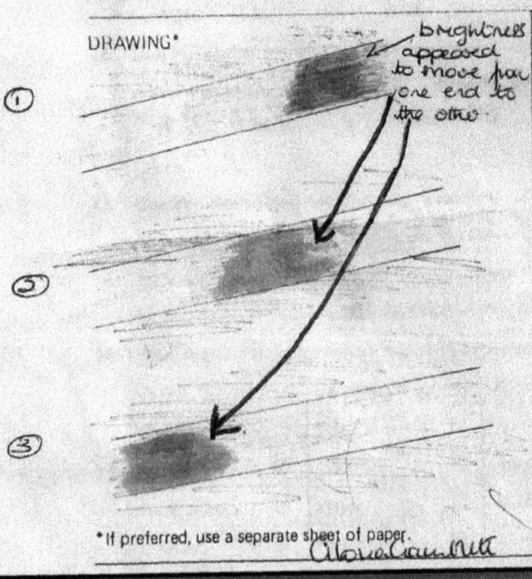

① brightness appeared to move far one end to the other

②

③

* If preferred, use a separate sheet of paper.

Your full name (Mr/Mrs/Miss/Ms) GLORIA GAUNLETT Age 39

Address HILLCREST

NEW INN PONTYPOOL GWENT.

Telephone No. P'pool (STD)

Occupation during last two years LOCAL GOVERNMENT OFFICER.

Any professional, technical or academic qualifications or special interests

Do you object to the publication of your name?
YES NO *Delete as applicable.

Today's Date 13.10.82

Signature Gloria Gaunlett

OCTOBER 1982

PORTSMOUTH WOMAN SIGHTS SATURN-SHAPED UFO

Also includes – UFOs seen over Gwent • 'Figure of Eight' UFO seen over Hyde, Cheshire, by a woman and her husband

UFO over Portsmouth

AT 3.15am on 8th October 1982, Mrs B Clasby, living in Compton Road, Portsmouth, was awoken by a throbbing electrical noise, accompanied by green wavy lines of light that illuminated the bedroom. Alarmed, she made her way to her mother's room but found her fast asleep. Looking through the window, she was staggered to see a large, glowing green coloured 'disc', with a dark Saturn ring around it, covered in tiny flashing lights, set geometrically in what looked like grid pattern, rather than random. **(Source: Ian Clasby)**

More UFOs are spotted

WESTERN MAIL, SATURDAY, OCTOBER 2, 19

THREE further sightings of unidentified flying objects in Gwent have been reported to the police — bringing the total to six in just over a week.

The new claims came on Thursday night in separate incidents in the New Inn, Pontypool and Griffithstown areas of the county, from "quite sensible and sane people," said a police spokesman.

The first report came from Mr Stuart Blake, who said he had watched white flashing discs in the sky with the naked eye and binoculars for 35 minutes from a friend's house in St Augustine Road, Griffithstown. This was at about 8.30pm.

Within an hour Mrs Doreen Phillips, of Gower Green, Croeyceiliog, saw a bright blue light in the sky which was said to be static and shimmering.

The final sighting came from Golf Road, New Inn, where Mrs Mary Gauntlett, her daughter and a friend watched a narrow green band of light moving across the sky.

Two policemen at Monmouth reported sightings last week. They said their UFO appeared to have landed at one stage.

'Oval shape with flames'

Snapped, mystery object over city

WHAT is it? A fireball, a UFO or what?

Loughor photographer Mr. John Ferris hasn't a clue. But he does know it's a shot in a lifetime.

He managed to photograph the mystery object — "It was an oval shape about the size of a small house with what looked like flames shooting out from the top" — as it fired over the Townhill area of Swansea at 3 p.m. last Wednesday.

He was sipping a cup of coffee in a city store restaurant when a woman pointed up to the sky and drew his attention to the object.

"I grabbed my camera and ___ed off the last shot on the film with my zoom lens. I didn't think anything would come out. It was a very overcast and dull day and whatever this thing was it was very bright," he said.

Overcast

"I'm mystified. I don't know what it is, but I know it is a shot in a lifetime. Someone else must have seen it."

Mr. Ferris was using 35 millimetre black and white film with his Pentax ME Super camera with 210 millimetre zoom lens. His photograph has been enlarged 170 times to show Pantycelyn Road, Townhill, with the object just behind it.

Swansea police said they have had no reports of any UFO sightings, but Gower weatherman Mr. John Powell said conditions were right for a ball of lightning.

"It was a stormy day and if ever you were going to see a ball of lightning or a fireball that was the day for it. The description seems to fit, but not having seen it myself I could not be sure," he added.

Mr. Ferris, of Heol Maes y Cerrig, Loughor, said: "I honestly don't know what it is. I've never seen a fireball or balled lightning so I can't say whether it was that or possibly a UFO."

● MR. JOHN FERRIS ... "It was oval, about the size of a small house."

UFOs over Newport, Gwent

On 14th October 1982, British Transport Police Officer — Peter Griffiths, was patrolling the car compound at the docks, on Thursday night, when he saw two bright, pulsating lights; one in the North, the other to the South. After watching them for a few minutes, he saw the one in the South change to red and green — then to a red glow, move towards the other 'light', and disappear into a bank of cloud.

(Source: *Western Daily Mail* – 'Car Patrol Officer sees UFO')

Mystery Light over Ipswich

A curious '*ball of white light*' was seen motionless in the night sky on 18th October 1982, towards the north-west direction of Ipswich, by a meteorologist who asked his name be kept confidential. The object then ejected a puff of smoke and changed to a '*red ball*' that was seen to move away towards the north-east. A spokesman for RAF Honnington was contacted. He confirmed that they had no aircraft in the area, but that it *"might have been a plane, lighting its re-heater, which allows for faster flying."*

(Source: *East Anglia Daily Times,* **19.10.1982)**

UFO OVER THE BRIDGE

Returning from Pembroke Fair on Saturday night two Pembroke Dock teenagers saw what they believe was an unidentified Flying Object above the Cleddau Bridge.

Michela Rigden (16), Lamados, Milton Terrace, and Lloyd Johnson (17), 25, Commercial Row, were walking along Milton Terrace at about 11.30 p.m. when they noticed a bright orange light in the sky above the Cleddau Bridge. At first they thought it was a very bright orange street light, but realising it was too high above the bridge, Michela ran to her home to fetch her sister Tracey.

When they returned the light had changed to a bright white colour. It disappeared behind a cloud but kept re-appearing for about five minutes, during which time a crowd of about nine stood at the top of Sloggett's Hill watching.

Michela, pupil at Pembroke School, accepts that people may be sceptical of the sightings. "I didn't believe in UFOs before, but I do now," she said. "It wasn't a helicopter. I've seen helicopters at night before!"

She admits to being a little frightened now but she says she wasn't frightened at the time. Although she hasn't read any books on the subject she intends to do so now and has bought a book on the subject.

This sighting is the latest of a series in recent years in Pembrokeshire.

Further sightings over Gwent

During the evening of 23rd October 1982, further UFOs were sighted over the Gwent area, at Bettws, Newport. John Clarke sighted something very unusual in the sky.

"I first thought it was an airplane, at around 10,000ft, but knew this wasn't the case, having been trained in aircraft recognition while in the army. I then saw a huge saucer-shaped object, perhaps 200ft in width, showing a blue flashing light and a still green light on the top of the object. I shouted for my wife, Rosemary, to come and have a look. It was in sight for 15secs, until lost from view as it headed away, towards Cwmbran."

A few minutes later, Mrs Marion Gladys Mason of West Roedin, Coed Eva, was driving home along Henllys Way, near St. Dials Junior School, when she sighted:

". . . a long oblong shape in the sky, roughly the size of a railway carriage, showing two small white lights at each end, with a small red light on the bottom", moving over the sky, at an estimated speed of 40mph."

Mrs Mason rushed home and watched the object through binoculars, before it disappeared over Cwmbran.

(Source: *Western Daily Mail*, 16.10.82/*South Wales Argus* – 'Flying saucer among Gwent UFO sightings')

'Figure of 8' UFO over Hyde, Cheshire

Mrs J. Shirovay, of Hyde, Cheshire, was awoken at 4.30am on 28th October 1982, and went to the window to look out.

"I saw a strange oval-shaped object in the sky over the centre of Hyde, with very bright hazy light at the edges, showing glints of red and blue as it moved up and down, and then swung from side to side. It also made a number of 'figure of eight' movements.

I woke my husband, who was astounded by its appearance. Actually, this was the second time I saw it. The first was on 17th October 1982, between 6.00am and 6.30am. Oddly, when an aircraft passed underneath it, the object stopped moving."

South Wales Argus 25.10.82

'Flying saucer' among Gwent UFO sightings

A RARE dry and clear Saturday night resulted in two Unidentified Flying Objects being reported to Newport police.

A flying saucer, 200 feet in diameter, was apparently spotted over Bettws, Newport, at 10.34pm by a trained ex-military observer. And about ten minutes later, a long "railway carriage" shape was reported over Cwmbran.

Mr John Clarke, a quality control inspector, of Frome Walk, Bettws, told the Argus he was putting on the kettle in his kitchen when he spotted the saucer outside his window.

"I first thought it was an aeroplane at around 10,000 feet, but I was trained in plane recognition while in the army and it wasn't anything I ever saw then. It was the fact that it was completely silent that got me," said Mr Clarke. "I looked out again and realised it was a huge saucer-shaped object, perhaps 200 feet across, with a blue flashing light and a green light not blinking at all on the top.

"It was in my sight for about 15 seconds and then it vanished over the house. I called my wife and then we both saw it heading away towards Cwmbran."

Mrs Rosemary Clarke, a factory worker, said: "It was the astonishing size which impressed me. That, and the lack of any engine noise. I didn't used to believe in such things, but it would be incredible arrogance to believe that we are alone in this universe.

"We are honest, hardworking people who had just spent an evening watching television. We never drink. I'll talk about it with people at work and see what they think," said Mrs Clarke.

Unknown to the Bettws family, a matter of minutes later Mrs Marion Gladys Mason, of West Roedin, Coed Eva, Cwmbran, was driving home along Henllys Way near St Dials Junior School.

She told police it was then she had her first sighting of a long oblong shape in the sky, roughly the size of a railway carriage. It had two small white steady lights on each end and one small red light at the bottom.

The UFO was still in her sight when she got home. She rushed upstairs and got her binoculars. She was able to estimate its travelling speed at around forty mph, before it turned over Cwmbran and disappeared.

Yesterday a Ministry of Defence spokesman in London said they would receive the Gwent police reports as a matter of course, and if they could not find a conventional explanation of the sightings they would interview the Clarkes and Mrs Mason.

Strange Encounters

NAME ...J Shirovay............................... Mr/Mrs/Miss/Ms

ADDRESS ...13 Bramall Street Hyde Cheshire.........

....

.... TEL: ....

AGE GROUP: 18 - 25, 26 - 39, 40 - 55, 56 - 70, 70+, AGE IF UNDER 18 ......

QUALIFICATIONS (Where relevant) ....

DATE OF ENCOUNTER ...28th of October 1982.........

TIME OBJECT/ENTITY <u>FIRST</u> SEEN ...0430.........

PRECISE LOCATION OF WITNESS ...Bedroom of house.......

...situated in Bramall st in Hyde.......................

....

....

<u>ACCOUNT OF EXPERIENCE</u>

O the morning of the 28th of October 1982, at 0430 on that morning I was awakened by somethin I don't know what. When through the bedroom window I saw a strange oval shaped object in the sky over the centre of Hyde, it was a very bright light hazy at the edges which showed glints of red and blue as it moved. IT was moving in a very unusual manner it went up and down then swung from side to side like a pendulam it also did several figure eight movements the object was in view for about ½ hr I woke up my husband who witnessed the light also it is not the first time that I have seen it I also saw the same object or something like it on the morning of the 17th of October between the hours of 0600 and 0630 the object went through exactly the same movements as described above. the first time it appeared to come from the direction of Ashton and the second time from the Mottram area the object when doing these strange movements stopped still when a aircraft flew under the light in the sky

I AGREE THE ABOVE ACCOUNT IS ACCURATE.

MY NAME MAY/MAY NOT BE PUBLISHED.

Signature ....

Date ....

W   WEATHER CONDITIONS

Cloud	Moon/Stars	Precipitation	
0	Yes/No	———	0.003
1/3	Yes/No	Rain/Hail/Snow	0.004
2/3	Yes/No	Rain/Hail/Snow	0.006
O/Cast	———	Rain/Hail/Snow	0.009

WITNESS DRAWING OF OBJECT/ENTITY

NOVEMBER 1982

'FLYING SAUCER' SEEN BY PILOT OVER PORTUGAL

Also includes – Motorist sights strange being • Kite-shaped UFO seen by schoolboy, over Cheshire • Employees at a factory, near Swinton, South Yorkshire, sight two UFOs moving across the sky • Strange 'light' seen over Dagenham

UFO over Portgual

SOMETIME between 10.50am and 11.50am on 2nd November 1982, Airline Captain Júlio Miguel Guerra – a flight instructor for the Portuguese Air Force, in 1982 – was flying a Chipmunk trainer in the region between Torres Vedras and the Serra de Montejunto mountain range, situated north-west of Lisbon. It was a clear sky, with unlimited visibility.

"The aircraft was at a height of around 1500-1600metres over Maxial, when a shining object was seen very close to the ground. It suddenly changed behaviour, as though realising my presence; ten seconds later is shot up to the same height of the aircraft, which would indicate a speed of 504km.p.h. It then commenced to fly around the plane in great sweeps and I was obliged to perform a series of tight curves so as to keep track of it. It came close enough for me to see that it resembled a ball of mercury. At various times the object had been very close to me and I was able to verify that it was round, with two halves, shaped like two tight-fitting skullcaps. I carefully looked at the lower one, which seemed to be somewhere between red and brown, with a hole or dark spot in the centre. The centre band looked like it had some kind of a grid, and possibly a few lights, but it was hard to tell since the sun was so bright and was reflected. It flew at a fantastic speed in a large elliptical orbit to the left, between 5,000ft to the South and approximately 10,000ft to the North, always from left to right, repeating this route over and over. I tried to keep it in sight."

Captain Júlio Miguel Guerra

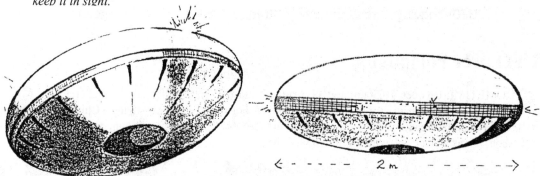

The object circled his small airplane for 15 minutes, while he was alone in the sky in his DHC-1 Chipmunk. He made this drawing the day after the encounter and submitted it, with his report, to the Portuguese Air Force. He was not the only witness, after reporting to his base what was happening (and receiving the expected badinage of comments, involving the sighting of footballs and the worse for drink). Two other Air Force pilots – Carlos Garcês and António Gomes – made their way to the location, and watched the object repeat its elliptical course, passing between the two planes on each return, for about 10mins. They estimated the size, given its proximity to the two aircraft of being about 8-10ft. Finally the object shot off across the sky, heading south-west, in the direction of the Serra de Cintra Range, before vanishing from sight. After landing, all three pilots filed detailed, independent written reports with the Air Force.

General José Lemos Ferreira – the Portuguese Air Force Chief of Staff, at the time – authorised the release of all the records to a team of scientists and experts, who conducted a lengthy scientific investigation. The group estimated that the unidentified object was flying at over 300mph vertically, and its velocity, when it circled Guerra's aircraft, was about 1,550mph. Since leaving the Air Force in 1990, after 18 years of service, Júlio Guerra has been a Captain with Portugália Airlines (TAP) – Portugal's largest commercial airline. He has 17,000 hours of flight experience, and in 2009, he received an aeronautic Science Degree from the Lusofona University of Oporto. (Courtesy Júlio Guerra).

(Source: CNIFO (UFO Investigation Group Lisbon) Case Report/*FSR* Volume 32 No 5 1987 'Close sighting by Portuguese Air Force Pilots' (November 1982) Jose Sottomayor and Antonio Rodrigues)

Close encounter with entity

We spoke to Mrs Dorothy Day about what she and her husband saw, while returning home along the A12, near Felixstowe, in Suffolk, during one late evening in November 1982.

"My husband was driving when we both noticed what we first thought was a man out with his dog, at the side of the road. As we approached closer, my husband shouted, 'What the hell is that?' I looked and saw a 'person', dressed in a silver suit, stood at the side of the road, with his arms hanging down by his sides, the fingers pointing to the ground. What really frightened us was the complete lack of any facial features. I locked the door of the car as we drove past.

My husband debated about going back to have another look, but I refused. We drove to the sanctuary of a telephone box and contacted a friend of my husband. He came out and the two of them went back to have a look, but there was no sign of what we had seen."

(Source: Personal interview)

Kite-shaped UFO

In November 1982, 11-year-old Damien Hulme from Stockport, Cheshire, was on his way home, after playing a video game, when he saw:

". . . a kite-shaped object, with blue and white beams – an orange light in the centre, and a number of flashing smaller lights surrounding the outside – hovering approximately 100ft above trees, near Hazel Grove."

Terrified, the schoolboy ran home.   **(Source: *Stockport Times*, 4.7.86)**

UFO over Mexborough

Over the years, we have had the pleasure of talking to Stephen and Kevin Pratt with regard to the 'Triple UFO photograph' taken by Stephen, in 1966. (Full details of the sighting can be found in Volume 3 of *Haunted Skies*, 1966-1967). Although some people have alleged this photograph was faked, we do not believe this to be the case despite claims to the contrary by some researchers, who have refused to enter into any dialogue with the brothers, but continue to insist that they are faked. Unfortunately, most people have forgotten that the circumstances of this photograph being taken were accompanied by the eye-witness accounts of both parents and other members of the family.

Stephen, who has kept in regular touch with us, over the years, was to tell of another sighting which took place on the 24th November 1982, while working night duty at the Stelrad factory, Swinton, near Mexborough, South Yorkshire.

> *"At about 6.30am, one of the workmen shouted for me to come and have a look outside. When I got there I saw two 'globes of light', like two full moons, with a third smaller, flickering red one above, moving through the sky, heading towards the town. Although the Sheffield Star covered the sighting, I kept quiet – not wishing to attract further ridicule towards myself and family."*

1982

NIGHT SHIFT WORKERS WITNESS UFOs OVER
STELRAD RADIATOR FACTORY / SWINTON - MEXBOROUGH
SOUTH YORKSHIRE. DATE 24TH NOV 1982 - TIME 6:30 AM
APPROX 50 FT ABOVE RAWMS LANE TRAVELLING MAGNETIC
NORTH OVER MEXBOROUGH

DESCRIPTION: LIKE TWO FULL MOONS IN THE BLACK SKY
BEING FOLLOWED IN THE DISTANCE BY A RED FAST
FLICKERING LIGHT

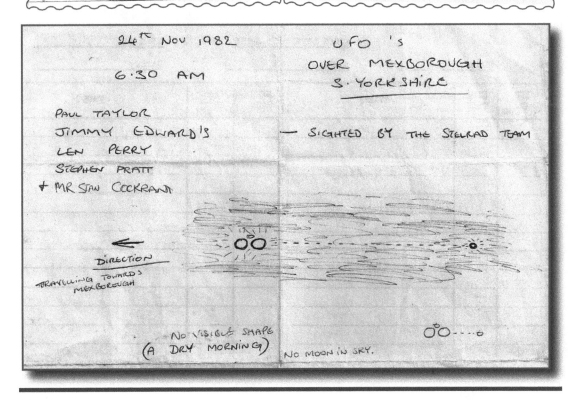

NO VISIBLE SHAPE OF A CRAFT BUT ESTIMATED ABOUT THE SIZE
OF A CAR. NOTE: THERE WAS NO MOON THAT NIGHT AND DRY
WITNESSES WERE: MR PAUL TAYLOR - PRESS LINE
MR LEONARD PERRY - PRESS LINE, MR JIMMY EDWARDS - PRESS LINE
MR STANLEY COCKRAM - LABOURER and many other
workers not wanting to be named.
REPORT WENT TO UFO INVESTIGATOR : WALT REID 'BUFORA'
                                        17 LANSHAW TERRACE
                                        BELLEISE LEEDS
                                        LS10 3NX

* 1998: Note Phil Mantel Bufora : House TOWER VIDEO, LEEDS, YORK
FILMED FEB 1998 SHOWS THE SAME TWO FULL MOON LIKE
OBJECTS — THE SAME LIGHTS AS SEEN BY FACTORY &
          SWINTON / MEXBOROUGH, S YORKS IN 1982.

1982 → /   1982
                DARK SKIES

NIGHT SHIFT WORKERS WITNESS
UFOs OVER STELRAD RADIATOR FACTORY
SWINTON / MEXBOROUGH, SOUTH YORKSHIRE.
DATE 24TH NOV 1982
TIME 6:30 AM
APPROXIMATELY 50 FEET ABOVE RAWMS LANE
TRAVELLING MAGNETIC NORTH OVER MEXBOROUGH

DESCRIPTION LIKE TWO FULL MOONS IN THE BLACK SKY
BEING FOLLOWED IN THE DISTANCE BY A RED FAST FLICKERING RED LIGHT

NO VISIBLE SHAPE OF A CRAFT BUT ESTIMATED ABOUT THE SIZE OF A CAR
NOTE - : THERE WAS NO MOON THAT NIGHT. AND DRY

THE WITNESSES WERE:
        MR PAUL TAYLOR   - PRESS LINE
        MR LEONARD PERRY   - PRESS LINE
        MR JIMMY EDWARDS   - PRESS LINE
        MR STANLEY COCKRAM   - LABOURER
                and many other workers - not wanting to be named

THE REPORT WENT TO UFO INVESTIGATOR   WALT REID - (BUFORA)
                                        17 LANSHAW TERRACE
                                        BELLEISE
                                        LEEDS
                                        LS10 3NX.

24th NOV 1982   UFO's
                           OVER MEXBOROUGH
6.30 AM   S. YORKSHIRE

PAUL TAYLOR
JIMMY EDWARD'S   — SIGHTED BY THE STELRAD TEAM
LEN PERRY
STEPHEN PRATT
+ MR STAN COCKRAM

← DIRECTION
TRAVELLING TOWARDS
MEXBOROUGH

NO VISIBLE SHAPE
(A DRY MORNING)   NO MOON IN SKY.

Strange 'light' over Dagenham, Essex

At 6.20pm on 25th November 1982, George Shadrake (50) of Ilchester Road – a metal worker by trade – was on the corner of Gale Street and Porters Avenue, when he noticed a strange 'light' in the sky above the houses, towards the north-east direction. This was completely separate from the moon, which was overhead. He stopped a woman passing by, and asked her to look at the object; she ignored him and continued on her journey.

(Source: Dan Goring)

DECEMBER 1982

FLARE-LIKE OBJECT SEEN IN SKY OVER AVELEY

Also includes – Bell-shaped UFO seen over Oldham, Lancashire
Triangular UFO seen over Nottingham

Flare-like object over Aveley

POSTMAN John Saville was heading along the B1335, westwards, north of Aveley, at 11am on 14th December 1982, when he sighted a pink, flare-like, object in the sky across open fields to his left.

> *"The 'flare' was trailing black smoke as it came towards me. About 40secs later, it vanished from view."*

Enquiries were later made by Dan Goring with the firing range officer, at Purfleet, some one-and-a-half miles from the scene of the sighting. He stated that the flares they used, fired from a Very pistol, only had a range of about 200 yards. The larger flares had a range of 1,000 yards. He confirmed, on that day, no flares had been fired.

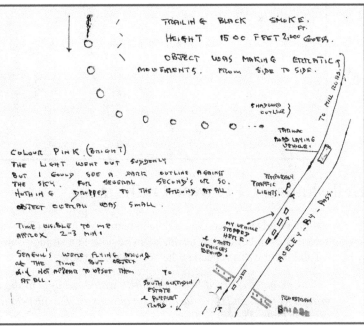

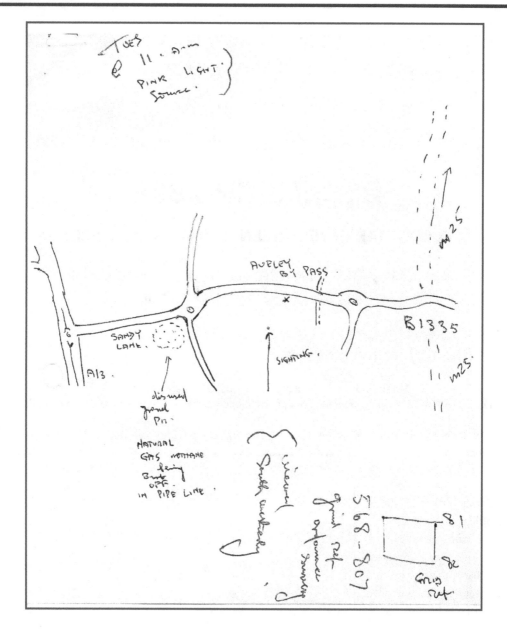

Bell-shaped UFO over Oldham

At 2.45am on 17th December 1982, Oldham man – Mr Avison (70) was finding it difficult to sleep, after having returned from holiday, in Spain, when he noticed a strange object in the sky through the bedroom window. Thinking it was a reflection, he opened the window.

> *"I saw an object shaped like a hand bell, with a red light at the top, orange coloured lights around its base, and two blue lights set into the middle, just stationary in the sky. Five or six seconds later, it vanished from view."*

The incident was brought to the attention of Dave Bezer, a few months later, by Mr. Avison, who described the sky as having a few clouds in it, following a wintry shower, and the object being over the direction of Oldham Boundary Park Hospital. Dave, once again, carried out a meticulous investigation into the matter. However, he was unable to identify what the object was.

Triangular UFO over Nottinghamshire

In December 1982, Mrs Anne Marsh was on her way to work, at Edwinstowe Leisure Centre, Nottinghamshire, when she noticed:

". . . a large, jet black, triangular object, with an orange light in each corner, motionless in the night sky. I carried on to work and pointed out the object in the sky to many people at the Centre. A short time later, it moved slowly away – towards the direction of Sherwood Forest."

(Source: Personal interview)

UFO TIMES

Number 2   July 1989

PROJECT PENNINE   -   POLICE VIDEO UFOS OVER M1?

PLUS - SHUTTLE ENCOUNTER - SKYWATCHER - NEWS, VIEWS AND REVIEWS

1983

Danish fishermen defy the British government's prohibition on non-UK boats entering its coastal waters. In the same month armed police shoot an innocent car passenger, in London, believing him to be an escaped prisoner.

First British breakfast time television programme, *Breakfast Time*, broadcast by the BBC. The wearing of seatbelts becomes compulsory in the front of passenger cars.

Red rain falls in the UK, caused by sand from the Sahara Desert in the droplets. The compact disc (CD) goes on sale.

The biggest cash haul in British history sees gunmen escape with £7 million from a Security Express van in London.

Margaret Thatcher, Conservative Prime Minister of the United Kingdom since 1979, wins a landslide victory with a majority of 144 seats

JANUARY 1983

UFO CRASH LANDING IN WALES, DEBRIS RECOVERED – MINISTRY OF DEFENCE DENIES THE INCIDENT

Also includes – Mysterious trench appears in Reading road • Two Plymouth women chase UFO, seen over naval airbase • Orange ball of light seen over Bradford Triangular UFO sighted over Swansea, seen by police and public

Mystery trench discovered, Berkshire

SOMETHING strange took place, during the night of 15th/16th January 1983, when people living in Milestone Avenue, Charvil, Berkshire, discovered a mysterious trench, which appeared overnight, cut into their access road.

One resident, Mr Halliday of Thames Drive, said:

> *"I couldn't believe it. The hole cut off Milestone Avenue, which is our only access road. It was like an elephant trap. Whoever did it took up five feet of tarmac and then dug a trench more than a foot deep; it has lovely neat edges."*

Local Berkshire County Council surveyor – Mr Qusklay – attended the scene and denied that this was anything to do with the Council and that if it had been, they wouldn't have dug up the road during the night, as it would have awoken the local residents.

We emailed Reading Library and asked them if they were willing to check the local newspaper for any further information on or about that date. When they advised us of the costs incurred for doing this, we had to decline.

(**Source:** *Reading Evening Post*, **19.1.1983**)

UFO over Plymouth

A trapezoid-shaped object, estimated to be 100ft across and 200ft deep, was sighted over Crownhill, Plymouth, in January 1983. Mr T. Tyler (then 13) and his mother, tells of being alerted by the younger sister, who saw it moving over the other side of Whiteleigh Valley, at rooftop height. They described is as:

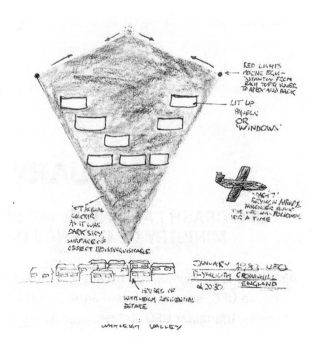

> "The top of it had two red lights, which moved from the object's two top corners, in sequence towards the apex of the upper point of the inverted cone, and then moved back down to the corner. It was last seen heading in a north-east direction. The newspaper, next day, told of two women who had tried to follow it. I also understand that it was seen over a naval airbase, which was a refitting yard for nuclear submarines."

(Source: WWW, 2013, *UFO Evidence*)

UFO debris found in Wales

During a visit to see our friend, Margaret Fry – Head of the Welsh Federation of Ufologists – in Abergele, North Wales, some years ago, we met up with UFO/Paranormal researcher – Gary Rowe, who brought our attention to an incident involving the discovery of a large amount of metal fragments found strewn over a farmer's field at Llanilar, near Aberystwyth (a village in Ceredigion, Wales, about 4 kilometers south-east of Aberystwyth) on 9th January 1983, which was the subject of an investigation by the police and MOD.

We visited the farm and spoke to Mr & Mrs Evans, who told us that a team of uniformed RAF men, Police and plain clothes officers, had searched the woods and recovered a large amount of debris, including what looked like an aerial and a large piece of metal (with a serial number stamped on it) from the wreckage. This had been scattered over four fields, consisting of extremely light pieces of shards of metal, some 5-6ft in size, but strong enough, in the final impact, to sever branches of trees in a nearby copse belonging to the Forestry Commission. The only Newspaper which covered the story, albeit briefly, without any other 'additional' follow-up (as far as we are aware) was the *Sunday Express*, (23.1.83) – 'Strange debris out of the sky', by Andrew Chapman.

An RAF spokesman said:

> "This debris certainly has nothing to do with us. We are examining fragments to try and place them together, in the hope of a clue to where it came from and what it was."

SUNDAY EXPRESS.

23RD JANUARY 1983.

strange debris out of the sky

by

ANDREW CHAPMAN

AN ASTONISHING sight greeted farmer Irwel Evans as he trudged across his fields to tend his newly-born lambs.

Hundreds of pieces of honeycombed metal foil were strewn over an area the size of three football pitches.

Huge twisted alloy plates, painted green on one side grey on the other, lay everywhere. And in a nearby copse branches had been sheared off trees.

Mr. Evans telephoned the police.

Soon his farm at Llanilar, near Aberystwyth, Wales, was like a film set from a spy thriller.

Police took away fragments of metal for analysis: A team of uniformed RAF men with plain clothes officers combed the land and nearby woods, using flashlights as darkness began to fall.

Baffled

Among the pile of debris taken away was an aerial and a large chunk of metal with part of a serial number on it.

Everyone concerned was convinced that whatever it was that covered Mr Evans's fields had fallen out of the sky at dead of night.

But after two weeks the riddle still remains. Police are baffled. So, too, are the RAF.

No-one in the close-knit Welsh community heard a plane that night. Nothing unusual showed up on RAF radar scanners.

Mr. Evans, 29, who farms his 260 acres single-handed, said: "Whatever tumbled from the sky broke up on impact.

"It must have been a fair size. Wreckage was scattered across four fields. Had it hit building there's no doubt the devastation could have been terrific.

"It must have come down the night before I found it for the area was clear in the afternoon when I checked the flock. Yet I heard nothing at all unusual.

"Although the pieces themselves were extremely light they must have fallen with some force to sever branches off trees. It is all very disturbing."

Mr. Emyr Hughes, secretary of Cardiganshire farmers' union, said: "I've asked the Ministry of Defence for an explanation, but so far have had no reply.

"The RAF say they had no aircraft out at the time this debris must have landed, nor where there any manoeuvres.

"Not only that, their radar scanners picked up nothing unusual."

Meanwhile, villagers are still speculating about the debris.

Could it be part of a large weather balloon? "No," say Aberystwyth police. "Too much metal."

Part of a satellite? "Unlikely. Any remains would be charred. We have no explanation as yet. It's baffling."

An RAF spokesman said: "The debris certainly had nothing to do with us. We are examining the fragments to try to piece them together in the hope of a clue to where it came from and what it is."

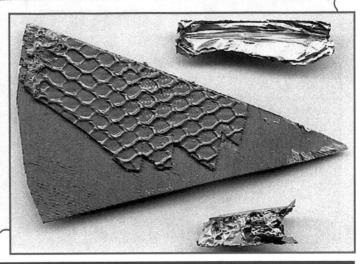

The matter became the subject of local speculation; some suggested it might have been a balloon (an explanation dismissed by the Police, because there was too much debris). Some thought it might have been a satellite – (unlikely, in the absence of any burning or impact to the ground). Others wondered if it might have been a UFO, although the evidence indicates, from its description, that it was likely to have been something manufactured by human hands, rather than any alien device.

Gary Rowe:

> *"Without doubt, this was one of the most important post-war UFO cases that I had come across. From substantive enquiries into the matter, after the recovery and analysis of some of the metal fragments found, I am convinced this was no aircraft, nor was it likely to have been any 'alien' spacecraft. The tests conducted on the metal revealed it to be a pure form of Durilium, with anomalies as used in fighter aircraft applications, particularly on the control surface, which suggests the object was an aircraft."*

The intriguing question is why there was no explosion, or bodies found? Apart from that, there was far too much material to have fallen off the aircraft without causing its destruction, which leads us to consider the likelihood of whether this was an unmanned aircraft, flown covertly; hence the 'official' denials, not only from the police but from the Civil Aviation Authority and MOD, that anything ever took place at all. More worrying are the numbers of reports of triangular UFOs seen during this month. Was it one of these that crash-landed?

The only other person who has taken an interest in this incident was Mark Olly – a Cheshire writer and archaeologist – who runs the archaeological unit CWP Archaeology (Celtic Warrington Project). His aim is to document all prehistoric and Dark Age remains in the Mid Mersey Valley, North Cheshire and South Lancashire, using Warrington as the central point.

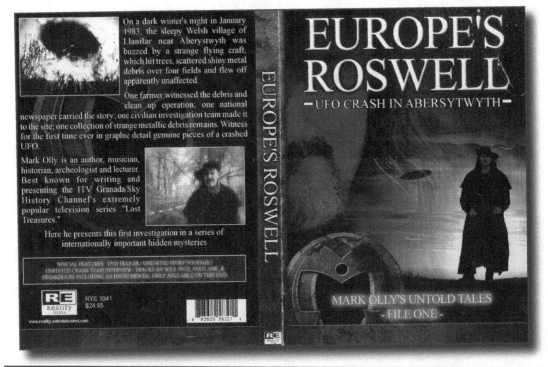

On a dark winter's night in January 1983, the sleepy Welsh village of Llanilar near Aberystwyth was buzzed by a strange flying craft, which hit trees, scattered shiny metal debris over four fields and flew off apparently unaffected.

One farmer witnessed the debris and clean up operation; one national newspaper carried the story; one civilian investigation team made it to the site; one collection of strange metallic debris remains. Witness for the first time ever in graphic detail genuine pieces of a crashed UFO.

Mark Olly is an author, musician, historian, archeologist and lecturer. Best known for writing and presenting the ITV Granada/Sky History Channel's extremely popular television series "Lost Treasures."

Here he presents this first investigation in a series of internationally important hidden mysteries

SPECIAL FEATURES: DVD TRAILER / UNEDITED STORY FOOTAGE / UNEDITED CRASH TEAM INTERVIEW / TRACKS BY SOUL PATH, FASTLANE & FREAKHOUSE INCLUDING AN INSTRUMENTAL ONLY AVAILABLE ON THIS DVD

EUROPE'S ROSWELL

– UFO CRASH IN ABERSYTWYTH –

MARK OLLY'S UNTOLD TALES
- FILE ONE -

RYE 1041
$24.95

www.reality-entertainment.com

This is a unique historical project for the North-West British Isles, revealing an unsuspected picture of the region in Dark Age times, which receives no funding of any kind. Mark produced a film, entitled Europe's Roswell – UFO crash in Abersytwyth – and should be commended for making a film of this mysterious event that still remains unexplained to this present day.

In 2013, we took the opportunity to talk to Mark about the film. He had this to say:

Mark Olly

"I got together with Mark Lloyd to make this film and he is a qualified researcher and works at the central library, at Aberystwyth. We managed to track down the one original newspaper article, which was sent to Gary Rowe. We traced it back to the magazine that had produced it and spoke to the journalist, Andrew, who had 'written-up' the article. He checked his notebook for source, but was surprised to find he had no record for where it had originated from, which means that if this hadn't been 'written-up', we would be none the wiser.

Something else of interest is that following a radio talk at Buxton, on UFOs, I was contacted by a woman, who said she was a student in Aberystwyth, at the time of the UFO crash. She said she had been looking out of her hotel window, one morning, when she saw, across the bay, a huge disturbance in the water. She then fetched a camera and had enough time to photograph a UFO coming out of the bay. This took place in 1983, and was important enough for me to ask her for a copy of the photo, which never materialised. My DVD was finished. I had no plans to reopen the case. It's worth bearing in mind the possibility that there may be a connection."

We wrote to the MOD asking them, under the FOI Act, if they could shed any light on the identity of the material, and received the following answer:

From: Mrs J Monk
Directorate of Air Staff – Freedom of Information 1

MINISTRY OF DEFENCE
5th Floor, Zone H, Main Building, Whitehall, London SW1A 2HB

Telephone (Direct dial) 020 7218 2140
(Switchboard) 020 7218 9000
(Fax) 020 7218 2680

Mr John Hanson
31 Red Lion Street
Alvechurch
Worcestershire
B48 7L6

Your Reference:

Our Reference:
01-03-2005-135811-007
Date:
16 March 2005

Dear Mr Hanson

I am writing concerning your request for information about an incident of metal debris being discovered on Farmer's land at Llanilar near Aberystwyth on 9 January 1983. Your request has been passed to this Department as we are the focal point within the Ministry of Defence for correspondence regarding UFOs.

I have made a search through all the UFO related files we have for the year 1983 and have found no documents relating to this alleged incident.

Sorry I could not have been more help.

Yours sincerely

J. monk.

'Dear Mr Hanson,

I am writing concerning your request for information about an incident of metal debris being discovered on farmer's land, near Aberystwyth, on 9th January, 1983. Your request has been passed to this department, as we are the focal point with the Ministry of Defence for correspondence regarding UFOs. I have made a search through all the UFO related files we have for that year, 1983, and found no documents relating to this alleged incident.

Sorry I could not have been more help.

Yours sincerely,

Mrs J. Monk.'

We wrote to the Heddlu Dyfed-Powys Police, asking if they had any information on the incident. Supt. Arfon Jones wrote back, telling us they were unable to assist with our enquiry, as they did not hold information as far back as 1983.

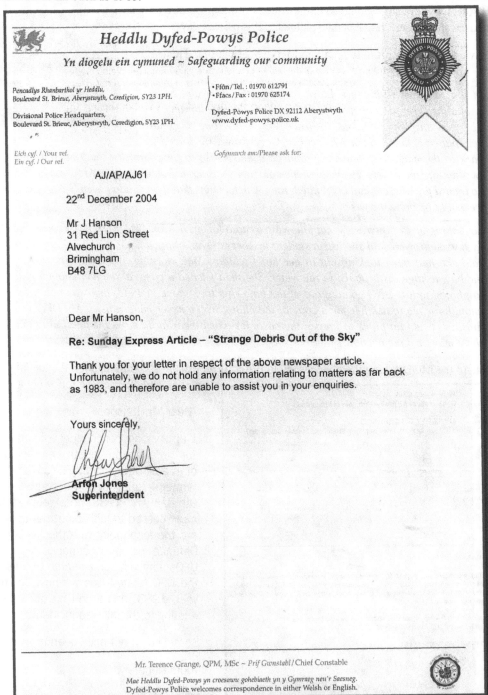

Heddlu Dyfed-Powys Police

Yn diogelu ein cymuned ~ Safeguarding our community

Pencadlys Rhanbarthol yr Heddlu,
Boulevard St. Brieuc, Aberystwyth, Ceredigion, SY23 1PH.

Divisional Police Headquarters,
Boulevard St. Brieuc, Aberystwyth, Ceredigion, SY23 1PH.

• Ffôn / Tel. : 01970 612791
• Ffacs / Fax : 01970 625174

Dyfed-Powys Police DX 92112 Aberystwyth
www.dyfed-powys.police.uk

Eich cyf. / Your ref.
Ein cyf. / Our ref.

Gofynnwch am:/Please ask for:

AJ/AP/AJ61

22nd December 2004

Mr J Hanson
31 Red Lion Street
Alvechurch
Brimingham
B48 7LG

Dear Mr Hanson,

Re: Sunday Express Article – "Strange Debris Out of the Sky"

Thank you for your letter in respect of the above newspaper article.
Unfortunately, we do not hold any information relating to matters as far back
as 1983, and therefore are unable to assist you in your enquiries.

Yours sincerely,

Arfon Jones
Superintendent

Mr. Terence Grange, QPM, MSc ~ *Prif Gwnstabl* / Chief Constable

Mae Heddlu Dyfed-Powys yn croesawu gohebiaeth yn y Gymraeg neu'r Saesneg.
Dyfed-Powys Police welcomes correspondence in either Welsh or English.

Heddlu Dyfed-Powys Police

Yn diogelu ein cymuned ~ Safeguarding our community

Mr Barry Taylor, BA, Dirprwy Brif Gwnstabl,
Pencadlys Heddlu Dyfed-Powys, Blwch Post 99,
Llangynnwr, Caerfyrddin, SA31 2PF.

Mr Barry Taylor, BA, Deputy Chief Constable,
Dyfed-Powys Police Headquarters, PO Box 99,
Llangunnor, Carmarthen, SA31 2PF.

•Ffôn/Tel. : 01267 226307
•Ffacs/Fax : 01267 226310

Dyfed-Powys Police DX 120325 Carmarthen 4
www.dyfed-powys.police.uk
e.bost/e.mail ~ acpo@dyfed-powys.pnn.police.uk

Eich cyf. / Your ref.
Ein cyf. / Our ref.   DCC.rg.152_04

Gofynnwch am:/Please ask for:

Mr J Hanson
31 Red Lion Street
Alvechurch
Birmingham
B48 7LG

20 December 2004

Dear Mr Hanson

Re: Sunday Express Article – "Strange Debris Out Of The Sky" 23/1/03

I refer to your letter received today, the contents of which I have noted.

I have forwarded your letter to Superintendent Arfon Jones, Divisional Commander for Ceredigion who will communicate with you in due course.

Yours sincerely

Mr B Taylor
Deputy Chief Constable

Mr. Terence Grange, QPM, MSc ~ *Prif Gwnstabl / Chief Constable*

Mae Heddlu Dyfed-Powys yn croesawu gohebiaeth yn y Gymraeg neu'r Saesneg.
Dyfed-Powys Police welcomes correspondence in either Welsh or English.

UFO debris found in County Clare

Oddly we were to come across another incident, involving the discovery of unidentified debris found on a farmer's land – this time in 1996, at County Clare, Ireland. This happened at the farm belonging to Mr John Clohessy, from Ballynacally, situated on the banks of the Shannon Estuary. He reported finding a number of pieces of curved panels, believed to be from the engine of an aircraft, spread over 30 acres of land.

The matter became the subject of conversation by aviation enthusiasts, who speculated that there was a connection with an aircraft, as the farm lies under the main transatlantic flight path out of Shannon Airport.

INCIDENT IN IRELAND

On Tuesday, 6 August 1996, *The Irish Times* published a curious article under the headline 'Specialists to examine debris'.

'Aeronautical specialists are to examine what are thought to be parts of an aircraft found on a farm in Co. Clare at the weekend.

'Mr John Clohessy, who farms near Ballynacally on the banks of the Shannon estuary, found the pieces of metal spread over 30 acres of land. The farm is on the main transatlantic flight path of Shannon airport. Local aviation enthusiasts believe that the main pieces of metal found are consistent with the curved panels on the engine of an aircraft. They also claim that the debris came from a military aircraft.

'A spokesman for Aer Rianta told *The Irish Times* yesterday it had the pieces of metal at Shannon. He said: "We got a report on

Sunday and the airport police were alerted, who collected the items from the farm. We informed the Irish Aviation Authority and understand an aeronautical investigator is coming to examine the objects. "He should be in a position to confirm or deny whether they are off an aircraft".'

According to researchers from the Dublin-based IUFOPRA Information Network, the material was spread over 30 acres of land, suggesting that whatever deposited it was either in violent collision with the ground (not likely - no mention of an impact site) or was travelling at a tremendous altitude in order to spread debris across such an area.

Most believe the material came from a military aircraft of some sort and firmly point the finger of suspicion at the United States, despite the fact that Ireland is a self-declared 'Neutral' country and a 'Nuclear-Free-Zone'. However, according to the *IUFOPRA Journal*: 'Rumours have

circulated for years about [Irish] Government complicity with USAF activities over Ireland. Some disclosures were made in the '80s, which revealed that USAF planes were allowed to cross our airspace secretly, some possibly carrying nuclear weapons.' Interestingly enough, sources close to UFO Magazine claimed members of the Irish Garda [police] assigned to the crash site were outraged

Soil samples were also taken by a local archeologist. A spokesman for Aer Rianta told *The Irish Times* that it had the pieces of metal at Shannon. He said:

> "We received a report on Sunday and the airport police were alerted, who collected the items from the farm. We informed the Irish Aviation Authority and understand an aeronautical investigator is coming to examine the objects. He should be in a position to confirm or deny whether they are off an aircraft."

We contacted members of the local UFO group, who remembered the incident, and although carrying out some initial investigations, concluded there might have been a rational explanation. Unfortunately, no documents or photographs of the locality were preserved. We wrote to the farmer, but never received any reply – likewise, enquiries with Aer Rianta were unsuccessful, despite two letters and emails sent to them we never received any reply.   **(Source: *The Irish Sun*, 6.8.1996 – 'Wreckage may be part of US Jet')**

UFO over New Zealand

Admittedly, while this object – which crashed and showered the land with shards of honeycombed metal – was probably an unmanned aerial vehicle type that did not appear to have contained any occupants, we wondered if there were any similarities with a UFO that was sighted on 24th April 1976, at Kaiwaka, New Zealand, by Mrs B. Mason and Mr B. Watt. The couple noticed a large red '*ball of light*' through the dining room window, crossing their farm at 9.30pm, illuminating the ground in red light as it did so – heading towards the direction of Arai Point. After looking at it through binoculars, they rushed to get a camera and took two photographs. Unfortunately, these did not turn out. Although there is unlikely to be any connection with the event at Llanlilar, the drawing intrigues us. **(Source:** *Xenolog 105*)

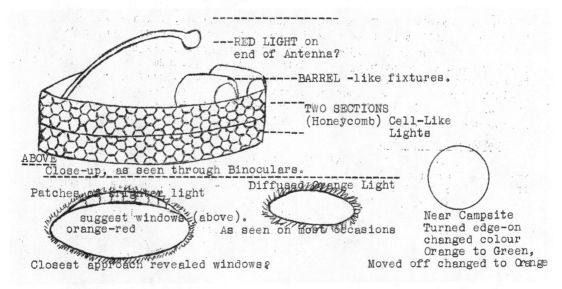

The day of 'bombs' from the sky

Western Daily Press Reporter

TWO bomb-shaped pods crammed with radio equipment crashed onto the Dorset village of Upwey yesterday from a training aircraft.

One weighing 5cwt missed market gardener **William Stanley** by 12ft as he ploughed his small-holding off Dorchester Road, Upwey, near Weymouth.

This was not the only occasion we were to come across reports of debris found on the ground. As we reported in Volume 4 (1968-1971) on or about the 25th March 1971, three large parts of an aircraft fell into the garden at 716, Dorchester Road, Upwey (a small village, situated in south Dorset) which narrowly missed Mr William Stanley – a market gardener – by a few feet.

PLANE PARTS CRASH NEAR MAN

A WEYMOUTH man narrowly escaped death this morning when a part of an aircraft fell from the sky landing only 12ft. away. Two other plane parts fell within 100 yards. Mr. William Stanley, a market gardener, was working on his grounds at Upwey, near the bottom of Ridgeway Hill. He said, "I was ploughing the land with a rotovator, so I couldn't hear it coming, but then there was a loud bang, like an explosion, which has

Four Chimney's garden

Lucille Désirée Ball

Coincidently, a famous name associated with Upwey is that of Lucille Désirée Ball – the American actress/comedian – who was proud of her family and heritage. Her genealogy can be traced back to the earliest settlers in the colonies. One direct ancestor – William Sprague (1609–1675) – left England on the ship Lyon's Whelp for Plymouth/Salem, Massachusetts. They were from Upwey, Dorset, England. Along with his two brothers, William helped to found the city of Charlestown, Massachusetts. Other Sprague relatives became soldiers in the US Revolutionary War and two of them became governors of the state of Rhode Island. Lucille Ball was born on 6th August 1911 and died on 26th April 1989 (aged 77). She received many prestigious awards throughout her illustrious career, including some received posthumously, such as the Presidential Medal of Freedom by President George H.W. Bush, on 6th July 1989.

(Source: *Wikipedia*, 2013)

Close Encounter for Ronald and Nancy Reagan

On the Presidents UFO website (13.8.2009) Grant Cameron writes about Ronald Reagan having had two UFO sightings, when Governor of California (1967-1975). The first occurred on the night that Reagan was invited to a party given by Hollywood actor William Holden. This sighting was corroborated by comedian Steve Allen, and actress Lucille Ball.

It is said that Ronald and Nancy Reagan arrived an hour late at the party. According to both Allen's and Ball's account, Reagan was very excited. He described how he and Nancy had seen a UFO, while coming down the coast highway to Los Angeles, and stopped to watch the event. Some unconfirmed stories stated that the object actually landed.

Lucy, in her account of the incident, stated:

> *"After he was elected President, I kept thinking about that event, and wondered if he still would have won if he had told everyone that he had seen a 'flying saucer'."*

Lucille Ball later discussed the incident with fellow Hollywood actress Shirley MacLaine, which appears to have confirmed a rumor circulated for years that this was not just a sighting but a close encounter. The only thing that varied was the location of the party – Ball told MacLaine that it was at Helen and Armand Deutch's house. (Armand had been a Hollywood producer and later member of Reagan's kitchen cabinet. Helen and Armand were considered one of Ron and Nancy Reagan's closest friends)

According to Ball, Reagan told her that the UFO landed and an alien emerged. It told Reagan to quit acting and take up politics. Shirley MacLaine had put most of the story in her 2007 book *Sage-ing while Age-ing.* MacLaine wrote the Ball account on page 142.

> *"Reagan had seen a craft when he was an actor, as he and Nancy were driving on Mulholland Drive in Los Angeles. Apparently the craft landed and an occupant descended, who then spoke to him telepathically. He never told me directly, but he did tell a party of people who were waiting for him at Helen and Armand Deutch's house. Lucille Ball told me he had arrived ashen and confused, and told her the story. She told me because, as a Democrat, she wanted me to know that Ronnie must have been crazy."*

UFO sighting over California

The other Reagan sighting occurred in 1974, just before Reagan ended his second term as Governor. The story was told by Air Force Colonel Bill Paynter, who became the pilot of Reagan's Cessna Citation jet plane following his retirement from the Air Force.

In a story Ronald Reagan told to Norman Miller, Washington Bureau Chief for the *Wall Street Journal*, the Governor's plane was making an approach to land in Bakersfield, California. It was during the descent that Reagan noticed a strange light behind the plane.

"We followed it for several minutes", Reagan told Miller. *"It was a bright white light. We followed it to Bakersfield and all of a sudden, to our utter amazement, it went straight up into the heavens."*

Paynter:

> *"It appeared to be several hundred yards away and was a fairly steady light; until it began to accelerate it appeared to elongate – then the light took off. It went up a 45° angle at a high rate of speed. Everyone on the plane was surprised. The UFO went from normal speed cruise to a fantastic speed instantly. If you give an airplane power, it will accelerate, but not like a 'hot rod', and that's what this was like."*

UFO Researcher – Stanton Friedman – interviewed Paynter, years later.

> *"I spoke with the pilot of his plane when Reagan was California Governor. I can't recall his name now, but Don Berliner, very up on aviation matters, immediately recognized the name. The pilot had 30,000 hours, which is a very high number. He confirmed that the sighting occurred and that the quotes in the National Enquirer were accurate."*

(Source: *Reagan and the Aliens*, Stanton Friedman, 16th September 2003, *'UFO Updates'* List)

Orange 'ball' over Bradford

On 12th January 1983, a strange orange '*ball*' was seen moving through the sky over Manchester Road, Bradford, by Mr Michael Brett, at 11.10pm.

> *"It was bright orange and flying from the direction of Lidget Green, towards the City Centre. A couple nearly crashed their car when they saw it."*

Airfield Press Liaison Officer – Squadron Leader Tony Ware – was contacted. He confirmed that there had been no flights after 10.00pm. It was not to be the last time that this sort of strange object was seen. There was a spate of similar objects seen all over the South Coast, during the later part of the 1980s.

(**Source:** *Bradford Telegraph and Argus*, **15.1.1983 – 'Orange glow in sky puzzle')**

ORANGE GLOW IN SKY PUZZLE

A STRANGE orange ball, slightly tapering at the edges, floated over Bradford City centre....

Mr. Michael Brett, 26, a builder of Larch Drive, Odsal, was waiting for a bus home on Manchester Road, on Wednesday night, when he saw the object moving from the direction of Lidget Green towards Bradford City centre.

"I couldn't believe my eyes" said Mr. Brett. "It was bright orange and glided off towards the city center."

Mr. Brett says a couple saw it too and the man, whose identity is not known, told him he nearly crashed his car looking at it.

The RAF are playing host to a Nato flying exercise this week, but Church Fenton Airfield Press Liaison Officer, Squadron Leader Tony Ware, said: "We had no exercise aircraft over that area that night."

Leeds and Bradford Airport closes down at 10 p.m., so aircraft movements seem unlikely to account for the sightings.

The weather did change at that time, a cold front arriving from the south west. Some quirk of the meteorological situation may account for the presence of this latest example in a long line of Unidentified Flying Objects sighted in the heavens by generations of Bradford skywatchers.

UFO sighting, Birmingham

In 1983, Steven Welsh was 19 years of age and living in Lozells – a suburb of Birmingham, 2-3 miles from the City Centre. He was employed as a hotel porter, at the 200 bedroom, 3 stars *Ladbroke Hotel, Union Passage, Birmingham, between 1979, and left in 1990 as a manager.

> *"One afternoon, in January 1983, I arranged to meet my cousin, Brian, at the Backyard Bar at the Grand Hotel, Colmore Row, Birmingham; I travelled to Birmingham City Centre on the 33 bus from Lozells. I walked through Union Passage – the location of the Ladbroke Hotel – with late shoppers and workers going home. As I went past the overhead hotel signage canopy, which obscures the skyline for approximately 15 yards, I saw an enormous lit spherical shape in the sky – the typical 'flying saucer' shape. I was stunned and stared at the object for what seemed minutes, but probably was only seconds.*
>
> *My first inclination was to beckon to the people walking towards me. I said 'Look at that'; there was no response from anyone. I repeated 'Look up there!' . . . still no response. I was getting frustrated that nobody was taking any notice of me, so I kept repeating the request. Eventually, I realised that there was no sound coming out of my mouth.*
>
> *I followed the object, still trying to get people to look at it, but everybody ignored me. I walked through Union Passage, and turned left at Union Street. I crossed the road and stood almost directly outside Rackham's department store, Cherry Street. The object had moved to directly in front of me, but probably 1-2 miles away. I stared in disbelief, and then the glowing object moved rapidly to my left and out of sight."*

Steven made his way to the Ladbroke Hotel and asked duty receptionist, Lin, if she has seen anything unusual; also if any guests had reported the sighting. She said no and looked at him in disbelief. The following day (Wednesday) Steven was due to attend the wedding reception of friends – Gwynne and Richard – at the *Yard Of Ale* Public House, in Birmingham City Centre. He received a phone call at home from his cousin, Brian, who said *'I've been trying to contact you, are you ok?'* Steve replied *'I'm ok. I'm going to Gwynne's and Richard's wedding reception today'*. Brian replied *'It's Thursday evening'*! Steve thought he was joking, but turned on the TV to see *Top of the Pops* was on, which is always shown at 7.30pm on Thursday. Steve stood there feeling very confused, wondering what had happened. Inexplicably, he was unable to account for having lost a complete day and missed the wedding of his good friends. He called them to explain, but was unable to tell why he had not turned up.

In 1991, after meeting his present wife, Mary, the couple moved to London before moving to Ashby-de-la-Zouch, a year later. Steven mentioned to his wife about his experience. She contacted a UFO investigator from the Leicestershire area to come and interview him. When they turned up at the house at the time arranged Steven felt unable to take part and the interview never took place.

Steven is now 50 years of age, and wonders if there is a connection with what happened in 1983. Since then he has suffered bouts of memory loss, time loss, a feeling of dread and intrusion, and experiences a total dread of anybody looking in his mouth; during visits to the dentist.

> *"I cannot touch my navel anymore and since then suffer from digestive problems. When I'm alone I do not feel alone. I woke up during an appendix operation, in 1985. I could feel the pain, but I was unable to tell the surgeon. It was the same feeling I had when I saw the object in Union Passage. My friends recall incidents to me, a few years after the experience; I cannot remember those years, which are mostly blank. I have never experienced a 'UFO' again. I have told family and friends about my experiences – some believe me, some don't. It doesn't really matter to me if they believe me or not. When I hear the stories in the media and the debates on whether 'we are alone in the universe or not', I feel a great sense of satisfaction in knowing that I already know."*

Not having met or spoken to Steven we are unable to comment, other than the account seems, on the face of it, to be genuine. We left our contact and email details on the website, hoping he would contact us, so that we could take the matter further, but we never received any answer. Unfortunately, without knowing a great deal more about Steven and his relevant personal/medical history, never mind other possible explanations to take into consideration, we felt we should leave it at that – an interesting report, which should be taken on face value only. Hopefully, others may come forward to corroborate the sighting – now over 30 years ago.   **(Source: www.reportaufo.com, UFO website 2013)**

Triangular UFO over Swansea

At 5.55pm on 19th January 1983, an '*aircraft-shaped object*' (moving far too slowly to be an aircraft) showing six lights at the front and three lights at the base, was seen heading over Swansea Airport, towards the Gower Peninsular.

At 6pm, the same day, Michael Troake – a Detective Sergeant, based at Morriston Police Station, Swansea – was carrying out enquiries into a spate of burglaries in the Winch Wen area, with his colleague – DC Gethin James. They were about to get into the CID car, when they saw a cluster of lights approaching their position in the sky:

DS Troake:

> *"What surprised me was the way in which the lights blocked out some of the stars, giving me an impression of an object that was long and rectangular in shape. As this massive, silent, transparent, object loomed overhead, I could see a number of blue flashing lights at its edges. All I could do was stand in awe, looking upwards, as this 'thing' – only about a hundred feet off the ground – headed slowly towards Swansea Bay."*

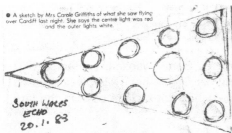

● A sketch by Mrs Carole Griffiths of what she saw flying over Cardiff last night. She says the centre light was red and the outer lights white.

SOUTH WALES ECHO 20.1.83

What Carole saw over Cardiff . . .

REPORTS of a giant triangular object hovering over South Wales are today being investigated by police.

POLICE PROMISE A SERIOUS PROBE ON GIANT UFO REPORTS

Descriptions of a sighting in Llandaff, Cardiff, match those made by six people in Swansea, including two detectives.

All say they encountered a giant triangular-shaped object with white lights along the border of the triangle. Some reports say it was larger than a jumbo jet and had a red light in the middle.

Mother of four Mrs Carole Griffiths, of Heol Penlan, Whitchurch, Cardiff, was being driven home from work at 7pm when she saw the object over the River Taff, close to Llandaff Rowing Club.

She said today. "My husband stopped the car we were so amazed. It looked like Concorde taking off but it was stationary in the sky. I normally pooh-pooh things like that when I hear about UFO."

● Mrs Griffiths — pictured at work today.

Griffiths's husband, John, ...

tises in Caerphilly, said the object seemed fixed in the sky. "I don't know what I was looking at — I have never seen anything like it before," he added.

South Wales police said they received a number of calls reporting UFOs between 6pm and 7pm yesterday.

The first sighting reported four flashing lights in the sky. Within minutes detectives reported watching a silent object, triangular in shape, drift west over Swansea.

They said it was flying at 1,000 feet, with three lights, two of which were pulsating. It was followed by a smaller similar object. The RAF received two similar reports.

A police spokesman said the reports would be treated seriously. "At present we have not got a clue, but inquiries will be made," he commented.

the Air Call Ltd — a communications company in Cathedral Road — said he saw a similar object above Pentwyn earlier in the evening.

A passenger in the car, Dr ... Pub, who prac...

That triangle is no 'plane—expert

THE MYSTERIOUS flying triangle that has been haunting South Wales skies this week, could not be an aircraft known to British aviation, according to a former RAF aircraft engineer.

Mr Joe Toland, aged 46, an engineer with the RAF for 13 years, was coaching Llandaff Major under 12's soccer team when he saw the object.

Airport's record year

CARDIFF Airport has sent out their biggest-ever summer holiday brochure this year.

It lists all the destinations, tour operators and airlines providing services and features the largest summer holiday programme the airport has ever run.

Twenty thousand copies have been distributed to travel agents throughout South Wales and, for the first time, to Bristol areas, including Gloucester and Cheltenham.

"We stopped playing to watch it," he said. "I couldn't fathom out why the lights were so far apart. It was close perhaps 600-1,000 feet up.

"It must have been 300 feet across, so it could not be an aircraft. The thing I really don't understand is that it made no noise."

UFO expert Mr Bill Riot, aged 35, of Llandough Castle Plain, Llandough, is convinced the triangle is a visitor from space.

"I have spent an awful lot of time looking at stars ...

unusual aircraft lights, though it was in the flight path from Rhoose Airport," he said.

"It must have been 300 feet across, so it could not be an aircraft. The thing I really don't understand is that it made no noise.

● THE sketch and headline that appeared with the report in Thursday's South Wales Echo.

What Carole saw over Cardiff . . .

What Carole saw over Cardiff . . .

taking notes for about a year now. I wouldn't say I'm a UFO freak, my interest is mainly scientific.

Mr Riot, who is an artist, sketched the object fly past his house last Wednesday night.

"What they are doing, who knows?" he said. "We have got to take this seriously.

"One imagines they are taking samples from a fertile earth while it is still fertile.

"There have been a lot of close encounters of the first nature in Wales. I believe they will soon make themselves known.

ever since I spotted a very strange UFO in Australia," he said.

"It most definitely is not a meteor as some people have claimed—I saw plenty of meteoric activity in Australia, and this was nothing like it.

"I am in the process of getting a book on sightings in Wales—I've been ...

SUNDAY MIRROR, February 20, 1983   PAGE 15

QUICK-DRAW KIDS TRACK A UFO

AN amazing UFO sighting by more than 200 people is being investigated.

Among those who spotted the "flying saucer" along a 40-mile stretch of South Wales coastline were two policemen, a class of schoolchildren and a football team.

The sighting—over a one-hour period—is one of the best-witnessed ever.

First to spot the triangular-shaped craft was 22 pupils at Cardiff's Ynys Wen primary school.

Spotters—Jonathan Hutchins, 7, and sister Lyndsay, 5

By STEVE BAILEY

They told their teacher, John Williams, who was astounded when the children later produced nearly identical drawings.

Twenty miles west, at Llantwit Major, football coach Joe Toland and a team of boys also got a clear view of the UFO.

Gethin Humphreys could hardly believe their eyes when the craft glided slowly overhead.

Sgt Tronke, 42, said last week: "I'm used to seeing aircraft in the sky but this was massive—much bigger than a plane.

"There was a large main cluster of lights at the front, shaped a bit like a boomerang, followed by a triangular group of lights.

"They were moving gracefully across the sky about 1,000 ft up." The two officers did not enter an official report for fear of ridicule from sceptical colleagues.

Ian Mrzyglod, of the UFO Research Association, said: "Simple lights in the sky are easy to explain away.

"But this was a gigantic solid structure ...

Sky-watchers agree on mystery lights

By Robert Lloyd

WHATEVER THE nature of the UFOs which passed over Swansea and other parts of South Wales two days ago, sky-watchers are agreed on one thing.

South Wales Evening Post 21.1.83

The objects were roughly triangular with flashing lights in each corner and moved silently and slowly across the sky.

And one Swansea woman has come up with her own artistic impression of what the UFOs which puzzled and astonished hundreds of people on Wednesday night looked like.

Mrs June Thomas, of Pentrechwyth Road, Bonymaen, Swansea, had just finished work as a cleaner at the Viscose plant at South Dock when she saw the mystery objects.

Mrs Thomas said today she discounted theories put forward by Swansea Coastguards that the lights she saw in the sky were meteorites burning up as they entered the earth's atmosphere.

"What I saw was two objects, very big objects, moving across the sky slowly and without any noise," she said.

"Call them flying saucers if you will, but they were definitely not planes or meteorites."

Another UFO spotter Mr Peter Trotman, of Bryncerdyn Road, Newton, Mumbles, said ...

METEORS! NEVER SAY ALL THE UFO SPOTTERS

UFO SPOTTER Mrs. June Thomas's drawing of the two triangular objects. The angles of the triangle are where Mrs. Thomas saw flashing lights.

he was astonished to hear the claim that the sighting was meteorites.

And Mr. Kenneth Needles, of Verdi Road, Port Talbot, said he was also sure the UFOs were objects of some kind.

Mr. Needles, who was in the RAF during the war, said: "To be honest, I have no idea what the UFOs were, but they can't have been aircraft."

An RAF spokesman at the Ministry of Defence in London said he had not yet received any official reports of the sightings.

He said: "When we do get official reports through we will investigate the matter. It takes time to check flight plans, but

my initial response would be to say the sighting was of aircraft flying in formation."

This theory, however, was dismissed by yet another UFO spotter, Mr. John Owen, of St. Catherine's Road, Baglan, who saw the lights in the sky above Porthawl.

He said: "What I saw was about 600 feet from the ground, huge in size and did not have any engine noise, not like any civil or military aircraft I know. Besides, it was only moving at about 30 m.p.h., far too slow for an aircraft.

"I cannot really say what it was . . . it was certainly phenomenal."

Wednesday night's sighting, which occured at a time when air traffic controllers at RAF Brawdy and Cardiff-Wales Airport reported no unusual aircraft flying over the area, was accompanied by one unusual event.

Electricity supplies to several hundred people in the Kittle and Bishopston area were cut off for a short while, but an electricity board spokesman said the black out was due to a temporary fault, probably caused by a branch hitting an overhead power line.

DC James:

"It was the most incredible thing I had ever seen . . . bigger than two football fields and covered in blinding lights, although I could just make out a smaller object in the shape of a 'V' following behind."

BLACK TRIANGLE UFO

PHIL JONES (48) – a local Government housing officer, from Swansea, contacted UFO Evidence WWW Internet, in August 2013, honouring his late father's wish (who passed away in April 2012) that details of his UFO sighting, which took place back in the late 1980s, could now be released into the public domain.

"My dad was a driving instructor and on this occasion he was leaving at 6.15pm to pick up a pupil.

As he left the house, he noticed a black triangular object in the sky – the size of a family car – slowly moving through the sky, above the top of the house next door.

The object was blacker than the night sky and had a small tube protruding from each corner, showing a bright light at each tip. The 'craft' was estimated to be no more than 18 inches high, and he presumed that if there had been anyone inside it, they must have been lying down or very small indeed.

As it moved over, approximately a foot above the house, it made a chugging noise as it crossed the road, heading in a north-west to south-east direction and Swansea Bay. It then appeared to adjust its height and missed the ridge tiles by inches, before descending back to its original course and was soon out of sight."

From the information supplied, we are fairly certain that this occurred in 1983, as Phil made reference to a number of police officers who reported having sighted a triangular UFO over Swansea Bay and the Gower Peninsula. (See page 236).

This was not the only time we were to hear of such a 'craft'. In 1988, a schoolgirl from Godmanchester sighted a similar object moving over, in broad daylight, not forgetting the Jessie Roestenberg UFO, seen in October 1954. In both of these incidents the witness sustained medical problems, caused by the apparent fields of radiation which surrounds these objects, fact not conjecture!

Mr John Hanson,
PO Box 6371,
Birmingham.B48.RW

Wednesday, 15 March 2000

Dear Mr Hanson,

Reading an article by Ms Emma Jones, in the South Wales Evening Post of 7th Mar ult., in which she said that you would like to hear of UFO incidents witnessed by members of the public irrespective of when or where they occurred. Consequently I would like to tell you of two such happenings.

As a student, attending an IT Course sponsored by Swansea College, I was required to undertake a project to demonstrate my IT skills and, of the varied subjects we could choose, I selected **Mysteries**. We were allowed to copy 2500 words of text from any authors or articles we chose, but had to include a minimum 500 word text of our own. For this portion of the work I chose to include my own experiences, an extract of which I enclose.

In researching this subject, I rekindled an interest that had prompted me to buy those various books from which I extracted the information. I trust this will be of interest to you and your group

Yours truly

Gerald Hopkins

The Dunes,
,Port Eynon
Swansea,
W/Glam., SA3.1NN

Before I close this narrative I wish to relate my own experiences of moving lights. Firstly whilst returning form an emergency call from a client during my working years, travelling homewards from Rhossili along Monksland Road one evening in the autumn and fading light, I glanced to my left and saw a translucent green light, rectangular in shape like a shop window. It was over the Lougher Estuary approximately 8-10 miles, as the crow flies and travelling eastwards. At that distance it appeared to me to be about the size of four large houses one on top of the other. There were no reports on anyone else seeing this and I did not report it.

Another such incident I saw was at the time of a refuelling exercise taking place in late evening in the Bristol Channel, during a fine autumn evening in 1983/4. I was standing on my front lawn watching the obstruction lights attached to the planes moving eastwards in mid channel about 13 or 14 miles away, when to my left and just above the height of the cliff tops to Oxwich Point on the seaward side, a set of lights in the form of a stretched out letter 'M' came towards me.

There was no sound of engines as it came nearer. The lights of Borva F/S Centre behind me must have attracted it. It came in further than the wreck buoys marking the Ivanhoe, at a height about 500 feet, and turned slightly parallel with the shore before zooming up and out of sight. There was no sound of engines at all, not even when it accelerated and climbed away. With a torch with a good beam I might have been able to see it! Perhaps next time.

The following day reports of flying saucer activity observed by residents, were published the local press and mention made of the refuelling exercises.

Mike explained, after switching-on the police radio, that he was just in time to hear the Force Control Room asking if any officers had seen a UFO. If so, they were to return to the police station.

When he and his colleague arrived back at the police station, they were met by a RAF officer, from RAF Uxbridge, who asked him a number of apparently pre-prepared questions about the incident. Michael later discovered, from newspaper accounts, that over two hundred people, spanning a forty mile stretch of coastline, had sighted the same UFO.

Five minutes later two objects – *'a long one, in front of another, displaying a large red light, with flashing white lights in the centre and tail'* – were seen stationary in the sky, over Llwynhendy, Llanelli, before heading off towards the Gower, a short time later.

A silver coloured, saucer-shaped object, showing four or five lights, flashing in rotation, was seen motionless in the sky, over a steel works in Port Talbot, at 6.05pm. A few minutes later, it was joined by a second UFO. The two of them moved off towards Swansea. The activity continued with a sighting by a motorist of three lights, set in a triangular pattern, with a pink light at each corner, accompanied by a faint humming sound, crossing the sky, at 6.35pm.

At 7pm, Mrs Carole Griffiths from Whitchurch, Cardiff, was driving home with her husband, John, and a friend, Dr. Nribendra Deb, when she saw a triangular object hovering over the *River Taff*, close to Llandaff Rowing Club.

> *"My husband stopped the car; we were so amazed it looked like Concorde."*

Mrs June Thomas of Pentrechwyth Road, Bonymaen, Swansea, had just finished work as a cleaner, at the Viscose Plant, South Dock, when she saw:

> *". . . two very big objects moving across the sky, slowly and silently – call them 'flying saucers' if you will, but they were definitely not planes or meteorites."*

Between 6pm-7pm, South Wales Police confirmed that they had received a number of reports from the public of UFOs seen over the county. From the nature of the sightings it is inconceivable to believe these were examples of meteorites, burning up in the Earth's atmosphere, according to one suggestion made by the local Coastguards.

**(Source: Jeffrey Horton-Jones/*South Wales Echo*, 20.1.83/*South Wales Echo*, 24.1.1983 –
'That triangle is no plane–expert')**

UFO over Swansea

Mr Roland Betts – a long-distance lorry driver from Killay, Swansea – had just uncoupled his trailer and was in Dunvant Road, high up on a hill, with a sweeping view of Swansea Bay, at around 6pm.

> *"As I got out of my vehicle, I was attracted by a large area of stars that were blocked out. There was a massive round object; I would guess at approximately 10-20,000ft in the air. It appeared to have lights around the perimeter and was absolutely silent. If it was moving, it was moving very slowly. For some reason, it didn't sink into my mind what it might be. I went into the house and told my wife that I had just seen an unidentified object in the sky. Imagine my surprise when she told me that a programme had just been interrupted by a news broadcast, relating to a UFO having been sighted between Swansea and Cardiff, by many people!"*

(Source: Personal interview)

FEBRUARY 1983

GREEN SPHERE FOLLOWS POLICE

Also includes – Orange sphere seen at Tamworth • 'Flying Saucer' seen over the
River Thames, by local man and his sons

Green spheres seen, Staffordshire

AT 10pm, in February 1983, two Special Constables from Stonehill Police Station were driving along the A51dual carriageway, at Stonehill, Staffordshire, when they saw:

". . . a green coloured sphere – the size of a motor car – pulling alongside, silently pacing the vehicle for a distance of approximately 200 metres, before it veered off the road, following the line of some hedges, towards Western Bank."

The Officers debated whether to try and follow the object, but chose not too.

In the same month, an off duty Special Constable was driving near Burton-on-Trent, accompanied by his wife, when they observed a '*green sphere*' approaching them from the road ahead, described as being the size of a car, at a height of 20ft off the ground, before passing directly over their car and disappearing.

(Source: Gary Heseltine/PRUFOS, Police Database)

Orange sphere seen, Tamworth

Although we do not know the exact time of the month this incident happened, it took place near Wiggington Park, Tamworth, between 9pm and 10pm, in February 1983, and involved Mr Mike Corns of Tamworth, who was walking home across the park, when he experienced a sensation that he was being watched.

"The hairs on the back of my neck were tingling. I turned to my left and saw an orange sphere of light gliding above the ground, about 200ft off the ground. I felt unable to walk. The sphere came up level with me and then headed off, towards Lichfield. Since that night, my belief in God and the Bible has changed."

(Source: Staffordshire UFO Group)

During the evening of 16th February 1983, an Otley man sighted a large oval-shaped object in the sky, near Farnley Hall. It gave off a fluorescent blue colour. **(Source: Graham Birdsall)**

'Flying Saucers' over River Thames, London

At Southend, Mr. Andrew Neagen from Shoeburyness, Essex, was driving along the seafront road, with his sons and a friend, when one of his sons drew his attention to a strange object he could see over the *River Thames*, heading towards London. Andrew told his son that it was probably an aircraft, but at his son's insistence stopped the car and they all got out to watch.

Andrew:

> *"I told them they had better take a good look, as they would probably never see anything like this again; it was massive in size, long, cigar-shaped and dull silver in colour. It had what appeared to be windows along its length. It then stopped moving. From the underside of the end pointing towards London emerged three saucer-shaped objects, which headed away over the Thames towards London. The 'cigar' then reversed its course and disappeared into the distance."*

Mike Perryman of *London UFO Studies*, who investigated the matter, said that the River Thames has been, and still is, the subject of intense UFO activity during that time. **(Source: Dan Goring/Roy Lake)**

MARCH 1983

DID RAF JETS TRY AND INTERCEPT UFO OVER BRIDLINGTON?

Also includes – Nursing sister followed by UFO – tree found badly burnt

UFO chased by RAF?

A T 6.58pm on 14th March 1983, Bridlington youths – Michael Hodgson and Stephen Harvey – watched a UFO fly over the fields, close to the Danescroft estate. It then went up the little forest on Pinfold Lane. A few minutes later it reappeared, being followed by a RAF Jet Fighter aircraft, which chased it all over the estate. Suddenly, it stopped over a car depot and disappeared from view.

At 7.05pm, the UFO was seen in the sky over Scarborough Road Garage, by Richard Duckett.

(Source: *The Bridlington Press*, March 1983)

'Wave' of Triangular UFOs seen over the United States

Although sightings for the UK seem to have died down, the same cannot be said for the United Sates, which was to experience a 'wave' of unprecedented duration, involving reports of a huge 'wing', 'boomerang', or 'V' shape, displaying multi-coloured flashing lights, seen moving across the sky. The activity appears to have been centred over New York and Connecticut and first came to notice on 17th March, when a huge, dark metallic object, with glowing lights, was noticed flying very low, over populated suburbs. Interestingly the lights were observed to change position to various configurations, including 'horseshoe', 'cross', straight line and a large circle.

Schoolboys log UFO sightings

I tried to throw some light on what three pupils from Burlington Junior School thought was a UFO over Bridlington.

The pupils, Stephen Harvey, Richard Duckett, and Michael Hodgson wrote and told me that a jet-fighter chased the mystery object until it disappeared over a car depot in the town.

I checked with the RAF but they too failed to come up with an answer and, although their aircraft may have been on mandatory night training flights at the time, their pilots had not reported anything strange in the Bridlington area.

The boys wrote to me: "On Monday, 14 March, we sighted something we thought was a UFO above the factories on Pinfold Lane. It was 6.58 pm when we first saw it. It was flying around over the fields on Danescroft Estate. It went up to the little forest on Pinfold Lane.

"Then, about 7 pm, it came again followed by a jet fighter. The fighter was chasing it all over the estate. Then, suddenly, the UFO stopped above a car depot and it just-disappeared.

"The third sighting was at 7.05 pm over Scarborough Road Garage and then it disappeared again. The first sighting was seen by Stephen Harvey and Michael Hodgson. The second sighting was also see by them. The third sighting was seen by Richard Duckett."

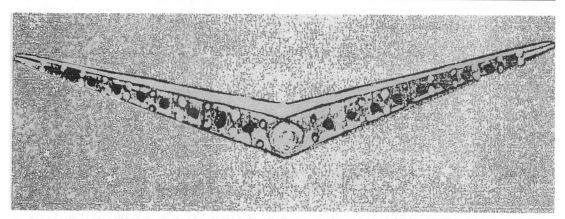

On 24th March, the object(s) was seen again – this time over Yorktown, by citizens and police officers. *The Port Chester Daily* newspaper told its readers about this under the headline of *'Hundreds claim to have seen UFO'*, the following morning. On 25th and 26th, a similar UFO was seen over the same locality.

(Source: *FSR*, Volume 31, No. 3, 1986 – The Wave of 'Wing' reports: More on the 'Boomerang':
As large as two football fields', by R. Perry Collins)

It appears that the object seen over Yorktown is no doubt identical to what was photographed in 1990 during an upsurge in sightings of what became labelled at the 'Triangular UFO'.

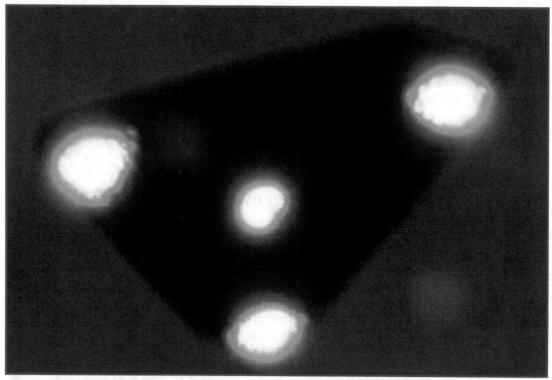

The photographer hereby releases this photograph into the public domain. All claims to copyrights have been surrendered. Picture taken 15 June 1990, Wallonia, Belgium by J. S. Henrardi

APRIL 1983

UFO SEEN OVER BRADFORD

Doughnut-shaped UFO over Bradford

MRS Maureen King and her twin sons – Gerald and Christian (13) – were having breakfast at Coopers Lane, Horton Bank Top, Bradford, on 25th April 1983. At 8.45am, Gerald pointed out something in the sky that appeared to resemble a doughnut in shape.

Maureen:

"It was black and grey and spinning. It carried on over the fields and we then lost sight of it."

(Source: *Telegraph and Argus*, 28.4.1983 – 'Pie in the sky')

Roy Lake, chairman of London UFO Studies (seen here with Michael Rutherford), is as keen now as he was then in the UFO subject. He is a most helpful man and like Dan Goring has given us various advice over the years with regard to specific cases.

MAY 1983

POLICE OFFICERS' CAR KNOCKED OUT BY UFO

Also includes – Housewife from Merseyside tells of seeing 'Flying Saucer' spinning over the roof of her house • UFO Display over Bradford, involving four lights

UFO over Hartcliffe, Bristol

AN object, described as showing flashing red, yellow, and sapphire blue, lights was seen moving across the sky, by a family from Hartcliffe (the scene of a number of similar incidents, over the years). After calling the police, two policewomen based at Broadbury Road, Knowle, arrived and told of seeing:

> *". . . an object, hovering over a hilltop, in the Hartcliffe area. We followed it for two miles, towards Dundry, where it stopped in mid-air and was then joined by another one, heading from the direction of Bedminster".*

It would appear that the police vehicle – then driven by the policewoman, in pursuit of the UFO – broke down, the next day, due to a faulty battery. Whether this was sheer coincidence can only be speculation.

The UFO was also seen by Police Sergeant Ian Lock, who was on patrol in Bedminster with PC Nigel Marsh.

Flying friend baffles police

By Mark Hanna

ULLO, ullo, ullo . . . What's going on up there then?

Bristol police have drawn a blank in their investigation into the mysterious unidentified flying object of Dundry Hill.

A family in nearby Hartcliffe have seen the UFO regularly for the past two years.

The father, aged 46, who asked not to be named, said it had flashing lights of red, yellow and sapphire blue, and moved across the sky.

The family calls it "our little friend" but have become embarrassed about telling other people about it.

But recently they reported it to the police.

Two police women were called out from Broadbury Road police station, Knowle, and followed the object for two miles towards Dundry where it stopped.

Then another UFO joined it from the Bedminster area.

"We waited and one of them went up in the air and flew away. It was a bit creepy and we left the other one there," they said.

The police women checked with nearby Bristol Airport and the Ministry of Defence and were told there was no trace of air traffic in the district.

20.5.83   20/5/83

BRISTOL JOURNAL

MAY THE FORCE BE WITH YOU?

Report by PETER HILL

THREE Bristol bobbies have had a close encounter of the 'force' kind.

In two baffling incidents they claim they spotted UFOs over south Bristol recently.

And in both cases they were no aircraft in the area at the time.

The 'flying squad' investigation started when two WPC's from Broadbury Road police station were called to a man's home in Hartcliffe.

He had reported a mysterious object flying over his home and said it had been coming and going for two years.

One of the WPC's said: "When we got there we saw a light and at first thought it was a plane but we couldn't make out the shape.

"Next we saw a light stopped and hovered a bit like a harrier as it turned around on the spot.

"We got in our car and followed it for two miles towards Dundry where it stopped.

"Then another one came from the Bedminster area and as we waited one of them went up into the air and flew away.

Creepy

"It was a bit creepy and we left the other one there."

After checking with Lulsgate Airport and the Ministry of Defence they discovered no aircraft had flown in the area at the time.

And to add to the mystery, when they tried to start their car the next day their battery was completely flat.

Sergeat Ian Lock and PC Nigel Marsh, of Broadbury Road Sta-

Police in UFO sighting mystery

tion were patrolling separately in Bedminster when the two WPC's made their first sighting.

"We heard the Hartcliffe call and looked into the sky," said Sgt Lock. "Coming over the hill from Knowle was a circular light which looked to be pretty high and heading towards Nailsea."

Sgt Lock said the light was moving faster than a normal aeroplane as it passed overhead and also gave off a white light.

"Five minutes later there was a roaring noise and a red flashing light from behind me," he said.

"I thought it was a low flying exercise but I checked and found out it wasn't."

PC Marsh added: "I saw a star and a planet stationary over Dundry but I did hear what sounded like a jet fly over Broadbury Road."

"We heard the Hartcliffe call and looked in the sky and saw, over the hill from Knowle, a circular light, which looked to be pretty high and heading towards Nailsea. Five minutes later, there was a roaring noise and we saw a red flashing light behind us. I thought it was a low flying Exercise, but checked and found it wasn't."

(Sources: *Daily Star,* Manchester, 17.5.83 –'Cop car's battery flattened by UFO'/*The Bristol Journal*, 20.5.83 – 'May the Force be with you'/*The Western Daily Press*, 17.5.83 – 'Flying friend baffles Police')

On the 20th May 1983, a cigar shaped object was seen in the sky, over Bexleyheath, by Mrs Margaret Fry and neighbours.

In the same month, a golden disc-shaped object was seen heading across the sky, over Cardigan Bay, by a father and daughter.

'Flying Saucer' over Merseyside

Mrs Barbara Hanhart from Wallasley, Merseyside, wrote to researcher Brenda Butler about what she witnessed, at 9.30am on 31st May 1983.

'Dear Sir/Madam,

The front page story on the News of the World, this week, gave me a feeling of contentment. So many stories are heard about UFOs but nobody in Authority, namely Defence establishments, seem willing to admit they are around. I was never really convinced either way about them, and admit to being rather sceptical about people's claims to them. I had just fed my cat on that beautiful sunny morning and was outside, putting an empty tin in the bin, when out of habit, I looked up at the guttering of the house, as the birds had been using the loft for breeding, when I noticed a mirror type reflection from the TV aerial, and stepped back to see what it was, and saw what looked like a small sun, spinning on the spot.

I gazed, fascinated, but without thought of what it could be. Suddenly, the object must have changed position, as it wasn't catching the sun any more – just standing still over the roof of my house. I shouted

DEVERAUX DAVE
WALLASEY
MERSEYSIDE
3-10-83

Dear Sir/Madam,

The front page story on the N.o.W this week gave me a feeling of contentment. So many stories are heard about U.F.O. but nobody in authority namely defence departments seem willing to admit they are around. I was never really convinced either way about them but admit to being rather sceptical about peoples claims to them. That is until Tuesday 31st May 1983 at 9.30 am.

I had just fed my cat on that beautiful sunny morning and was outside putting the empty tin in the bin when out of habit I looked up at the guttering of the house as the birds had been using our loft for breeding and I used to watch the birds flying underneath the weather board with feathers and twigs for their nests.

I noticed a mirror type reflection from the TV aerial and stepped back to see what was glinting in the sun. It looked like a small sun spinning on the spot. I gazed fascinated but without thought of what it could be. Suddenly the object must have changed position as it wasn't catching the sun anymore but just seemed to stand still over the roof of the house. My first words were "bloody hell its a flying saucer." I saw it clearly although it was small it must have been about the height of the aeroplanes which we often see here on their way to Manchester or L'pool. It was in two parts it had a circular top three supporting legs and a circular base it

③

was metallic and all I could think of was how the round shape looked so true against the blue sky. It stayed still about ten seconds. I watched as it lifted and moved into the small patches of puffy cloud which was here and there but I could still see the glint in the sun. It went a full half circle before sitting behind a small thin cloud. I couldn't make out what it was doing until a few moments later a commercial airline diagnoly crossed it's path. It had obviously been thinking of a way to get out of the path of the plane. It was about the same height and I'm sure the pilot must have registered something in the sky to the left of him. I think the plane may have been going to a local airport because it wasn't that high on the skyline. When the plane had passed the 'object' slowly

④

passed back over my roof into a little heavier cloud and I lost sight of it.

I awoke my Husband who was sleeping after night work and being half asleep didn't take much notice. I went back downstairs and considered ringing our local Radio but as I didn't even have a witness (except the cat) I was frightened of feeling a little foolish. I told a couple of people as I took my son to school when I had found a bit of courage but they laughed and thought I was seeing things. I stood outside many morning's willing another one to show up I knew what I had seen but I wanted someone else to see it.

A couple of months went by and one evening my husband and I were talking to our elderly neighbour. I told him what I had seen months before. As I waited for him to

⑤

smile, his face ~~was~~ went a little pale and he
said he believed what I had seen as he had
a similar experience near the beginning of the
year. He was drawing his front curtains
when he saw what he thought was the moon
until it started changing colours and moved
off.
About six weeks ago two ladies saw a
similar object over our local Town Hall about
7 in the evening. They mentioned this to my
Mother, who, until that moment confessed she
thought I was barmy.
My concern over these objects is the fact that
they seem to be pretty busy over an area
which house's a Nuclear Plant namely
Capenhurst. The only other reason for coming
to this area is to join the dole queue.
In seriousness though I wonder about that

⑥

plant and all it entails.
Nuclear Fuel has got to be the fuel of the future.
Is it a possibility that another world may have
run out or exhausted certain supply's? Sounds far fetched?
I wonder how many security dept's would be
willing to admit that these objects are here
for a reason
I wonder how many more would tell you to rip
this letter up and treat it as the words of a
crank?
I know what I saw. Now you know too.
Why can't someone investigate some of these
sighting's and publish the truth. This world
belongs to us all not just to the military
What in "The World" do these beings want? I'd love
to know. Your's Sincerely
Mrs. Barbara Hanhart

out, 'What the bloody hell? It's a 'flying saucer'!' It was in two parts – a circular top, three supporting legs, and a circular base. The outside of the object was metallic; I estimated it was about the height of an aircraft in the blue sky. After about ten seconds, it lifted and moved into a small patch of puffy cloud. A commercial aircraft then crossed its path diagonally. I'm sure the pilot must have seen it. When the plane had passed, the object slowly passed over my roof into a little heavier cloud and I lost sight of it. I told my husband and others what I had seen. They laughed at me and suggested I must have been seeing things. Some months later, I happened to mention what had taken place to my elderly neighbour. His face went pale and he told me he had seen something similar, which he took to be the moon, until it started changing colour.

UFOs over Bradford

At about 3.15am on 27th May 1983, Mrs Meg Steward of Hunters Park Avenue, Clayton, Bradford, sighted four unusual '*lights*', motionless in the sky. She watched them for 20 minutes and then went back to bed. The next day, she contacted the *Telegraph and Argus* to report the matter. A spokesman for the Meteorological Office suggested the lights were being reflected from the ground into the sky. (What lights would these be?)

On 28th May, UFO researcher – Graham Idle – went to see Mrs Steward, who complained about the poor quality and inaccurate information contained within the newspaper report.

> "My sighting involved four large, bright orange/red, oval lights, with two smaller 'star' like lights to the rear of the larger objects. The one on the right disappeared after five minutes. Ten minutes later, one of the smaller ones then shot off across the sky to join up with the remaining larger object. As it did so, there was a frightening flash of light – so bright it hurt my eyes, before disappearing from sight."

(Source: Graham Idle, *Telegraph and Argus*, 27.5.1983 – 'Seeing lights')

JUNE/JULY 1983

SOUTHAMPTON MAN SIGHTS SAUCER-SHAPED UFO – HE IS LATER WARNED TO KEEP QUIET

Also includes – Crop circles discovered in Wiltshire – the Media takes an interest.
Dan Goring, from the Essex UFO Society, visits the location –
Ian Mrzyglod, from *Probe*, also attends • Did Aliens land at Wigan?

The 'Men in Black'

DURING the course of our investigations into UFOs, we were to come across a number of reports involving visits to the witness's house, by black-suited men – now popularised in modern-day folklore as being members of the 'Men in Black', who, some suggest, are aliens in disguise. While others suspect they are officials from a covert government department, whose objective is to cause fear and intimidation to those concerned. One man who chose not to be intimidated was Graham Herring from Southampton, Hampshire – a keen radio ham, for many years.

> *"At 1.46am, in July 1983, I was transmitting on the FM wavelength, at my home address. Suddenly, the night sky was illuminated by a powerful light. Wondering what on earth was going on, I rushed to the window and looked out to see a glowing orange saucer-shaped object, moving slowly through the air, about a hundred feet off the ground. I stood in disbelief, watching the object, which I estimated was about 150ft long and 50ft in width. After losing sight of it, I sketched what I had seen onto one of the wireless logs. I then contacted the* Southampton Echo *newspaper, and told them what I had seen.*
>
> *A few weeks after the incident, I received a visit at the house by two well-dressed men, who showed me their identification badges, explaining they were from the Home Office."*

After discussing what he had seen, they took possession of the original wireless log, with the illustration of the object on it, and threatened him to keep quiet about the sighting, although their actions did not make sense as, by then, the story had been published by the local newspaper and the *News of the World* (9.10.83).

Still more revelations in the story that gripped the nation

UFO LANDS IN SUFFOLK

And that's OFFICIAL

HOW we told you of the UFO

THE SI

A FORMER senior Ministry of Defence backed the News of the World's dem: the gigantic cover up on the UFO tha Britain.

"I must speak out," he said. "The Ministr know far more than they are prepared to s they have an obligation to tell the occurred that night in a British v

The official spoke as two other ast came to light following our dramatic week of the UFO landing in Tanghai RAF Woodbridge, Suffolk, These were

● Secret Service agents "invented" as part of an elaborate plot to hus incident at 3 a.m. on December 27, 1980.

● An American airman is convinced he was brainwashed by interrogators to blot out all memory of the alien craft.

The Defence Ministry official was an Assistant Under-Secretary of State—a post that allows access to top secret papers.

BAFFLED

He is still bound by the Official Secrets Act, so cannot be named.

He said: "It is in the public interest to push this hard. What worries me is not what the Ministry may be concealing.

"It's the alarming possibility that they may be trying to brush under the carpet something stupendous which has got them as baffled as the rest of us."

The ex-official claimed that reports of "little green men" leaving the UFO at Tangham Wood would not be disputed by the Ministry.

He said: "It will probably pay official circles to let you go on down this line. On past form, public interest will peter out in a week or two.

"The Ministry and others can then settle back on their haunches and hope it doesn't happen again."

What the man from the Ministry really thinks happened is amazing.

He reckons top-secret space experiments could have been carried out over England—and something may have gone drastically wrong.

Farmers and foresters living in the remote countryside **KNEW** something mysterious had hap-

Drawing annotations:
CAME FROM NEW PLAYER? AREA CIGAR SHAPED not too round.
TIME 1.46 monDAY MORNING
20 to 30 FEET LONG
BRIGHT WHITE LIGHT?
REDDY YELLOW GLOW
STREET LIGHTS WENT no way
REMAINED STOPPED FOR 1-2 mins
WENT out Chopper
LOW HUM HIGH ABOVE GROUND 150 - 200 FEET
MADE DOGS BARK MOVED OFF AT VERY FAST SPEED
NORTH BY NORTH WEST

GRAHAM'S UFO sketch from memory—he says the originals were seized

INVADED FROM SPACE

PEOPLE from all over Britain have reported UFO sightings since the News of the World's exclusive story last week.

Engineer Mr Leslie Frost, 48, claims to have seen monster spaceships in 1980 near his home at Hopton, Norfolk.

He says: "What I saw on August 20, 1980, could not have been built by human beings.

"We don't have the technology to put into the air a vast structure 600ft long by 120ft tall—which my engineering training tells me must weigh 35,000 tons, compared with the 2,000 tons of the Space shuttle.

"Yet I saw two of these, plus a triangular smaller machine along the lines of the illustration in last Sunday's News of the World. I watched these machines for half an hour with my wife from our garden."

CB enthusiast Graham Herring says his radio log has been seized by Government men—because he sketched a UFO in it.

Promised

Graham, 34, made two drawings of a cigar shaped object which hovered near his home in Hinkler Road, Southampton, three months ago.

His account of the mystery aircraft appeared in his local newspaper.

Shortly afterwards two men came to my home and said they were from the Ministry," said Graham.

"They were very interested in my sketches of the UFO and asked if they could borrow them to show some experts. They promised they would return them—but they never did."

Graham made new sketches from memory.

Mr and Mrs Roy Webb and their daughter Hayley, 15, had an uncanny experience near where the UFO landed in Suffolk—and on the same night.

Said Mrs Webb: "We were driving home to Mertlesham, near Woodbridge at 2.30 a.m. when Hayley said, 'Look at that star—it's following us.'

"We could see a bright white light keeping level with us as I drove along at 30 mph.

"When we stopped, the light stopped, hovering above us without a sound. Then in the blink of an eye it went up and away very fast."

Hovered

That same night, near the same spot on the same road, a white light terrified Robert Newstead.

"It followed me all the way home to my cottage near Beccles," said Robert.

"It hovered about 6ft in the air and a few feet behind me, not making a sound. I was scared."

Graham Herring's illustration bears a strong resemblance to the UFO, photographed over Erdington, Birmingham, in 1978, not forgetting the object sighted over Belfast some years previously.

(Source: Personal interview)

Above: UFO photographed in Birmingham, 1978.
Right: Object sighted over Belfast

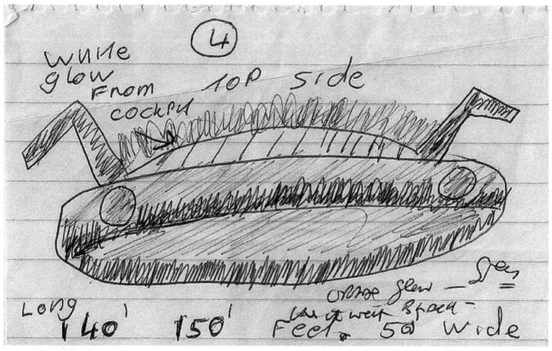

Another drawing made by Graham Herring from memory – his original having been confiscated by 'men from the Home Office'.

Corn circles discovered, Wiltshire

In an excellent article written by Ian Mrzyglod – entitled 'Driving Us Round in Circles', and published in the *Probe Report* – he expressed the feeling that it was against his better intentions to get involved further, because – first, sufficient coverage had previously been given to the circles in an earlier edition of the *Probe Report* and elsewhere, since 1980 and secondly, articles published on cornfield circles in a UFO journal could create a link between them and UFOs, which Ian believed did not exist.

We believe that there is a connection between the movements of UFOs and simplistic circles found in farmers' fields. Regretfully, we do not have the space in this book to cover, fully, 'crop circle' events brought to our attention – as reported UFO activity has to take precedence. Because of this, we shall try and cover as much as we can, knowing the amount of interest which still attracts media coverage to this present day.

On 1st July 1983, Dan Goring – editor of *Earth-link* – was on holiday in the West Country, during mid-July 1983, with his friend Robert, when they decided to visit some previously publicised crop circles. These were made up of a large circle and four smaller ones, spread equally around the outside in a field of barley south of the B3098 road, approximately three quarters of a mile west of *Bratton, visible from the famous Westbury White Horse hill.

---

*Bratton Camp was also the location of a multi-national Crop Circle surveillance project, in the summer of 1990, organised by Pat Delgado and Colin Andrews, called *Operation Blackbird*. Television and newspaper media from many different countries were there too, as well as security guards, military personnel, and a small group of dedicated UFO witnesses, including Rita Gould (internationally known and respected psychic) along with other participants and witnesses from the first Crop Circle surveillance project, held the previous June, near Cheesefoot Head, in Hampshire, named *Operation White Crow*, also organised by Pat Delgado and Colin Andrews.

Dan:

> *"In each circle the barley, about 3ft high, had been laid flat in a clockwise direction, spiraling out from the centre. Joining the small circle to the larger ones were rough paths, clearly made by people who had visited the location before we had."*

We now know that Ian Mrzyglod, from *Probe*, and some of his members, also made a visit to the Westbury White Horse site on 6th July 1983, and that a thorough investigation was carried out by them into the matter.

Over 25 years later, following a visit to Cradle Hill, Warminster, by Ian – who now lives in the United States – he was pleased to see that many friends and former colleagues arrived to see him, including former Councilor Terry Chivers, whom we had the pleasure of talking to, over the years with regard to his involvement with the *Probe* group.

The Wiltshire Times covered the event on 8th July 1983. On 9th July, members of *Probe* travelled to the Westbury White Horse site, to obtain photographs for further analysis, and met up, once again, with Dr.

Terence Meaden of the Tornado & Storm Research Organisation, based in Trowbridge, Wiltshire. Later that afternoon, during a visit to Cley Hill, just outside Warminster (the scene of several circles in 1982) a formation of five circles was discovered, but this was not released to the Press.

This was followed by a report in the *Daily Express* (11.7.1983) of the appearance of the first set of five circles. As a result of this, both BBC and Independent TV featured the circles on the early evening news and breakfast TV. Various theories were put forward to explain the marks; some said they were rutting deer, others mating badgers (or even over enthusiastic couples, chasing each other around in circles). Other explanations included mother foxes, teaching their offspring to hunt in circles, helicopters flattening the corn, practical jokers, and whirlwinds. As time went by, human nature being what it is, the matter was soon forgotten.

Left: Francis Shephard with the chain that was used to re-create the Westbury/Bratton circles. HOAX?
Right: A whirlwind trail photographed in the same field as the circles. WHIRLWINDS?
(Photos: Left – Credit Wiltshire Times.
Right – Ian Mrzyglod.

J. Allen Hynek

"HAD ANY GOOD LOCAL REPORTS LATELY?..... WE NEED A LIFT HOME"

10   DAILY STAR, Tuesday, July 12, 1983

STAR BINGO! MORE NUMBERS EVERY WEEK. ONLY IN TH

IT'S ALL HOT AIR!

By CHARLES LANGLEY

A WHIRLWIND—not a spaceship — was responsible for these five mysterious holes in a cornfield, experts agreed yesterday.

The five flat patches look as if a heavy object, supported by four legs, dropped into the field at Westbury, Wiltshire.

But yesterday at the Met Office in Bracknell, Bucks, a weather expert said it was all hot air.

Star solves UFO riddle

He explained : "A bare patch in a cornfield will heat up to a higher temperature than the surrounding corn and send a column of hot air up to 200 feet in the air.

"The hot air is then caught by a breeze and it begins to spin causing a small local whirl-wind that flattens the corn."

And the chief investigator of the British Unidentified Flying Object Research Association, Jimmy Randalls said: "We have seen so many of these marks

Circles of mystery... the puzzling holes in U F O country   Picture: CHRIS WOOD

...village lies within the famous "Warminster Triangle," which is to UFOs what Cowes is to yachting.

But even there, five mystery circles that have suddenly appeared in a fresh green cornfield have got everyone guessing.

It looks almost as if E.T. has come back to earth.

The biggest hole is 50ft in diameter. The four others, 14ft in diameter, are neatly positioned around it to create four corners, just as though a spaceship has landed.

Swirling

The corn inside has been flattened close to the ground in a swirling, circular manner, as if by a giant fan or whirling blade.

What has been baffling everyone since 40-year-old farmer Stan Pointer reported the strange sight is that there were no signs of entry by tractor or motor vehicle.

Theories have been flying around like saucers from outer-space.

Stan's wife, Janet, believes the circles were made by a whirlwind. "They can do funny things in a cornfield like this," she said.

But her husband said: "I've never seen anything like this in my life.

Some people say that deer are to blame. But Mr Alan Shepperd ,on whose land the circles lie, says: "It is the wrong year for deer to be rutting, which could make them flatten an area."

Sightseers

Police in Westbury are not ruling out practical jokers. But a spokesman said: "Whoever did it, if they did, put in a lot of hard work and study to get the circles right."

Even that seems unlikely, though. There are several marks linking the circles now because sightseers have walked all over the spot—but there were no clear marks at first, says Mr Sheppard.

One person who doesn't think for a moment that ET has made a flying visit is Steve Duffy, the helicopter pilot who flew me over the field yesterday.

"This is a good old can job," he said, grinning. "You can see where someone walked round and round with a ruddy grass mower."

Councillor Terry Chivers and members of the Probe Group

On 12th July 1983, the *Daily Express* published details of further crop circles being found; this time, at Cheesefoot Head, near Winchester, Hants. These were similar and consisted of a large central circle, about 60ft across, and four 'satellite' circles, measuring 12-15ft across.

Dan Goring:

> *"On July 19th we decided to pay another visit to the top of the White Horse to take photos, before leaving for home, when we were astonished to see that some new holes had appeared alongside the first set, made up of five circles; the first about 32ft across, while the smaller ones were 11.5ft across – the barley being flattened in an anticlockwise direction."*

At some stage, Alan Shephard and his son, Francis, contacted a newspaper (believed *Wiltshire Times*) and admitted being responsible by forming the marks in the corn with a heavy chain. Ian contacted Francis and spoke to him. Francis told Ian that he was responsible for the second set of circles found at Westbury Bratton.

Emphasizing the painstaking lengths that Ian went to with his investigation into matters like this was the discovery of an American newspaper clipping, showing Francis wearing a Warminster T-shirt, which seemed strange as he had earlier declared that he was sceptical of any UFO theory behind the formations being made in the crop. Ian speculated whether the Shephard family was deliberately attracting publicity, in order to promote their own farm produce, but felt this was not the case after having gone to the farm on 18th August 1983, and speaking to Francis's daughter. She explained that the American journalists, in which the T-shirt article appeared, had wanted a sensational story, and that the T-shirts were one of a batch, printed two years previously.

Further enquiries revealed the *Daily Mirror*, who felt they had been 'scooped' by the *Daily Express* and other tabloids, sent a team to duplicate nearly perfectly the neighboring five circle formation, by dragging a chain to recreate the impressions – except their circles were smaller and they had a clockwise spiral. The *Mirror* team then took away their photographs, waiting for the *Daily Express* to report on the circles, and then, presumably, own up to the stunt, which would no doubt have 'scored some points' against their rivals. Unfortunately, the 'hoax' never came to anything.

Ian also spoke to Bob Rickard, of the *Fortean Times*. He spoke to the reporter from the *Daily Mirror*, who explained how they had created the hoaxed circles by measuring them with a length of cord, tied to a swing ball pole and using a compass to calculate the position of the four smaller circles, which took 24 minutes to complete.

Another theory was offered. Were the crop circles an attempt to rekindle dwindling interest in UFO activity around the Warminster area? Sadly, those halcyon days of the 1970s were gone. Groups had ceased to exist. Even Arthur Shuttlewood struggled to get his books published and publishers were now becoming wary of publishing books on the UFO subject.

Ian makes us laugh when he considers possible explanations by summing up the clues available, which indicate the person responsible must have *"a reasonable knowledge of UFOs – enough to know of UFO nests, must live in the West Country, or have easy means of commuting, to enable early morning starts to the task, and must need psychiatric attention."*

He theorised further by speculating that if the circles failed to appear, then the whirlwind theory would be quashed and the hoaxers would have been responsible.

UFOs galore over Yorks

YORKSHIRE Evening Post 20/7/83

By CHRIS CHILD

Somebody up there could be watching North Yorkshire — more than 30 sightings of UFOs have been reported in the county's East Pennines area since January, it was revealed today.

Details of the sightings come from Mr. Mark Birdsall, research officer of the Yorkshire UFO Society, who said March and April was a particularly active time for such incidents.

Mr. Birdsall, 24, of Lovell Towers, Leeds, said UFOs had been seen at Grassington, Skipton, Carlton, Addingham and Gargrave, among others.

He said that the east Pennines was Britain's best area for UFO sightings.

Mr. Birdsall said that during March and April there were two strange incidents at Grassington.

One involved a large circular object, glowing white and flashing, hovering above a woman as she walked down her garden path.

In the other case a man heard a high-pitched siren noise early one morning and discovered an orange glow in some trees.

When the glow had vanished the trees were exposed and one was found to be badly scared. A sample of the bark was analysed by Leeds University, which reported that it had definitely not been damaged by lightning.

Two people who saw an object hovering very low over Carlton Moor have had their photographs examined by experts who say there is definitely something on the negatives.

Mr. Birdsall added that the most dramatic sighting, made by two police officers at Crence near Skipton in April, 1981, was still being analysed.

The two officers took photographs of an object, about 60 feet in diameter.

UFO researcher Mr. Mark Birdsall with one of his maps showing sightings in Yorkshire.

On 21st July 1983, Grassington, North Yorkshire Police Officer – Tony Dodd, of *Contact International* – was featured in an article published by the *Craven Herald*.

Close Encounters – Pemberton, Wigan

An unusual incident took place at 11pm on 22nd July 1983, at Wigan, Lancashire according to *Northern UFO News,* written by Jenny Randles. It involved three women, who were sat outside their houses, during a hot summer's evening. Their husbands were working the night shift. Unfortunately, the identity of the witnesses and the location of where this happened are not known, which is frustrating.

At 11pm, one of the women noticed a bright *'star'* in the sky over the flats in the western direction. At midnight,

Little did he suspect that by the last third of the 20th Century, twenty-six countries had reported the presence of approximately 10,000 (90% of which were located in southern England). Many of the formations appearing in that area were positioned near ancient monuments, such as Stonehenge. According to one study, nearly half of all circles found in the UK, in 2003, were located within a 15km (9.3 miles) radius of Avebury. Archeological remains can cause crop marks in the fields, in the shapes of circles and squares, but they do not appear overnight and they are always in the same places every year. The scientific consensus is that crop circles are almost entirely man-made, with a few possibly due to meteorological or other natural phenomena.

(Sources: *Weekly World News*, USA, 16.81983/*Wiltshire Times*, 26.8.1983/*Swindon Evening Advertiser*, 19.7.1983/*Daily Express*, 12.7.1983/*Bristol Evening Post*, 18.8.1983/*Daily Express*, 11th 12th and 15th July 1983/*Probe Report*, Volume 4, No. 2, October 1983/ Dan Goring, *Earth-link*, September 1983)

ARE THESE UFOs?

CRAVEN could be providing an underground base for extra terrestrials.

This is the theory of UFO investigator Tony Dodd who lives at Wharfeside, Grassington.

And the far-from-eccentric Tony does not rely on fantasy for his argument, he believes he has the truth to substantiate his claims — like the picture of two blurred objects hovering over the area recently.

"This area has a very high percentage of the national sightings," said Tony. "I took this picture of something flying around at night.

"The majority are seen at night, they have been seen many times around here. I have seen 60 or 80 ('fires') machines in the last ten years.

"If you see one at a distance it appears just as a ball of light, but as it moves closer the definition improves.

"The ones in the picture were a ball of light. They were the usual common balls, and were about 400 yards away."

Sightings

Tony is the official North Yorkshire investi-

gator for the UFO tracking organisation Contact International, and he is trying to find out why there are so many unexplained sightings in this area.

"I feel because this is one of the hotspots, as far as sightings go, there are bases located in certain places where they go underground," he said.

In his time as an investigator, Tony has had encounters with different types of spaceship, but one, in particular, stands out in his memory.

"There was an occasion when one came right across my car flying low.

"It was a giant triangular shaped object, a great triangle of light. I flashed a torch at it and they turned round and came back.

"At one time I was a bit apprehensive, but I have been so close to these things they they know I am there. There never been any aggression at all.

"There are strange things flying around at night, but where they come from is another thing.

"I can't believe they are anything that has been produced by us, purely and simply because there has been one sighted in the atmosphere travelling at 22,000 miles an hour.

they seem to be nuts and bolts."

Tony says there is a long history of UFO activity in this area, but that only around 10 per cent of the sightings are ever reported.

He said: "What we are trying to do is find the common factor which could tell us why it is they are here. I wish people would report the sightings — not just the distant blips, but something which could give us something to work on."

Anyone who has any information about UFO activities in the area should contact Bernard Walsh at the Craven Times, and he will put them in touch with Tony.

Machines

"They seem to be more prevalent on winter nights. A lot of the ones I have seen have been way below cloud level. They tend to move more frequently North to South.

"They are huge machines these, and, although they are nothing like anything that has been made on earth

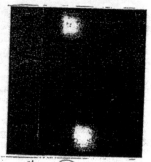

"UFOS Report MF18283
CRAVEN HERALD
SKIPTON.
21/7/83"

the *'star'* began to move northwards and elongate, now resembling a spinning top and changing colour to red. Fifteen minutes later, the object was seen to curve across the sky towards Winter Hill.

At 2am a Jack Russell terrier, belonging to one of the women, ran off into the house (apparently agitated). This was followed by the sound of what was described as a sucking, croaking noise, repeated four times, something the women said *"they never wanted to hear again in all their lives"*.

Then a terrifying *'figure'* appeared on nearby waste land, frightening the women – who ran back into their houses.

The *'figure'* was described as being of normal height, wearing a one-piece suit, with what looked like a goldfish bowl on its head. *'It'* had a glass visor, with a ridged tube – like an elephant trunk – and a box on its chest into which this led. Around the face end of the tube were lumps. The right arm was held stiffly; the other held the box.

One of the women awoke her son, who lived opposite, and he tried to film the area but the flash failed to work. The police were called and arrived at 2.35am. It was said that although they treated the call with great humour, they realised, from the state of the women, that something had frightened them.

This was one of those incidents that begged further investigation. Exactly where in Pemberton did this happen? Was there any examination carried out on the waste land where the entity was seen? Were any after-effects sustained by the women? Was a report sent to the MOD? Were there any other witnesses?

We made an appeal in the local newspaper, during late March 2013, hoping to discover more details, and also spoke to veteran UFO researcher – Bill Eatock – who remembered hearing of the incident, but had nothing further to add.

DAILY MIRROR, Thursday, July 28, 1983

'Spaceship' scares wife

DEFENCE experts were asked yesterday to investigate a housewife's close encounter with a UFO which terrified her.

Mrs Patricia Stark, 25, says she saw a huge spaceship fly over her house as she opened her curtains after midnight.

She said at her home in Penroy Avenue, Bridgwater, Somerset, yesterday: "First one part of the object would glow and then grow dark, and then another part.

"It was silent with no bright lights and no smoke, but it was absolutely huge—about the size of three large aircraft.

"I was petrified."

Her husband Brian, 28, said: "We have reported it to the Royal Naval Air Station at Yeovilton, Bristol Airport and the Ministry of Defence."

(Source: Jenny Randles, *Northern UFO News*, No. 100, Jan/Feb. 1983)

On 28th July 1983, a Bridgewater, Somerset, woman reported seeing a UFO cross the sky, just after midnight.

AUGUST 1983

FURTHER CROP CIRCLES FOUND IN WILTSHIRE

Also includes – Close encounter at Basingstoke for local fisherman
Ex-RAF serviceman sights 'silver crosses' flying over Birmingham
Revolving disc seen over Ilkley

Further crop circles found at the Westbury White Horse

O N 6th August 1983, members of *Probe* met up in Warminster for a social gathering and decided to visit the Westbury White Horse, to show a visitor from London what crop circles looked like. When they reached the location they were stunned to see, placed next to the original set of five, another smaller formation, showing a large central circle, surrounded by four smaller ones. On the way back from Warminster, while passing the village of Upton Scudamore, they discovered a single circle in the field (map reference 872465) roughly 60ft in diameter.

Ian Mrzyglod summarized what had happened since early July.

> *"Two sets of five were discovered in Westbury Bratton, one set of five in Longleat, just outside Warminster, at the foot of Cley Hill, another in the Devil's Punchbowl, at Cheesefoot Head, and the fifth in Wantage. There were also single circles found at Westbury, Bratton, and Upton Scudamore, outside Warminster. All were formed without anyone apparently being seen."*

Close encounter, Basingstoke

Mr Alfred Burtoo from North Town, Aldershot, had served in the Queen's Royal Regiment, in 1924, and Hampshire Regiment, during World War II, and was known locally as an historian and member of the local Archaeology Society, with previous employment as farmer and gardener, and of also having lived in the Canadian outback.

At 12.25am on the 11th August 1983, he decided to go fishing along the side of the Basingstoke Canal, accompanied by his dog, 'Tiny'.

After chatting briefly to a Ministry of Defence policeman on his beat, near Government Road, he headed toward his regular fishing site, about 115 yards North of the Gasworks Bridge, and sat down opposite the water spout, about 100 yards away from the road bridge.

He then undid his fishing rod holdall and took out the bottom joint of his fishing umbrella, pushed it into the soil, and tied the dog to it. While unpacking his tackle box, he heard the gong at Buller Barracks strike one o'clock.

He then set up the rod rests, and cast out his tackle, and sat down watching the water for fish movements, but after about fifteen minutes, decided to have a cup of tea and stretch his legs. He was putting the cup to his mouth when he noticed a vivid light coming toward him from the south, over North Town.

> *"It wavered over the railway line, came on again, and then settled down. The vivid light went out, though I could still see a light through the boughs of the trees. I thought, well that can't be an airplane; it's too low, because it was at a height of about 300ft. I set the cup down on the tackle box and lit a cigarette, and while smoking it my dog began to growl; I then saw two 'forms' coming toward me.*

When they were within five feet of me they stopped and looked at me, and I at them, for a good ten or fifteen seconds. Tiny, an obedient dog, had stopped growling by this time. They were about four feet high, dressed in pale green coveralls from head to foot, wearing helmets of the same colour, with a blacked out visor. The one on the right beckoned me with his right forearm and turned away, still waving his arm. I took it he wished me to follow, which I did. He moved off and I fell in behind him, with the chap on the left behind me.

We walked along the towpath, until we got to the railings by the canal bridge. The 'form' in front of me went through the railings, while I went over the top, and we crossed Government Road – then went down on the footpath. Going around a slight left-hand bend I saw a large object, about 40 to 45ft across, standing on the towpath, with about 10 to 15ft of it over the bank on the left of the path. I thought, 'Christ, what the hell's that?'... didn't think about UFOs at the time. When we got down there, the 'form' in front of me went up the steps and I followed. The steps were off-line to the towpath and we had to step onto the grass to go up them. Portholes were set in the hull,

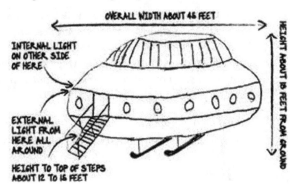

and the object rested on two ski type runners. Going in the door, the corners weren't sharp; they were rounded off. We went into this octagonal room. The 'form' in front of me crossed over the room and I heard a sound, as if a sliding door was being opened and closed. I stood in the room to the right of the door, and the 'form' that had walked behind me stood just inside, between me and the door. I don't know whether it was to stop me going out or not . . . I stood there a good ten minutes, taking in everything I could see. The walls, the floor and the ceiling, were all black and looked to me like unfinished metal, whereas the outside looked like burnished aluminum. I did not see any sign of nuts or bolts, nor did I see any seams where the object had been put together.

What did interest me most of all was a shaft that rose up from the floor to the ceiling. The shaft was about four feet in circumference, and on the right-hand side of it was a Z-shaped handle; on either side of that stood two 'forms', similar to those that walked along the towpath with me. All of a sudden a voice said to me, 'Come and stand under the amber light'. I could not see any amber light, until I took a step to my right – and there it was, way up on the wall, just under the ceiling.

I stood there for about five minutes, and then a voice said, 'What is your age?' I said, 'I shall be seventy-eight next birthday'. After a while I was asked to turn around, which I did, facing the wall. After about five minutes he said to me, 'You can go. You are too old and infirm for our purpose'."

Alfred left the object and walked down the steps, using the handrail, noticing it had two joints in it, and came to the conclusion it was telescopic. He then walked along the towpath, but about halfway between the object and the canal bridge, he stopped and looked back, noticing the dome of the object resembled an oversized chimney cowl and was revolving anticlockwise.

> *"I then walked onto the spot where I had left my dog and fishing tackle, and the first thing I did when I got there was to pick up my cold cup of tea and drink it. And then I heard this whining noise, as if an electric generator was starting up, and the thing lifted off and the bright light came on again. It was so bright that I could see my fishing float in the water, 6ft away from the opposite bank of the canal, and the thin iron bars on the canal bridge. The object took off at a very high speed, out over the military cemetery in the west, and then a little later I saw the light going over the Hog's Back and out-of-sight. This was around 2am."*

Mr Burtoo carried on fishing until 10am, at which point two Ministry of Defence mounted policemen rode up to him. After some general conversation about the various fish caught, he told them about the UFO. One of them said:

> *"Yes, I dare say you did see that UFO. I expect they were checking on our military installations."*

At that moment, a man from the canal lock yard came along and advised the MOD policemen that horses were not allowed on the towpath, and so the conversation was cut short. Mr Burtoo continued fishing until 12.30pm and returned home at 1pm. He told his wife, Marjorie, and a friend of hers, that he had seen a UFO, but refrained from telling them he had been taken on-board.

The story of Alfred Burtoo's encounter made headline news in the local paper, two months later, as a result of him having written to the *Aldershot News*, initially, inquiring if anyone had reported an unusual light at the time of the incident. The newspaper then notified Omar Fowler – the Chairman and Investigations Coordinator of the Surrey Investigation Group on Aerial Phenomena (SIGAP) who subsequently interviewed Mr Burtoo in October. Unfortunately, enquiries made by Omar to trace the two mounted men, and other possible witnesses, were unsuccessful.

Omar Fowler

In the following month Tim Good interviewed Alfred, in the presence of local reporter – Debbie Collins – from which it was ascertained:

> *". . . the shape of the central room as being octagonal, with a low ceiling, and that the floor appeared to be covered with a soft material of some kind, because he was unable to hear his footsteps. The internal lighting did not appear to emanate from any particular source, with the exception of the beam of amber light, underneath which he was asked to stand. The lighting in general was rather dim. There were no dials, controls, seats, or other objects seen, apart from the central column with its Z-shaped handle. The temperature inside the craft was a little warmer than outside, which would make it about 65F."*

He noticed a faint smell, similar to that of decaying meat. No facial features could be detected, since these were covered by the visors. The pale-green, one-piece, suits also covered the hands and feet, and appeared to be moulded onto their thin bodies, like plastic. He did not notice if the gloves covered the fingers. There were no belts, zippers, buttons, or fasteners. All four beings were of the same size and unusually thin shape. Had any females been present, Mr Burtoo felt sure he would not have failed to have noticed! The beings spoke in a kind of *'singsong'* accent, similar to *'a mixture of Chinese and Russian'*.

Mr Burtoo, in fact, felt convinced that they originated here on Earth.

> *"I do not think they come from outer space, for we are told by scientists this planet is the only one with water."*

Top UFO Expert Confirms Man's Astounding Claim:

I Was Taken Aboard an Alien Spacecraft and Examined Like a Bug

A 77-year-old man says he was taken aboard a spacecraft by four-foot-tall aliens wearing green suits and helmets — and a top UFO expert who has lectured to British government leaders says his astounding story is true.

Recalling his terrifying abduction, Alfred Burtoo of Aldershot, England, revealed that the strange squat creatures examined him under an amber spotlight, then told him: "You can go. You are too old and infirm for our purposes."

Burtoo said the phenomenal encounter with otherworldly beings occurred early in the morning last August 12, as he was fishing in a canal.

"I spotted a light in the sky coming toward me," he recalled. "I thought: 'It can't be an airplane, because it's only 300 feet off the ground. I wonder if it's a helicopter?'

"It landed behind some bushes, which blocked my view. Then I saw two shapes emerge from the bushes.

"They were about four feet high and dressed from head to foot in pale green coveralls. They had helmets of the same color, with their visors blacked out. I stood frozen to the spot in terror.

"It must be a terrible dream,' I told [...] em. [...] hem. It [...] raft ...

up into the air and shot away [...]t tremendous speed," Bur[...]oo recounted.

Timothy Good, who has lectured on UFOs before a top British government commission probing UFO reports, told The ENQUIRER,

ENCOUNTER with aliens terrified Alfred Burtoo.

GREEN-SUITED aliens drew Alfred Burtoo into their craft and examined him.

"I am convinced this man is telling the truth."

Good, who has also lectured on UFOs at universities throughout England, said he interviewed Burtoo more than 12 times over several months and subjected him to a battery of questions. Burtoo always told the same story, exact in every detail. Good also investigated Burtoo's background.

"There is no doubt in my mind that he was taken aboard an alien craft," concluded Good, who's also an author and consultant to the British Broadcasting Corp.

Omar Fowler, chairman of the Surrey Investigation Group on Aerial Phenomena, which includes pilots and scientists among its members, added: "This is really an exciting case. I believe it to be genuine."

— *JOHN COLLINS*

July 17, 1984 **Page 14** NATIONAL ENQUIRER

Tim Good:

> *"Alfred Burtoo suffered none of the side effects sometimes reported by close encounter witnesses, such as temporary paralysis, nausea, diarrhoea, skin disorders, eye irritation, and so on; nor is he aware of any amnesia or time lapse. But he told me that he did feel 'different' after the experience. He ate little for a while, resulting in some loss of weight, and felt less inclined to go out. He also found difficulty getting to sleep, due to continually turning the events over in his mind. But he had few regrets about his extraordinary experience, which in my opinion ranks as one of the most convincing close encounter cases I have investigated."*

Man goes fishing — is caught by flying saucer

ANGLER ALFRED BURTOO has quite a different tale to tell after his fishing trip to a remote canal.

It was he who got caught — by little green men who took him aboard their flying saucer.

The astonishing incident occurred at Aldershot, England, where experts are convinced of the validity of his story.

Comments Omar Fowler of the Surrey Investigation Group on Aerial Phenomena: "I've been investigating UFO sightings for 16 years, and this is the most sensational thing that's ever happened."

Burtoo, 77, accompanied by his dog, Tiny, was fishing in the canal when, he says, the flying saucer landed.

"I saw a bright light coming towards me, and it hovered just over the railway line," he recalls.

"It then settled on the bank. I went to have a look, and two figures dressed in pale green suits came towards me.

... He's examined by little green men

"They were about four feet tall and had dark visors covering their faces.

"One of them beckoned me, and I followed them to the steps.

"I wasn't afraid — I was more curious than anything."

Burtoo then describes going aboard the UFO.

"It was made of a kind of burnished aluminum, and I climbed some steps and went inside," he says.

"I walked across the room, and one of the aliens spoke to me in a kind of sing-song voice, with an accent something between Russian and Chinese.

"He asked me to stand under the amber light. I

ALFRED BURTOO points to where flying saucer landed.

By HAROLD LEWIS

couldn't see it at first, because there was a kind of black tube blocking my view.

"Then I saw it and went and did as I was told.

"After a few moments, they then asked me to turn around, which I did. They asked me how old I was, and

I told them the truth.

"Then they said I could go, because was I too old and infirm for their purpose."

Burtoo left the spaceship and was halfway along the towpath when it took off.

Burtoo says: "I didn't believe in flying saucers until this hapened to me."

Believed

Although Burtoo told his wife, son and a neighbor about his close encounter, he didn't report it officially, because he didn't think he'd be believed.

There have been dozens of unexplained reports of unidentified flying objects in the area during the past 15 years.

Says Fowler: "I was very skeptical about his story when I went to interview him.

"But he came out with things he couldn't possibly

have known about unless he'd been studying UFOs for years.

"I'm convinced his story is absolutely true and this actually happened."

| 24 | January 24 '84/EXAMINER |

Mindful of the possibility that he had finally confessed the story to be a hoax, Tim Good wrote to Alfred's wife, Marjorie, and asked if this was so. She replied:

"It was not a hoax. What Alf told you was the absolute truth. My friend, who was with me when Alf came home, can verify what he said. He looked absolutely shaken and he told both of us about his experience that he had with the UFO. My husband was not a man who believed in fantasies, or had hallucinations. He was down-to-earth, and you can take it from me that Alf never changed his mind on the story of what he had seen and experienced."

Ministry of Defence spokesman – Peter Hucker, of Secretariat (Air Staff) 2a – said in a letter to Tim:

"I was interested to see the report of Mr Burtoo's alleged encounter. We have no record of corresponding reports which might support this story. There was certainly no report submitted to us by the MOD police concerning the incident . . . MOD interest in the subject is limited to those sightings which are directly relevant to the air defence of the UK . . . The majority of reports received here are often weeks old, and we simply cannot devote public funds to the detailed investigation of such sightings when no threat to National Defence has been demonstrated."

Omar Fowler concluded in his 'write-up' of the incident that he was dealing with a genuine man, who was not prone to fantasizing, didn't seek any publicity, and had little interest in UFOs until the encounter. It was only when he wrote a letter to the newspaper, enquiring if anyone had seen *'strange lights'*, during the night in question, that the focus of Press attention was put on him. Omar tells us that Alfred lost over a stone in weight, through worry rather than fear, his last comment to him being:

"I don't care who believes me or not. I know what I saw and I don't care a damn about what anyone thinks."

Hilary Porter from Beams:

"I have been periodically checking out this area, walking the canal path and exploring nearby, and have found that the whole place is even more restricted (and has been so, long before 9/11 or 7/7) and there is a soldiers' presence in many locations around here, including SAS dressed in black, all fully armed everywhere you go; and its been like this for 15 to 20 years now, so what is it they DON'T want us to find out?"

Alfred Burtoo, who maintained it had been the greatest experience of his life, died on 31st August 1986, aged eighty.

(Sources: Omar Fowler – 'A landing and close encounter, near Aldershot, *FSR* 29, No. 2/ *Guardians of Planet Earth*/*Above Top Secret*, Timothy Good)

The Fry Report

In April/May 1982, Greg Childs – a researcher for Terry Wogan – telephoned Margaret Fry and asked her if she would be willing to take part in a new TV Chat show. Margaret agreed, believing that this would be an ideal opportunity to tell the viewers about her sighting of the 26th July 1978, which involved at least 13 of her neighbours. Margaret agreed to take part and made her way to the studio, accompanied by those neighbours and Timothy Good.

Margaret describes the visit to the Television Centre, at Wood Lane, in 1983, and of meeting up with people like Wayne Sleep and also Meat Loaf's wife, who sat next to her. Her hope that she and the others would be taken seriously was somewhat diminished by the

Greg Childs, the producer, with Margaret Fry at White City Television Studios, 1983

appearance of Terry Wogan and David Frost, wearing some sort of yellow masks, who, according to Margaret:

> *". . . deigned not to talk to us, or the studio audience; when I showed them the photo I took of a UFO over the Serpentine, Hyde Park, Terry – without bothering to look at it – declared it was a seagull!"*

Margaret left the studio regretting they had gone. Sadly, despite many thousands of UFO sightings later, and the passing of now 30 years, UFOs and the witnesses who are involved, are still being subjected to ridicule by the media . . . Nothing has changed.

Newspaper article for August 1983

August 1983 appears to have been the centre of attraction to the Press, as can be seen from the various newspaper articles devoted to the UFO subject. Here are some of them . . .

Telegraph & Argus, Monday, August 8, 1983

AS I READ IT   by JOHN HEWITT

Close encounters of the blurred kind . . .

HAVE you been abducted by aliens, recently?

According to "flying saucer" investigator Jenny Randles, you might have been whisked into a spacecraft and never remembered the experience.

If it was a spacecraft. If it was a real experience.

Let's begin at the beginning, which is what Jenny Randles hardly ever does in her usually sensible but irritatingly rambling book The Pennine UFO Mystery (Granada £1.50).

As readers of the Telegraph & Argus will be only too well aware the Pennines area (including Bradford) had been fertile ground for recent UFO sightings, especially, for some reason during November 1980 and the summer and autumn of 1981.

Silent lights explained

A pulsating white ball was seen to rise above the trees at Wyke Woods; above Woodside estate a whole string of lights moved in a jerky fashion across the sky then vanished in a blinding flash of light; a golden triangle with a dark centre appeared to descend behind powerlines at Hipperholme; at Scammonden Dam a brilliant white light moved across the sky, halted, pulsating, then shot off across the sky to disappear in seconds.

"It was strange, I felt so calm and so peaceful," reported the observer. Jenny Randles seizes upon this feeling of other-wordliness or unaccountable time-lapses which crop up again and again in reports of UFOs. Is it a vital clue to the mystery?

It needs to be said that Jenny Randles is no UFO-nut. She is Director of Investigations of the British UFO Research Association whose Manchester branch went to a great deal of trouble to prove (at least to their own satisfaction that reports of silent multiple lights in the sky were in fact aircraft which were gliding in against all the rules with their navigation lights switched off.

So her account of the puzzling case of Todmorden policeman Alan Godfrey carries more weight. On November 28, 1980, PC Godfrey was nearing the end of his night duty at 5.5 a.m. when he saw what at first he thought was a well-lit bus.

He drove his Panda car to within 100ft. of the thing and stopped, amazed. It was dome shaped, 20ft. across, 14ft. high and hovering 5ft. above the road. Two thirds of the way up was a line of five windows contrasting darkly with the bright fluorescence of the object. Though frightened, he made a sketch. The next thing he knew, the object was gone and he was 100 yards further done the road.

Later he recalled hearing a voice in his head which had said: "You should not be seeing this. This is not for your eyes".

A pain in the head

The UFO investigators persuaded him to be hypnotised by two highly-regarded experts, neither of whom were told anything in advance of the nature of the incident.

Under hypnosis, PC Godfrey recalled that he was carried into a room, presumably inside the "flying saucer". He was met by a bearded man wearing a skullcap and a white sheet, whom he referred to as Joseph, who was accompanied by what seemed to be eight three/four-foot high robots.

He was placed on a bed-like table of black leather and examined. When he tried to look at one of the machines there was a sudden pain in his head. Bracelets were attached to his right arm and left leg and plugged in, and he was asked questions. He then reawoke in his car.

His story is so banal, it is incredible, and yet he clearly believes it. The whole hypnotic session could easily be dismissed as a particularly vivid dream, except that it mirrors so closely the accounts of many other people "abducted by aliens".

Is it clear evidence, then, that the aliens have landed and are closely observing us without being too obvious about it?

Jenny Randles, to her credit, isn't as keen as some of her colleagues to opt for science-fiction solutions.

She suggests there are two separate but linked phenomena at work. The bright, ball-shaped lights appear to be true physical objects, often seen in connection with powerlines or reservoirs which suggests an electrical origin.

Perhaps they emit some form of radiation or energy which affects the consciousness of observers, and is picked up by people who are particularly sensitive — or psychic.

It causes them to hallucinate, so that they conjure up little playlets involving aliens and glittering spacecraft, memories which appear totally real, even under hypnosis.

The suggestion has much to commend it. The deeper one explores the puzzle of UFOs, the greater the similarity there is with other so-called psychic phenomenon — ghosts, water divining, precognition, telepathy, spiritualism. It would also explain why several groups of people in Lancashire reported seeing a vast spacecraft flying overhead, while other people at the same time saw absolutely nothing.

Battles in the sky

It may be significant that people in earlier years have reported UFOs in forms which were familiar to them. In medieval times there were fiery crosses and battles in the sky; at the beginning of the century it was cigar-shaped flying ships, in the twenties phantom aeroplanes; now it is "flying saucers" and aliens with pointed chins and almond-shaped eyes.

I am not going to pretend there aren't holes in Jenny Randles' hypothesis. It does not explain why extraordinarily similar reports come in from all parts of the world, from a huge variety of cultures; nor why reports seem to come in waves.

But she clarifies the issue in two ways. She insists, quite rightly, that unidentified aerial objects do exist; that there is a case to answer. And she tries to guide us away from the too-marvellous, too-seductive option of believing in beings from the stars. There could be another answer.

Unidentified — but not inexplicable

A space invader they all want

DAVID BROWN and the meteorite — sadly it's only a replica

Story by BRAD WILLIAMS

A MYSTERIOUS object came flying down from outer space startling three Cleveland railwaymen.

They heard a brief roaring sound overhead. Then a dull thud in the ground at the siding they were working in just outside Middlesbrough.

They rushed to investigate thinking that the noise sounded like a alien body that had fallen to earth.

They ran past a signal box and came across a hole, the width of a saucer and a few feet deep. One of the men put his hand in it but quickly snatched it back when he discovered it was hot.

A few minutes later he tried again and this time managed to unearth a beautiful meteorite. Measuring five inches by six and weighing one and a half pounds, it was clearly an astonishing find.

Soon after the historic discovery in March 1881 experts realised that

they were dealing with one of Britain's best specimens from outer space.

Today boffins at the British Museum would love to get their hands on the shell-like stone.

And dozens of local extra-terrestrial enthusiasts would like to catch a glance of Middlesbrough's extraordinary treasure.

As far as railway technician David Brown of Granville Road, Linthorpe, is concerned the whereabouts of Middlesbrough's missing meteorite was almost more of a mystery than its origins.

The 24-year-old space researcher first discovered that Middlesbrough had made a name for itself as a meteorite landing site when he visited the Natural History Museum in London.

"There is a large display map, and on it were the words MIDDLESBROUGH in big white letters. But they only have a plaster cast of the meteorite. So I went to my local library and they knew very little about it," explains David.

His tireless trail of discovery led to the Yorkshire Museum in York where the meteorite finally came to rest. They have a fully documented account of the strange incident 102 years ago.

It was confirmed that the meteorite is exceptionally well preserved because it did not age as it came through the earth's atmosphere.

But David Brown firmly believes that the specimen should be back in the town it landed. Instead there is an unsatisfactory replica.

There is a plaster cast of it in a cupboard at the Dorman Museum,

but it should be put on display. I'm sure there is a great deal of interest in it, so why should it be 90 miles away?"

Now he wants to start a public appeal to establish who owns the space object, and to find out how space in Cleveland could be made for it.

But Dr. Robert Hutchison, curator of meteorites at the British Natural History Museum, says he'd like the specimen to be on display in London.

"The configuration of the Middlesbrough meteorite is very good and we would very much like to add it to our collection. Only 20 meteorites have dropped and been found in this country in the last 200 years," said Dr. Hutchinson.

A spokesman for the Yorkshire Museum stressed that there were plans to allow the meteorite to out of its glass case. Not now, or any time in the future.

Close, but not an encounter

UFO's that puzzled a Middlesbrough family may have been satellites, according to amateur astronomer Timothy Barker.

The Turnbull family of Laburnum Road, Overfields, were fascinated by a starry spectacle for two nights and were convinced the objects flashing across the sky were not just shooting stars.

They said the objects moved across the sky with most travelling from north to south.

But Timothy, 18, of Acklam Road, a member of the Cleveland Astronomical Society, said the family probably saw some of the telecommunication satellites orbiting high above the Earth.

"You can see them any night of the week and some of them are as bright as stars," he added.

Strange 'blobs' in the skies

STRANGE phenomena which light up the eastern skies have been spotted by West Yorkshire folk over the weekend.

The Yorkshire UFO Society has been inundated with calls, particularly from people in Bradford and Halifax, reporting sightings.

One woman from Halifax claimed she lay paralysed as a bright blob of light came within two feet of her bedroom window and remained there for four to five minutes.

A Keighley man said he saw a brilliant coloured dumb-bell shape hovering over Keighley Tarn for five minutes on Friday night.

The society keeps their names confidential, but T & A photographer Ronnie Patchett, of Bingley, said he spotted a ball of fire over Chellow Dene which seemed to set like the sun before going into eclipse at 11 p.m. yesterday.

Mr. Mark Birdsall, of the U.F.O. Society, said the close encounters were possibly due to a meteorite shower which began last Thursday.

The sightings could be pieces of rock which pass very close to the earth. "This has been going on for a few days now," he said.

"The sightings only last for a brief time. It is a question of being in the right place at the right time," he added.

The shower is expected to continue for a few more days. Mr. Birdsall said now is an excellent time to watch out for sightings.

TOPICS TONIGHT
By Argus

UFO? Do you know?
SCEPTICAL colleague John Hewitt had a sight of a somewhat unusual UFO on Tuesday morning.

"I caught sight of it from Bolling Road, Ilkley at 7.45," he says. "I thought it was a balloon at first travelling at perhaps 500 feet or so more or less following the railway line.

"But if it was a balloon it was an odd one. It was disc-shaped and metallic, turning so that it kept flashing in the sun. At the speed of a light aircraft it kept a straight course and was lost to sight in the bright morning sun.

"My first thought was that it was being towed by a plane, but I could hear no noise and no plane was visible.

"So what was it? It looked manufactured and possibly scientific."

Did anybody else see it and can they solve the mystery?

England – Aug. 18, 1983

Anyone see this UFO?

Sir, — I wonder if you [r]e had any reports of UFO sighted last [w]ednesday night [A]ugust 10) at about 11 [p.]m.?

[M]y son was driving [ho]me on his motor bike [fro]m Gosforth to Cald[e]rbridge and as he was [pass]ing the Boonwood he [th]ought a glimpse of [some]thing in the sky. He [tho]ught it might be a [sho]oting star, so he [pul]led in to have a good [loo]k. He had stopped just [bef]ore a turning which [lea]ds to Wellington.

[T]here in the sky, hov[er]ing above the two [hou]ses there, was this [en]ormous UFO. He said [it] was about 150ft above [the] roof level, and must [ha]ve been 200ft long. It [ha]d a big white light at [the] bottom and green [flas]hing lights along the [si]de. My son said he got [a] very good look at the [obj]ect and could see its [out]line and everything

He was very frighten[ed] and just sat there watc[h]ing it until it eventual[ly] swerved away an[d] headed towards Wasdal[e].

Telling a friend ye[s]terday at the golf cours[e] she seemed very inte[re]sted and asked wh[at] time this was. Appa[r]ently she was drivi[ng] back from Whitehav[en] with her husband and [as] they came into Cal[d]erbridge she saw the[se] green flashing lights [in] the distance toward[s] Gosforth.

She asked her husba[nd] what he thought th[ey] were and he said: "O[h] it's just a plane." S[he] said it was far too lo[w] for a plane, but then th[ey] were in Calderbridge a[nd] lost sight of the obje[ct]. She thought nothi[ng] more about it until I r[e]lated my tale.

I would be intereste[d if] anyone else saw an[y]thing on that night.

UFOs over Birmingham

At 10.30pm on 13th August 1983, Ex-RAF Bomber Command serviceman – Geoffrey Osborne from Solihull, West Midlands – was conducting a 'sky watch' with his son, on a clear, dry night, having already plotted the movement of twenty one meteors and ten satellites, when:

"I noticed three disc-shaped objects – yellow on the inside of red rims – hurtling across the sky in an 'L' formation, from the south-east direction, heading north-west. Within ten seconds, they had reached the other side of the sky.

Just before they vanished, I saw the disc at the rear cross over the one in front of it before returning to its original position. While we were discussing with great excitement what we had seen, all of a sudden, two large 'silver crosses of light' appeared from the south-east, apparently following the same path taken by the previous objects.

Highwood Avenue
Solihull
West Midlands

13th. February, 2000

Dear Mr. Hanson & m/s Holloway,

Thank you for your letter and enclosure of the Newspaper article, which makes interesting reading. Unfortunately; I, my Wife and Son can add very little to what I have already mentioned in my first letter, however, there are certain observations I can make.

The Silver Crosses that we saw were of a crucifix shape, a strange shape indeed, they had no other colour, unlike the Disc's. They were silver presumedly; because of Sun reflection which shows their height above the earth. The Disc's and Crosses could be seen by the naked eye, but only as points of light, and as you know, meteors cannot deviate from their line of approach. With our powerful binoculars, the disc's had an apparent diameter of 4 to 6 inches, the crosses were at least two feet, which means they must have been enormous in actual size, and the disc's correspondingly smaller.

Certain aspects of your newspaper article are intriguing in that so many sightings appear to be so numerous in shape and colours. I know there has been many bogus accounts made over the years, but conversely, so many have been made by highly responsible unimaginative & professional people of all walks of life that U.F.O.'s must be an actuallity.

I concur with your view, that you are not convinced that they come from outer space. My reasons may not be the same as yours, the distances involved and what goes with it being my main one. However, you mention them going between dimensions and vanishing, this would involve a fourth dimension which I have no quarrel with, however, I have a problem with the Atom Bomb theory, because U.F.O phenomenon has been with us for decades before atomic energy was envisaged, in fact,

I telephoned Birmingham Airport and asked to be transferred to the department that deals with UFOs, and then told an official what I had seen. At 11am, the next morning, an official from Birmingham Airport telephoned me to tell me that a man in Sutton Coldfield had

reported having seen two 'silver crosses' constantly rotating around each other, moving over the town. When I asked him if the UFOs had shown on Radar, he declined to assist me any further."

(Source: Personal interview)

verses 4 to 24. which makes one wonder what exactly was seen by the viewers, but apart from this hypothesis, U.F.O. sightings have been recorded to my knowledge most of my life and in fact long before.

A theory of mine which I have expressed over the years, which has been met on some occasions with incredulity, that U.F.O.'s could have come from this planet Earth...from thousands of years in the future, this of course means TIME TRAVEL. too futuristic for some? but surely no more so than space ships traversing thousands of trillions of miles? however, both our ideas face the dilemma of EINSTEIN's theory of Relativity 1916 of the formula E=MC squared, which shows that the speed of light can never be reached by man, as the more energy used to attain light speed, the greater the Mass becomes, so you use more energy to overcome that problem, but again the Mass doubles proportionate to the distance incurred and does so in a never ending cycle. This must mean for both of our views; that somehow, the U.F.O. travellers discovered another relativity formula that overcomes Einsteins. I could go on, but I have no wish to bore you with my ramblings.

I wish you well for when you publish your book and look forward to reading it in the future.

Yours sincerely

Geoff. Osborne.

G.W.Osborne.

Domed Disc UFO over Shipley

On the same evening (13th August 1983) a motorist was parked up, enjoying the view over Shipley, West Yorkshire, when he saw a bright pulsating light crossing his line of vision, at eye level. As it approached closer, he saw a *'light'* pulsating every two seconds, on top of a disc-shaped object, with a shiny domed revolving top and dark underside.

It passed out of sight in about 2-3 minutes.   **(Source: West Yorkshire UFO Society)**

Ghostly Police Officer

During the afternoon of 18th August 1983, Joan Maloret from Portsmouth, Hampshire, was out walking near the Pallant Crossroads, in the centre of Chichester, West Sussex, when she noticed a figure standing on the opposite pavement, directly across from her position.

> *"He was a male and dressed in an old-fashioned police uniform; the jacket was tight, and the helmet clearly discernible. I thought it was someone in fancy dress. Suddenly, to my astonishment, he just disappeared in front of me."*

Joan was so intrigued she carried out some research and established that this location was regularly used by a policeman, on traffic duty, many years ago.

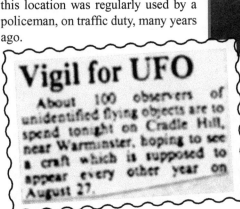

Vigil for UFO

About 100 observers of unidentified flying objects are to spend tonight on Cradle Hill, near Warminster, hoping to see a craft which is supposed to appear every other year on August 27.

On the 27th of August 1983 a 'sky watch' was held on Cradle Hill, involving a hundred people.

UFO over Ilkley

At 7.45am on 30th August 1983, Ilkley resident – John Hewitt – reported having sighted what he first took to be a balloon, following the railway line. As it came closer he saw a revolving disc-shaped object, with a metallic outer surface, reflecting the sun, as it slowly spun in the air, at an estimated height of about 500ft off the ground.

John then contacted the *Telegraph and Argus*, who published his sighting on 31st August 1983 – 'UFO do you know'?

UFO mystery

....And this is what the Adel sky-watchers saw

By TONY HARNEY

This is the first startling picture of the Adel UFO that has baffled Leeds residents.

Yet three days after scores of families in the Adel area of Leeds watched the strange flickering lights hovering and banking in the night sky for over an hour there was still no official explanation of the sightings today.

This picture, taken by an Adel resident, shows just what the sky watchers saw.

Armed with a tele-photo lens amateur photographer Michael Tebbs, an insurance broker of The Meadows, Adel, took a series of time exposure photographs of the mystery lights.

Hovered

Mr. Michael Tebbs ... the man who took the startling picture.

UFO ... this picture taken by Mr. Michael Tebbs shows the strange lights hovering over Adel.

YORKSHIRE EVENING POST
Thursday September 15, 1983

"A friend rang me from Oakwood and asked if I could see the lights and both my mother and myself looked out of the window of our house.

"We sat and watched the lights for about an hour, turning red, blue, green and white. At first I thought it must be a plane until it disappeared at tremendous speed and then returned hovering and banking in the sky," he said.

"At the same time there were other lights flashing across the sky and then we saw something which looked like a fireball flash across the night sky.

"I am not a UFO nut and can only say what I saw, but of course I have no idea what it was."

Since the Yorkshire Evening Post first received reports of the strange sighting there has been no explanation forthcoming for their presence in the sky despite widespread inquiries by the paper.

A spokesman for the Air Traffic Controllers at Leeds Bradford Airport said: "It was certainly not one of our aircraft.

"We had nothing in the sky at this time. We did receive reports of the lights, but could not trace or see anything from here.

"One thought at the time from our senior air traffic controller was that it might have been an aircraft climbing from Manchester Airport into our area and they do sometimes seem to stand still in the sky."

Mr. Graham Birdsall, chairman of the Yorkshire UFO Society, said investigators would be interviewing some of the witnesses.

● Starting next week – YEP spotlight on UFO sightings in Yorks.

SEPTEMBER 1983

A POSTMAN SIGHTS A LANDED UFO, WHILE ON HIS ROUND

Also includes – Ex-RAF Serviceman sights UFO over Poole • Strange lights seen over Bradford, making a humming noise, by local resident • Company director sailing on his yacht sees four 'lights', forming a square • Massive silver 'disc' seen over Waterloo Bridge, London; according to witness, hieroglyphics were seen under the base of the object • Close encounter in Lancashire for Mr Thomas Schofield

Landed UFO, Kings Lynn

IN mid-September 1983, a postman was driving his van along the A47, between Wisbech and Kings Lynn, at 10.45pm, when he was astonished to see a bright, cage-shaped, object resting on the ground in a nearby field.

He slowed down and further scrutiny revealed it was emanating bars of blue, red, and green light.

He stopped the van, got out, and made his way towards the object, which had eight bars to each side.

> *"Each bar seemed to vibrate a very bright colour, as it moved anticlockwise – blue, green, and red. My eyes began to smart with the intensity of the light. After about five minutes, the 'cage' slowly rose upwards and then disappeared in front of my eyes.*
>
> *I got back into the van and recommenced my journey, but felt that someone or something was sitting next to me. This feeling lasted for about 15 minutes."*

(Source: Contact UK)

UFO over Poole

At 5.30am on 19th September 1983, Mr Ernest Tucker from Sandbanks Road, Poole, who had seen service with the RAF Volunteer Reserve in World War Two, sighted a roughly spherical 'light', about a quarter of the size of a full moon, appearing to move towards Hengistbury Head (another of those localities which was to see more than its fair share of UFOs, over the years). It appears a woman living at Branksome Chine (also in Dorset) saw the same object, although she described it as *'a thing with lights on, with a tail like appearance'*.

By the time police officers arrived, there was nothing to be seen. The sightings were later explained away as likely to have been a satellite, flare, or Venus.

(Source: Frank Marshall, BUFORA/*Evening Echo*, 19.9.1983 – 'Weird object reported over coast')

UFO over Bradford

At 3.30am on 21st September 1983, a mysterious *'bright light'* was seen in the sky over Harden, Bradford, by local residents, for over two mornings running. The *'light'* was described as being a yellow glow, accompanied by a humming noise. After a short time it moved away, before being lost from view as it went over the horizon. The matter was reported to the police, at Keighley.

(Source: Graham Idle, *Telegraph and Argus*, 24.9.1983 – 'Woman tells of UFO riddle)

Four lights over Felixstowe

At 7.55pm on 25th September 1983, a company director was sailing his yacht out of Felixstowe Harbour, towards the direction of Harwich, when he noticed what he thought to be lights of an aircraft, moving east to west, at low height. As they came closer, *"I saw four lights, forming a square, heading towards the land."* **(Source: Michael Lewis, BUFORA)**

UFO over Waterloo Bridge

Victoria McLennan has no problem in remembering her UFO sighting, as it took place on her 18th birthday, at 5pm on 29th September 1983.

"I was on my way to meet my brother in Covent Garden, travelling in the back of my boyfriend's MG sports car, with my best friend sat in the passenger front seat. The road was quite busy, at the time, as we drove over the bridge with about 60 people crossing over it. Suddenly, we saw, directly in front of us, a massive silver disc. It almost dropped out of the sky in front of us, taking up a large area, hovering on its side. I could see portholes all around the centre and what looked like lights on inside.

Some of the windows looked dull, as though people were looking through them. The craft was shining a lilac light from its underside. As it hovered I noticed there was writing under it, which looked like hieroglyphics, resembling what looked like a swastika in red, but I believe, if my memory serves me right, the 'arms' may have been going in the opposite direction from a swastika. There was a car in front of the MG; a little boy was jumping up and down on the back seat, with excitement. We presumed he had also seen the craft. He was almost pointing at me and I nodded at him to confirm he had also seen it, although his parents didn't seem to react.

Some of the people crossing the bridge had obviously seen it, as they stood there with their fingers pointing up to it; others just walked on, like nothing was there. I sat there with my mouth wide open, speechless – then it disappeared – no trail, no sound and no smell. I turned to my boyfriend and said, 'Did you see that?' and he said 'No'. I said to my friend 'Did you see that?' Her mouth was wide open. She just nodded. I confirmed we had both seen the same object but was amazed that my boyfriend hadn't seen it, as it was massive – you couldn't miss it. I checked the papers for a few days, after thinking there would be a report – but nothing. The car engine turned off. We had to restart it."

(Source: Personal interview)

Close Encounter, Lancashire

Thomas Schofield – a coalman by trade, from Cranshaw Booth, Rossendale, in Lancashire – was on his way home, between 8.30pm and 9pm, in September 1983, after having just closed up the garage leading into the coal yard, situated just off Forest Bank Road, near to the junction with the A56 Burnley Road.

". . . when I became aware of some movement behind my left shoulder; I turned around and was staggered to see two 'figures', dressed in what appeared to be highly polished clothing – like chrome – standing about 25 yards away from where I was stood, now transfixed. They

Thomas Schofield

were wearing helmets that resembled straight cylindrical tubes. No facial features were evident.

When one of them turned, they made a distinctive rustling noise – then they walked away, carrying what looked like a long polished metal bar, the same colour as their suits."

A short time after news of the incident had been published, Thomas was contacted by somebody from the United States, who told him he was writing a book on UFOs and asked for permission to 'write-up' the incident. It was only by chance that Thomas later came across the finished article, dated 15th May 1984, which proclaimed in its attention grabbing headlines 'Military Alert as UFO Aliens invade' and included such phrases as 'A Blitz of UFOs' and 'trembling witnesses and menacing alien creatures marauding on the ground', leaving Thomas feeling betrayed that his account of what had taken place was sensationalised out of all character.

"The strange thing is that my wife, Mary, who was very sceptical about UFOs, was with me a few months later when we saw what we thought was an aircraft in trouble, one late

01706217124.
passed aug 2003.

12 Forest Bank
Craw craw booth
Rossendale
Lancs.
9-10-2000

Dear John,

Thank you for your letter and map.

When it arrived the envelope had come unstuck. I hope nothing has been lost in transit.

Please feel free to use the sketch.

The time when I saw the figures, was between 8-30pm and 9-0pm. It was just starting to go dark and I needed a light in the garage door way, in order to reverse the truck in. It was late in September.

The helmets struck me because of their simplicity, just straight cylindrical tubes with what appeared to be flat tops.

No aperture was evident on either one.

Both figures were covered in their entirety by silver chromium, the objects they held were of a similar colour.

I immediately searched the area, but saw no sign of their passing.

Yours faithfully,
Tom Schofield

Forest Bank . . . scene of the incident

evening. Rushing outside we saw a flame coloured object, hovering above trees, about 30ft away from the house. It then changed into a bright 'ball of light' and appeared to descend over the side of Cribden Hill, about a mile to the South. As it fell downwards, two small lights dropped away from it."

VALLEY OF THE UFOs

NEWS OF THE WORLD
INVESTIGATES

Faceless men and flying saucers—32 reports so far

IT was dusk when coalman Tom Schofield's day suddenly turned to terror . . . as two silver-suited aliens loomed up behind him.

He had just arrived home from work in the village of Crawshaw Booth — overlooking the eight-mile Rossendale Valley running between Burnley and Todmorden.

He told me: "I was closing the garage door when I saw something from the corner of my eye. I looked over my shoulder and they were there."

Tom, 48, leaned forward, his hands tightening their grip on a mug of tea.

"I can still see them clearly," he said. "There were two figures in silver suits—like the chrome of a car bumper, brilliantly polished and without a crease.

"I just kept looking at them. Then suddenly I realised they didn't have any features. They didn't have faces.

Probed

"Their heads seemed to be covered with helmets.

"One of them turned towards me and I heard their clothing rustle.

"They were carrying something between them. It looked like a metal bar."

Tom looked away for just a second. When he turned back, the visitors had gone.

The case of the silver aliens is one of 32 hair-raising sightings from

12, Forest Bank
Crawshaw booth.
Rossendale
Lanes.
BB4 8NN.

23. 7. 2000.

Dear Mr. Hanson,

Thank you for your letter dated 12.7.2000.

I can quite understand your reluctance to accept reports of sightings, out of hand!

The enclosed copy of an American report, will show you what I mean.

The man who phoned me said he was writing a book to be published in the USA.

I told him, word for word, the story I gave to the News of the World reporter.

By a quirk of fate, I acquired a clipping from an American news paper sent by a relative, to a lady in Crawshawbooth.

You may well imagine how I felt after reading it.

My wife Mary, always very sceptical about stories of sightings, did however see for herself, not long after the garage episode.

Late one night we were watching the television, it was summer and very warm,

Sitting, near the centre of the room. I suddenly became aware, of what I first thought to be a aircraft in trouble. It appeared to be flame coloured, high above large trees, which are only some 30 feet away from the houses.

We both immediately ran outside, entire to see a bright ball of, now to my surprise white light, very similar to the one in the Free Press report.

It appeared to be descending the side of Cribden Hill about 1 mile away to the South.

We saw it for only a few seconds, as it disappeared, two small bright lights seemed to fall away from it.

Regarding the Police Officer "Harry Harris", I cannot say, not knowing either man.

I enclose a copy of my clipping to explain.

Also please find, some old snaps of the locality.

Please do not hesitate to contact me, if you have any query, at all.

I will be glad to hear from you.

Yours faithfully.

Tom Schofield

OCTOBER 1983

TRIANGULAR UFO SEEN FLYING OVER KIDDERMINSTER

Also includes – Dome-shaped light seen over Keighley, by schoolgirls
UFO Display over Essex • UFO over Manchester • Green UFO seen over Reading
brings car to a halt • UFO paces car along the A49 in Shropshire . . .
woman passenger taken ill • UFO over Leeds

Triangular UFO seen

IN October 1983 people living in Blackpole, on the outskirts of Worcester, looked up with astonishment, when a triangular object, showing a brilliant light in the middle, with a number of smaller lights around its *'body'*, making a noise like an old piston engine aircraft, passed over the suburb.

Are we really expected to believe the explanation offered by the Birmingham Edgbaston Observatory that they had seen a weather balloon?

UFO over Yorkshire

Rachel Whiteoak (11) and friend Vanessa Brook (9) from Utley, near Keighley, were returning home from Utley Recreation Ground, Keighley when they saw a dome-shaped bright light on the hill, near the Steeton Jubilee Tower, as darkness fell on 7th October 1983. Frightened, the children made their way home, where Vanessa told her brother Russell (12) what they had seen. As they were putting

Vanessa's cycle away around the back of the house, Rachel looked up and saw the light again in the sky. The children described it as:

> *". . . a plain white, like a bowl, cut flat, with a triangle cut out of the top, with a spire and a red glowing square on the outside."*

Mark Birdsall – the Yorkshire UFO Society's Research Officer – confirmed that they had received other reports of UFOs being seen in the Keighley area and that, two hours after the sighting, a large red object was seen over Beck Hill, Leeds.   **(Source: Mark Birdsall, Yorkshire UFO Society/*Keighley News*, 7.10.83)**

UFO Display over Essex

At 7.15pm on 10th October 1983, Mrs Carole Ashton was stood at the rear of a dairy farm, run by her husband, Francis, at Hatfield Peverel, six miles north-east of Chelmsford, Essex, watching the night sky, when she noticed several lights towards the south-east, bearing 130°.

> *"My curiosity was aroused. I stood watching as they approached closer. I saw a red light first, followed by several others – yellow, white, and blue in colour, before they merged into one mass of light, containing what appeared to be six separate lights made up of multicoloured smaller lights. A group of four then split away, heading northwards; one of them shot off southwards, to meet up with others. My attention was now focused on a dome or half moon-shaped object, with merging lights on is base, slowly descending through the sky. By now, my husband and children had joined me."*

An investigation, later held into the incident, revealed the house clock to have lost 15 minutes of time, and that heavy interference was seen on the television set, during the incident taking place.

(Source: Steve Chetwynd/Mike Wootten, BUFORA)

UFO over Manchester

In the early hours of 14th October 1983, Mr William Skelton from Harpeyhay, Manchester, got up to let the cat out, when he saw:

> *". . . what looked like an upside-down pudding bowl, with an orange globe projecting from its left-hand side, darting about – as if looking for something. Another globe appeared from its left and repeated the same action, for a few minutes, before moving in a half circle, then heading upwards into the sky, at a fantastic speed – far too fast for any human to have survived."*

(Source: Brenda Butler)

Close Encounter, Reading

At 6.15am, the same morning (14th October 1983) a young woman was driving in a north-west direction, along the A327 towards Reading, between Arborfield and Shinfield, when she noticed a bright light in the sky – first on her left, and then on the right. Thinking it to be an aircraft she carried on, but then the car lights and radio failed, with the car coming to a halt. Looking upwards, she saw the *'light'* descending towards her position in a series of circular movements.

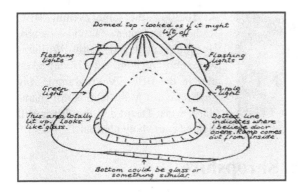

"As it approached closer, I realised that it wasn't any aircraft. The light from it was incredible, illuminating the road and car, making my skin appear green. There was a large green light on the left-hand side and a purple one on the right; it circled the car. For a minute or two I had the feeling I was going to go inside, and wondered how I would get out.

It then hovered in front of me, close enough to see that the surface was grey aluminum in colour, with a width that covered the road in front of me. Suddenly, it shot upwards into the sky and disappeared from sight. The lights and radio on the car came back on.

When I arrived home I discovered that the journey, which should have taken me twenty minutes, had lasted forty minutes. When I checked the clock in the car, it was fifteen minutes slow."

(Source: Gordon Creighton)

★ SUNDAY MIRROR, October 16, 1983   PAGE 5

DJ DAVID STIRS UP UFO FEVER

UFO fever hit Britain yesterday, after a close encounter by radio star David Jacobs.

Callers jammed BBC switch boards after Jacobs mentioned briefly on his Radio Two show that he had seen a mysterious ball of light as he travelled to London on the M1.

The callers reported similar sightings and pieced together, they gave the path of the UFO as a great swathe from Yorkshire, through the Midlands to the West Country.

Jacobs was returning from the 35th Any Questions anniversary pro-

By STEVE BAILEY

gramme in Mansfield, Nottinghamshire, with panelist, politician Shirley Williams.

He said: "It was extraordinary. I've never seen anything move so quickly.

"Suddenly, a brilliant white light with a 'tail' shot from left to right in front of us, at a height of about 250 to 300 feet—then disappeared."

The spot where 57-year-old Jacobs saw the light was between M1 junctions 21 and 22 in Leicestershire, at 10.30 pm on Friday

night. His driver saw the phenomenon, too, and thought it might have been a shooting star.

Jacobs said: "It was travelling too low and too fast for that to be a possi-

Trail of the UFO

The UFO path plotted by spotters along the length of Britain from Yorkshire to Devon

bility." Shirley Williams and fellow panelist Jonathan Porritt missed the light from their rear seats.

Shirley said: "David was clearly taken aback. He

gave a sharp intake of breath, and his first words were 'My goodness. That's impossible'."

Listeners' calls confirming or adding to Jacobs' sighting came from as far away as Seaton in Devon and Market Weighton in Yorkshire.

There were so many that the popular broadcaster had to appeal to people to stop telephoning Broadcasting House because the switchboard could not cope.

Air Traffic Control at nearby East Midlands International airport recorded nothing on their radar

Did Jacobs believe in UFOs? He said later: "There's no way I would close my mind to anything like that—and this is the first time anything like this has happened to me."

David Jacobs

Jonathon Porritt

Shirley Williams

At 10.30pm the same evening BBC Radio 2 presenter *David Jacobs, †Jonathon Porritt and ‡Shirley Williams were returning home from having taken part in the BBC TV Programme *Any Questions?* at Mansfield, Nottinghamshire, when David and the driver Bill sighted something unusual.

Paced by a UFO at Whitchurch, Shropshire

Just over a week later, on 21st October 1983, a married couple who were driving north along the A49, from Shrewsbury to Weaverham, Cheshire, at about midnight, saw a disc-like object, projecting strong beams of light, flying over trees ahead of them. These beams of light entered the car and struck the feet of the occupants. The wife claimed she could smell burning and suffered an attack of hypertension and became very ill. At Taporley, they thought they saw the object again, shooting across the road in front of them, accompanied by a swishing sound. At Cuddington the object reappeared, now highly visible as a fluorescent white oval, showing a slight dome on top, displaying two green, two red, and a brilliant amber light, set horizontally. The UFO stayed with the car for some time, before finally being lost from sight. Was there a connection with other UFO sightings that had taken place along this same stretch of road?

(Source: *Northern UFO News*, Case number 8317)

UFO over Leeds

At 9.30pm on 22nd October 1983, Shadwell, Leeds, residents – Michelle Forest and her friend, Lynette Reaney – were walking towards their car, which was parked in the *Red Lion* Car Park. They noticed a bright *'light'* high in the clear sky that appeared to be moving, *'dancing up and down'*, while heading in a north-south direction. As it did so, it occasionally flashed with light. They watched it for about 15 minutes and were convinced it was no aircraft. **(Source: *UFO Update Quest*, July/August 1984)**

---

*David Lewis Jacobs, CBE (born 19 May 1926) is a British actor and broadcaster who gained prominence as presenter of the 1960s peak-time BBC Television show *Juke Box Jury* and Chairman of the BBC Radio 4 political forum, *Any Questions?* In *Journey Into Space*, he played the lead role of 'Jet Morgan'. As someone who used to thoroughly enjoy listening to this *Radio Luxemburg* weekly science fiction series, I never knew this part was played by David Jacobs until now!

†Sir Jonathon Espie Porritt, 2nd Baronet, CBE (born 6 July 1950), is a British environmentalist and writer, best known for his championing of 'Green' issues and his advocacy of the Green Party of England and Wales. Porritt appears frequently in the media, writing in magazines, newspapers and books, and appearing on radio and television regularly. He has also written a number of books on 'Green' issues, including *Seeing Green*.

‡Shirley Williams, Baroness Williams of Crosby PC (born 27 July 1930) is a British politician and academic. Originally a Labour Member of Parliament (MP) and Cabinet Minister, she was one of the 'Gang of Four' rebels who founded the Social Democratic Party (SDP) in 1981. In 2001–2004, she served as Leader of the Liberal Democrats in the House of Lords, and served as Adviser on Nuclear Proliferation to Prime Minister Gordon Brown from 2007 to 2010.

NOVEMBER 1983

POLICE SERGEANT TONY DODD SIGHTS UFO OVER SKIPTON

Also includes – UFO seen over Bradford

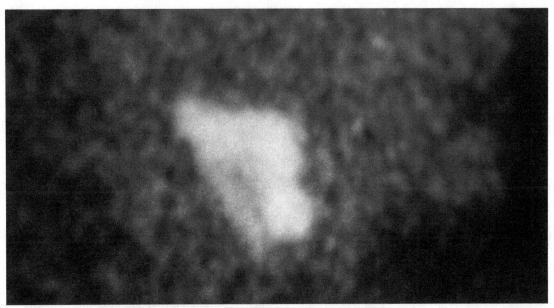

Tony Dodd took this photograph of an object, part of a series, over Beamsley, North Yorkshire in November, 1983

UFO over North Yorkshire

AT 7.55pm on 7th November 1983, Police Sergeant Tony Dodd and his wife, Pauline, were driving between Bolton Abbey and Addingham, near Skipton, North Yorkshire, when they sighted *"a large, disc-shaped UFO, resembling a spinning top"* approaching the vehicle from their right, at low altitude, estimated as being four times the size of their car, before passing almost directly over the car roof and disappearing behind nearby trees. Moments later, the same UFO reappeared and swept towards the car, once again. PS Dodd pulled the car over to a stop, and took a series of photographs of the object as it moved away into the distance.

The photographs were later sent to a research facility called Ground Saucer Watch, in Arizona, that specialise in the analysis of reported UFO images. Their conclusion, after analysis, was that the photographs had recorded a genuine UFO on film – one of the few to meet their strict criteria. They estimated the object was 30ft in diameter and was near spherical in shape. **(Source: Tony Dodd)**

UFO over Bradford

Just over a week later, on 16th November 1983, Mrs J. Gibson of Bullroyd Drive, Bradford, was making the tea at 5.43pm, when she spotted a bright cream object, with white edges, above the horizon, about 150ft above Great Hopton Road.

> *"It appeared to wobble as it hovered. It was larger and brighter than the nearby school floodlights, which were on at the time. A minute later, it shrank to a small dot – like on a TV screen – and disappeared from view."*

At 5.45pm, Mr & Mrs M. Mattox from Roundhill Close, Bradford, were shocked to see a bright oval-shaped *'light'* moving through the sky, estimated to be a third of the size of Bradford City's floodlights. At some stage the object disappeared behind houses, only to reappear and then disappear for good.

(Source: *Bradford and Telegraph Argus*, 18.11.1983 – 'Flying floodlights')

DECEMBER 1983

UFO SEEN OVER LEEDS

Also includes – Boat-shaped lights seen over Worcestershire

Strange lights over Leeds

DURING the early morning of 3rd December 1983, Keith Longbottom was walking to work over a stretch of wasteland, known locally as 'The Hollow', which terminates at Meanwood Road, Potternewton Road, in Leeds. Beyond the main road are factory buildings of the Yorkshire Switchgear Engineering Company. (Behind this was an escarpment called the 'ridge' – the scene of a UFO landing some years previously). Keith was about 200 yards from the Meanwood Ridge, when he noticed what he took to be a star in the sky, moving along in strange, jerky movements, approximately 30° off the horizon. The illustration provided shows what was unlikely to be an aircraft.   **(Source: Mr Mulligan)**

Boat-shaped lights over Worcestershire

At 7pm on 3rd December 1983, a formation of red, green, and white lights, *'resembling a boat in shape'*, was seen motionless in the sky over Severn Beach, for about 10 minutes. *'It'* then picked up speed and disappeared, accompanied by a soft purring noise, the witness remarking on the fact that the intermittently flashing lights seen, changed to white as it flew away.

At 10.05pm on 12th December 1983, a five sided object, showing white and green lights at its rear, was seen moving across the sky, at about the height of a low flying aircraft, over Lower Almondsbury.

A report from the USA for the same date

Geraldine R. Shields (aged 15) of 703 Granite Ridge Road, Hull, Wisconsin, told Portage County Sheriff's Department deputies that she had seen a circular or disc-shaped object, hovering over her house, between 9pm and 9:30pm on 12th December 1980. She described the object as being:

> *". . . about 25 to 30ft in diameter, with a low crown, making a high-pitched sound, and was displaying red, yellow and white lights. The sound woke up a baby in the house, and I had to cover the baby's ears because of the noise. The object appeared three times and, at one point, pictures fell from the wall and the house vibrated."*

The deputies, who did not sight anything themselves, said that another girl in the house also observed the object and Geraldine was visibly shaken from the incident.

(Source: Stevens Point, *WI Daily Journal*, 13.12.1980)

At 3.30pm on 20th December 1983 – a cold, overcast day, with moderate wind – a round, white-fluorescent green object, like a headlamp, was seen stationary in the sky over Stoke Gifford. It then veered off to the left, changing colour from green to white, expanding as it did so to oval in shape, before vanishing from view. At 4.46pm 21st December 1983 an object, resembling burning acetylene, was seen heading across the sky over Thornbury, Bristol – gone out of view in ten seconds. **(Source: Peter Tate)**

At 5pm on 25th December 1983, a number of UFOs were sighted over Rangeworthy, Gloucestershire, involving a deep golden yellow *'light'*, seen moving slowly south-east through the sky, ejecting fragments. A similar phenomenon was reported over Wickwar, Chipping Sodbury, and Godrington, described as resembling a *'small sun'*, *'sodium street lamp'*, or *'star'*. Could this have been space debris, burning up, as it hit the atmosphere?

At 9.18pm the same day, this time over Oxford, two police officers observed four white tubular-shaped objects, silhouetted against a clear sky, moving silently in a west to east direction, whilst stood at the rear of St. Aldates Police Station in Oxford. The altitude of the objects was estimated to be 1,000ft and speed of 150 mph. **(Source: MOD Files)**

The Yorkshire UFO Society – Graham Birdsall (1954-2003)

One man that we had the pleasure of talking to on many occasions but never meeting personally was Graham Birdsall, who back in the 1980's, founded the Yorkshire UFO Society – with his brother, Mark. Later he became editor of the *UFO Magazine* (UK) and, built the publication into the most successful and influential magazine of its kind.

Graham was also a friend and mentor to many of the best-known (and lesser known) ufologists around the world. He produced many UFO conferences and was widely respected for his commitment to the UFO cause. He should never be forgotten.

Graham:

> *"I have been involved in this for 35 years and have been asking the questions about whom they are and why they are here. But now I've realised the question we really should be asking is, who are we and why are we here?"*

Pontefract-based veteran UFO researcher, friend and author of several books on the UFO subject, Phil Mantle, who has been assisting the authors of *Haunted Skies* was himself a member of that UFO Society. We asked him why there were few audio/visual recording of the early conferences. He had this to say . . .

> *"During those early days of UFO conferences, the facilities to video proceedings would*

have been a great idea but would have been costly; remember domestic video cameras were not in common use. We could have used them, but it would have been very costly in contrast to the way in which we now, as a matter of course, film the conferences."

PHILIP MANTLE

1 Woodhall Drive, Batley,
West Yorkshire, England, WF17 7SW
Tel/Fax: 01924 - 444049

**British UFO Research Association
Mutual UFO Network**

Fortunately, Phil was able to take many, now unique, photographs of some of the people involved, which we are proud to present, as it sets the scene beautifully for that bygone period.

Philip Mantle with Hilary Evans

In 1983, The Yorkshire UFO Society arranged a coach trip to visit the Oxfordshire based Contact UK Conference. Unfortunately due to circumstances beyond their control the trip was aborted.

Graham Birdsall, holding the burst tyre that foiled the outing to Oxford

INTAKE HIGH SCHOOL

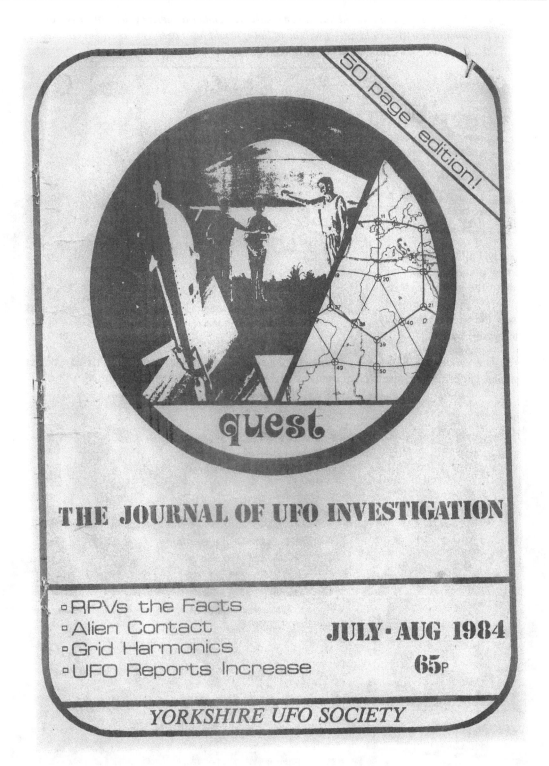

1984

In April of this year WPC Yvonne Fletcher is shot and killed by a secluded gunman, leading to a police siege of the Libyan Embassy in London.

Michael Jackson is accidentally severely burned at the filming of a Pepsi commercial. Space Shuttle Challenger is launched on the 10th space shuttle mission. Astronauts Bruce McCandless II and Robert L. Stewart make the first un-tethered space walk.

A year-long strike action begins in the British coal industry. Sinn Feins Gerry Adams and three others are seriously injured in a gun attack by the Force. Indian Squadron Leader Rakesh Sharma is launched into space, aboard the Soyuz T-11.

British comedian Tommy Cooper suffers a massive heart attack and dies, while live on TV. Aboard the Space Shuttle Challenger, astronaut Kathryn D. Sullivan becomes the first American woman to perform a space walk.

Band Aid (assembled by Bob Geldof) records the charity single 'Do They Know It's Christmas?' to raise money to combat the famine in Ethiopia.

JANUARY/FEBRUARY/MARCH 1984

TRIANGULAR-SHAPED OBJECT SEEN OVER KEYNSHAM

Also includes – Cone-shaped light over Dorset

O N 3rd January 1984, a triangular-shaped object, pink in colour, was seen flying across the sky over Keynsham, at 5.33am. According to the witness:

"It shot off in different directions along straight lines, heading in a south to north direction, before vanishing from view over in 45 seconds."

The following day, a silver triangular-shaped object, showing approximately ten dull glowing lights, was seen floating silently through the air over Kingsdown, Bristol, before changing direction and out of view in 30 seconds. According to the witness, it resembled a flock of birds in formation.

Cone-shaped light over Dorset

On the evening of 19th January 1984, Mrs Maxine Allenby and her son, Robert, were driving along the main Lyndhurst Road, at Hinton Admiral, near Christchurch, on their way home to Ashurst, when they saw what they took to be a low flying aircraft. The object, showing a mass of cone-shaped light, made a steep dive and passed across the road ahead, before moving out of view, behind trees, in the direction of Walkford. They contacted the police at New Milton, and Air Traffic Control, Hurn Airport, but were told that they had not received any other reports. **(Source: Nicholas Maloret)**

UFO over Heysham, Lancashire

At 5.32pm on 27th February 1984, a woman from Heysham, Lancashire, was drawing the curtains when she sighted an object, like a butterfly, moving past the window. It was described as:

". . . big as the full moon and had alternating perfect circles of grey, black, and silver. A minute later, it was lost from view."

(Source: NLUFOIG, Gordon Barraclough)

March 1984 Yorkshire UFO Society holds their conference – here are the photographs!

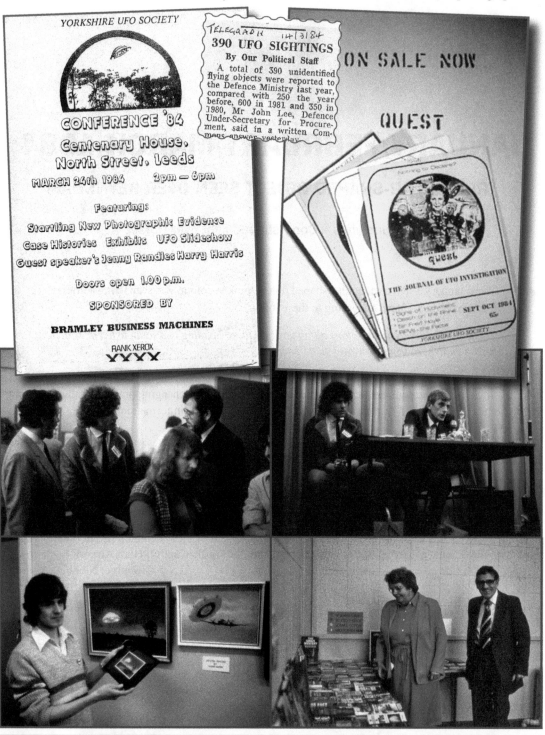

APRIL 1984

UFO OVER STOKE-ON-TRENT

Also includes – Orange spheres seen in Wales – helicopter scrambled – was one of these seen landing at a USAF Airbase, details of which were classified Top Secret for over 30 years? • Did RAF scramble Jet Fighter after UFO was seen over London airspace? • UFO sighted over Blairgowrie, Scotland, by local man, followed by a visit of mysterious strangers to the village • UFO seen over Middlesex, police officers attend and witness phenomena – medial problems incurred
and a visit by government officials

UFO over Stoke-on-Trent

AT 11.30am on 4th April 1984, reporter Geoffrey Newson was talking to Jane Perry – the executive officer of the *Etruria Festival, when they were stunned to see a 60ft diameter, grey disc-shaped object, moving through the sky, over Stoke-on- Trent.

> *"Under it was a fast revolving cone-shaped object. After about 45 seconds, it descended to a few hundred feet, before accelerating rapidly away. We watched it slowly move across the 180 acres of industrial wasteland site, which was under development for a pleasure park. At times, the lower revolving section seemed to expand. It looked like a fat ice-cream cornet. I then reported it to the police."*

---

*Etruria was the fourth and penultimate site for the Wedgwood pottery business. Josiah Wedgwood, who was previously based in Burslem, opened his new works in 1769. It was named after the Italian district of Etruria, home of the Etruscan people, who were renowned for their artistic products. The site covered 350 acres (140 ha) and was next to the Trent and Mersey Canal. As well as Wedgwood's home, Etruria Hall, it included the Etruria Works which remained in use by the Wedgwood enterprise until 1950. Much of Etruria became derelict with the move of Wedgwood after the Second World War and the subsequent closure of the nearby Shelton Bar steelworks. Large-scale regeneration began in the 1980s with the Stoke-on-Trent Garden Festival. Since the Festival closed at the end of 1986, the site has been given over to the Festival Park commercial and retail development. Etruria is also home to *The Sentinel*, the local evening newspaper for the Stoke-on-Trent area. The press hall there is responsible for printing several newspaper titles, including *The Sentinel*, and many northern editions of *The Daily Mail*. *The Sentinel* had previously been based in Hanley.

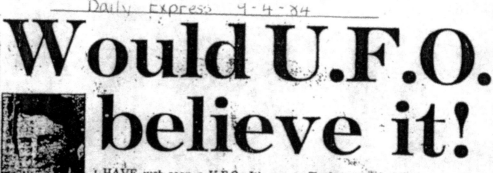

Daily Express 9-4-84

Would U.F.O. believe it!

i HAVE just seen a U.F.O. It's as simple — and as complicated — as that.

As a Pressman the only thing I feel, flying saucer spotters have in common is that they are all "other people." It never, it seems, happens to you.

Now I am one of them — and my troubles have started.

The facts are the easiest part : I watched a 60ft. diameter grey disc arrive over Stoke-on-Trent with a fast moving, revolving cone beneath it.

After about 45 seconds it descended a few hundred feet, hovered and then moved away accelerating rapidly.

I reported the event to the local police, but then the calls started coming in . . .

From UFO spotting officials, from Pressmen like myself from people who just described themselves as "watchers."

"They'll never believe you," said some of the callers. They are not wrong.

Fortunately I had a reliable witness. For the UFO first appeared at 11.30 a.m. last Wednesday, through the window over the right shoulder of Jane Perry, 29, the highly efficient executive officer of the Etruria Garden Festival.

Together we watched it slowly move across the site where 180 acres of industrial wastelands are being turned into a pleasure park.

We saw it descend and hover for about 15 seconds before moving off. At times the revolving section beneath seemed to expand, giving the overall appearance of a large fat, ice cream cornet.

To make my dilemma worse the police said no-one else had reported the sighting. So if anyone out there has the answer, I would like to know.

UFO over Cornwall

They were not the only ones to sight a UFO on that day. Newquay man Roger Knight (18) was driving home from his girlfriend's house in Holywell, Cornwall, just before midnight on 4th April 1984, when he saw:

". . . two dazzling white lights, with a third red light below, in the sky; it was stationary and about 150ft above me. I turned the car radio off and stopped the car. I wound down the window and listened .There was no noise. Suddenly, it started to come down the hill towards me. I became worried and drove away."

(Source: *Cornish Guardian*, 5.4.1984 – 'Midnight sighting of UFO')

UFOs seen over North Wales

At 2am on 14th April 1984, married couple Margaret and Ron Fry, living in Llangernyw, Abergele, North Wales (population 460) were disturbed by the sound of a huge army helicopter flying overhead and the flashing beacons of police cars.

Wondering what on earth was happening, the couple got dressed and went outside, where they spoke to various residents who told them that, at midnight, two orange *'balls of light'*, or spheres, were seen passing low through the sky, over Glan Collen. The helicopter then took off and landed in the local school playing field. Their curiosity aroused, Margaret stood watching the proceedings, involving army personnel, heading into the field with equipment on their backs.

We were amazed to learn that one of these objects landed in a field a few feet away from farmer Williams, and his 14 year-old son, and then moved up the slope before flying upwards, once again. (Margaret tells of other reports, involving a similar light source, which explode to reveal what appears to be structured craft.) We had ourselves come across many other sightings, involving these mysterious orange *'balls'*, which are sometimes accompanied by larger craft.

Margaret:

> *"This is what farmer's wife, Mrs Evans, and her son, saw from their farm lower in the valley. The orange light exploded in pale mauve sparks. Out of this emerged a helmet-shaped, grey craft, which was seen to descend slowly behind a hillock, at Cwm Canol, further down the valley. I interviewed dozens of people from Llangernyw and Gwytherin. In addition to them, a team of Venture Scouts, from Staffordshire/Derbyshire borders, on holiday at Cwm Canol Farm, witnessed what happened. Their leader telephoned the police. My investigation revealed that the second 'ball of light' was seen to head off towards the direction of Gwytherin Hamlet and change to a rocket shape, where it was seen by a couple returning home, at midnight, descending behind a hill at Ty Newydd Isa Farm."*

Declassified File released – UFO over RAF Lakenheath

On 19th April 1984, a senior air traffic controller (SATCO) was supervising his deputy and an assistant at an unidentified airbase in East Anglia. According to the report, the deputy was in contact with a light aircraft, preparing to land on runway 22, when the SATCO noticed lights approaching the other runway.

The unidentified object came in at speed, touched down on runway 27, then departed at terrific speed, in a near vertical climb, according to the files. It was described as:

> *". . . a brilliant, solid 'ball of light', bright silvery in colour".*

An F-15 Eagle seen here at RAF Lakenheath

The file noted that *'witnesses do not wish to be identified, in case their professional integrity is questioned'*.

One is bound to ask what exactly went on here and why this was kept secret for so many years. We sense there is much more to this matter than we shall ever probably find out about. We do not even know what airbase it was. The fact that an unidentified object of presumably alien origin landed, albeit briefly at a UK airbase, is surely a serious matter that begs further investigation.

Although this appears to have been kept from the public's attention, brief details were published by *International UFO Reporter*, in March 1986. They identified the airbase as RAF Lakenheath, but gave the date as 18th April. According to their information, a rectangular UFO was seen hovering silently only 100ft above the side of a road, near the airbase, showing red, green and white lights.

From the same agency, with what appears to be the correct date, at 4pm on 19th April 1984, air traffic controllers at an eastern airport in England, witnessed a glowing sphere that looked like:

> "... *masses of silver paper, 'crinkled up', touch down on a cross runway, then rocket skyward in a manoeuvre judged impossible for aircraft. It climbed 3,000ft in under a second.*"

(Source: *International UFO Reporter*, March/April 1986, p.5/Declassified File PRO)

Royal Air Force Station Lakenheath is located near the town of Lakenheath, in Suffolk, 4.7 miles north-east of Mildenhall, Suffolk, and 8.3 miles west of Thetford, Norfolk. On the night of 28-29 November 1942 Australian born RAF Flight Sergeant Rawdon Middleton, was posthumously awarded the Victoria Cross for valour, when, despite serious face wounds from shell-fire during a raid on the Fiat works at Turin, and loss of blood, he brought the damaged aircraft back towards southern England. With fuel nearly exhausted, his crew were then ordered to bail out. Middleton was killed when the Stirling,  BF372 OJ-H, crashed into the English Channel. The last line of his Victoria Cross Citation reads: *"His devotion to duty in the face of overwhelming odds is unsurpassed in the annals of the Royal Air Force"*.

RAF scrambles Jet Fighter?

Was there any connection with another UFO reported during the same evening, followed by an apparent military response, which occurred at 9.30pm on 19th April 1984, according to Robert Baker – a UFO Investigator from the London area who told of seeing:

> "... *a brilliant white sphere gliding silently through the sky, over West London, which paused in flight and made a zigzag turn, in order to prevent crossing the path of incoming and outgoing commercial flights. Within a few minutes a plane – resembling a Canberra Jet Reconnaissance Bomber – came over, cutting across the busy flight paths into Heathrow*

Airport. It flew around apparently looking for the UFO, which had extinguished its lights and flown away by then. Twelve minutes later, an RAF fighter plane – a Jaguar or Hawk – appeared from the East and flew around the area, at terrific speed, very low, before executing a manoeuvre strictly forbidden, lighting its afterburners, and then did a 'U' turn and headed eastwards."

What happened at Blairgowrie, Scotland?

Blairgowrie is one of the largest towns in Perthshire and is situated to the north of the city of Perth on the banks of the *River Ericht,* Blairgowrie.

Blairgowrie is the gateway to Glenshee, which caters for year-round sports including skiing, golfing, mountain biking, abseiling, hang gliding and paragliding. Close by, the village of Meikleour boasts the Meikleour Beech Hedge, which was planted in 1746 and is officially recognised as the tallest hedge in the world.

One of the things that it isn't known for was a bizarre incident that happened on 25th April 1984, involving then local resident Sidney Freeman, and his mother – Gwendoline – when, following the arrival of a group of mysterious strangers, a UFO was sighted over the house.

Strangers arrive in the town

Sidney:

> *"At the time I was living with my mother, Gwendoline, and father, Donald, in Riverside Road, Blairgowrie.*
>
> *One afternoon, my father asked me to come and have a look through the window. I looked out and saw a group of ten to fourteen people, all male, dressed in black three-quarter length coats, white shirts, and wide brimmed hats. Four of the men were elderly and had long pigtails and beards. The rest were middle-aged and young boys. We watched, with great surprise, as this highly unusual group of what looked like a religious gathering, walked up to the next door neighbour's back garden and entered the back of the house, after being invited inside by the daughter – whom we knew well.*
>
> *Three hours later, they came out of the house and walked off towards the town."*

Donald and Sid had no wish to be nosy, but being friendly with the woman who lived in the house they were concerned about what this was about. Knowing that something rather odd had taken place, Sid had to pass-by her walking back from town, just a day or so later. When she noticed that Sid seemed concerned, she asked what the matter was.

Taken aback, Sid tried to explain why he was puzzled by what he saw on that day, describing the strange *'figures'* they had seen walking up her garden path. It soon became clear that as far as she was concerned, no-one, and certainly not any mysterious men, dressed all in black, had entered her house either on that or any other day. On hearing this, Sid was staggered, embarrassed, and rather concerned. Sid apologised to her and returned home and told his mother and father what had transpired.

UFO seen hovering over nearby tree – Blairgowrie

At about 5.30pm on 25th April 1984, a pleasant, warm day, Sidney Freeman was in the front garden, weeding. His mother – Gwendoline– was sat in the back garden doing some weaving work, with the family collie dog nearby. Suddenly the dog, apparently agitated by something, ran into the kitchen with its tail between its legs.

Gwen:

> *"Seconds later a strange cloud of light, enveloped me so bright it blinded briefly. A forsythia bush directly in front less than five feet away, began to shimmer with bright light.*
>
> *A beam of light, then flowed upwards from the bush, and travelled between two fir trees, before passing over the roof of the garden shed. The beam rose upwards, to a silvery shape hovering over the house. Stepping to one side I was able to obtain a better view of the object, realising that, as I did so, I was confronting a truly awesome phenomenon, resembling some sort of 'spaceship'."*

Gwen later described this as:

> *". . . a large, bulbous-shaped object, with a long tail. Beneath the tail section, a light illuminated five V-shaped downward pointing 'ports'. The front of the 'spaceship' then lit up and I noticed a lip or flange surrounded the circular area. Suddenly the port lights were extinguished and the whole object began to rock from front to back."*

Sidney Freeman, confirmed his mother's account.

> *"I heard my mother shouting for me to come and have a look. I gazed upwards and saw my mother, pointing in the sky. I followed her gaze and saw a brilliant 'light', glinting in the sunshine, hovering over a tall beech tree at the lower end of our next door neighbour's garden.*

> *In a matter of a split second, it shot upwards and was gone. My mother told me what she had seen – 'a 'light' had dropped down, enveloping me. I felt overcome with joy – then the 'light' left me. It lit-up the forsythia bush in front of me. It was large and bulbous, with a long 'tail'. Beneath its 'tail' were five 'V'-shaped projections, pointing downwards. I could see a number of lights dancing all over the 'spaceship' – probably the reflection of sunlight catching it. There was a 'lip', or flange – something like a knight's visor flap on the helmet – a shield, in other words. The 'ship' then*

*moved out of the reflective angle of the sun and tilted, nose down, at which point I shouted
out to you'."*

At this stage, Gwen's husband – Donald – arrived home from work. Sid and his mother explained what had
taken place. Intrigued by the incident, they attempted to estimate the size of the object seen. They judged
it to be 150ft in length, floating about 80ft above ground. The overall shape was reminiscent of a Yale key.

The Police are called

Sid telephoned the Blairgowrie Police, and two officers arrived shortly afterwards. One officer remarked
that this object had previously been reported *"further up the Glen and from RAF Leuchars, where it had
given them a lot of trouble that afternoon, and that other people had also sighted it"*.

The officers then searched all over the back garden, taking soil, along with leaf samples, from the forsythia
bush – the area where Mrs Freeman had been sitting. After about two hours the policemen left, telling
the family that they would keep them informed of the outcome of the investigation – which has never
happened.

Why, it may be asked, the secrecy? Attempts in the early 1990s by UFO investigator – Ken Higgins – to
locate police reports of the incident, met with no success. No-one at the police station remembered the
incident, and Ken was informed that any documents relating to it would have been transferred and probably
destroyed, and that the officers had been moved elsewhere.

A visit from two strangers

One evening, a few weeks after the UFO sighting, the door bell rang.

Sidney:

> *"I went with my mother to the door, where we were greeted by two strangers, dressed in
> what looked like old-fashioned clothing from the 1920s. The man was wearing a dark, brown
> pin-striped suit, with a trilby hat to match. The woman wore a heavy coat, cut in herring-
> bone design, and was wearing what looked like a 'bowl of fruit' hat on her head. Both
> their eyes were prominently black. They told my mother, in
> conversation, that she wasn't to speak anymore of what she
> had seen and that, if she did, she would be doing the work
> of the devil."*

At this stage, Sidney told them to leave. The last he saw of them was as
they headed away from the direction of the village, along the river bank.

We established that Sidney possessed a background history of other
UFO sightings, stretching back to childhood, but felt that this did not
influence the version of events given by him – obviously a very genuine
man, who appears to have been one of many who sighted the UFO.

Sidney also told us that some time after the event, while working in the
local ironmonger's shop, in Blairgowrie, a woman customer came into
the premises.

"She handed me a cooking pot and asked if the pot base could be mended, as it had a hole burned into it. As I went to take hold of the pot handle, what I can only describe as looking like a long wavy line of rainbow coloured plasma – not a static discharge – left me and went into the pot. I knew that the woman had seen it, because she literally froze with fear before running out of the shop along with her daughter. I never saw them again."

Mystery Helicopter over the house

The family's strange encounter was to be only the start of a series of unexplained events.

One morning, Sid and Gwen heard an unusual *'rumbling'* above the house which grew louder until it became deafening, and the whole bungalow seemed to vibrate.

Sid:

"Looking towards the river from the back door, we were shocked to see a military helicopter, hovering some 40ft above the river. Underneath it were slung two half globe-like spheres attached to a box; one was coloured black, and the other orange/red. They were hovering so close to us we could even see a small red light on one of the boxes; they hovered for quite a long time over the River Ericht, *only 30ft in front of the bungalow. It seemed the crew was scanning the area around our home."*

Sid, now employed as a local reporter, for the *Scotsman* telephoned the RAF station, at Leuchars, to find out if they knew anything about this incident.

After some initial difficulty, he was informed that the helicopter was simply *'on manoeuvres,'* and that there was nothing for the family to worry about.

Two days later, however, they were startled by the reappearance of the helicopter and were struck by the fact that it repeated the earlier tests. Significantly, the RAF had never chosen Blairgowrie previously, in order to carry out exercises, nor have they found it a suitable spot since.

Not surprisingly, the events which occurred were to have a profound effect on the Freeman family. Gwen began to exhibit the power to heal by touch – an ability known to have been developed by some individuals following a UFO encounter.

Ron Halliday

Accounts of mysterious 'Men in Black' (or MIBs, as they are known) who visit people who have witnessed UFO activity, are matters that we have come across many times during our research. These 'people', whoever they are, appear to be more concerned with preventing the information being passed to the Media and have often threatened or intimidated people to keep quiet – sometimes bizarrely after Press publicity – which doesn't make sense, but these 'people' aren't bound by such restrictions.

(Sources: Ron Halliday, *UFO Scotland: The Secret History of Scotland's UFO Phenomenon*, p125.
Authors own interviews with Mr Freeman)

UFO over Middlesex –visit by the Men in Black?

The following evening, at 9.45pm on 26th April 1984, a spinning, multicoloured object, throwing off globules of light, was seen darting about in the sky over Stanmore, near Harrow, Middlesex.

As a result of a telephone call to the police, made by Gerri Ashworth – who was accompanied by neighbours Terri West and Ruth Novelli – at least seven officers attended the scene, at 10.22pm. They included Police Constable Richard Milthorpe and PC Paul Isles.

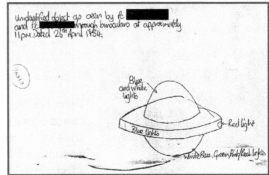

Terri:

> *"I was stood outside with Gerri; Ruth had gone indoors. All of a sudden this 'light' came out of the sky, about the width of the garden (approximately 30ft) – the colour of the moon – and struck the garden I was standing in, before rippling backwards into the UFO."*

Ruth Novelli:

> *"I saw what looked like a star, initially; it was changing colour and moving up and down, and from side to side. It was quite scary and really weird. I felt very strange. I have never seen anything like that before."*

PC Richard Milthorpe:

> *"It was circular in the middle, with a dome on top and below. The middle section contained blue lights, with a red one on the far right-hand side. The dome on top had blue and white flashing lights, while the dome underneath was blue, green, white and pink.*
>
> *I estimated it to be about a mile away, moving erratically in the sky, up and down and to and fro. It gradually got further away, until it eventually faded from view."*

Policeman tells of night he had a close encounter

By Vic Gibson

Terri West

We were not surprised to hear, from conversation with Terri, that the incident, which she felt privileged to have witnessed, had led to some dramatic changes in her life. Such traits of behaviour were to become an all too familiar ingredient of UFO/Paranormal experiences.

The following day, Terri noticed her face was burning – as if she had been too long in the sun.

> *"It was very red. Even now, when I get hot, you can see a visible line down my face. I never had this problem before my sighting; worse, I was forced to seek medical attention, when it was discovered that one of my eyes was damaged with a fixed pupil."*

There is little doubt in our opinion that this medical condition was caused by one side of the face being exposed to the ultraviolet radiation given off by the object – an opinion based on other UFO sightings we had come across, over the years. In addition to the physical after-effects, Terri reported:

> *"Strange things began to occur around the house. I came down, one day, and discovered that the glass window bowl of the washing machine had been blown outwards, onto the floor, and electrical appliances continued to run, despite them being unplugged from the wall! My character changed completely, as a result of the 'encounter' previously. I had little interest in furthering any academic study and used to skip school regularly. Now I have two Degrees, and have broadened my own scientific and cultural horizons. I can't say that what we saw was any alien spaceship, or alien beings. I can only tell you what happened on that evening and afterwards."*

Ruth:

> *"The weirdest part of the whole episode was when a local UFO enthusiast called me, a few days later. He said, 'You should be prepared for men in black suits, and a shiny black car, coming to your door in the coming days. They'll tell you they are from the Ministry of Defence but they're not' before adding, 'They'll ask you lots of questions about what you saw, but they quickly get tired'.*
>
> *Of course, I thought he was completely 'round the bend'. That was until three weeks later. I arrived home from work and my neighbour asked if we'd been expecting any visitors that day; she said a black car, with three men in dark suits, had been at my house and left, when they realised nobody was home. She knew nothing of the phone call I'd had from the UFO man. It was extremely spooky and I only wished I'd been in when they'd called."*

It goes without saying that if it wasn't for the courage of people like Terri, Ruth, and so many hundreds of others we were to meet, over the years, our knowledge of the UFO subject would have been far more minimal.

(Source: Personal interviews/*Stanmore and Harrow Newspaper*/*Harrow Observer*, 4.5.1984)

MAY 1984

UFO SEEN OVER HALIFAX

Also includes – UFO seen over Portland • Black 'pencil' UFO seen over
foundry chimney, at Skipton

Strange 'star' – Halifax, Yorkshire

O N 9th May 1984, Trevor Peel from Lightcliffe, Halifax, and Iris Martin, were out walking, during the evening, when they saw a strange looking *'star'* in the south-western sky, at an altitude of 90°. Trevor looked at it through a pair of binoculars and saw that there were twelve small lights, spinning around it. This was also witnessed, the following evening, at the same time.

(Source: Graham Birdsall)

UFO over Portland

At 9.25pm on 12th May 1984, Mr George Davey of Portland, Dorset, was closing the bedroom curtains, when he saw a large bright *'disc'* shoot across the sky.

> *"It had what appeared to be a tailpiece, about six times the length of the diameter of the object. It was travelling in an east to west direction. I lost sight of it somewhere over the Portland Bill direction."*

(Source: Nicholas Maloret)

UFO over Skipton, Yorkshire

At about 2.30pm on 23rd May 1984, John Lee (18) was tending a large flock of sheep, south of Skipton. It was a perfect day, with sunshine, very little cloud and no wind.

John noticed what he first thought was a large kite, just to the North of Skipton, in the direction of the Glywed Foundry, which houses Skipton's largest chimney and structure. He soon realised that the object, which was similar in description to a *'black pencil'*, was far too large to be a kite. John then called Mrs L. Watson – the farm owner – to come outside. She came over to him; at this point the object began to move, heading over the *Cracoe area.

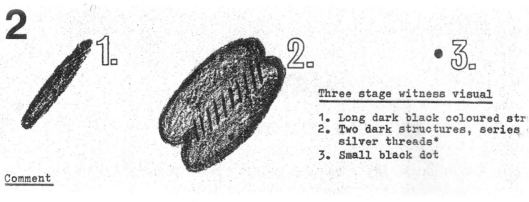

Three stage witness visual

1. Long dark black coloured str
2. Two dark structures, series
   silver threads*
3. Small black dot

Comment

Visitors from Space?

SKY LIGHTS: The lights of what is claimed to be a UFO in the Yorkshire Dales. The small light on the left is thought to be connected with the main group.

Off-beat encounter

A POLICEMAN'S photograph of strange bright lights near a cliff in the ... picture was certainly not an official police picture or report.

ON A CLEAR MORNING in March, a long, low, and managed to get shots of what they con... shining object with three intense white lights cluded was a UFO. spaced along its side, hovered in front of Cracoe. The police officers have allowed us to reproduce...

---

*Cracoe has been the subject of interest by UFO researchers, going back to the early 1980s, when local Police Constable Derek Ingram took some photos of strange lights, seen shining off the rock face. The officer drove over to the fell but saw nothing that might have explained what he saw. An investigation, made later, revealed that the culprit was a combination of white light, reflecting from white and green lichen, Yorkshire grit rock, quartz crystals and water – although this explanation could not have been the answer for what John Lee had seen. In addition to this, Philip Mantle was out sky watching with Graham Birdsall, and others, one cold and dismal evening, when Philip saw a bright light stationary in the sky over the fells. By the time he brought the matter to the attention of Graham, it had gone. (Source: Andy Roberts http://thewhyfiles.net/cracoe)

John ran back into the house and picked up a pair of binoculars. He looked through them and saw the *'black pencil'* was spiralling upwards, at an angle of 65°.

> *"There appeared to be two dark structures, joined by a series of silver threads. The object was rounded at both ends and very long. It was moving very slowly. It was shining, as if the Sun was catching on gloss black paint."*

About ten minutes later, the object had gained tremendous height and now looked like a tiny dot in the sky towards the south-east.

An investigation carried out by the Yorkshire UFO Society (who produced a magazine, entitled *Quest – The Journal of UFO Investigation*, detailing incidents investigated by Graham Birdsall his brother, Mark, and Philip Mantle, along with others) told of a UFO sighting that took place at 3pm, the same day, over Hunslett. **(Source: Mark and Graham Birdsall)**

Diamond-shaped UFO over Saunton Sands, Devon

We realised that we had forgotten to put this sighting in, which was brought to our notice after an appeal in the newspaper, some time ago. If ever you can sense the fear when someone is telling you about what they saw, this would be one of those occasions.

Mrs Jan Bullock contacted us, wishing to bring our attention to an incident that involved her husband, John, who was previously Officer-in-Charge of Barnstaple Fire Station, on 4th August 1983.

She said:

> *"He and three fire crews, and some estate workers, attended a vast area of gorse fire, early evening, at Saunton Sands, and while they were fighting the fire, a huge craft hovered above their heads for about 20 minutes. My husband likened it to the UFO in 'Close Encounters'. Whilst it was hovering, smaller craft left the large one and disappeared at an astonishing speed, then later returned. When the UFO left, that also disappeared at the same speed.*
>
> *When he arrived home the look on his face was one I had never seen before, despite all the*

Road Traffic Accidents and scenes he has witnessed. He said 'You will never believe what I have just seen', and he was quite shaken. He got in touch with RAF Chivenor to ask them if anything 'unusual' was going on; had they picked anything up on radar etc., but they said they had not, and nothing more was said about it. I will also add that none of the other people would talk about it either. Everyone said that no-one would believe them; indeed, when my husband has told others they don't believe him either, yet they all know that he is the very last person to make anything up like that. Also the next day, in the national newspapers, there were dozens of reported sightings over South Wales."

We spoke to John Bullock, who was initially reticent of getting involved but confirmed everything his wife had told us, an attitude, we felt, dictated by fear of attracting ridicule, although John felt it important that somebody knew what had taken place.

An appeal was made in the local newspaper, asking for any witnesses to come forward, from which we received an email from Ian Parker.

"I read with interest your piece in the North Devon Journal *(23.12.2010) about the UFO sighting on Saunton Down. I was also a fireman and was on Saunton Down when the incident occurred. While working on the Down, Concord flew over at approximately 10pm (we were, at that time, in its flight path) and we all looked up, when we heard the familiar sonic booms. It was a clear night and we saw a large diamond-shaped object in the sky. What we actually saw was the object blocking out the stars as it slowly and silently moved across the sky in the direction of Lundy Island. When it was out over the sea, it appeared to hover but, after a few minutes, a number of single lights came out from the larger object, at great speed and raced across the sky. They then paused, as though hovering before returning quickly to the main craft. This behaviour went on for at least an hour. I also remember the Officer-in-Charge radioing down to the fire appliances, parked on the main road, to switch off the blue flashing lights so as not to attract the craft's attention.*

The next day there was a report in (I think) the Western Morning News, *reporting further sightings of the same craft. One was from South Wales, looking across the Channel in our direction, by a police patrol unit. The Fire Officer in charge that day reported the sighting to RAF Chivenor, but they said that nothing had been picked up on radar that night. I can't remember the date this happened, but I will never forget that night."*

Another retired Fire Fighter who contacted us was Vernon Dayman, who was stationed at Woolacombe, for 27 years – the last ten as Station Commander before retiring in 1995.

"We had been called to a gorse fire at Saunton Down, along with other crews – probably from Braunton & Barnstaple. It was a clear night and my first sighting was of three lights, forming a triangular shape. The size and distance were difficult to ascertain, but it passed slowly over my head before disappearing. Shortly afterwards, I was amazed to see several (about eight or nine) very bright white ball-shaped lights, which appeared to be over the Woolacombe area; they looked as though they were hanging like baubles in a random manner, in close proximity to each other. They remained visible for probably three or four minutes before finally forming into a straight line and heading out over the sea. Several members of the Woolacombe fire crew confirmed the sighting at the time, but were probably too embarrassed to say anything."

JUNE/JULY 1984

FLASHING RED 'LIGHTS' OVER UTTOXETER

Also includes – UFO, showing wing like protrusions, seen over Portsmouth
Crop Circles discovered, West Sussex • UFO over York Minster Cathedral –
Did a UFO cause a blaze? • UFO seen over Bristol Airport

Flashing Red 'Lights' – Uttoxeter

DURING the early hours of 21st June 1984, a 65-year-old housewife of Highwood, Uttoxeter – unable to sleep – was looking through the wide-open window, when she saw what looked like a plane approaching from an easterly direction. As it came closer, she was astonished to see what looked like

". . . a circle of flashing red lights, surrounding a constant red light, travelling faster than anything I had ever seen before, changing into a triangular-shaped object."

(Source: Declassified MOD Records, 2009)

UFO over Portsmouth

Robert Clasby, of North End, Portsmouth, was looking out of his bedroom window, at 11am on 14th July 1984, when he noticed:

". . . a peculiar white cylindrical object in the northern sky, showing a number of pointed wing like protrusions. Within seconds it moved up into the sky and was gone out of sight."

(Source: Personal interview/Nicholas Maloret, WATSUP)

Crop Circles found, West Sussex

On 7th July 1984, a quintuplet set – one of many appearing around that time – were found below Cradle Hill and Seaford, near Alfreston, West Sussex, close to the home where The Deputy Prime Minister, The

Right Honourable Sir Dennis Healey, lived. Sir Dennis said that his wife had seen a bright red *'light'* over this area, from their nearby home.

> *"I am the last person to believe in UFOs, but trying to find a rational solution to this problem is a bit difficult. I'm totally baffled. I am expecting now to come across little green men, although I suppose it might be even worse if they were members of the Conservative Cabinet who had landed, or if the aliens turned out to be Press officers of the Conservative Chancellor."*

(Source: *Daily Mail*, 4.8 .1984 – 'Healey's Comet: or are there UFOs at the Bottom of Dennis's Garden?'/*Daily Express* 23.7.1984)

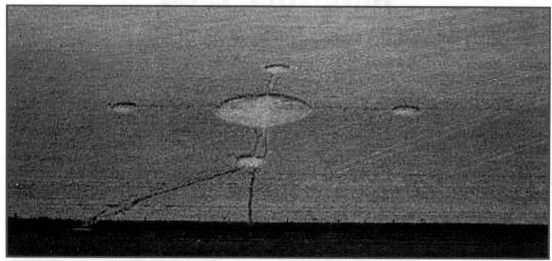

UFO seen over Bristol – and plotted on radar!

Bristol was again the scene of another UFO sighting. This took place just after midnight on the 14th July 1984 and involved Police Sergeant William Smith who was directing traffic at the scene of a road traffic accident. Suddenly two flare like objects appeared in the sky; one blue the other white, before arching downwards to the ground. In another part of Bristol Sgt John Sparrow was on duty when sighted what looked like a red flare coming down from the sky with a white light behind it. A few miles further away at the City's airport Air Traffic Controllers plotted an Unidentified Object crossing the radar screen at about a thousand feet and at 60 knots. It then disappeared but then reappeared close to the edge of the Bristol Chanel before disappearing for good. Despite a lengthy search of the area by the coastguards and RAF Helicopters nothing was found.

(Source: Peter Tate/*Sunday Express* 15.7.1984 'Red flare sparks night time riddle')

UFO causes blaze at York Minster Cathedral?

At 10.30pm on 15th July 1984, van driver Eddie Adcaster, from Huntingdon, was outside his house when he noticed:

> *". . . a glowing orange object – resembling a zeppelin, without any undercarriage or propellers – moving fast across the clear sky, from the York direction. It then flew away and left a white vapour trail behind it, before vanishing into a single cloud. Soon afterwards, I saw what appeared to be a short but severe electrical disturbance, with beams of light – looking like rockets – moving across the sky."*

At 2am on 16th July 1984, taxi driver – Bill Whitehead – was parked on the St. Sampson's Square taxi rank, when he saw:

> *". . . a flame coloured object over York Minster, with what looked like a 'charge' coming out of the base".*

Was this the cause of a fire that started in the *Cathedral requiring the attendance of the Fire Brigade, under the direction of Divisional Commander Alan Stow? He told the *York Express* newspaper (18.7.84) *"We have not eliminated anything from our enquiries at this stage: all possibilities are being investigated"*

Despite a stream of phone calls to the police, reporting having seen a UFO in the locality, churchmen and the police dismissed this as an explanation. Minster spokesman – Canon Michael Bowering – allegedly said *"That's very interesting. Have these chaps seen opticians recently? I look forward rather more to*

---

*In 741 the Minster was destroyed in a fire. It was rebuilt as a more impressive structure, containing thirty altars. In 1137 the structure was damaged by fire, but was soon repaired. An accidental fire in 1840 left the nave, south-west tower and south aisle, as roofless and blackened shells. On 30th December 2009, more than 30 firefighters worked with specialist craftsmen to rescue one of England's stained glass treasures, when a fire broke out at York Minster's restoration workshop and stone yard.

Mystery 'Zeppelin' seen by York pair on night of blaze

By Nick Ingelbrecht

TWO York men believe a UFO attack may have been responsible for the blaze at York Minster.

One, a York taxi driver, claims he saw a fast-moving Zeppelin-like object sending down a flame-coloured charge while it was over the Minster.

The other man, a van driver, made a separate sighting of the UFO earlier that night, and produced a drawing of what he saw, which has been exclusively obtained by the Express.

Van driver, 55-year-old Eddie Acaster, of 86 North Moor Road, Huntington, and taxi driver, Bill Whitehead, aged 44, of Lock Cottage, Haxby Road, said they kept their UFO sightings secret until now for fear of being ridiculed.

But they came forward with their bizarre story in the hope that other people may have seen something similar, and that the UFO theory may shed some light on the mystery of the Minster fire.

Sightings

Eddie made his sighting at 10.30pm on Sunday night last week from outside his house.

He said he saw a Zeppelin-like object moving fast in a North Easterly direction from York.

He said it was glowing molten-orange in the clear skies, and had a white vapour trail following behind.

He stood watching it for about a minute before it vanished into a single cloud in the sky.

Soon after, there was a short but severe electrical disturbance, said Eddie.

"I have never seen lightning like it. It was too straight for lightning — lightning is jagged.

"It was like a rocket directed towards a ship.

"The 'lightning' was definitely aimed," said Eddie, who was an Army crack-shot during his service with the Green Howards.

Possibilities

Eddie said the object he saw was like a Zeppelin without an undercarriage or propellers.

The description is similar to that given by taxi driver Bill Whitehead.

He was on the St Sampson's Square taxi rank at around 2am, Monday morning, when he claims he saw the UFO over the Minster.

"I thought it was a UFO. It was flame coloured.

"It looked as if there was a charge coming out of the bottom of it. To me it seemed like a flame — unless it was lightning," said Bill.

He added: "It was strange. There was no noise coming from it. I thought it was a barrage balloon at first, but they don't travel at that speed."

One of the men investigating the Minster blaze is Divisional Commander Alan Slow of York fire brigade. He told the Express: "We have not eliminated anything from our inquiries at this stage. All possibilities are being investigated."

Puzzle

Local airports said they had nothing in the air at the time of the reported sightings.

Inquiries were made at RAF Linton-on-Ouse in respect of that base and those at Topcliffe, Church Fenton, Dishforth, Elvington, and RAF Leeming; Teesside airport, Leeds Bradford and Newcastle had no aircraft coming or going at that time.

Bill Whitehead said around six other people were in St Sampson's Square at the time he made his sighting.

They may be able to confirm the story.

Report your sighting to the Express by dialling York 39929.

Eddie Acaster's drawing of the UFO, seen disappearing into a bank of clouds.

EDDIE ACASTER: Bizarre theory of how Minster fire was started. Picture by Darren Hartas.

seeing the official fire report when it comes out. I'm an agnostic", while the police adopted a more or less similar response to the suggestion that the blaze was caused by a UFO.

Common sense dictates otherwise. *The York Express* newspaper was deluged with phone calls from people who claimed to have seen a *'saucer'* or *'silver ball'*-shaped object in the sky.

1. One woman pensioner from Bootham, who declined to be identified, said *"At first, I thought it was part of the Moon; it was orange in colour and shaped like a rugby ball"*.

2. Mr Bramwell Taylor, of Haworth, reported having seen *"what looked a silver 'ball' flash parallel across the sky, at just above house height"* on the evening of 15th July 1984. Another woman told of seeing what she said looked like *"a strange object, flying across the sky. I heard a swish every few seconds, followed by this orange coloured light."* Other reports described what looked like an orange ball of fire. One woman even saw *"what looked like the face of a short person, reflected in her front window"*.

3. Earlier that night, Mrs Susan Taylor, and her husband, were returning home to Chestnut Crescent, Holme, after having been to Manchester. As they drove over Spalding Moor, her husband stopped the car and pointed to an object in the sky, which they described as *". . . pointed at the top, like a spinning top, and red in colour; seconds later, it was gone from view"*.

4. A week before the fire, Poppleton housewife – Mary Philips – reported having sighted *". . . a single cloud in the sky, with 'flying saucers' coming and going from it, for over an hour"*.

Triangular UFO over Nuclear Power Station

In October 1984, George Lesnick (a Fairfield, Connecticut, Police Officer, for 29 years), UFO researcher Phil Imbrogno, of CUFOS, Chicago, and Dr. Allen Hynek, were interviewed by Lee Spiegal, of NBC radio, following a 20 month long period, involving numerous sightings of triangular UFOs, reported over the eastern United States.

After the show, they were contacted by a security guard at a nuclear plant, who told them of a huge UFO sighted by him and his colleagues. A time and place was arranged for a personal meeting. When George and Phil arrived at the location nominated, they were met by a total of six guards – all of whom told the same story. During the evening of 24th July 1984, personnel at Indian Point Nuclear Facility saw a huge white 'V'-shaped object, displaying two rows of lights, which was seen descending through the sky to an estimated height of 500ft, before then approaching the facility – at 100yds away. According to witnesses, it was diamond-shaped and approximately 450ft in length. It was seen to change in colour to blue, to red, to green, and then to amber in colour.

It then hovered almost directly over the plant, making a low humming noise, and was observed by 15 guards, and an order was given for shotguns to be issued. The UFO then flew to within 30ft of Reactor Number Three. As it did so, the Plant's alarm and communication systems shut down. Somebody contacted the Army at nearby Fort Smith, explaining what was happening. After about 15 minutes the UFO slowly drifted away, before accelerating upwards and heading in a north-west direction. It is alleged that a request was also made for an armed helicopter to come and shoot down the UFO but, before the command was given, the UFO moved away and left the area. This incident was investigated further and another twenty more witnesses were found to the sighting.

Despite this overwhelming evidence, the Plant authorities denied any such knowledge! Enquiries to ascertain if the security cameras picked up the UFO were also doomed to failure, when it was established the cameras were not loaded that evening. How convenient was that?!

Local Police in Peekskill received numerous UFO sightings, during the same evening. One of them – Sgt. Karl Hoffman, said the UFO he observed included *'a dozen white lights'*, in 'V'-formation, that slowly moved towards the power plant at Indian Point.

It appears that the security guards were then advised not to discuss the matter again with the investigators, as further attempts to speak to them were unsuccessful. Carl Patrick, from the Plant's information office, when questioned by investigators about the UFO, had this to say:

> *"I can neither confirm nor deny that the guards fired upon it, but they did what was necessary to protect the Plant."*

Emphasising the way in which the authorities played their part in defusing and minimising reports like these, following media interest, was a newspaper article about the sightings, published in February 1985, by Jim Montavalli – editor of the Fairfield Advocate. Jim then asked George and Phil to appear on his weekly television programme – 'What do you think?' screened on 20th March 1985. As the programme ended, an immense *'ring of lights'* was seen above the Bridgeport studio. These *'lights'* were then seen to move across the sky over New Haven and into Central Connecticut. Motorists heading along many routes pulled in with amazement. This was no UFO but eight aircraft, equipped with red lights, moving at a height of 5-7,000ft. Despite enquiries made, the identity of the aircraft, or their pilots, was never established. It appears that these were, in fact, light aircraft, as this was confirmed by another pilot, who was sent up to investigate from Danbury Municipal Airport. This was no coincidence, but an attempt by the authorities to create an impression that sightings of genuine UFOs could be explained away, rationally, as man-made phenomena – an art in which they appear to be well practised.

Indian Point power plant

A period photograph of Dr. Allen Hynek is shown with Bill Dillon, whose spectacular sighting took place in 1957 (see *Haunted Skies* Volume 1) while a pupil at Ramridge School, in Bedfordshire. Bill has also been a source of much inspiration to the authors of this book and has kindly provided us with some examples of visuals he has recorded, together with his own artwork, which we take great pride in showing.

Robert Hastings:

Allen Hynek with Bill Dillon (right) BUFORA Conference in High Wycombe 1980's

"Although my own research has been exclusively devoted to UFO activity at nuclear weapons sites, UFO sightings at commercial nuclear power plants have been reported worldwide, for over four decades. These incidents are obviously integral to the UFO-Nukes Connection. A short, far from complete, compilation of them appears below – including the widely-reported sighting of a UFO that hovered over the stricken Chernobyl nuclear plant, near Kiev, in Soviet Ukraine, after one of its reactors exploded in April 1986."

(Source: NUKE PLANT GUARDS REPORT HOVERING UFOs, *Journal News*, New York, UFOs – DID ALIENS BUZZ INDIAN POINT PLANT? *Reporter Dispatch*, **White Plains, New York)**

AUGUST 1984

UFO LANDING AT STONEHENGE

Also includes – Crop Circles discovered

UFO landing at Stonehenge Wiltshire

THE *Biggleswade Chronicle* (10.8.84) told its readers about a strange incident that had befallen members of the Waistell family, who were driving past Stonehenge, on the A303, just before 11pm on 10th August 1984, when the sky turned a dark golden colour, followed by the appearance of a white *'star'*, which turned red and then green in flight. A short time later, while still on the A303, the family saw what appeared to be a large domed object, with yellow lights streaming from windows in its side, standing in a field close to a road sign pointing off to *'Quarley. Turning around, they headed back to have a closer look, but whatever it was had gone.

June 21st Solstice © Reverend Barker 2013

After proceeding on their journey – still on the A303 – they saw further examples of strange *'lights'* in the sky; they included a flashing *'star'*, seen to split into two bright yellow *'stars'*, and a strangely shaped object, with lighted windows, which split into two white *'lights'*, turned red and raced off across the sky – the activity over by midnight.

*Quarley is a village and civil parish in the Test Valley district of Hampshire, England. It is about 7 miles west of Andover and, according to the 2001 census, had a population of 161.

UFO seen over field, Essex

On the same night (10th August 1984) a nurse from Bishop's Hill, Marks Tey, six miles from Colchester Essex, was on her way home, at 11pm, with her boyfriend, when they saw:

> ". . . *a large orange object, surrounded by twelve lights hovering over a nearby field.To our surprise, at least nine separate lights moved away from the UFO – some red, the others blue/ green – and moved around the outside of our car*".

The nurse, who asked that her personal details be withheld, telephoned the police – who did not take her seriously. **(Source: Brenda Butler/Ron West)**

Further Crop Circles found – Wiltshire

During the same year, another crop circle was found at the site of the White Horse, Bratton, near Westbury, Wiltshire (51° 16N, 2° 11W) and a second one directly south, at Cley Hill, near Warminster (51° 12N 2° 11W).

Crop Circle found – Hampshire

In August 1984, farmer's wife – Mrs Barbara Hall, of Corhampton Lane Farm, Corhampton, Hampshire – was out riding her horse, during the first week, when she came across a single circle, swirled into her

husband's wheat field, at grid reference: SU 590 204. She went home, gathered her camera, and took this photograph, showing her son. It measured approximately 40ft in diameter and was swirled in a clockwise direction. The Hall's saw another two formations on their farm; these were to the North, during 1987 and 1988. Others in the area, also nearby, appeared during 1990 and 1995.

'Flying Saucer' over the Thames & the Aethurius Society

John Holder, the previous chairman of Chelsea Financial Services – a highly educated man, with three Degrees, including a PhD in Biotechnology – was with two companions, one of whom we believe was George King of the Aetheuris Society during 1984 when they sighted a *'saucer shaped object'* flying over the *River Thames*. Coincidently, *John was an advisor to the United Nations, in 1977, during a debate on UFOS. (Full details can be found in *Haunted Skies* Volume 7.)

Richard Lawrence, Executive Secretary at The Aetherius Society, who has assisted the authors previously with information pertaining to the role of the Society, has published a book on the UFO subject in 2010 entitled UFOs and the Extraterrestrial Message. He was interviewed recently and asked about whether Governments had lied about UFOs?

> *"Following the Second World War, governments have lied for decades about UFOs and tried to cover up the truth. There is no doubt about this whatsoever, as my book demonstrates. There could be various reasons for this, but the main one, I believe, is that they have not wanted to admit their ignorance to the public at large, and thereby lose their authority with the people. Another reason often cited is to avoid mass panic. Yet another one is because the superpowers have each wanted to be the first to make contact for strategic, military reasons. It is likely that even leaders of nations have been kept in the dark by those mysterious figures who wield power behind the scenes. For example, based on a memo released under the*

---

*After completing a PhD in Biochemstry at Hull University, John originally started work as a teacher but then moved into the city to work for Hambro Life. On seeing an opportunity to rebate to clients some of the commission payable to financial advisers, John founded Chelsea Financial Services in 1983.Although the firm started slowly with many fund groups refusing to deal with them, CFS shone through and discount broking was born. Advice was originally given to customers but when the Financial Service Authority wanted clear water between execution-only business and advice, Chelsea Investments Limited was formed. Dr John Holder is also Chairman of the Mind Body Spirit Festivals and an International Director of The Aetherius Society.

Public Records Act, Sir Winston Churchill, then Prime Minister of Great Britain was misled about flying saucers by officials. The UFO phenomenon is certainly as ancient as the oldest records on Earth and, I believe, pre-dates even these. The Sumerian records are said to go back hundreds of thousands of years and they refer to gods who descended from the sky. The Hindu scripts, which were passed down orally for, some say, many thousands of years, have an exact Sanskrit word for a celestial spacecraft, vimana. The Bible is comparatively recent but has several examples of UFOs within its pages."

WESTERN DECEMBER 19 1984

We did not cause U.F.O. say BBC

710

Mystery UFO could herald new sightings

THE U.F.O. sighting in the West Dorset area of Rampisham last weekend could not have been caused by the nearby BBC overseas transmitting station.

That was the view this morning of the station's transmitter manager Mr. Mike Axford.

"When we are operating our equipment under test conditions, or if there is a fault, there are sometimes lights and sounds emitted from the aerials which could make people wonder," he said.

"But I can definitely state that there was nothing occurring at the station at the time of the Saturday sighting which could have produced such an effect."

The mystery object, seen by several people, from the main Yeovil to Dorchester road, was round with a domed top which rotated slowly high in the sky

THE sighting on Saturday of a mysterious unidentified flying object over Rampisham in West Dorset could be the forerunner of a series of similar visitations according to a local expert.

Mr. Andrew Child, of Portwey Close, Weymouth, and his wife Pam spotted the strange object in the sky at about 4.40 p.m. as they drove along the main Yeovil to Dorchester Road, near the Yetminster turn-off.

The couple watched the UFO for some ten minutes as it hovered about four miles away over Rampisham.

Other drivers stopped and shared Mr. Child's binoculars for a closer look at the object, and all agreed it was unlike anything they had seen before.

Mr. Child described it as about the size of a medium jet plane, but it was round and with a domed top. They could not see markings or lights, and it did not

move other than to rotate slowly.

There have been many sightings of UFOs in Dorset over the years, and local investigator of the British Unidentified Flying Object Research Association, Mr. Frank Marshall, of Shrubbery Lane, Weymouth, says they often come in groups.

"It is quite likely that now there will be whole series of UFOs seen in the area," he said.

Mr. Marshall has been investigating reports of sightings for 25 years but has never had a good view of a UFO himself.

"It is almost as if they play ducks and drakes with me, as I keep just missing being in the right place at the right time," he said.

"The object the Childs saw was grey and without colour and movement, apart from rotating, which is unusual," he said, "although one UFO was seen over Brixham

some years ago which hovered for most of the day."

Mr. Marshall added that the area around Rampisham and Eggardon Hill has become well known over the years for mysterious happenings.

"The ignition and even the lights of cars often cut out completely there for no apparent reason," he said. "And near Beaminster a few years ago three cars went dead for something like half an hour before they could be restarted.

"There are a lot of Roman roads in the area, and some theories have been put forward about lay lines."

Mr. Marshall is now awaiting the official explanation from the Ministry of Defence.

"Official explanations are often more ridiculous than any sighting report," he said. "But I would certainly like to hear of any other sightings in the country."

THURSDAY

UFO

SEPTEMBER-DECEMBER 1984

SIGHTING REPORT FROM COUPLE

Also includes – UFO seen over Dorset – did it affect the witness's car? –
Includes other reports from the same area

UFO over Bromsgrove

ROBERT Price contacted us with regard to what he experienced, in October 1984, while driving home from Bromsgrove, along the A448 dual-carriageway, leading to Redditch, Worcestershire, at 9pm, one evening. He was accompanied by his two work mates.

> *"As we drove past the junction with Foxlydiate, on our right, I saw a black mass, showing five faint lights, shoot across the front of the car from the left. I can't really remember exactly what happened after that, but was surprised to hear, later, that I had stopped the car a short distance down the road."*

Coincidently, during conversation with a police officer's wife, who lived close to the junction, we were told that she had been walking home, late one evening, near to Foxlydiate Wood, close to the dual-carriageway, when:

> *"I was shocked to see what looked like a ghostly figure, about six feet in height, wearing something resembling a black cloak. He, or 'it', actually slid past me, causing great fear. I will never forget what I saw as long as I live."*

UFO over Hampshire

During the same month, a married couple from Hayling Island, in Hampshire, were driving home, one evening, along West Lane, between Daw Lane and a house named 'Littlewood', on their right, near to Hayling. They reported 'two bright lights'. (See sighting report.) **(Source: Nicholas Maloret)**

000081

GROUP	A.P.R.A.	BUFORA REF.	YEAR	NUMBER	INVESTIGATOR		CASE SUMMARY	
/INVEST REF:	000031				EVALUATOR		DATE	1·10·8
							TIME	8-9 pm
RETURN FORM TO:-	A.P.R.A. U.F.O. INVESTIGATIONS		66ᴬ ST. ANDREWS ROAD, SOUTHSEA, PORTSMOUTH PO5 1EU.				LOCATION	
							EVAL'N	
							UFO CLASS	
							CLOSED	

UFO SIGHTING ACCOUNT FORM

SECTION A

Please write an account of your sighting, make a drawing of what you saw and then answer the questions in section B overleaf as fully as possible. Write in **BLOCK CAPITALS** using a ball point pen.

My husband and I were returning home between 8-9 one evening. I'm really not sure what day it was but in the middle of the week when suddenly I spotted these two bright lights my husband slowed down (but didn't stop) and we opened the window to make sure we weren't seeing a reflection off the windows. We studied them going brighter and a lot larger but it was nothing like we've seen before and was not a plane light one was going at a slow speed and the other one was faster then slower. My husband has since said that it was raining and it was a strange night very dark one half of the sky and very light the other half but it didn't feel normal a strange feeling which we couldn't explain.

Please continue on a separate sheet if necessary. P.S (Neither of us drink)

DRAWING*

Your full name (Mr/Mrs/~~Miss/Ms~~) mrs A Varley & Mr D .... Age 41 & 44

Address.......... Brights Lane
Hayling Island Hants

Telephone No................(STD.....)

Occupation during last two years. (mrs) Housewife
(mr) Caretaker

Any professional, technical or academic qualifications or special interests

....

Do you object to the publication of your name? YES
*Yes/~~No~~ *Delete as applicable.

UFOs over Dorset

On 18th December 1984, Mrs J. Taylor telephoned BUFORA member – Frank Marshall – to tell him her husband had seen what appeared to be a 'shooting star' moving across the sky, at 6am, while starting up the car.

A few minutes later, Mrs Taylor left for work, at Harrison Hospital. As she drove along the outskirts of Charminster, near Lockers Garage the lights and engine of the car began to falter, followed by the appearance of a bright *'light'*, seen heading across the sky in front of them.

At 4.40pm on 19th December 1984, Mr and Mrs Childs of Parkway Close, Weymouth, were driving along the Dorchester-Yeovil Road, near Melbury, when they noticed a grey elliptical object in the south-west part of the sky, which was rotating slowly around its axis. Two other cars stopped to watch the phenomena. The incident was later reported to the *Western Gazette*. This may have been the same *'light'* reported by a motorist, and his wife, who were on the M5, near Hatch Bredon, at 4.40pm, the same late afternoon.

Mrs Sherman of Preston, Weymouth, contacted Mr Marshall, following publication, to tell him that the UFO seen by Mr and Mrs Childs was a hang glider, which regularly flies over the locality. Frank continued his enquiries and discovered that gas filled balloons and kites had been launched from Melbury Osmond – a couple of miles from where the 'Childs' had reported seeing their UFO. Whether these were the explanation for what the couple saw, we cannot say.

(Source: Frank Marshall)

THE UFO REGISTER

Date	Time	Location	Description	Class
3.1.84	8.00pm	Bristol	Triangle of pink light	CEI
4.1.84	9.00pm	Otley	Yellow diamond shaped light	CEI
7.1.84	10.00pm	Walsall	Coloured lights	LITS
11.1.84	5.00pm	Birmingham	Coloured lights	LITS
14.1.84	5.00pm	Birmingham	Coloured lights/spinning	LITS +
14.1.84	2.30am	Eccup	White stationary/moving lights	LITS +
17.1.84	8.45pm	Boston Spa	4 orange lights in formation	N/L +
17.1.84	7.15pm	Leeds	Yellow light moving slowly	N/L +
17.1.84	12.23am	Leeds	Glowing ball of yellow light	N/L +
18.1.84	2.30am	Leeds	Yellow light	CEII
21.1.84	10.00pm	Skipton	Small circular grey object/lights	CEI +
9.2.84	7.20am	Leeds	Small ball of white light	CEI
12.2.84	Teatime	Otley	Blue & red cigar shape	CEI
23.2.84	3.30am	Scarboro	Large intense white light/dumbell	CEI
29.2.84	12.20am	Skipton	Glowing circular of white light	CEI +
4.3.84	1.15am	Batley	Circle of yellow & white lights	CEI +
10.3.84	8.15pm	Batley	Circle of red,green and blue lights	LITS @
8.4.84	8.30pm	Halifax	12 points of white light/stationary	LITS
26.4.84	9.45pm	Harrow	Bright light changing colour*	CEI
4.5.84	11.00pm	Threshfield	Cluster of pulsating red lights	CEI
8.5.84	10.53pm	Scarboro	Brilliant white falling light	D/D
23.5.84	2.30pm	Skipton	Large black cigar shape	D/D
23.5.84	3.00pm	Hunslet,Leeds	Small black circular shaped object	CEI
31.5.84	10.20pm	Chesterfield	Dark shape/2 white lights/beams**	CEI
1.6.84	12.00am	Skipton	Dark circular shape	N/L
4.7.84	11.00pm	Keighley	Red ball of light (large)	N/L
4.7.84	11.05pm	Riddlesden	Spherical shaped red light	CEI
5.7.84	8.45pm	Earby Moor	Large glowing cigar shape/very low	N/L
6.7.84	U/K	Carleton Moor	Yellow ball of light	LITS +
6.7.84	10.45pm	Keighley	Three glowing white lights-moving	CEI
9.7.84	U/Kam	York	Dark 'zeppelin shaped oval'	LITS s/e
16.7.84	12.00am	Leeds	Large white light/2 smaller lights	LITS s/e
16.7.84	11.50pm	Leeds	Two fast moving white lights	

All the above documented reports are copyright of the Yorkshire UFO Society except:- *T.Good **BUFOS

The symbols after the classification rating indicate YUFOS Research Division analysis/evaluation. Reports not bearing any symbol do not necessarily indicate UFO report (true). YUFOS reserve the right to re-examine case files, once total evaluation has taken place and the reports still cannot be identified, a new symbol will be used to indicate 'true UFO report'.

UFO SYMBOLS

+ = Aircraft   @ = Astronomical event/image etc   s/e = Satellite   V = Venus
H = Helicopter   B = Balloon   F = Flares   K = Kites   RP = RPVs   HX = Hoax
M = Moon   S = Searchlights   " = Birds   C = Clouds   ML = Missile launch
SL = Streetlights   SE = Sun effect   CH = Car headlights   SP = Stars/planets.

M.I.B.

THE UFO REGISTER

A TERM USED BY QUEST FOR THE COLLECTION OF PURPORTED UFO DATA

36

1985

British Telecom announces it is going to phase out its famous red telephone boxes.

US President Ronald Reagan is privately sworn in for a second term in office.

Nelson Mandela rejects an offer of freedom from the South African government.

The Provisional Irish Republican Army carries out a mortar attack on the Royal Ulster Constabulary police station at Newry, killing 9 officers in the highest loss of life for the RUC on a single day.

An earthquake, measuring 8.0 on the Richter magnitude scale, hits Santiago and Valparaíso, in Chile, leaving 177 dead, 2,575 hurt, 142,489 houses destroyed and about a million people homeless.

The United Kingdom has its first ever national Glow-worm Day.

Fire engulfs a wooden stand at the Valley Parade stadium in Bradford, England, during a football match, killing 56.

Scientists of the British Antarctic Survey announce discovery of the ozone hole.

Space Shuttle Discovery completes its mission. The first Nintendo home video game console in United States is released by the System Arrow. A Douglas DC-8 crashes after take-off in Gander, Newfoundland, killing 256 – 248 of whom were US servicemen, returning to Fort Campbell, Kentucky, from overseeing a peacekeeping force in Sinai. (Source: Wikipedia)

Ron West of the Essex UFO group

In August 2013, thanks to the help of Brenda Butler, we received a huge amount of archived UFO material which had been collected by Essex-based UFO researcher, Ron West. There were hundreds, if not thousands, of sighting reports and illustrations, covering the period of UFO history from 1988 to 1996. Unfortunately, there was little for the period of 1985, other than a few brief references. Our thanks also go to the lady who has looked after the material since Ron passed away, despite suggestions to the contrary as to its disposal.

The woman, who is well-known to us, does not want to be named.

UFO SIGHTING ACCOUNT FORM

SECTION A

Please write an account of your sighting, make a drawing of what you saw and then answer the questions in section B overleaf as fully as possible. Write in **BLOCK CAPITALS** using a ball point pen.

AT ABOUT 9-15 pm I WAS IN THE KITCHEN OF MY HOUSE WHICH FACES NORTH. I HEARD A THUD SOUND OUTSIDE WHICH SOUNDED LIKE SNOW FALLING OFF THE ROOF ONTO THE KITCHEN BAY. THINKING IT MIGHT BE YOUTHS THROWING SNOWBALLS FROM THE LANE AT THE BACK I WENT OUT TO HAVE A LOOK. I LOOKED TOWARDS THE LANE AND THEN NOTICED A VERY BRIGHT LIGHT SOME DISTANCE AWAY TO THE NNW OVER THE COTTAGE OPPOSITE. IT WAS MOVING SLOWLY TOWARDS OUR HOUSE AT A HEIGHT OF ABOUT 500ft. THINKING IT WAS SOME KIND OF AIRCRAFT I CALLED MY 3 DAUGHTERS AND THE SHOUTED OF MY WIFE AS THE OBJECT CAME NEARER. THE BRIGHT LIGHT SEEMED TO GO OUT AND WHEN ALMOST OVERHEAD WE COULD SEE AN OVAL OR KITE SHAPED CRAFT WITH RED/AMBER CENTRE LIGHT, FOUR GREEN LIGHTS AND SURROUNDING TWINKLING BLUEY COLOURED TINY LIGHTS. IT MOVED SLOWLY SSE OVER OUR ROOFTOP AT ABOUT 500ft. WE WENT INDOORS AND LOOKED OUT OF THE SOUTH FACING LOUNGE WINDOWS AND SAW THE 'OBJECT' AGAIN, MOVING ON THE SAME COURSE. IT

Please continue on a separate sheet if necessary. WENT OUT OF OUR SIGHT IN THE DISTANCE AT ABOUT 9-30pm. THERE WAS NO NOISE R THE OBJECT.

DRAWING*

Like blue/green fairy lights.

Centre light red/ amber

Green lights

Dark holes or vanes.

DIRECTION.

* If preferred, use a separate sheet of paper.

Your full name (Mr/~~Mrs/Miss/Ms~~)

JACK STUTTARD Age 47

Address 246 BRIERCLIFFE RD BURNLEY

Telephone No. 30653 (STD)

Occupation during last two years HEADTEACHER

Any professional, technical or academic qualifications or special interests CERTIFICATE IN EDUCATION

Do you object to the publication of your name? *~~Yes~~/No. *Delete as applicable.

Today's Date 4th MARCH 1985

Signature Stuttard

Published by the British UFO Research Association (BUFORA LTD.) for the use of investigators throughout Great Britain. Further copies may be obtained from BUFORA Research Headquarters, Newchapel Observatory, Newchapel, Stoke-on-Trent, Staffs., England. Form R1

JANUARY 1985

KITE-SHAPED UFO OVER BURNLEY, SIGHTED BY HEAD TEACHER

Also includes – Star-shaped UFO seen over Somerset • Triangular UFO seen over Gloucestershire • Cars breaking down at Winterbourne Abbas

Kite-shaped UFO over Burnley

HEAD teacher Jack Stuttard from Briercliffe Road, Burnley, Lancashire, was in the kitchen of his house, at 9.15pm, one evening in January 1985, when he heard a thud, as if a load of snow had fallen onto the roof. Thinking it might have been youths, throwing snowballs, he went out to investigate and noticed a very bright light, moving slowly over the roof of the house opposite, approaching his direction.

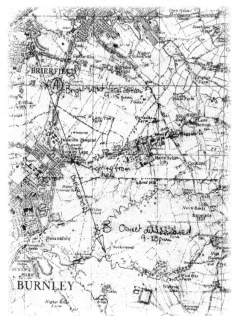

"I called to my wife, Merle, Nicola (15) and twins – Clare and Michelle (13) – to come and a have a look. We watched this very peculiar object, which we first took to be some sort of aircraft, moving overhead. It was kite-shaped, with a flattish base, showing a large amber red light in its centre, with green lights at each of the four points of the craft. Around the edges was a number of twinkling blue/green fairy type lights. Around the central light were what looked like several grey triangular vanes, or holes, as it passed silently overheard. We noticed a peculiar thing – the normally busy road to the south side of the house had gone very quiet, as if the traffic had stopped moving."

(Source: Peter Hough /Personal interviews with authors)

WE REALISE WE ARE ON A FLIGHT PATH AND OFTEN NOTICE AND HEAR AIRCRAFT IN NNW/SSE AND REVERSE DIRECTION. THIS OBJECT WAS MUCH LOWER THAN NORMAL FLIGHTS OBSERVE. WE THOUGHT AT FIRST IT WAS SOME LARGE AIRSHIP TYPE CRAFT AS IT APPROACHED BUT OVERHEAD IT APPEARED FLATISH UNDERNEATH WITH SORT OF GREYISH METALLIC VANES (SEE DRAWING) OR HOLES.

THE CHILDREN NOTICED THE LACK OF SOUND. I SAID THAT WE WOULD HEAR THE ENGINE WHEN IT HAD PASSED OVER PERHAPS, BUT THERE WAS NO ENGINE NOISE AT ALL. THIS IS WHEN WE BEGAN TO THINK ~ WHAT WAS IT ?"

FLIGHT PATH — SEE MAP

HEIGHT :- APPEARED TO US ABOUT 500ft - DIFFICULT TO JUDGE.

ONE OF THE STAFF AT MY SCHOOL ALSO SAYS THAT AT ABOUT 9-15 ON THE SAME NIGHT HER HUSBAND AND HERSELF ALSO HEARD A FUNNY THUD SOUND ON THEIR ROOF. THEY SHOUTED UPSTAIRS TO THEIR DAUGHTER TO ENQUIRE WHY SHE WAS NOT IN BED AND HAD SHE KNOCKED SOMETHING OVER? SHE WAS IN BED AND HAD HEARD THE NOISE ON THE ROOF. THEY WENT OUTSIDE TO EXAMINE THE ROOF BUT COULDNT SEE ANYTHING AMISS. THEY DIDNT LOOK UPWARDS TO THE SKY OR SEE ANYTHING STRANGE. THEY LIVE ALMOST AT THE POINT WHERE I SAW THE OBJECT FIRST)

On 4th January 1985, Mrs G. Trott was at her home address in Station Road, at 11.15pm, when she saw a brilliant star-shaped object in the sky due south of Ilminster – totally unlike any star she had ever seen.

(Source: Frank Marshall)

Further publicity was still being given to the events that had taken place at Rendlesham Forest – now only a mere 5 years ago. Who would have guessed that over 33 years later, the incident was still to be the source of not only interest but controversy!

From Ron West of Essex Group: *10/1/85. Higham Ferrers. Northants. 01.30. Dia-Black. 3 Red. Hovering.* (no other details).

40, Station Rd,
Ilminster,
Somerset.

Dear Sir,
I wish to report an unusual sighting I saw in the sky 5-15 on Saturday evening due South from Ilminster, it was like a massive star very brilliant, there was no other star in the sky.
Yours.
G. Trott. (Mrs.)

GRASSROOTS

'Despite a massive cover-up, News of the World investigators have proof that the mysterious craft came to earth in a red ball of light. An American airman who was there told us there were three beings in silver space suits aboard the craft . . .' More seriously, they produced a supporting statement from a named American Air Force colonel, which we reprint on the right. And an American UFO expert who said 'You can't hide the truth for ever.' Which is where Ian Ridpath takes up the investigation.

A flashlight in the forest

FOUR Christmases ago, something remarkable was said to have occurred outside the US Air Force base at Woodbridge, near Ipswich. News of the event leaked out slowly, finally hitting the headlines in October 1983: "UFO Lands in Suffolk — Official," screamed the front page of the News of the World.

The story was sensational. It told of a group of American airmen who were confronted one night with an alien spaceship in Rendlesham Forest, which surrounds the air force base. According to the story, the craft came down over the trees and landed in a blinding explosion of light.

The airmen tried to approach the object, but it moved away from them as though under intelligent control. The following day, landing marks were found on the ground, burns were seen on nearby trees, and radiation traces were recorded. There was even talk of aliens aboard the craft, and allegations of a massive cover-up. It had all the ingredients of a classic UFO encounter.

The News of the World's informant was a former US airman. He was given the pseudonym Art Wallace, for he claimed that his life had been threatened if he talked. Yet here he was freely giving interviews to newspapers and television.

While his fantastic story might be doubted, it was impossible to shrug off a memo written by the deputy base commander, Lt. Col. Charles I. Halt, to the Ministry of Defence, which was publicly released in the United States under the Freedom of Information Act. Halt's memo, reprinted in full here, is not as sensational as Wallace's story, but it is prime documentary evidence of a type rarely encountered in UFO cases.

UFO researchers in Britain could scarcely believe their luck: this was The Big One, final proof that We Are Not Alone. The News of the World paid £12,000 for the story. A book was recently published about the case, and American TV crews have been filming at the site in recent weeks.

All that evidence, backed up by the word of the US Air Force, could not possibly have a rational explanation.

Or could it? Here are the facts that you have not been told.

Soon after the News of the World story appeared, I went in search of local opinions about the case. I made contact by telephone with a forester, Vince Thurkettle, who lives within a mile of the alleged UFO landing site. "I don't know of anyone around here who believes that anything strange happened that night," he told me.

So what did he think the flashing light was in Rendlesham Forest? I was astonished by his reply. "It's the lighthouse," he said.

That lighthouse lies at Orford Ness on the Suffolk coast, five miles from the forest. Thurkettle plotted on a map the direction in which the airmen reported seeing their flashing UFO, and found that they were looking straight into the lighthouse beam.

Could this really be the answer? I visited the site with a camera crew from BBC TV's Breakfast Time. On the way there, the cameraman was sceptical about the lighthouse theory. I didn't blame him.

It was gone midnight when Vince Thurkettle took us to the site of the alleged landing, and it felt spooky. The area had by now been cleared of trees as part of normal forest operations, but enough pines remained at the edge of the forest to give us a realistic idea of what the airmen saw that night.

Sure enough, the lighthouse beam seemed to hover a few feet above ground level, because Rendlesham Forest is higher than the coastline. The light seemed to move around as we moved. And it looked close — only a few hundred yards away among the trees. All this matched the airmen's description of the UFO.

The conclusion was clear. Had a real UFO been present as well as the lighthouse, the airmen should have reported seeing two brilliant flashing lights among the trees, not one. But they never mentioned the lighthouse, only a pulsating UFO — not surprisingly, since no one expects to come across a lighthouse beam near ground level in a forest.

So startlingly brilliant was the beam that the television cameras captured it easily. The formerly sceptical

Triangular UFO

On 14th January 1985, David Williams and his wife, Jill – from Mitcheldean, Gloucestershire – were driving along the A40/B4224 road, after having just left Ross-on-Wye, at 1.45am; when a triangular, red *'light'* appeared and flew in front of their car, moving from left to right as they travelled along the road, for at least 15 minutes.

THE GUARDIAN Saturday January 5 1985   9

Colonel Charles Halt's memo on official American Air Force notepaper was headed "Unexplained Lights", dated 13 January 1981, and sent to the RAF. It said:

1.   Early in the morning of 27 Dec 80 (approximately 0300 L), two USAF security police patrolmen saw unusual lights outside the back gate at RAF Woodbridge. Thinking an aircraft might have crashed or been forced down, they called for permission to go outside the gate to investigate. The on-duty flight chief responded and allowed three patrolmen to proceed on foot. The individuals reported seeing a strange glowing object in the forest. The object was described as being metallic in appearance and triangular in shape, approximately two to three meters across the base and approximately two meters high. It illuminated the entire forest with a white light. The object itself had a pulsing red light on top and a bank(s) of blue lights underneath. The object was hovering or on legs. As the patrolmen approached the object, it maneuvered through the trees and disappeared. At this time the animals on a nearby farm went into a frenzy. The object was briefly sighted approximately an hour later near the back gate.

2.   The next day, three depressions 1½" deep and 7" in diameter were found where the object had been sighted on the ground. The following night (29 Dec 80) the area was checked for radiation. Beta/gamma readings of 0.1 milliroentgens were recorded with peak readings in the three depressions and near the center of the triangle formed by the depressions. A nearby tree had moderate (.05-.07) readings on the side of the tree toward the depressions.

3.   Later in the night a red sun-like light was seen through the trees. It moved about and pulsed. At one point it appeared to throw off glowing particles and then broke into five separate white objects and then disappeared. Immediately thereafter, three star-like objects were noticed in the sky, two objects to the north and one to the south, all of which were about 10 degrees off the horizon. The objects moved rapidly in sharp, angular movements and displayed red, green and blue lights. The objects to the north appeared to be elliptical through an 8-12 power lens. They then turned to full circles. The objects to the north remained in the sky for an hour or more. The object to the south was visible for two or three hours and beamed down a stream of light from time to time. Numerous individuals, including the undersigned, witnessed the activities in paragraphs 2 and 3.

CHARLES I. HALT, Lt Col, USAF
Deputy Base Commander

cameraman was convinced. My report was shown the following morning on Breakfast Time, much to the dismay of UFO spotters and the News of the World reporter.

The lighthouse theory soon had its supporters and its detractors. But there were still too many open questions for the case to be considered solved. For instance, what about those landing marks?

Some weeks later I returned to Rendlesham Forest in search of answers. The landing marks had long since been destroyed when the trees were felled, but I now knew an eyewitness who had seen them; Vince Thurkettle. He recalled for me his disappointment with what he saw.

The three depressions were irregular in shape and did not even form a symmetrical triangle. He recognised them as rabbit diggings, several months old and covered with a layer of fallen pine needles. They lay in an area surrounded by 75ft tall pine trees planted 10ft to 15ft apart — scarcely the place to land a 20ft wide spacecraft.

The "burn marks" on the trees were axe cuts in the bark, made by the foresters themselves as a sign that the trees were ready to be felled. I saw numerous examples in which the pine resin, bubbling into the cut, gives the impression of a burn.

Additional information came from other eyewitnesses — the local police, called to the scene by the Woodbridge air base. The police officers who visited the site reported that they could see no UFO, only the Orford Ness lighthouse. Like Vince Thurkettle, they attributed the landing marks to animals. The case for a landed spaceship was looking very shaky indeed.

What had made the airmen think that something had crashed into the forest in the first place? I already knew from previous UFO cases that a brilliant meteor, a piece of natural debris from space burning up in the atmosphere, could give such an impression. But I was unable to find records of such a meteor on the morning of December 27.

Here the police account provided a vital lead by showing that Col. Halt's memo, written two weeks after the event, had got the date of the sighting wrong. It occurred on December 26, not December 27.

With this corrected date, I telephoned Dr John Mason, who collects reports of such sightings for the British Astronomical Association. He told me that shortly before 3 am on December 26 an exceptionally brilliant meteor, almost as bright as the full moon, had been seen over southern England. Dr Mason confirmed that this meteor would have been visible to the airmen at Woodbridge as though something were crashing into the forest nearby. The time of the sighting matched that given in Col. Halt's memo.

Finally, I turned to the question of the radiation readings. I learned that readings like those given in Col. Halt's memo would be expected from natural sources of radiation such as cosmic rays and the earth itself. In short, there was no unusual radiation at the site.

As for the star-like objects in the final paragraph of Col. Halt's memo, they were probably just that — stars. Bright celestial objects are the main culprits in UFO sightings, and have fooled many experienced observers, including pilots. The object seen by Col. Halt to the south was almost certainly Sirius, the brightest star in the sky.

If it seems surprising that a colonel in the US Air Force should identify a star as a UFO, consider the alternatives. Is it likely that a bright, flashing UFO should hover over southern England for three hours without being spotted by anyone other than a group of excited airmen? And if Col. Halt really believed that an alien craft had invaded his air space, why did he not scramble fighters to investigate?

UFO hunters will continue to believe that an alien spacecraft landed in Rendlesham Forest that night. But I know that the first sighting coincided with the burn-up in the atmosphere of an exceptionally bright meteor, and that the airmen who saw the flashing UFO between the pine trees were looking straight at the Orford Ness lighthouse. The rest of the case is a product of human imagination.

"We stopped the car three times, to satisfy ourselves it wasn't a reflection. When we halted, so did the light. When we arrived at Mitcheldean, it moved over the top of the Rank Xerox factory."

(Source: Pete Tate/*Probe*, Ian Mrzyglod)

385

UFO INTERNATIONAL
SIGHTING REPORT

File Reference: Form R1

Encl No

Please read this form carefully before completing and continue on a separate sheet of paper if necessary. DO NOT COMPLETE ANY QUESTION UNLESS YOU ARE SURE OF THE ANSWER.

1. Name: *DAVID WILLIAMS.*   2. Occupation: *PRODUCTION ENGINEER* Age: *33*

3. Address: *7 TUSCULUM WAY*   Tel No: *0594 543361*
    MITCHELDEAN
    GLOS GL17 0HZ

4. Date & Time of Sighting: *1.45 AM TO 2.00 A.M. (14.1.85)*   Day of Week: *MONDAY.*

5. Location: *ALL THE WAY BETWEEN ROSS-ON-WYE & MITCHELDEAN (A40 & B4224 ROADS)*
    (please give map reference if at all possible)

6. Weather Conditions: *COLD, FROSTY BUT EXCELLENT VISIBILITY.*

7. Did the sighting take place during: ~~DAWN/DAY/EVENING~~/NIGHT

8. Colour of Object: *LIGHT RED*

9. Shape of Object: *TRIANGULAR*

10. Give details of any noise the object may have made: *NO NOISE AT ALL*

11. What was the apparent speed of the object: *STATIONARY* /~~SLOW~~ /
    VARIABLE, ACCORDING TO SPEED OF CAR   FAST / ~~VERY FAST.~~
    MY WIFE WAS DRIVING.

Drawing of Object

THE COLOUR SHOWN IS THE APPROX. COLOUR OF THE OBJECT, ALTHOUGH THERE WAS NO BLUE OUTLINE

DIRECTION OF TRAVEL

overhead

A   B

Place an A to indicate where the object was first seen, in relation to the horizon and a B where it was last seen.

12. Duration of Sighting- hours: *00*   minutes: *15*   seconds: *00*

13. Give details of protrusions such as aerials, lights, etc:
    (continue on a separate sheet of paper for sketches or drawings)
    NO PROTRUSIONS.

14. Give details of any movements the object may have made:
    ~~~~ *AS DESCRIBED IN 11.*

15. If you took photographs or made any kind of measurement please give details:
    NO PHOTOS OR MEASUREMENTS.

16. Give details of any unusual effects you may have noticed on people, animals, plants, electrical equipment, etc:

NONE, EXCEPT THE UFO APPEARED TO TRACK THE HEADLIGHTS OF THE CAR.

17. Please give a detailed account of your sighting. Include any details that you think are important or that are not covered by the questions: (continue on a separate sheet of paper if necessary)

WHILST TRAVELLING HOME EARLY THAT MORNING THE OBJECT WAS FIRST SIGHTED BY MY WIFE, WHO WAS DRIVING THE CAR. THROUGHOUT THE WHOLE JOURNEY THE OBJECT WAS IN FRONT OF OUR CAR, SOMETIMES ON THE L.H. SIDE & SOMETIMES ON THE R.H. SIDE. WE STOPPED THREE TIMES & GOT OUT OF THE CAR & TURNED OFF THE HEADLIGHTS, IN ORDER TO PROOVE IT WAS NOT A REFLECTION OR SOME OTHER NATURAL PHENOMENON. WHEN THE CAR WAS STATIONARY SO WAS THE OBJECT. ON THESE THREE OCCASIONS WE VIEWED THE OBJECT CLEARLY FOR ONE TO TWO MINUTES EACH TIME.
IN MITCHELDEAN THE OBJECT LAY OVER THE RANK XEROX FACTORY. THE FACTORY IS LARGE & HAS ITS OWN STREET LIGHTING

18. Please list the names and addresses of any other witnesses, to this sighting:

① JILL WILLIAMS.
WIFE.
SAME ADDRESS

② A. STEWART
9 KHILL ROAD   6LI
MITCHELDEAN
GLOS

19. Who was the first person you told of this sighting and how soon after the event: MY FATHER — WITHIN SECONDS — IN FACT HE HAD A GLIMPSE OF THE OBJECT FOR ABOUT ONE SECOND BEFORE IT MOVED AWAY.

PERSONAL DETAILS WILL NOT BE RELEASED TO ANY THIRD PARTY WITHOUT PRIOR CONSENT.

Date: 19. 3. 85.   Signature: D. J. Williams

Thank you very much for taking the time and trouble to complete this form and helping UFO INTERNATIONAL.

Cars breaking down – Winterbourne Abbas

Garage owner Andrew Hall, of North Mills Recovery Service, was driving back to Bridport, Dorset, after having collected a damaged Ford Transit van, accompanied by Mr Peter Chubb, at 9pm on 27th January 1985. At a point where the road bends, while travelling at about 45-50mph, the engine on the breakdown truck and vehicle being towed cut out – the lights then failed. The two men got out and tried to figure what had happened, with the aid of torches. As they lifted the bonnet, the lights came back on again. Mystified, the men continued on their journey.

As a result of some publicity in the local newspaper – the *Echo* – regarding the incident, Mr Barry Chilvers, from Weymouth, contacted the newspaper and complained of having experienced a similar problem with his Toyota car, while driving along the same stretch of road, at 9.15pm on 27th January 1985.

"I was driving back from Dorchester and had reached Monkton Hill, when all of a sudden my lights dulled and then flashed on and off, several times. I thought the car was going to fail altogether. As I reached the top of the hill, the lights came back on again."

It is interesting to note the incident took place along a ley line, which runs from Flower Barrow Hill Fort, near Tyneham, through Maiden Castle, Nine Stones at Winterbourne Abbas, Eggardon Hill Fort, and Pilsdon Pen near Marshwood – places of interest that were to be brought to our attention, involving reports of UFOs sighted and vehicle interference, although it was learnt, in recent years, that on one occasion, interference of this nature was caused by malfunctioning MOD Microwave Transmitters.

**(Source: Frank Marshall/*Dorset Evening Echo*, 23.1.85 – 'Mystery of breakdown at Stone Circle –
Second Car affected by mysterious cut-out')**

FEBRUARY 1985

UFO SEEN – STAFFORDSHIRE

Also includes – UFO over Surrey • Close encounter North Wales • Reports from London and Cornwall

O N 2nd February, a glowing orange cigar-shaped object was seen over Clacton-on-Sea, Essex, at 7.40pm.

At 3.30pm on 3rd February 1985, teenager Nicholas Gregory received a telephone call from two friends, after they sighted a bright light travelling across the sky, heading towards the direction of Keel. Nicholas went outside and saw the object himself.

Approximately 30 minutes later, over Wolstanton Marsh, Newcastle-under-Lyme, the strange light was also observed by footballer Mervyn Edwards. The Cheadle police, who was contacted about the incident, confirmed they had received another report of a similar object, seen over Tean Road, on 2nd February, at about 8pm. (**Source:** *Stoke-on-Trent Evening Sentinel*, **4.2.1985 – 'Wolstanton boy sparks UFO alert'**)

UFO over Epsom, Surrey

At 6.40am on 6th February 1985, Molly and Billy Crafter (72) from Ashley, Epsom, Surrey, were astonished to see a brilliant object, eastwards, in the clear morning sky over the Croydon area.

> *"It was stationary for about 30 seconds and then moved upwards, before veering to the left. As its speed increased, the lights dimmed."*

The couple reported it to the local newspaper – the *Banstead Herald* – who published their story on the 8.2.1985, 'Bright sky light – my story'.

The local Ewell Astronomy Group suggested the couple had seen an aircraft, heading straight towards them!

Molly and Bill would, by now, be passed; however, their sighting is recorded.

Close Encounter – North Wales

At 3am on 8th February 1985, David Thomas (19) from Pwllheli, Wales, was walking back home from a night out. As he trudged along the four and a half mile journey back to the village where he lived, on what was a cold night, with a light covering of snow, he heard a humming noise – like the noise an electricity generator would make. Wondering what the source of this noise could be, he decided to investigate further and made his way across a field. As he did so, the noise increased in volume.

> *"Something seemed to be obscuring the starlight. I looked intensely and saw a large, dull, black thing, hovering about two and a half feet above the ground. It was about 25ft across and 20ft high. I could see what looked like antennae, or stabilisers, sticking out of it. There was what looked like a drawbridge like hatchway and windows at the top. I didn't see any sign of lighting, but the object showed a dull, almost muted, fluorescent glow."*

As he stood there in the darkness, watching the strange humming object floating above the ground, his attention was caught by a movement to one side of it. He looked and was astonished to see a group of smaller shapes, humanoid in form, making their way across the field towards him. His first instinct was to flee. As he turned around to do so, he was confronted by one of the strange humanoid shapes blocking his escape route. Frozen in fear, the next thing he became aware of was a hand like grip on his arm and then being propelled forwards, toward the object.

David:

> *"They spoke to me, but not like a person speaking. It was like they were talking to me in my head. They were saying, 'You're alright. You are ok.'"*

David was transported forwards in some manner, as his feet were not on the ground. He is not sure how he entered into the object, but the next thing he became aware of was finding himself in a large bare room, on his own.

According to a description of these *'alien occupants'*, later supplied to Margaret Fry, they were wearing what looked like octagonal helmets, featureless, apart from two dim lights, positioned where their eyes should have been. They were wearing grey suits, with gold coloured belts, and straps which looked similar to braces, black knee boots and gloves. David remarked on the similarity between these entities and the *'robots'* depicted in the 1950s Hollywood science-fiction films, due to the way in which they would move their arms and legs in a rapid, stilted fashion.

After about 15 minutes, he was then led into what appeared to be a control room. This contained three or four TV consoles or screens, positioned on the wall. David believed the *'beings'* were letting him know telepathically that he was being decontaminated and prepared for a time change. He was then aware of the *'craft'* taking off, although there was no sense of motion. David says:

> *"I sat there, watching the big screen showing planets passing by – Jupiter, Saturn, and out to beyond Pluto, where the 'craft' docked with a mother ship."*

He was then taken for a medical examination aboard the larger 'craft'.

One of his *'captors'* produced a long instrument, which was pointed at one end (this instrument is claimed to have been responsible for burn marks found on David's body, the following day).

David:

> *"They checked me all over and seemed to ponder over my private parts for a while. I don't know whether they were trying to work out whether I was a male or female."*

Probes were then placed on his head, chest, and around the neck. He was aware that his heart rate was increasing and then decreasing, as if on command from his abductors.

He was then asked telepathically if *'they'* could have permission to remove his eyes for further examination. He refused.

David Thomas

An arrow indicates where David Thomas' encounter took place

A music tape-cassette was removed from his pocket by one of the *'beings'* and apparently examined in one of the consoles in the room. David recalls the irony of hearing a heavy rock anthem pounding its beat across the most alien of scenes. The *'aliens'* told him telepathically that they originated from a planet beyond the constellation of Lyra. They breathed pure oxygen and disliked the polluted atmosphere of the Earth. They also told him that they had a temporary base in Greenland, but had been forced to destroy a number of bases on the Moon to avoid discovery by probes and visits from Earth.

Further *'conversation'* took place, in which the *'aliens'* admitted they had captured the Voyager spacecraft for analysis, which they declared as being very primitive.

At some point he was taken from the larger *'craft'* to the smaller one, and was then aware of finding himself back on the lonely field in North Wales.

David experienced a feeling of dizziness and was sighted in this condition on the road by a passing police patrol car. The officer stopped the vehicle and asked David if he had been drinking, or taking drugs. After

Philip Mantle seen here with David Thomas (right)

ascertaining this was not the case, the officer took David home in the police car, arriving there at 5.30am.

Following his return, he experienced a delayed reaction from what had, after all, been a traumatic encounter, and discussed it with his mother.

Just over a week later, following telephone enquiries made, David and his mother drove to the Oxfordshire headquarters of Contact UK International on 17th February 1985.

During various interview sessions conducted with the guarantee that his name and personal details would be kept confidential, David told the investigators that the *'aliens'* said they would return to the Earth at a future date and seek him out, once again.

As a result of David's continuing breakdown in health, which involved constant nightmares and his obvious distress following the UFO incident, his mother contacted a psychologist, who suggested hypnotherapy. After a course of these sessions, David was finally able to come to terms with his encounter.

The incident was investigated by Margaret Fry, of Contact UK International – a personal friend of the authors – whose own spectacular sighting of a UFO took place on 17th July 1955. This has been fully documented in Volume 1 of *Haunted Skies*. We would also like to credit Philip Mantle for his investigation into the same case.

Margaret confirms that David was very reluctant to show her and Philip Mantle the site of where the incident took place, but on learning that Philip had travelled a great distance to see him, showed them the site but became very agitated, and as far as Margaret knows, has never been there again. Margaret wonders if experiences like this can be traced back through individual generations of people. She told us about the following strange incident, which took place in the 1870s, although she took great pains to remind the reader *"I am not that old!"*

1870 landing, North Wales

Whispering sands is a stunning beach on the North Wales peninsula, near Aberdaron. The name originates from the noise made by the sand as you walk on it. Although we do not know the exact location of the smallholding, it involved Mrs Edwards, a widow, and her son, Willie, who was living in a small village called Saron, just above the beach. Mrs Edwards asked Willie to collect some driftwood from the beach – as the annual fair at Pwllheli was being held the next day – so baking could be done.

Willie walked down from their little wooden bungalow to the beach, whilst his mother walked to the nearest village – Aberdaron.

Willie's mother returned from the fair at 5pm, and went into the house. After seeing no sign of her son, she went down to the beach and found the huge bundle of driftwood neatly stacked at the edge of the woods. Nearby, she discovered a huge round circle, or hole, in the sand. Mystified, and now alarmed, Mrs Edwards walked to Aberdaron to fetch the police.

After explaining her son's failure to light the fire, and his unusual out of character absence, a police officer returned with her to the family home. By that time, the marks in the sand had been washed away. After being unsuccessful in tracing his whereabouts, the officer suggested the worse may have happened and that the poor youth had been drowned.

About three weeks later, whilst she was cooking over the fire and still coming to terms with her grief – in walked her son. He said wearily, *"Look Mam, I am very tired. I will tell you after I have had my nap"*. With that, he sat down and fell asleep. His mother remarked how different he looked; his hair was rough and he seemed to be in some sort of trance.

The next day, he explained what had transpired.

> *"I had collected a huge bundle of driftwood and stacked it where the woods met the beach, a few weeks ago, when I heard a funny noise coming from the Whistling Sands. I walked down on the sands and a huge black 'thing' landed near me. Two little men 'dressed like doctors' came out of a door in it and walked toward me. They were talking, but I could not understand a word that was said. They were not big men, but they forcibly carried me to the craft and took me in.*
>
> *It had gone 'straight up – not sideways, straight up and up'; they then landed. I did not know where, but they took me immediately into a great big building, where they put me on a table and took something from me. They would not have taken me there if they did not want something from me, would they? Everybody I saw there was smiling at me and they were more forward in everything. The colours of the place were amazing to me."*

In conversation with Margret about the matter, in late August 2013, she told us that currently, along with another member of the Welsh Federation of UFO Researchers, she is offering support to a young man with regard to what she describes as *"the most appalling complaint of alien abduction she has come across so far"*. This involves a young man, who lives in North Wales. He claims of being taken against his will, many times over, by what he perceives to be an alien source for *'breeding purposes'*. He tells of seeing two women aboard the *'craft'* – one in her 40s, from the Cumbria area; the other in her 20s, from the Midlands – who were picked up by the aliens.

The young man was hoping to have identified the home addresses of the girls concerned, and then contact them to see if they had also suffered a similar experience to him, which would have corroborated his account. However, he has been unsuccessful so far. This was not the only time we had come across similar reports, involving other humans seen onboard the *'craft'* who had been picked up previously. On one occasion, the 'abductee' later met up with one of the persons he had seen at a UFO meeting.

We cannot prove categorically that the 'intelligences' behind acts such as this are representative of an alien race, because we do not know. What we do know is that many thousands, if not millions, of people worldwide, have experienced similar traumas through what are generally referred to as alien abductions, and will continue to do so. Instinct, rather than attempts to rationalise incidents like this, suggest we are dealing with something very real and frightening in its implications. If only people had the choice!

Margaret Fry:

This story was handed down to the family of Mrs Edwards, now living at Ruthin, but from the village of Aberdaron. She was a lady of 87 years and she recalls her grandmother first telling her this story, in 1914. She described how Willie had to put up with a lot of ridicule until one evening, when he was in a pub – in walked a man from Aberdaron and, upon hearing this yarn being repeated yet again, he said:

> *"Hang on a minute, I was too far away to see the 'craft' on Saron beach, but I did see it rise up from that area from Aberdaron and go straight up into the sky."*

> **(Source: Margaret-Ellen Fry – 'Who are they?' Credit Margaret Hainge-Lloyd)**

UFO over Suffolk

On 9th February 1985, an Ipswich housewife was stood in her front porch, at 10.30am, when she was astonished to see an orange flickering or pulsing oval-shaped object in the sky, directly in front of her – the size of a dinner plate, showing lights at the top and bottom – about 2-3,000ft away.

> *"It appeared to hover at times and then shoot away, at great speed, and return to its original position. As it did this, it also changed its shape and brightness. I last saw it heading eastwards, towards the direction of Woodbridge."*

> **(Source: Brenda Butler files)**

Motorist encounters strange 'ball of light'

On 10th February, a Mount Joy woman motorist, on her way to work in Cornwall, reported having sighted a strange globe of light that appeared to have followed her for some distance.

According to Ron West, at 10.15pm on 12th April 1985, a number of red, blue, white and green, lights were seen hovering in the sky over Cricklewood, London.

At 2am on 16th February 1985, two police officers were on duty in East Seaford, Sussex, when they sighted four red and white lights, forming a star-like formation, moving silently across the sky, at a 70° elevation. The object was estimated to be one mile from the officers' location.   **(Source: Declassified MOD Files)**

Is it or isn't it?

THIS puzzling picture was taken by 13-year-old schoolboy Ryan Hodges (above), of Mayenne Place, Devizes.

Ryan, a second-year pupil at Devizes School, was attending motor - cycle scrambles near Axminster on February 10.

The scramble took place at Trinity Hill, in the Otter Vale.

At about 12 noon Ryan was taking photographs of the surrounding countryside, from the hill top, when his attention was drawn to a white object with red bars at the top, which was travelling through the sky like a very fast aeroplane.

He took this picture, and the object (arrowed) eventually disappeared behind some hills in the distance.

The object was said to have been seen by at least one other person at the scramble, and Ryan says he saw it for at least two minutes. The weather was bright and sunny.

This picture is a greatly-enlarged print from a colour negative. Ryan handed it in to our Devizes office and photographer COLIN KEARLEY produced this print.

Kearley has examined the negative and says it has not been tampered with in any way, nor did there appear to be any processing fault on the negative.

CORNISH GUARDIAN, THURSDAY, FEBRUARY 14th, 1985

'My UFO shock' — shaken driver

A SHAKEN 28-year-old woman was yesterday puzzling over the UFO-type object which she says petrified her as she drove to work.

The woman did not want to be named, and said: "People will only think I am a nutcase, but I am not."

It was at about 5.45pm one day last week that the woman, who lives in the Colan area, joined the Quintrell Downs-St. Columb Road road at Mount Joy.

"Suddenly I saw a bright yellow light, about 10ft long, oval in shape, by my offside hedge," she said. "Although brilliant, it did not radiate light, other than a mellow glow on a cottage wall. It was so powerful that it obscured my vision up the road.

"It hovered close to the hedge, then seemed to shrink, went pitch black and moved from side to side across the road.

"It shrank to the size of a large football, changed to bright luminous green with a red glow in the centre, and finally went almost purplish before vanishing.

"Quite suddenly the light appeared again on my right, further down the road, and followed the same pattern of changing colour and size before disappearing.

"This happened six or seven times over a stretch of half a mile. I was doing about 20mph, and I was getting mesmerised. All the time it was getting weaker and slower.

By the time I reached White Cross and saw it on the opposite side of the junction I was in such a panic that I turned off my route into the minor road just to get away from it."

The woman, who is married, reported the incident to police, who checked the area and found nothing. They suggested it might have been a weather balloon. "But I know it was not that," she said.

"I know, too, that it was not a white fireball as I have seen one before. It exploded in my kitchen, and I had two other people with me to confirm what had happened."

The woman was certain that the phenomenon was not the result of reflections from her windscreen.

After work, the woman was too frightened to drive back along the road alone. She waited for her husband, and also for another car to be travelling in the same direction.

"I was absolutely petrified," she said. "I had not drunk any alcohol before I left for work, and I do not take hallucinatory drugs."

MARCH 1985

PLYMOUTH WOMAN SIGHTS UFO

Also includes – UFO sightings from Gwent, Wembley Stadium, London, Nottinghamshire, and a UFO landing at Leeds

A T about 7pm on 3rd March 1985, on a dry clear night, Plymouth woman – Mrs Rosemary Maben – was looking up into the night sky at Venus, when:

"Just below the planet, another smaller bright object appeared – approximately three-quarters of the size of the planet – which then began to move quickly towards the north-west direction, until out of sight. I looked back at where it had come from in the sky and noticed a tall dense column of black, blue and white, smoke had appeared – which then followed the same course as the previous object."

(Source: Personal interview)

At 11pm on 14th March 1985, an unusual object was seen in the sky over Newport, Gwent, by a teenage boy, who contacted the police. A police officer from Alway Police Station went outside and saw an object in the sky, at a 45° elevation, moving from east to west. **(Source: Declassified MOD Files)**

It is claimed that on 5th and 17th March 1985, an object – shaped like a banana – was sighted in the sky, over Wembley Stadium. However, we have no further details.

(Source: Paranormal Database, 2013)

Similarly, on the 17th March 1985, Ron West tells of a disc-shaped object seen low

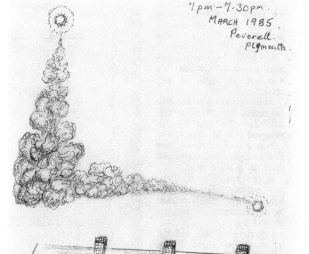

Rosemary Maben's sketch of what she encountered

2 2 MAR 1985

Family 237 spots UFO

A UFO emitting rays of green and red light was reported near an Oxfordshire village last week.

Three strange lights were seen low on the horizon in the north of the county on Thursday night.

The Walters family, of Valentia Close, Bletchingdon, claim the lights appeared at 7 p.m. and disappeared once, before shining in a different part of the sky until 8.30 p.m.

The family says that at one stage the lights emitted star-like rays in green and red.

Lorry driver Mr Alan Walters, 48, said: "The lights were very low in the sky and stood still for most of the time.

"There were green and red rays intermittently coming out of them before they petered out and re-appeared in the sky elsewhere."

He said: "I am very sceptical about UFOs but this was not any type of aircraft."

The curious sight was also witnessed by Mr Walters' wife Sue, 41, and his 15-year-old son Michael.

Police at Woodstock saw similar lights but dismissed them as a helicopter.

A spokesman at Kidlington police HQ said the lights were probably caused by atmospheric conditions around a star.

Upper Heyford airbase reported no night flying exercises at the time.

down in the sky, at 9.30pm, moving slowly over Sutton-in-Ashfield, Nottinghamshire. In the middle of the same month, the *Oxford Times* told of strange lights being seen by lorry driver Mr Alan Walters, and his family.

Yorkshire UFO Society Conference

At 4am on 23rd March 1985, an orange globe-shaped object was reported hovering in the sky over Dulwich, London. Later that day, the Yorkshire UFO Society held its annual conference at Centenary House, Leeds. It was attended by Tim Good and Jenny Randles. Investigator of the Year Award was presented to Philip Mantle.

A MAJOR EVENT IN LEEDS
Yorkshire UFO Society and Quest Magazine

Case Histories   UFO Slideshow

Exhibits   Refreshments

quest

CONFERENCE '85
Centenary House, North Street, Leeds

MARCH 23rd   1.15pm – 6.00pm

Featuring: Startling New Evidence

Guest speaker's

M.I. BIRDSALL   TIMOTHY GOOD

Jenny Randles

plus   GW BIRDSALL   PHILLIP MANTLE

Doors Open 12.15pm

Admission   Adults 75p   Children 50p

YORKSHIRE UFO SOCIETY
12 Miles Hill Street,
Leeds LS7 2EQ.

Leading UFO researchers alleged governments are involved in an international cover-up over "unexplained atmospheric phenomena". Report by JOHN WEBB. Pictures by JIM MORAN

Weekend **PEOPLE**

Graham Birdsall (centre) presents trophies to Mark Birdsall (left) for UFO research and Phillip Mantle, Investigator of the Year.

Timothy Good selects slides in his photographic evidence.

'Real truth' about aliens

ALTHOUGH most people's heads were fairly close to the clouds in Leeds on Saturday, those of one particular group of seekers-after-truth were definitely right in them.

The term "unexplained atmospheric phenomena" (UAP) would have been taken by most to describe the fact that it was still raining hard as it had been the evening before. To this group, however, the term meant something entirely different.

UAPs — nothing to do with OAPs — is the vogue word for unidentified flying objects; that is, those in the know now believe those flashing lights in the sky are neither flying nor objects.

Nor are they likely to disgorge little green men waving laser guns, PEOPLE learned at the Yorkshire UFO Society's major conference at Centenary House, Leeds.

The leading figures in UFO research gathered to swap notes at the conference and compare reports of latest sightings; the theme of the gathering was to discuss an alleged international cover-up by governments who are desperate to hide the real truth from us poor unsuspecting citizens.

The centre piece of the day's entertainment was a talk and slide-show from the suave Timothy Good, who has travelled world-wide interviewing key witnesses and discussing the subject with pilots, astronauts, scientists and politicians.

Does he get annoyed when people scoff at his investigating and suggest his chairs are possibly not all at home?

"I sympathise with their feelings but I get a bit annoyed when people who know nothing about the subject say that I am wasting my time. There is a good deal of evidence, which if they looked at it would soon make them change their tune," he said.

When presented by the loquacious Mr. Good, who New Society has described as a sort of "interstellar Melvyn Bragg," there is at least enough to make a reasonable person think again.

Mr. Good's passions are two-fold: UFOs and music. For 14 years he was a violinist for the London Symphony Orchestra and he is now a session musician for television programmes and pop groups.

He believes governments around the world are hiding the truth about alien bases on earth. "I don't think these aliens suddenly come from other galaxies to the earth. I believe they are here all the time, possibly using us all as some sort of guinea pigs."

The society handed out its awards for the year; investigator of the year was Phillip Mantle of Batley. He is on call for much of his spare time to look into sightings.

"Most of the sightings are fairly easy to assess, either aeroplanes or satellites; only five per cent end up being unidentified," he said.

He travelled to Wiltshire last summer to investigate curious marks on a cornfield, which earned national newspaper publicity. After talking to local people, he decided the flattened corn was probably a fraud.

Another speaker, Jenny Randles, gave up a full-time teaching post to take up UFO research and has now produced several books on the subject. She is persuaded by the weight of evidence that something fishy is definitely going on. But she says the concept of flying saucers is now rejected by many ufologists.

"I don't believe there is anything physically flying around with intelligent life aboard; but there are phenomena which we cannot explain."

UFO painter Robert Cherrey with some of his works.

YORKSHIRE EVENING POST
Monday March 25 1985 **5**

Now an even closer encounter with the ET kind

An internationally-known UFO researcher and adviser to the House of Lords on the phenomenon claimed in Leeds that extra-terrestrials have bases on earth.

Mr. Timothy Good, who has studied encounters with unidentified flying objects for 30 years, also claimed that Government intelligence agencies were aware of their presence.

Mr. Good, a professional violinist, was one of the guest speakers at a conference organised by the Yorkshire UFO Society in Leeds, entitled "Seeking the Truth." It was attended by a mixture of phenomena faithful and sceptics.

Mr. Good, of Bromley, Kent, produced dozens of documents marked "top secret" — leaked to him from the American FBI and CIA — as well as a host of other stuff now available in the U.S. through the "Freedom of Information Act."

The papers, dating from the 1940s, told of mystery incidents involving the military and civilians throughout America and even included a highly-secret instruction to American Air Force pilots on the different approaches to UFO's and unidentified aircraft violating American air space.

Mr. Good gave detailed information about Encounters of the Third Kind — actual contact between people and alleged alien craft.

He described many animals found in deserted areas with surgical wounds and claimed there were in America 49 strong reports of landed UFO's which had been covered up by the American authorities.

Mr. Good also showed a recent Russian Government report on UFO's and other documents relating to experiences in countries such as France and Iran.

He said he was not prepared to guess where the spacecraft came from, but said he was convinced some of them had bases on earth and craft and bodies of aliens were now in the possession of the American military.

On the local scene Mr. Mark Birdsall, the Yorkshire society's research co-ordinator, reported that in 1984 there had been 52 reports of UFO sightings, of which 14 had been identified.

UFO landing, Leeds

On 28th March 1985, the *Bradford Star* newspaper – 'Strange Night Lights triggers UFO theory' – reported an extraordinary story, involving a UFO landing and its alien occupants.

Our enquiries made into this newspaper cutting revealed that on 2nd July 1984, a couple from Thorpe Edge, who declined to be identified, were awoken by a bright *'light'*, during the early hours of the morning. They saw a *'craft'*, standing on four legs, in nearby *Calverley Wood. The couple fetched a pair of binoculars and were amazed to see four small, almost *'reptilian'* humanoids, near the *'craft'* – apparently engaged in collecting specimens from the ground.

We know that Anne and Darren Chanter, her son from Bradford, and Mr Paul Bennett, were involved in this investigation, during late August 2013. We spoke to Anne about the matter. She had no problem in recalling the event, despite it being over 25 years ago. Following the initial telephone call to her from the woman concerned, she made her way to a remote farmhouse overlooking Calverley, Pudsey, near Leeds, where she spoke to her at some length, and was shown the location concerned. Soil samples were taken but they revealed nothing of any value when analysed. **(Source: West Yorkshire UFO Group)**

---

*Calverley is a village in the City of Leeds Metropolitan Borough in West Yorkshire, England, on the A657 road, midway between Leeds city centre and Bradford. In the 1086 Domesday Book it is shown as Caverleia, also Caverlei.

Anybody out there? Philip says yes

Unearthly goings on in places as far apart as Normanton and Wiltshire, have led to Philip Mantle, 27, of Lady Ann Road, Batley, being awarded the title of UFO Investigator of the Year.

The award was made to Philip, who has been a member of the Yorkshire UFO Society for three years, at a recent meeting of leading figures in UFO research in Leeds.

Philip is on call virtually anytime when he is not working, as an engineer for a Morley graphics firm, and has been swept off to the scenes of sightings all over the country.

On one occasion this involved a 500 mile round trip to Wiltshire.

After interviewing many local people he decided that the incident was probably a fraud. This is by no means uncommon as

Philip Mantle. — (R.N.).

only five per cent of the sightings investigated are thought by enthusiasts to be UFOs.

Philip's interest in mysterious flying objects was aroused in his youth, when he was a keen astronomer. He gradually became more interested in studying UFOs than the stars.

One of the strangest incidents Philip has investigated, occurred only a few miles away in Normanton, when a woman phoned to say that her grandchildren had seen a large silver object, shaped like a Mexican hat, land in a field.

Three strange figures emerged, but were scared away when the children approached, she told Philip.

Anyone who has witnessed what they believe to be a UFO sighting, should contact Philip on Batley 444049.

APRIL/MAY 1985

POLICEWOMEN SIGHT UFOs IN BRISTOL

Also includes – Close encounter for motorcyclist in Oldham, Lancashire
UFO over Bradford-on-Avon, Wiltshire • Egg-shaped UFO seen over the Isle of Wight
UFOs knock out radio communications at army base, Otterburn and a UFO seen
over Connecticut

A T 5.15pm on 14th April 1985, a married couple living in York, accompanied by their two teenage daughters, sighted a number of small silver *'bubbles'* in the sky, towards the north direction. They faded away, leaving six, which appeared to move in and out of a circle for about a minute, before heading away, one by one, at great speed, south-eastwards. **(Source: Brenda Butler files)**

May 1985. Policewomen on duty in Bristol – a locality which was to attract numerous reports of UFOs during this period – reported having sighted mysterious flashing lights, making roaring noises, as they sped through the sky.

Close encounter, Oldham – and a visit from the 'MIB'

At 4.30am on 9th May 1985, Douglas Oliver was riding home to Oldham, along the A580 East Lancashire road, after having been to see his girlfriend in Liverpool. He stopped in a lay-by and lit a cigarette, and then heard a humming noise coming from a nearby field. He walked over to have a look and saw, about 100ft away, a silvery-white glow, out of which two 'figures' appeared.

According to Douglas, who was interviewed by Mr Douglas Oliver (no relation) – then a member of BUFORA and head of BUFOS – he had this to say:

Police girls chase light in the sky

TWO policewomen who spotted flashing lights in the sky have set off a UFO hunt.

A first they feared they were "seeing things," but soon after their experience male colleagues reported more flashing lights, this time accompanied by a roaring noise.

Now police in Bristol say they are baffled by the sightings after they failed to trace the mystery objects through the Ministry of Defence and local airport.

Daily Express

17-5-85.

"The 'figures', some 5ft tall, advanced to within 7-8ft, allowing me to see them clearly. Both wore a lurex type material, which sparkled in the glow of the 'craft' and the lights of my motorcycle, which were still on. Both had short blonde hair, and looked perfect human beings. One was male; the other female. They were wearing wide belts, with an egg-shaped canister on the right-hand side."

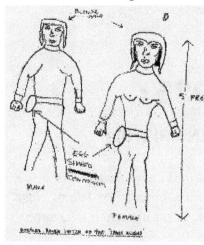

Douglas began to back away, at which point the *'woman'* said to him, *"Don't be afraid".*

Douglas asked her where they were from. She replied, *"From the Third Solar system".*

He then said, *"But there is only one".* She replied, *"Yes, in your Galaxy".*

Douglas asked, *"Why are you here?"* She replied, *"We had to land for minor adjustments".*

Douglas said, *"How does it work?"* She replied, *"Power is based on magnetic fields and gravitational pull. You wouldn't understand. We must go".*

Both persons turned and walked back to the glowing object. Douglas then heard the humming sound increase in volume and a silvery cigar-shaped object took off at tremendous speed, at a 45° angle. Douglas maintained that he later contacted Manchester Airport enquiring about any flights logged for that time, and was told there were none.

On 13th May 1985, Douglas was at his home address when he received a knock on the door, at 11.10am. As he opened the door, he was confronted by two men, who had parked a black car outside. They were described as *"both in their early 40s, dressed in black shoes, black hats, and white shirts."* They told Douglas they knew about his encounter and that he had contacted the airport, and said:

"You should say nothing to anyone for your own safety".

Douglas became angry and told them to clear off.

According to Douglas he received a second visit a few days later, by a RAF Officer, who advised him similarly.

(Source: Douglas Oliver, *New BUFORA Journal,* **August 2002, Issue 9/Peter Hough, MUFORA/**
The UFO World 87, **Jenny Randles, BUFORA)**

Yorkshire UFO Society stake out on the moors!

In this year the Yorkshire Post published an article about the Yorkshire UFO Society, which included a reference to the caravan that was used during their investigations.

There is a part of North Yorkshire known as Flying Saucer Alley because of peculiar sightings over the years. REGINALD BRACE joined investigators in search of UFOs but sadly only managed to intercept a wink from Jupiter.

Something bright was winking through a cloud, but it was only good old Jupiter, on the blink as usual

ONE of the ironies of Ufology is that few, if any, of its disciples have actually seen an Unidentified Flying Object.

Graham Birdsall, 31, founder and president of the Yorkshire UFO Society (motto: Seek And You Will Find) has been involved in UFO research for 18 years and is still waiting the first sight of anything that defies explanation. "That's the worst thing about it," said Mr Birdsall, who was drawn into the world of aerial phenomena at the age of 13 when he saw a ball of light skimming over a Leeds roof top. He now accepts it was probably a passing aircraft.

"I have interviewed hundreds of people over the years who have told me about sightings. I would have given my right arm to share. That's typical of every UFO investigator in the country. Jenny Randles, one of Britain's leading writers on UFOs, has never seen a damn thing. Yes it is frustrating — but you carry on."

One of Mr. Birdsall's colleagues, Philip Mantle, said: "It's similar to fishing. You go to a river you know is stuffed with big fish, but it's the beggar ten pegs up who gets one. You need patience — and if we didn't think our patience would be rewarded one day we would pack it in."

Our close encounter of a convivial kind took place in a wind joined caravan on the remote moorland above the village of Carleton, near Skipton, which is serving as the base for the Yorkshire UFO Society's nine day, round-the-clock Skywatch. It is a publicity exercise designed to draw attention to the society's activities but there is always the hope that something amazing will happen. After all, this is the area of Yorkshire known as Flying Saucer Alley or the Warminster of the North because of a number of odd happenings over the years.

So far the Skywatch sightings have been largely routine. A reddish glare last Friday night could have been the work of some local wit bent on confusion, and although several pairs of binoculars were trained on what looked like a tadpole with lights in the small hours of Sunday, the consensus of opinion leaned towards nothing more peculiar than a light aircraft.

The trouble with Ufology today is that there is usually a solution. It was different in the Fifties, Sixties and Seventies when talk of little green men and shimmering saucers caused many a fluttering in extra-terrestrial dovecotes. To some extent the mystery has gone. People are still seeing strange things in the sky but the source could be Venus — the Queen of UFOs — Jupiter, Mars or merely the moon peering through a cloud, fireballs, meteors, satellites, bits of space debris, weather balloons, aircraft with strobe lights, helicopters using night sun searchlights or remote pilotless vehicles.

"Sometimes we upset witnesses with our analysis of what they have seen but we are open-minded and realistic," said Graham Birdsall. "We obliterate 98 per cent of sightings. This leaves two per cent, unexplained, and it is that two per cent which keeps us interested. If I thought there was an explanation for everything I would save myself

two or three thousand pounds a year, take more holidays and live a normal life again with my wife and three daughters.

"You can't come up with an explanation for the hovering object seen by two policemen at Cracoe Fell in 1981; the Mexican hat shaped craft and three men in silver suits reported by a miner's wife from Normanton; the woman on the Skipton-to-Clitheroe road startled by a battery of lights over her car; the courting couple disturbed by a similar phenomena; the North Yorkshire farmer driven off the road by a glowing craft suspended over his car.

"Several people came to us and reported seeing a large Blimp shooting purple rays over the Vale of York shortly before the York Minster fire in 1984. They included people at a bus stop, taxi drivers and a tourist from Scotland. When they publicised their sighting they were ridiculed. So were we, but we are used to it. People once laughed at the idea of man walking on the moon. We think our York report is just as worthy of investigation as lightning, particularly when the nearest thunderstorm was several miles away from the Minster."

Several police officers have reported weird sights in and around Carleton and Elslack Moors in North Yorkshire and Mr. Birdsall places great store on their observations.

"Objectivity goes right out of the window when you get policemen talking about noiseless UFOs with nuts, bolts and portholes," he said. "The only logical conclusion to some of the things which have been seen is either a secret piece of airborne craft

or an intelligence unknown to man. The more I see of the latest space hardware the more my leanings increase towards unusual surveillance craft, still in their infancy. But you cannot discount the extra-terrestrial possibility."

When he is not peering at the sky, collating research material, editing the YUFOS magazine Quest and addressing meetings, Mr. Birdsall slaps tickets on cars as a parking meter attendant in Leeds. His companions on the Skywatch include Mr. Mantle, 27, a Batley engineer; Paul Chaplow, 18, an apprentice panel beater from Leeds, and Robert Cherry, 31, a Leeds postman.

They eat ham sandwiches, fry sausages, make coffee and talk UFO language which includes classifications like CE I, II, III and IIII (close encounters with varying degrees of intimacy), D/D (daylight disc), N/L (nocturnal light) and LITS (lights in the sky). Around them are the trappings of your dedicated Ufologist: cameras, telescope, video equipment, binoculars and CB radio.

With midnight an hour away we clambered out of the caravan to see if anything was happening in the heavens. Something bright was winking through a cloud, but it was only good old Jupiter, on the blink as usual.

Gaps between the scudding clouds revealed star formations but nothing moving. Not even a satellite tonight, and definitely no chance to echo the immortal words "Beam me up, Scottie." Not that the assembled Skywatchers were expecting too much. As Philip Mantle said, Ufologists have to be patient as they wait for the Big One.

Operation Skywatch: from left, Graham Birdsall, President of the Yorkshire UFO Society, Paul Chaplow, Investigator, Mark Birdsall, Research Co-ordinator, and Philip Mantle, Overseas Liaison Officer, on the lookout for UFOs at Carleton, near Skipton.
Picture by BRUCE ROLLINSON

UFO over Bradford-on-Avon, Wiltshire

At 10pm on 17th May 1985, a large bright orange ball of light was sighted in the sky above Great Chalfield Manor, near Holt, by a couple driving along Leigh Road. It remained motionless for about a minute, before moving across the sky behind a house, followed by the appearance of three orange flashing lights in the sky. The couple contacted the police at Devizes to report the matter, and later received a visit from the MOD.

At 10.45pm on 18th May 1985, a flying disc was seen heading slowly across the sky, over Birmingham.

(Source: Ron West)

UFO over Isle of Wight

We spoke to Eric Spanner, a long-term resident living on the Isle of Wight, who described what he saw, at 9pm on 19th May 1985.

> *"I was out walking on the Downs – a high point overlooking Upper and Lower Ventnor, with the sweep of the Channel behind – when I noticed a bright light, resembling a large flare, just above the horizon. I watched as it gently moved across the sky about half a mile away, approaching the shoreline to the north-west, when it then headed inland, about 60ft off the ground, following the contours of the land, accompanied by a faint whining noise. It then settled over a house in Down Road, allowing me to see an egg-shaped object, 8ft in diameter or so, showing two diffused fluorescent lights, with an aura or halo around its rim, before rising up vertically and heading up the valley, tilting as it did, showing the top two lights, set in a now black body. My God! I thought its heading towards me. Fortunately, it passed overhead and I lost sight of it."*

(Source: Personal interview/Kathleen Smith, *UFOLOG*)

UFO over Otterburn

In the same month, Territorial soldier Robert O'Callaghan, from Gateshead, was taking part in an exercise held at the Ministry of Defence, Otterburn Training Range, manning an observation post overlooking a small hill, at the valley entrance, with a colleague, at midnight.

> *"He was the first to notice and bring to my attention, a number of white lights in the sky, which seemed to curl around the hillside directly in front of us, then rose in height until they reached the brow of the hill, before moving upwards into the sky – where we lost sight of them. Because we were expecting an 'enemy attack', we tried to contact the HQ by using our mobile 49 radios, but they wouldn't work at all; the batteries were dead, although they had been brand new and checked, a short time previously. So we sent a messenger to HQ and were stunned to later discover all of their radios and communications had been immobilized."*

(Source: Barry King)

USA: UFO seen over Connecticut

Between 9:30pm and 10:15pm on 26th May 1985, more than 200 people telephoned local and state police to report a huge object, with bright lights, flying low over the highway, near the towns of Newtown and Southbury in Connecticut.

The sightings took place around Interstate 84 – one of the most heavily travelled highways in the north-east. Those witnesses that called state police in Southbury were told that it was nothing more than a group of ultra-light aircraft from Candlewood Airport, flying in close formation and hanging coloured lanterns from the bottom of the plane. The police also told witnesses that the aircraft were painted black, so all that could be seen were the lights. Many of the witnesses to the phenomenon found it very hard to believe the official explanation. **(Source: NICAP, Philip Imbrogono http://www.ufocasebook.com/i84encounter.html)**

At 2am on 31st May 1985, Potters Bar businessman Gaetano Avogadro – a former Italian resistance fighter – and his wife, Irene, were at their home address, working late. Suddenly, a bright light went past the curtains. The couple looked out and saw a completely silent object, covered with lights, flying very low across the sky. **(Source: *Potters Bar Press*, 6.6.1985 – 'Was it really a UFO?')**

JUNE 1985

EGG-SHAPED UFO SEEN OVER WILTSHIRE

Also includes – UFO over Cwmbran • UFO sighting by Chinese pilots and
UFOs seen over Tyneside

ON 2nd June 1985, a black egg-shaped object, sighted in the clear blue sky above Bromham, near Melksham was photographed by the witness, moving from the direction of Marlborough, towards Bath. **(Source: *Wiltshire Times*, 16.5. 2008)**

UFO over Cwmbran

On 5th June 1985, Jane Thomas of Cae Dewen Two Locks, Cwmbran – a secretary with Torfaen Council – was on her way to the bathroom to fetch a glass of water, at 2am, when she saw, through the window:

> *". . . a large, square-shaped object, hovering in the sky over Twmbarlwm. It then started to 'bounce', before seeming to change shape and ascend rapidly. I saw two large lights travelling towards the object."*

(Source: Margaret Fry/*Cwmbran Star*, 7.6.1985 – 'Did Jane see UFO?')

At 9.55pm on 8th June 1985, a red glowing, oblong-shaped object, was seen moving slowly through the sky over Hertfordshire. **(Source: Ron West)**

China: Pilots sight gigantic UFO

On 11th June 1985 at Lanzhou, Gansu Province, China, a Chinese Civil Aviation Administration Boeing 747 encountered a UFO on the Peking to Paris flight that almost forced the captain to make an emergency landing.

Flight CA933 was over Lanzhou, the capital of Gansu Province, at 2240 hours, when Captain Wang Shuting and his crew first observed the object. The UFO flew across the path of the airliner at its altitude of

33,000ft, at a very high speed. The object illuminated an area of twenty-five to thirty square miles and was huge, with an apparent diameter of six miles. It was elliptical in shape and had an extremely bright spot in the centre, with three horizontal rows of bluish-white lights on the perimeter. The sighting lasted for two minutes. **(Source: Timothy Good, *Above Top Secret*, p. 212)**

UFOs over Tyneside

During the evening of 14th June 1985, scores of people from the Newcastle area telephoned the police, reporting seeing UFOs over the City. The local radio station Metro's switchboard became jammed with callers, following a report from a couple at Denton Burn, who complained that while out driving, they were *'buzzed'* by a UFO. Mr William Strain – forecaster at the Newcastle Weather Centre – told people there must have been an explanation for these occurrences and that he didn't subscribe to the idea of visitors from outer space.

> *"Often, when people have seen a UFO, it's sparks from the Metro, reflected on low clouds."*
> (The Metro was not running that night).

Enquiries made with RAF Boulmer and Newcastle Airport revealed nothing out of the ordinary, while Inspector Steven Ransome, of Northumberland Police, confirmed they had not received any reports of UFO activity. **(Source: *Newcastle Evening Chronicle*, 14.6.1985 – 'UFO riddle over City')**

On 23rd June 1985, Secretary Cheryl Kilcoyne and her husband, John, sighted a silver sphere in the sky above Heaton Norris, Stockport, in Cheshire.

FIVE CLAIM UFO SIGHTING

SECRETARY Cheryl Kilcoyne looked up from her magazine and spotted a silver sphere in the evening sky above Heaton Norris.

She rushed to an upstairs window with husband John and three friends and studied the 'space invader' for six minutes as it moved across the sky, swooping occasionally and then climbing again.

"It was level with a plane on the flight path to Manchester Airport, but moving a lot slower and glinting as it caught the sun," explained Cheryl.

The sighting, at 6.50 p.m. on Sunday, took place at her mother-in-law's home in Bower Avenue, Heaton Norris.

Cheryl, 21, of Cambridge Road, Heaton Chapel, said: "It must have been a genuine UFO, I don't see what else it could have been. The amazing thing was that over dinner I had been describing a UFO I sighted nine years ago in Macclesfield, it looked exactly the same."

Wendy Ostcik, 18, of Broadstone Road, Heaton Chapel, watched its movement with Cheryl. "I know people who have seen them but this was my first sighting and am not convinced they do exist."

However, a spokesman for the British UFO Research Association in Warrington poured cold water on the report: "From what you have described it sounds as if it could have been a silver balloon or a weather balloon, possibly caught in the aircraft's slipstream. Ninety per cent of sightings, particularly at this time of the year, can be explained."

JULY 1985

'FLYING FERRIS WHEEL' UFO OVER WINCHESTER

Also includes – Egg-shaped UFO over Portsmouth • Ghostly car seen by police officers at Winchester • UFO display over Glasgow, witnessed by Close Encounters Group UFO seen over Falmouth, Cornwall, by woman out walking

PENSIONERS Jack and Patricia Collins from Fox Lane, Stanmore, Winchester, were driving home late on the 6th July 1985, when they sighted an unusual object, travelling across the sky.

Patricia:

"It was a huge circular thing, and was divided out like the spokes of a wheel. Around the outside of these were very bright lights – like huge light bulbs – and other lights in the sections. It was so bright – like something out of a fairground – and was hovering about 30ft off the ground, over fields. When we arrived home we called the Police."

(Source: *Southampton Reporter*, 19.7.1985, Colin Andrews)

UFO over Portsmouth

Another sighting of a similar object took place at 2.52pm on 13th July 1985, involving local UFO Researcher Nicholas Maloret (WATSUP).

"I was in my rear garden at Lockway Road, Milton, Portsmouth, on the afternoon of 13th July 1985. It was a fairly hot afternoon, with a blue, cloudless sky, when I saw this bright pinpoint of light in the East, 45° off the horizon. I thought it to be an aircraft, to begin with, until it passed overhead, at a height of about 1,000ft, when I saw an egg-shaped object, with sunlight glistening on its upper surface and a dark grey underneath, head towards the West, where I soon lost sight of it."

Mrs Fountain-Fernley from Chesterfield, Derbyshire, wrote to the MOD, asking them for any information about the incidents at Rendlesham Forest, and received this answer:

MINISTRY OF DEFENCE
Main Building Whitehall London SW1A 2HB
Telephone 01-218 (Direct Dialling)
01-218 9000 (Switchboard)

Mrs E Fountain-Fearnley
Hillcrest
2 Norton Avenue
Shuttlewood
Nr Chesterfield
Derbyshire S44 6RA

Your reference

Our reference D/Sec(AS)12/2/1

Date 2 July 1985

Dear Mrs Fountain-Fearnley

 Thank you for your letter of 15 April. You may find it useful if I explain that the sole interest of the United Kingdom Ministry of Defence in reported sightings of Unidentified Flying Objects (UFOs) is to establish whether they have any bearing on the defence of the country.

 There is no organisation in the Ministry of Defence appointed solely for the purpose of studying reports of such objects, and no staff are employed on the subject full time. The reports we receive are referred to the staff in the Department who are responsible for the air defence of the United Kingdom, and they examine the reports as part of their normal duties.

 Since our interest in UFOs is limited to possible defence implications we have not carried out a study into the scientific significance of these phenomena. Unless there are defence implications we do not attempt to identify sightings and we cannot inform observers of the probable identity of the object seen. The Department could not justify the expenditure of public funds on investigations which go beyond the pure defence interests.

 We have to recognise that there are many strange things to be seen in the sky, but we believe there are adequate explanations for them. They may be satellite debris re-entering the earth atmosphere, ball lightning, unusual cloud formations, meteorological balloons, aircraft lights, aircraft at unusual angles or many other things.

 The only information we have on the alleged "UFO sighting" at Rendlesham Forest in December 1980 is the report by Colonel Charles Halt, of the United States Air Force. We are satisfied that the events described are of no defence significance. I enclose a copy of Colonel Halt's report which may be of interest.

Yours sincerely

Winchester – Ghostly Car seen by Police!

Retired Police Officer Brian James contacted us with some information, relating to a visit made by a police colleague to the house of Winchester resident Joyce Bowles, but still remains puzzled as to what it was that he and another officer followed in the summer of 1985.

"I was on traffic patrol with PC Marshall, who was driving at the time. About mid-afternoon, we were travelling along St. Cross Road, out of the city, and turning left into Five Bridges Road (known locally as Ghost Corner) when we saw, ahead of us, a red saloon car. It was about 200 yards in front of us, when it turned left into a track leading up to a house and out buildings. Both Harvey and I were familiar with this property and its owner but did not associate this car with the property, so we decided to investigate. When we turned left into the track, there was no sign of a car.

We looked everywhere around the property and in buildings, but this car had vanished off the face of the Earth. We could not explain this occurrence and we had no previous knowledge of any such like happenings. We never did establish why Five Bridges Road was called Ghost Corner, but obviously, something had taken place at this location in the past. Needless to say, we both kept this occurrence to ourselves for a long time before saying what we had seen; otherwise we would probably have been ridiculed."

UFO display over Glasgow

At 12.30am on 13th July 1985, Brian McMullan Junior, GS and Brian McMullan – members of the Glasgow based band C.E.IV – were stood outside their bass player's home in the north side of Glasgow, waiting for a taxi to arrive on what was a clear night, and looking up into the night sky. They had been out there for some 20 minutes, when GS shouted *"What the hell is that? Did you see that?"*

They looked up and saw a *'small fuzzy amber coloured ball'*, high in the northern sky, about the size of a bright star, which, within seconds, began to increase in size while descending. Brian Junior looked at it through binoculars and then passed them to his father, who had this to say:

"It came down across our position, heading south, in a slow skipping movement. You could see the top, as it seemed to lean back, then the bottom, as it dipped forward. It continued in a straight trajectory. These movements could be seen easily with the naked eye, but when using the binoculars the sight was phenomenal. We all agreed it gave the impression that you could almost touch it! As it disappeared low over the city, we rushed into the house to waken the fourth band member. He obviously wasn't too pleased he had missed the 'overhead' views.

We stood around, discussing exactly what each of us had seen; the whole sighting had lasted about 30 seconds. When I first saw the fuzzy 'ball' high in the sky, it was red-orange, but as it approached closer it changed to bright amber. It reminded me of a hot poker, taken from a fire and cooled down. I definitely received the impression that it was slowing down through the atmosphere and 'cooling' in some way! Small dark individual lines seemed to be dancing all over the surface. City lights were amber, but this object was not reflecting these. The fact that we saw the same colours on top of the object proves this point.

The amber colour, shape and movement, conveyed this to be an object of complete beauty. When close up, I kept thinking the design was perfection. No sound whatsoever came from the object and I think this added to the mystic of it all. I could see no door/window lines, or any lines showing a possible join anywhere. I've often thought that if a model of this object were to be made, it would have to be one piece of amber glass, blown to shape. We all had different ideas regarding the surface. One band member swore it was reflective, like perfect mirror glass, and the other thought it to be transparent."

The following report is taken from notes 'written-up' by Brian Junior, the morning after the sighting.

"After a few minutes GS grabbed my arm and brought my attention to a light, moving slowly in the distance behind a neighbour's tree. As it emerged from the top of the tree, it became obvious that it was an aircraft. At the same time my dad was pointing out some flashes high in the sky to the North. Another light appeared close to the aircraft we had just viewed. This was another aircraft and I remember, at the time, we all thought that they were dangerously close!

A few moments later GS pointed to the North and shouted, 'Did you see that?' My dad saw it, too, and made a comment. I looked up and saw nothing, but as we all moved around the side of the house for a better view, I then spotted an orange circular object.

It was big, about the size of a 5p piece, held at arm's length. As I looked through the binoculars, the object filled my view completely. I felt it was like aluminium and seemed to glow an amber colour. I watched through the binoculars for around 7 to 8secs. Most of this time I was attempting to take it all in! I remember saying, 'My God – I don't believe it! It's a flying saucer shape!'

At this point my dad shouted to get CR out, so GS ran back into the house. As they came back out (CR half sleeping!) it shook me back to reality (like I was paralysed watching it) and I handed the binoculars to my dad. He began describing what he was seeing. GS just stood quietly gaping at the object; this surprised me, as I would have expected him to be running around excited, like his normal self. He, too, was frozen to the spot. I can only guess we were paralysed through the awesome wonder and close proximity of the object, or the object itself could project this feeling!

Immediately after the sighting I felt sickly and couldn't stand properly. It took at least 5mins before I felt normal again. Standing around afterwards, it seemed half an hour had passed – yet it was only minutes. My watch alarm had gone off at exactly 1.01am. This I thought unusual, but honestly can't put any real credence as to why this should happen!

As it passed above our heads and across the city, it remained high above the flats in the distance, about the same height again as the flats. The circumference of the object seemed to match the width of the 20 high multi-storey flats. Calculations would have the object around 500ft above ground, with a circumference of about 60ft.

The speed could not be calculated with any accuracy, but because of the close proximity and the time it took to pass overhead, we guessed it must have been approximately 80mph. During the week that followed, we attempted to work out where the object was heading. Using maps and judging by the angle and direction (SSW) we estimated it would be very close to the ground, around 20 miles south of the city. That would be the Fenwick Moor area, adjacent to the M77 Motorway."

Brian and his father are keenly interested in the UFO subject and have participated in 'sky watches', attended meetings, and written articles for various UFO magazines and journals, over the years. They are to be congratulated on the preparation and documentation of a thorough report, which contains a wealth of details relating to the sighting of something out of the ordinary, but fairly commonplace to the pages of this book. We wish them well and good luck.   **(Source: Personal interviews/Philip Mantle)**

Philip Mantle seen here with Brian McMullan Junior and father, Brian McMullan

At Islington, in London, a green cigar-shaped object was reported over the locality, at 2.20am on 16th July 1985, heading northwards.   **(Source: Ron West)**

An unconfirmed source tells of a UFO being chased by two RAF Tornadoes over Mansfield, Nottinghamshire, at 1.30am on 24th July 1985.   **(Source: WWW UFO Evidence)**

UFO chased by Jets over Zimbabwe

Reading Evening Post.

- 2 AUG 1985

'UFO' gives fighter

237

jet planes the slip

TOP ZIMBABWE air force officers are convinced they have had a visit from outer space that showed them a clean pair of heels when chased by air force jets.

Air force fighter planes were scrambled last week after a "bright flying object" was sighted over southern parts of the country.

Air force commander. Azim Daudpota said: "This was no ordinary unidentified flying object and scores of people saw it".

Two air force Hawk jets

moved to intercept the UFO, which streaked from 7,000 feet in less than a minute.

The orange-coloured UFO was tracked from the southern border town of Beitbridge to the southern city of Bulawayo, where air force and aviation and meteorological experts kept it in sight.

Daudpota said he was quite prepared to believe the UFO might have been a remote-controlled airship.

Bulawayo Airport control tower officials said the UFO seemed rounded with a short cone above it. No one managed to capture it on film.

Towards the end of the month another pursuit took place, involving Fighter Jets being scrambled – this time over Zimbabwe – after a bright orange flying object was sighted, by many people, and reported to the authorities.

Was there a connection with what Mrs Elsie Lee of Norton Avenue, Shuttlewood, Bolsover, and a member of the Yorkshire UFO Society, saw at midnight on the same date? Elsie described seeing:

> ". . . a star-shaped object, with red and blue flashing
> lights, in the sky for over two hours."

She called the police and PC Mark Turner arrived. He and Elsie watched the object for about 35 minutes, before it moved away towards the direction of Dronfield.

The sighting was reported to the local *Derbyshire Times Newspaper*, who published her story on 9th August 1985 – 'Spaced out Elsie's starship Enterprise'.

Elsie spots UFO in colour

UFO investigator Elsie Lee wants information from anyone who may have seen an object zipping round the night skies above north Derbyshire last week.

Mrs Lee, of Norton Avenue, Shuttlewood, near Bolsover, says she and a policeman saw an unidentified flying object through her binoculars at 1.45 am last Wednesday.

"It looked like a large and exceptionally bright star and was shining red and blue," said Mrs Lee, an investigator for the Yorkshire UFO Society.

"I was later stunned to see that the 'star' had disappeared. There was not a cloud in sight, so it could not have been obscured."

She claims she next saw the object 60 degrees to the left of her first sighting, and 20 minutes later it had moved back to the right.

Mrs Lee then called the police and says Pc Mark Turner watched the object get smaller and disappeared toward Dronfield.

Pc Turner said last night: "It seemed to be moving very slowly in a straight line. She was quite struck on it being a UFO but it just looked like a star to me".

SHEFFIELD + DoNCASTER TELEGRAPH (1985)

MONDAY JULY 29th

AUGUST 1985

UFO SIGHTED OVER BIRIMGHAM

Also includes – UFO seen over Cornwall • Close encounter in Florence • Triangular
UFO over New York • UFO over Petersfield

UFO over Birmingham

ON 10th August 1985, a resident of Selly Oak, Birmingham, was looking out of the window, at 1pm, when he noticed what he took to be a kite in the near distance. He said:

"As it moved nearer, I was astonished to see that it appeared self motivated and elliptical in shape, showing circular central indentation, and was reflecting the sun's rays. It was spinning around slowly and heading towards the Woodgate Valley Park and Birmingham University area."

The witness, who was previously sceptical of such matters, reported it to the Birmingham Group – UFOSIS.

At 8.10pm on 14th August 1985, a flashing silver and black heart-shaped object, rotating anticlockwise in the air, was seen over Fishponds, Bristol. **(Source: Peter Tate, Bristol)**

UFO over Falmouth, Cornwall

Marjorie Walker from Falmouth, Cornwall – a mobile hairdresser by trade, at the time – told of a very strange object she saw in 1985, while out walking her dog along a public footpath above the beach, with views of Pendonise Point, with its castle on top.

"As we walked along, I was surprised to see what looked like a small bubble. Within the blink of the eye, a large orange disc appeared, hovering three to four hundred yards ahead of me, over the sea. It was the size of two double-decker buses, one on top of the other, shaped like a ring, filled with an orange milky substance that was pulsating. I said out aloud, 'It's a UFO'.

I saw a young woman approaching with a wheelchair and toddler. I asked her if she could see the thing over there. She looked and said, 'Oh my God, what is it?' I was amazed how calm I felt. A little further up I saw two men, leaning over a fence. I went up to them and pointed out the object. Like the woman before, their first words were 'Oh my God, what is it?'"

The sighting of the object is as clear now as it was then, and changed Marjorie's outlook on life. She had a question to ask the scientists, who tell us these things don't exist, *"When are you going to wake up?"*

Close Encounter in Florence, Italy

We were to learn of an incident which took place on August 8th 1985, in picturesque Florence, Italy. The sighting reminded us of what Gloucestershire man John Hickman had seen over Tewkesbury, in November 1972. Whether there was a connection we cannot say, but it seems of much value to outline what happened.

It involved Signora Domenica Cantone, who was then living in a sixth floor apartment with her husband – a Police Inspector.

Unable to sleep, owing to the heat of the night, she went out onto the balcony, at 3.30am, and saw an object approaching silently from her left-hand side.

> *"The strange thing halted on a level with the balcony, a few metres away from me, and directly above a small football pitch alongside the building. I then saw an egg-shaped body of a silvery hue, surmounted by a transparent glassy cupola, through which I could see houses on the other side. Inside the cupola I saw two 'men'; they were talking to each other. Every now and then they broke off their conversation and gazed fixedly at me. All I could see was their heads, each of which was surmounted by two great 'ears' (possibly part of the caps in which their heads were swathed). Suddenly, from the base of the object emerged three 'legs' or 'arms', the same colour and luminosity as the body of the UFO."*

At this point Domenica was (understandably) seized with panic, thinking she was going to be abducted and *tried to wake her husband, but was unsuccessful. She then ran back to the balcony, where she was in time to see that the UFO had already started to pull up its *'legs'*, while the two men still gazed at her. Moments later, the object departed silently away and at speed, emitting a vivid light that was so intense that it hurt to look at it.

It was now 4am; 30 minutes had elapsed since she had first seen the object. She went back to bed, after shutting all the windows and blinds, but was unable to sleep again that night. It was said that two years on, she was still terrified and slept with the windows barred.

This matter was investigated by Fabrizio Villa and Calogero Orlando of the National Ufological Centre, in Italy (CUN, Italy) who discovered that two days after the sighting, some boys found marks on the sports field alongside the building. These consisted of three circular imprints, with a deeper area containing rubble and what appeared to be fragments of compressed carbon, with an outer area of greyish powder. We

---

(*The failure to wake a family member is a trait of behaviour we have come across previously, involving sightings of UFOs. This may lead some people to suggest that this was not happening on a physical plain but in a dream like state. If this was the answer to all such reports, then why is, on other occasions, people who are awake elsewhere see the same UFO, not forgetting the onset of physical ailments which can follow incidents like these?)

are not sure how the Press became involved, unless the Police Inspector reported the matter to his HQ, but the locality was to be the source of much attention by people who came to have a look after it happened, no doubt presuming the UFO had landed.

(Source: *FSR* **– A CE-111 Encounter in Firenze, summer 1985(?), Volume 32, No. 3, 1987)**

Three white lights were seen stationary in the sky over Croydon, in Surrey, at 11.40pm on 23rd August 1985. Was this another example of the Triangular UFO, or was there another explanation?

(Source: Ron West)

USA: Triangular UFO seen again and a news blackout!

On 25th August 1985, New York Journalist *Greg Boone was on duty with ten other newsmen, at the Poughkeepsie Journal. At about 9.35pm, they received a radio message reporting a giant *'boomerang UFO'* had been seen in the sky heading south, on Route 9.

This sighting took place during the Dutchess County Fair, attended by approximately 20,000 people, many of whom were travelling home along that highway, heading south from Rhinebeck, New York, about 18 miles north of Poughkeepsie – about 75 miles north of New York City.

Greg was told that the craft was huge and heading south, and might be visible from their office windows on the 3rd floor. He and two editors dashed to the northern window of the managing editor's office and, sure enough, at a distance of approximately five miles, they saw a dark shape, about 100ft above the ground, with amber and red lights slowly growing bigger as it headed their way.

Greg:

> *"It was big, slow moving, and in no way was supposed to be flying over residential areas. Folks up there have shotguns and use them at the drop of a hat! It is very old republican territory. Folks still beef about Pearl Harbour like it was yesterday. On the highway, thousands and thousands of people were so alarmed that they bolted from their cars to gander at this craft. I stood there and watched as the craft suddenly got within a couple of miles and then shut off its lights, aft to fore, before pivoting port, travelled east a bit, then startlingly made a hard starboard turn and headed straight for us! This thing got huge and, believe it or not, flew right over top of us by about 40ft. It had to be 200ft wide and was jet black. The illumination of the street lights did not reflect anything off its surface that we could determine. Wanting to get a better glimpse of it, we dashed to the other windows to see if it had passed overhead – couldn't be seen – and we realised it might be hovering over us. Sure enough, that's what it did! We dashed to one of the bathrooms facing east, and that's when the craft turned east again and glided over the more heavily populated section of the city, noiselessly, and was gone."*

According to Greg, tens of thousands of people sighted this UFO, including journalists, police officers, and military personnel.

Greg:

> *"Well, we're sitting there, screaming at the photographers and reporters that this will be the story of the century. We had access to AP, Gannett, etc., and USA Today, which we mainly put out. Nope. Word came down from on high that not one word was to be mentioned. This was a solid object that hovered, manoeuvred, and was seen by tens of thousands, pictures taken, and no mention anywhere. Next day, some 'menacing' chaps showed up in our editorial office. I got in trouble for staring back just as menacingly."*

*Greg Boone is a writer, pencil sketcher, inker, and publisher. He worked for the Gannett News Service, several popular magazines and comic books. He is also the author of The UFO Mafia. Boone's work is found in DC Comics, Batman Annual #13, several issues of Thrasher Magazine and Thrasher Comics, Defiant Comics' Good Guys, Acclaim Comics Bloodshot, Time Walker and Shadow Man, Tekno Comics, Neil Gaiman's Lady Justice and Boone's popular books Evol Baby, Monster Posse, RADREX series. A UFO researcher and journalist, Boone is a one-man-gang, able to write, pencil, ink, and publish. Working in radio and global communications networking, Boone spends his time in science research and is returning to comics. His newest novel is entitled The UFO Mafia and he is already in negotiations with film companies for development into a major motion picture feature.

(Source: WWW Internet, 2013)

This was the first time that craft flew over our newspaper, but wasn't the last. A year later (in 1986) a huge saucer-shaped craft did the same thing. We all bolted outside – this time on the roof of the building – and saw a circle of lights, about a half mile wide, hovering over a local monument that rests on a hill that couples go to 'pitch woo'. It was there for about 10mins and cops, people, all saw it. Then the remarkable part, as I dashed downstairs to get my trusty telescope from my van to get a closer look, I suddenly looked straight up and another large boomerang object was directly overhead!

Three people were in the parking lot at that time with me, and we stared at it and then it kicked in orange afterburners.

I recall six laterally on its aft section, took off like a rocket due west, at high speed, and then did a hard bank port that surprised us and must've taken off south-west, at over 500mph easy. You could HEAR the afterburners kick in overhead and this thing, at about 100ft high, was about 100ft wide. It wasn't the source of the circular lights, but we suspect the boomerang-shaped object chased away the circular object. That's two UFOs in one, at night, close up – again multiple witnesses. I've seen these craft about six times and way back, in 1980, a friend got pictures of it – the first time I'd heard of it, and we developed the film at the newspaper ourselves. Nothing unusual but definitely the boomerang shape, and we figured just another test aircraft that region is famous for – testing. Yet again, 'Mum was the word' and there was heck to pay if you pressed the issue at the evening editor's meeting."

For those that believe this classification of UFO was the product of the 1980s, the reader is reminded of a sighting in June 1960, involving Tommy Dunford, from Wiltshire, whose report can be found on page 156 and 157 of this book. (Also covered in Volume 2 of *Haunted Skies*). We did email Greg, but as of yet have not received any reply from him.

In addition to this sighting was the recovery of a sketch drawn by ex-RAF serviceman Mr S. Victor Yeakes, who sighted a wedge-shaped object over Felixstowe, in 1953. (See page 98 in Volume 1 of *Haunted Skies*) Once again, it illustrates that triangular UFOs are not the product of the 1980s.

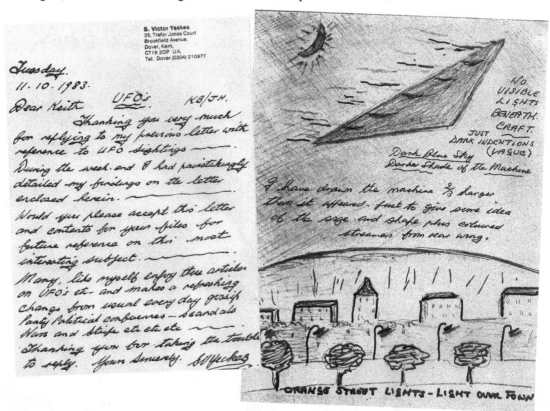

UFO over Petersfield

On 31st August 1985, Dorothy Smith from Woodbury Avenue, Petersfield, was awoken at 3.45am by the family cat. Looking outside to see what the commotion was all about, she was shocked to see:

> ". . . a brilliantly lit object, looking like a gondola, lit up with electric light, hovering over the fir trees, four gardens down. I watched it for 30mins and then rang the Meteorological Office, at Bracknell. They told me it was nothing to do with them, or the Military. Could it have been some kind of experiment?"

(Source Personal interview/*Petersfield Post*, 1.8.1985 – 'A not so very far away encounter')

SEPTEMBER 1985

UFOs SEEN OVER OXFORDSHIRE

Also includes – Close encounter at Bagshot Heath, Surrey

A SILVER coloured *'disc'* was sighted stationary in the sky over Edmonton, in London, at 8.15am on 1st September 1985. At 9.30pm, the same day, a pink coloured object, with glittering lights, was seen low down in the sky, before suddenly disintegrating and disappearing from view over Rogate, West Sussex, by Mr and Mrs Peggy Jones-Parry, while returning home.   **(Source: Ron West)**

UFOs over Oxfordshire

According to Derek Mansell of Contact International UK, Oxfordshire, he received seven separate reports of strange objects seen in the sky, at 9.05pm on 9th September 1985. They occurred over Oxford, Bicester, Boars Hill, Kidlington and Wheatley, involving what was described as a fairly low silent swept wing object, showing an unusual light pattern.

Two days later, on 11th September, between 8.50pm and 9.04pm, a mysterious *'light'* was seen circling the sky over Wheatley, before fading away. On the same day (11.9.1985) between 9.30pm and 9.45pm, a married couple from Bicester spotted two orange-yellow *'discs'*, moving at speed across the sky, heading towards the direction of Oxford.

> *"One was travelling in a straight line; the other, weaving from side to side."*

On 12th September 1985, two Abingdon housewives reported having sighted a huge metallic object moving across the sky, at 11.5am. As it did so, two aircraft were seen to pass underneath it. The women watched it for 35 minutes, before it was lost from view. On the same day, three men in Marston Link Road, Oxford, saw several shining objects moving slowly across the sky, heading eastwards. Other witnesses were three nurses, who reported having sighted three large silver *'discs'* heading west to east across the sky. Still more witnesses to unidentified flying objects seen on this day included two motorists, who were travelling along the M40, near High Wycombe, when they sighted five luminous objects, at low height in the sky, about the size of footballs, travelling one behind the other.

**(Source: Derek Mansell, Contact UK, *The Oxford Times*, 4.10.1985
– 'Fresh Spate of UFO sightings over County')**

Close encounter – Bagshot Heath, Surrey

On 15th September 1985, butcher David McMurray and his wife, Susan, were driving home to Farnborough, Hampshire, along the A322, towards Bagshot, after having visited friends at Guildford, Surrey, with their two children – Paul, aged five months and Katy, 16 months.

They tuned off the main road at the 'Gordon Boys School roundabout', heading for Farnborough along Red Road (B311) and had only gone about a quarter of a mile when, as they turned a slight bend, saw the amazing sight of a saucer-shaped object, hovering over the road, about 50-60 yards away from their position. The light given off by the object was so bright that David was forced to turn his eyes away.

David:

> *"As we continued to approach it, another similar object appeared from behind trees to our left and travelled alongside our car, just behind the trees skirting the road. At this point we noticed another car, which had been behind us, come to a stop and pull off the road. The first object then shot off skywards and disappeared. I decided to continue our journey and drove for about a mile where there was a new property development, hoping for the chance to run to a nearby house. I stopped when I reached this point and got out, but Sue locked the door and refused to leave the car, the children being fast asleep at this time. The UFO had also stopped and was visible above the tops of trees across the other side of the road. I could see that it had a brilliant red light on one side and green light the other. Around the craft were a number of dazzling white lights, but no sign of any movement or rotating lights. I had an impression 'it' was watching us. I heard a buzzing noise, as if someone had started up an electric sewing machine. About a minute and a half later, the object suddenly accelerated away and was gone – now just visible as a star-like object in the sky."*

David jumped back into his car and drove up the slight hill to obtain better view, but saw nothing. He

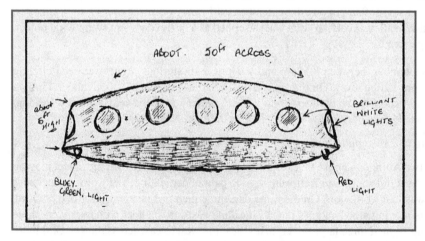

then returned and saw that the driver of a white Volvo was sat there, with the interior light on, but inexplicably did not stop to talk to him.

The family then made their way to the nearest police station and reported the matter. David also telephoned West Drayton Air Traffic Centre and Heathrow Airport Control Tower.

The next day the whole family found themselves having overslept, not waking up till 9.30am. David went out to start the car. However, he found the battery flat, but managed to obtain some assistance from a nearby garage to get it going.

The following day (16th September 1985) David developed a severe headache and, after being examined by his local Doctor, was referred to the Hospital, where an ECG test and blood pressure checks were carried out but found to be normal.

Following on from these symptoms, David became aware of a *'hollow feeling'* in his stomach and *'shaky'* legs. This condition persisted for 8-9 days, by which time Sue also complained of the same symptoms.

David McMurray

Other medical problems were to manifest. David found himself experiencing disturbed sleep, accompanied by memory flashbacks of the UFO incident, and these coincided with memory lapses. He then noticed an outbreak of small red circles, about one and a quarter inch in diameter, on his body. The first one appeared on the side of his neck and lasted for a few hours. As this faded away, another appeared.

Family tell of two sightings

Clouded in mystery —one of the flying saucers as David saw it in his sketch

OUR UFO TERROR

By BILL DAVEY

A FAMILY had a bizarre close encounter on a day out—with two UFOs.

The first flying saucer put butcher David McMurray and wife Susan in a spin when it hovered in front of their car.

Minutes later a second "space-craft" flew into view—and now the strange sightings are being probed by experts.

David and Susan were driving home across Bagshot Heath, Surrey, to Farnborough, Hampshire, with their two children Paul, 5, and Katie, 18 months.

David, 35, said: "I saw something hovering above the road in front of us. I could not believe my eyes.

"It was a huge saucer-like craft about 50ft. long with brilliant lights coming from portholes around the centre. Then it suddenly took off." When a second craft began to tail the family's car David stopped, got out and went to investigate. But it too, took off.

David said: "The whole family were weak and trembling for days afterwards."

Susan, 25, a hairdresser, said: "When David tried to start his car the battery was drained." She added: "I saw the two things with my own eyes. It was an incredible experience."

One UFO was also spotted five miles away by salesgirl Lyn Brookes, 24, of Wokingham, Berkshire.

She said: "It hovered in one spot for about five minutes.

Down to earth—Susan, Katie and David

Watching

"I was really frightened. It was as if it was watching me."

Now David has sketched the strange craft and is sending his drawing to the Ministry of Defence who are to investigate.

UFO expert Omar Fowler, 54, has also seen the drawing and said: "I have no doubt this report is genuine."

Heathrow Airport say none of the strange craft could have been planes.

UFO-watchers believe the area is a target for flying saucers.

Even stranger and worryingly was the fact that red rings, which had previously appeared only on the left-hand side of his body – neck, shoulder, trunk and groin, had repeated themselves during the period event, plus 17-22 days on the right-hand side of his body, in a similar pattern. He also became aware that, at odd moments in his mind, he was explaining the function of various mechanical and electrical domestic appliances, such as the electric light switch when in the house, and the mechanism of the car and engine while out driving. The strangest thing of all (if they can, indeed, get any stranger) was a message running through his head almost continuously. *'Epsilon 44L-47L'*

On a return visit to the location of where he had witnessed the UFO, David had an overwhelming urge not to make his way towards where he had seen the 2nd UFO and left the scene.

Mr Omar Fowler, who investigated this matter – then Chairman of SIGAP (Surrey Investigation Group) and also a consultant for *FSR* – was able to track down details of other witnesses who had seen unusual things that evening.

25 OCT 85
UFOs? Nothing new

THE reports of the bright lights or UFOs reported in your editions of September 20 and October 18 are not new.

My father, travelling from Lightwater to Woking when he worked with horses, was considerably frightened some time in the late 1920s by a bright light, which he described as being of dazzling brightness, which travelled parallel with him across the common from Lightwater Manor, disappearing abruptly near the Gordon Boys School junction with Red Road.

He was cycling at about 4.30-5 a.m., as was his habit in order to feed the horses before work. He was the most unimaginative man in the world, just a simple country man.

It was talked about in our family for years whenever anything of a supernatural happening was under discussion.

I was about 18 at the time and remember it well. He was, he said, "shaking with fright." — J. Davies (Mrs.), Brahms Road, Brighton Hill, Basingstoke.

The first was Mr and Mrs Webb. They were driving along the M4, towards the direction of the Wokingham turning, about 12 miles from the Bagshot Heath incident, at 8.45pm, when they saw a bright red glowing object shoot across the sky from the direction of Bagshot. Later on, at 11.45pm, Lynda Brookes and her boyfriend sighted a strange red and white flashing object in the sky, over the Wokingham area.

Mrs Brooks told Omar: *"I was really frightened. It was as if it was watching me. My Great Dane dog was disturbed and whining."*

On 12th January, the following year, David went to Stanmore, in London – the home of *FSR* Consultant Dr. Leonard Wilder – after arrangements were made for him to be hypnotized by him in the presence of Dr. Bernard E. Finch, Gordon Creighton, and other interested parties. After introductions were made, the matter was discussed, followed by Dr. Wilder placing David onto the couch and then the session began. David outlined the initial encounter with the UFO and made the following references – *'the Guardians from Epsilon 44L 47L 44L'*, which was mentioned many times by him during that session. [David was to find himself facing another traumatic experience on 26th January 1986, details of which will be found in due course.]

Reports of motorists being followed by unusual lights along rural roads form a common background to the Volumes of *Haunted Skies*, whatever the era.

(Sources: Close Encounter on Bagshot Heath Page 2, *FSR* Volume 31, 1986/*SundayMirror* 29.9.1985 'Our UFO Terror'/*FSR* Volume 31 No 6 1986, Omar Fowler/Gordon Creighton)

According to declassified MOD documents, on 8th September 1985, a *'beam of light'* from behind a row of trees was seen spinning around the sky, followed by a round object, described as having a circumference to that of a house, with a ring of red lights around its base, each being about one and a half inches in diameter, and was seen to rise from the ground. This was accompanied by a humming noise, which increased in volume and show of lights. It was last seen heading east across fields from the Bransholme estate, flying at a height of about 50ft. The sighting occurred around 1am, with the movement lasting about 15 minutes. Reports from the night suggest that conditions were favourable for flying, with good visibility. According to the Ministry of Defence, at the time of the sighting a military exercise, involving flares, was taking place in the East.

At 8pm on 27th September 1985, two police officers observed a large object, displaying four white lights in a delta formation, showing a red light underneath as it passed over the Long Clawson area of Ashby-de-la-Zouch. The UFO flew at a low altitude and was virtually silent as it across the sky. Only when it was directly overhead did the officers detect a slight humming noise. **(Source: MOD Files)**

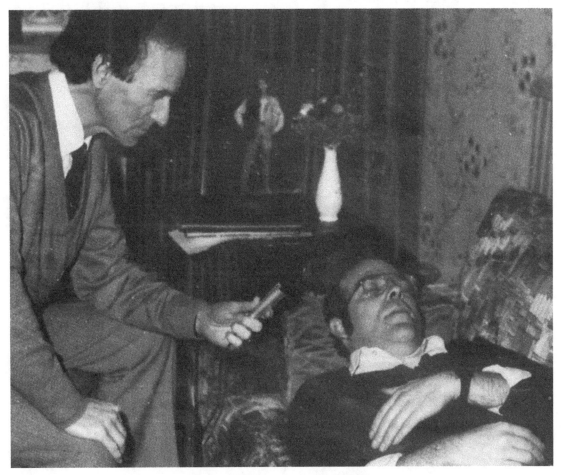

Dr. Leonard Wilder hypnotising David McMurray

Camberley News, Surrey.

16 OCT 19..

UFO SPOTTED BY MUM AND DAUGHTER

A MOTHER and her teenage daughter watched in amazement as a light brighter than any star swung backwards and forwards in the night sky.

Mrs. Joyce Rapley and her daughter June (19) are convinced that the bright yellow light they saw from a bedroom window at their home in Ambleside Road, Lightwater, was not a star or an aeroplane. They believe they spotted a UFO.

Their sighting comes exactly a month after Farnborough butcher Mr. David McMurray and his family saw what appeared to be a massive spacecraft in the nearby Bagshot Heath area.

The "close encounter" experienced by the McMurrays, of Broomhill Road, was later backed up when two other sightings were reported on the same evening, one in the Bagshot area and one over Wokingham.

The activity has led local UFO expert Mr. Omar Fowler to speculate that Bagshot Heath could have been singled out by aliens as an area for special study.

Attention

He said the activity of the light seen by Mrs. Rapley and her daughter was "typical of UFO activity."

Mrs. Rapley woke at 6.05 a.m. on Tuesday and got up

to let out the family dog. Even without her glasses on, her attention was caught by a brilliant light shining in the sky in the direction of Chobham.

Explaining away the light to herself as a particularly bright star, Mrs. Rapley crept back upstairs to bed, saying nothing. But June awoke quite independently and with sharper eyes could see at once that the light was not a star.

Mrs. Rapley said: "She said, 'Good God, look at this'."

June added: "I was staring at it for ages. It went from one side to the other and back and forward. I went to

get a camera, but when I came back it was gone.

"I looked to see if there were any red lights like an aeroplane. You could not hear anything. At that distance you would hear an aeroplane's noise. I opened the window."

Invaded

June, who works at Lenthéric Morny in Camberley, said she deliberately left off the lights. Even so, she said she wondered if the occupants of the UFO realised she had gone downstairs to get her camera.

She added: "I could see the shape of it; a dome shape like a hat."

Mrs. Rapley (55) said:

"Getting up without my glasses on I had just thought that is a bright star, although I couldn't see any other. Then my daughter pointed it out and I thought 'Good God, we are being invaded'."

She continued: "The swinging from side to side was very conspicuous, like someone swinging a lamp from side to side."

The couple said they had wondered whether or not to say anything, but if no one did, nothing would ever be confirmed. They would like to know if anyone else saw the light.

Mrs. Rapley said: "I did not believe before. I was very sceptical. You think like

everyone else the reports are just someone thinking they have seen something, but having seen it like that it makes you wonder.

"I said I wondered where they are coming from, but I suppose there are so many planets."

June now plans to keep her camera at the ready beside her bed in case the light should reappear.

Mr. Fowler said: "The movement of the light is typical of UFO activity. We have had reports over the years from Lightwater, Chobham and Bagshot Heath areas of strange noises and lights. It is not new, but nevertheless it sounds very interesting."

June Rapley and her mum looking out for more mystery manifestations.

Coming and going in a twinkling

WHILE walking my dog at about 7.35 this evening, (October 20), I saw a twinkling light in the sky towards Pool and Carn Brea. It was like a star, but much bigger and brighter, travelling at a high speed away from me. It then disappeared. After a few seconds, the "object" reappeared, towards Portreath, disappearing again to reappear towards the Redruth area.

This is the third time in six months I have seen this object in the sky, always travelling at high speed, disappearing then reappearing in a split second in an entirely different location.

Has anyone else seen this object, or can anyone explain it to me?

My son saw it once when with me, but it disappeared so quickly he was unable to explain it. It did not reappear that evening.

It is far too fast for a plane, and changes direction too often. It is too big for a falling star.

I would love to think I've seen a UFO — but if it isn't, then what is it?

Mrs. I. Warren
(Not prone to fantasy)
Camborne

OCTOBER/NOVEMBER 1985

DOMED UFO SEEN OVER SURREY, BY MUM AND DAUGHTER

UFO SEEN NEAR RUGELEY POWER STATION STAFFORDSHIRE

Also includes – A report of UFO sighted by police officers

A T 3am on 4th October 1985, three orange lights, forming a triangle, were reported in the sky over Fulham, in London. **(Source: Ron West)**

UFO over Surrey

On 15th October 1985, Lightwater, Surrey, resident – Joyce Rapley – put the dog out, at 6am, when she noticed a strange *'light'* in the sky. Thinking no more of it, she went back to bed. Unknown to her, daughter – June – was also awake and happened to glance out of the window, when she saw:

> *". . . a very strange light in the sky, resembling a hat or dome-shaped object swaying from side to side. I rushed to get my camera, but by then it had gone."*

(Source: Omar Fowler, SIGAP/*Camberley News*, 18.10.1985 – 'UFO spotted by Mum and daughter'/personal interview)

On the the late evening of 25th October 1985, PC Laurence Milligan and Mathew Scott, observed a red and green flashing UFO, for 45mins, over Sunningdale, Windsor, Berkshire, after having responded to a report by a member of the public. Eventually, the UFO disappeared in a north-westerly direction. Enquiries revealed that it had been seen over the Virginia Water and Harpsford Avenue areas of the town. Checks were made with RAF Waddington, but proved negative.

(Source: *Windsor, Slough, and Eton Express*)

At 8.30pm on 9th November 1985, three red lights, forming a triangle, were seen moving slowly across the sky over Loughborough, Leicestershire. **(Source: Ron West)**

UFO mystery stumps police

An unidentified flying object was seen from Virginia Water by a postman and police on Sunday evning.

Postmaster Jim Mason was outside his home in Harpesford Avenue when he saw it through his telescope.

"Red and green lights were flashing on it, but it was not moving," said Mr Mason, who watched if for 15 minutes.

"It was shaped like a star, but it was not a star — it was something out of the ordinary."

Keen on studying the sky on a clear night Mr Mason said: "It was due north west to the recreation ground opposite."

Mr Mason alerted the police, and Constables Laurence Milligan and

by Edward Bubb

Matthew Scott of Sunningdale also saw the object through Mr Mason's telescope for a further 45 minutes before it disappeared.

"It was very similar to a

plane's navigation lights, but it did not appear to be moving," said Constable Milligan. He said the object was stationery although there were lots of planes around at the time.

It was reported to the Royal Air Force Aeronautical Information Service at West Drayton which has a department taking details of UFOs.

I confirm that UFO sighting

I READ your article (Egham News, Oct. 24) on the sighting of a UFO. When I saw it, it was at an earlier time, about 2.20 p.m. I saw it approaching the bridge at Kitsmead Lane (near the tank testing factory). It was a NW direction.

I was coming home for a visit. (I go to boarding school). The object was silver. It was gleaming in the sun. It was not quite a cigar shape, but more rounded.

At the time of sighting I remarked to my father, who was driving, but we dismissed the thought as an airship or something British Aerospace might be testing, because it isn't far away. When I tried to look at it again later, I could not see it.

I do not think it was an airship. It would be a different shape and would not reflect the light, like metal. I do not think it was an aeroplane because I would have seen the tail section.

P. WINGROVE
Chantry's
Knowle Grove Close,
Virginia Water

In November 1985, Paul Hopley of Brereton, Staffordshire, was walking across the local football field, with his mother and grandmother, at 10.30pm, when a yellow coloured object, some 25-40ft in diameter, rose up over the nearby hill of Diners Knob and stopped 50-60ft above their heads, changing colour to orange as it did so, before heading away towards the direction of Rugeley Power Station.

> "It appeared to be wafer thin, and showing intense shades of colour which moved about like liquid. Just before it reached the power station it shot upwards into the sky at a 90° angle."

(Source: Mark Heywood, Staffordshire UFO Group/ Graham Allen/Irene Bott)

DECEMBER 1985

LANCASHIRE COUPLE CHASED BY UFO

Also includes – Ball of red light seen over Bristol • 'H'-shaped UFO over London.
Was it the same UFO that 'buzzed' a pilot?

O N 20th December 1985, a *'ball'* of red light, constantly changing colour from red to white, was seen heading southwards across the sky over Filton, Bristol, at 6.45pm, by local resident Martyn Baker, which apparently followed the M32, towards Bristol, at a height of between 600-1,000ft – extremely unlikely to have been an aircraft according to the witness, who was able to look at it through binoculars.
(Source: Peter Tate, Bristol)

Followed by a UFO

A local businessman was driving home from Darwin, in Lancashire, with his son, at 5pm on 28th December 1985, near Belmont, when they saw a strange white *'ball of light'* in the sky, with fuzzy edges, some 500ft above the ground, over Egerton. To their horror, it began to follow them along the Darwen Road, before heading towards the nearby Delph Reservoir.

When the couple arrived home at the family farm, they saw the wife and daughter inside the house and began to unload the suitcases. Suddenly, the UFO appeared behind them. Frightened, the father and son dashed into the house, where they continued their observations of the UFO until 8pm, when it disappeared. This was followed by the appearance of two *'lights'* that came over a nearby hill, criss-crossed over, and went out of sight. The family strongly rejected a suggestion put forward that they had seen Venus!

**(Source: Steven Balon/*Bolton Evening News*, 31.12.85 – 'Family terrified by UFO',
& *Evening News* 6.1.1986 – 'UFO chased us at 50mph, say couple')**

A glowing white cigar-shaped object was seen over Clacton-on-Sea, in Essex, at 11.10pm on 28th December 1985.
(Source: Ron West)

'H'-shaped UFO over London

Anthony Chiverton was on his way to deliver a Christmas parcel to his sister – then living in London, during December 1985.

As he and his two friends drove along the Edgware Road, towards London, he noticed a dark grey object in the sky through the window and remarked to his colleagues how peculiar it was. The party stopped the car and got out.

> *"We stood there for about ten minutes, watching it shoot across the early morning skyline. It had a distinctive shape – like that of a letter 'H' or letter 'I', depending on which way you looked at it – and was covered in lights. On returning home, late Saturday night, I told my family what I had seen. They listened but I don't think they believed me. I am pretty sure, the next day, there was a report in the local newspaper from the pilots of an aircraft, who alleged that they had been 'buzzed' by a UFO either leaving or entering airspace over the Airport, which would have been the same time we saw the UFO, although they didn't mention the unusual shape."*

(Source: London UFO Studies)

1986

After three successive monthly falls in unemployment, the jobless count for December 1985 increased by nearly 15,000 to 3,181,300. Game show Catchphrase begins on ITV, hosted by Roy Walker, along with the computer Mr. Chips. The United Kingdom and France announce plans to construct the Channel Tunnel, which they hope to open by the early 1990s.

Buckingham Palace announces the engagement of Prince Andrew to Sarah Ferguson.

Rioting erupts overnight in prisons across Britain. The worst disturbances come at Northeye Prison, in Sussex, where a 70-strong mob of prisoners takes over.

April 26th 1986, Chernobyl explosion.

Estate agent Suzy Lamplugh vanishes after a meeting in London.
John Stalker, Deputy Chief Constable of Greater Manchester police, is cleared of misconduct over allegations of associating with criminals.

Economists warn that a global recession is imminent, barely five years after the previous recession. First episode of medical drama serial 'Casualty' airs on BBC One TV.

On the 25th December, more than 30 million viewers tuned in for the episode of the TV series, East Enders, which first went on air nearly two years before.

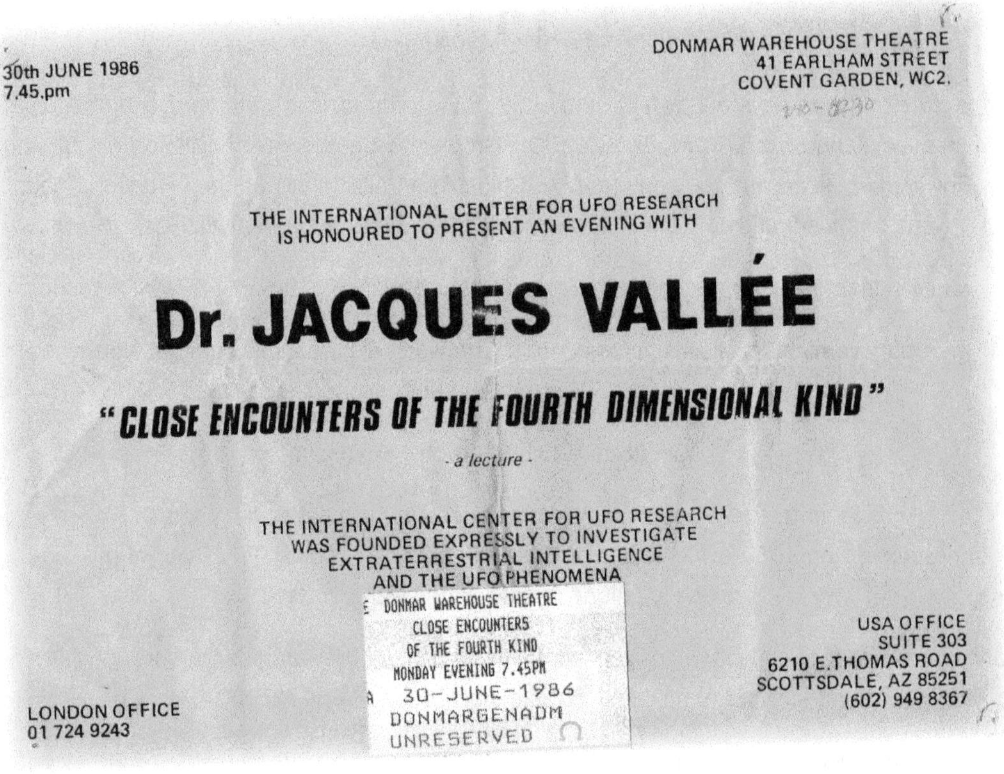

30th JUNE 1986
7.45.pm

DONMAR WAREHOUSE THEATRE
41 EARLHAM STREET
COVENT GARDEN, WC2.

THE INTERNATIONAL CENTER FOR UFO RESEARCH
IS HONOURED TO PRESENT AN EVENING WITH

Dr. JACQUES VALLÉE

"CLOSE ENCOUNTERS OF THE FOURTH DIMENSIONAL KIND"

- a lecture -

THE INTERNATIONAL CENTER FOR UFO RESEARCH
WAS FOUNDED EXPRESSLY TO INVESTIGATE
EXTRATERRESTRIAL INTELLIGENCE
AND THE UFO PHENOMENA

DONMAR WAREHOUSE THEATRE
CLOSE ENCOUNTERS
OF THE FOURTH KIND
MONDAY EVENING 7.45PM
30-JUNE-1986
DONMARGENADM
UNRESERVED

USA OFFICE
SUITE 303
6210 E.THOMAS ROAD
SCOTTSDALE, AZ 85251
(602) 949 8367

LONDON OFFICE
01 724 9243

JANUARY 1986

MYSTERIOUS STAR LIKE OBJECT OVER SUSSEX

Also includes – Police sight UFO over Scotland • UFO photographed by Shuttle crew
Flying 'Boomerang' UFO over USA • Yorkshire UFO Society
Taxi driver sights UFO over Wales

Mysterious red 'star' over Sussex

ON 5th January 1986, a resident of Furnace Green, Crawley, Sussex, sighted a large red *'star'* in the sky, at about 11pm, over Tilgate Park, which turned white before disappearing shortly afterwards.

(Source: *Crawley and District Observer*, 8th January 1986 – 'UFO man tells Police')

UFO over Scotland

During the evening of 6th January 1986, an object – described as resembling a *'luminous flying clothes pole'* – was seen over Armadale, by local police officers – Police Sergeant Jimmy Begg, and Police Constable Tommy Murphy.

A search of the Avondale Drive area failed to find anything of significance, after the glowing object was seen to disappear into a nearby housing estate.

(Source: *West Lothian Courier*, 10.1.86)

Was this the same UFO seen by pensioner Stan Hebson, from Trinity Drive, Northside, Carlisle, Cumbria, at 7.15am on 7th January 1986? (See newspaper clipping)

WEST LOTHIAN COURIER, Bathgate, England
Jan. 10, 1986   CR: T. Good

POLICEMEN SPOT UFO

LOCAL police were investigating the sighting of a UFO reported by two of their own officers.

The officers, Sergeant Jimmy Begg and P.C. Tommy Murphy, stationed at Armadale, saw the UFO, described as a "luminous flying clothes pole" in the sky above the town on Monday evening.

"I glanced up to the sky and saw an orange-red object travelling at around 60 m.p.h. falling to the ground," said Sergeant Begg. "It looked like a luminous flying clothes pole and didn't burn out. It continued to glow as it disappeared into a housing estate."

The officers, who saw the object from their patrol car from nearly a mile away, described it as six inches in diameter and three feet long. Sergeant Begg saw the object for around five seconds, P.C. Murphy for two.

The policemen later scoured the Avondale Drive area but could find no sign of the object. No residents in the area reported anything strange.

CUMBERLAND EVENING NEWS, Carlisle, England – Jan. 7, 1986 CR: T. Good

Stan has a close encounter

A COUNTY pensioner has had a close encounter of the UFO kind.

Stan Hebson, 71, was gazing from his window at Trinity Drive, Northside, when he saw a bright light in the sky.

"I saw a large, cigar-shaped UFO facing over the Solway towards the Scottish side.

LOOKED

"It was about 7.15 a.m. and it was above the level of the street lights."

Retired fork lift truck driver Stan says it was a dark morning and there were no stars showing.

He said: "It didn't move at all. I watched it for three minutes through my binoculars. I put them down, and when I looked up again it had vanished.

"There is no way it could have been a plane because it wasn't moving."

Stan says he will report his sighting to the British Flying Saucer Bureau.

Flying Boomerang, USA

At 9pm on 9th January 1986, at Hartford, Connecticut, USA, a number of cars stopped along Interstate 84 to watch a silent boomerang-shaped object – estimated to be the size of a Boeing 747, displaying white, red, blue and green lights – moving low through the sky. It then hovered for 15 seconds before heading off to the west. The boomerang seen over Hartford and New Britain was also seen by dozens of witnesses in Torrington, Connecticut. A family reported a UFO, with 10 white lights, hovering directly over their house, engulfing their home in a brilliant white light. They were so frightened that they fled to the basement.

**(Sources: Larry Hatch, U computer database, case # 14294,
citing Dale Goudie, CUFON;
Philip J. Imbrogno, Contact of the 5th Kind)**

Recently, there has been quite a lot of talk about an old photo that was taken on the shuttle Columbia, in January 1986. The photo in question — STS61C-31-002 in NASA's archives — depicts a triangular object, gliding past the shuttle in the Earth's upper atmosphere. NASA's description of the photo is that it's simply *"a small piece of thermal insulation tile [that] floats in space near the Shuttle Columbia. The cloudy surface of the earth is used as a background."*

Yorkshire UFO Society

In this month The Yorkshire UFO Society applied for a £100 grant from Leeds City Council, towards the cost of its annual conference in Leeds, due to be held on 22nd March 1986. One of the guest speakers was Tim Good. Unfortunately, the funding application was turned down. Mark Birdsall, co-ordinator of research, explained the Society was a non-profit-making organisation.

(Source: *Yorkshire Evening Post*, **22nd January 1986 – 'UFO men seek cash landing')**

CONTRARY to public opinion, UFOs are regularly seen over major cities and Bradford is by no means an exception.

The Yorkshire UFO Society has on record many startling encounters over Bradford and its surrounding satellite towns and villages.

Reports of strange incidents is nothing new to this area, yet how real is the phenomenon and can it all be placed in categories which support a more down to earth explanation? The evidence suggests not, and we must point out that the following documentation has been analysed by some of the leading UFO researchers in this country and much of the data suggests an unknown intelligence.

Reports of UFOs continue to build up in our files relating to the Bradford area, but we must go all the way back to 1960 to find a classic example of how the subject displayed itself to a couple of innocent witnesses. This report, compared with recent encounters, will amply show how little the UFO has changed in the eyes of the un-knowing witness.

Froze

Two women had left a house in the Low Moor area and were heading on foot towards High Fernley. Suddenly they became aware of a dark grey saucer shape just above a nearby hillside. Around the centre of the object a series of brightly lit 'portholes' were very evident. No sound could be heard even though the object was just two hundred feet away, hovering motionless just above some advertisment boards. The couple froze for a moment, and watched the very large craft move silently towards the Pennines.

There is nothing in the report to suggest a hoax or mis-identification of any known airborne object.

How physical is the phenomena and do UFOs constitute a threat to the public? A

MARK BIRDSALL, Research Director of the Yorkshire UFO Society, describes recent sightings, and concludes that Bradford is on a major UFO flightpath. Mark, a 28-year-old computer operative, formed the YUFOS with his brother in 1981. It now has some 200 members, 40 of them in Bradford.

terrified witness living in the King's Road recalls: "The year was 1967 and I was aware of a loud, puisating, whirling sound outside my bedroom. The time was 2.30 a.m. I turned my bedroom light on and the sound grew louder. At this point my bedroom light started to flicker. I looked outside the window and couldn't believe my eyes! An enormous domed saucer was moving slowly across the street. It sent shivers down my back. It was bright silver and had a series of flashing lights around a raised dome. I would estimate its size to be no smaller than 150 ft. It was incredible."

The modern era of UFO sightings and the lengthy investigative methods and procedures YUFOS undertake to solve such mysteries are today 'dogged' by man's own advanced technological achievements in aviation. Today there are so many unusual objects to be seen in the skies. But could anything explain the object which hurtled towards Bradford on November 7, 1981?

Many witnesses as far afield as Huddersfield spotted a strange sphere cruising at tree top level and spinning rapidly. As it approached south Bradford, people observed a smaller sphere entering the large windowed ball.

1981 was perhaps Bradford's year in so far as UFO sightings are concerned. But few of the witnesses to the following daylight

DATELINE:- 26 January 1986   Location:- Connahs Quay,Clwyd,Wales

There was quite a wave of UFOs in Wales during 1986,mostly investigated by the tireless CONTACT UK investigator and UFO repeater witness Margaret Fry.One of the most fascinating was this one.It occurred at a small town on the Dee Estuary,very near the English border and just two miles from Oakenholt,the village where the Sunderland family had their world famous CE 4 experiences.The site of a large former steel works and an active major power station dominates the area,which is interesting as many of the local area UFOs have been observed over these locations. At 8.20 pm on this particular night a taxi driver first saw the object and jumped from his car in surprise.It was described as 3-4 car lengths in size,a rounded oval (although more 'dome like' when seen from the side).It was low enough for a perfect view of the underside as it glided over,revealing steady white lights in a ring round the edge a bright blue light at the rear and three 'slits' pouring out white light in the base.In her investigation Margaret Fry tracked down three people able to sketch the object independently,from other locations in the town.Their drawings clearly do show the same very graphic and most unusual object.The metallic nature of the body,the frosted appearance of the windows and bright blue of the light were all remarked upon.No sound was heard by any of the observors.Some speculation has been offered about a 'Stealth' aircraft under secret test,since an RAF base (Sealand) is only a few miles across the border.However, naturally this was denied - as was all official knowledge of what might lie behind these impressive sightings.

UFO over Wales

On 26th January 1986, a taxi driver from Connah's Quay, Clwyd, Wales, was on duty at 8.20pm, when he was astonished to see an object in the sky, which he described as being three or four car lengths long.

"As it glided overhead I was able to see some steady white lights around the edges of its underside, a bright blue light at the rear, and three slits pouring out white light in the base."

Margaret Fry carried out an investigation into this matter and was able to track down other people living in the town, who had seen the same UFO.

FEBRUARY 1986

TRIANGULAR UFO SEEN OVER LIMA, BY WIFE OF AIR FORCE PILOT

Also includes – UFO sighted by woman living near USAF Base – letter written to Gordon Creighton at *FSR* • Fireman sights UFO over Southend. Was a helicopter scrambled? UFO alleged to have been seen over Irish Sea, by Prince Charles

Triangular UFO seen over Ohio, USA

CASES involving what appear to be structured objects, rather than wraithlike in their presentation, have always interested us. However, space prevents us from covering everything we came across. As the reader will see during the late 1980's there were many UK sightings of what became labelled as the 'Triangular UFO'. These are just two of them:

At 7pm on 8th February 1986, a young couple driving on State Route 117, in Lima, Ohio, spotted a dark triangular UFO, with three bright lights, hovering over some trees near a farm. The object was estimated to be 50-60ft long and made no sound. Their sighting lasted for five minutes.

(Source: John P. Timmerman, *International UFO Reporter*, **July-August 1986, p9)**

On 12th February 1986, the wife of an Air Force pilot – an intelligent woman, with a Nursing Degree, from Lima, Ohio, was awoken at 12.33am by an indescribable noise. The woman got out of bed and checked her daughter, who was still asleep. She then noticed an unusual

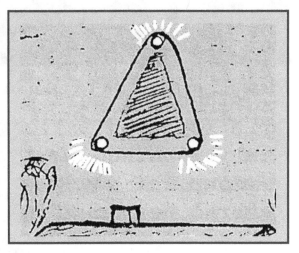

glow, silhouetted against the light from a nearby oil refinery plant, and went outside to find the cause.

"I saw a large triangle, with a bright light at each apex, and dark mass inside; it was massive and heavy.

I went back inside the house and awoke my husband. By the time he came out to have a look, it had gone."

Enquiries by the Airport Police, and other sources, failed to obtain any explanation as to what it was that she had seen. **(Source: John Timmerman, CUFOS)**

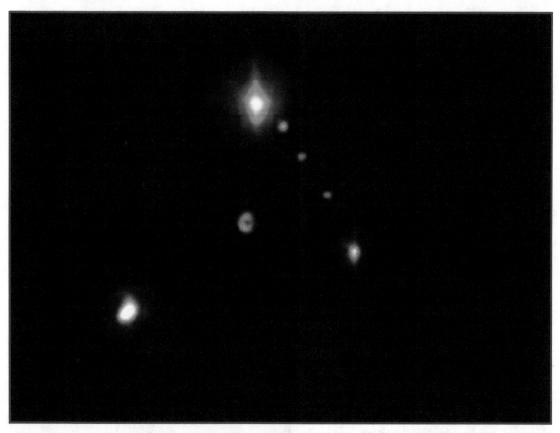

Close Encounter with UFO, USA

In July 1986, Gordon Creighton – editor of *Flying Saucer Review* – received a letter from a retired nurse (then aged 72) living in California, who told him of a very strange and rather disturbing account which had happened on 26th February 1986.

The woman concerned asked Gordon not to identity her name or location, which is of course her prerogative, but it would have been helpful to have identified the exact location. This is what she had to say in the letter:

"I live in a 96-unit compartment complex out of town. The complex is of two storeys, with many tall pine trees around. My own apartment faces the back, where there is a lot of lawn, green pine trees, and ground cover of ivy and Virginia creeper. There is a high wall running

the full length of the property at the rear, so it is very private. Many young working people live here in the complex, and also airmen from the nearby USAF Airbase and their families.

It is my habit to awaken early at sun up and go to the kitchen and make a cup of tea, and then take this back to the bedroom and enjoy it while planning the day or read. On that morning I was sitting in an easy chair, still in my nightgown, in the act of pulling up my socks. As I raised myself up, facing the window, a long grey mottled object floated slowly by at windowsill level. It was perfectly silent. My first thought was to run to the window and see what it was, but instantly I became paralysed. I couldn't move. My head fell back against the wall and my eyes closed; some very strange thoughts went through my head. A few minutes elapsed and I now realised I could move again. I went to the window and high in the pine tree was a pale grey object. It wasn't perched on a limb but motionless in space, between the branches. For some unknown reason I felt that this object knew I was in the window watching it. Suddenly, it tipped on its side and silently floated away towards the south direction, following the course of the bigger one. Just as I turned to leave the window another object appeared, moving at a height of about 2-3 inches above the lawn and heading right towards me.

I stood staring, as it came closer. It was about 3ft long and some six inches in diameter. When it was 6-8ft away from me it slowed down, almost to a stop. The middle third of it slid back, allowing me to see a dark, mechanical-looking apparatus inside and two bars of a golden colour – one on each side of the opening. I estimated them to be about half an inch wide and a foot long.

Suddenly, seemingly out of nowhere, five or six more of these 'weapons' appeared behind the lead one. The lead one opened up and I saw a curl of smoke float across the dark opening. This struck me on the front of my head and rendered me unconscious. I have no memory of leaving the window or the room. When I came to, some time later, I found myself by the front door of the building and heading towards my bedroom. The experience left me with a constant headache that lasted for eleven days and nights. From the hairline above the forehead and towards the back, over an area the size of the palm of my hand, still continues to hurt every few days – aspirin is useless."

Gordon gave her the details of some highly qualified individuals, living in the States, who would be prepared to help her.

On 26th September he received another letter from the woman, in which she gave him some additional information:

"As the headaches were of concern, I didn't pay much attention to an itchy spot that I found in the left groin area. I eventually became annoyed and curious, because I couldn't feel anything there, so I took a mirror and found a perfect ring or circle – a bit smaller than a 25cent piece – and very red inside the ring. It appeared as though some sort of suction had been applied, for the blood appeared to be just under the surface of the skin.

The circle has gradually disappeared after a few months, the itch has gone. The headaches are diminishing in frequency. I kept thinking if these were 'weapons' – following the larger craft – what they could do to the nearby Strategic Air Command Base and the aircraft there."

(See David McMurray page 368 for comparisons.)   **(Source: *FSR*, Volume 32, No. 2, 1987)**

UFO over Southend

Fireman John Knights was sat in his living room, talking to his colleague – Ian McGrath – in Boundry Road, Eastwood, Southend, at 5.30pm on 17th February 1986, when he noticed:

> *". . . A silver 'long thin pencil' object in the sky, with a pointed tail at the base – more like a missile than a jet aircraft – slowly crossing the clear sky, approximately 20 miles away."*

After it dropped out of sight, leaving a vapour trail behind it, a *'military'* helicopter appeared and flew over where the object had gone. Enquiries with Southend Airport revealed a helicopter was flying about in the area that evening. Was it scrambled to intercept the UFO, or is there a more mundane explanation? We will probably never know.   **(Source: Ron West/Brenda Butler)**

UFO over Irish Sea

On 23rd February 1986, it was the turn of Royalty, once again, to sight something unusual, according to a number of newspapers, who told of a *'red glowing UFO'* seen by the pilot of a RAF VC10, bringing Prince Charles back home from California to England. It was said that the incident occurred while the Prince's aircraft was nearing the end of the 12 hour flight, and involved the sighting of a UFO by five different aircraft, over the Irish Sea. Although four other pilots also reported seeing what we presume to be the same UFO over the same stretch of the Irish Sea, no trace of the *'unidentified aircraft'* was ever found, despite an investigation launched by the authorities. We wrote to the Prince in 1997, asking for further information, but were advised by his Secretary that *"He didn't want to comment on the matter."*

UFOs GET THE ROYAL SEAL

FASCINATED . . . the Prince wants UFO news

WHILE investigating the subject of flying saucers we came across an odd fact concerning Prince Charles; he held a secret garden party a year or so ago in order to discuss with enthusiasts and experts the whole UFO business.

Both Charles and Prince Philip have an abiding interest in the subject and the Prince of Wales, in particular, is fascinated by most aspects of the paranormal.

"His interest was and remains very strong," says director of UFO investigation Jenny Randles. "At the time of the party he was under pressure and so I was asked not to talk about it to journalists. I see no reason why I shouldn't now."

Miss Randles, who says that Prince Charles's gathering was attended by such weird fellow enthusiasts as Michael Bentine and Uri Geller, gives us a reason for the Royal Family's obsession with visitors from space.

Keen

She says: "It all goes back to the day when a UFO landed at Broadlands in Hampshire, the home of the late Lord Mountbatten." (This last piece of information is not necessarily regarded without a modest degree of scepticism by your diarist).

Miss Randles continues: "That's when the interest started. The Prince is particularly keen to be kept in touch.

"He is on the mailing list of the magazine Flying Saucer Review."

The MOD said: *"Prince Charles' pilot did report seeing a bright flash, but we are satisfied there was no danger to the Prince's aircraft".*

Coincidentally (or not) another glowing red light UFO was seen moving across the sky over Windsor Castle, a few days later, in early March, attracting further media attention, with alleged sightings of a mystery craft, *'the size of a Mini'*, seen flying close to the battlements.

EXCLUSIVE

By MARTIN BRUNT and BILL DAVEY

PRINCE Charles is at the centre of a bizarre UFO mystery.

The Prince had a close encounter during a flight home from the United States last week.

The pilot of his RAF VC-10 radioed air traffic control to say he had been startled by a "glowing red object" in the sky.

Incredibly, FOUR other aircraft reported sighting the "UFO" over the same stretch of the Irish Sea.

Visit

An immediate investigation was launched—but no trace of the unidentified aircraft was been found.

Other explanations—such as meteors or debris from a satellite—have also been ruled out by experts.

Charles was nearing the end of a 12-hour trans-Atlantic flight after a five-day visit to the U.S. when the incident happened.

A source at West Drayton air traffic control near London's Heathrow airport said: "The object was reported by five different aircraft, including the Prince's.

CHARLES IN UFO RIDDLE

Sunday Mirror 2 March 1982 J.M.

Pilot shocked by close encounter

"The pilot described seeing a red glowing object. The light from it lit up his cockpit.

"We just don't know what it was. It's a complete mystery."

And an air traffic official at Ireland's Shannon airport said: "The pilot saw a bright flash in the sky.

"An immediate check was made on all aircraft, but none was missing.

"Whatever the pilot saw, it certainly was not another aeroplane."

A Ministry of Defence spokesman confirmed: "Prince Charles's pilot did report seeing a bright flash, but we are satisfied there was no danger to the Prince's aircraft."

Philip's a 'saucer' watcher

PRINCE PHILIP has been a keen UFO follower for the past 30 years.

Creature

UFO expert Tim Good, an author and lecturer, said last week: "It may not be pure coincidence.

"It is likely that any creature from outer space that is more advanced than us would be aware of the significance of a Royal flight."

And former diplomat Gordon Creighton, the editor of Flying Saucer Review magazine, said:

"I've no idea what this object could have been, but it would be wrong to dismiss it. There are beings in space watching us very closely."

Philip—follower

He is a keen reader of the magazine, Flying Saucer Review.

And he once invited a man who claimed to have seen a UFO landing to come to Buckingham Palace to tell his story to a Royal aide so the official could report to Philip who was on tour in Australia.

March 1982

ANOTHER UFO!

by Royal Appointment

A mystery craft over Windsor

AN oval-shaped UFO has been spotted over Windsor Castle.

---EXCLUSIVE---
by MARTIN BRUNT

The mystery craft flew close to the battlements in broad daylight.

CHARLES IN UFO RIDDLE

Despite the sensational approach made in the newspapers, we ascertained that the object was debris from space, or a meteorite, which was confirmed by Dr. Ann Cohen – astronomer at Jodrell Bank Radio Telescope. Apparently Armagh Observatory received many calls from the public, including UFO enthusiast/journalist Miles Johnston, reporting the sighting of the flaming object as it passed over the UK. It is clear that this story was 'whipped up' and various people misquoted. We understand that Prince Charles was asleep at the time!

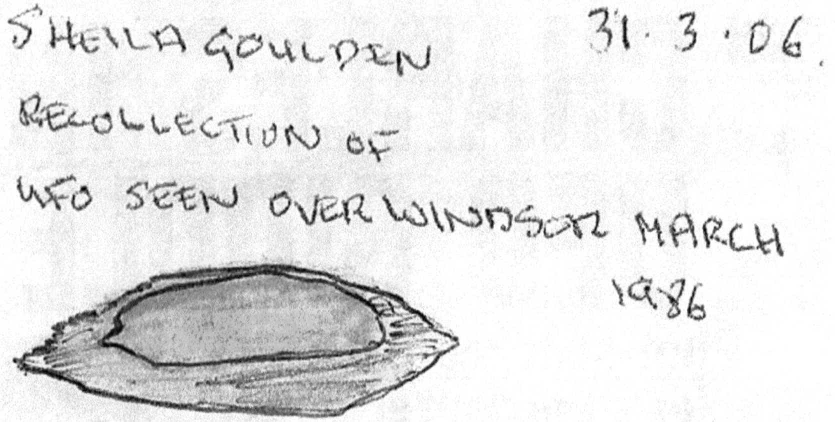

SHEILA GOULDEN   31·3·06.
RECOLLECTION OF
UFO SEEN OVER WINDSOR MARCH
                              1986

TONY GOULDEN   31·3·06
RECOLLECTION
OF UFO SEEN IN WINDSOR
MARCH 1986. WHEN HE WAS 17 yrs
                              OLD.

MARCH 1986

USA PILOT CHASED BY UFOS – WAS A PLANE DOWNED BY THE OBJECTS?

Also includes – UFO sighted over Windsor • Close Encounter Carleton Moor

Aircraft chased by UFOs over Ohio

ON 1st March 1986, a number of white and blue lights were seen descending out of a larger object in the sky, over Payne Field Army Base, Seattle, Washington. Some people thought they might have been parachute flares, released during an exercise, although a women sergeant on the base denied this to be the explanation.

According to Dale Goudie at MUFON, who carried out an investigation into the matter, an event which took place just before the mysterious falls of lights may have had some bearing. It involved Shawn Kiaer and his instructor, who were flying a light aircraft over Snoqualemie Pass, when the men saw two amber *'balls of light'* approaching them head-on, and took evasive action to prevent a collision.

To their surprise, they realised they were now being followed by the two lights. They tried to contact the control tower, but their transmission was momentarily blocked. Radio reception then retuned to normal, as the two *'balls of light'* accelerated into the distance and disappeared from view. Set against this backcloth of events was a report from two witnesses of a mid-air collision, between a light plane and another aircraft, over *Black Diamond. According to them, one of the aircraft exploded in mid-air.

The Federal Aviation accepted that an aircraft/explosion had taken place but disregarded the testimony offered by the witnesses, after failing to locate any wreckage of the mysterious aircraft.

(Source: Dale Goudie, MUFON)

---

*Beginning in the 1880s, Black Diamond was a rural coal mining area, developed by the Black Diamond Coal Mining Company of California, which owned and operated the mine. Black Diamond is located at 47°19 4 N 122°0 53 W (47.317802 -122.014793). A look at the Internet, in 2013, at the UFOs Northwest Web site, reveals a disturbing number of sightings (approx500) recorded over Washington State, between 2006 and the present.

UFO over Windsor

In early March 1986, Sheila Goulden, living in Windsor, was with her son, Tony, when they saw:

> "... *a bright yellow or white light, with a reddish colour outside – similar to a magnesium flare – travelling in a horizontal position above the rooftops of warehouses, about a mile away from their home, flying on a parallel course to the River Thames, away from Windsor Town and Castle.*"

(Source: *Sunday Mirror*, 2.3.1986 – 'Charles in UFO Riddle')

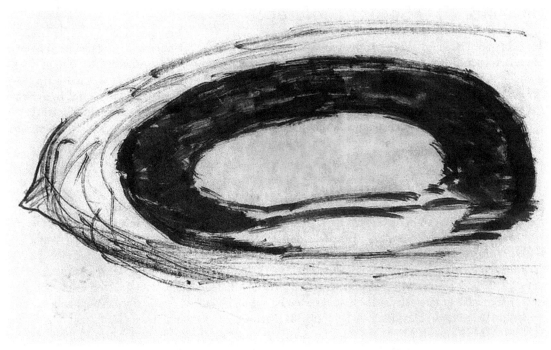

Object sighted by Sheila Goulden and her son in Windsor, March 1986

West Yorkshire UFO Society investigator – Philip Mantle – made an appeal in the local newspaper, asking for any information about a UFO seen over Morley, Leeds.

UFO over Morley?

THE YORKSHIRE UFO Society would like to hear from anyone in the Morley area who saw a large circular object with multicoloured lights in the skies over Morley recently.

Mr. Philip Mantle, an investigator with the society, said a woman from Bradford who was travelling home along the Bradford/Wakefield Road around 8.30 p.m. on March 24 initially saw a row of lights.

She and her husband were looking towards Leeds when they saw the unidentified object and they pulled into a layby near the Tingley Working Men's Club to observe it further.

The object appeared to be moving towards Leeds and was about two or three miles away and a number of other people in cars pulled into the layby to look at the object, Mr. Mantle added.

Mr. Mantle said the society was trying to locate the other car drivers and anyone else in the area who saw it.

Anyone who saw the object can contact Mr. Mantle on Batley 444049.

Yorkshire UFO Society conference

This conference included a reference to four UFO reports, brought to their notice during the previous year, between August 11th and September 8th. According to Mark Birdsall, on 21st August 1985, a red glowing *'spinning top'* was sighted hovering over a farmhouse, north of Skipton. On the 31st August a boy ran home in a terrified state, after sighting a strange shape over Carleton Moor. He had to be treated by a doctor, after suffering a temporary loss of vision. Other reports from the Carleton Moor area told of a UFO seen to just miss striking a radar installation on the moors, on 14th August 1985, and that American personnel spent three days on the moors looking for something.

Project Hessdalen, Norway

Another speaker at the conference was Odd-Gunnar Roed from Tonsberg Norway a leading researcher for UFO Norway and Project Hessdalen. Hessdalen is a small valley in the central part of Norway. At the end of 1981 through 1984, residents of the Valley became concerned and alarmed about strange, unexplained lights that appeared at many locations throughout the Valley. Hundreds of lights were observed. At the peak of activity there were about 20 reports a week. As no official institute with governmental support in Norway seemed to be interested in these strange lights, five individual researchers began their own research project in 1983: Project Hessdalen. A field investigation was carried out between 21st January and 26th February 1984. Fifty-three light observations were made during the field investigation. Lights are still being observed in the Hessdalen Valley, but their frequency has decreased to about 20 observations a year. An automatic measurement station was put up in Hessdalen in August 1998.

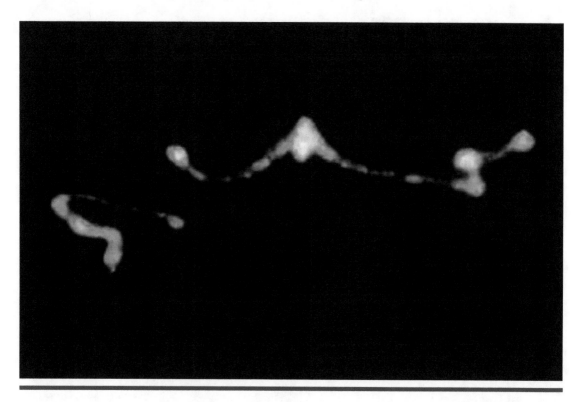

Odd-Gunnar Roed was asked what he thought these strange lights could be:

> *"Well that is almost an impossible question to answer. First these lights appear intelligent then on the other hand they don't appear to be that intelligent as they are travelling through this remote valley doing absolutely nothing. We never witnessed anything of a structured nature, only lights. However, the local people have reported close encounter type cases and close-up UFO sightings of cigar shaped objects. We have had the lights react to us, for example, we decided to turn off our instrumentation and the sightings increased, when we decided to turn it back on again the sightings decreased. This was when we decided to do this not when we actually hit the switch. It is very difficult to answer this question but I would go as far as to call these lights natural phenomena."*

YORKSHIRE UFO SOCIETY

CONFERENCE 86 "THE MATERIAL EVIDENCE"

CASE REPORTS, POSITIVE PROOF OF OFFICIAL DECEPTION, FRIGHTENING EVIDENCE OF PHYSICAL CONTACT BETWEEN YOUNGSTERS AND THE PHENOMENON. IF YOU WANT TO LEARN MORE ABOUT THE UFO ENIGMA IN A SHORT SPACE OF TIME THAN YOU COULD POSSIBLY LEARN IN A YEAR, COME TO CONFERENCE 86, YOU WON'T REGRET IT!

Case Research, Exhibitions, Maps,

INTERNATIONAL SPEAKERS

O.G.ROED OF UFO-NORGE (NORWAY'S PREMIER UFO ORGANISATION WILL GIVE US A BRILLIANT ACCOUNT OF HOW ONE TINY REMOTE PART OF HIS COUNTRY IS NOW THE CENTRE OF WORLD-WIDE ACTIVITY DUE TO REGULAR AND SPECTACULAR UFO SIGHTINGS WHICH IS NOW BEING EXAMINED BY SCIENTISTS AND UFO RESEARCHERS FROM AS FAR AFIELD AS THE UNITED STATES. WE PROMISE YOU THIS PART OF THE CONFERENCE ALONE WILL BE WORTH YOUR ATTENDING, THE PHOTOGRAPHS ARE MAGNIFICENT!

Odd-Gunnar Roed

TIMOTHY GOOD IS BRITAIN'S FOREMOST LECTURER ON UFOs AND RETURNS TO LEEDS BY POPULAR DEMAND. HIS DEEP STUDY OF THE SUBJECT, ILLUSTRATED BY A SERIES OF AMAZING DOCUMENTS WHICH HAVE BEEN AT ONE TIME 'TOP-SECRET' WILL HAVE YOU ON THE EDGE OF YOUR SEATS. TIMOTHY IS ADVISER TO THE HOUSE OF LORDS ALL PARTY UFO STUDY GROUP, AND HIS RECENT BOOK, 'GEORGE ADAMSKI – THE UNTOLD STORY, HAS BEEN WELL RECEIVED THROUGHOUT THE WORLD.

Timothy Good

Jenny Randles

JENNY RANDLES IS BRITAIN'S FOREMOST AUTHORITY ON UFOs, AND IS CURRENTLY THIS COUNTRY'S ONLY FULL TIME 'UFOLOGIST'. 'UFOs – A BRITISH VIEWPOINT' 'UFO REALITY' 'THE PENNINE UFO MYSTERY' 'SCIENCE & THE UFOs' AND THE EVER CONTROVERSIAL 'SKYCRASH' ARE JUST SOME OF HER BOOKS WHICH HAVE PLACED HER IN-TO THE CATEGORY OF 'MUST BE SEEN – MUST BE HEARD! HER KNOWLEDGE OF HOW THE AUTHORITIES IN PARTICULAR ARE HANDLING THE ENIGMA IS STAGGERING.....

SATURDAY 22nd MARCH 1986 1 – 5.00pm

Centenary House, North Street, Leeds

How to find us!

ADULTS _____ £1.50

SENIOR CITIZENS _____ £1.00

CHILDREN _____ £1.00
[Doors open 12 noon]

Display, Books, Film, Slides & More!   Details: Leeds 460179

APRIL-JUNE 1986

UFO SIGHTED OVER LANCASHIRE
BRITISH PILOT ENCOUNTERS UFO OVER CAMBRIDGE

Also includes – Cigar-shaped object seen Derbyshire • Strange lights over Devon
UFO seen over Hartcliffe, in Bristol

UFO over Lancashire

AT 9.50pm on 4th April 1986, a resident of Dukinfield, Lancashire, was outside his house when he heard a *'whoopmh whoomph'* sound – not unlike the sound of helicopter blades, threshing the air (which he believes was caused by displaced air pressure in his eardrums). This was followed by a fizzing, hissing, sound. He looked upwards and saw what looked like:

> *". . . a blue and white burning rock, with a fuzzy outline, about the size of a full moon, moving slowly and steadily across waste ground and railway sidings, at low height; it was in view for about 90 seconds. It then vanished by the foothills of the Pennines."*

(Source: Georgina Mills, MUFORA)

Cigar-shaped UFO over Derbyshire

On either the 3rd or 14th April 1986, a motorist was driving up Swinscoe Hill, Ashbourne, at 7.15pm, when he saw several cars parked in the lay-by. Thinking there had been an accident, he pulled up. He was astonished to see a cigar-shaped object in the sky, showing a red light at the front, with searchlights at the rear.

Ashbourne News Telegraph, Derbyshire, England. Oct. 23, 1986

Hunt For Witnesses In UFO Inquiry.

UFO enthusiast Mr Peter Ann has received a report of yet another "sighting" in the Ashbourne area and is anxious to contact a group of people he thinks may have seen something unusual.
Mr Ann, chairman of the Derby and Derbyshire branch of the National UFO Investigation Society. says a woman claims to have seen a suspicious object while she was driving down Swinscoe Hill at about 7.15 on Sunday.
She saw something in the sky, which featured a square of four red lights and there seemed to be two white lights at either side. The woman did not think it was a plane, although it was definitely travelling across the sky.
She also noticed three or four people standing on the hill, looking up towards the sky, and it is these people Mr Ann wants to contact. Mr Ann can be reached on Derby 559293.

On the evening of 17th April 1986, Marylyn Preston Evans, of Saltash, Plymouth, Devon, was contacted by a friend, who told her that they had sighted a most unusual object in the night sky, which was described as:

> *". . . the size of a lorry, showing twenty bright lights, with a triangle of red lights on the back.*
> *It flew over Saltash, towards St. Austell."*

Mrs Evans telephoned the RAF at Mount Batten, and the Coastguard; neither could offer any idea as to what it was. Whilst there is little doubt this may well have been a genuine sighting, the admission by Marilyn that she was a contactee for spacemen, would not have convinced many of the readers on this occasion.

(Source: *Western Morning News*, 23.4.1986 – 'Watch this space'/Dennis Harriman,
National UFO Investigation Society)

UFO over Cambridge

A RAF pilot was piloting a Chipmunk, at 2,500ft, over Cambridge Airport, at midday on 7th June 1986. As he descended towards the runway, on what was a warm sunny day, he saw a bright point of light, which he thought, at first, might have been a balloon, reflecting the sunlight, at an estimated height of 1,500ft above the south-east perimeter of the airfield.

As he approached in a turn, the *'light'* began a rapid acceleration, heading towards the south-east, moving in a diametrically direction to his – giving an impression that the ground was spinning. The *'light'* was last seen heading towards the Gog Magog Hills, before vanishing from sight. The pilot (in 1987) – a Company Director and holder of a Masters Degree, from Oxford – still ponders as to the nature of what it was he saw on that day. **(Source: Jenny Randles, BUFORA – 'The UFO World 87')**

UFO over Bristol

At 6.35pm on 13th June 1986, two bright *'lights'* were seen crossing the sky over Hartcliffe, Bristol, before being lost from view as they turned sharp right and disappeared into clouds. This was witnessed by a couple living on the 9th floor of a block of flats, who contacted Air Traffic Control, at Bristol Airport, who in turn sent a copy of the original 'log' to UFO researcher Mark Birdsall, of the Yorkshire UFO Society who had written to them about the matter.

On 17th June, we learn of a sighting over South Africa – thanks to Cynthia Hind. Also on this date were reports of a strange flashing *'light'* over Bournemouth.

On 30th June 1986, Jacques Vallee came to London to give a talk, and Patrick Moore was on the warpath!

'Flying Saucers' from Mars

In the same month Chris Allen published the fruits of several years' research, uncovering the real author of *Flying Saucers from Mars*. This book was published in 1954, by Cedric Allingham, but his true identity was never ascertained due to him being taken ill shortly after the book's release. According to his publisher,

CASES OF L I T S

The Booysens Triangle, 1986 (Case N° 22)

On 17th June, 1986, six people (names known to the Editor) were present in the Booysens residential area of Johannesburg, South Africa, when they observed an object moving across the sky. The time was 2110 and the sighting lasted for approximately 15 minutes.

The observation was made by all witnesses who at first thought it was an aircraft as it moved at a steady speed and in a straight line from NNE to S.

The sky was clear and moonless with some very high cirrus cloud, but stars were clearly visible through the thin cloud. The only source of illumination was the street lights.

The light source was larger than a match-head and slightly smaller than the full moon, and initially the witnesses thought it might be a Jumbo jet.

However, they all felt it was travelling slower than a 747, but as the altitude was greater than 10 000 ft (3 000 m) and there was no noise, they ruled this out.

They felt that the object was huge, well over 1 000 ft (300m) across.

They discussed reporting the matter to the newspapers but two of the witnesses did not want to be involved so the idea was abandoned.

They watched the papers for other reports for several days but none appeared and the matter was left at that.

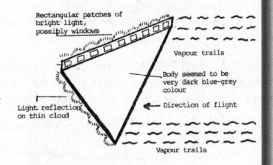

The object they saw looked like this :-

Rectangular patches of bright light, possibly windows

Vapour trails

Body seemed to be very dark blue-grey colour

Direction of flight

Light reflection on thin cloud

Vapour trails

Editor's Comments

Although this report is not in great detail and I cannot identify what was seen at the time, we are including it in this issue as it ties in with the recent Belgian flap of 1990 (March 30/31st) when the Belgian Air Force scrambled two F-16's to investigate an object picked up on radar and seen visually.
The object had a distinct triangular shape.

SKY HI!

MARS: The planet has been particularly bright in our skies. Now we will have to wait till 2003 when Mars will be the closest yet — 35 million miles away.

Mr Allingham had gone abroad to convalesce and had passed away. It is the shared opinion that this was of course Patrick Moore, whom we once spoke to about a visit to Warminster, after it was alleged he had seen a UFO.

PETER TORY

I see no hoax, says Patrick

PATRICK Moore has been accused of perpertrating a major hoax involving flying saucers.

He's hopping mad about the suggestion and has threatened to sue anyone who brings the matter to public light.

Well, it is being brought to public light. And, dare one say, it is a rather intriguing story.

Some years ago — in the fifties — a book was published by one Cedric Allingham, called Flying Saucer From Mars. It was a best-seller.

The author claimed in its pages that he had witnessed the landing of a UFO in Scotland and that he was taken on board and whisked around the Solar System.

This wonderful tale, told as it was in the rather less sophisticated times when man had not yet vaulted into space, very much excited Fleet Street.

The papers tried, indeed, to track down the amazing Mr Allingham so that he could tell them in some detail about his wonderful celestial voyage.

Alas, the publisher's Muller's, claimed that Mr Allingham was dying in Switzerland. And that he was unable to speak.

Plain

This week, however, a magazine called Magonia — it is dedicated to paranormal matters, and the like — will claim that Cedric Allingham never existed.

And, further, that the author of the book was none other than our much respected astronomer, the eccentric Patrick Moore.

Says Jenny Randles, director of investigation for the British UFO research association: "It's as plain as anything that he did it. The magazine has spent

five years, on and off, researching this. Patrick Moore did it as a joke and to upstage another author who was making absurd claims. Moore has always regarded UFOs as 'absolute rot'."

However, Patrick Moore himself, possibly fearful for his revered reputation, will have nothing to do with it. He said to us : "I can't be bothered with these people.

"It's the closed season for nuts. Thank you. Goodbye."

IF YOU'RE DYING TO HELP . . .

A BIZARRE DIY advert is showing on television in (where else?) Texas. A man in overalls in a carpenter's shop extols the virtue of—Do It Yourself Funerals. While it stops short of showing him making his own coffin, the man says: "Make this your last DIY venture. Save the family all the trouble."

Only in the mad old USA I fancy.

SONG SCORES HIT IN THE BOER WAR

IF Margaret Thatcher wonders how her people feel about the South African regime, she ought to take into consideration the recent ascent to the top of the music charts of The Chicken Song by the Spitting Image team.

Our cuts correspondent tells us that the catchy little ditty on the flipside — entitled I've Never Met A Nice South African — has been a major factor in that infuriating record's strange success (400,000 copies sold in the UK and demand still steady).

"I've got directory inquiries in less than 30 rings; I've even heard a decent song by Paul McCartney's Wings," goes a typical verse. "But I've never met a nice South African."

A jaunty chorus of Boer voices responds with : "And that's not bleddy surprising, mate" and goes on to confess to murder, general subnormality and appalling BO.

It would be reasonable to suppose that a couple of million people have heard it by now. The Commission for Racial Equality, who would expect to be alerted to any formal objection to such blatant prejudice, have heard not a peep of protest.

Patrick wrote to us some years ago, telling us he had 'pulled the plug' on the Loch Ness Monster, UFOs and Ghosts – and then rang us to ensure we understood that he had stopped becoming involved in such subjects. He then rang us again to reiterate what he had written to us. He was a man of character who, although publically made it known that he did not believe in UFOs, actually believed in the existence of unidentified light phenomena.

On the 28th of June 1986, Moira Bishop and her husband Alan, sighted three bright objects in the sky over the village of Stedham, West Sussex at 1, 3 and 6 O'clock positions. After about five minutes the lights moved away in a sweeping arch across the sky heading northwards and were out of sight shortly afterwards.

(Source: *Midhurst & Petworth Observer,* **3.7.1986, 'Lights in the sky')**

'Media is under mystery influence'

2379

REVELATIONS that mysterious influences caused the press to ignore a startling theory about aliens on Earth are soon to be made by Rickmansworth's UFO expert, Gordon Creighton.

Mr Creighton, a retired diplomat, will publish the revelations and repeat the theory in the magazine *Flying Saucer Review,* which he edits from his home in Cedars Avenue.

In June there had been wide media interest in which the French astronomer and physicist, Dr Jaques Vallée, expounded his belief that visiting aliens do not come from outer space but break through into our world from another dimension.

Dr Vallée, who was Steven Spielberg's adviser for *Close Encounters of the Third Kind* and was the model for the French scientist Lacombe in the film, said many aliens were already here, unrecognised and observing the human race.

He added, however: "When we do see them arrive or depart, it's listed as a UFO sighting."

Mr Creighton is now sure that the aliens used a form of telepathy to deter the media from publishing Dr Vallée's theory, as only one newspaper reported the lecture.

He says: "This is alien control, and the aliens are not necessarily benevolent. I think this control is responsible for the mess the world is in.

"I also think the aliens are most anxious that they shouldn't be rumbled. For that reason they spread the theory that aliens were extra-terrestrial, rather than from another dimension."

Mr Creighton, who has previously told of spacecraft being found crashed with dead aliens inside, intends putting forward the multi-dimensional theory and discussing the press blackout in *Flying Saucer Review,* probably in the same issue as he explained the recent circular depressions in cornfields in Hampshire and Wiltshire.

JULY 1986

CHESTERFIELD MAN SIGHTS UFO OVER CITY

Also includes – Schoolboy sights glowing object over Chesterfield • A UFO is filmed crossing the River Thames at Abingdon • A UFO is seen over Torquay, and a bricklayer from Kent sights a silver, saucer-shaped object

Orange glowing object over Chesterfield

MELVYN Broadhurst from Holme Hall Estate, Chesterfield, happened to be looking out of his window on the evening of 5th July 1986, when he noticed an orange glowing object, a few yards away, moving silently over treetops, at Ashgate Woods.

> *"I thought it was searching as if to land, so I dashed downstairs and saw it going in the direction of Linacre Road, towards Ashgate Hospital. It was oval-shaped, the size of a Mini car, very bright yellow, with a bright blue flashing light on top.*
>
> *I watched it for about 20 minutes, before it went into clouds, out of view"*

The Hartcliffe area of Bristol was to be the scene of numerous reports of strange phenomenon, over the years.

UFO over Walsall

Lichfield Post newspaper reporter – Steven Sharma – was then aged 14, in the summer of 1986.

> *"I was walking home along Princess Street, Walsall, and in the process of turning left into the street where I lived, when I noticed the traffic was slowing down. I saw many drivers looking upwards and pointing. I looked and saw what I can only describe as a giant blazing silver bullet, or lozenge shape, hovering in the sky over the Gas Works at Pleck. I felt frozen with awe, rather than fear, and stood there, mesmerised, just watching. By now the queue of traffic had spread backwards to the railway bridge. I carried on watching for a short time*

and then ran back home, where I burst into the house and literally dragged my family outside, who were just in time to see it rush off across the night sky, before it was lost from view."

(Source: Personal interview)

Bell-shaped UFO over Cheshire

In July 1986 at Stockport, Cheshire an off duty police officer was cleaning his camera at home, when he suddenly noticed a strange bell-shaped UFO in the sky above his home and took a single photograph of the object. The officer later learned there had been a series of reports from members of the public in the Stockport and Greater Manchester area.

We emailed Stockport Central Library hoping to obtain further details of this matter in late August 2013.

(Source: *Stockport Times*, 4.7.86.)

UFO over Abingdon Berkshire

On a visit to the *Barge* Public House in Honey Street, Alton Barnes, Wiltshire – the focal point of public interest during the mid-1990s, after a number of crop circles were found in the local area – we became acquainted with Vince, who was responsible for painting the magnificent ceiling inside the bar, which overlooked the bedecked walls on which were pinned the latest crop circle photographs and miscellaneous information.

Vince told us about a UFO, captured on film by Abingdon man Maurice Ridgley, in 1986, who we managed to eventually trace, in 1998.

Maurice:

> *"It was a Saturday morning, in June or July 1986. My son Jeremy, and I, were in the garden which backs onto the Thames, when we noticed a strange object in the sky. It looked like a giant upside-down Volkswagen Beetle.*
>
> *I shouted for my wife to come out and have a look, then ran into the house and picked up my JVC Video camera and took a short of clip of film, lasting a minute, before it suddenly accelerated upward into the sky."*

Mr Ridgley contacted RAF Benson immediately after the sighting, and was told nothing untoward had shown on the station radar. He then telephoned *Central TV* (then based in Oxford) who sent a reporter around to the house to interview the family, and left – promising to get back in touch. Rather oddly, he was never heard of again, nor was any publicity ever given to this incident.

We contacted *Central TV*, hoping to obtain a copy of the film, and were told that they had no knowledge of any such incident, or anybody that had been to see him from their office.

After viewing the film, we felt it should be examined by someone with specialised equipment and contacted Mr Ashley Windsor, of Mask Technology, Newbury, Berkshire, who agreed to examine it, free of charge (unfortunately, owing to demands of other clients; namely the *BBC* and the Crown Prosecution Service

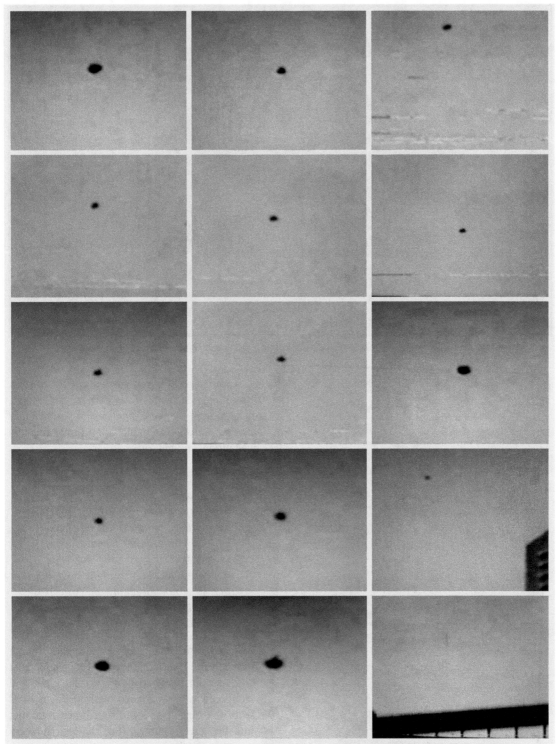

Screen shots of part of the video taken by Maurice Ridgley from his back garden in 1986 of an object over the Thames

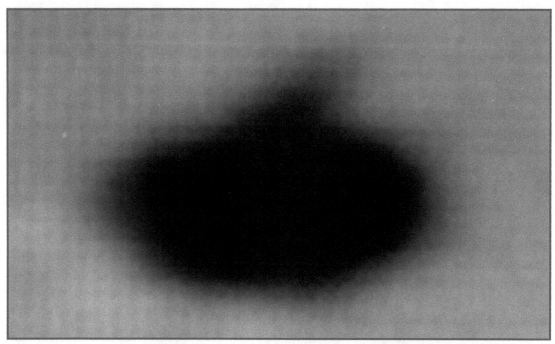

A close-up of one of the screen shots from the video taken by Maurice Ridgley with his JVC video camera

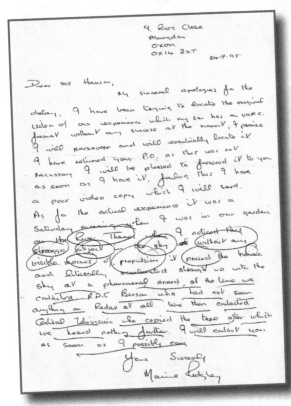

the examination was not carried out for at least 18 months) – a matter for which he apologised, and suggested *"it could have been a parcel net of black balloons"* – an explanation firmly rejected by Maurice, and his son.

Maurice:

> *"It had what looked like two swiveling gantries. We watched it for about 10-12 minutes. If it had been balloons, why didn't it move about in the sky? It was following what appeared to be a straight course across – not forgetting the way it suddenly shot straight up into the sky. I don't believe it was balloons."*

Was it a parcel net of black balloons? Having watched the film many times over, we felt that this was not likely to be the explanation, and wondered what was seen to drop downwards from the object, at some speed, and plummet into the River Thames. (See the last frame in sequence on the previous page).

UFO over Torquay

On 18th July 1986, Roger Tibbenham had just closed the bar at the RAF Association Club and was stood outside, taking in the air, when:

> *"I saw a circular saucer-shaped object, showing a number of bright lights around its outer edge – like a flat dish – tumbling over and over in the sky. I watched it as it flew from the Chelston area, towards St. Mary Church. I ran back into the Club and pulled one of the members out – Pam Pook. She and I stood watching it in amazement, before it went out of sight in ten seconds."*

(Source: *Herald Express*, Torquay, Devon, 20.7.86 – 'Rogers UFO Tumble over Torquay'/Personal Interview)

Did RAF scramble jet fighters?

On the evening of 23rd July, a spherical-shaped object was seen darting about in the clouds behind St. John's Roman Catholic School, Earlham Road, Norwich, by Mrs P. Fletcher. Other witnesses included Mr & Mrs Williams, who saw it over Winchester Tower, close to the Bowthorpe and Hellesdon areas. Interestingly, Mr & Mrs Williams pointed out that during their sighting, between 7pm and 8pm, two fighter planes appeared and seemed to be carrying out some investigation, although this is, of course, speculation.

(Source: *Eastern Evening News*, 30.7.1986 – 'Could it be a UFO?'/ *Eastern Evening News*, 4.8.1986 – 'Yes it was a UFO')

EXPRESS, Derby, England – July 24, 1986

Experts puzzled by UFO reports

by Express reporter

EXPERTS are baffled by sightings of cigar-shaped UFOs all over Derbyshire.

Mysterious pulsating lights have been spotted at Sinfin and there have been over a dozen other sightings.

On one occasion a bright white light shot out of the side of, well could it be ... a spaceship?

Beam

Mr Denis Harriman, regional co-ordinator of the National UFO Investigation Society, said reports have flooded in from all over the county.

"Whatever it is seems to travel very slowly, has a red light at the front and a white beam at the back.

"From what I've heard it could be anything from 100-500 feet long," he said.

Some objects look like a star until seen close up and over Windley a craft of metallic appearance was seen which hovered over trees and shot away as the witness approached.

And a bright orange light has been spotted flying from Melbourne to Windley, reputedly as big as a Wessex helicopter.

A spokesman for the Derby Astronomical Society said the brightness of Venus in recent weeks could account for some sightings. Derbyshire Police confirmed they had received reports of strange sitings, but could offer no explanation.

Another *'flying saucer'* was seen in the same month – this time over Priory Park, Kent – involving bricklayer John Bolton. He noticed a bright flashing *'light'* in the sky, at 4pm, and brought it to the attention of his workmates, who watched the *'silver saucer-shaped object, with a domed top, as it hovered in the sky for some 20 minutes'* before heading off towards the Thames Estuary, where it disappeared from sight.

(Source: Ron West/Brenda Butler)

At 8.50pm on 29th July 1986, Derek Mason and his two children, from Hull, reported having sighted a long tube-like object, showing grey and white light patches, with a bright light on the back, fly at speed through the sky. **(Source: *Hull Daily Mail*, 30.7.1986)**

Magistrate sees a UFO launch a rocket!

BIDEFORD magistrate John Garnsey and his wife, Jennifer, talked this week about the UFO they saw in the sky over Westward Ho! They, and 15 other people enjoying a barbecue, watched it for ten minutes before it disappeared.

Mrs Garnsey said: "It was drifting in a low arc across the sky. It was bright yellow and shaped like a Zeppelin.

"The weirdest part of it was that it appeared to release a bright orange rocket while we were watching.

"It was completely silent. We thought it might have been an aircraft or a helicopter, but there was no noise.

"I have always been sceptical about UFOs and I don't think what we saw came from Mars or anywhere like that. I am sure there must be a logical explanation."

However, the RAF said it had no aircraft flying in the area on the night the object was seen, July 16.

And the barbecue party swore blind that they had not been drinking . . . .

AUGUST 1986

NORTH DEVON MAGISTRATE SPOTS UFO DURING BARBECUE

Also includes – Artist sights UFO over Wisbech, in Cambridgeshire
Spinning UFO over Barnsley • Teenager followed by UFO

UFO over Bideford

WE spoke to John Garnsey – a local magistrate from Bideford, North Devon – who still remains puzzled as to what it was that he and a number of other guests saw, during the early evening of 7th August 1986, while attending a barbecue at his home address.

"A 'light' appeared and began to slowly drift across the sky. After about 10 minutes, it discharged a bright 'light', which shot off across the sky – like a rocket. A short time later, the original 'light' faded away. It wasn't any flare or aircraft, I'm convinced of that."

(Source: Personal interview)

'Flying Saucer' over Keighley

Towards the end of the month, Keighley pensioners – Edith Spencer (90) and Margaret Snowden of Delph House, Parkwood Rise – were enjoying a cup of tea in their 9th floor flat, when they heard a buzzing sound outside. They were astonished to see an oval-shaped object flying towards the tower block, from the direction of Haworth, and Oakworth Moors.Edith:

"It was black on top, with a silver rim around its centre."

(Source: *Bradford Telegraph & Argus*, 20.8.1986 – 'Afternoon cuppa disturbed by a UFO')

On 21st August 1986, Tim Good gave a lecture at Beckley Village Hall, Sussex. Admission cost £3.25, which included wine and a light buffet!

UFO over Wisbech

Artist James Aish, from Tydd St. Giles, near Wisbech, Cambridgeshire, was looking out of his bedroom window, one summer's day in 1986, when he saw a *'flying saucer'* . . .

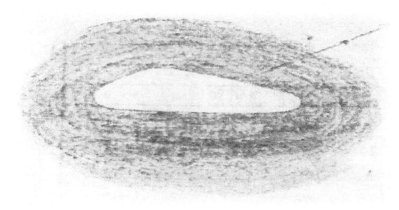

". . . as clear as day. It was shaped like a disc, with some sort of control tower just off the centre."

We spoke to James (now in his late 70s, still working as a personal security officer) who had no difficulty in remembering the incident, which was to shake his belief in life in general.

"There was something written on it – like a marking – but it was too far away to make out. It could have been a cockpit or something. When I told people, they laughed at me."

(Source: Derek Newman, East Anglia UFO & Paranormal Society)

We now know that a UFO was reported as seen over Bristol, on 13th August 1986 – a matter that was brought to the attention of Graham Birdsall, who wrote to the Airport. *(Their reply is opposite.)*

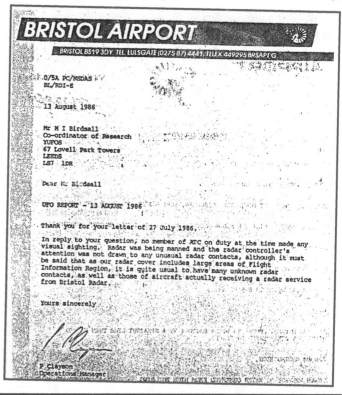

Spinning UFO over Barnsley

Mr John Brook, of Berby Street, Barnsley, was on his way home, at 10.50pm on 22nd August 1986, when he saw a strange object in the sky.

"It looked like it was spinning on its axis. Suddenly a bright 'light', with a fluorescent tint to it, shone down onto me.

It was so bright that I had to shut my eyes. I felt a tingling sensation all over and the hairs on the back of my neck stood up. I turned and ran home, as fast as I could."

The object was seen hovering about 50ft off the ground, over the Co-op Dairy, in Summer Lane.

Followed by a UFO

Oldham teenager – Lynne Murray (16) – was on her way home, at 9.40pm on 27th August 1986.

"I heard a horrible noise, like a sucking sound, and looked up, seeing lights in the distance – red, green and blue, flashing alternately. I was so scared I ran, but it came over the top of me. It then disappeared but reappeared. It was three to four houses long. I ran and it seemed to chase me, until I reached my friend's home – Claire Smith, in Manor Road – who offered to walk me the rest of the way home. When we arrived there, it appeared above the house. We could hear the noise again. We waited inside until it had left."

JP sees UFO

A UFO resembling a Zeppelin has been spotted over the Westcountry. The phenomenon was seen by a barbecue party in North Devon.

Mr John Garnsey, a local magistrate, said: "It was most weird. I thought it might be a plane, but it made no noise. We watched it for over 10 minutes drifting across the sky.

"It seemed to discharge a rocket from it then disappeared across the horizon."

Seventeen witnesses at the party watched the UFO — and Mr Garnsey insisted: "We hadn't been drinking!"

His wife Jennifer said: "It was travelling slowly across the sky. All of a sudden another bright light like a rocket flashed from it.

"It was completely silent. We thought it might be an aircraft or a helicopter, but we couldn't hear an engine."

The mysterious craft was spotted near Westward Ho! A spokesman at nearby RAF Chivenor said: "Our helicopters weren't flying in the area at the time."

It was suspected that an RAF Sea King helicopter might have been practising without lights that night. But a spokesman at RNAS Culdrose, where the RAF training unit is based, said: "We definitely had no aircraft in the area at the time."

(**Source:** *The Oldham Advertiser*, 28.8.86 – 'Teenager in close encounter')

'Oval flying saucer' shocks Margaret

Rain theory over that silver UFO

by Sue Riley

A UFO enthusiast has come up with a theory for the silver UFO seen by two Keighley pensioners.

Mrs. Margaret Snowdon, 60, of Delph House, Parkwood Rise, was having a cuppa and a chat with neighbour Mrs. Edith Spencer, 90, when their conversation was interrupted by a strange buzzing.

Looking out the window they saw a weird, oval-shaped object flying towards Keighley from the direction of the Haworth/ Oakworth moors.

It was black on top with a silver rim around its centre and disappeared towards Keighley town centre as quickly as it came.

David Barclay, of Shipley, who writes about UFO's, said as the sighting occurred just before a downpour, it could be linked to the theory of barometric pressure.

It is thought that pressure in rocks produces electricity, which in turn produces a glowing aeroform.

Mr. Barclay is currently forming a group in the Aire Valley to study all aspects of the paranormal.

Believe

Mrs. Snowdon said she saw the UFO "as plain as anything."

"I didn't believe in flying saucers but I do now," she said.

Keighley police said they had received no reports of any other sightings in the town.

The Aeronautical Information Service at RAF West Drayton said there had been no reports of phenomena in West Yorkshire.

SEPTEMBER 1986

FISHERMEN SIGHT UFO OVER DAVENTRY

Also includes – Strange black cloud seen over Dagenham
Glowing orange 'ball of light' seen in sky close to Gatwick by local housewives
Cylindrical UFO seen over Edinburgh

A MYSTERIOUS pulsating light was seen in the sky over Scunthorpe at midnight on the 2nd of September 1986– 15 degrees above the horizon. Ten minutes later it moved away eastwards.

(Source: BUFORA)

UFO over Skipton Yorkshire

On September the 4th 1986 Kingsley Wiggin (14) from West Bank Road, Skipton North Yorkshire was outside at 7.35am when he saw a glowing object like a bright star hovering over the Rockwood estate. By the time he had called his father it had gone. **(Source: Yorkshire UFO Society)**

UFOs over Coventry

Brothers Clive and Joseph Goode, from Walsgrave, Coventry, were at the Country Park in Daventry, setting up their fishing equipment, as the sun rose on 23rd September 1986, when they sighted:

> *". . . a large UFO, followed by five smaller ones, making a whirring noise, heading from the direction of Long Buckby, before being lost from view in the sky over the Preston Capes area".*

A police spokesman suggested that the objects could have been caused by condensation from a jet aircraft, which had just passed over! On the same date hundreds of people telephoned the authorities in Luxemburg and Belgium reporting having sighted five or six bright green lights travelling about 500ft off the ground.

A week later, brilliant lights were seen in the sky over Daventry Country Park, travelling towards Preston Capes, by Company Director, Pauline Dunn, and her husband, Stanley. **(Source: Personal interview)**

ANGLERS SPOT UFO

● THEY'RE coming . . . Brothers Joseph and Clive Goode tell of their close encounter. Picture: Pete Spencer.

TWO fishermen are convinced that visitors from another world passed over Daventry this week.

They are challenging experts to explain the appearance of six Unidentified Flying Objects over the Country Park early on Tuesday morning.

For brothers Clive and Joseph Goode claim they saw "aliens" as the sun was rising over the reservoir.

"I stood there absolutely dumbfounded. I've never seen anything like it," says Clive who lives in Walsgrave, Coventry.

They say that six objects came across the sky from the direction of Long Buckby. They were in formation with a large object at the front.

The UFO's made a whirring noise and two of them left wispy trails in the sky, the brothers claim. Geese on the reservoir were "going crazy" as the objects passed and disappeared in the direction of Preston Capes.

By
John Howes

Clive and Joseph were spending their first day fishing at the Country Park and had set up tackle at about 6 am, before the sun rose.

The objects appeared shortly afterwards at about the height of low clouds, and were out of sight within a few seconds.

"It happened so quick," says Joseph who works on the production line at British Leyland. "I reached for my camera, but it was too late.

"If you'd seen it yourself, you wouldn't have believed it. I wish it wasn't true because I spend a lot of time out fishing and this has put me right off," he told the Weekly Express.

"I have always been interested in UFO's but I never really believed they existed. If anyone tells me this was a balloon or a jet-fighter, they have got to be joking," adds Joseph.

He says that a jet-fighter passed over

several minutes before the UFO's — but that the unidentified objects were travelling much faster than any planes.

The brothers say they were fishing a fortnight ago at Stanford near Lutterworth when they saw a bright light moving in the sky. They believe that the Ministry of Defence could be testing new weapons in the area.

"It was something unexplained. Do we have something that far advanced?" asks Joseph.

Sgt Tony Picketts of Daventry Police says he will be advising aviation authorities of the sighting and they may wish to launch an investigation. He is not aware of any defence exercises in the area.

He says he believes the objects may be caused by condensation from a jet aircraft which had just passed over. He says when pilots adjust the throttles, there is a "blip" in condensation trails which give the appearance of smoke rings.

And he urges anyone else who saw the objects to report the sightings to the police.

Strange black cloud over Dagenham

On 24th September 1986, Anne Hooker of Bonham Road, Dagenham, in Essex, was outside her house, when she noticed a very strange jet black cloud, motionless in the clear night sky, towards the southern direction.

She was later interviewed by Dan Goring, who told us how frightened she had been (even while relaying the account). Dan regards her as a genuine woman. Sadly, Anne would have now passed away, so we have used her name and hope this will not offend her relatives.

UFO near Gatwick Airport

In September 1986, a glowing orange *'ball'*, surrounded by a pale orange aura, was seen moving slowly through the night sky, close to Gatwick Airport, by housewife Ursula Scratchley and her companion, Penny Crowder. They contacted Air Traffic Control at Gatwick Airport, to report the matter, but were told nothing had shown on Radar. **(Source: Personal interviews/UFOTREK)**

Cylindrical UFO over Edinburgh

Edinburgh resident – Mrs Yvonne Westgarth – was looking out of her north facing window, in South Edinburgh, on 30th September 1986, when she saw:

> *". . . a white cylindrical object with a black band around its centre, flying silently through the sky, just above rooftop height, before it disappeared out of view, towards the west-north-west."*

The incident was later explained away as being the enlarged distorted mirage of a Boeing 757, landing at Edinburgh! **(Source: Personal interview)**

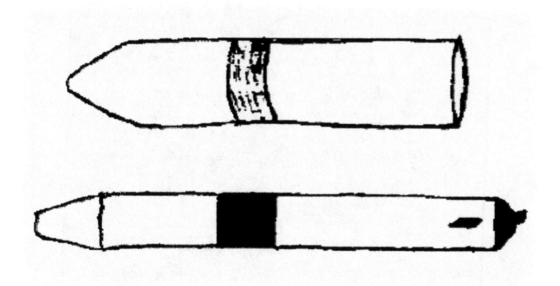

OCTOBER 1986

STRANGE PHENOMENA OVER DAVENTRY

Also includes – UFO seen over Sutton Coldfield Hospital • British Rail workers
at Felixstowe sight spheres of light crossing the sky • UFO lifts car from the ground
in Italy • In the UK a Police Sergeant reports his police car was turned
upside-down, while on patrol

A LARGE rectangular object, flashing with lights, was seen slowly moving across the sky over Rhyl, North Wales, on the evening of 2nd October 1986.

Preston Capes, Daventry, was the source of another UFO sighting – this time on 8th October 1986, involving Mrs Daphne Underhill, from Woodford Hales, whom we spoke to about the incident.

> *"We were getting ready for bed, when my husband called me to have a look out of the bedroom window. I looked out and saw an orange and red coloured circular object, fairly high in the sky. Then part of it broke away – not smooth but jagged in appearance – and shot off across the sky towards Preson Capes. Several minutes later it reappeared in the sky, but soon faded from view."*

(Source: Personal interview/*Weekly Express*, 9.10.86 – 'Village is UFO Focus')

On the early morning of 9th October 1986, a huge cigar-shaped object, estimated to be 400ft long by 60ft in width, was seen by three nurses and a doctor, at Goodhope Hospital, Sutton Coldfield (apparently tracked on Radar). **(Source: John Hurley, Birmingham, UFOSIS)**

UFOs over Suffolk

On 27th October 1986, British Rail workers – Eric Wallis and Michael Scaffe – were working in the shunting yards, in Felixstowe, at 3.45am, when the ground in front of them was flooded with bright blue light. Looking upwards, they saw:

> *". . . A bright blue 'globe of light' with silver flames streaking from it, crossing the sky."*

UFO over the A12, Suffolk

Other sightings of what appears to have been the same UFO came from Ufford and Ipswich, which also included a sighting of *"a white 'ball of light', which passed overhead, making a humming noise"*, according to former teacher – Janet Richards – who was driving along the A12, at Blythburgh, with her daughter – Cathy. A similar report was obtained from qualified pilot and nurse, Melanie Hartley, of Bury St. Edmunds, who was driving home at 11pm, near the village of Fornham All Saints, Suffolk, with her two daughters in the back, when their curiosity became aroused after seeing a bright *'light'*, reflecting off the bonnet. When they looked upwards, they saw:

> *". . . a saucer-shaped object (the length of three double-decker buses) hovering in the sky".*

UFO lifts car from ground

The following day (28th October) a huge black triangular-shaped object was seen, at 6.15pm, hovering over the local harbour at Viareggio, Italy, by a couple out driving. They described it as showing a light at each corner, and actually drove underneath it. As they did so a loud boom was heard, at which point the engine on the car revved and then died. Frighteningly, the rear end of the car was picked up and then dropped onto the ground as they passed from underneath the object – the occupants feeling that they had been in a lift, which had dropped downwards. The object was then seen to move away towards the mountains. The couple went to the police and reported the matter. Not surprisingly, they suffered physical after-effects in the form of severe headaches, which lasted several days. Other witnesses reported having seen strange lights on the same evening. **(Source: Moreno Tambellini, CISU)**

In 1983 a similar situation happened in the States during 1983 involving Mrs Catherine Burk. See page 70.

Police car is lifted up and overturned

Oddly we were to come across another mysterious incident, involving a vehicle which appears to have been completely picked up and then slammed into the ground. It involved retired Detective Inspector Roger Tucker, from Kidlington, near Oxford. (He was 19 when he joined the Police Force in 1959).

We went to see Roger on 16th November 2012. This is what he had to say:

> *"I was promoted to Sergeant, collar number '1977' on the 5.1.1978. At the time the accident occurred, I was posted to night duty and driving towards Aylesbury, on the A41, at about 3am in early September 1978, in a brand new Ford Escort, which had 35 miles on the speedometer. It was a clear, dry night, with excellent driving conditions, so I switched off the car headlights.*
>
> *I had my overcoat on, with the collar turned up.*

The next thing to happen was that I was aware of being upside-down and pointing in the other direction, towards Bicester. I began to crawl out from the window, but was prevented from doing so by the epaulette, on the left-hand side of the traffic coat, catching something in the car, but managed to free it and crawled out onto the road. My first feeling was of relief. I remember thinking how wonderful the first 'suck' of water was from a rain puddle on the tarmac, as it had started to rain, accompanied by that peculiar refreshing smell of rain on the dry road. I had an impression of the local surroundings being very blue, reminding me of an old-fashioned TV screen – a Royal blue colour.

A lorry pulled up in front of me. The driver got out and helped me to my feet, after advising him I wasn't seriously injured, although my back was in agony. I then asked him where he was going; he told me Bicester. I looked around at the police car and was shocked to see that the top of the vehicle had been squashed down. The roof was now 15-18ins above the top of the windows. There was a massive dent in the roof. I stood there in shock, wondering how the bloody hell this had happened, as I had not struck any other vehicle or obstacle in the road. (It was now 3.10am)

I made my way over to the nearby cottage and knocked on the door. A woman opened the door and spoke to me. She said words to the effect, 'You were quick, I've just phoned the police – the crash awoke me.' I explained that I was the officer concerned.

A short time later, PC Michael Horne arrived and we stood pondering on what had caused the car to flip over onto its roof with significant force. He checked the side of the road grass verge and nearby trees, and could find no sign of any collision with the police car, or skid marks, and was just as perplexed as I was as to what had caused the car to end up like this. An ambulance arrived and took me to John Radcliffe Hospital, at Oxford, where I was treated for the back injury. A police inspector then took me home.

DRUG SQUAD OCT. 1972 AGED 32yrs

Detective Inspector Roger Tucker, above in 1972 and right, in 2012.

I still have no idea what it was that caused the accident. It was suggested that the car had skidded on a patch of oil, but this wasn't true. Strangely, another officer, who attended the scene, told me he had seen a mysterious blue light in the sky, over the locality of the accident, as he was on the way there. Was there a connection with what I had seen? I believe there was a period of time that I was unable to account for."

NOVEMBER/DECEMBER 1986

CYLINDRICAL UFO OVER EMLEY MOOR

Also includes – UFO sighted at sea by police officer • UFO over Canada
Fish-shaped UFO

AT 4am on 2nd November 1986, a huge cylinder-shaped craft was seen by a number of eyewitnesses, hovering in the sky over the Emley Moor TV transmission mast, Holmfirth. Police officers arrived on the scene at around 4.20am and watched the UFO, which they estimated was hovering at a height of 1,200ft above the mast, showing bright white lights at either end, for several minutes. An unnamed officer said:

> *"On first seeing the object it was totally static in the sky, not moving in any direction, but appeared to be hovering".*

Another said:

> *"It did not move in any direction, though it appeared to wobble and distort".*

It is thought that nine people saw the UFO, which appeared to be changing colour from red to green before it flew off in an easterly direction. Officers reported the sighting to the Civil Aviation Authority, which could offer no explanation. It was confirmed that it was not a commercial or private aircraft.

(Source: Declassified Ministry of Defence documents/*Wakefield Express City Newspaper*)

UFO sighted at sea by former police officer, 1986?

Retired Police Officer Alan Blue:

> *"I was serving on-board the training ship* Malcolm Millar *with about 50 plus crew. Some 'off duty' called on deck to experience a massive cubic grid, made out of what appeared to be laser light! It was from horizon to horizon and awe-inspiring and out of this world. It lasted for some time and we could all see it. It was off the French coast, in the region of the Channel Islands, in daylight, with no fog – very odd. I was officer of the watch, but when I asked what I should enter in the log, the skipper directed that no log entry was to be made! So there is no official record of a very strange and unexplainable event. Do you have any explanation?"*

We spoke further to Alan, hoping that he might have remembered the date. He looked through his logbook and found there are two possible dates!

> *"The first is 16th November to 29th November 1986: Sail Training Ship* Malcolm Millar *on a voyage Portsmouth, Southampton, St. Malo, Fowey, Cowes, Southampton – this trip was 572 miles logged, 14 days aboard, of which there was 24 hours of night sailing at sail.*

> *The second is 7th to 20th October 1990. The route was Falmouth, St. Malo, Bruges, Portsmouth, Southampton – this trip was 748 nautical miles logged, 14 days aboard, of which 28 hours night sailing at sea. It is so long ago that I would be guessing to try to say which one it was. On both of these cruises I was a watch officer. On each trip there were 39 trainees, aged 16 to 25 years. The rest of the crew, on each occasion, was made up of past trainees, plus volunteers, plus permanent crews, making a total of about 50 people."*

UFO over Canada

Was there a connection with what was seen the following day – 17th November 1986 (presupposing that the *'cube'* was seen on the 16th) involving Japan Airlines flight JAL 1628, captained by Kenjyu Terauchi, which was flying from Iceland to Anchorage, Alaska, carrying a cargo of wine from Beaujolais, and over Fort Yukon at 6.10pm (Anchorage time) when he and his crew sighted flashing lights moving alongside them, while cruising at 35,000ft?

Captain Terauchi:

> *"There were three of them in formation – yellow, amber, and green. I descended to 31,000ft, accompanied by this 'thing' which was as big as aircraft carrier. It seemed to play tag with us for about 30 minutes, but was lost from view as we circled to land at Anchorage."*

The co-pilot – Takanori Tamefuji – compared the numerous lights or flames to . . .

> *". . . Christmas assorted lights – a salmon colour (red or orange) – and white landing light, just like a landing light, weak green, ah, blinking. The intensity wasn't constant but rather it pulsated – became stronger, became weaker, became stronger, became weaker – different from strobe lights. The lights were swinging in unison, as if in good formation flight . . . close (formation) of two aircraft, side by side. I had no doubt that I was seeing some sort of aerial object, or objects, just ahead and to the left of the airplane."*

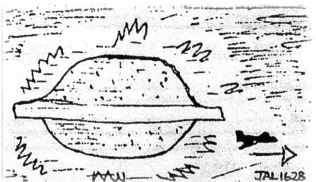

He compared the clarity of the lights to seeing night flight head-on traffic, at which time it is only possible to see the lights on the approaching aircraft and without seeing the total shape. Upon seeing the lights, he first thought that he was seeing two small aircraft. However, they were very strange because there were too many lights and it was so luminous. Subsequently, he had

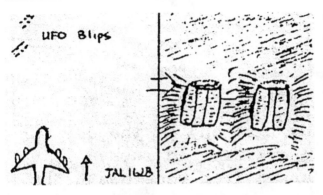

the feeling that it was larger than a normal aircraft.

The flight engineer, who sat behind the co-pilot Yoshio Tsukuba, had a poorer view of the lights. He recalled that when he first saw them he was looking . . .

". . . through the L1 window at the 11 o'clock position (about 30° to the left of straight ahead) and saw clusters of lights undulating; the clusters were 'made of two parts . . . shaped like windows of an airplane' (i.e., arranged in square or rectangular clusters). The lights in front of us were different from town lights. They were white or amber in colour."

This was a sighting that attracted the attention of the world media – *The Times* even covered the incident.

Some months later, the Federal Aviation Administration published a full *report (which cost $200).

The Mutual UFO Network launched an investigation into the incident, after confirming from Jim Derry – the FAA Security Officer – that the witnesses were normal, professional people, and not given to hallucinations.

Captain Terauchi

Terauchi speculated that . . .

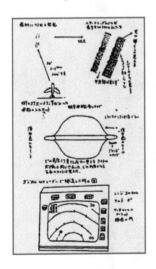

"The spaceships fired jets to kill the inertia (actually, momentum) of their high-speed manoeuvre. After this manoeuvre, from the left of the plane to the front, the ships appeared as if they were stopped in one place in front of us. At this time, one 'ship' was above the other. Three to seven seconds later, a fire – like from jet engines – stopped and became a small circle of lights as they began to fly level flight, at the same speed as we were, showing numerous numbers of exhaust pipes.

However, the centre area of the ship(s) where below an engine might be, was invisible. [From] the middle of the body of a ship sparked an occasionally (sic) stream of lights, like a charcoal fire, from right to left and from left to right. Its shape was square, flying 500ft to 1,000ft in front of us – very slightly higher in altitude than us. Its size was about the same size as the 'body' of a DC-8 Jet, and with numerous exhaust pipes."

---

*After a three month investigation, the FAA formally released their results at a Press conference held on 5th March 1987. Here Paul Steucke retracted earlier FAA suggestions that their controllers confirmed a UFO, and ascribed it to a *'split radar image'*, which appeared with unfortunate timing. He clarified that *'the FAA [did] not have enough material to confirm that something was there'* and, although they were *'accepting the descriptions by the crew'* they were *'unable to support what they saw'*.

In 2013 Philip Mantle sent us a photo of a UFO, taken by Mr Richard Cooke on 6th July 1997, over Chichester, UK. Was this the same UFO seen by Captain Terauchi? See also Page 207 'UFO over Portsmouth'.

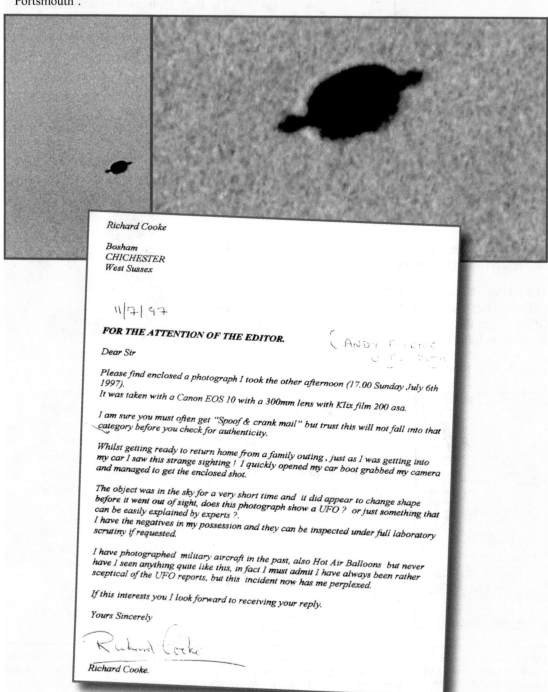

Richard Cooke

Bosham
CHICHESTER
West Sussex

11/7/97

FOR THE ATTENTION OF THE EDITOR.

Dear Sir

Please find enclosed a photograph I took the other afternoon (17.00 Sunday July 6th 1997).

It was taken with a Canon EOS 10 with a 300mm lens with Klix film 200 asa.

I am sure you must often get "Spoof & crank mail" but trust this will not fall into that category before you check for authenticity.

Whilst getting ready to return home from a family outing , just as I was getting into my car I saw this strange sighting ! I quickly opened my car boot grabbed my camera and managed to get the enclosed shot.

The object was in the sky for a very short time and it did appear to change shape before it went out of sight, does this photograph show a UFO ? or just something that can be easily explained by experts ?.
I have the negatives in my possession and they can be inspected under full laboratory scrutiny if requested.

I have photographed military aircraft in the past, also Hot Air Balloons but never have I seen anything quite like this, in fact I must admit I have always been rather sceptical of the UFO reports, but this incident now has me perplexed.

If this interests you I look forward to receiving your reply.

Yours Sincerely

Richard Cooke.

Fish-shaped UFO seen

A strange fish-shaped object was seen in the sky over Peynton, Stockport, on or around the 5th December 1986, by Miss Barnes – then living in Dickens Lane.

Oddly, the authors of this book photographed a fish-shaped object in the sky from their home in Alvechurch, in August 2013, which was no doubt an advertising balloon that had broken free.

It was the turn of Marlpool Garden, Kidderminster, residents to report something unusual at 12.50am on 9th December 1986, when a freak whirlwind caused damage to fences, accompanied by a noise – like sirens, or whirring.

According to Mr Derek Perks, his daughter – Rachel – told of seeing *"four different shaped objects, motionless over the town"*, just before the damage occurred.

(Source: Kidderminster Times, 11.12.1986 –
'Residents mystified as havoc hits homes')

At 4pm on 19th December 1986, Kathleen Richardson from Chockleys Meadow, Leegomery, Telford, Shropshire, and her husband, sighted:

> *". . . a large, round object, dark on the bottom and silver bright on the top. It was wavering around in the sky and some way off."*

RAF Shawberry confirmed there had been no flying in that locality.

(Source: Shropshire Star, 20.12.86 – 'Couple see a strange shape in the sky')

A group of between six to eight UFOs were sighted over Bradford, trailing orange glows, as they headed quickly across the horizon, at 7.25am on 23rd December 1986, by at least four people – some of whom contacted the Leeds/Bradford Airport, who confirmed nothing was showing on their radar.

(Source: Bradford & Telegraph Argus, 23.12.86)

It is interesting to note that following the matter being brought to the attention of the media, a journalist from the *Sunday Mirror* contacted Gordon Creighton, Editor of *Flying Saucer Review*, and spent some considerable time discussing the incident and the work of *FSR*. Although the article was reproduced accurately by the *Sunday Mirror*, they did not include any mention of the role played by *FSR* in investigating sightings like this. Gordon found out, later, that they had been inundated with letters from the public, after publication of the incident, but these letters were never forwarded onto him.

The fish-shaped object photographed in Alvechurch by the authors in 2013 believed to be a errant advertising balloon!

Fish tailed UFO – 1995

At 1.30 a.m., 20th October 1995, Nancy Wilson living in Baxterley, Staffordshire got up to fetch a glass of water. While on her way back to bed, she glanced through the rear bedroom window and saw: *"A glowing silver object resting on the canopy roof. I tried to wake my husband, without any success. I looked back and saw a fish tailed object moving rapidly away from the house. It was the weirdest thing I had ever seen in my life."* An examination of the roof, revealed a dozen or more 'plastic poppers' used to waterproof the tops of the screws, which fixed the elderly sheets of translucent plastic onto the battens underneath, were open. In addition to this, we found four small 2 inch triangular impressions in the plastic, created from downward pressure rather than upwards, along the edges and top sheet, and, when marked out on a plan, showed what appeared to be a facsimile of the shape of the UFO, as reported by Nancy – thought provoking in its implications! We later spoke to a local taxi driver, who had dropped a fare off, a couple of miles away from Baxterley, at 1.30 a.m., the same morning. He described having seen *"a bulbous light crossing the sky"*.

Haunted Skies Spotlight
ALLEGED REPTILIAN – DAVID DANIELS

Part 1 Tucson, Arizona: 1984 – Lt. Colonel Wendelle Stevens

THE first part of our story begins in an American prison, sometime in 1984, and involves USAF Lt. Colonel Wendelle Stevens (born 18.1.1923) – who was very well respected and an internationally known leading researcher of the UFO subject. Sadly, he passed away on 7th September 2010.

Wendelle Stevens was born on 18th January 1923, and raised in Minnesota. He enlisted in the Army shortly after High School and graduated from the Lockheed Aircraft Maintenance & Repair School, Aviation Cadet Training and Fighter Pilot Advanced Training as a 2nd Lieutenant in the US Army Air Corps. After that, he attended the first Air Corps Flight Test Pilot School, at Kelly Field, where he learned to fly all the aircraft used by Air Corps at the time, as well as other US Navy aircraft.

During a long, distinguished career in the military, one of his assignments was the supervision of a highly classified team of technical specialists, who were installing hi-tech data, collecting equipment aboard the SAC B-29s for the *Ptarmigon Project* – a research project photographing and mapping every inch of the Arctic land and sea area. This equipment was designed to capture, record, and analyse, all EMF emissions in the Arctic, photograph all anomalous phenomena, and record all disturbances in the electrical and engine systems of

the aircraft – looking for external influences caused by UFOs. This information was then couriered nightly to Washington.

Wendelle was a retired USAF fighter pilot and committed over 54 years of research into the UFO subject, including the collection of more than 4,000 actual UFO photographs. He wrote and co-authored over 18 books on extensive UFO contact cases. He also organised, prior to his death, in 2010, *The International UFO Congress* of which he was a director of since its inception.

(For tributes paid to Wendelle, please see http://www.openminds.tv/wendelle-stevens-passes-214/)

Arizona Department of Corrections Tucson, 1984: At the time, in 1984, Wendelle was serving a term of custodial imprisonment, the charges of which have no relation to either the integrity of the man or of the subject of this book. Wendelle was expecting retired FBI Agent Jim McCoy, of Tuscon, to visit him. (He had sat on the APRO Board of Governor meetings with him before the death of Jim and Coral Lorenzen). After hearing his name called over the speaker system, Wendelle went over to the centre, presuming Jim had arrived early, but found he was not there yet – so sat down to wait for him. Glancing around he noticed a Catholic priest, sat talking to some visitors, who he described as being *"a youngish man, 6ft 2ins in height, with sandy hair, clipped short military style, slender and healthy looking."* The 'priest' got up, began to bless people, and walked up to where Wendelle was sitting, and went to sit down.

Father David Daniels

Wendelle:

"Excuse me, Father, but I have a visitor coming to see me".

He replied, 'I am your visitor'. 'No', I said, 'I am waiting for Jim Mcoy', and pushed the chair back under the table. He said, 'I have come to see you. My name is Father David Daniels'. Being a Catholic I asked him where he had come from, as I didn't recognise his vestment. He replied, 'Yugoslavia, by way of New York'. I told him I didn't know any priests in Yugoslavia. Daniels replied, 'Actually I came from London, through Yugoslavia'. He then sat down and took out a cheap plastic pen – a 'Bic banana' and paper, and started to make notes.

I grew suspicious, knowing that most American priests are not allowed to own any personal possessions, until after being ordained and given the Pope's ring. Their friends usually give them the only expensive things they may properly possess – a good fountain pen, a good leather wallet, and an expensive crucifix. They are also usually given a good leather bound bible, with gold tipped pages. This priest had a cheap pen, a miniature 25 cent notepad, and a cheap crucifix, wrapped around a Gideon's Bible – the kind that are put into hotel rooms for free possession by tenants passing through, which made me somewhat suspicious of him. I asked him for identification and he showed me an American passport. It had his photo and signature, with the permanent address given of *414N 44th Street, New York – an easy one to remember with all the fours."

(*Authors note, 2009. This address is a hotel in New York)

At this stage, Jim McCoy entered the room; Wendelle told Daniels that he would have to leave, which he did, blessing people as he walked away. Wendelle told Jim about his suspicions and asked him to wait for him outside the prison and follow him. Jim later told Wendelle that he had seen *"Daniels leave the prison, get into an old car, and drive to downtown Tuscon, where he parked the car and gave the keys to the owner of a pizza shop. He then caught a bus downtown and got out in front of the Congress Hotel, opposite the Railway Station – a cheap hotel, then costing $10 a night."*

Tuscon: Daniels visits prison again

The following day Wendelle was in his cell, typing, when he received a visit from the Chief of Chaplains of the prison complex, who told him he had another visitor. He made his way over to the visitor's centre, thinking it was his daughter, Cece, bringing him some mail, but instead there to greet him again was David Daniels. Wendelle asked him what he wanted, as he had not asked for any priest. Daniels replied, *"I came*

From:	<S18195A@aol.com>
To:	<johndawn@hansonholloway.fsnet.co.uk>
Cc:	<CeceSt@aol.com>
Sent:	20 July 2005 21:14
Subject:	David Daniels

Dear John:

Oh Boy! This may take some time to tell. I first met "Father" Dasvid Daniels when he came to see me in prison.

I was expecting retired FBI Agent Jim McCoy, of Tucson here, to visit me as he had sent me word that he would be out on this particular Friday. I had known McCoy for years and knew him very well. We both sat in the old APRO Board of Governors Meetings here in Tucson while APRO was active and before the deaths of Jim and Coral Lorenzen. Bob Deaan was another Senior Board Member at the time.

At about ten minutes to 12:00 I heard my name called over the speakwer system to come to the visitors center for a visitor. I thought Jim McCoy had arrived a little early and went on over to the center. He was not there yet but they let me in anyway as "my visitor" had arrived.

As I entered the room I noticed a Catholic Priest sitting at the first table talking to some other visitors. Not seeing McCoy I went on past to the back of the room where I could see all who entered, to wait for McCoy, and sat down at a vacant table. He was slow in arriving.

As I waited I saw the Priest get up from the table in front and begin blessing people at every table as he came toward the back. When he got to my table, he pulled out a chair and began to sit down. I said, "I am sorry, Father, but I have a visitor coming." He said, "I am your visitor." I said, "No, I am waiting for Jim McCoy, I am sorry", and I pulled the chair back to the table. He pulled it out again and repeated, "I am your visitor. I am Father David Daniels, and I have come to see you!"

"To see me? Where are you from?" I was a little confused. because I was Catholic and I did not recognize his order. Each order of Catholic Priests has some distinguishing part of their vestments, and I thought I knew them all.

He repeated it had taken him some time to get here, but he had come a long way to see me. I said, "Where did you come from?" and he said, "Jugoslavia", by way of New York."

I said I didn't know anybody in Jugoslavia, and no Priests or Catholic Orders from there.

He said, "Actually I came from London, through Jugoslavia", and he pulled the chair out again and sat down. He took out a small pocket notebook and a pen, a Bic Bananna, and started to make a note. This made me even more suspicious because what Catholic Priest, who is not allowed to own property, has anything but an expensive pen given to him by his family.

The notebook was a tiny one you buy in the discount stores for 25 cents. His Crucifix wrapped around the bible he was holding was different from any I had seen before. It was of a dark wood, a little bigger than most, and bound with silvery metal around the edges. He had it wrapped around his Bible, which I suddenly recognized as the Green Grosgain version put into hotel rooms by the Gideons. This roused my suspicions even more and I asked to see some identification, which he promptly produced in the form of an American Passport.

It had his picture and a signature in it, and a permanent home address of 414 N. 44th St., New York, NY, an easy one to remember by the number of 4s in it. Now the name David Daniel, two first names, struck me as odd. It also had an endoresenent written in cursive in English, on the first page, which read, "Please extend the usual courtesies of the Church to the bearer." and was signed in Cursive by an indistinct name, Vicar of (and I do not remember the next word) but he said it was the head of his Anglican Order in London. That explained the vestments, which may have been correct but unfamiliar to me.

About that time I saw Jim McCoy enter the room at the far end and I said to Father Daniel that I would have to spend some time with my anticipated vuisitor. and that he should leave.

He got up and said he would be back and he went around the room blessing people again and then went out the door.

Needless to say, I expressed my suspicions to Jim and he said he would see what he could find out, and I gave him the Name, address and number pundched in the tops of the pages of that passport, which I had memorized. I suggested Jim wait out in the parking lot and try to see how the priest got to the prison. He thanked me and left and the Priest came back.

Jim waited as suggested and told me later that the Priest came out of the building and got into an older car that he was driving and drove out of the parking lot and back to Tucson and downtown. Jim cautiously followed him to a Pizza parlor in the south city center, where the Priest parked the car and got out and went in and gave

20/07/2005

to get you out. You have some important work to do and you cannot do it in here". Wendelle told him he did not want to leave and, even if he could escape, he would be a fugitive and told him he had no intention of escaping, as he was innocent of all charges.

Daniels replied:

> "You are not thinking right. I can take care of that".

He then said something very strange:

> "I was going to join you in Harare(Rhodesia) to meet Cynthia Hind, to go down to Pinetown, South Africa, to interview Edward White on his contact with the Koldasians."

Wendelle was surprised by this declaration, as the only person he had ever told was Cynthia Hind – not even his daughter knew his destination. Daniels continued the conversation by adding:

> "I wanted to get an introduction to your courier, Varig Flight Captain Rodolfo Casellato, and ask him to take me to Mirassol to meet Antonio Ferreira, one of his ET contacts."

Wendelle:

> "I was flabbergasted, as I had not told anybody this information. Daniels stayed for about an hour and then left. The next day, my daughter, *Cece, visited with my mail. I was very much taken aback when she told me she had received a visit from a priest, at the family home, and that he had also been seen near my own house, in Tucson. She asked me why I had given him her address. I told her I hadn't. By now, I was sure he was no real priest, but an impostor. I asked him how he had found my daughter. He replied, 'That was easy. I had hoped she would give me a letter to Captain Casellato. I wanted to get to Brazil, unnoticed'."

Wendelle was to receive another final, further visit, from Daniels at the prison, when he confronted him and told him his passport was faked. In 2013 we emailed Arizona Prison and asked them if they had any knowledge of having employed a Father David Daniels to work in their facility from 1984 onwards.

It was chilling to see there were currently 122 inmates on death row, two of whom were women, their crimes made grim reading. In a reply from the facility, Alfred Harris, administrative assistant from the prison, confirmed they had no knowledge of any Father David Daniels being employed there from 1989 onwards, which of course does not cover the period asked for. Presumably their records don't go back that far.

Cece Stevens

*Cece Stevens has studied the paranormal for most of her adult life. After a near death experience from a serious car accident, in 1973, Cece found her natural birth talents heightened to an even greater degree. She has studied Astrology since she was introduced to it when she was 15 years old, and has three books to her credit on the subject, as well as several other fact books. In

From: <S18195A@aol.com>
To: <johndawn@hansonholloway.fsnet.co.uk>
Cc: <CeceSt@aol.com>
Sent: 24 July 2005 17:09
Subject: Re: David Daniels

Dear John:

Yes, I would love to see a copy of Brenda's report on David Daniels. I shall continue with my narrative acount of his visits to me.

He came back to the prison, to see me the next day. Saturday, still a visiting day, and I went over to the Visitor's Center, thinking my daughter Cece had come out to bring me some mail. When I got there it was not Cece, but David Daniel.

He was a smiling youngish looking man, sandy haired, about 6' 2" tall. slender and heaalthy looking, like he worked out regularly. He wore his hair clipped short, military style.

He greeted me with, "You know we should be friends. We were born under the same signs. As a matter of fact we have the same birthday!" I said, "What is yours?" and he replied, "18 Jnuary, as I said, like yours."

This seemed incredible , and I asked to see his driver's license. He responded by handing me his passport again, and I opened it and looked at the front page with his picture and signature. Sure enough, it showed an 18 January birthdate, but just 20 years after mine, showing him born in 1943, making him about 40 years old.

I said, "Just what are you doing here, Father?" And he said, "I came to get you out. You have some important work to do, and you can not do it in here." I said, "Look, I do not want any help. If they opened the doors wide, I would not leave. I have my home andd my business to think of, not being a fugitive unable even to use my right name." He said, "You are not thinking right. I can take care of that."

Then he said ssomething strange. He said, "I was going to join you in Harare (Rohdesia) to meet Cynthis Hind, to go down to Pinetown South Africa to interview Edward White on his Contactw with the Koldasians.

I had told nobody about that, not even my daughters. And then he added, (equally surprising), "I wanted to get an introduction to your courier, Varig Flight Captain Rodolfo Caselatto, and have him take me to Mirassol to meet Antonio Ferenia on his ET contacts with whom he fathered an alien hibrid daughter.

This really floored me as I had told nobody about that case which I was still writing up. He stayed for about an hour andd then left.

My daughter Cece came out the next day, Sunday, with my mail, and she said that a Priest had come to her home to ask about me. She said my neighbors had seen him at my home in Tucson, looking it over. She asked me why I had given him her confidenfial address, and I said I had not done so.

She said he had bought a couple of my pictorial coffee table books on the Pleiadian Contact Case in Switzerland. He watched Cece go into a bedroom in her house where she kept them. That same night he came back about midnight and tried to open that bedroom window from the outside, but the neighbor's barking dogs discouraged his efforts and he left

He never told me he was a Pleiadian, but he had a very special interest in that case. He came back to Cece"s again and bought more Pleiadian pictorials.

On the Following day, a non-visitor day, I was in my cell typing, when I heard a key knocking on the small glass port in my cell door, and I looked up to see a round face with round spectacles peering in. I went to the door and opened it to see a short portly man in a while shirt and blacluntrousers out there with the Priest.

He said he was the chief of chaplains for the prison complex, and that Father Daniels had come a long way to see me, and he introduced us. I could see that the Priest was pretending to meet me for the first time and had extended his hand. I shook hands with him and said, "Glad to meet you, Father."

The Chief of Chaplains took us over to the Visitor's Center and unlocked the door and lock us in. He put us in a sound protected Attorney-Client room and locked us in, saying someone would come to let us out in an hour.

When he left, I asked the priest again, "Just what are you doing here? I have asked for no Priest?" And again he said, "To get you out. You have some important things to do."

I repeated my statement that I would not leave if they opened the doors wide! I considered myself innocent of the charges and would show them so by being the best model prisoner until I was officially released. And I really was, which I think was why the Warden granted an exception and allowed me to have a typewriter in my cell.

By now I was quite certain that this man was no real Priest. I asked him how he found my daughter, and he said, "Oh that was easy. I had hoped she would give me a letter to Captain Caselato. I wanted to get to Brazil

24/07/2005

unnoticed."

He seemed to know everything I had been doing.

A couple of weeks after he left Tucson, Cece got a letter from Christina, Capt. Casellato's daughter living in New York, saying she had met the nicest young man, a young clean-cut man who drove a red Ferari sport car, and took her to elegant expensive restaurants. She had introduced him to her father when he was in town, and they got along well

While we were in the Attorney's room in the Visitor's Center, I asked him how he got in on a non-visitor's day, and he said, "You know your Yard Captain's name is Daniels? I said yes, and he raised his eyebrows.

I got word that Jim McCoy would be out to see me that coming weekend, and he did come out. He advised me that the Priest's passport number was in fact one assigned to the American Embassy in London, but that it was not "properly issued".

Now I knew that my Priest was an imposter!

He came to see me one more time and I told I knew his passport was invalid, and that if he ever came back I would turn him and have him detained.

That was the last I ever saw of him.

The next I heard was that he was back in London and was staying with Brenda

With all my respects...

Wendelle Stevens

From: <S18195A@aol.com>
To: <johndawn@hansonholloway.fsnet.co.uk>
Cc: <CeceSt@aol.com>
Sent: 25 July 2005 19:34
Subject: Re: Emailing: brenda1, brenda

Dear John:

I have remembered a couple more items about David Daniels.

The permanent home addess shown in his passport, 414 N. 44th Street, Nw York, is not a residence address.

This fellow may have been in prison at one time, because when the Chief of Chaplains brought him to my cell, he remarked on the efficiency of the design, and asked the prison Chaplain if he could go in and look around. The Chaplain looked at me and raised his eyebrows.

I said, "Go ahead.", and he went in and made the best and most thorough cell shakedown i had ever seen – even better than most trained guards. When he finished he said, "Yes, this is pretty tight. Nothing in here."

I thought that odd and still do.

I wonder if Christina Casellato still lives in New York, since her father's strange death, and if she ever got a picture of the man. I will have to ask Cece if she has heard from Christina since that time.

All my best...

Wendelle

1990, while working in her bookstore, Cece had a profound experience and was given her native name 'Raven Hawk'. She has a drum, named 'Thunder', which she uses to make it rain. She made the front page of the *Tucson Citizen*, when asked by a reporter to prove she could cause rain. Rain, hail and snow fell to the ground that day. She made the cover of the newspaper. In 2009, she did her first record album – 'Awakenings' – an album designed to calm and relax with. It has been a privilege to correspond with Cece – a delightful woman – and her late father, Wendelle.

Without their valuable contributions to what should now be regarded as an important part of UFO social history of the modern day UFO phenomena, we would be worse off.

Part 2 – New York: Suspicious fire

Following Wendelle's release from prison, Daniels later came to visit Wendelle and his daughter, Cece at their home address, in New York. Just prior to him leaving for England, a number of books on the Pleiades were placed onto the lounge carpet and set on fire; fortunately, the fire was extinguished before the house was burnt down.

Cece, 2013:

> *"I remember the break in and also the times that someone else was there, inside, while I slept. I would wake in the morning and find cigarettes in an ashtray next to my bed! In my living room – quiet threats is what I read from it. My daughter had someone following her to and from school, lots of hard times then."*

```
                              Jan. 23.85

Dear Brenda,
      Hi, let me introduce myself, I am Wendelles
daughter Cece Stevens. I have read your letter, and
have seen to it that dad, and George Green also have
a copy of it.
      From the sounds of it you have had your share of
D.D. from the start. From the story that you told
the only few things that I can add to that is he
told me that he was from a planet called "Titan"
which is one of the moons of Saturn. He wouldn't
say what his mission was. And also he told me that
he was the " long lost illigitimet son " of my dad,
and that I owed it to him to give him money for food
and bed and board. Needless to say things got worse
as by now I am sure that your friend knows about.
      I usually don't scare easily, and made that clear
to the point. David was in turn more afraid of me
is what I felt to be the case.
      My house was broken into three times while David
was here, and also my fathers. I could never find
anything missing, so I was left to belive that it
was a scare tactic. Finally I called the police on
him, and have a few connections of my own. Suddenly
david fled the city, and has not been seen or heard
from til Mr. Trente letter came.
      To say the least we were stunned to see that D.D.
is saying that we are indorcing him!!! We would like
to see him in jail.
      DO NOT TRUST our dear D.D., as he will prey on it
and use ut against you.
```

Cece also described another incident, involving Daniels, who had been disturbed by dogs, barking, after trying to open the bedroom window. She believed he wanted to examine some books on the Pleiadian race, kept in the house, including recently purchased books on the Switzerland contact case (relating to 'Billy' Eduard Albert Meier – citizen of Switzerland and contactee).

It was never our intention to become involved in researching the backgrounds of claims made by people like Billy Meir, Adamski, and others, of their association with members of alien races, purely because of the lack of space available to cover what appeared to be quite involved investigations. Apart from that it appears impossible to categorically prove or disprove either way the claims made by these people. It seems the same situation exists with David Daniels and his female associates and their various visits made to a number of countries, seeking out people who were then very much involved with UFO investigation.

While there were people like Brenda Butler, who found him charismatic and believed he was an alien representative of the Pleiades race that had come to Earth to teach others, especially following his amazing transition from human to reptilian – many others did not share the same feelings and expressed hostility towards him rather than the opposite.

We have no reason to disbelieve Brenda's version of events, however strange they may be, but human nature dictates that unless one actually witnesses for themselves events like these, then they will always be treated with scepticism and suspicion.

pg. 2

Please excuse my typing, it has been several years since the last time I used one, and I'm a bit rusty.

David was living with a man in Tucson here, and I shall see what I can find out from that end, and conduct a bit of an investagation of my own. If I come up with anything I shall pass the information on to you. And if you could please let me know of anything that you should come up with. Also could you please let Mr. Trent see this letter, and if you wouldn't mind, I would rather D.D. not know, as I don't care to have him harassing me any farthur.

D.D. told you an outright lie about my father selling any secrets of any kind. He didn't sell any of the sort.

David knows how to pump people for information, and then make them belive that he is psychic, and or lead you into thinking that he is with the government. It is just one of his many scare tactic's that he is so fond of useing on people. Our dear D.D. has a split personality, and suffers from delusions of granger. It saddens me that he is useing our good name and running it in the mud with his own reputation. I wish ther was some way that I could stop all of that.

I am curious Brenda, as to what D.D. had to say about me. I won't be surprised if it all is bad.

Did D.D. happen to mention to you as to when his birthday was? I know that this is an odd question, and it has nothing to do with Astrology at all, but does tie in with a few lose ends around here. I

pg. 3

would really be curious to know what you have found out. Day, month, and year. Do you think that you can find this out for me? Thanks.

I am sure that you shall be hearing from my dad in the near future, and possibly George. They each have their own story to tell. Funny part is that none of our stories match up. Each one is a different version. To my dad he was a quiet priest, and did not swear or smoke, or drink. To another gentleman friend Bob, he was like a monk, and would not talk, but sat and basically watched Bob. Then to George he was average Mr. Joe Blow off the street. And to me he swore like a sailor, smoked like a steam ship, and was ill tempered because I wouldn't go along with his scam. I wanted proof and he couldn't prove a thing, so I called him a fraud.

I spoke to Bob just now, and he told me alot of things that are to long to go into at this point.

I should think that if your Ministry of Defence should get in touch with our police Department, an have a sheet run on D.D., I think that they would be surprised as to what they would find.

enough for now, will await your next letter.

Sincerly yours,

Cece Stevens
9650 E. 31st. Street
Tucson, Az. 85748
U.S.A.
phone (602) 886-2182

The Koldasians

A man, named Edwin, claimed that he was able to receive messages from Outer Space and was the subject of much attention by Carl Van Vlierden – a Field Investigator for MUFON, living in South Africa.

Cynthia Hind – Another pioneer of UFO research

Vlierden told South African UFO researcher Cynthia Hind – a field investigator for MUFON – that he was planning to compile the messages into a book, due to be published in 1982.

Cynthia grew up in Namaqualand, South Africa, and served in the South African WAAF. She married an RAF Pilot and went to live in Northern England, before immigrating to Zimbabwe, some years later.

Cynthia's first UFO book, entitled *UFOs – African Encounters*, was published by Gemini, Salisbury, Zimbabwe, in 1982. Some of her best UFO investigations in Africa have been published in the *MUFON UFO Journal* over the intervening years. When an important UFO case warranted, she did not hesitate to fly or drive to the site and carry out a full-scale investigation, with the assistance of local qualified scientific advisers.

Mrs Hind was a member of the Soroptimist, serving as President of the Harare Club in 1979-1980, and National President of Zimbabwe in 1984-1986. Starting in 1988 as Editor of *UFO AFRINEWS*, she had mailed her newsletter worldwide to interested people. Cynthia had seven newsletters issued since 1988, and various articles on UFOs published in Australia, Brazil, Britain, France, South Africa, USA and Zimbabwe, including the *MUFON UFO Journal*. She contributed chapters on African UFOs to the following books: *UFOs 1947 – 1987*, edited by Hilary Evans and John Spencer, *Phenomenon*, edited by John Spencer and Hilary Evans, *The UFO Story* 1990, edited by Timothy Good, and *UFOs – The Definitive Casebook*, by John Spencer.

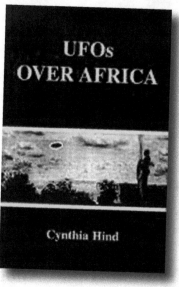

Her last book, *UFOs over Africa*, was published in June 1997. It sums up, in detail, a lifetime of work spent in careful investigation of a host of the most unusual cases, including the strange appearance of silvery-suited aliens and unique light phenomena at the La Rochelle estate, the abduction chronology of two Johannesburg women and, for the first time, tells the complete story of the Ariel school UFO landing with first-hand accounts by over a dozen young students.

In Cynthia's book, *UFOs – African Encounters*, she outlines how Edwin, while working as a radio mechanic in a factory south of Durban, in 1960, formed a friendship with a new worker – George – at the same factory. George (whose last name is not disclosed) is described as being well-built and powerful. He had a pleasant face, dark hair and eyes; he was about 35 years of age.

An example of just how strong he was occurred at work, when George moved a heavy machine that had taken five men to manoeuvre along the factory floor. One evening, while fishing at their regular spot – Patterson's Groyne – George produced what looked like a radio set, consisting of two vertical rods, joined by a horizontal piece, some one and a half metres high. When this was switched-on, a strange language was heard.

Some 15 minutes later, a light appeared in the sky. A voice (in English) was then heard on the radio, from a man who told them his name was Wy-Ora and commander of the spacecraft from KOLDAS, which was part of the Confederation of Twelve Planets. Wy-Ora told Edwin that George was one of their races and that his real name was Valdar. His (George's) role was finding a suitable person on Earth to spread information about beings from Outer Space.

Following a demonstration of the craft's capabilities, Edwin expressed concern that he was too young to form such a group, but George convinced him otherwise.

Edwin:

> *"Until Valdar left, a great deal of his time was spent in the library, reading and studying. He was particularly interested in the different Earth religions and attended church services as an unbiased and deeply interested observer."*

He also told Edwin

> *". . . that there were hundreds of space beings, like himself, living on Earth; they remained there for one to five years, before being recalled to their home planets."*

In 1962, Valdar told Edwin that he was going to leave and invited him to go to Richards Bay, where – after handing him a little black box – instructed him to shelter behind a sand dune, in order to protect himself

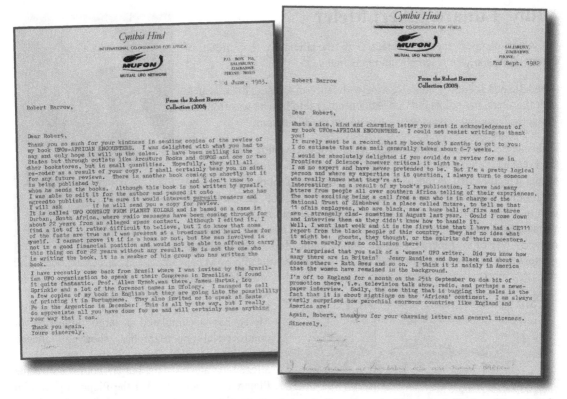

from the effects of the spacecraft, which landed nearby. A disc-shaped object, described as 50 meters in diameter, with a dome on top and observation window, then landed. Edwin says he saw a *'figure'* inside the dome. Goodbyes were made and then George left. Cynthia Hind, who published details of the matter in her book, *UFOs – African Encounters*, was undecided whether to believe Edwin's version of events given the lack of proof, and of the fact that she never met George.

We pondered if George 'Valdar' was David Daniels, taking into consideration his interest in Earth religions, but as these events took place nearly 25 years before Daniels came to the UK, clearly this was unlikely to have been the same person – (unless you believe Daniels was an alien, with an undetermined life expectancy).

Cece Stevens

Cynthia Hind informs the reader, in her UFO magazine – *AFRINEWS*, 1990 – that Carl finally published his book, relating to the claims made by Edwin and George, entitled *The Twelve Planets Speak*. (Wendelle confirmed to us that Daniels travelled to Harare, Zimbabwe, and met UFO researcher – Cynthia Hind – who told Wendelle, in a letter written to him, that Daniels had asked her to take him to see Edwin White – the contactee in that case – but she refused to do so, as Edwin did not want to be involved in any publicity with anybody). We have no documentary evidence so far to link Daniels with a visit to see Cynthia Hind, but we would be surprised if he hadn't made contact with her.

'Billy' Eduard Albert Meier

Billy has claimed regular contact with the Plejaren – a group of extraterrestrials, who resemble human beings.

Wendelle had spent considerable time with Billy, discussing these issues, over the years, but points out that Daniels never told him he was from the Pleiades – just that he was very interested in the Pleiadians.

A farmer born in the town of Bülach in the Swiss Lowlands, Meier joined the French Foreign Legion in his teens, but says he soon left and returned home. He travelled extensively around the world pursuing spiritual exploration, covering 42 countries over 12 years. In 1965, he lost his left arm in a bus accident in Turkey. In 1966, he met and married a Greek woman, Kalliope, with whom he has three children. The nickname 'Billy' came by way of an American friend, who thought Meier's cowboy style of dress reminded her of 'Billy the Kid'. This anecdote was told by Meier himself in an interview with Bob Zanotti of Swiss Radio International, in June 1982.

Beamships used by the Pleiadian races. Image created using the bitmap program from line drawings in the Billy Meier case in 'UFO Contact From The Pleiades' by Wendelle Stevens.

Pleiadian Type 1 7 Meter Diameter 3 Person Crew	Pleiadian Type 2 7 Meter Diameter 3 Person Crew	Pleiadian Type 3 7 Meter Diameter
Reddish bottom Emits humming sound	White top dome Reddish/orange ports	Gold/silver finish Dimensional travel
Pleiadian Miniscout 5 Meter Diameter 1 Person Crew	Pleiadian Drone 3.5 Meter Diameter Pilotless robot	Large Pleiadian Ship ~20 Meter Diameter
Dark gray metallic Atmospheric only	Silver/gold finish Reddish bottom ring	18 ports around rim Red/orange bottom
Lyrian Beamship 7 Meter Diameter 3 Person Crew	Vegan Beamship 8 Meter Diameter	DAL Universe Ship ~8 Meter Diameter
Dull gray sections Sits on light beam	Silver/gray finish Sits on efflux	Silver/metal finish Lands flat on ground

Meier has accumulated a large collection of controversial photographs, showing alleged spaceships (called beam ships) as well as alleged extraterrestrials, human beings called the Plejaren). Meier says that the Plejaren gave him permission to photograph and film their beam ships, in order to produce some of the evidence for extraterrestrial visitation. Meier's claims are both believed and disputed by UFO sceptics and enthusiasts. Meier began accumulating his collection of photographs in the 1970s. His photographs were featured in various newspapers and magazines from around the world, such as the *Quick Magazine* (German), *Blick* (Swiss) *Argosy* (USA) and *Il Giornale dei Misteri* (Italian).

'Billy' Eduard Albert Meiers claimed his first extraterrestrial contacts occurred in 1942, at the age of five, with an elderly extraterrestrial human man, named Sfath. Contacts with Sfath lasted until 1953. From 1953 to 1964, Meier's contacts continued with an extraterrestrial human woman from another universe, named Asket. Meier says that after an 11-year break, contacts resumed again (beginning on 28th January 1975) with an extraterrestrial human woman, named Semjase – the granddaughter of Sfath.

Billy also claims to have visited other worlds and planets, along with another universe, with these extraterrestrials.

Meier claims that he was instructed to transcribe his conversations with the various extraterrestrials, most of which have been published in the German language. These books are referred to as the *Contact Notes* (or *Contact Reports*). Currently, there are eleven published volumes of the *Contact Reports* (entitled *Plejadisch-Plejarische Kontaktberichte*). Some of the *Contact Reports* were translated into English, extensively edited and expurgated, and published in the out-of-print, four-volume set *Message From The Pleiades* by Meier case investigator Wendelle Stevens. There are also many contact reports translated into English (unedited) by Benjamin Stevens.

Meier's discussions with the Plejarens are highly detailed and wide-ranging, dealing with subjects ranging from spirituality and the afterlife to the dangers of mainstream religions, human history, science and astronomical phenomena, ecology and environmental dangers – in addition to prophecies of future historic trends and events.

An additional aspect of the Meier case is the highly controversial book the Talmud Jmmanuel. It is said to be the translation of ancient Aramaic scrolls that were discovered by Meier and a colleague, in Jerusalem, in 1963. The book claims to be the original teachings and life events of the man named Jmmanuel (called Jesus Christ by historians and Christians). Extensive study has been made of the book by James Deardorff.

Some of the most important evidence for Meier's claims comes from his large collection of photographs. These include images of metallic discs floating above the Swiss countryside, the 1975 docking of Apollo-Soyuz, pictures of celestial objects from a non-Earthly vantage point, pictures of apparent extraterrestrials, prehistoric Earthly scenes, and scenes of a devastated future.

1978 – Lt. Colonel Wendelle Stevens carries out an investigation into the claims

In 1978, the photographs, films, sound recordings, and Meier himself, were the subject of six years of investigation by Lt. Col. Wendelle Stevens (ret.) and an American team of analytic experts (see documentary *'Contact'*). Stevens employed a wide range of investigative techniques, such as photogrammetric and computer analysis of photographs, tonal and dynamic analysis of recorded sounds, recreation of models, and extensive lie-detector tests on Meier and his acquaintances. Stevens' findings were largely supportive of Meier's claims. Stevens himself thought the case was genuine, but his findings were largely ignored by the UFO community.

1985

Wedelle C. Stevens
P.O. Box 17206
Yucson, Arizona 85710

1 July 1985

My Dear Helen:

I just received your letter and have set it out here for immediate amswer, because I consider it highly important and directly concerned with what is happening. May I first ask of you a favor? I owe Brenda a letter but have been waiting for her book which I ordered from Arcturus for 3 months, because they sold out the first shipment and have been waiting for a re-supply. I wanted to see if I had any questions before writing. Arcturus says the resupply may arrive any day now. In the meantime, if you would kindly send her a xerox copy of this letter it will answer some of her questions also. To begin with I have instructed my daughter to send you a copy of the Prelim- inary Investigation Report, which describes the scientific aspects of the case. You may send her a check or money order after you receive it, or if it is not what you seek, you may return it. That is a documentation of the <u>reality</u> of the contacts.

There is no doubt in my mind that there were real contacts, real photographs, and very real evidence. I can not say that all is real, because over time and with enough interference, and acts of necessity as well as acts of preservation, it is not always possible to separate the legitimate from the spurious on the parts of many agencies of all kinds. If this sounds like double-talk is is because there is so much inter- ferrence that it finally becomes difficult to distinguish the true realities. Besides the Pleiadians themselves intruducing false leads to keep things from being finally proved, for many good reasons, we have many others doing the same thing for different reasons. I published that 542 page report to release, <u>in proper context</u> what I knew of the case after investigating it for 6 years and living in the household with the witnesses for more that 100 days. I know them fairly well. All that you can read...

What you will not find properly explained, because of the confusion introduced, is the real reason for contacting this Earth humanity at all. Their study of planets is actually much broader and many other intelligent beings studied are never contacted, also for very good reasons. But in our case they have a direct interest and they feel a responsibility because, according to them, their ancestors (and ours also in a way) set themselves up as Gods over the primitive survivors of their own earlier coloniz- ations here who had been reduced to savagery by cataclysmic events. The last great wave of immigration was some 70,000 years ago when 70,000 (merely coincidence) IHWH came here from the Pleiades and colonized and ruled for 10,000 years before evacua- ting the planet again, taking many with them. Those left here degenerated into savagery once more when all of their technology was lost. Great civilizations have emerged and failed many times since then, but always the IHWH returned in greater or lesser force, usually being treated as Gods by the primitives here, which they often acknowledged and even fostered.

Remember now, they were not the only ones. There were others doing something similar elsewhere on this planet involving other races. The IHWH were interested in the white race, their primary descendents, which they tried to keep from racial mixing, hence the strong prohibitions on miscegnation and the myth of the chosen race. Only the white race has this myth. You will find the IHWH mentioned only in white race literature, the term IHWH being the unpronounceable name for deity was corrupted to the English term Jehova. The Jehovas were men, like us, who came from the sky, who preyed on the primitive belief that they were Gods. We have educated too many people in the world today for those primitive beliefs to stand the tests of logic. How can an all-loving all just God kill the innocent firstborn in every family in punishment for something they knew nothing about and had no control of??? What all just God promises vengence on his own creation which if the beliefs were true he could make any way he chose, and if so why make bad ones or weak ones??? If the myth were true, why did he create any failures???

The Pleiadian team visiting Switzerland sought to reveal the falsehoods instituted in those fundamental beliefs, and put there deliberately to control men for political power alone, to aggrandize a few, the politicians and the priesthood at the expense

of the many. Of course this was seen as, and in fact was, an attack on fundamental
Christian beliefs. They/did not deny the greatness of Christ, whom they knew as
a highly advanced spirit who took incarnation here in a physical body to help free
the earth humans from this bondage to the IHWHs, but even HIS real teachings were
taken over by the religious hierarchial system and bent to conform to their purposes.
This was merely another form of political domination which was able to absorb and
dilute the truth to such an extent that they made it a part of their old religious
mythology. Even the great Roman Empire was able to incorporate it into their political system and convert it to an instrument of power, the very antithesis of the
true Christ consciousness.

Another thing we did not report in the technical coverage was the identification
of Meier as early as 6 for indoctrination into a need to know for himself what he was
to believe and why. He was led through every major religion and many minor ones in
the course of a 20 year preparation, participating in them from the inside in order
to know for himself what they were all about. All this preceeded their revelation to
him that he had accepted a mission before his birth to try to demonstrate the fallacies
that had developed in Earth Religions, carefully fostered by elements of political
control to maintain their political power, but which in fact enslaved the mind and
actually retarded progress and evolutionary development because we were forfeiting
our natural intelligence to the manipulations of a few.

In an interesting play on etymology, they explained that it was no accident that we
have substituted the word RELIGION (meaning re-connecting [to the past]) for RELEGION
(meaning re-revelation [the proper meaning intended]).

Naturally advocating any of this was going to get him into trouble with literally
everybody, and it took years of persuasion to get him to accept it. Then they allowed
him to take photographs of their ships impossible to duplicate and equally impossible
to prove false. This was intended to get some attention for what he might reveal later.
The forces in power recognized the threat early and began to bring all forces to bear
to stop the action and to discredit the witness. He barely survives the most energetic
efforts to discourage him. He has survived 11 asassaination attempts on his life,
plus many other offenses against his family and his property. In most cases his mir-
aculous escapes were actually facilitated by the Pleiadians. I myself was involved in
one which you will read about in the book.

The Pleiadian concept of God is not anthropomorphized or personified in any way.
They acknowledge great spirits, advanced in evolution, but not as Gods. They have The
CREATION, of which everything is a part, and the sum of the parts is The CREATION.
Manifestation is the CREATION experiencing itself in polarity. They find no single
part any greater than any other part because they are all the CREATION in itself. This
comes as a blow to man's claimed superiority in creation. It is like saying that the
heart is superior to the lung when neither can survive long without the other. Under
this concept vivisection of our younger brothers in the animal kingdom is murder!

To demonstrate how truths are corrupted in time by the machinations of less than
benevolent humans, he was taken back in time, either actually, or in some special
technical recreation that appeared to be reality to him, to the later days of Christ
to observe and hear for himself what was being taught, and he found it quite different
from what our bible interpretations say today. He found that the politics of the
churches, the Council of Constantinople, the Roman Government, the Aristocratic families of Italy, the King of England and a host of others have changed virtually everything in the original teachings, leaving little of the lesson intended. His mission
was to appeal to all to think again for themselves, accept no dogma, no declarations
of superior knowledge, and nobody elses' concepts of reality, but to think and KNOW
for themselves. It is as simple as that. And therein is the great danger to him. He
was to point out that in the eyes of CREATION no-one and no-thing was superior to any
other and that all enjoyed the same favor in CREATION. What we do to another, we do
to ourself because we are all equal parts of creation.

The philosophy is interesting and in fact fits much better into a universal multi-
planetary belief system such as others advocated by other extraterrestrial visitors
than the concepts we presently hold. There is much food for thought here. I am reminded
of Bill Herrmann's church trying to try him for heresy because of his contacts with
the creatures from Reticulum because having no Christ, they had to be devils...

My very best regards,

Wendelle C. Stevens

Tucson, Arizona 85710

14 November 1985

Dear Ms. Mynne:

I am terribly behind on my mail, and am just trying to catch up on urgent matters at the moment.

I am very concerned about the mail problem. I am sorry you did not receive your book, the Pleiades Report of Investigation yet. It was mailed on schedule when I advised its dispatch, and has not come back here either. Usually if they are misaddressed or are undeliverable for some reason, they come back to me.

I have sent another in case it does not show up there. If you get the first one perhaps you know somebody else who will be interested in buying it. I have only a few copies left and they will be finished and sold out. I only printed 2,000.

I still owe Brenda Butler a letter too. You said here that she did not receive her copy of the Pleiades Report of Investigation either. I have therefore sent her a replacement copy also. If it does arrive perhaps she can find another interested party who wants to buy it. I just wish there was a better way to control the mail.

I bought a copy of Brenda's book from Arcturus Books, and found it extremely interesting and very well handled. I am convinced there is still more to that story than we have learned so far. I liked it so well that I have bought several more copies for Christmas presents.

Yes, I did receive the letter you wrote in July. I just had not answered it yet. I seem to never catch up on the mail.

I have several projects in work that seem to absorb all my writing and correspondence effort.

I shall be looking forward to buying a copy of your book when you get it done. It sounds like a very interesting treatment of a most delicate problem.

All for now, my friend...

W. C. Stevens
Wendelle C. Stevens

PS: maybe the postman thought your new address was too long to bother forwarding the book —— ha!

Some UFO researchers, such as Stanton Friedman and Jacques Vallée, publicly dismiss the Meier case, while others believe the Meier case to be the most thoroughly researched and validated UFO case in our history. Some critics have provided examples of faked photos, similar to what Meier produced, and have pointed out that some of his photos correspond to scenes that were subsequently found in science fiction books, paintings and television programmes. Meier claims that some of his photos were altered by intelligence agencies and slipped into his collection in order to discredit his UFO testimony. *Kal Korff has been particularly vociferous in dismissing the Meier case, pointing to proof of Meier's fakery obviated by finding light-direction and focal discrepancies consistent with cut-and-paste and model techniques.

Examination of the UFO photographs taken by Billy Meir

Photographic analysis was performed on Meier's photographs and films in the late 1970s, when Meier first started to publish his photographs. In a report entitled *"Preliminary Photo Analysis"* written by Design Technology of Poway, California (contractor with NASA's Jet Propulsion Laboratory and the US Navy) signed by Physicist Neil M. Davis (1978)

It contained test results from the analysis of one of the controversial photographs taken by Meier, using microscopic examination, density contour plots, and examination for evidence of double exposure, photo paste-up, model at short range suspended on a string etc – in short a hoax.

They stated *"Nothing was found to indicate a hoax"* and concluded *"Nothing was found in the examination of the print which could cause me to believe that the object in the photo is anything other than a large object photographed a distance from the camera."* They also recommended that the print was a second generation photograph and a more detailed analysis of the photo can only properly be made on the original film.

Recreations of Meier's images were created by photographic effects specialist and stop-motion animator Alan Friswell, for the June, 2005 issue of *Fortean Times* magazine. Friswell had employed techniques used in the pre-digital age of film special effects, as modern processes would, in Friswell's opinion, have been "unsporting". Using "old fashioned" tricks, such as foreground miniatures and photographic cutouts,

---

*Kal K. Korff. At the age of 16-17, Korff was, in fact, very interested in the Billy Meier UFO case after having heard about it for the first time from Col. Wendelle Stevens. It is claimed he insisted that Stevens take him to Switzerland to meet Billy. Stevens refused to do so, due to the fact that Korff was still a minor and that federal law required all minor American citizens who are leaving the USA always to be accompanied by a parent or legal guardian.

Friswell crafted copies of Meier's UFO pictures, but claimed that his pictures did not in any way confirm that Meier was a hoaxer, as without personal experience of the events, he had no right to draw conclusive opinions one way or the other.

Meier's relationship with his wife, Kalliope, ended acrimoniously and in 1997, Kalliope stated in an interview that the UFO in the photos looked like models that Meier had made himself, with items like trash can lids, carpet tacks and other household objects, and that the stories he told of his adventures with the aliens had been entirely fictitious. She agreed when asked by an interviewer that the infamous "wedding-cake" UFO looked like the lid to a trash barrel.

She has also claimed that one of the pictures taken of an "extraterrestrial female" was actually an acquaintance, covered in tanning foil. Also, she claimed that photos of the extraterrestrial women – Asket and Nera – were really photos of two of the *'The Golddiggers'*, dancers Michelle Della Fave and Susan Lund. These photographs were among a series of photos that had apparently been tampered with. Michelle Della Fave alleges that pictures of her were illegally used by Billy Meier to support his claims of having been visited by female extraterrestrials. Close examination of the photos of Michelle Della Fave and the photos of extraterrestrials – Asket and Nera – reveals distinct differences in the facial structures of the women.

In a report entitled *"Analysis of the Wedding Cake UFO"*, an independent researcher attempts to determine the size of the UFO in one of Meier's photographs by analyzing the reflections of surrounding objects on the metallic surface of the UFO. With the aid of 3D modelling computer software satellite imagery and a scale model of Meier's property, they determined the UFO in the picture was an object greater than 9ft in diameter.

The metal samples

In a video made, *'Contact: An Investigation into the Extraterrestrial Experiences of Eduard Meier'* a metallurgist's examination of Billy Meier's metal revealed:

> *"We have little marker bars here that we can line up on each peak as they come up. This one indicates that we have silver there. Over here, let's see, we've got some copper; a small amount of copper. That looks about all that's in here at the moment."*

In 1979, Meier sent Marcel Vogel – a chemist working at IBM – crystal and metal samples, claimed to have been received from the Plejarens. Vogel examined these samples with a scanning electron microscope and reported:

> *"When I touched the oxide with a stainless steel probe, red streaks appeared and the oxide coating disappeared. I just touched the metal . . . and it started to deoxidize and become a pure metal. I have never seen a phenomenon like that before."*

Vogel also claimed that another metal sample he examined contained nearly every element in the periodic table, stating:

> *"Each pure element was bonded to each of the others, yet somehow retained its own identity."*

At 2500 magnification, Vogel claims the sample was:

". . . metal, but at the same time . . . it is crystal! It's a very unusual combination from a metallurgical standpoint. I've shown these to metallurgists and they shake their heads. The most unusual thing you'll see, purity of these metals in adjacency to one another without their cross contamination. They're very sensitive to marking; the soonest I've exposed them to intense light from my microscope the metal oxidizes very rapidly and just breaks down. I've never seen that before."

(Source: Wikipedia)

Wendell Stevens' book – 'UFO... *Contact From The Pleiades'*

In Wendell Stevens' book *UFO . . . Contact From The Pleiades: A Preliminary Investigation Report* (1982), page 424:

> *"Looking at the piece by X-ray diffraction, for elemental analysis, he found a single element deposit of Thulium (Tm, Atomic Number 69, Atomic Weight 168.934), a rare transition element in the Lanthide series, and also of Rhenium (Re, Atomic Number 75, Atomic Weight 186.2), another rare metal".*

Further down the page is also the following paragraph:

> *"Looking at that part spectrographically, the Thulium, remarkably, showed only the primary band spike for that element – no secondary bands existed. All of the elements examined spectrographically had missing bands in their spectra, which should have been there if they were normal spectra. This indicates that the elements are put together in a very unusual way from normal Earth technology. The spectrographic bands are entirely different, beyond what one would consider an isotope. The bands showed a very high elemental purity and no secondary bands and no catalyst. Most of the specimens studied showed the same un-Earthly characteristics. Due to the disappearance of the metal samples and no peer review process being adhered to, it is not possible to scientifically verify Vogel's claims today."*

Specimen disappears!

On page 426 of the book – the specimen was being carried by Dr. Vogel, in a small plastic envelope, to the Ames Research Laboratories for further tests. Inexplicably he reported that the metal specimen simply disappeared, leaving the envelope completely undisturbed.

Rodolfo Casellato

A couple of weeks after he left Tucson, Cece received a letter from Christina – the daughter of Rodolfo Casellato – a Varig Airlines Flight Captain, then living in New York (to whom we wrote, but never received any answer). She told me:

Wendelle C. Stevens
P.O. Box 17206
Tucson, Arizona 85710
U. S. A.

30 December 1984

My Dear Mr. Trent:

Thank you for your letter of 15 December. I know that my daughter has written you also, the day she recieved your letter. I am amazed, shocked and disgusted at what this impostor David Daniel did to you. However you are not alone. I too have been ripped off by this man. He came to see me three times in the robes of an Anglican Priest, pretending to be a holy father. He said that the Anglican Church had secretly accepted the fact that the angels of the bible were nothing but extraterrestrial UFOnauts visiting Earth then, and that they were still arriving today. He said that he had verified my reportin and therefore wanted to buy a number of books, and I sold him perhaps 2 dozen at bookstore wholesale prices. He took those books to a number of UFO researchers and gave them as gifts from me, implying that we were friends, or were working together and persuaded them to take him in for a time. I never knew or heard of the man before he came and bought the books.

When he first came to me, saying he was from England, and that he had just arrived, I had the presence of mind to ask to see his passport, and I memorized the number and address. For your information here they are: U.S. Passport number D779918, Social security No. 359-32-2884, Permanent address: 44 E. 74th Street, New York city. The man's birthdate in the passport was 18 January 1947 (my own day and month). All of these numbers are easy to remember. By the time I discovered anything wrong he was already gone. So I had his passport checked. It is a fraud iindicating issue by the U.S. Consul in London. I also saw in the front cover, a hand written indorsement by a Bishop of the Anglican Church in London. Does he indorse passports? I believe that not only the PP is fradulent but that the indorsement, the Soc Sec number and the perm. address alre also wrong. Then I began hearing from my own friends who were taken in on the same scam. He is a very strange man. It seems that he may still be in England. Would you kindly advise my good friend Brinsley Le Poer Trench of this situation and advise him to alert his coleagues in the House.

I am dreadfully ashamed about all this but I am hearing about it just as you. He certainly has no mandate from me, and I hope they catch him soon. He has told some people he is my son, and others that he was in one or another of my commands when I was in the Air Force, all of which is totally untrue.

Now I want to thank you for all your effort concerning the books, but you must agree that they are not good books. They were never intended to be good books. Their style just happened. They are fairly informative reports, and that is just what they started out to be. How they ended up in hard covers is another story. I do not seek to re-print them. I grant all requests to extract from them with the exception of the Pleiades material which is controlled by the people who made the movie of that case. For the rest, they are only copyrighted to prevent mis-use of the material. All of them are true to the best of my knowledge. Anybody can go back to any of them and find what I found. In that sense I published them as documents. I printed only 2 or 3 thousand copies of each, no more than enough to make the information available to other researchers. I have no plans to reprint any of them, as there are other cases to put the money into.

Since you have been so kind and friendly, I would like to ask of you one little favor: Could you give ma a mail address for Mr. Peter Paget, author of THE WELSH TRIANGLE. I am interested in the Mrs. X in the last chapter because I have a couple of cases of bio-genetic engineering invol-ving women that I must check with him on for possible im-portant correspondences.

I am also interested in the old man abductee who was rejected because he was too old. Has his whole story ever been written up by anybody yet?

All for now. I am truely sorry for your inconvenience, and I regret the unfail imposition on your good will and that of all my other friends as well. I wish I knew who he really is. The FBI, Immigration, local Police and other agencies here are all looking for him also. If you see or hear of him again, may I suggest calling the U.S. Consul's office to report his whereabouts.

Again My apologies, and thanks for writing. George Green is looking for him also.

Wendelle C. Stevens

"I have met a nice, clean-cut, young man, who drove a red Ferarri sports car and took me out to elegant, expensive, restaurants. I have introduced him to my father, when he visited. They seem to get on well."

(Authors: It is suspected this was David Daniels).

1976 Brazil: The Klermer case

On 21st January 1976, Erminio Reis – a Jehova's Witness Minister, at the time – and his wife, Bianca, alleged that while driving from Rio de Janeiro to Belo Horizonte, in Brazil, they were abducted – car and all – aboard a big *'Flying Disc'*. They remained three days and two nights aboard in conversation, and being shown around the *'craft'* the whole time. The Minister tried to convert the ET, but was himself converted, and he went on to teaching yoga in Sao Paulo. The contacts are still ongoing! The name of one of their main contacts was Karran, which – erroneously – was mistaken, by some, to be the name of the planet.

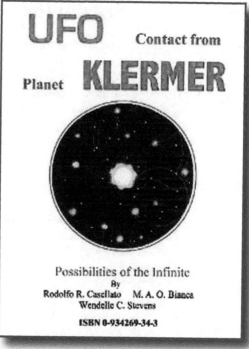

UFO **Contact from**
Planet **KLERMER**

Possibilities of the Infinite
By
Rodolfo R. Casellato   M. A. O. Bianca
Wendelle C. Stevens
ISBN 0-934269-34-3

"We saw that they were two men, very tall – a little over 2.0 meters. They were wearing white overalls, and they were coming up to us while they were talking. They were smiling, with beautiful white teeth. The skin was like a bronze colour. I also noticed, when they came closer, that skin colour I had never seen before. They were very beautiful people, with large green eyes – oblique, but the eyes were positioned a little different from our own. Our eyes end at the side of the head in a point, but their eyes were just the opposite. The point was close to the nose and not at the side of the head. They looked like oriental eyes, but in reverse. We see oriental eyes pulled to the sides, but theirs was reversed and pulled to the front, towards the nose, and the round end was at the side of the head. They were very nice looking. They had nice long, black hair, worn to the neck, and neatly cut, horizontally, across the bottom."

Wendelle:

"Rodolfo was then flying a regular route from Sao Paulo to New York and back, weekly. He was interested in UFOs and did some investigative follow-up for me on Brazilian cases. He found Erminio Reis in the *Klermer case. He had just visited another witness in an important case for me and was returning home to Sao Paulo, in 1988 or 1989, with some positive evidence, when his car was sideswiped by a heavy vehicle. He was knocked off the road and crashed into the ditch, mortally injuring him. He died at the scene, after telling witnesses to 'get the briefcase to Stevens'. They, of course, found no briefcase in the wreckage, the car, or anywhere in the vicinity of that car.

David Daniels wanted Casellato to take him to Mirassol to meet Antonio Ferreira in that case, involving abduction for genetic experiment, which produced a hybrid daughter being brought back to Antonio to see her father. I understand from Casellato's daughter Christine that Daniels made contact with Casellato, in Brazil, but I have no more details on that."

Part 3 – Great Britain: 1984

The next part (no doubt there are many other parts which lay undiscovered, surrounding the activity of Father David Daniels) took place towards the end of 1984, when Brenda Butler received a telephone call from her colleague – BUFORA Researcher, Dot Street – on 24th November 1984, who told her that she had received a visit from a man, who claimed he was an alien from the Pleiades, and that he wanted Brenda to go up to see him, at Dot's house. Although Brenda was reluctant to make the 20 mile journey at that time of the day, fearing it was a ploy just to see her, she agreed to do so, because of Dot's insistence. (We understand that Daniels had originally written to Jenny Randles about meeting up with Brenda and Dot).

From a diary kept by Brenda Butler – March 1985

"My second encounter with someone from the Pleiades is a meeting I will never forget. This meeting lasted for 3-4 months. David Daniels had apparently come to Earth in a spacecraft and landed somewhere near Cornwall. He said he had to come to find me. There were nine of them that landed and five would come to find me. They had to walk into someone's body – a human. Instead of coming to mine he arrived on Dot's doorstep. I arrived at 6.30pm; Dot introduced me to a tall, thin, good looking man, with long thin hands and fingers, pale complexion, blonde hair, and pale blue eyes. I learnt his name was David Daniels. He told me he was from the Pleiades. Dot asked me to go into the kitchen; she said she had seen him walking up the garden path, earlier, while in the company of her daughter.

As she turned around, he was stood next to them. I asked her why she had let the man in if she had felt frightened. She replied, 'I had no choice. I went into the living room and met him, straightaway I felt a strong bond between us. He showed me some star charts and maps. We talked a great deal, but because Dot kept picking arguments with him, he suggested we go for a walk, which we did. All the time he spoke about his home on the Pleiades. He said he had landed in Arizona before he came to the UK. He also told me that his purpose on the Planet was to gather together a column of people for the big landing to come. I was the one he was going to teach. I asked him when this was going to happen he replied, 'many years time we will find you' Over the next few weeks, I made many visits to see David and talk to him. He said if he didn't leave Dot's place he would soon die. He asked if he could stay with me, but I told him I didn't have the room.

Over the next few weeks I made many visits to see David and talk to him. On one occasion after we arrived late at her house after having been out in the car, Dot told David to pack his bags in the room while she talked to me. She complained that David had kept appearing and reappearing in front of her, and that all he ate were pounds of sweets and green vegetables. I went up to see David, he told me he had to get away from Dot, because they didn't get on and then asked me to lock the door – I didn't feel frightened in any way and did as he suggested. He then started to shake; all of his veins stood out to about an inch, his body, face and hair changed to what looked I can only describe as a creature with green snake skin, this metamorphous was only for a few seconds, during which time he talked in a strange language.

During further conversation, David told her that he had been sent to the planet with eight others, to collect

Wendelle C. Stevens 47475
Santa Rita ACTC-T
10,000 South Wilmot Rd.,
Tucson, Arizona 85777
U.S.A.

26 January 1985

My Dear Brenda:

I was delighted to recieve your latter. My daughter Cece brought it out to me yeaterday. The above address will get mail to me here at prison, but be advised that every bit is opened and photographed before I get it. My visits are restricted and I can not be sure that this will get out to you. Cece told me she had written you also. She tends to exagerate a little but mostly what she says will be correct to some degree.

Yes, I am very concerned for anybody DD contacts. He came here as a priest, telling me he was on a confidential mission for the Anglican Church, who had recognized the reality of the UFO phenomenon, and that the angels of the Bible were in fact UFOnauts visiting Earth then as they do now. I told him I did not believe such a thing, and then I asked what diocese he was from and which rectory he was staying in. He said he had not checked in with local church authorities because his mission was confidential. Now he was dressed like a priest, looked like a priest, and acted like a priest, taking time to bless almost every table in the visiting room as he worked his way down to where I was waiting. We were now sitting at a table with his Bible in front of him and a rosary and Crucifix around his neck. I even felt quite embarrassed to ask him for some evidence of his mission. He produced a passport that showed that it had been issued by the U.S. Consulate in London, and it had a hand written endorsement in the front signed by a Bishop of the Anglican Church in London. Not even knowing who the Bishop was I could not question that, but I did notice one thing that jumped right off the page at me. His birthdate was the same day and month as mine but for year 1947. Had I been a little more observant then I would have also noticed that there were a lot of 7s and 4s in the numbers (passport, address, etc.), but when I remarked on the birthdate, his only remark was, "Now do you wonder why I am here?" It was very mysterious. He was quite psychic and I discovered he was picking up my thoughts, so I tried to concentrate on different things. When I asked where he came here from he said Jugoslavia, that part of his mission took him there first. I remembered that the passport issue date was recent and there were only about 7 stamps in it. It was issued in London, had an exit visa, an entry and exit in france, another stamp (Austrian I think) and an entry and exit for Jugoslavia, and an entry stamp for the U.S. That part seemed true and so I didn't immediately question the rest.

That meeting was rather formal and he proceeded with "his mission", asking how the South African book was comming along (I am publishing Van Vlierdens book on the ET contacts with Edwin) and then said that he had planned to meet me in Rhodesia. Now this really amazed me because though I had planned to go to Natal to look all the principal witnesses in the eye and examine the evidence there before I printed the story, ... I would have to go through Cynthis Hind in Salisbury to get to Edwin, so that would be my first stop -- but I had told no one, not even my daughter,of these plans. How did the Anglican Church know? He mentioned other things that convinced that he had a remarkable source. I thought he must be intelligence too, but who's???

That story here would also fill a book and so I will jump forward till my sources verified that the passport was fradulent and I confronted him with it. By now he had been in my home, convincing the renter that he had my permission and "borrowed" a few books. Later somebody broke into my daughter's house and took a full case of books which I now suspect was DD.

He asked about a book on a Brazilian case I am putting together for Dr. Buhler, and I had told very few about that. He even went to Brazil and looked Buhler up. When he knew I was aware of his false identity, he told me that he was an ET and that he was here to get me out of prison because they had a "mission" for me. I told him that I had my own mission and didn't want any other. He went to Colorado and looked up two people I was doing business with, telling them that I had sent him. One was whose name was apparently used also to further his tricks, as I am afraid he may be using yours now wherever he may be.

Would it be possible to get word to Admiral Hill-Norton and to Lord Clancarty that I did not send him, nor authorize him in any way, and was in fact ripped off like everyone else he meets. I do not know who he really is or where he really comes from. I worry about his next victims. I may have gotten off light with only a few hundred dollars loss.

Thanks for the flyer on your book. I have ordered a copy from Arcturus, who is waiting for their next shipment to fill the order. I read in one of Lou Farish's newsclips that you have a tape of part of the meeting or contact event involving Col. Holt. I would like to attend one of your lectures and hear that. May I suggest that you make a copy to take to your lectures and keep the original in a safe place and used as little as possible. I have had many things stolen from me at lectures. I can't wait for your next book to come out. If you do publish another, may I also suggest that you have that audio tape impressed on a plastic page in disc format and bind it in the back of the book to give others a chance to hear the live event. That ought to add something special to the book at a reasonable rate. I believe you can get such pages made up 2,000 at a time for about .40 per page, and you could add this to the price of the book.

Thanks for the information on Peter Paget. I had already written to that address which I got out of the book on the Welch Triangle and they did not answer. I hope he has not run into trouble.

DD is collecting nothing for any book for me. I have no 500 page book in work. I do have one 368 page book for Buhler on the contacts at Mirassol, Brazil; and the South African contacts investigated by Carl vanVlierden, 305 pages and a couple more similar documented reports, not well written but informative and verifiable by anyone who wants to do so. I didn't sell any secrets and didn't write about any. I have not broken any oaths of secrecy. Everything I have released was outside those oaths and was developed privately at my own expense.

Thanks for the clips on Mr. Bertoo. I had missed those. Do you happen to have a mailing address for Mr. Omar Fowler, the investigator of that case.

Welcome to the club. Nothing gets published that does not draw fire. You may have a thousand very pleased readers and only a couple dozen antagonists, but the attackers are militant and have a lot of energy (and help) and will do almost anything. They will even carry out their threats as Bill Herrmann found out. A sad commentary on our humanity. It is no wonder that there is very little open contact with ETs. We are dangerous to them and ourselves too...

I will have to close as like you, I have many letters to write. I will write Mr. Trent in a couple days also.

I am pleased to make your aquaintence and thanks for writing. If there is anything I may do for you do not hesitate to ask.

My very best respects,

Wendelle C. Stevens

PS: May I give George Green your address? He travels a lot and may be able to fill you in more next time he is in London. He is definitely OK....

a column of people for the landing, and that Brenda would be told when and where this would take place. By this time, Dot was very unhappy and ordered David to leave. Brenda asked Dot to let him stay one more night, in order to make some arrangements, the following day, to find him other accommodation – to which Dot agreed.

"Dot telephoned me in the morning, telling me that when she had got up, David had gone. At this point I heard somebody outside my house; when I opened the door, it was David. I was very happy to see him and telephoned Dot to say he was at my house. She told me she never wanted to see him again, as all he wanted to talk about was the stars and the Pleiades. He seemed happy in the caravan. I don't think he ever slept, but walked about all night long.

The neighbours became frightened of him and told me to tell him to go. He burnt the heater in the caravan during the time he was living in there, and completely ruined the inside. He never came to the house to use the toilet, or wash his clothes – yet he was spotlessly clean, so were his clothes. He came into the house to eat. His meal usually consisted of green vegetables and sweets, along with a drink while he used the phone, but this only took place at night-time. He made numerous telephone calls to his 'people' and his government. The telephone numbers made by David never showed up on the telephone bill, as promised to me by him.

One night I overheard a conversation made by him, while on the telephone.

The gist of it was 'yes, she is a Librian – seems to be alright – very knowledgeable. She will make a good leader when the time comes. I will teach her what she needs to know'.

We spent a lot of time together, which upset my partner, Chris Pennington, as he and David did not get on at all. One afternoon we had been out for a walk with the dog. He was very wary of David, who accepted him but advised me to keep the dog at a distance.

Glimpses into Pleiades cultures and a dying planet

David invited me into the caravan, after telling me that it was time to be shown 'things'. He told me not to be afraid and lie on the bed, as I would see things I should know. He touched my head and I saw a beautiful blue diamond, with facets in it. I felt myself going into a trance-like state and remember seeing lovely people, dying of starvation, disease and devastation, nearby cities in ruins. He asked me what I was seeing and I described it to him. He told me that this was once the Pleiades and germs from their planet had found their way into the city. As they were unable to combat the disease, this was one of the reasons why they had come to Earth to collect soil samples and vegetation. Unfortunately, they had unintentionally brought some of these germs with them, which were causing problems on Earth.

Blue crystal is used again – Pyramids being built

On another afternoon I visited the caravan and after being shown a blue crystal, which David wore around his neck, was touched upon the head once again. This time I saw monasteries, with monks looking down from a giant height, into a valley, where people were gathering crops – many of which were dying through lack of water. Through this facility of communications, I was also shown tunnels, with people living in them, and a UFO landing site in Peru.

Further sessions included seeing the Pyramids being constructed, block by block, involving hundreds of people using steps to carry out the work.

David also confided in me that women were taken aboard one of their 'craft' and impregnated by an alien being and that subsequently, when the baby was born, it was brought up as a hybrid. Some of the women involved stayed to rear the babies, while others were returned to their homes with no knowledge of what had happened to them.

One day, following one of our long talks, David said to me 'I think you should see me as I really am', and then asked me to lock the door. At that stage I still thought of David Daniels as being a human, rather than a reptoid. David took off his sweater and made several very deep breaths, and changed into a reptilian. I wished he had given me more warning, as I didn't have any sweets available for him and wasn't sure how he would react without them; this time, his arms, hands, face and head, changed into what looked like a snake, with a reptilian face. He then spoke to me in a weird language, prior to changing back to human form. The first thing he asked for were some sweets. When I told him I hadn't got any, he asked me to pass him a box, kept on the side, out of which he took a small yellow stone that he held to his throat and forehead before placing back into the box. Within a few minutes he was back to his original human form. He told me that his real name was Kar (pronounced Ka).

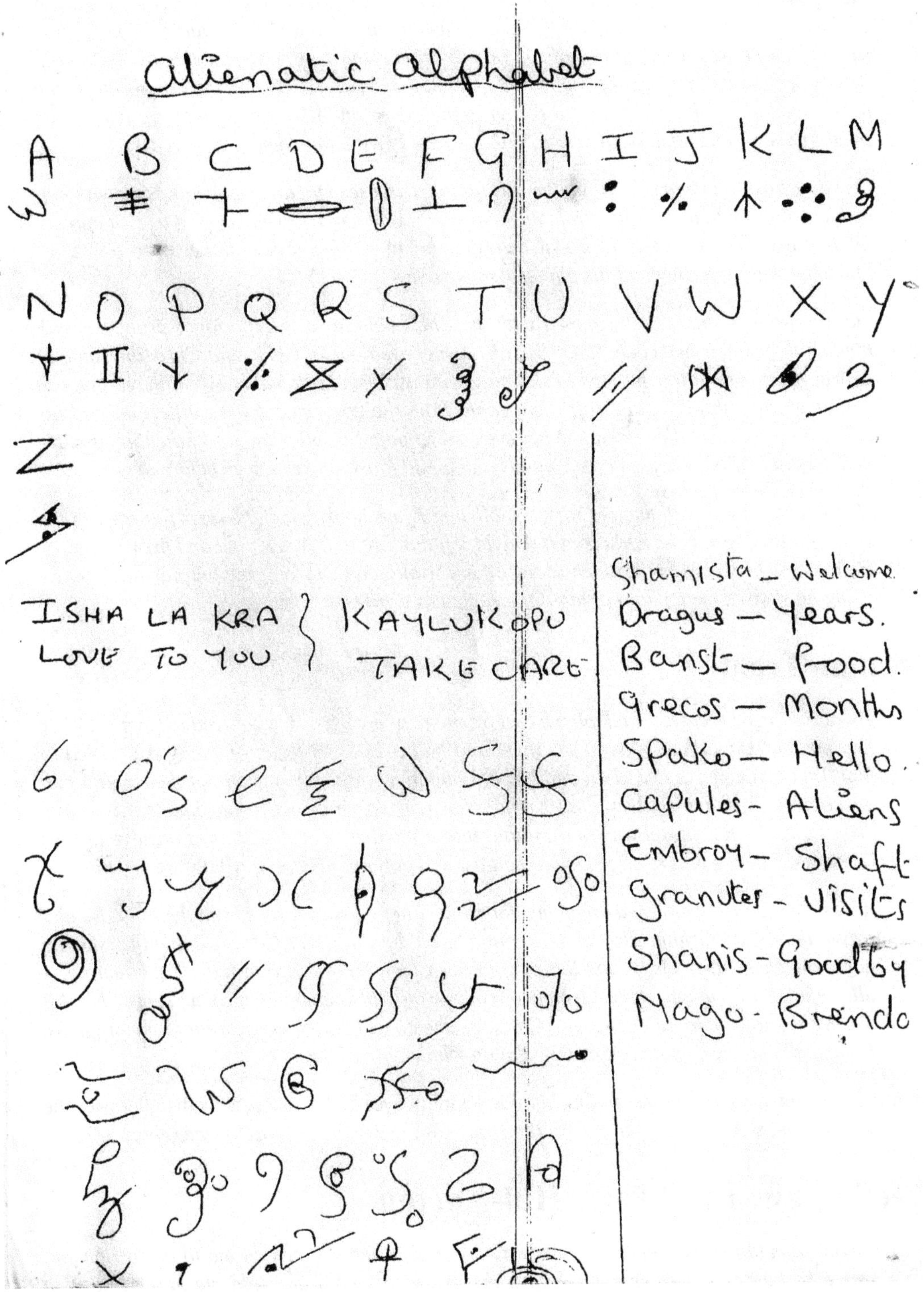

alienatic alphabet

A B C D E F G H I J K L M

N O P Q R S T U V W X Y

Z

ISHA LA KRA } KAYLUKOPU
LOVE TO YOU } TAKE CARE

Shamista — Welcome.
Dragus — Years.
Banst — Food.
grecos — Months
Spako — Hello.
Capules — Aliens
Embroy — Shaft
granutes — Visits
Shanis — Goodby
Mago — Brenda

I took David to see my friends – John and Alison Day. (Details of their UFO sighting can be found in volume four of Haunted Skies). When we arrived at the couple's home, John shouted at me to get David out of the house. David and I were shocked at this outburst. Alison, who was throwing what appeared to be salt around the room, joined in by telling me to remove him. At this point, David recognised John as an 'Alien from another planet' – the inhabitants of which had been at war with his people for many hundreds of years.

One day, I asked David if he would be willing to go and see Dot and make things up with her, as I felt she should also benefit from this knowledge. He agreed to go, as long as Dot agreed. On that evening we met up with Dot, but after thirty minutes they both began to row, after David tried to explain about his planet – so we left.

During the time that David stopped with us, Chris continued to experience problems with him, as they didn't like each other. David was very jealous of Chris and Chris the same of David. After about three months of stopping with us, David told me he would have to leave and meet up with his 'spacecraft', as people from the government were after him and his colleagues. He also told me that he believed somebody was following and watching him. He had the capability to read people's minds and could finish off sentences before they could.

He went to church with me and took a bible and hymn book, which he later returned to the vicar, explaining why he had taken it. David left that night. It was a cold and frosty evening. He told me he would be in touch soon; others would come to visit me but not stay. Before going he showed me a photo of himself, dressed as a priest.

Norman Trent

Two days later I received a telephone call from one of my friends, who lived in Norfolk. They told me that David had been to see them and had asked him to leave, being frightened of him. This couple gave David an address in London to stay with a friend of theirs, who had an interest in 'shape-shifters'. My friend, Norman, drove David to the London area and dropped him off. Norman was to complain that a number of strange things occurred at his home address and that strange people had tried to get into his house, who were not human.

A week later, Suzanne turned up on my doorstep. She told me she was from the Pleiades and stayed the night. Suzanne also spoke about a 'craft' landing near Cornwall, but that she did not know David Daniels. I took Suzanne to meet Dot, but the two of them didn't get on at all. Before Suzanne left, she told me two others would also come to meet me soon. She also warned me to be careful of Dot and Chris, as she considered them a threat to my progress. Ironically, neither David nor Suzanne got on with either of them.

(Trent was to later write to Brenda, telling her that Ralph Noyes had expressed his disquiet over the role of the man – Daniels, and was going to *"warn the House of Lords UFO Group to steer clear of him"*).

Meeting The Lord Peter Hill-Norton

David phoned me on regular intervals. On one occasion, he invited me to go to London, where he had been sleeping rough in a disused warehouse, and told me he had been in contact with Ralph Noyes and was going to stay with him. He asked me to go over to the piece of waste ground, opposite my house, and recover his maps and bag, which he had buried before he came to see me. He instructed me to contact Ralph Noyes and tell him I had recovered the items and that they were intact.

I went over to the waste ground and discovered a tunnel going down into a bunker, with beds and crockery in it. I found his material in a hole beside the tunnel, and took them home. Inside the bag, which was soaking wet, I discovered a bible, a cross, and photographs of a priest, who looked like David. In addition to this, I found a brown teddy bear in the bag, but no clothes or money.

Ralph Noyes

I telephoned Ralph Noyes and asked if I could speak to David. Ralph denied he was there, so I told him to tell David, when he saw him, that 'mission had been accomplished – all correct, even brown teddy bear'. Ralph asked me what all this was about. I said, 'Just give David that message, please'. Ralph said he would if he saw him.

The following day, David telephoned me to say he was at Ralph's, and thanked me for delivering the message.

Ralph spoke to me next, and questioned me about what had taken place while David was staying with me. I was flabbergasted when Ralph told me David had shown himself to him as something not from this world. He also mentioned having been shown some spacecraft. I confirmed this was correct, and Ralph expressed some concern that our telephones were being monitored. Ralph said that his phone was monitored when he worked with the MOD.

I went to London, where I met with David Daniels at the train station, and we made our way to the MOD. Following our arrival there, we were both searched by the security men, who also checked our case and my handbag. We were escorted into a large room, which contained three chairs and a long table. The Lord Hill-Norton came in about five minutes later. He introduced himself and asked how could he help? David spoke about his planet and the Pleiades. The Lord Hill-Norton seemed very interested in all of this. I tried to talk to him about the Rendlesham Forest case, but he seemed disinterested and continued talking to David. He then said 'I wish I could help in some way, but because of my pension and job, dare not'.

After we left, we walked around and caught the train back to my house. David stayed with me for a week, although he kept saying it was dangerous for me and him.

In further conversations with David Daniels, he mentioned about the 'Middle Earth

The Lord Peter Hill-Norton

people' – a race of people living under the earth. Their existence is apparently known to the Government. The people that live under the earth, in tunnels and caves, originally came from another planet to live. When humans eventually began to live in large numbers on our planet, these inhabitants escaped to live under the ground.

David returned to stay with Ralph Noyes and I understood they got on well together. Ralph told me he had learned a lot from him.

2013 – Nick Pope confirms this meeting took place and that Lord Hill-Norton met David Daniels.

Ralph Noyes was former Head of DS8, the forerunner of Sec (AS) 2a (UFO Desk) at the MOD. In 1985, he wrote a novel based on the Rendlesham Forest incident, entitled *A Secret Property*. He also reported his own sighting of: *". . . three yellowish-white 'balls of light' flying in triangular formation, which stopped and hovered in the sky, near Elstree Studios, one night in May 1985."* Like Hill-Norton, Noyes was convinced that the MOD was hiding something, but discovered nothing further than the standard line that Halt's report had been examined and dismissed as *'of no Defence interest'*.

Contacted by New Scotland Yard

Following a visit to see the two of them, I received a telephone call from Ralph to say that David had left, as he feared for Ralph's safety. David then contacted me by telephone, asking me if any 'Agencies' had contacted me; I told him 'no' and asked him why. He said 'Well, they will – don't believe them. They are after me and have set me up. I have to go now' and he put the phone down. About ten minutes later the phone rang. A man asked for Brenda Butler. When I confirmed this, he told me he was a Detective Inspector White, from New Scotland Yard, and that they were looking for a David Daniels. Inspector White also mentioned he was from MI5. I told him that I would telephone him back to confirm his telephone number as relating to New Scotland Yard. After I had done this, I spoke to Detective Inspector White and asked him why they thought I knew David Daniels. He said to me 'We found your name and details on a UFO book, which was in his possession'. I denied knowing David, but the man told me they had proof that I knew him. I asked him what he had done wrong. The Inspector replied, 'The FBI and CIA are after him for stabbing a man to death'.

I told the Inspector that this didn't necessarily prove that David was guilty. The Inspector advised me that if David contacted me, I should phone him straightaway, as he was regarded as a very dangerous man and the authorities needed to find him.

Hardly had I put the phone down when it rang again. This time it was somebody from the FBI. The Agent told me that it would be in my interests to tell them where David was. I pointed out I didn't know where he was. The Agent replied that they knew he had definitely been staying at my house and that they would visit me, in order to obtain a statement if required. I then admitted he had stayed with me, but I did not consider him dangerous or a criminal. The Agent said 'You leave that up to us to decide'. I asked him why the FBI would be interested, if he had killed a man in London. He told me you have a right to know. I said to him 'I don't believe he has killed anyone. I think you are interested in him for other reasons'. The man replied 'You haven't heard or seen anything' and put the phone down.

After these developments, I wondered what I had got myself into. The events seemed more in keeping with a movie film than reality."

We emailed New Scotland Yard, in 2009, and asked them if they could confirm that Daniels was wanted for murder. They declined to give any information, stating that such information was covered under the Data Protection Act – which seems odd. If he was still wanted for murder, one would have thought that somebody would have contacted us, curious as to why we had emailed them under the FOI Act on this matter. Surely, for such a serious offence as this, details would still be on the Police National Computer; even if they were not, it seems astonishing that no check was made on 'cold cases' currently on file.

We did consider whether Inspector White was fictitious but discounted this, bearing in mind that Brenda had rang New Scotland Yard and had spoken personally to Inspector White (who has the same surname as contactee Edward White). It is possible that this is mere coincidence, but we suspect differently.

Brenda appears to be the only one that held David Daniels in high respect, as the reader can see; others bitterly regretted having been involved with him. We, of course, never met him but often wonder how many others were to meet him, through the years? Were those associations benevolent, or malevolent, in nature? We shall probably never know.

The CIA and FBI

Brenda:

> *"I was astonished when the telephone went again – this time it was Inspector White, asking me if I had cooperated with the CIA and FBI. I told him I couldn't help any further. He said to me 'We must find this man. He and his companions are considered very dangerous. I will be in touch again soon'.*
>
> *The next day, David phoned. He asked me if somebody had phoned or been to see me.*
>
> *I told him they would trace his telephone call, and to be careful. I told him what they had told me and David said: 'They were trying to capture me and the others, as someone has told the authorities about us and our 'craft'. Fortunately, no one knows the location of the landing site, or the pick-up point'.*
>
> *Two days later David contacted me again, telling me he dare not come to see me again, as I was under surveillance. A fortnight later David telephoned and said he was awaiting his 'ship' to come and collect him, and his colleagues, back to his own planet. I never heard from Inspector White, the FBI, or the CIA, again."*

Other members of the Pleiades arrive

About a week after Daniels left Leiston, a woman called to see Brenda Butler at her home, and introduced herself as Oriana, from the Pleiades. She told Brenda that there were nine of *'them'* altogether, and was taken to see Dot, but she didn't like her.

A few days later, two people turned up at the house – Michael and Oriana O'Legion – who claimed to be *'star'* children from the Pleiades. They were interviewed on *East Anglia TV* as being *'star'* children from the Pleiades. Brenda confirms having seen them on TV, wearing some beautiful outfits. (Attempts to recover this film from *East Anglia TV* proved unsuccessful.)

Oriana then left, the following day, but over the course of the weeks, two others from the Pleiades – 'Tara' and 'Tron' – arrived to see Brenda, but did not stay. A fourth woman, called 'Suzanna', came to see Brenda, and was taken to see Dot but they didn't get on.

1979 Antonio Carlos Ferreira – Who was he?

The Mirassol UFO Incident is the name given to an incident, in which it is said that Brazilian security guard Antonio Carlos Ferreira was abducted from his workplace – a furniture factory in Mirassol, São Paulo – on 28th July 1979.

According to his own accounts, Ferreira was approached at his place of work, at 3am, by three humanoid figures who tranquilized him with a light-emitting gun before taking him aboard a smaller ship, which ferried him to a larger craft further away. Once on board the ship, Ferreira states that he was positioned in front of a large television-like device and presented with a variety of images, before being forced to mate with an alien woman, after which he was tranquilized again and returned to his place of work.

Ferreira described his abductors as being approximately 1.2 meters tall, with pointed ears, slanted eyes, and human-like mouths. They lacked eyebrows or eyelashes and spoke in a language that superficially resembled Japanese. Some are said to have had dark skin and red curly hair, while others are said to have had light skin and straight black hair. He described their ship as being spherical, with three undercarriage-like legs protruding from the bottom, and as having an interior that was lit by bright red and green lights that grew more intense as they approached the craft's ceiling.

Ferreira states that he encountered the aliens again, in 1982, at which time their craft is said to have landed close by him, so that the alien woman from the first encounter, and a childlike alien, could observe him from a distance. Ferreira is said to have experienced a third encounter later, in 1982, in which he was taken into the hangar of an alien craft, via a green beam of light, before being injected with a yellow substance. He said he was then taken to meet the two aliens once more, the younger of whom he was led to believe was his child. Other encounters are said to have followed, to a total of 16 between 1979 and 1989.

(Source: Wikipedia)

Australia connection – 2000: Honolulu and implants

The Reverend Glennys Mackay JP is an ordained spiritual minister, clairvoyant, medium, healer, meta-physical teacher and lecturer of the UFO Phenomena. She is still actively involved with research within the Queensland UFO Network, and the Australian National Director of MUFON.

While living in New Zealand, Glennys has claimed contact experiences every night, right throughout the 1970s. She claims a lifetime of close encounters with beings described as the *'tall whites'*. These are mostly multiple witness encounters, including one that happened in 1968, when she was cured of terminal cancer.

In 1978 she witnessed a large UFO in the back paddock, behind her house, and was later told the exact date of the fall of the Berlin Wall by ET beings. Glennys has spent six-and-a-half years travelling around Australia, and in this time she has collected many stories from the indigenous communities who reported contact with *'star'* people.

In October 2000, she emailed UK UFO researcher – Bob Stewart – who has expressed an interest in David Daniels and told him of a trip around Honolulu and its outer islands, involving her and 14 other people, travelling in two coaches. During that trip she met a mystery man and his partner Jane – about 5ft in height – who had disturbed their group.

He told her his name was David Sutherland and that they were staying at a local hotel. Enquiries made later revealed no trace of any such guest.

Glennys:

> *"They could read our minds and corrected our thoughts. They would not let us photograph them. One of the girls – Lynn – did this from a distance, and the resulting photograph only showed a blur, with gold and green light where the top of the torso was. While I was with them, I felt something going in between my shoulder blades. When I got back to the hotel, I asked a friend to have a look. She discovered a pin prick and could feel under my skin something like the thickness of two matchsticks and half the length."*

We contacted Glennys, in 2013, and initially discussed this matter with her. We had hoped to learn more about the other members of the group, with a view to speaking to them about Sutherland. From the description given of this man, it is likely that he was David Daniels. Here is what she had to say on the matter:

> *"I took a group of friends from Brisbane on a sacred tour to Hawaiian Islands. The night before we left I received a phone call from a man requesting to join us on the tour. I explained we were leaving the next day, and perhaps he could join us on our next trip? He asked, 'Where are you staying?' My inclination was not to tell him, but I said, 'Outrigger Hotel, Hobron, Waikiki.' He replied, 'I will see you then.' I asked him where he was phoning from. He replied, 'Gold Coast'. I asked for his name. He said, 'David Sutherland'."*

Glennys arrived in Honolulu at 5.40am, and made her way to the hotel. It was agreed that, after a rest, the group would meet down at reception, at around 10am, and pick up the two 8-seat vans. At around 9am, the phone in her room rang. The reception desk told her that Mr David Sutherland was downstairs to see her. She went to reception and met . . .

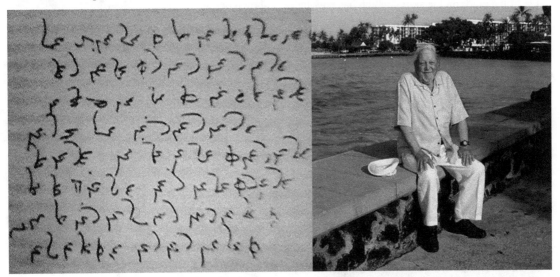

This, sent to Brenda Butler on November 8, 1980, from Colonel Wendelle Stevens. Right: Wendelle seen relaxing in Hawaii.

"a tall young man that looked anything from late 20s to mid 30s, about 5ft 10ins to 6ft in height, accompanied by a very small thin young girl, with very white skin – like she had never been out in the sun. When I spoke to her, she would look at David and he would answer. She never spoke. Over the next four days, they shared the van with us. When we stopped for lunch they would not join us, but would wonder off. When we tried to get a photo of them, they seemed to disappear out of our range. They would always sit in the back of the van and there were times when he would collect our thoughts. I asked them where they were from and where they were going when they left. They said 'Norway'.

We realised there was no way they could have arrived into Honolulu from Australia at the same time – as ours was the only flight. When questioned by some of the ladies as to where they were staying, they gave a name of a hotel in Waikiki but checking later on, we found no so such person stayed at that hotel."

As mentioned previously, photographs taken of the couple showed only the bottom of their legs and feet.

Disturbingly, following the deliberate and unlawful introduction of what appears to have been some sort of undetermined device, inserted into her left shoulder blade (apparently by Sutherland and his female companion) Glennys informs us that *'eleven other occupants of the same party'* also experienced the same trauma.

While having a bath and massage by her friend and partner, to relieve the pain felt by the *'implant'* in her back, Glennys says she felt *'it'* move.

Brenda Butler – The French Seven

Somebody else who told a similar story was Brenda Butler. She maintains she also received one of these tracking devices, when aged nine, and that it was highly visible on her left shoulder for some years. She also complains that it moves around from the left ear to the shoulder. Some years ago an illustration was made of the mark on the skin – which has now faded – shown below.

When someone placed a Geiger counter on the object situated on her left shoulder, it went off the scale.

A few years ago, while having a MRI scan at Ipswich Hospital for suspected Angina, the nurse insisted that

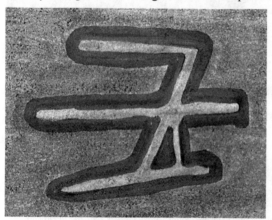

she take off the jewelry from around her neck, as it was showing on the image monitor. Brenda, who does not wear jewelry, denied wearing any necklace. The anomaly shown on the image screen was explained away as being a technical fault. The machine, which had a history of 100%, then broke down and required attention, before being put back into service.

Brenda went to see the doctor, some years ago, after continuing discomfort in the neck and shoulder. He examined her and asked about the mark on the shoulder and whether she had ever had any surgery using precision instruments, to which she replied in the negative.

INDEX

(Also includes source references)

B

COPYRIGHT/PERMISSIONS

DISCLAIMER

These books have cost us a great deal of money to produce, but we strongly believe that this information forms part of our social history and rightful heritage. It should therefore be preserved, despite the ridicule still aimed at the subject by the media. *All previous titles – pictured above – are currently available.*

If anyone is willing to assist us with the preparation of any illustrations, it would be much appreciated. We can be contacted by letter at **31, Red Lion St, Alvechurch, Worcestershire B48 7LG**, by telephone **0121 445 0340**, or email: **johndawn1@sky.com**

For those that may wish to consider publishing their own books or magazines, our typesetter, Bob Tibbitts, is available to offer his design, layout and typesetting services – producing a final press-ready pdf file which can then be used for professional printing. He can be contacted on email: **isetcdart@tiscali.co.uk**